THE ROUTLEDGE COMPANION TO MEDIA AND RISK

This collection presents new work in risk media studies from critical humanities perspectives. Defining, historicizing, and consolidating current scholarship, the volume seeks to shape an emerging field, signposting its generative insights while examining its implicit assumptions.

When and under what conditions does risk emerge? How is risk mediated? Who are the targets of risk media? Who manages risk? Who lives with it? Who are most in danger? Such questions—the what, how, who, when, and why of risk media—inform the scope of this volume. With roots in critical media studies and science and technology studies, it hopes to inspire new questions, perspectives, frameworks, and analytical tools not only for risk, media, and communication studies, but also for social and cultural theories.

Editors Bishnupriya Ghosh and Bhaskar Sarkar bring together contributors who elucidate and interrogate risk media's varied histories and futures. This book is meant for students and scholars of media and communication studies, science and technology studies, and the interdisciplinary humanities, looking either to deepen their engagement with risk media or to broaden their knowledge of this emerging field.

Bishnupriya Ghosh teaches postcolonial theory and global media studies at the University of California, Santa Barbara. Much of her scholarly work, including the two books, *When Borne Across: Literary Cosmopolitics in the Contemporary Indian Novel* (2004) and *Global Icons: Apertures to the Popular* (2011), investigates contemporary cultures of globalization. She is currently working on two monographs on speculative knowledge: a book on spectral materialism in global cinemas (*The Unhomely Sense: Spectral Cinemas of Globalization*) and a comparative study of epidemic media in the United States, South Africa, and India (*The Virus Touch: Living with Epidemics*).

Bhaskar Sarkar, Associate Professor of Film and Media, UC Santa Barbara, is the author of *Mourning the Nation: Indian Cinema in the Wake of Partition* (2009). He has published a wide range of articles in edited collections like *World Cinemas, Transnational Perspectives* (2008), *International Communication* (2012), and *Figurations in Indian Film* (2013), as well as in journals such as *Rethinking History, positions: asia-critique, Cultural Dynamics*, and *Transnational Cinemas*. He is also co-editor of *Documentary Testimonies: Global Archives of Suffering* (2009), *Asian Video Cultures: In the Penumbra of the Global* (2017), and two journal special issues, "The Subaltern and the Popular," *Journal of Postcolonial Studies* (2005) and "Indian Documentary Studies," *BioScope* (2012). He is currently working on two monographs: *Cosmoplastics: Bollywood's Global Gesture*, and *Pirate Humanities*.

THE ROUTLEDGE COMPANION TO MEDIA AND RISK

Edited by Bishnupriya Ghosh and Bhaskar Sarkar

NEW YORK AND LONDON

First published 2020
by Routledge
52 Vanderbilt Avenue, New York, NY 10017

and by Routledge
2 Park Square, Milton Park, Abingdon, Oxon, OX14 4RN

Routledge is an imprint of the Taylor & Francis Group, an informa business

© 2020 Taylor & Francis

The right of Bishnupriya Ghosh and Bhaskar Sarkar to be identified as the authors of the editorial material, and of the authors for their individual chapters, has been asserted in accordance with sections 77 and 78 of the Copyright, Designs and Patents Act 1988.

All rights reserved. No part of this book may be reprinted or reproduced or utilized in any form or by any electronic, mechanical, or other means, now known or hereafter invented, including photocopying and recording, or in any information storage or retrieval system, without permission in writing from the publishers.

Trademark notice: Product or corporate names may be trademarks or registered trademarks, and are used only for identification and explanation without intent to infringe.

Library of Congress Cataloging-in-Publication Data
A catalog record for this title has been requested

ISBN: 978-1-138-63893-8 (hbk)
ISBN: 978-1-315-63750-1 (ebk)

Typeset in Bembo
by Wearset Ltd, Boldon, Tyne and Wear

CONTENTS

List of Figures   ix
Notes on Contributors   xi

1. Media and Risk: An Introduction   1
   Bishnupriya Ghosh and Bhaskar Sarkar

PART I
Historical Perspectives   **25**

2. Has Risk a History?   27
   Gaspar Mairal

3. Risk: The Origin of the Word in Medieval Commerce and Poetry   46
   Wolf Kittler

4. Insurance and the Language of Risk in Early Modern Political Thought   79
   Emily C. Nacol

5. Hazardous Individualism   91
   Jason Puskar

PART II
Expertise   **105**

6. Risk Media in Medicine: The Rise of the Metaclinical Health App Ecosystem   107
   Kirsten Ostherr

7. The Algorithm Dispositif: Risk and Automation in the Age of #datapolitik   118
   Davide Panagia

8 The Perils of Migration: Countervailing Mediations of Risk at the EU's
  Maritime Frontier 130
  Charles Heller and Lorenzo Pezzani

9 Mediating Expertise: Uncertain Risks of Electromagnetic Pollution 148
  Rahul Mukherjee

PART III
Times 163

10 Preparedness Documents After the Fact 165
   Lindsay Thomas

11 "Is there a Ghost in the Computer?" A Spectrology of Uncanny Risks 177
   Projit Bihari Mukharji

12 New Media At Risk, or When The Future Ain't What It Used To Be 191
   Timothy Murray

13 Into the Beyond: A Conversation with Michael Madsen 207
   Michael Madsen, Bishnupriya Ghosh, and Bhaskar Sarkar

PART IV
Scale 217

14 Chernobyl, Risk, and the Inter-Zone of the Anthropocene 219
   Adrian Ivakhiv

15 Risk, Law, and Media: A Case of Climate Change 232
   Ariel C. Nelson and Janet Walker

16 Media/*Meteōra* 259
   Greg Siegel

PART V
Virtuality 275

17 Red Dot Sight 277
   Colin Milburn and Rita Raley

18 The Safety 293
   Jordan Crandall

19 Tunnel Risk and the Mediation of Border Security Spectacle 303
   Juan Llamas-Rodriguez

20	Floating Architectures: Fantasises of Safety in Oceanic Riskscapes *Melody Jue*	315
21	Corrections to the First Draft of History *Raqs Media Collective*	328

PART VI
Affect   345

22	Social Media and the Social Question: Speculations on Risk Media Society *Joshua Neves*	347
23	Your Brain on Screens: Neuronal Risk and Media Addiction *Thomas Lamarre*	362
24	*Risk*'s Fraught Mediascape *Jeff Scheible*	377

PART VII
Legitimacy   389

25	'One little seed blowing in the wind': Risk Media in Trans-species Biogovernance *John Shiga*	391
26	Reflections on Risk, Media, and the Reasonable Animated by a Trial by Jury *Lawrence Cohen*	411
27	Cruising Risk, Surviving Desire *Daren Fowler*	425
28	Skin Out of the Game: Virtual Gambling in Novel Spaces *Alexander Mirowski and Edward Castronova*	438

PART VIII
Disciplinary Modulations   451

29	Risk as Aesthetic Virtue *Vinzenz Hediger*	453
30	Notes on Dissent and Risk *Ricardo Dominguez*	468
31	Trigger Warnings and the Disciplining of Cinema and Media Pedagogy *Lucas Hilderbrand*	472

32 "A Path So Twisted"—Staying Off the Straight and Narrow 487
    Jack Halberstam

33 The Risk of Tolerance: Feminist Killjoys, the Creative Humanities, and the
    Belligerent University 495
    Karen Redrobe

    Index *513*

FIGURES

3.1	Map of the Mediterranean	47
8.1	Analysis of March 29, 2011 Envisat satellite image showing the modeled position of the "left-to-die boat" (yellow diagonal hatch) and the nearby presence of several military vessels who did not intervene to rescue the migrants	134
8.2	Chain of events in the "left-to-die boat"	135
8.3	The frantic tangle of Automatic Identification System (AIS) vessel tracks in the Mediterranean following the April 18 shipwreck	137
8.4	Map comparing the operational zones of Italian Navy's Mare Nostrum and Frontex's Triton	138
8.5	Map representing the main nationalities of "illegal border crossers" for the central Mediterranean route	141
9.1	King interviewing Reynard in 1993 on CNN's *Larry King Live*	149
9.2	Dutt with Garg (a gesture of solidarity)	157
9.3	Garg outside her house l0oking at the cell tower	157
9.4	Cigarette in cell phone's antenna ad spoof	160
10.1	One of Powell's presentation slides documenting a taped conversation from "Remarks to the United Nations Security Council"	171
10.2	Picture of the documents discovered in "the homes of an Iraqi nuclear scientist" from "Remarks to the United Nations Security Council"	172
13.1	Photograph of viewers inhabiting the installation at the Louisiana Museum of Modern Art	208
13.2	Signs of danger: alien contact. (Screenshot)	210
13.3	Approach to Onkalo (*Into Eternity*, 2010)	210
14.1	Soviet propaganda poster. "The October Revolution announced a new era in human history! The great family of the October Revolution opened for the world the epoch of domesticating the cosmos!"	221
14.2	Video game enthusiast "stalkers" in the Zone	225
14.3	Prypiat, Ukraine, 2016	226
15.1	The Our Children's Trust website as media assemblage	233
15.2	Nelson Kanuk explaining the effects of ice sheets banging into his house	239
15.3	The eroding riverbank in Nelson Kanuk's community	240
15.4	Kanuk measuring land subsidence	240
16.1	Photo Credit: NASA	259

16.2	Photo Credit: NASA	260
16.3	Photo Credit: Wikimedia Commons	260
16.4	Photo Credit: NASA	267
17.1	Advertisement for the American 180, *Gun World*, February 1974	279
17.2	anon, image macro created at I Can Has Cheezburger?	285
17.3	"The Father, the Son, and the Holy Fonz," *Family Guy*, 2005	287
17.4	Banksy, *Armored Dove of Peace*, 2007	289
19.1a and b	*What Lies Beneath* foregrounds the labor of human agents even when promoting technologies. (Screengrabs)	309
19.2a and b	Camera position and framing convey the physical toll of shutting down tunnels, reinforcing the myth of exceptionality promoted by CBP agents	310
20.1	Vincent Callebaut Architectures, Lily Pad	320
20.2	Botanical City, Shimizu corporation	321
20.3	Wetropolis, sky view	325
22.1	Mark Leckey's 2010 *GreenScreenRefrigeratorAction* provocatively engages the intimacies of the Internet of Things	352
22.2	Stilled YouTube video of "Google Deep Dream Zoom: 'Inside an Artificial Brain,'" is one of hundreds of such visualizations uploaded by users	353
22.3	The Facebook scandal is defined by Mark Zuckerberg's congressional testimony rather than years of privacy breaches or the company's role in shaping new interface intimacies	357
23.1	The 2014 anime series *Ai Tenchi Muyō* duly includes the television animation advisory over its opening sequence: "For the sake of your health, when you watch TV anime, please try not to approach the screen, and keep the room well illuminated"	368
23.2	The 2015 anime series *Himouto! Umaru-chan* comically associates watching television up close in a darkened room with other excessive and addictive behaviors, such as junk food	368
24.1	Lady Gaga interviews Julian Assange in *Risk*	377
27.1	Player-controlled tongue licking gun-dick to full magazine from Robert Yang, *The Tearoom*, 2017, video game	428
27.2	The erotic aestheticization of risk in *Mens Room: Bakersfield Station*, directed by Joe Gage, Titan Media, 2004	432
27.3	The distancing glances and affects that blur the line between erotic caution and desperate fear from William E. Jones, *Tearoom*, 2007, film	433
28.1a	The original appearance of the AK-47 weapon	441
28.1b	An unobtrusive skin for the AK-47	441
28.1c	An ostentatious skin for the AK-47	442
33.1	"Toleration" (Herman Kirn, 1883, Wissahickon Valley Park)	496

CONTRIBUTORS

Edward Castronova is Professor of Media at Indiana University. His scholarly work specializes in games, technology, and society.

Lawrence Cohen is Professor of Anthropology and of South Asia Studies at the University of California, Berkeley. His current research is on Indian national biometric identification and security and what happens when a nation becomes a database. Prior research in urban India has focused on dementia and the postcolonial sociology of the family; on sexual pleasure and violence in the constitution of a provincial, "backward," ethos; and on the molecular structure of globalization emergent in the ethics of transplant surgery.

Jordan Crandall is a media artist, writer, and performer. He is Professor of Visual Arts at University of California, San Diego. He was recently awarded the Vilém Flusser Theory Award for outstanding theory and research-based digital arts practice, given by the Transmediale in Berlin in collaboration with the Vilém Flusser Archive of the University of Arts, Berlin. He is currently completing a new project called AUTOCADE, a work of speculative literary fiction, driven by philosophical and technoscientific inquiry, that envisions the effects of artificial intelligence and automotive robotics on social and cultural life.

Ricardo Dominguez is a co-founder of The Electronic Disturbance Theater (EDT), a group who developed virtual sit-in technologies in solidarity with the Zapatistas communities in Chiapas, Mexico, in 1998. In 2007 Electronic Disturbance Theater 2.0 with Brett Stalbaum, Micha Cardenas, Amy Sara Carroll, Elle Mehrmand, and Ricardo created the Transborder Immigrant Tool (a GPS cell phone safety net tool for crossing the Mexico/U.S. border). The project was under investigation by the U.S. Congress in 2009–2010 and was reviewed by on Fox News as a gesture that potentially "dissolved" the U.S. border with its poetry, http://tbt.tome.press/

Daren Fowler is a doctoral student in the School of Film, Media & Theatre at Georgia State University. Their research examines the aesthetic politics of queer media and activism, with particular focus on the continuing AIDS crisis and its visual investment in the body and materialism.

Bishnupriya Ghosh teaches postcolonial theory and global media studies at the University of California, Santa Barbara. She has published on literary and popular cultures, global media and environmental studies in journals such as *Screen*, *Public Culture*, *The Journal of Postcolonial Studies*, *Representations*, *boundary 2*, and *Bioscope*. Much of her scholarly work, including the two books, *When Borne Across: Literary Cosmopolitics in the Contemporary Indian Novel* (Rutgers UP, 2004) and *Global Icons: Apertures to the Popular* (Duke UP, 2011), investigates contemporary cultures of globalization. She is currently working on a comparative study of epidemic media in the United States, South Africa, and India (*The Virus Touch: Living with Epidemics*).

Jack Halberstam is Professor of Gender Studies and English at Columbia University. Halberstam is the author of six books including: *Skin Shows: Gothic Horror and the Technology of Monsters* (Duke UP, 1995), *Female Masculinity* (Duke UP, 1998), *In A Queer Time and Place* (NYU Press, 2005), *The Queer Art of Failure* (Duke UP, 2011) and *Gaga Feminism: Sex, Gender, and the End of Normal* (Beacon Press, 2012) and, most recently, a short book titled *Trans*: A Quick and Quirky Account of Gender Variance* (U of California P, 2018). Places Journal awarded Halberstam its Arcus/Places Prize in 2018 for innovative public scholarship on the relationship between gender, sexuality and the built environment. Halberstam is currently working on several projects including a book titled *Wild Thing: Queer Theory after Nature* on queer anarchy, performance and protest culture the intersections between animality, the human and the environment.

Vinzenz Hediger is Professor of cinema studies at Goethe University Frankfurt, where he directs the Graduate Research Training Program "Configurations of film." He is a Principal Investigator at the Cluster of Excellence "Normative Orders" and a member of the Mainz Academy of Sciences and Literature. His publications include "Films That Work. Industrial Film and the Productivity of Media" (AUP 2009, with Patrick Vonderau) and "Nostalgia for the Coming Attraction. American Movie Trailers and the Culture of Film Consumption" (forthcoming from Columbia UP).

Charles Heller is a researcher and filmmaker whose work has a long-standing focus on the politics of migration. In 2015, he completed a Ph.D. in Research Architecture at Goldsmiths, University of London, focusing on the politics of mobility across the Mediterranean Sea. He is currently a postdoctoral fellow at the Graduate Institute, in Geneva, where is conducts research supported by the Swiss National Fund (SNF).

Lucas Hilderbrand is Professor of film and media studies, visual studies, and gender and sexuality studies at the University of California, Irvine and author of the books *Inherent Vice: Bootleg Histories of Videotape and Copyright* and *Paris Is Burning* (Queer Film Classics series). His essays have also appeared in *Camera Obscura*, *GLQ*, *Film Quarterly*, *Journal of the History of Sexuality*, *Jump Cut*, and other venues.

Adrian Ivakhiv is the Steven Rubenstein Professor for Environment and Natural Resources, a Professor of Environmental Thought and Culture, and Coordinator of the EcoCultureLab at the University of Vermont. His research and teaching are focused at the intersections of ecology, culture, religion, media, and philosophy. His books include *Shadowing the Anthropocene: Eco-Realism for Turbulent Times* (Punctum, 2018), *Ecologies of the Moving Image: Cinema, Affect, Nature* (Wilfrid Laurier UP, 2013), and *Claiming Sacred Ground: Pilgrims and Politics at Glastonbury and Sedona* (Indiana UP, 2001). He is a fellow of the Gund Institute for Environment and of the Rachel Carson Center for Environment and Society, and a former president of the Environmental Studies Association of Canada. He blogs at Immanence: EcoCulture, GeoPhilosophy, MediaPolitics (blog.uvm.edu/immanence).

Melody Jue is Assistant Professor of English at UC Santa Barbara. She has published articles in *Grey Room*, *Women's Studies Quarterly*, *Animations*, *Humanities Circle*, and *Green Planets: Ecology and*

Science Fiction. Drawing on the experience of becoming a scuba diver, her monograph *Wild Blue Media: Thinking Through Seawater* (forthcoming with Duke Press) develops a theory of mediation specific to the ocean environment.

Wolf Kittler is Professor in the Department of Germanic, Slavic, and Semitic Studies, and in the Comparative Literature Program at the University of California, Santa Barbara. He has taught at the universities of Erlangen-Nürnberg, Freiburg im Breisgau, Konstanz, Munich, and Cornell. His publications include books on Franz Kafka and Heinrich von Kleist, and articles on literature, philosophy, the history of science, techniques, law, warfare, and media from antiquity to the present. His area of expertise is cultural history.

Thomas Lamarre teaches in East Asian Studies and Communications Studies at McGill University. He is author of numerous publications on the history of media, thought, and material culture, with projects ranging from the communication networks of ninth century Japan (*Uncovering Heian Japan*), to silent cinema and the global imaginary (*Shadows on the Screen*), animation technologies (*The Anime Machine*) and television and new media (*The Anime Ecology: A Genealogy of Television, Animation, and Game Media*, 2018).

Juan Llamas-Rodriguez is Assistant Professor of Transnational Media in the School of Arts, Technology, and Emerging Communication at the University of Texas at Dallas. His research focuses on media infrastructures, creative labor, border studies, and Latin American film and television. His work has been published in *Feminist Media Histories*, *Film Quarterly*, *Jump Cut*, and the *Journal of Cinema and Media Studies*.

Michael Madsen is a Copenhagen-based conceptual artist and documentary filmmaker. He is the director of several documentaries such as award-winning film, *To Damascus: A Film on Interpretation* (2005), *Into Eternity: A Film for the Future* (2010), and *The Visit: An Alien Encounter* (2015), and the founder and artistic director of art projects such as "Sound Gallery" (a 900-square meter diffusion system underneath the Town Hall Square, Copenhagen, 1996–1998) and "The Search" (an interactive multimedia installation at the Louisiana Museum's 2018 Moon Exhibit). The latter is part of Madsen's new documentary project, *The Search*, which will feature understandings of Earth life as a crew leaves our damaged planet in search of a new one.

Gaspar Mairal is Professor of Social Anthropology at the University of Saragossa (Spain). He received a doctorate in Social Anthropology in 1990 from the university of Madrid. He has researched and published extensively on historical anthropology, collective memory, water studies and risk, both in English and Spanish. His most recent work is consecrated to the cultural history of risk.

Colin Milburn is Gary Snyder Chair in Science and the Humanities and Professor of English, Science and Technology Studies, and Cinema and Digital Media at the University of California, Davis. He is the author of *Nanovision: Engineering the Future* (Duke UP, 2008), *Mondo Nano: Fun and Games in the World of Digital Matter* (Duke UP, 2015), and *Respawn: Gamers, Hackers, and Technogenic Life* (Duke UP, 2018).

Alexander Mirowski is a doctoral candidate at Indiana University's School of Informatics, Computing, and Engineering. He is a historian of technology and in particular of games; he is interested in game communities, the governance structures in which they are situated, and games as platforms for cultural, economic, and political activity.

Projit Bihari Mukharji is Associate Professor at the University of Pennsylvania. A historian by training, his work explores the histories of science, medicine, and technology in modern South Asia. He is particularly interested in the ways in which the subaltern, the everyday, and the lowbrow haunt the histories of science and technology. Mukharji is the author of *Doctoring Traditions: Ayurveda, Small Technologies and Braided Sciences* (Chicago, 2016) and *Nationalizing the Body: The Medical Market, Print and Daktari Medicine* (London, 2009).

Rahul Mukherjee is Assistant Professor of Television and New Media Studies at University of Pennsylvania. His research and teaching interests are in environmental media and global media. He is presently completing a book project titled *Radiant Infrastructures* regarding environmental implications of radiation-emitting technologies. He has been part of two collaborative projects, one concerned with circulation of local music videos through memory cards in India and the other dealing with ICT (platform jumping) practices in Zambia.

Timothy Murray is Director of the Cornell Council for the Arts, Curator of the Rose Goldsen Archive of New Media Art, and Professor of Comparative Literature and English at Cornell University. His books include *Medium Philosophicum* (2019), *Xu Bing's Background Story* (2016), *Digital Baroque* (U of Minnesota P, 2008), *Zonas de Contacto* (Educal 1999), *Drama Trauma* (Routledge, 1997), Mimesis, Masochism & Mime (Michigan UP, 1997), *Like a Film* (Routledge, 1993).

Emily C. Nacol is Assistant Professor of Political Theory at the University of Toronto. She specializes in the history of early modern political thought and political economy, with a focus on the problems of risk and uncertainty in seventeenth- and eighteenth-century British political and economic writing. Her first book, *An Age of Risk: Politics and Economy in Early Modern Britain* was published in 2016 by Princeton UP.

Ariel C. Nelson is a Staff Attorney at the National Consumer Law Center focusing on credit and background reporting and criminal justice debt issues. She is a contributing author to NCLC's *Fair Credit Reporting*. Previously, she litigated environmental and administrative law cases as a staff attorney/clinical teaching fellow at Georgetown University Law Center. She also served as a law clerk to the Honorable Judge David O. Carter of the U.S. District Court for the Central District of California and to the Honorable Judge Dorothy W. Nelson of the U.S. Court of Appeals for the Ninth Circuit. She holds a BA from the University of California, Berkeley and a JD from Harvard Law School.

Joshua Neves is Assistant Professor and Canada Research Chair at Concordia University (Montréal). His research focuses on global and digital media, cultural and political theory, and problems of development and legitimacy. He is the co-editor (with Bhaskar Sarkar) of *Asian Video Cultures: in the Penumbra of the Global* (Duke UP, 2017), and author of *Faking Globalization: Beijing's Media Urbanism and the Chimera of Legitimacy* (Duke UP, forthcoming).

Kirsten Ostherr is a media scholar and health researcher at Rice University in Houston, Texas. She is founder and director of the Medical Futures Lab, author of *Cinematic Prophylaxis* (Duke, 2005) and *Medical Visions* (Oxford, 2013), and editor of *Applied Media Studies* (Routledge, 2018). Her research on trust and privacy in digital health ecosystems has been featured in *Slate*, the *Washington Post*, *Big Data & Society*, and *Catalyst*.

Davide Panagia is Professor of Political Science at UCLA. He is a political theorist with multidisciplinary interests including contemporary political theory and the history of political thought, aesthetics, media studies, cultural theory, literary studies, and cinema. His work specializes on the relationship between aesthetics and politics. His most recent book publications include *Rancière's Sentiments* (Duke UP, 2018), *Ten Theses for an Aesthetics of Politics* (Minnesota UP, Forerunners, 2016) and *Impressions of Hume: Cinematic Thinking and the Politics of Discontinuity* (Rowman and Littlefield, 2013). His current research project, #datapolitik, is a study of police powers in the age of cybernetics.

Lorenzo Pezzani is an architect and researcher. In 2015, he completed a Ph.D. in Research Architecture at Goldsmiths, University of London, where he is currently Lecturer and leads the MA studio in Forensic Architecture. His work deals with the spatial politics and visual cultures of migration, with a particular focus on the geography of the ocean. In 2011, Heller and Pezzani co-founded Forensic Oceanography, a collaborative project that has developed innovative methodologies to document the conditions that lead to migrants' deaths at sea. They also launched the WatchTheMed platform, a tool enabling nongovernmental actors to exercise a critical right to look at the EU's maritime frontier. They have authored a number of human rights reports, including "Report on the Left-to-Die Boat" (2012); "Death by Rescue" (2016); "Blaming the Rescuers" (2017) and "Mare Clausum," all of which have had a major impact both within the fields of migration and border studies, nongovernmental politics and the public sphere. Based on their research, they have lectured internationally and generated a number of theoretically innovative articles published in several edited volumes and in a number of international journals such as *Cultural Studies, Postcolonial Studies*, the *Revue Européenne des Migrations Internationales, ACME, Spheres*, Global Media and Communication, Philosophy of Photography, *New Geographies* and the *Harvard Design Magazine*. Their videos "Liquid Traces" (2014), "Death by Rescue" (2016), "The Crime of Rescue," and "Mare Clausum" (2018) have been exhibited internationally, including at the HKW, the Venice Biennale, the MACBA and the MOMA and the ICA.

Jason Puskar is Associate Professor of English at the University of Wisconsin-Milwaukee, and the Associate Dean of the Graduate School. He works on American literature and culture from the late nineteenth to the early twentieth centuries, with emphasis on media studies, economics, and business history, and the history of science and technology. He is the author of *Accident Society: Fiction, Collectivity, and the Production of Chance* (Stanford, 2012), and is currently completing a book on the cultural history of binary switching before computers.

Rita Raley researches and teaches in the Department of English at the University of California, Santa Barbara. She has published on subjects ranging from tactical media, machine translation, and electronic literature to Global English and universal alphabets.

Raqs Media Collective (1992, Delhi, India) is a contemporary arts practice that follows its self-declared imperative of "kinetic contemplation" to produce a trajectory that is restless in its forms and exacting in its procedures. Raqs articulates an intimately lived relationship with time in all its tenses through anticipation, conjecture, entanglement, and excavation. Conjuring figures of cognitive and sensory acuteness, Raqs' work reconfigures perceptional fields, alters the terms of somatic co-presence and demands that everyone looks at what they take for granted, anew.

Karen Redrobe is the Elliot and Roslyn Jaffe Professor of Cinema and Modern Media and the Director of the Wolf Humanities Center at the University of Pennsylvania. She is the author of *Vanishing Women: Magic, Film and Feminism* and *Crash: Cinema and the Politics of Speed and Stasis* (Duke UP, 2010), and editor of *Animating Film Theory* (Duke UP, 2014). She is working on a new book, *Undead: Animation and the Contemporary Art of War*, and a co-edited collection, *Deep Mediations*, with Jeffrey Scheible.

Contributors

Bhaskar Sarkar, Associate Professor of Film and Media, UC Santa Barbara, is the author of *Mourning the Nation: Indian Cinema in the Wake of Partition* (Duke UP, 2009). He has published a wide range of articles in edited collections like *World Cinemas, Transnational Perspectives* (Routledge, 2008), *International Communication* (Sage Benchmarks in Communication, 2012), and *Figurations in Indian Film* (Palgrave Macmillan, 2013), as well as in journals such as *Rethinking History, positions: asia-critique, Cultural Dynamics,* and *Transnational Cinemas*. He is also co-editor of *Documentary Testimonies: Global Archives of Suffering* (Routledge, 2009), *Asian Video Cultures: In the Penumbra of the Global* (Duke UP, 2017)), and two journal special issues, "The Subaltern and the Popular," *Journal of Postcolonial Studies* (2005) and "Indian Documentary Studies," *BioScope* (2012). He is currently working on two monographs: *Cosmoplastics: Bollywood's Global Gesture*, and *Pirate Humanities*.

Jeff Scheible teaches in the Film Studies Department at King's College London. His work is interdisciplinary and comparative, theorizing and historicizing contemporary media and visual culture. His first book, *Digital Shift: The Cultural Logic of Punctuation* (University of Minnesota Press, 2015), received the Susanne K. Langer Award from the Media Ecology Association. His essays have appeared in *Film Quarterly, American Literature, Canadian Journal of Film Studies,* and more. He is currently editing a collection with Karen Redrobe titled *Deep Mediations*.

John Shiga is an Associate Professor and Chair of the School of Professional Communication at Ryerson University in Toronto. He has published work on intellectual property, the history of digital audio, acoustic memory and interspecies communication. He is currently working on a cultural history of sonar in which he explores the role of acoustic sensing in the militarization, industrialization and commodification of ocean sound.

Greg Siegel is Associate Professor of Film and Media Studies at the University of California, Santa Barbara. He is the author of *Forensic Media: Reconstructing Accidents in Accelerated Modernity* (Duke UP). His essays have appeared in *Cabinet, Communication and Critical/Cultural Studies, Discourse, Grey Room,* and the anthologies *Rethinking Disney: Private Control, Public Dimensions* (Wesleyan UP) and *Television: The Critical View*, 7th ed. (Oxford UP).

Lindsay Thomas is Assistant Professor of English at the University of Miami. Her current book project, *Training for Catastrophe: National Security and the Use of Fiction After 9/11* (forthcoming), argues the national security state uses fiction to train people to accept catastrophe as part of everyday life. She is also co-director of WhatEvery1Says, a computational text analysis project exploring the shape of contemporary public discourse on the humanities.

Janet Walker is Professor of Film and Media Studies at the University of California, Santa Barbara, where she teaches and researches in the areas of documentary film; feminist, trauma, and memory studies; and media and environment. Her books include *Trauma Cinema: Documenting Incest and the Holocaust* (UC Press, 2005), *Documentary Testimonies: Global Archives of Suffering* (with Bhaskar Sarkar, Routledge, 2010) and, most recently, *Sustainable Media: Critical Approaches to Media and Environment* (with Nicole Starosielski, Routledge, 2016). She is the co-recipient of a 2017–2019 Mellon Sawyer Seminar award for a project entitled "Energy Justice in Global Perspective" and is writing a book on media mapping and critical environmental justice.

1
MEDIA AND RISK
An Introduction

Bishnupriya Ghosh and Bhaskar Sarkar

The impetus for this volume came from our participation in two research residencies: "Speculative Globalities" (Irvine, spring 2009) and "Risk@Humanities" (Ithaca, 2012–2013).[1] During our stint at Cornell, two visiting senior scholars from two distinct disciplinary formations caught our attention with their presentations on risks associated with the HIV–AIDS crisis: William Leiss et al.'s, one of the foremost experts on risk communication and policy, and Michael Warner, known for his seminal work on queer theory and the public sphere. Prior to their visits, we read Leiss' (2008) co-authored study of the Canadian policy debates around blood donation from MSM (Men Who have Sex With Men) groups, and Warner's (1995) controversial first-person piece in *The Village Voice* on negotiating risky sexual practices in the pre-antiretroviral era.[2] While both addressed individual and social entanglements, there were clear differences in the way they approached questions of moral responsibility and ethical obligations in handling risk. In many ways, these differences brought us to this project.

In the co-authored article, Leiss et al. considered alternative time-frames for MSM donor deferral (policyspeak centered on abstinence) to replace the then-current lifetime ban on blood donation from MSM. Should members of this community be allowed to donate blood, if they practiced abstinence for ten years, five years, or even one year? Leiss understood the lifetime moratorium, which made blood bank shortages worse, as hailing back to the panic around contaminated supplies during the early years of the HIV–AIDS crisis. However, one year seemed too short a period to get rid of a "residual risk" even after "various safeguards for blood [were] applied" (58). In his estimation, the ten- or five-year deferrals seemed safe enough.[3] In the lively discussion that followed, the points of disagreement reflected a generation gap around making abstinence a policy instrument, and called attention to divergent assumptions about the constitution of risky social groups, the veracity of survey-driven evidence, and problems of "knowing" intimate sexual practices. Seminar participants also questioned the moral imagination underlying such studies, a normalizing imagination which shadows biopolitical governmentality. When pressed, Leiss insisted on the transparency of communication between reasonable and responsible folks, especially in the context of a social crisis. This liberal investment in the well-informed and committed citizen–subject, an idealization of post-enlightenment political theory, keeps at bay the uncertainties of behavior, disclosure, data collection, and knowledge.

A few months later, we had the opportunity to discuss with Michael Warner his reflections on negotiating desire, especially risky sexual behavior, in the midst of an epidemic. Writing in 1995, Warner poses the question—"how much risk is acceptable?"—from the perspective of a gay male subject. This essentially trans-individual perspective, which embodies the daily heartbreaks and struggles of living in the shadow of death, troubles all normative imaginations with their proscriptions and prescriptions, including melancholic attempts from within the gay community at denouncing promiscuity, closing down bathhouses, and extolling abstinence. Warner presents his own risky behavior to underscore the impossibility of fully regulating lived sexual practices—those everyday becomings whose value to individuals is not calculable. His point is that the standard discourses of risky behavior cannot address non-normative subjectivities, their self-evaluations, or their ethical self-relations.

Both Warner and Leiss engage similar questions of ethical risk management. For Leiss, the MSM donor deferral policy represents not the contest between right and wrong, but the contest between two rights: the right to receive uncontaminated blood squares off against the right to be free of unreasonable discrimination. When risk is low, what amount of precaution is reasonable and what amount of risk is acceptable? Leiss' notion of community is predicated on the marking out of MSM groups as the source of risk for the collective. Warner writes from within the eye of the storm, as it were: as a gay male subject figuring out what remains of a life whose self-defining practices threaten its continuity, he implodes the identitarian collectivity to embrace the singularity of experience. It is the singular that turns quantification into an infeasible undertaking. And yet, so much of social scientific research on risk, even when it attends to the qualitative dimensions, slips into a will to quantify. Policy studies that work with survey data about population groups to make biopolitical interventions cannot avoid the aggregation of non-normative singularities into an isolable particularity. This instrumentalizing reduction delivers the normative as a manageable target. Warner foregrounds indeterminacy as a constitutive element of risky phenomena: that is, the persistence of the uncertain in the social despite all attempts at rational governance.

Our discussion of these public engagements with risk by two reputed scholars brings to the fore several dimensions of isolating, measuring, assessing, and managing risk: in this case, the erasure of difference and the occlusion of uncertainty. Crucially, it also highlights the processes of mediation which shape the seemingly value-neutral survey and the highly personal testimonial. While attentive to variation, the first continues to bulldoze difference within the social group in order to establish its core identity, a reduction that then allows for stereotyping and pathologizing "a lifestyle." This erasure of difference typifies risk management that disavows radical uncertainties. In contrast, the testimonial historicizes the subject in terms of its concrete locations and practices, insisting on the non-normative nature of subjectivity. Lifestyles are inimitably different, even within a avowedly localized context such as New York's West Village. In the first case, mediation abstracts and isolates particularities, producing a standardization of even non-normative population types. In the second, any such standardization is ruled out. The testimonial form refuses the censorship of communities in crisis by recording the episodic oscillation of carnal expressions caught between the protection of the self and the intractability, even resilience, of desire.

The essays in this volume collectively explore the conjunction of risk and media/mediation. Everyday life is replete with instances of such a conjunction. For many contemporary subjects, the day begins with a highly communicative morning run: lightweight wearable devices register and record vital statistics such as heartbeat and blood pressure levels. The body appears in discrete quantified fragments, generating information streams that track latent damage. One may live for years with imperfect lungs or increased blood pressure, but when one receives and processes embodied signals of those states, they become legible as risk. A large market for digital health apps offers techno-moderns all kinds of options for reading and interpreting these signals. Personalized biosensors, connectivity infrastructures, and data storage facilities organize the dispersed labor of biomedical self-tracking within a brisk economy, presenting new risks. Beyond the consumerist care of the self, "self-quant" communities build and organize platforms, protocols, and technologies in order to modulate risk at the most intimate scales.[4] Every now and then, a crisis erupts in the techno-economic complex of personalized risk mediation to explode all illusions of individualized control over the quantified self. In a recent privacy scandal, Facebook agreed to shut down its

Onavo VPN because the Onavo app had mined user health data from smartphones, including screenshots of Amazon purchase histories. Apple instantly blocked the Facebook Research app from its App store, and Facebook removed the app from the Google Play Store.[5] The furor once more drew attention to the data mining that aggregates and sells consumer information. For consumers, techno-economic integration enables connectivity as well as vulnerability; again and again, the individual user suddenly becomes aware of her statistical capture as population aggregate. These intricate functions of the human–machinic apparatus—from reading embodied signals to sensing technological vulnerability—highlight the centrality of *mediation* to risk. This is what the present volume is about.

Why Media and Risk?

Risk is the qualitative perception of possible harm. Conceptions of danger or peril prevail across cultures and hearken to ancient times. With the expansion of speculative trade and commerce in the early modern period, risk began to circulate primarily in its economic sense: potential harm rendered as financial loss. With the emergence of probabilistic knowledge in the eighteenth century and its institutionalization in the nineteenth, risk became a bona fide calculative rationality: specialized instruments facilitated quantitative analyses of the possibility and extent of future loss. Whether a venture was high risk or low risk depended not on probabilities alone but on the expected returns.[6] The twentieth century was the century of risk management and speculation: the basis for the rapid expansion of stock markets and venture capital, such enterprises were so successful that a hubris of control took hold of capitalist societies. The triumph of increasingly sophisticated financial instruments mobilized riskier ventures, capitalizing on risk for bigger gains and aggravating the very volatility that they sought to mitigate. Just as better mountain climbing gears encourage more dangerous expeditions, so too, living with and seeking out intensified risks became a driving force for the twentieth-century zeitgeist. As Joseph Schumpeter noted, capitalism expands through innovations, through the "creative destruction" of extant systems. The sprawling speculative economies of the late twentieth century led to spectacular growth; yet the unbridled opportunism of these decades, feeding off pyramid and Ponzi schemes and runaway derivatives based on formulas that nobody quite understood, led to greater instabilities. In the twenty-first century, new uncertainties arising from increased market volatilities, technological instabilities, and environmental damage posed challenges to the efficacies of the risk calculus. As modern fictions of stable advancement and progress began to unravel, and discourses of precarity, catastrophe, and doomsday proliferated, uncertainty became intrinsic to contemporary life. This profound shift was as cognitive as it was affective.

As this rough and ready account indicates, mediated risk has become inimical to our lives. Whether it dwells in recursive events such as credit card hacks, weather warnings, or travel alerts, risk media channel and intensify perceptions. By risk media, we mean all the forms and processes that arise from the conjunction of risk and media/mediation. On the one hand, risk media constitute and communicate risk: without mediation, there are no risk perceptions. On the other, media and mediation often introduce new dangers or intensify already existing risks.

This mutual determination of risk and media is one of the core features of modern societies that compel an acute awareness of living with risk. The sociologist Ulrich Beck (1986) argues that the modalities of living with risk have become habitual to modern industrial societies; on the other hand, the constant incidence and identification of risks prime modern consciousness to find risk cues everywhere.[7] A society in which the processes of modernization have proliferated and intensified risks comes to see itself over time as a "risk society." But how are the risks registered—how does that society "see itself" as such? And what kind of agency arises from such self-recognition? This is where risk media come in. The most common example of risk media are statistical data and their visual representations. In rendering and vivifying inert numbers into compelling patterns, even feelings, risk media galvanize preparedness. People prepare to safeguard themselves according to their exigencies and capacities: middle-class homeowners stock up on batteries, canned food, and water; the 1 percent invest in exploratory plans for interplanetary settlements as planetary damage accrues; and the undocumented consolidate fugitive networks in the absence of social security dispensations. One of Beck's main insights concerns present risks of which we remain unaware. Invisible pollutants, he argues, seep into skin, membrane, and organ, but such infiltration remains latent until the lungs throw a spasm or the skin breaks out in rashes, until harm becomes palpable as symptom. When more "cases" emerge in a demographic field, the deepening sense of collective harm instigates public scrutiny, facilitating macro-level recognition of a risk pattern. The data collection and case studies that follow impel a *self-reflexive* impression of imminent danger. Mediation is constitutive of this intensified risk perception.

Media/Mediation

Risk is virtual, an outcome always on the horizon. *We require mediation to render risk legible.* Risk perceptions depend on mediatized forms, from tables, bar diagrams, and graphs (generated via regression analyses) to color-coded emergency alerts (chromatic transcriptions of threat levels) to geospatial models (generated by live-tracking of winds, currents, moving landmass, etc.). Risk mobilizes media technologies and infrastructures: expanding air traffic control grids or sharing surveillance intel, for instance, seek to contain risks. And yet, such expansions and connections often exacerbate the spread of risks: leaked information or a localized glitch in air traffic control can turn into a massive catastrophe. Designed to mitigate, warn, and shield, these media fields of risk bring a sense of anxiety into daily life—the feeling of being caught in a grid, of constant vulnerability, of not knowing when and where a new threat will emerge. Mediation can therefore amplify and accentuate risk: think of swift-moving conspiracy theories, thickening gossip cultures, and the speedy virality of social media. Further, media technologies penetrate all aspects of planetary life so thoroughly at the current juncture that media environments become inherently risky. Whether it is the extractive technologies whose invasive probes transform the ocean floor; or the digital reengineering of genetic codes that render biological matter malleable; or indeed data mining and bot activity online that manipulate social relations, media, in recreating geological stratum, biological substrate, or social affiliations, also renders them more volatile. Mediation, then, indicates processes or events that are not reducible to media technologies or forms: it intervenes in extra-medial ontologies. As a creative process, rewriting genetic codes changes biological matter; equally creative are the collective micro-actions of sharing, tweeting, and annotating that turn the original record (such as the video of a brutal beheading or lynching) into a social force. These ontologies have ambiguous and complex impacts: the modified genetic codes promise great medical benefits, but they also have capacities for social harm (e.g., the dangers associated with eugenic experiments); likewise, a violent video may circulate as an extreme instance of social aggression *and* fuel copycat aspirations that transform what is portrayed in the video into a potential risk scenario for many. That is to say, risk communication remains a subset of risk mediation.

In recent years, theorists of media have focused on mediation not just as an epistemological event—in the sense of reflection, representation, or even figuration—but also as a process that transforms actual lived worlds. This has led them to interrogate some of the foundational dualisms of western philosophy: subject/object, ideal/material, human/nonhuman, natural/artificial, and so on. While such oppositions have traditionally provided the basis for media studies arguments about subjects making media, or media violence impacting subjects, or artificial intelligence taking over human consciousness, now they seem archaic. In the wake of digital media, genomics, and an intensifying environmental crisis, we have become hyper-aware of the interpenetration of the biological, the digital, and the geological. The interpenetration itself is nothing new: it is just that the new scientific insights and technological inventions call attention to entanglements of human–nonhuman and living–nonliving relations. For Sarah Kember and Johanna Zylinska (2014), the accelerated thoroughfare between information and flesh exemplify such entanglement. However, they remind us that humans and nonhumans have always co-emerged with technology; put differently, technologies are "media," dynamic substances with their own material properties, that enable the human lived worlds. The invention of fire or the wheel, for instance, irrevocably changed not just human lives but human–nonhuman relations. The same is true of the Internet. Mediation, then, is the process or event in which humans emerge with technology.

But before such new materialist invocations of mediation, there was the cultural materialist conceptualization of the term. In its most influential articulation, Raymond Williams (1985) already departs from the political valence of mediation as arbitration or indeed just the interaction of two opposing forces. Rather, he draws our attention to the materiality of the interaction that is "substantial," with "forms of its own" (72). Mediation is not a "neutral process of the interaction of separate forms, but an active process in which the form of the mediation alters the things mediated, or by its nature indicates their nature" (73). While the phrase "mediation alters the things mediated" seemingly suggests an ontological transformation, Williams goes on to characterize mediation as "an activity which directly expresses otherwise unexpressed social relations" (73). Hence, we might think of mediation as an epistemological category offering forms of what Fredric Jameson (1988) described as cognitive mapping. But as Richard Grusin (2015) points out, Williams holds on to a natural–social dualism so that mediation remains an intermediary to the nonhuman or natural world without becoming a "property of the nonhuman world itself" (137). Grusin argues that mediation never jettisons the epistemological role that was important to Williams. But beyond the epistemological, for Grusin, media and media technologies also operate "technically, bodily, and materially to generate and modulate individual and collective affective moods or structures of feeling" (125); that is, media refashion or translate individual experiences, relating or connecting them to each other. Grusin, then, returns us to the ontological paradigm of mediation which involves interactions between humans, *and* between human and nonhuman systems.

Taken together, the insights of Williams, Kember and Zylinska, and Grusin push toward a deeper understanding of mediation that is pertinent to thinking risk. Risk no doubt emerges in material contexts; and risk perceptions, whose established forms are epistemological, have ontological effects. But there are also those embodied risk perceptions that remain sensory, affective, or intuitive, skirting reflective and deliberative modes and occluding legibility. If these multiple levels of apprehension come into play for a risk to be recognized as such, then only a more capacious paradigm of mediation will do. In stressing knowing-without-knowing as a supplement of conscious perception, such a paradigm helps develop what remains recessed in Beck's articulation of the latency of risk. The latency arises as much from the possible incidence of harm in the future as from its multidimensional apprehension which complicate explicit formulations.

The present volume engages this expanded sense of risk mediation in 30 analytical and two creative pieces. The contributors amass a dazzling array of risk media: contracts, policy documents, legal decisions, patents, political tracts, theological doctrine, love poetry, novels, low-brow print media, digital apps, news across mediums, electronic health records, films, television shows, emergency indexes, cellphone footage, art installations, social media posts, blogs, websites, video art, painting, and dance. Our main goal is to articulate methods, approaches, and concepts with respect to different spheres in which risk surfaces.

Risk and Media Across Disciplines

Scholarship that takes up the conjugation of risk and media remains largely within well-etched disciplinary boundaries, be that expertise in specific kinds of risk (e.g., technological, biological, financial, or social) or expertise in specific media (e.g., mass print cultures, television, biomedia, digital media). The disciplines that have been most accomplished in conceptualizing the intersections of "risk" and of "media" across the typologies of risk fall within the social sciences: communications studies, social psychology, and sociology. The interdisciplinary studies of risk assessment, risk perceptions, risk behaviors, risk amplifications, risk mitigating policies, and risk communications have all been generative endeavors with substantial impact in the public sphere. Essays in the iconic collection *Mad Cows and Mother's Milk* (Leiss and Powell 1997), for instance, discuss the ripple effects of mass mediation that enabled 11 cases of bovine spongiform encephalopathy (commonly known as mad cow disease) to snowball into a transatlantic ban on British beef. Drawing on the social amplification of risk framework (SARF) that was developed in the late 1980s to study the dynamic social processes underlying risk perceptions, these essays marshall quantitative data to show how specific mass media reach large audiences.[8] Feelings are crucial in such analyses of fear cascades and emotional contagion: in *The Perception of Risk* (2000) and *The Feeling of Risk* (2010), social psychologist Paul Slovic presents psychometric calculations of risk to understand collective risk perceptions. Quantitative data and rhetorical analyses together produce risk as a collective experience; the subject is always in-the-aggregate, it always represents a social group.[9] The volume *The Risk Society and Beyond* (Adam et al. 2000), of which Beck is a co-editor, explores the challenges that risk poses for social theory; while some of the essays trace the evolution of Beck's ideas, others (notably the one by Scott Lash) tease out the analytical limitations of risk society, offering alternative frameworks for understanding risk's recalibration of the social. In its address of broad questions, this volume comes closest to ours, but the questions remain primarily occupied with social categories and domains; the mediality of risk media receives short shrift. Joost Van Loon's *Risk and Technological Culture* (2002) is a more sustained interrogation of new risk cultures within information societies, and plays close attention to the role of cybernetic media. But the book's subtitle, "Toward a Sociology of Virulence," indicates its focus on recognizably sociological phenomena (waste, epidemics, cyber-risks, and riots) that arise from new technological risks.

Within the critical humanities, the question of how risk and its management shape subjectivity and agency by inserting individuals and communities into biopolitical, financial, and technological regimes is of paramount importance. Scholars and artists interrogate how goals such as security, solvency, and the care of the self, which promise freedom or, more expediently, protection, effectively lead to a capture of the subject; in response, these thinkers explore possible modes of flight. Several essays in the volume *The Aesthetics of Risk* (2008), edited by John Welchman, examine the ways in which the modern subject "is caught up in an ever-expanding network of predictive and proactive stratagems for the management of risk" (9). Drawing attention to probability theories, "promiscuous alliances" with evidence-based fields such as "law, medicine, political statistics, and polling," the volume argues that we have become "hyper-actuarialized citizens" as "involuntary parties to the model-based predictive orchestration of the world events" (9). A primary impetus of the volume is to explore dissent and exit: how to escape the "hydra-headed nooses of fiscalized social control that snatch the administration of risk away from us" (9). Hence, the "aesthetics of risk" refers to critical explications of ensnarement in regimes of control as well as to speculative explorations of exit. As Welchman notes in his introduction, during the Romantic period, the economic well-being of the subject generated a sense of the "expressive" self that no institution could capture and discipline. The Romantic artist as dissident is the first among a series of moderns in this history of the arts. Since then, the performative dimension of risk-taking recurs as artistic practice. Refusing commercial incorporation, the historical avant-gardes, in particular, would stake their own dissident claims on the future. In these discussions, risk aesthetics emerge across walks of life: a creative forming, building, and making that courts danger in the name of art.

Moving beyond the "artists taking risk" perspective, recent scholarship has begun to examine the aesthetic dimensions of risk management. Scholars and artists like Nicholas De Genova (2017), Kelly Gates (2011), Derek Gregory (2011), Marcus DeSieno (2018), and Eyal Weizman (2017), among others, have examined the aesthetic–performative aspects of security whether at the national border or at work: the ubiquity of walls and barbed wire fences, cameras and searchlights, identity cards and biometric devices; or emergency drills, credit checks, and cybersecurity training. This analysis of security spectacles has its cognate in the gleeful detection of breaches and transgressions as well as the fantasies of border crossings: intellectual maneuvers that accept the persistence of uncertainty—indeed, that tap into uncertainty as a productive social force (da Costa and Philip 2008; Galloway and Thacker 2007; Sampson 2012; Serres 2007). In such approaches, living with uncertainty makes possible a broader set of agencies than risk control systems and their foreclosures would permit. Perhaps this intellectual drive—along with the historical conjuncture of 9/11, the financial crash of 2008–2009, and extreme climate patterns—explains why contemporary humanistic thought is preoccupied with crisis and precarity rather than with risk (Berlant 2011; Butler 2004; Nixon 2011). The etymology of crisis ("to decide" in Greek) points to a forking path scenario; the final outcomes are contingent upon decisions made at the crossroads. However, as Janet Roitman shows (2013), the very narrativization of crisis apportions blame in ways that deflect attention away from structural causes. Precarity refers to endemic vulnerability with no foreseeable end; the Latin etymology suggests abject dependence and supplication. And yet, as Guy Standing (2011) points out, the utterly marginalized and seemingly meaningless lives introduce new social risks, destabilizing established sociopolitical orders. In both situations, while the conditions are dire, the upshot remains open-ended. By contrast, popular imagination tends toward the language of the catastrophe: to think of the coming catastrophe is to eliminate risk, to accept it as *fait accompli*, to arrive at an apocalyptic finitude.

More thoughtful reflections move in two directions. First, critical approaches attribute systemic failures to a burgeoning crisis of capitalism, a system driven by the relentless need to expand and an increasingly unsustainable logic of extraction (Cooper 2008; Harvey 2006; Postone 2012). Among scholars more attentive to mediation, Richard Dienst (2011) argues that the financial imprudence necessary to shore up demand and support excess capacity leads to "bonded" existence: people everywhere are ensnared in debt relations that control and govern their lives. Benjamin Lee and Edward LiPuma (2004) show how opaque financial instruments such as derivatives, in seeking new speculative gains, orchestrate an instantaneous global market across all sectors, including food, clothing, and housing, thereby intensifying and globalizing risks. Second, there is the more affirmative search for uncharted, even unforeseen, potentialities (Casarino and Negri 2008; Haraway 2016; Milburn 2008). It is this affirmative gesture that gets taken up in its ample speculative force, and across a dizzying array of human endeavors, by the anonymous collective, an uncertain commons. In its manifesto *Speculate This!* (2013), written in the shadow of the global financial meltdown and in the midst of the Occupy movements worldwide, the group poses a more playful and open-ended "affirmative speculation" against forms of predatory speculation at work in real estate and financial markets. While affirmative speculation is more invested in exploring the fullness of possibilities without being circumscribed by narrow teleologies and short-term returns, the more opportunistic practices of "firmative speculation" seek to privatize the commons, capitalize on every prospect, and close off many future possibilities to develop the few pathways with the highest pecuniary yields. For example, social risk perceptions about race ghettos or elite enclaves mobilize speculative commercial projects working in cahoots with municipal governments, incorporating mechanisms of gentrification and segregation in the blueprints for urban development. However, a community's vital energies scuttle all such plans in terms of tactical claims to space, from the more established practices of squatting as challenges to property codes, to innovations like breakdancing and *parkour* asserting the irrepressible capacities of the "street" body.

The Routledge Companion to Media and Risk is in conversation with these multiple strands of scholarship and creative work. As is wont with such volumes, there are points of congruence with the extant literature as there are clear, and, hopefully generative, divergences and developments. The intent is threefold. First, to reflect on and elaborate the categories and assumptions that underwrite the discourses of media and risk. For when unthought, these elements frequently occlude processes of mediation. For instance, risk markers (such as biohazard insignia or signage marking nuclear waste sites) are often presumed to be universally legible across locations and times; but they are in fact culturally and historically determined. As Michael Madsen asks in *Into Eternity* (2010), his film about the nuclear waste storage facility in Onkalo, Finland, what signage might serve as adequate markers of a risk that persists over deep timescales—in this case, the half-life of radioactive matter? Second, to tease out the mediality of risk media that materializes risk patterns across various social domains. What we do not do is to turn media into mere evidence of risk; for risks do not simply pre-exist, but emerge through mediation. Nor do we organize the volume along risk typologies (environmental, financial, social, technological and so on): in focusing engagement with the social domain of risk's incidence, such typologies deflect attention away from the mediatic unfolding of risk. What we do is to distribute the chapters, each of which is a situated study of a particular type of risk, into sections that are organized according to categories that highlight (a) the contours of this sub-field (intellectual/institutional histories; pedagogical implications across disciplines) and (b) the parameters, processes, and stakes that comprise the riskiness of a risky event (time, scale, affect, virtuality, expertise, legality/legitimacy). Third, to consolidate risk media studies from a humanistic perspective, thus answering the question: what do the humanities have to offer to understanding risk?

Social science research tends to adopt positivist approaches and evidence-based analyses. Even when qualitative aspects are the being analyzed, researchers deploy sophisticated methodologies that approximate the qualitative with quantitative analytics (for instance, the proxy variables of econometric modeling). Not everything can be translated into quantitative data without doing serious violence to what is studied. Policy-oriented studies have an obligation to come up with concrete recommendations. With a view to pragmatic outcomes, risk perception/communication studies projects address rather specific and practical concerns arising in one domain; the bracketing of intersectional complexities appears neutral and objective, masking inevitable ideological operations. Piracy is dealt with as a legal issue, when it is primarily a social and cultural phenomenon precipitated by technological change; quarantine, always overdetermined by a broader logic of segregation and securitization, becomes purely a matter of public health security; terrorism, a complex political imagination involving not simply retribution but also a fight for justice, is reduced to a pure threat from an unjust enemy exterminable by any means (Sarkar 2016). In other words, risk researchers are beholden to positivist articulations that narrow down, abstract, and simplify a dynamic situation to its partial and, therefore, more manageable representation.

While generally unable to establish clear causalities or produce unambiguous conclusions, the frameworks and methodologies of the humanities allow for engagement with the contradictions, elisions, and excesses of the social field, so that one has a fuller, more nuanced understanding of what is at stake in a risky situation. In addition to seeking more complex answers, humanities research adopts a more critical–interpretive stance interrogating its analytical categories and questions; these meta-reflections often recalibrate the initial problematic, allowing other possible solutions to surface. Thus, while not good with short-term decision-making, the humanities enrich public policy debates with insights about "the big picture," including what is missed, overlooked, or willfully erased. In his rumination on agency in the Anthropocene, the historian Dipesh Chakrabarty (2009) questions the separation of human history from natural history. Climate change has brought into focus the natural "parametric conditions" that determine human action; the histories of acidifying oceans, of evaporating ozone layers, of melting glaciers reveal the human to be a geological agent that ultimately threatens its own existence. Chakrabarty's insight, that the historical critique of socialism or capitalism that has occupied historians thus far is simply not adequate to understanding current environmental crises, has helped shift the terms of the environmental debate.

In situations that seem dire—when a threat looms with inevitability, or when damage is irrevocable—and any intervention appears futile, philosophers, artists, and activists take positions and actions that involve risk. While dangerous and without immediate reward, these gestures take on significance at the performative level: they enact, mediatize, and explicate the social relations that constitute, control, and capitalize on risk, seeking to reframe the event, alter the terms of the debate, and shift public perception/opinion. A spectacular example comes from the annals of the Plachimada protests against the Coca-Cola factory in the early 2000s. The women householders of Plachimada, a village in the southern Indian state of Kerala, complained that the operations of the factory were contaminating groundwater and drying local wells. Morning after morning, they demonstrated before the factory gates with colorful but tellingly-empty plastic pots, even as legal battles raged in the courts with varying success. As Bishnupriya Ghosh (2010) notes, the quiet performativity of the quotidian plastic pot, now iconic of thirst and deprivation, countered Coke's mythos as the "refreshing drink for all seasons," inspiring national and global solidarities against the offending soft drink giant. Ultimately, the plant was permanently closed. Challenging power and the crushing logic of decline, such interventions pry open alternative futurities—in this case, the restoration of a water commons.

The social sciences have a hard time with uncertainty at both practical and philosophical levels. After all, the taming of uncertainty via the instruments of probability theory remains among the most spectacular successes of this epistemological domain. But this will to mitigate uncertainty comes at the cost of reducing it to manageable risk involving a finite set of possibilities. The humanities, in contrast, have always placed human affairs in relation to larger forces that escape calculation: whether that is a greater community, the unconscious, nature, chaos, or the divine, we cannot understand this force-field in strictly positivist terms. The big Other is incalculable in its effects. The humanistic disciplines have developed rich frameworks to understand how these powerful forces move, what forms they take, and why they induce intense fascination and fear. The engagement with this force-field amounts to a recognition of *radical uncertainty* and a willingness to live with it.

The core project of modernity was the institution of a rational subject whose disenchanted gaze brought uncertainty within the calculus of reason: the secular confronting divine enchantments, technologies controlling wild natures, states organizing their unruly populations into governable constituencies. However, subjects had to contend with moments of great upheaval in their lives, moments which in their unanticipated and unimagined experientiality induced shock, loss, and incomprehension.

In grappling with the incredulous question—"how could this happen to us?"—traumatized subjects indicate a failure to comprehend, let alone come to terms with the experience. Indeed, the experience is not really experienced fully until it can be assimilated into a coherent narrative: the subject requires mediation to overcome the latency of trauma. We might say that the temporality of trauma is the obverse of the temporality of risk. If the former is about the completion of an event that occurred in the past, the latter involves the anticipation of an event that will probably transpire in the future. Thus both trauma and risk displace the modern subject from the certitude of a linear, continuous, and teleological becoming. In their interpretive and speculative dimensions, the humanistic disciplines are more equipped to address these disruptions and detours just as they are able to engage philosophical/cosmological concerns that extend into indeterminacy.

The balance of this introduction seeks to bring out the interventions of the volume in two ways. First, instead of privileging separate risk domains (biological, social, economic, technological), we situate our contributors in relation to certain interdisciplinary vectors that arise from the extant literature on risk mediation. Second, we flesh out the organization of the book along categories that highlight the mediality of risk mediation.

Risk Histories

This volume opens with a section on the genealogies and etymologies of risk. Although the standard narrativization of risk histories leads to the emergence of probability as the mathematical revelation of the world's "inner springs," as Ian Hacking (1990) notes, the chapters in this section together refuse such a linear history. Risk as a conceptual category surfaces at different points in global history: one could pen its civilizational histories from the Arab world, from China, from Mediterranean shores, from the Americas. Ancient practices of divination, reading aleatory arrangements of signs to foretell futures, are the earliest speculative methods for encoding the future. Bones, stars, and stones, all become risk media and are read for what they forecast or forebode. So are playing cards, dice, and roulettes that parallel, and sometimes precede, the emergence of risk in maritime customs. Writing about one of the first etymological traces of risk (*rizk*, in Arabic, appears in 120 verses in the *Qu'ran*) in his essay, Gaspar Mairal notes that risk materializes as social custom as early as the seventh century AD.[10] Arab traders journeying across great deserts put their trust in Allah; it is only later that risk as "God's provision" would lose its positive valence in a process of secularization. Two legal traditions, the *qirad* (Arabic) and the *commenda* (Latin), would contour relations between merchant seafarers in southern Europe (Genoa, Pisa, Venice, Marseilles, and Barcelona) in the thirteenth century. Risk media such as contracts and notarial documents record the appearance of *risicum* in Latin. Entering this history of merchants, mariners, and notaries as they encoded dangers on the oceans, Wolf Kittler understands speculative encoding to take full contractual form when the center of power shifts from southern Europe to Great Britain in the seventeenth century. But well before that, the concept had unexpectedly seeped into other fields: for instance, thirteenth-century love poetry. Such permeations inspire tracking risk across incongruent imaginations, mediums, and social sectors; and in discrete objects such hoary traveler's tales, playing cards, or insurance contracts.

In the early modern period, a more continuous history of risk congeals around the global trade in people and goods. We know that trade ventures would pave the way for massive colonial systems that brought most parts of the world under European hegemony. As Anthony Giddens (1990) argues, European expansionism dis-embedded multiplicities of time (standardized in the meridian or the calendar) and money (standardizing exchange value, currency, trading rules), promoting a universal system at the expense of the pluriverse. Global interconnectedness generated a sense of control through economic and technological standardization as well as increasing vulnerabilities. Whether that was the outbreak of cholera in mid-nineteenth century London (traced to British soldiers returning from colonial India) or popular rebellion against European commodities (British tea chests flung into in the Boston harbor), the fallout from global interconnections called for a calculative judgment and new technologies of control. Giddens describes this ricochet between risk and uncertainty as the double-edged character of modernity. A postcolonial supplement would point out that there were no comparable risk contracts for the colonized communities that were exposed to great peril because of the systematic destruction of local practices, expertise, and institutions: the 1943 Bengal Famine is just one of many such instances of endangerment.

As the modern world transitioned from mercantilism to capitalism proper, risk became more important as a fulcrum of economic entrepreneurship. Modern banking systems (the earliest instances being British and Dutch) and global institutions for underwriting loans (such as the Lloyd's Coffee House in London) made economic speculation a global force. Emily C. Nacol, in her contribution to this volume, focuses on two tracts to trace the early dissemination of risk into public cultures: Daniel Defoe's *An Essay on Projects* (1696) and Adam Smith's *Wealth of Nations* (1776). While the former makes the case for small-scale social endeavors as morally proper economic activity, the latter argues for securing public confidence in the formation of joint-stock companies. Jason Puskar follows this cultural history to the nineteenth-century appearance of "hazardous individualism," an orientation involving excessive, even irrational, risk-taking. The figure of the hazardous individual, argues Puskar, adds a romantic edge to liberal capitalist subjectivity, complementing the period's normative ideal, the reasonable individual agent who would approach risky ventures armed with probabilistic calculation.

Probabilistic thought matured, notes Lorraine Daston (1995), by expanding its scope well beyond "simple games of chance," and folding in extant resources such as John Graunt's mortality tables (now the basis of regression analysis) (237–238). By the mid-nineteenth century, the mathematical tracing of future harm had become the new creed in controlling risks across various sectors. And yet, within these new sureties lurked the human capacity for unreason; and without, the as-yet-unimagined possibilities. By the beginning of the twentieth century, probabilistic frameworks reached their apogee in the economic and financial institutions of risk. As economist Frank Knight would argue in *Risk, Uncertainty and Profit* (1921), a classic in risk studies, runaway speculation and market volatilities called for informed judgment based on extensive statistical knowledge. And yet, writing in the decade when the certitudes of Newtonian mechanics gave way to quantum physics, and when the devastation of World War I destabilized global markets and called into question the entire project of modernity, Knight had to contend with intractable forms of uncertainty that the risk calculus could not domesticate. Risk discourse encoded futures in terms of known possible states and their likelihood of occurrence. However, it was not possible to pin the future down entirely in terms of a probability distribution among identifiable options; unimagined future states could always transpire. While offering such a radical conception of uncertainty, as an economist, Knight stressed the need for experienced professionals armed with specialized risk instruments and housed in financial institutions. Uncertainty was acknowledged and erased in one stroke.

Risk Institutions

Risk management professionals continue to claim that they have the expertise to navigate situations where risk inheres in not knowing which among a set of known states will materialize, as well as those unlikely situations where the full array of possible states are not known. Today, we recognize these professionals in the hedge fund managers, insurance agents, and actuaries who parcel out and bundle risk. With the advent of new information technologies that enhance data collection, aggregation, and storage, financial expertise is at once highly specialized and personalized, remote and dispersed, instantaneous and abstract. The complexities make this domain so obscure that no human agent can have full cognizance of all its aspects; as the idea of expertise is rendered increasingly vacuous, so the layperson's insecurities and anxieties escalate. Speculative bubbles and financial crashes since the early twentieth century are the crisis points that deepen the suspicion of financial expertise, compelling the humbling recognition of unknowable states beyond statistical forecasts. New risk media—new data, new algorithms, new enactments—keep us immersed in financial lifeworlds with the promise of a better grasp on futures, even as they intensify uncertainties through derivative contracts, accelerated transactions, and viral amplifications.

This conflictual experience of risk experts and institutions calls attention to one of the main features of Beck's risk society: the distrust of specialized expertise in social perceptions of risk. Cass Sunstein (2005) characterizes the split between lay and expert risk analyses as the difference of the populist from the technocratic. This is not to suggest that expert analysis is more technological; on the contrary. Risk devices from Geiger counters to health apps have equipped publics with handy risk instruments. What Sunstein argues is that expert risk analysis privileges the techniques of risk measurement and assessment, while the populist takes public injury as its *raison d'etre*. In the case of the 2008 financial crash, those who lost homes and pensions felt duped by the experts. Yet expertise remained indispensable: the experts who failed to avoid the meltdown continued to receive astronomical payoffs so that they could now fix the problem. The ensuing government bailout of the "too big to fail" banks still invokes great bitterness. This is but one instance of the populist sense of injury. The very experts and institutions on which people depend become embroiled in the widespread capitalization of risk—be that opportunistic leveraging in the derivatives market, underplaying industrial toxicity, or embezzling disaster relief resources. The conflict between expert and laypersons, argues Beck, is a core aspect of our techno-modern condition.

The problems of indeterminacy and unknowability produce anxiety, alarm, even panic. Throughout the twentieth century, that vulnerability has only escalated in the wake of massive and periodic technological failures. Paul Virilio (2007) argues that every technology—device or system—is an accident waiting to happen; he speculates that the catastrophe toward which we hurtle is the mirror image of the originary Big Bang, thereby evacuating all human responsibility from the scene of the accident. In contrast, Greg Siegel (2014) analyzes how forensic media forms such as airplane cockpit black boxes record and help reconstruct high-speed accidents, enabling experts to assign causes to establish responsibility. These reassuring narratives displace disruptive chance and unimaginable uncertainties with their causality, thereby allowing the formulation of safety protocols at the levels of technological design, manufacture, and use. Despite these retrospective inscriptions of catastrophic accidents as outcomes of avoidable failures, deep anxieties about the possibility of recurrence persist in the popular imagination. Indeed, Charles Perrow (1984) ascribes the technological accident to the increasing complexities built into large-scale technological systems: the accident becomes a "normal" event in the sense that no measure of safeguards can eliminate a residual chance of occurrence. In the case of the Three Mile accident of 1979, multiple failures in nuclear reactors generated the radiation leak; Chernobyl and Fukushima are subsequent notable instances of nuclear accidents. Such failures have inevitably led to inquiries that reveal the limits of both risk communication and scientific expertise. At Fukushima, the model for forecasting tsunami impacts on the nuclear power plant, based on time series data from a Chilean experience, failed to account for a tsunami of the mammoth proportion that actually hit the plant (Suzuki 2011). In the case of the Three Mile accident, one operator who had a hunch about the cascading effects of a single glitch across the system did not communicate it to others. Hidden from view, such lapses in calculation and communication aggravate public distrust; at other times, a chasm opens up when lay perceptions are brushed asides as irrational or unscientific. Risk communication scholars note that residents of the Love Canal neighborhood near Niagara Falls had complained of animal deaths and black ooze since the late 1950s (after Hooker Chemical had dumped toxic waste in the 1940s). Such rumors are also risk media, anecdotal evidence collated in popular epidemiology. The actual controversy broke as late as the 1970s, once mass media reportage (newspapers and television) reached larger audiences, provoking outcries for cleanup (Mazur 1998). In such accounts, mass media amplify risk perceptions and leverage particular instances into collective experience. In this volume, Rahul Mukherjee's chapter on electromagnetic (EMF) emissions "felt" by residents living close to cellphone towers in India explode into controversy in 2010. In transmitting their knowledge to large audiences and social networks, lay publics mediate expertise. Confronted by public outcries, the experts are called upon to explain themselves—to come clean about their assumptions and predictions, errors and oversights. Mukherjee's essay suggests electronic mediations and digital infrastructures have had transformative impacts on the interface of expert and lay knowledge. As the boundaries of the classical public sphere implode, individuals or social groups participate enthusiastically in the making of risk media. Greg Siegel's essay explores the increasing power of lay risk perceptions of the potential meteor collision of 2013. While NASA's Near Earth Object Hazard Program missed signs of danger, enthusiasts with personal devices captured the zooming superbolide, circulated the footage online, and turned the near miss into a mass experience of potential catastrophic risk. In her contribution, Kirsten Ostherr demonstrates how digital affordances enable new collaborations between the public and the experts. In her generative case study, clinicians and patients together formulate medical risk through the platform of the Electronic Medical Record (EMR). Changing media landscapes alter what comes to be understood as specialized knowledge and where that knowledge must reside.

Both medical and legal institutions are heavily implicated in the modalities of commercial and scientific risk. In many ways, the legal profession is a conduit for risk's incursions into quotidian lives. The question of who or what is responsible for harm becomes legal quagmire in both spectacular and everyday experiences of risk. It is not easy to establish causality in every case; not all "publics" have the clout to hold institutions, corporations, or states responsible; and the worries about the impact of newly set precedents on future liabilities derails risk attribution. In this collection, John Shiga's perusal of the patents, court decisions, and news of a Canadian case regarding agricultural biotechnologies (Monsanto versus a farmer who reused seeds) establishes the interface of legal and popular mediations of risk. As technological capacities to probe and extract at molecular scales expand, legal institutions face new challenges: how can states adjudicate new relations arising among human and nonhuman bodies in a transgenic landscape? Ariel C. Nelson and Janet Walker, in turn, address the legal difficulty of adjudicating future harm to coming generations based on the documentation of present environmental damage. They consider a media-rich initiative, Our Children's Trust, under whose auspices 21 young persons sued the Government of the United States for violation of public trust. The court's decision to let the case proceed, argue Nelson and Walker, is indicative of the strength of new collaborations between experts (a climate scientist was one of the plaintiffs) and lay publics that clearly mark who is most at risk from accelerating environmental damage.

The complications in the face-off between expert and lay risk knowledges find elaboration in other essays in the volume. Lawrence Cohen's ruminative exploration of his role as juror and notetaker ushers us into the courtroom spectacle of a mother who sued Abbott Laboratories for drug side effects inflicting her child. Deeply ambivalent about the legal instruction to assess the reasonableness of the mother's risk perceptions, Cohen questions the assumptions behind the process of risk responsibilization. Lucas Hilderbrand and Karen Redrobe's essays track risk perceptions in university settings. Whereas Hilderbrand considers pedagogic risks for disciplines such as film and media studies in the crucible of the classroom, Redrobe focuses on humanities cultural work at risk in context of the "belligerent university" that is increasingly reliant on military funding for research. In a more personal vein, Ricardo Dominguez pauses on high-risk conjunctures throughout his career as an academic to question the myth of the university as a safe space for free thought and action. Recurring throughout the volume are similar reflexive gestures, some more explicit than others, assessing risks in academic life and practice; one might also discern a direct lineage of activist art from Dominguez (at the U.S.–Mexico border) to Heller and Pezzani (in the Mediterranean), this volume).

Risk Socialities

Criticizing the individuation of risk and the consequent assigning of blame, anthropologist Mary Douglas (1992) situates risk as a cultural–political project that organizes the social field. Underlying the risk calculus is moral judgment that separates irrational risk-taking behaviors from prudent rational choice. Predicated on structural inequities, social differentiations inform which behaviors must be checked, who becomes a scapegoat, and where blame is placed. These differentiations emerged early in the history of risk, back when the standardization of probability entered the legal domain. As probabilistic instruments underwrote legal contracts covering aleatory contexts, insurance practices that hedged against risk in socially productive ventures were considered legitimate, in opposition to gambling and other unproductive, addictive vices that courted risk. Tracing "contract law" in the eighteenth century, Pat O'Malley argues that probabilistic risk became a moral affair when creative speculation with "reasonable foreseeability" was carefully distinguished from ruinous speculation (2003, 231). Gaming wagers, which exemplified the latter, invited regulatory legislation such as the English Gaming Act of 1744; whereas insurance wagers were legalized because of their foundations in calculative rationality.

As Michel Foucault's work on social normativities and repressions suggests, legislative measures instilling a norm—an ideal reasonable commerce defined in opposition to an idle wild speculation—tend to spawn brisk illegal business and illicit pleasures. Alexander Mirowski and Edward Castronova's contribution to this volume focuses on skin gambling to convey the complexities of gaming wagers and their legalities. A mode of buying and selling the outer layers that style online game players (guns, shirts, boots, hats) from secondary trading sites, skin gambling generates shadow revenue streams that are not sanctioned by the original game designers. These online merchandise are risk media that spring up elsewhere when a trading site is closed, their itinerant illicitness producing pleasure—a renegade creative rush fueled by regulation. A second essay on videogames as virtual risk environments explores the erotic charge of heavily policed sexual activity. Looking back at police raids on gay sex in public spaces, Daren Fowler considers cruising in gameplay premised on "high-risk behaviors." When a player starts having sex with a stranger after assessing the scene (a park, a toilet, or tearoom), the possibility that it might be a policeman could be as much an enticement as a deterrent: risk drives allure. This immersion in risk-as-pleasure derives its force from the systematic regulation of sexuality that Foucault examines in his *oeuvre* on disciplinary power.[11] The "irrational subject," the social scapegoat, straddles the domain of the illicit: the game is legitimate, a consumer commodity, but the desire, articulated against imposed norm, is explicitly queer.

Other essays in the collection complicate the history of what constitutes cultural dissent against the processes of normalization. Jack Halberstam looks at the culture of humorous repartee and insult that was once a staple in queer socialities, but that now comes under rigorous analysis; such modes of wit are neither tenable nor "normal" in the present recalibration of queer with trans★ communities. Halberstam's reading of two films as queer media history underscores the role of media industries in the production of social risk that is then challenged and negotiated in the larger public culture. Vinzenz Hediger makes a similar move in his historical analysis of artistic risk-taking and its complex relations to both art and global media markets. What is articulated against the commodity form accrues another kind of value: aesthetic virtue. Both Halberstam and Hediger demonstrate the instability of social risk over time: old acceptances become impossible speech, brave deviations from formulaic media production consolidate status and reputation. Both track the performativity of high-risk ventures, individual and collective. Also attentive to the cultural–political dimensions of risk media, Jeff Scheible takes us to an encounter between Lady Gaga and Julian Assange in a sequence of Laura Poitras' *Risk* (2016). Assange, iconic of the political consequences of too much information but also accused of sexual predation, confronts the affective force of Lady Gaga's questions. In the context of the #MeToo disclosures, the encounter proves to be as uncomfortable for the spectators as it is for the actors. Media are inherently risky, as we know from the infamous leakiness of the Internet; they generate potentialities (such as spilled secrets) which threaten not only state but also public, and even personal, security.

It is not just the disciplinary apparatus that is at stake in the production of social risk. Risk emerges also in the apparatuses of security that measure and regulate current circulations of information, goods, and people. Risk analyses parse big data to separate high risk (the infected, the elderly, the young, the racially-marked, the foreign) from low risk (usually, propertied and productive citizens) population groups, producing targets for protection and containment. On the basis of such demographic parceling, states adopt a broad-based paradigm of securitization against all manner of harm, from terrorist threats to microbial infractions. In her contribution to this volume, Lindsay Thomas examines the U.S. government's preparedness programs in which imagined containment addresses *all* threats (terrorism, microbial contagion, food insecurities), giving rise to what Andrew Lakoff and Stephen Collier call "vital systems preparedness."[12] Scenario building for military games places high social risks in a relatively near future; one must always invest in security, for "they" are always coming. Calculations give way to fiction, to virtual futures in which risks escalate. Crucial to security regimes are new and emergent technologies of surveillance that track and visualize dangers. Charles Heller and Lorenzo Pezanni's "counter-risk analysis" of the surveillance by Frontex (the European Border and Coast Guard Agency), tracking refugee boats in the Mediterranean, reveals how some boats in distress are caught on radar but allowed to capsize. This looking away at maritime borders—an instance of what Foucault describes as letting (some) die to make (others) live[13]—epitomizes the high social costs of security. Juan Llamas-Rodriguez also examines border security spectacles, focusing on drug-trafficking at the U.S.–Mexico border. As the physical infrastructure and medium for illicit circulations, the narco-tunnels produce capital while undermining the territorial sovereignty of the United States. Their flagrant illegitimacy galvanizes the mediation of tunnel security across various platforms: as narco films and television shows, artistic interventions, even border patrol videos. Across these essays, risk media infiltrate bodies, goods, and geophysical spaces in the name of public security—and simultaneously register their irrepressible fecundities.

Crucial to the operations of the security paradigm, the same publics who are being protected are also constantly subjected to surveillance in what Davide Panagia names the #datapolitik. Exploring the implications of the "track and trace" regimes of control for contemporary political ontologies in his chapter, Panagia argues that algorithmic power now organizes, i.e., mediates, all human action. Colin Milburn and Rita Raley follow a similar logic in their essay on "red dot sight," the optical mechanism in firearms that tracks shooting targets. The "red dot" focalizes movement, suturing the firearm user to an anticipated but as yet not fully known target: whether the target is a threat becomes immaterial, all that matters is the precision with which one hits it. As a risk technology, the red dot ontologizes the injury to come, makes it practically inevitable; simultaneously, it legitimizes killing via a discourse of technical efficiency. In his chapter, Tim Murray examines the informatic pull of futurity in three new media art works in which the artists playfully rewire the technological control of bodies and movements. As installations, the works induce new reflexivity about our dreamlike integration with machines. Together, these discussions of new technologies that control movements and regulate spatial sense-perceptions of objects establish the constitutive force of risk media environments: they are embedded in us, even as they embed us in them. Far from the domain of institutional risk, the risk media are now in our heads, in our muscles and viscera, under our skin. Structuring human perception and behavior, they contour what we might name risk worlds.

Risk Worlds

Risk media's impact on human perception is widely studied across disciplines from cognitive psychology to behavioral economics. Notable among these studies is the previously mentioned social amplification of risk framework (SARF), focused on processes that transform particular risks into collective experiences. The Decision Research Group's psychometric "cognitive maps" of risk attitudes and perceptions assemble and aggregate multivariate data to analyze subjective processes underlying risk perceptions: for instance, researchers track how people respond to specific "imagery" (general icons such as biohazard signage or specific ones such as oil-soaked pelicans) and "terms" (such "toxic," "poisonous," "hazardous," "deadly") associated with specific hazards in order to understand the emotional life of risk (Pidgeon 2003). Scholars such as Cass Sunstein zero in on the mechanics of emotional contagion in their work on the ripple effects and fear cascades structuring collective risk perception. In this scholarship, risk perceptions are always subjective—full of biases and orientations—even as risk analytics appear neutral and objective. While qualitative research methodologies analyze a range of subjective responses to received visual and linguistic indices (such as the iconic mushroom cloud), the analysis limits possible variations to a range of pre-given interpretations. Humanistic inquiries, too, carry out rhetorical analyses of subjective responses, but they attend to what is commonly comprehensible *and* what flies under the radar or is, at best, apprehensible. Interpretive frameworks drawn from fields such as psychoanalysis, narratology, and semiotics facilitate investigations of what does not fit (the trace, the aberration, the uncanny) as well as what fits too readily (habits, reflexes, pat reactions). Silences and ellipses, stutters and repetitions, gestures and ticks: all indices of the unconscious or of embodied cognitive capacities through which perceptions of past or coming trauma emerge.

A common stake across humanistic inquiries is the formation of the subject. Where the social sciences model recognizable social behaviors, humanistic interpretations also theorize the inaccessible spaces of the mind and body that are just as crucial to the subject's emergence. Milburn and Raley's essay underscores the phantasmatic dimension of the red dot: the technology derives its force from the desire for total efficiency through human–machinic action. Integrated into the weapon and neurologically conditioned to inflict injury, the biotechnical subject inhabits perceptual worlds with risks that are sensible but not fully comprehensible. The red dot example entails what affect theorists define as pre-personal spatial and sensory intensities: your lungs throw a spasm when a shadow crosses a dark alley because the form jogs an embodied memory that has settled into nerves and muscles. Such intensities are "infra," they are not quite visible. Nor are they conducive to generalization: singular subjects will respond differently to the most commonly understood risk signals. As Thomas Lamarre explains in his contribution to this volume, neuroscientific research on the impact of media usage on the brain repeatedly points to the difficulty of aggregation across media users. Ripple events such as Japan's "Pokémon Incident" of 1997, when a number of children fell ill from watching one television episode, do not yield sufficient data on why certain groups are more at risk than others. Brains are singular in their formation; subjective responses, arising from the embodied mind, cannot be understood in the aggregate. Even as subjects share common risk environments, every individual inhabits a singular risk world.

To elaborate: media are environments in which risks emerge. At one level, media are biotechnical and geospatial, structuring all human responses to danger; at another, media are historical and situated in specific locations. Whether it is watching too much television, or following the red dot, or jumping out of the way when one hears a screech of brakes, the social habitus of risk frames the subject's relation to media technologies. These encounters with possible harm—how the cues are received, what reactions they elicit—depend on both social frames and individual wirings. What, then, is the nature of the risk world that each subject inhabits? "Worlds," as we know, are dwelling places as deeply geophysical as they are social, and each subject occupies a specific configuration—here, a singular risk world. The layered configuration of a risk world, while rather tangible, is likely to elude full consciousness. All the same, these intensities of palpable risk feed into the shared risk environments, catalyzing collective formulations that we understand to be socially legible risk perceptions. People who live in toxic wastelands often speak of "knowing" it in their bones before they come to a shared recognition. They read the signals from nature—dead animals, withered plants, noxious fumes—that have not yet congealed as anticipatory warnings in collective understanding.

In this volume, Adrian Ivakhiv's essay on the radiation event of Chernobyl explores the interacting layers—a natural region (the forested area of north-central Polissa), a territory (the Ukrainian Republic), a system (the Soviet industrial complex)—that come together as a risk landscape. Chernobyl boggles the mind: Ivakhiv introduces us to the manifold risk media that this uncontainable hyper-event inspires, and that together seek apprehension of its material parameters and deep timescales. In a similar move, Michael Madsen places us in the deep timescales of radiation exposure. His speculative documentary, *Into Eternity* (2010), presents an audio-vision of invisible potentialities: sounds of dripping water in a dark granite cave make haptic the possibility of waste that leaks into body and bone. The medium of film stretches in this encounter with radical uncertainty: we are left with recordings of risk landscapes that supplement the visual with phenomenological cues—a layered soundtrack, a deliberately haptic camera, and a narration inviting speculation. Beginning with this evocative work, our interview with Madsen explores his media musings on possible encounters with the radically unknown. Such encounters pose fundamental questions about negotiations with the other, lay perceptions versus expert knowledge, and the possibility of risk mediations that are legible across space and time.

Notwithstanding the singularity of each individual risk world, shaped in the confrontation of the biological with the technological, risk worlds are also nested within social, political, and economic matrices. This location within the social field determines a risk world's relative riskiness: as we are reminded every day that, because of their specific entanglements, some subjects of risk are more vulnerable than others. Some buy tony property within gated communities, supplementing it with insurances and other protections; they enjoy all the security. Having little recourse to such safeguards, large populations keep on struggling in high-risk areas—violent neighborhoods, low-lying terrain threatened by sea-level rise, or the fringes of toxic waste sites. It is an ugly story, all the more disconcerting in its familiarity. The social dissonance of risk worlds imbues risk experiences with differing temporalities. In some risk worlds, the threats are still anticipatory. In others, the catastrophe is here, and the scramble for survival has begun. In still others, calamities of the past that portended shared futures were discounted as isolated natural disasters affecting communities of little world historical significance. Current work on climate refugees documents devastations of the past, legible only now as signs of a larger catastrophe already in the making: Amitav Ghosh (2016) writes eloquently about the many storms and seascape changes across the Bangladesh deltas in the 1970s and 1980s as early warnings of climate change. The poor who lost their homes, drifted and migrated, were never counted as climate refugees. Accounts of such extreme privation "elsewhere" now arrives as a two-fold shock: as news of the suffering of others, and as the shape of a proximate future for those who are relatively secure in the present. Melody Jue's chapter in this volume calls attention to the contradictions in risk mitigation plans for sinking islands, arising from the incongruous risk apprehensions of planners and island inhabitants. Large architectural firms offer futuristic models of "floating islands" designed to replace sinking land masses, replacement sliding into real estate upgrade in a striking instantiation of what Naomi Klein (2007) has called "disaster capitalism." Jue focuses on the shocking estrangement that affected inhabitants experience from encountering playful island futures while living out a catastrophe.

In their visual essay, "Corrections to the First Draft of History," Raqs Media Collective turns this shock of estrangement into an aesthetic strategy. The cultural form they invoke is the reading primer: while the content is simple and straightforward, it is still an enigma to the child reader. For Raqs, the relation between what we know for certain and what we do not know is similar to the silences and sounds that accompany the written text. The closing frames feature ink sketches of familiar objects—a pocket watch, a sundial, a donkey (or is it a mule?)—on the pages of a newspaper carrying data from India's financial markets, as if the sketched images are "corrections" to the stock and fund valuations from the world of speculative finance. In the South Asian context, the donkey invokes a host of associations: beast of burden, dumb, obstinate, loud, and so on. Its unheralded appearance on the market pages, like the arrival of an unexpected guest, defamiliarizes the humdrum fluctuations of stocks and shares: shifting the terms of interpretation, it complicates meaning, challenging our ability to know. Does the donkey index the Indian country bumpkin's infantile simplemindedness that blocks a cosmopolitan worldliness? Or the traditional Indian's blind adherence to archaic customs and values even as market logics infiltrate every aspect of life? Or, perhaps, the plebeian Indian's obduracy in the face of rapid global transformations? Or does it point to something altogether different? Just as we cannot be sure that it is not a mule, we cannot pin down the precise labor of signification that this beast of burden performs. Nor can we be sure of the meaning/intervention of the larger Raqs piece, except that its performative mediation of risk/uncertainty makes us experience instability, indeterminacy, and unknowability.

A theme that recurs throughout our mapping of the terrain of risk mediation has to do with the double-edged nature of connectivity and speed, security and surveillance, propinquity and access. This ambiguity generates a deep anxiety: that which enables also renders vulnerable. But this introductory emplotment would remain incomplete without an account of the pivotal role that digital infrastructures have assumed in worlding the present. As media theorists note, the materiality of infrastructures becomes manifest mostly at moments of disruption: we become aware of communication satellites or Internet cables when connections fail, when there are glitches in the system. Since digital technologies are fragile and unstable, the risk of breakdown is non-trivial: everyday operations require a certain level of working knowledge—minimally, the ability to troubleshoot, and ideally, the capacity for minor repairs. And thus, riskiness and vulnerability begin to shape aspirations for digital expertise: from the basic rewiring and repurposing of gadgets that shore up unsanctioned piratical practices to the more ambitious pursuit of skills with an eye on the high-tech job market. Writing about contemporary middle-class Indian aspirations in his contribution to this volume, Projit Bihari Mukharji analyzes the proliferating "computer ghost stories" in low-brow literary publications, avidly read by daily commuters on trains coming in to metropolitan areas. Personal computers and handheld smart devices in modest middle-class and lower middle-class environs are virtual portals to "the world," but they also plunge users into a sea of trouble—bugs and viruses, weak connections and loose wires, slow speeds and cable faults. Within the new popular genre, these technological roadblocks get articulated with middle-class aspirations in the figure of the computer ghost. As cultural figurations of blocked messages, lost connections, and frozen screens, not to mention slow commuter time, everyday exhaustion, and the humble environs that the would-be techno-moderns strive to leave behind, the ghosts index the untimeliness of lived experiences in relation to the promises of a high-tech, high-speed, sparkling-clean digital future.

With people becoming more adroit at navigating the protocols and modalities of digital platforms, lives are lived out more and more online. While social media and online gaming platforms spawn new participatory cultures, they also expose users to all manners of risk, from data theft to cyberbullying. In his chapter, Joshua Neves reflects on anxiety as the major affect arising from inhabiting social media risk worlds; in fact, people are now diagnosed with Social Media Anxiety Disorder (SMAD). The affective, personal risk is not all that there is to it, for social media can increase social risks by entrenching anti-sociality. Contra social media's celebrated contribution to social movements (such as the Arab Spring), Neves argues that social media concourse can intensify segregation as users interact, out of habit or nudged by algorithms, with those most like them. "Homophily," a term invoked to explain social segregation in the 1950s, becomes useful once again to understand the isolated and anonymous lives of social media users living in virtual gated communities. This loss of control over one's social media existence, and the simultaneous illusion of free individual agency which masks that loss, together present a conundrum that is at the heart of Jordan Crandall's dystopian short story, "The Safety." Set in a near future when the only legal options for cars are the self-driving models, Crandall satirizes a totalizing technocracy in terms of its drive to bring all human variation and imperfection under punitive autocratic control. We are left with fantastical worlds shorn of all things aleatory, of every random variation, of every whiff of chaos—worlds so seemingly predictable that they appear without vitality and steeped in incalculable loss. Sometimes playful, sometimes ominous, an unreasonably reasonable future knocks at the door.

★ ★ ★

Beyond the introduction, the *Routledge Companion to Media and Risk* is divided into eight sections. The first section, which signposts a few salient moments in the evolution of risk mediation, and the last, which dwells on the place of risk media in disciplinary and institutional settings, provide reflexive scaffoldings—where it all comes from, and where it can go—for the field that the volume seeks to shape and consolidate. These two sections bookend the other six, each organized around an overarching concept that pinpoints and explicates one constitutive aspect of risk mediation. More to the point, these six concepts together foreground the explicitly medial aspects—i.e., the *mediality*—of risk mediation. Our wager is that organizing the volume around concepts that embody the parametric, processual, and modal aspects of risk mediation (time, scale, virtuality, and affect), or that refer back to some of the institutions and norms that ground risk mediation as social practice (expertise and legitimacy), helps to keep mediality at the center of the collection's collaborative project. The eight sections are as follows:

Historical Perspectives: The concept of risk has multiple genealogies that have developed along uneven etymological itineraries, in diverse social and institutional settings, and via evolving media forms with distinct technological substrates. The essays track these histories along desert caravans from the seventh century onward (Mairal), in medieval commerce and poetry (Kittler), in early modern political thought (Nacol), and in nineteenth-century cultures of individualism (Puskar). As a whole, the section frames the volume's contributions in terms of historical perspectives that complicate standard accounts of risk's cultural and conceptual origins, broadening the geographies of risk's emergence, deepening the timelines of risk's evolution, and proliferating the media objects that ontologize risk.

Expertise: Encounters with risk give rise to competing perceptions in which formal, institutional expertise is often at odds with ground-level intuitive or tacit knowledge; in classic studies of risk societies, risk frequently arises in the knowledge gap between expert and lay understandings. The essays by Mukherjee, Heller and Pezanni, Ostherr, and Panagia variously track the techniques and apparatuses that comprise the mediality of risk expertise—radiation detectors, surveillance, electronic medical records, algorithmic cultures and big data. If these assemblages of expertise shape and control bodies, movements, and activities, they also provoke myriad negotiations on the part of the governed around questions of competence, data mining, political intent, and accountability. Whereas traditional risk discourses foreground dispassionate scientific objectivity as the basis for expertise, our contributors show how profoundly interested and contentious—i.e., political—expertise is.

Times: As danger that is currently imperceptible or anticipated in the future, risk is inherently a temporal projection. Generating a need for security that recalibrates the present, risk presents a range of future scenarios, some more livable than others. In this preoccupation with futurity, the essays in this section all turn to time, examining how the temporal aspects of risk are rendered via the medial properties of state documents, low-brow literature, digital art installations, and speculative documentary enactments. Mediations of risk take on complex temporal configurations: looped feedback between different moments in time, layered experiences of time, or catastrophic ruptures. The contributors interrogate how preparedness regimes evacuate the present in the name of securing against future damage (Thomas); examine how ghost stories provoke the shock of the uncanny to situate readers within the untimely globalities of our contemporaneity (Mukharji); demonstrate how new media art installations scuttle the biopolitical teleologies of military–industrial technologies through their tactical rewiring (Murray); and explore how the documentary form (Madsen) might project forward into deep timescales such as the half-life of radioactive waste or deal with temporal ruptures caused by startling eventualities (such as alien visitation, or abandoning a damaged planet).

Scale: Scaling between levels is intrinsic to the ontologies of risk; certain risks emerge from the mutual imprinting of the global and local, the expansion of the molecular to the planetary, or the folding of the microbial, the human, and the geological into each other. Media technologies and infrastructures get implicated in such operations of scaling: sometimes performing an epistemological function (e.g., amplifying local fears, making them relevant at a planetary level), at other times introducing new danger via the ontological capacities of digital mediation (e.g., a viral electronic worm inducing financial havoc). The essays examine the intersecting and nested risk landscapes of a multi-scalar event unfolding over time (Iakhiv); the difficulties of translation (across conceptual frameworks as well as across material forms) in moving between rights-based human-centric systems (courts, legal dispensations) and environmental futures (geological damage affecting coming generations) (Nelson and Walker); the harnessing of a singular risk event as the basis for a more general and pervasive intervention involving the institutions of research, security, and surveillance (Siegel)—a harnessing that is enabled by a risk "complex" arising from the intersection of scientific investigation, popular reception, and the digital circulation of the event.

Virtuality: As a key aspect of risk, the virtual highlights the anticipatory and imaginary or derivative status of the coming harm. Risk is imaginary not because it is not real, but because living with risk entails preparing for a state yet to come—one that is logically assessed and understood via probabilistic calculation or felt through intuitive perceptions. Risk can also be derivative not because it is unoriginal or fake, but because it arises as a second-order possibility, an offshoot of an original event; in this sense, risk inheres in the unpredictability surrounding subsidiary outcomes, and maybe amplified by attempts to capitalize on uncertainty and to make it more productive. In its speculative capacity, risk's virtuality helps us flesh out a range of possibilities for what is not yet fully known but is nevertheless a part of the coming reality. In facilitating opportunistic actions based on tentative intimations of the future, the virtuality of risk becomes a condition for the performative materialization of simulated states. The critical essays together reflect on risk's constitutive role in the ambiguities of reality. Whether it is the red dot that motivates—in the process of ensuring—the efficient elimination of a virtual target (Milburn and Raley); the security spectacle that exaggerates discrete border infractions to justify the vast security apparatus (Llamas-Rodriguez); or the architectural designs that conjure playful island futures in the face of ongoing, traumatic sea-level rise (Jue), risk mediations are part virtual (participating in future states) and part actual (building the present in context of those possibilities). Mobilizing the vacillations that risk introduces into planning, interpretation, and evaluation, the two creative pieces in this section—a dystopian sci-fi short story (Crandall) and a visual essay (Raqs Media Collective)—defamiliarize commonly recognized forms (the real, as we know it), allowing us to access the unthought assumptions and buried implications of everyday habit. In bringing us out of the normative sense of the real, virtuality queers our relationship to it.

Affect: Despite the will to rational management of partially predictable future states, risk perceptions rely heavily on affective and sensory faculties. Marshaling pre-personal intensities, affect arises as spatial, embodied responses to the muscular, neurological, and sensory cognition of cues such as movements, textures, temperatures, and vibrations. Think of a burning smell or noxious gas that promptly spurs a sense of corporeal danger; or the anxieties female gamers face as participants in massively multiplayer online games. Foiling all presumptions of an objective calculus, the persistence of the affective returns subjects to unsettling risk worlds. The anxieties and non-optimal behaviors that issue from this embeddedness are not signs of failure; rather, they point to a vulnerability that is intrinsic to existence. Putting to question the facile bundling of risk feelings as unreason, affect as an attribute of risk mediation enables a different kind of knowledge—a conditioned response, an intuition. Focusing on the subjective and singular, two of the essays show how media technologies concretize risk in affective terms, and at the medial registers of the visual, audible, haptic, and kinesthetic (Lamarre, Scheible). A third contribution foregrounds affects arising from circulation in social media networks, and from the human-machine interface (Neves). While appreciative of the sociality enabled by these platforms, we also worry about the spurious algorithmically-nudged click-bait communities hounded by gas-lighting and trolling activities.

Legitimacy: Technological innovations are the conditions for progress; but in opening up new frontiers, such developments introduce unanticipated challenges for governance. As the objects, institutions, and practices constituting the purview of Law change, the inadequacy of extant laws and the turgid pace of legal reform generates confusion. In perhaps the most salient example of such creative disruptions, the seismic shifts induced by the affordances of digital media technologies have produced new uncertainties for the media industries. The discourses of piracy, in demonizing the emerging practices of recording, copying, sampling, and dissemination as threats to the viability of this sector, effectively shift the focus of conversation from the need for a new paradigm of intellectual property to the management of the risks posed by piratical practices. Similarly, in the case of pharmaceuticals, apprehensions about the dangers to public health from spurious knockoffs displace conversations about the greedy over-reach of medical patents. Two of the contributors in this section (Shiga and Cohen) directly address the failings of the Law in its encounter with new transgenic substances (resilient transgenic seeds, leased rather than sold to farmers for one-time use, bring intellectual property rights into conflict with farmers' expectations about their rights) and with faith-based interpretations of medical risk associated with a new drug (interpretations that kept the plaintiff from going to court for many years, and put to question the logic behind her lawsuit). In both court cases, it is the legal codes and their underlying assumptions that come under pressure: as if, in the course of legal mediations, the risks to property/rights and to patient consumers have been transferred onto the Law. Fowler, Mirowski and Castronova explore the unsanctioned productivities of regulatory structures in generating illicit pleasure and value. Focusing on the interactivity of videogames, these essays examine the crucial role of risk in propelling desire and motivating gamers' moves—whether in the context of illegal trading online or of criminalized public sex.

Disciplinary Modulations: The contributions in the concluding section address head on the implications of interrogating risk mediation from critical humanities perspectives in various institutional and social settings. In a sense, the propensity for reflexivity that threads through this volume, but remains recessed for the most part, is made explicit in this section, and then elaborated with respect to cultures of creative–intellectual production. Three of the essays reflect on the risk media conjunction in the context of academic life and the university: the impact of the institutionalization of trigger warnings on classroom pedagogy (Hilderbrand); the military's regulation of the university's operations via research funding (Redrobe); and academics' embrace of intellectual dissent as a risky mode of interrogating, and seeking transformation of, the university's missions, its power matrix, and its place in the world (Dominguez). The two remaining essays analyze risk-taking practices in commercial domains that are nevertheless subject to high aesthetic and political expectations. As Hediger shows, aesthetic risk-taking itself becomes a strategy for augmenting value (a yoking inspired by the logic of market renewal, and frequently reduced to gimmick or sensationalism). Halberstam, for her part, focuses on risky humor and jocularity in queer public cultures that, in disavowing seriousness and respectability in their regulatory functions, once forged a mode of engagement that was creative, improvisational, and open. But now, a generational shift has changed that queer public sphere into an acutely self-policed space of rigid categories and acrimonious exchanges.

This volume takes as its point of departure the gambit that interdisciplinary conversations on risk and media generate new questions, perspectives, frameworks, and analytical tools for not only risk studies and media studies, but also for social and cultural theories. We offer the following 32 pieces in this spirit of productive collaboration.

Acknowledgments

This volume owes its evolution to multiple communities of collaborators and interlocutors. Our deepest gratitude goes to our fellow dreamers in the Speculative Globalities residency research group (2009) at the University of California Humanities Research Institute, Irvine: Colin Milburn, Rita Raley, Cesare Casarino, Geeta Patel, Sudipta Sen, and Aimee Bahng have contributed to the framing of this collection in more ways than they know. The Institute's Director, David Theo Goldberg, was an early and enthusiastic supporter, funding several meetings beyond the residency. While at Irvine, Kaushik Sunder Rajan, Bill Maurer, Kavita Philip, Jim Tobias, Adriene Jenik, Elinor Kaufmann, and Lucas Hilderbrand helped shape our thoughts. At UC Santa Barbara, the College of Letters and Sciences, the Critical Issues in America Program, the Center for Nanotechnology and Society, the Interdisciplinary Humanities Center, the Department of English, the Department of Film and Media Studies, the Orfalea Center for Global and International Studies, and Arts & Lectures made it possible to continue the conversation. For our UCSB chapter, we'd like to thank Rita Raley, Greg Siegel, Rahul Mukherjee, Janet Walker, Wolf Kittler, Charles Wolfe, Alan Liu, Barbara Herr Harthorn, Chris Newfield, Giovanni Vigna, Constance Penley, Mark Juergensmeyer, Victor Faessel, Anne Cong-Huyen, Lindsay Thomas, Roman Baratiak, and Kathy Murray. The presenters/interlocutors at the Risk Media conference (2012) and the workshops as part of the year-long series "Speculative Futures: Risk, Uncertainty, and Security"

(2011–2012) deserve a special shout out for helping us muddle through the vast interdisciplinary scholarship on risk: Michael Madsen, Priscilla Wald, Karen Beckman, Peter van c. Wyck, Kathleen Woodward, Andrew Lakoff, Thomas Streeter, Marieke de Goede, and Helen Nissenbaum. Finally, the contours of this volume began to take shape at Cornell University's Society for the Humanities, while we were members of the year-long research residency "Risk@Humanities" (2012–2013). Many thanks to Tim Murray, the Society's Director at the time, and fellow seminar participants, especially William Leiss, Michael Warner, Ingrid Diran, Annelise Riles, and Elisabeth Anker. We are grateful to friends who have seen us through the stages of this project, especially Pooja Rangan, Dan Reynolds, Joshua Neves, and Lisa Cartwright; to our graduate assistants, Lisa Han and Nicole Dib, for their editorial work; and to Sukanya Ghosh, for shepherding the always wayward images. We could take the risk because you all have persevered with us.

Notes

1. The first residency was hosted at University of California Humanities Research Institute (UC Irvine), and the second, at The Society for the Humanities at Cornell University.
2. See also, Daniel Halperin's (2007) discussion of Warner's piece.
3. The conclusions are based on comparisons of estimated residual risks for the two deferral periods along with their confidence intervals/uncertainty ranges: "at a reasonable level of confidence, we simply cannot say that the risk, as measured, is actually higher or lower" (Leiss et al. 2008, 58). The tendency to settle for the longer period of donor abstinence thus reflects social biases rather than scientific findings.
4. The self-quant communities organize in meetings and conferences as well as online (https://quantifiedself.com/). See also, Gina Neff and Dawn Nefus (2016) and Deborah Lupton (2016).
5. A report by TechCrunch in early 2019 showed how the Onavo code was repurposed for use in a Facebook Research app (gathering data from smartphone users, 13–35). Apple blocked the app after the discovery: see, Josh Constine, "Facebook will shut down its Spyware VPN app Onavo" (https://techcrunch.com/2019/02/21/facebook-removes-onavo/). Retrieved March 4, 2019.
6. $E(X)$, the expectation of a venture X, is the particular value of X multiplied by the probability $p(X)$ for the realization of that particular value of X. That is, $E(X) = p(X).X$. If the probability of a return is very low, the venture can still be considered low return even though the actual value of the return is high; conversely, if the probability of return is high, but the actual return amounts to a loss, the venture is high risk. The point is that the nineteenth-century calculations of expected returns from a venture took stock of not only the probabilities (the chances of particular outcomes) but also the actual outcomes.
7. Ulrich Beck published *The Risk Society: Towards a Self-Reflexive Modernity* first in German (1986) and later in English (1992); see also, Beck's *World At Risk* (2008) and Francis Ewald (1991), "Two Infinities of Risk."
8. See selections in Nick Pidgeon, Roger E. Kasperson, and Paul Slovic eds., *The Social Amplification of Risk* (2003).
9. Paul Slovic, *The Feeling of Risk: New Perspectives on Risk Perception* (2010); see also, Paul Slovic and Ellen Peters' distinction in "Risk Perception and Affect" (2006).
10. Earlier histories also document the encoding of risk in maritime trading social customs: Babylonian traders parleying ware in the Mediterranean embedded protections against potential loss in the Code of Hammurabi (c.1750 BC) while Chinese traders in the second and third centuries distributed valuable goods across vessels while traversing river rapids, as safeguard against loss.
11. Michel Foucault's work on the disciplinary ranges across many of his works, the most relevant of which for our purposes, here is *The History of Sexuality: An Introduction (Volume I)*, 1976; *The History of Sexuality: The Uses of Pleasure (Volume II)*, 1984; and *Abnormal, 1974–1975* (2004).
12. See, Andrew Lakoff (2008), "The Generic Biothreat, or, How We Became Unprepared," *Cultural Anthropology* 23.3 (2008): 399–428; Claudia Aradau and Rens van Munster, *Politics of Catastrophe: Genealogies of the Unknown* (2011); and Peter Adey and Ben Anderson (2012), "Anticipating Emergencies: Technologies of Preparedness and the Matter of Security."
13. Foucault elaborates the racial logic of security in *"The Society Must Be Defended": Lectures at the Collège de France, 1975–1976* (2003).

Works Cited

Adam, Barbara et al., *The Risk Society and Beyond*. Sage Publications, 2000.
Adey, Peter and Ben Anderson. "Anticipating Emergencies: Technologies of Preparedness and the Matter of Security." *Security Dialogue*, vol. 43, 2012, pp. 99–117.
Aradau, Claudia and Rens van Munster. *Politics of Catastrophe: Genealogies of the Unknown*. Routledge, 2011.
Beck, Ulrich. *The Risk Society: Towards a Self-Reflexive Modernity*. Sage Publication, 1986, 1992.
Beck, Ulrich. *World At Risk*. Polity, 2008.
Berlant, Lauren. *Cruel Optimism*. Duke UP, 2011.
Butler, Judith. *Precarious Life: The Powers of Mourning and Violence*. Verso, 2004.
Casarino, Cesare and Antonio Negri. *In Praise of the Common: A Conversation on Philosophy and Politics*. U of Minnesota Press, 2008.
Chakrabarty, Dipesh. "The Climate of History: Four Theses." *Critical Inquiry*, vol. 35, no. 2, 2009, pp. 197–222.
Cooper, Melinda. *Life As Surplus: Biotechnology and Capitalism in the Neoliberal Era*. University of Washington Press, 2008.
da Costa, Beatriz and Kavita Philip. *Tactical Biopolitics: Art, Activism, and Technoscience*. The MIT Press, 2008.
Daston, Lorraine. *Classical Probability in the Enlightenment*. Princeton UP, 1995.
De Genova, Nicholas. *Borders of Europe: Autonomy of Migration, Tactics of Bordering*. Duke UP, 2017.
DeSieno, Marcus. *No Man's Land: Views from a Surveillance State*. Daylight Books, 2018.
Dienst, Richard. *The Bonds of Debt: Borrowing Against the Common Good*. Verso, 2011.
Douglas, Mary. *Risk and Blame: Essays in Cultural Theory*. Routledge, 1992.
Ewald, François. "Two Infinities of Risk." In Brian Massumi ed. *The Politics of Everyday Fear*. U of Minnesota P, 1991, pp. 221–228.
Foucault, Michel. *The History of Sexuality: An Introduction. Volume I*. Vintage Books, 1976.
Foucault, Michel. *The History of Sexuality: The Uses of Pleasure. Volume II*. Vintage Books, 1984.
Foucault, Michel. *Abnormal: Lectures at the Collège de France, 1974–1975*. Picador, 2004.
Foucault, Michel. *"The Society Must Be Defended": Lectures at the Collège de France, 1975–1976*. Picador, 2003.
Galloway, Alexander and Eugene Thacker. *The Exploit: A Theory of Networks*. U of Minnesota P, 2007.
Gates, Kelly A. *Our Biometric Future: Facial Recognition Technology and the Culture of Surveillance*. New York UP, 2011.
Ghosh, Amitav. *The Great Derangement: Climate Change and the Unthinkable*. U Chicago Press. 2016.
Ghosh, Bishnupriya. "Looking Through Coca-Cola: Global Icons and the Popular." *Public Culture*, vol. 22, no. 2, 2010, pp. 333–368.
Giddens, Anthony. *Consequences of Modernity*. Stanford UP, 1990.
Gregory, Derek. "From a View to Kill: Drones and the Late Modern War." *Theory, Culture & Society*, vol. 28. no. 7–8, January 2011, pp. 188–215.
Grusin, Richard. "Radical Mediation." *Critical Inquiry*, 42, Autumn 2015, pp. 124–148.
Hacking, Ian. *The Taming of Chance*. Cambridge UP, 1990.
Halperin, Daniel. *What Do Gay Men Want?: An Essay on Sex, Risk, and Subjectivity*. University of Michigan Press, 2007.
Haraway, Donna. *Staying with the Trouble: Making Kin in the Chthulucene*. Duke UP, 2016.
Harvey, David. *Spaces of Global Capitalism: A Theory of Uneven Geographical Development*. Verso, 2006.
Jameson, Fredric. "Cognitive Mapping." In *Marxism and the Interpretation of Culture*. U of Illinois P, 1988.
Kember, Sarah and Joanna Zylinska. *Life After New Media: Mediation as a Vital Process*. MIT Press, 2014.
Klein, Naomi. *The Shock Doctrine: The Rise of Disaster Capitalism*. Picador, 2007.
Knight, Frank. 1921. *Risk, Uncertainty and Profit*. Houghton Mifflin Company, 1933.
Lakoff, Andrew. "The Generic Biothreat, or, How We Became Unprepared." *Cultural Anthropology*, vol. 23, no. 3, 2008, pp. 399–428.
Lee, Benjamin and Edward LiPuma. *Financial Derivatives and the Globalization of Risk*. Duke UP, 2004.
Leiss, William and Douglas Powell eds. *Mad Cows and Mother's Milk: The Perils of Poor Risk Communication*. McGill-Queens UP, 1997.
Leiss, William et al. "MSM Donor Deferral Risk Assessment: An Analysis Using Risk Management Principles (A Report for Canadian Blood Services)." *Transfusion Medicine Reviews*, vol. 22, no. 1, January 2008, pp. 35–57.
Lupton, Deborah. *The Quantified Self*. Polity, 2016.
Madsen, Michael. Dir. *Into Eternity*. Producer, Lise Lense-Møller, 2010.
Mazur, Allan. *A Hazardous Inquiry: The Rashomon Effect at Love Canal*. Harvard UP, 1998.
Milburn, Colin. *Nanovision*. Duke UP, 2008.
Neff, Gina and Dawn Nefus. *Self-Tracking*. MIT Press, 2016.

Nixon, Robert. *Slow Violence and the Environmentalism of the Poor*. Harvard UP, 2011.
O'Malley, Pat. "Moral Uncertainties: Contract Law and Distinctions between Speculation, Gambling, Insurance." *Risk and Morality*, edited by Richard V. Ericson and Aaron Doyle. U of Toronto P, 2003, p. 231.
Perrow, Charles. *Normal Accidents: Living with High-Risk Technologies*. Princeton UP, 1984.
Pidgeon, Nick. *The Social Amplification of Risk*. Cambridge UP, 2003.
Pidgeon, Nick et al., eds. *The Social Amplification of Risk*. Cambridge UP, 2003.
Postone, Moishe. *Perspectives on the Global Crisis*. Duke UP, 2012
Roitman, Janet. *Anti-Crisis*. Duke UP, 2013.
Sampson, Tony. *Virality: Contagion Theory in the Age of Networks*. U of Minnesota P, 2012.
Sarkar, Bhaskar. "Media Piracy and the Terrorist Boogeyman: Speculative Potentiations." *Positions*, vol. 24, no. 2, 2016, pp. 343–368.
Schumpeter, Joseph. *Capitalism, Socialism, and Democracy*. Harper Perennial Modern Thought, 2008.
Serres, Michael. *The Parasite*. U of Minnesota P, 2007.
Siegel, Greg. *Forensic Media: Reconstructing Accidents in Accelerated Modernity*. Duke UP, 2014.
Slovic, Paul. *The Perception of Risk*. Earthscan, 2000.
Slovic, Paul. *The Feeling of Risk: New Perspectives on Risk Perception*. Earthscan 2010.
Slovic, Paul. "The Psychology of Risk." *Saúde e Sociedade*, vol. 19, no. 4, December 2010, pp. 731–747.
Slovic, Paul and Ellen Peters. "Risk Perception and Affect." *Current Directions in Psychological Science*, vol. 15, no. 6, December 2006, pp. 322–325.
Standing, Guy. *Precariat: The New Dangerous Class*. Bloomsbury Academic, 2011.
Sunstein, Cass. *Laws of Fear: Beyond the Precautionary Principle*. Cambridge UP, 2005.
Suzuki, Tatsujiro. "Deconstructing the Zero-Risk Mindset: The Lessons and Future-Responsibilities for a Post-Fukushima Japan." *Bulletin of Atomic Scientists*, vol. 67, no. 9, September 2011, pp. 11–18.
uncertain commons. *Speculate this!* Duke UP, 2013.
Van Loon, Joost. *Risk and Technological Culture: Toward a Sociology of Virulence*. Routledge, 2002.
Virilio, Paul. *The Original Accident*. Polity, 2007.
Warner, Michael. "Unsafe: Why Gay Men Are Having Risky Sex." *The Village Voice*, January 1995.
Weizman, Eyal. *Forensic Architecture: Violence at the Threshold of Detectability*. MIT Press, 2017.
Welchman, John. ed., *The Aesthetics of Risk*. JRP/Ringier, 2008.
Williams, Raymond. "Mediation." In *Keywords: A Vocabulary of Culture and Society*. Oxford UP, 1985.

PART I

HISTORICAL PERSPECTIVES

2
HAS RISK A HISTORY?

Gaspar Mairal

Within current risk scholarship, there has yet to be a widely accepted consideration of risk as historical. Niklaus Luhmann, an influential risk studies scholar, missed a "historical–conceptual" study on risk. Similarly, in his frequently cited book, *Against the Gods*, Peter Bernstein does not use the word "history," and instead describes his work as "a remarkable story of risk" (Bernstein; Luhmann).

This chapter traces risk as a cultural–historical concept with its own genealogy. It seeks to establish, with some accuracy, a sense of how the modern-day concept of risk emerged. This requires precise conceptualization of terms that distinguish risk from related older terms such as "fortune," "hazard," "danger," "peril," "fate," and so on.

The early intuition of risk in the seventh century and the emergence of probability calculus in the sixteenth century at the hands of Pacioli, Tartaglia, and Cardano share a way of looking at the future; in both cases, we find that the approach begins by limiting possibility—in one case by describing God's providence as an assurance of success and a source of confidence in the outcome, and in the other by setting bounds on the event and then splitting it up to allow calculation. The methodological comparison I have drawn here is key to understanding how the two ways of conceiving probability, and ultimately risk, were historically constructed and related, first as narrative and then as calculus.

The Mediterranean Origin of Risk

The etymology of risk takes us first to the seventh century and to the Arabic word *rizq*, an original conception of risk that was present in the *Quran* as a religious principle. In the text, God was said to give a provision of spiritual and material goods to good believers, especially before the undertaking of a long and uncertain voyage by desert or sea. The *Quran* contains a large number of references to the *rizq* and provides this term with a large semantic field. The *Encyclopaedia of Islam* defines the Quranic *rizq* as follows:

> Rizk, and the nominal and verbal forms derived from it, are very frequent in the Kur'an, especially in reference to the *rizk Allah*, God's provision and sustenance for mankind from the fruits of the earth and the animals upon it.... Hence one of God's most beautiful names (see al-asma' al-husna) is al-Razzak, the All-Provider.
>
> *(Bosworth and McAuliffe)*

This original risk, in its Islamic–Arabic version, relates to navigation. The routes of caravans across the desert are the first context to locate the *rizq*. Those who were starting a long journey across huge and empty spaces like the deserts of the Arabian Peninsula, the Middle East, or North Africa, put their trust in God to get the *rizq* both for themselves and for the goods they transported. In addition to their caravans, the Arabs also crossed the Indian Ocean and the Mediterranean Sea with their ships. Navigating the desert and the sea were quite similar activities in regards to *rizq*. The desert, the sea, the ice, and the sky are the largest empty extensions that humankind has conquered throughout its history. These historical achievements gave impetus to human creativity through new knowledge, techniques, and products, as well as war and domination. Risk, in particular, took part in one prominent historical episode: the expansion of Islam. After three centuries, the Arabic–Islamic expansion had created a world of its own, which included the creation of new routes through the sea, another empty expanse. The new geographical and historical knowledge that the Arabs developed thanks to the Greek legacy and the influence of Persia, India, and China, supported new concepts—which no doubt included risk—in the context of multiple technical advances.[1] Borrowing devices of navigation such as the compass from other empires, the Arabs carried out conquest and created the notion of the *rizq* as the first historical precedent for the modern concept of risk.

The *rizq* refers to the spiritual blessing that all believers and their possessions can receive from God before starting a long and uncertain journey. Thus, the *rizq*, or "provision of God" is a relational quality that links God to a person and his goods. This relational process, coming from God and passing through faith and good actions to the believer and his possessions, would be the first version of risk; it implied trusting the outcome of a long journey by land or sea through this gift or God's provision. As Mikel de Epalza writes: "The risk in business is part of the trust in God, who would complement the insufficiencies of human calculations in the insurances, because he is the best of all suppliers, in all and always, Ar-Razz par excellence" (de Epalza 68).

The semantic field of the Arabic word *rizq* clearly demonstrates its relational nature, because nothing and nobody owns the *rizq*; instead, it comes from the relationship between God and the individual—a relationship that is also transferred to his properties. The future, conceived exclusively as uncertainty, is relativized by this belief in God's provision for both people and their belongings. Here we can see the semantic core of the *rizq*: it is the idea that someone, God at the beginning, guarantees persons and their possessions safety when they participate in a long and uncertain journey. When maritime voyages became increasingly common in the Arab world, the *rizq* was developed as a conceptual tool to manage the human and commercial exchange across the new routes in the Mediterranean Sea. The Mediterranean was an Arab sea from the ninth century until at least the twelfth-century Christian Crusades. Later, the maritime cities of South Europe such as Venice, Genoa, Pisa, Marseille, or Barcelona established their commercial routes.

Prior to the Greeks, Jews, and Romans developing maritime contracts like the *chreokoinomia*, the *isqa*, and the *societas*, the Arabs had already developed the *qirad* or loan, which applied to caravan's trades across the Arabian peninsula.[2] By the eleventh century, the merchants and seafarers in the ports of southern Europe also developed a kind of contract called *commenda*, which was intended to govern the commercial relations in the Mediterranean Sea for several centuries. In this encounter between the two legal traditions of *qirad* (Arab) and *commenda* (European), there was also a transfer of words and concepts, including the Arabic *rizq*. The transposition of *rizq* into Latin as *risicum* can be detected at the beginning of the thirteenth century in notarial documents in which *commenda* contracts were formalized. This hypothesis is the most plausible explanation of how the concept of risk arose and was applied for the first time in Europe. The conceptual transit from the Arabic *rizq* to Medieval Latin *risicum* also brought with it an important semantic shift, as this maritime trading concept would progressively become a negative one. This shift seems logical in a contract that had to deal both with advantages or benefits and losses or misfortune. The necessity of compensating someone for losses added content to the new word, *risicum*. The *rizq* or provision that, in a Arabic context, could be good or bad, thus became a new concept that referred to the contingency of a loss or damage in medieval Mediterranean sea contracts. From this point forward, the notion of risk would retain a negative connotation in Western World.

One of the earliest occurrence of the term *risicum* or in other words of a European version of the Arabic *rizq*, comes from a maritime contract dated in Genoa in 1248: "debet dicta navis in mari varari ad meum risicum et fortunam de omni casu" 'The said ship shall sail the sea at my own risk and fortune in events' (Villain-Gandossi 81).[3] This short sentence has a great historical value since it certifies the birth of risk in Europe. This term appeared in the context of maritime navigation and sea contracts. This initial use resembles a short narrative: if the ship or its cargo suffers some damage from any event at sea, the person who "commends" will take responsibility for this damage. Risk is thus always identified in a particular context of travel.

We can also emphasize how the possessive "meum" determines that the risk or fortune depends on someone, and therefore, it is not a thing in itself, but rather a relationship between people and objects, ideas, or situations. Thus, what produces risk is an object of risk—here it is the sea—and what is affected is the object at risk—a ship. The risk is always the relationship between two objects, and this relationship is expressed narratively in the following terms: "debet dicta navis in mare varari ad meum risicum et fortunam de omni casu" 'the said ship shall sail the sea at my own risk and fortune in all events' (Villain-Gandossi 81). In this very early form, risk is therefore contextual and relational as a narrative.

On the other hand, there are several authors (Golding; Villain-Gandossi) who have attributed the preserved text of the first policy of maritime insurance to a ship called Santa Clara, sailing from Genoa to Majorca in 1347. Georgius Lecavellum claims to have received 107 pounds of silver from Bartholomeus Bassus as a free and friendly loan that he was committed to return. He also made the commitment to undertake the risks of navigation via a direct route between Genoa and Mallorca in the following manner and by the stipulated amount: "I assume personally all risk and responsibility for the stipulated amount until the boat reached Mallorca, sailing direct route in the aforementioned form" (Golding).

Now we have an insurer who receives an amount of money from a ship owner, to be deducted if the ship and its cargo arrive at port without suffering damage within a period of six months. If it is damaged, he will have to pay double the amount received in addition to compensation for the damage, while putting up all his properties as a guarantee. Thus, insurance was born as a commercial activity specialized in the exchanging of risk and became a commodity valued at a stipulated amount. This fact put risk in more objective terms, since it was not only an adventure but also an amount of money, which corresponded. An initially religious and quite rational notion about the future was thus transformed into an intangible commodity.

The opening of routes in empty and unknown spaces like the sea raises an old problem: how we can give some content to the future? With the support of new technical resources of navigation as the rose of the winds, the calculation of latitude, the compass, and the books of navigation, the *rizq* offers an alternative to myth or divination for representing the future by projecting the person and their properties toward the events to come. A merchant could travel from a starting point, across a route, to a destination thanks to this "provision" of God. We know that from the thirteenth century beyond, merchants and traveling traders settled in ports and fair cities, and they stopped going from place to place with their goods. Caravans or traveling trade gave way to a kind of business in which a sedentary merchant played the key role in managing affairs from an office by hiring correspondents, agents, and partners to represent him in other places and countries. This change was part of a wider birth of mercantile capitalism, which included, among other things, the invention of the bill of exchange, double-entry accounting, and banking. New kinds of maritime contracts such as the Arab *quirad* or the Christian *commenda* appeared in the Mediterranean Sea so that all kinds of goods could be moved easily across the sea. On the other hand, this process brought a new separation between people and their goods and, in this way, the triple relationship with God was broken. Here we can identify a first secularization of risk, something crucial in the history of the concept.

When Risk Navigated to the Americas

By the end of the fifteenth century, scientific knowledge, based in the geography and cosmography of that time, provided the background capabilities for sailing to the West. The notion of the Earth as having a spherical form—though opposed to the Church's doctrine and outside the general beliefs of this epoch—had been demonstrated by the ancient Greeks and then accepted by a minority of scholars, including Columbus himself, who used the Spanish word "riesgo" in documents.[4] In 1498 in Seville, Columbus signed a sea contract with Antón Mariño, who had to supply the so-called Isles of the Indies: "Furthermore, all such stores as the said Antón Mariño may embark to take to the said isles of the Indies out of the funds received in respect of this contract, shall go at risk of their Majesties, whether of the sea or of corsairs, etc." (Varela 184).

Here, the word "risk" is a pre-established formula in a contract; we already know that these formulas were used in the medieval Mediterranean *commendas*. The expression "a riesgo" 'at risk' is equivalent to the Latin "ad meum risichum," which was documented in Genoa in 1248. The argument that titles this passage can be corroborated with an original document signed by Christopher Columbus himself. Thus, the notion of risk passed from the Mediterranean to the Atlantic and then to a new continent, the Americas. Moreover, we can apply the same previously explained conceptual model to this usage of the word risk. Risk is a probability relationship established between two types of entities: objects of risk and objects at risk. Here we have a concrete object at risk (the "stores"), and two explicitly mentioned objects of risk (the "sea" and "corsairs"). Here, risk is the probability that the supplies are lost or damaged in the case of big storms or an attack by corsairs. In those cases, the losses or damages would be covered by the King and Queen.

Following Columbus, many other voyages made the oceanic crossing from Spain to the Americas a permanent route for the Spanish fleet throughout the sixteenth century. This route, named *Carrera de las Indias* or *Route to the Indies*, has been one of the most significant paths in the history of maritime navigation. While important for many reasons, it was essential in the development of the so-called art of navigation. The treatises of navigation that were written and published in Spain at this time were numerous and very influential in England and France. In one, which is of particular interest because the author was not only a scientist but also an experienced seaman, the Spanish word "riesgo" is used more than 20 times. I have not found any other text from that time in which the word risk attains such a complex, wide, and precise usage as in the *Itinerario de Navegación* written by Juan Escalante.

Juan Escalante de Mendoza was a Spanish navigator who participated actively in the *Carrera de las Indias*, crossing the Atlantic Ocean several times. In 1595 he was appointed Chief of Naval Operations in the Nueva España's Fleet.[5] He died in 1596 in Panama at age 60. In 1575, he completed his *Itinerario de navegación de los mares y tierras occidentales* (*Itinerary of Navigation of Western Seas and Lands*). This is a work of great originality and extraordinary value for several reasons: First, it is a treatise of navigation that goes beyond the very significant division at that time between pilots—people with experience in navigation—and cosmographers, who were scholars with mathematical, astronomical, and cartographic education and who in some cases never sailed. After a good number of oceanic voyages, Escalante combined his vast experiences and his great knowledge in the art of navigation. We should thus recognize his text as the most complete treatise on navigation between Europe and the Americas to be found in the sixteenth century. In the treatise, Escalante creates a character, called "the pilot," who embarks from Seville together with a young sailor named "Tristán" who is traveling to the Americas for the first time. This "pilot" is a very experienced navigator who answers Tristán's questions on how to navigate the same voyage. This narrative is original in its description of all the vicissitudes that a seaman may find in his Atlantic Ocean crossing.

Escalante's narrative is very appropriate for the investigation of risk, since he uses the term abundantly. Furthermore, he places risk in contexts that contain descriptions of the events that this pilot/Escalante had lived through in his numerous voyages. This style of narration is much richer than those of contracts or accounts and transmits a certain verisimilitude. Risk is now linked to actions to be taken, to events that can happen and, above all, to futures that can be prevented.

At the beginning of Escalante's book, he explains his reasons for writing his treatise:

> to write a long account with all advice and rules which I understand are necessary, so that any discreet man when navigating could know where he is going to and so he could prevent the shipwrecks and be able to sail with the lesser possible risk.
>
> (Escalante de Mendoza 25)

Risk is clearly a central notion in Escalante's narrative, associating the navigator's safety with a lesser risk. What is more important is that risk is now a general concept that makes no distinction between things and people, since the new object of risk is the whole of the ship including, of course, its crew. This is a very significant development in the history of risk which, on the other hand, continues to be a matter of navigation as it was for the medieval *risicum* or Columbus' *a riesgo de*. The application of risk to human life was not very typical in medieval narratives, when goods and merchandise were the main issues. In contrast, Escalante's narrative uses a different idea of risk in which human life, rather than an interest, is the priority. Escalante writes: "If the ship is sunk the captain and sailors on board do not lose or risk any interest, but their souls for not doing well their jobs" (Escalante de Mendoza 34). It seems that Escalante wished to make clear the priority of life over any other material interest, vindicating the crew who owned neither the ship nor its cargo. To risk (*arriesgar* in Spanish)—this is the first time that I have registered the use of the verb—is something that corresponds to people and not to things. This is a very significant remark.

Prevention is an essential aspect of any modern conceptualization of risk, as Escalante was already aware. To prevent means to anticipate, and thus to have some knowledge about something that has not yet happened but could happen. This idea was a part of the Arabic notion of risk. Prevention also demands some kind of action, and this aspect would become increasingly important with the future development of insurance, navigation, calculation of probabilities, modern engineering, preventive medicine, and so on. However, Escalante's *Itinerary of Navigation of Western Seas and Lands* written in the sixteenth century already refers to action as the best way to prevent a damage. We can see it in the words used by Escalante to explain how to steer a ship and manage the sails in a tempest: "And if the 'nao' was suffering great storms and fearing of a heavy sea which could sink it, for the prevention of that risk no small sail should be placed across" (Escalante de Mendoza 34).[6]

We can observe here that an estimate of risk is something yet to happen in Escalante's account; as it does not yet exist, it can be avoided. Risk as a conditional future is a story within a story. Nevertheless, the action of managing risk is a story in the present. The grammatical construction permits the creation of overlaid times, and risk is always conditional upon the present. The actions that are proposed by Escalante, such as "navigate with small sail" or "not to place across any small sail," are expressed in the present tense, while risk is estimated in the conditional "could sink."

The positive value of using the notion of risk is in its capacity to promote safety, as Escalante emphasizes, but also for its selective character. According to Escalante, there are occasions in which we can choose, from among various risks, the lesser one. "Because between two risks which could be represented one must always choose the best and less inconvenient" (de Escalante de Mendoza 199). There is another important point to be emphasized here—it is the expression: "two risks which could be represented." The symbolic nature of any representation can be appreciated in this text, for it alludes to selecting from two possible representations. So risks always come from "something" which, not having a factual existence, demands its representation through language. This "something" is an imagined damage expressed by a representation, which is a narrated probability. If the damage occurred, we would then have a fact, and risk would no longer be a probability.

Reality substitutes its representation, but the representation—risk in this case—exists to promote an anticipated action in an attempt to avoid damage.

This summarizes the meaning of risk in Escalante's *Itinerario de Navegación*, but it does not express that of Columbus' contracts, where the use of risk was about the same as in medieval documents. This temporal comparison leads us to presume that oceanic navigation evolved significantly between 1492 and 1575, thanks to the extraordinary shift that came with the *Carrera de las Indias*. Risk, as described by Escalante, is a holistic notion, although it was still to be found in the maritime navigation. After the *Carrera de las Indias* the concept of risk undergoes a new and transcendental semantic shift. If the original risk was attributed to someone (God) who guaranteed a thing or a person, now this guarantee is not necessary because risk is just the probability that something, which is estimated to be harmful or undesirable, will happen. So after the concept of risk was emancipated from God with the contract and with insurance, it adopts a new referential frame which still includes damage and navigation, but whose attribution is more global. Of course, contracts and insurance policies in which risk is calculated and valued would persist, but risk would also become a concept with a wider usage and more extensive referential frames.

When Risk Set Foot in the Americas

All of my previous narratives have dealt with the oceanic voyages; I have mentioned only very briefly some events that occurred or could have occurred on land. I now turn to the "new world" and to the new experiences encountered by the first Europeans who set foot there, after the Vikings' ephemeral presence in North America. In this section, I am also interested in written sources, as they contain allusions to risk and permit us to reconstruct the context in which it arose.

Columbus' documents include several accounts of indigenous people encountered in travel and would use a variety of contradictory ideas and prejudices; among them is one that is directly related to risk. In this account, the native populations were also an object of risk. Columbus wrote to the Catholic kings, telling them about his incursions into the Caribbean islands in search of gold and other riches. He also alluded to the perils of that expedition—its wounded or ill members risked falling behind and being attacked by the Indians:

> it was a great disadvantage to let here the sick crew in an open place with huts, and the provisions and maintenances which are ashore, inasmuch as these Indians have shown themselves to the discoverers and they look very simple and without malice, and yet, because they come here to visit us everyday, it seemed to us that it was a good idea to put at risk and venture that people and those maintenances loose, something that a single Indian could do setting fire to the huts, as they come and go by night and day; so we maintain guards in the fields while our settlement is open and without a defense.
>
> *(Varela 124)*

Here we have the expression "*meter a riesgo*" 'to put at risk,' attributed to people rather than to merchandise or ships. Nevertheless, the probabilistic usage of the term risk is similar to previous cases: the context changes, but not the meaning. A shortened version of this narrative can be analyzed in the following terms: If an ill person suffers the fate of falling behind in an "open place with huts," there is a probability of being attacked by the Indians. The same account refers to the Indians' pacifist character, which permits us to evaluate them more as a risk than as a peril, and thus their attacks more as a probability than as a certitude. Following these considerations, we can conclude that here we have a notion of risk with wider semantic implications.

I use the concept of metonymy to characterize the development of a narrative in which risk was evolving; it is even more interesting to jump from one historical context to another thanks to the contiguity of spaces and activities. We saw earlier that the notion of risk developed in the oceanic navigation in the sixteenth century; something similar happened when those navigators set foot on land and, in many cases, remained there forever. They would not have an immense sea before them, and they would not need good ships or the best arts of navigation. Instead, they encountered another amazing and luxuriant space to stimulate their imaginations, with new riches to be taken—something like a paradise. However, this new experience also included the presence of human beings.

The first descriptions to shape the new world in writing were the so-called *relaciones* (accounts) and the *hojas volantes* (flyers) which gave details of all these conquests. I have already used some of them. Certainly, after decades of violence and the extermination of some native populations, the Spanish Empire consolidated and constituted itself as an extension of sixteenth-century European society. This new society needed printing and literature. I wish to consider the creation of a new world narrative and its close connection with wild nature and natural disasters. Let us mention a good example.

In 1538, Juan Sánchez Portero wrote one of these *relaciones*, addressed to the King of Spain. Here we have what is probably the first detailed description of a volcano in the Americas—the Masaya volcano in Nicaragua, at that time called "hell." This volcano was one of the fantasies that so inspired the conquistadores. In this case, it was believed that the volcano provided a way to locate an abundance of gold and other precious metals. Again, the myths and legends accompanied the explorers in their adventures and discoveries. Juan Sánchez Portero wished to obtain favors from the king of Spain, and so it is understandable if he exaggerated the story. But, in any case, he gives us a good example of how to enter a volcano and describes it as an object of risk:

> And specially I found myself in the entry point to the Masaya volcano which is located in that province … afterwards I and three other comrades came down the volcano with thick ropes, putting our lives at the greatest risk and danger of death, as there were five hundred "estados" of depth down to the bottom.
>
> (Serrano and Sanz 28)

The entrance to this volcano is presented as a very difficult operation requiring a lot of materials and preparation time. The descent into the crater is a very risky act with great danger. The expression used by Sánchez Portero suggests a gradation from risk to danger; if we follow the account, we can appreciate how risk is attributed to the action of entering into a volcano, the volcano itself being an object of risk.

The volcano as a natural disaster was unknown in Spain and even in Western Europe, where eruptions in South Italy (Vesuvio) and Sicily (Etna) had not occurred since antiquity.[7] Thus, volcanic activity became a very powerful object of risk to identify the new world in the European imaginary. In 1541, a volcanic disaster destroyed the city of Guatemala, and a description of this catastrophe was published almost immediately in Mexico City. This description is usually considered the first example of a primitive journalism. In addition, this publication was one of the first writings to be printed in the Americas.

The introduction of the press in the Americas took place in Mexico thanks to the Crombergers, a family of German printers who had settled in Seville at the end of the fifteenth century. They were, after the conquest of Mexico, the most important book dealers for the first Mexican libraries. The Crombergers sent the press to Mexico in 1539 under the management of printer Juan Pablos. Soon after, in 1541, this press published the *Relación del espantable terremoto que agora nuevamente ha acontecido en la ciudad de Guatemala*, (*Account of the Frightening Earthquake that Happened Newly in the Indies in a City Called Guatemala*), a very important document confirming that a new narrative of risk, with some journalistic features, was conveying news about the natural disasters (Rodríguez).

The *hojas volantes*, or flyers, were the first antecedent of journalism in the Americas until the publication of the *gacetas* (gazettes) in the eighteenth century. Those flyers narrated important events containing information that had to be disseminated promptly. This obviously would have been impossible without the press. The texts were relatively brief and circulated as leaflets. Their narrative structure was quite similar to the news, and they became—with some limitations if we consider the high proportion of illiterate people—a kind of substitute for the traditional announcements of town criers. This flyer printed and distributed in 1541 is the earliest known of its kind, and it is in fact the first example of journalism on the new continent. This natural disaster—the consequence of a big storm that demolished one of the Agua volcano walls and released a lake within the crater—devastated the city of Guatemala in 1541. In fact, this was not a volcanic eruption but rather a huge inundation, so it is surprising that this document refers to an earthquake in its title. This might be a mistake or an example of how the word "earthquake" acquired a general usage to describe any natural disaster of great proportion. The author of the story was Juan Rodríguez, who signed as "escribano" (clerk).

> Account of what happened in Guatemala Saturday, 10th of September 1541 at two o'clock in the morning. It had rained on Thursday and Friday, though not long or heavily, and the Saturday was as described. But at two o'clock in the morning there came a great deluge of water from the top of the volcano that rises above Guatemala, so suddenly that there was no chance to avoid the deaths and damage caused. The mud slide, which drove water, rocks and trees before it, was so large that those who saw it were most astonished.
>
> (Rodríguez)

This narration of the "frightening earthquake" demands very special attention, as López de Mariscal proposes:

> The "story of the frightening earthquake" becomes an edifying narrative which tries to move its readers to the contrition of their sins. As the story goes mouth-to-mouth or it is being remade by different emitters, other fantastic elements which reinforce its exemplariness are attached.
>
> (López de Mariscal 57–65)

Later on, this tragedy became a narrated fact in many other books, which adopted it as a transcendental event with a great significance.[8] Here again we find a story, more or less firsthand, followed by other narrations that remake it in their own way. In all cases, these authors are following the example of the original flyer in 1542 and trying to strengthen it. The flyer already mentions in its title that this event was a "great example for we all to emend our sins and be prepared for the time when God calls us." This appreciation, clearly documented by López de Mariscal, has great value in unveiling a kind of "matrix" narration: that is, narration with a pattern to inspire a number of future stories whose main intention, in echoing this first one, would be to face the probability that this disaster would be repeated.

Games of Chance: from Narrative to Probability Calculus

In all its forms and expressions, risk is a way of lessening uncertainty and thus it takes its place among the key ideas which forged modernity.[9] Risk allowed the transition from a future imagined as possibility to one imagined as probability, and this proved the inspiration for many leading figures of different ages facing widely varying situations of need: the Muslim theologians and caravans of the seventeenth century; the Mediterranean jurists, notaries, and mariners of the fourteenth century; and the conquistadors, chroniclers, and writers who first described the New World in the seventeenth century could all be said to have been moved by the urge to master the unknown, and all did so within a specific chronotope. Thus, they opened up and maintained routes that crossed the wastes of desert and sea. It is no accident, then, that the deserts of the Near East and the Mediterranean Sea provided the stage for the emergence of the new context. When the Portuguese and Spanish first embarked upon their transoceanic voyages of discovery, they made a giant leap by projecting an incipient and fairly sketchy understanding forward in their timeframe so that it became possible to imagine future events in space. This understanding was originally religious in nature, but it later developed into the kind of commercial knowledge that could be written down in a contract.

In addition to the experience of past time, mankind is also aware of future time, of that which is yet to come. The first and most basic characteristic of this timeframe is that we cannot in principle know what the future holds in store, for we have no experience of what has yet to be. This is, then, a state of uncertainty, and any event we may imagine in the future will by its very nature be merely a possibility. Anything is possible in the future. The first response to futurity was magical: with the aid of supernatural forces, men could see what had yet to occur, curing uncertainty with foresight. The magic of divination, soothsaying, and oracles was that the person vested with prophetic powers could see into the future. Magic was mankind's first bid to conquer the uncertainty of the future. Believers could not see for themselves, but they could receive messages from those who had the magic or supernatural power to see. As explained above, Islamic theology changed divination by introducing the idea of divine reason to foresee the outcome of future events. This new idea replaced visions with faith in one God: seeing was no longer believing.[10]

This was a crucial step, which was taken by both Christianity and Islam, and we must consider it in both its temporal and epistemological dimensions. A vision opens up an existential truth, and for the visionary it makes the unreal real. In this way, it annuls the effects of time, because there is no mediation between uncertainty and certainty and the vision transports the visionary from one time and place to another with complete immediacy. Faith, however, is a kind of belief that does not require visions, because it is derived from the rational theological principle that only God can know what will happen. Faith is, then, more rational than the pure belief expressed by the visionary. This epistemological shift in the nature of belief was rooted in the replacement of magic by true knowledge, which came directly from God. The rejection of visions, though still within the framework of religion, allowed believers to imagine or represent a reality that was still only dimly known—namely, as the space to be crossed on their journeys and voyages, and the events that might occur during the crossing.

Foresight is in some sense ontological, because it tells the believer what his future was, for it has been seen. Faith, however, recognizes that only God can know what will happen, and in doing so it assumes that there is still time before the event occurs, or to put it another way, it assumes that the future exists but is unknown to man. The only way to bridge the gap is to build a construct of time, which is none other than probability. Knowledge of probability allows us to glimpse into the unknown, achieving a relative understanding of what has not yet happened.

The origins of the game of chance go back millennia. Objects like plum and peach stones, pebbles, and knucklebones were thrown for divination in antiquity, as well as for play. Throwing the talus or astragalus bone of an ox or sheep, commonly known as the knucklebone, was without a doubt the most common method of dealing with chance. In the same way that the concept of risk developed as a more rational alternative to soothsaying, the calculus of probability developed from dice, which was historically both a game of chance and a means of foretelling the future (Reith). According to F. N. David, dice must have been created thousands of years ago by progressively shaping and smoothing the rounded side of knucklebones to obtain a more or less flat surface.

In *Games, Gods and Gambling*, David raises the historical problem of why it took so long for the notion of probability to emerge:

> We may speculate as we please about number, about the rules of the various games of chance about the use and misuse of the religious auguries, but there is no denying that the real problem which confronts the historian of the calculus of probabilities is its extremely tardy conceptual growth—in fact one might almost say, its late birth as an offspring of the mathematical sciences.
>
> *(David 5)*

Here I am also attempting to answer this question, although my response differs from the partial answers offered by David in his otherwise excellent book. According to David, it took a very long time to formulate the idea that the odds of winning or losing are the same when the dice are thrown, even in the highly specific and material context of games of chance. The random nature of reality has been recognized since the remote past, but the notion of equiprobability took far longer to emerge.[11]

> The random element was introduced before recorded time, and there are enough references in the literature before the birth of Christ to indicate that this random element—surely the goddess Fortuna herself ... was pursued with assiduous fanaticism. Why then was the concept of the equally-likely possibilities in die-throwing so long delayed? It is a question which one must, perhaps, try to answer in terms of the emotions rather than the intellect.
>
> *(5)*

This seems to me a problem that merits some reflection. Until now I have argued that narrative probability emerged before the invention of its mathematical calculation, and in doing so I have assumed that the use of the Arabic term *rizq* from the seventh century onward allowed an initial assessment of likely outcomes before setting out on a long journey or voyage. Today we may consider this a very simple problem, one which can indeed be solved merely by the application of common sense, but this is to ignore the abstract quality of the concept in question. The history of science tells us that there was always a religious dimension to humanity's early forays into abstract thought, for example in ancient cosmologies. Hence, the context in which we should place our problem is that of religion, and we need to recognize moreover the capacity of certain religions for rationalization at a certain period in their development. Émile Durkheim argued that science itself has its origins in religion, because this was for centuries the only school of thought capable of addressing key existential problems like the nature of death, the passage of time, the origin of life, the meaning of existence, the formation of the cosmos, or our place in nature. Another of these questions was about the meaning of the future. A part of the answer may be deduced from the arguments described above: the problem raised by David is both theological and rational, and to understand this we must recognize the existing compatibilities between the two. At a time when science was not yet an independent branch of knowledge, the problems of existence took on a pre-scientific quality. This is what happened in the Islam of the seventh century. By asserting that the future was in the hands of God alone, the theologians made a break with divination, returning humanity to a condition of uncertainty. However, in the face of this renewed uncertainty and the random nature of future events as demonstrated in the roll of dice, religion provided the individual with a way out, though it called upon and required faith. God offered the faithful a providence or *rizq* before they set out on any journey with an uncertain end. Hence, the Muslim traveler, whether as part of a caravan or aboard a ship, could enjoy a relative certainty, which came from God, with regard to the success of his venture. Probability expressed via *rizq* thus had an abstract dimension—a manifestation of faith in God. The probability of *rizq*, as seen in the theological abstraction lacking scientific context, was gradually transformed into an increasingly secularized and expert concept thanks to cartography, astronomy, navigation, improved shipbuilding and design, and later law and economics.

It was through these last fields of knowledge that maritime contracts and insurance policies were made, documenting the existence of narratives of risk based on a notion of probability, though probability was still essentially a descriptive notion at this time. As it became more secular, the notion of risk took on a more concrete form in the formula *ad meum risicum* included in contractual instruments, which later manifested as a specific sum of money in the early insurance policies made in the fourteenth century. If risk was initially inherent in the person, it came to be inherent in goods. Naturally, the concept still expressed the likelihood that something, by now exclusively something bad, might happen to a vessel and its cargo. This is in itself a narrative form, which several centuries ago anticipated the first glimmerings of mathematical probability developed in the sixteenth century by thinkers like Luca Pacioli, Niccolò Fontana Tartaglia, and, above all, Gerolamo Cardano. Probability is a time structure, or to put it another way, a means of narrating what could happen. Before it could be couched in mathematical terms, such narratives existed in the form of travelers' tales and belief in a God who offered the faithful a degree of certainty with regard to the future.

Concluding his argument, David offers a revealing explanation of why it took so long to arrive at the mathematical formulation of probability:

> In other words I suggest that the step did not come at that time because the philosophic development which opened so many doors for the human intellect engendered a habit of mind which made impossible the construction of theoretical hypotheses from empirical data.
>
> *(26)*

Before probability found its way into the observable realm through the game of dice, allowing the formulation of theories based on recorded data, it already treaded the opposite path; its incipient formulation inherent in certain abstract, theoretical concepts mixed with certain practices associated with long journeys and navigation. It was out of this mix or practical application that the first narratives of risk expressing a probability of adverse outcomes or loss emerged. In this light, probability was not discovered inductively, as David believed, but deductively, as historical analysis shows. In the same way that narrative probability emerged out of a theologically based notion of uncertainty and rational glimpse of the future, mathematical probability arose through recognizing the random fall of the dice and a subsequent understanding of equiprobability. I will now demonstrate this secondary development through a numerical calculation.

In its primitive Arabic version, risk developed through the Arab adoption of numerous innovations including the compass, chess, and astronomy arriving from the East, especially China and India. This is the case with what we in the West call Arabic numerals, though they in fact came from India. Around AD 800, Muhammed Ibn Musa al-Khwarizmi, whose name was Latinized as Algoritmi or Algaurizin, started using a system for writing numbers consisting of nine digits and zero (David 29). The next step was taken with the exchange of knowledge driven by the intense maritime trade of the Mediterranean, particularly between the city states of Italy and the Arab lands on the southern shore of the Mediterranean and the Middle East. It was Leonardo de Pisa (1170–1250), the son of a merchant who had made his fortune representing the city of Pisa in Barbary, who would write the first mathematical treatise in Europe to use Indian–Arabic numerals. The *Liber Abaci* or *Book of Calculation* was concerned with arithmetic and accounting, and its considerably expanded second edition was completed in 1228. Close to 300 years would pass, however, before the mathematical knowledge built up in Italy after de Pisa's *Liber Abaci* would be compiled as a book. This was Pacioli's *Summa de arithmetica, geometria, proportioni e proportionalita* (*Summa of Arithmetic, Geometry, Proportions and Proportionality*) which was printed in Venice in 1497.[12] In this work, Pacioli provides an example which would be the starting point for the subsequent invention of probability calculus. We may state the problem as follows: A and B are betting on a game of bowls and decide to continue playing until one of them has won six rounds. However, the game ends when A has won five rounds and B three. How should the stakes be split between them? Pacioli's solution is to divide the pot into eight parts, of which A should receive five and B three. However, his answer was questioned by later authors, who missed something that Pacioli could not have known: probability. Let us pause for a moment to consider Pacioli's problem from a narrative rather than a mathematical standpoint.

The story contained in the problem can be told in the following terms: two people are playing bowls and they agree that the first to win six throws will take the pot. In doing so, they have imagined a future in which one of them will be the first to make six rounds and will walk off with the stakes. It would be another matter entirely, if A and B had simply started playing without agreeing any particular outcome and had then split the pot after eight throws in proportion to the rounds won by each one, five to three. In this case, Pacioli's solution would have been correct. However, the game between A and B contained a future aspect of which Pacioli was necessarily ignorant. Pacioli's critics saw that the split should take account of this dimension, because it too formed part of the event. The problem, however, was how to do so, and it was here that the principle of probability began to emerge.

Girolamo Cardano (1501–1576) is a more widely known figure, because he wrote an autobiography describing his rather uneventful life. Very much the Renaissance man for the breadth of his knowledge and interests, he did not publish what would become his most famous work, *Liber de Ludo Aleae* (*On Casting the Die*), which was written in the 1560s but did not see the light of day until 1663, almost 100 years after Cardano's death. The key part of this work for our purposes is contained in Chapter IX "On Casting a Single Die." According to Cardano, all games of chance must be based on "equal conditions" in all circumstances of play, including betting, results, or the situation of the players.[13] When a single die is cast, any number of the six appearing on each face has the same odds of coming up. Hence, we may say that each of the six possible results are "equiprobable." This statement reveals the dawning of probability, because it refers to a calculation performed on the set of possible results. "I can throw 1, 3 or 5 the same as 2, 4 or 6. Therefore, the odds will fall according to this equality if the die be true" (Cardano).

Let us consider the narrative content of Cardano's proposition. The possibility of an event is a discrete whole and, therefore, any of the six possible faces could come up when the die is cast. This possibility is a complete uncertainty. The step that Cardano takes is to dissect this possibility, which ceases to be a whole and is split up into its constituent parts: the six equally probable possibilities. This division of a possibility, in itself a mathematical operation, creates or entails a chink in the curtain of uncertainty, because it succeeds in establishing that, rather than just any outcome, the cast of a die will produce one of six equally probable results. This is Cardano's key contribution, which does not change the event in itself (the casting of a die), but rather the statement of the event. While the notion of risk had provided a way of conceiving the future in terms of the probable rather than the possible (as in before setting out on a long journey), this new view of the casting of a die had the effect of transforming possible outcomes into numerical probability. Mathematical probability was thus present in Cardano's conception of probability as referring to a calculus of the possible outcomes of a game.

Cardano not only splits the discrete whole represented by the possibility of an event's numerical occurrence, he also defines its bounds by establishing six as the maximum number of equally probable outcomes in dice rolling. My interest here lies in the conversion of a narrative event, the casting of a die, into a series of numbers. Cardano made this transformation by dissecting and delimiting the possibility of an event's happening, an exercise for which the die is admirably well suited. The inductive invention of probability thus took longer than its imaginative deduction in the context of Islamic theology and then in maritime contracts. It was this gap which drew the attention of David and Hacking, who wondered why it was that such a long time had to pass before anyone succeeded in stating even a rudimentary theory of probability.

Daniel Defoe and *A Journal of the Plague Year*

Daniel Defoe is a towering historical figure to me because his work bridges the gap between narratives of adventure and narratives of risk. This becomes clear if we compare the two kinds of story which make up the most creative and least political part of his extensive writings. To begin with, Defoe engaged in journalism, writing stories based on a version of the facts. In addition, he makes use of incipiently scientific tools like archival documentation and statistics. The first type is exemplified by *The Storm*, published in 1704, and the second by *A Journal of the Plague Year*, published in 1722.

Natural disasters are present in Defoe's work. *The Storm* was a journalistic piece about a hurricane that had formed somewhere in the Caribbean and struck the English coast on the night of November 26, 1703, when winds of 70 miles per hour or more wreaked havoc, causing the deaths of some 8,000 people. The storm lashed Southern England from around midnight until the early hours of the following day. Defoe published his account of the catastrophe just a few months later in the summer of 1704.

The truthfulness of the written account is the principle on which a text like *The Storm* is founded. The author witnessed the historical events and tells his tale as they actually happened.[14] This was without doubt Defoe's intention, and his essay epitomizes early journalistic reporting. The first task to be addressed in writing any eyewitness account is to find direct sources and testimony, and Defoe not only turned to the press but did something unheard of at the time. Just a few days after the storm, he published announcements in two newspapers, *The London Courant* and the *London Gazette*, in which he asked for help from anybody who could produce written testimony of the destruction caused by hurricane. Defoe doubtless received numerous such responses, enabling him to write his book, which would have been impossible otherwise because his own personal observations of the hurricane's vast swathe of destruction must have been very local. By seeking eyewitness reports, Defoe was proposing something absolutely new, which was to create a socialized account written up by the author using shared information obtained from multiple sources. Journalistic reportage and ethnography are the two forms of narrative that have always made the greatest use of both personal observations by the author and eyewitness accounts. Writing in the early years of the eighteenth century, Defoe made use of both techniques to write his account of the great storm.

His reaction to this natural disaster may be considered a milestone in the history of literature and journalism. On the very day of the hurricane, Defoe left his house to walk the streets of London and see its effects with his own eyes, minutely examining the aftermath *in situ*, noting down what he saw and interviewing survivors. His aim was to bear witness to the facts and to describe the experience of those who were caught up in the calamity through their own testimony. His account was published only a few months after the events and is, indeed, a model of what we would now call reportage. The closer in time, the greater the credibility of the description. This was the maxim that allowed Defoe to produce a realistic descriptive narrative based on eyewitness testimony.

Moreover, some of his principles would later become necessary conditions for the development of narratives of risk. "Before we come to examine the Damage suffer'd by this terrible Night, and give a particular Relation of its dismal Effects; 'tis necessary to give a summary Account of the thing itself, with all its affrightning Circumstances" (Defoe *The Storm* 25). Defoe's expression, "a summary account of the thing itself" is a declaration of a new kind of narrative intent, and it also brings the narrator into direct contact with the events he is reporting. Journalism emerged in the seventeenth century as a means of recounting events as they occurred from day to day, in contrast to the genre's precursors, which had never appeared with such regularity. In his account, Defoe employs a day-by-day or even hour-by-hour chronicle of events as they happened. The onset of the storm was first felt in the increasing violence of the wind, presaging the devastation and ruin to come. In Defoe's words:

> On the Wednesday Morning before, being 24th of November, it was fair Weather, and blew hard; but not so as to give any Apprehensions, till about 4 o'Clock in the Afternoon the Wind increased, and with Squalls of Rain and terrible Gusts blew very furiously.... On Friday Morning it continued to blow exceeding hard, but not so as that it gave any Apprehensions of Danger within Doors; toward Night it increased: and about 10 o'Clock, our Barometers inform'd us that the Night would be very tempestuous; the Mercury sunk lower than ever I had observ'd it on any Occasion whatsoever, which made me suppose the Tube had been handled and disturb'd by the Children.
>
> (Defoe The Storm 26)

In order to dramatize his account and engage the interest of his readers, Defoe used a very literary time structure in which something terrible begins, then occurs, and finally ends in death and destruction. In this we may identify a seed of sensationalism and, though only in part, of narratives of risk. This way of describing events has marked the history of journalism, which developed through a narrative time structure based on these same elements, applying a purportedly experiential methodology of immediate involvement and seeking at all times to achieve the maximum verisimilitude and credibility to convince the reader of the story's truth. As time would show, however, not every account presented as following these principles actually does so. Defoe's narrative style in *The Storm* embraces qualities like eyewitness testimony, documentary sources, and realism that are intrinsic to any narrative of risk, but it still lacks the necessary future projection. Defoe would add this final ingredient in his *A Journal of the Plague Year*.

London at Defoe's time can only be understood in terms of its maritime connections as a great metropolis and entrepôt for goods and people of all kinds. According to Jack Lindsay, Defoe was the first to call London the "Monster City," and he put its population at this time at around a million and a half inhabitants (7–8). However, modern estimates suggest a figure between 575,000 and 674,000 people, though this would have easily made it the biggest city in Europe.

With London's population growing at breakneck speed despite the high mortality rate caused by disasters and dreadful conditions of public health and violence, a new kind of science was appearing in the form of demographic measurement. It was John Graunt of London who made the first descriptive statistical analysis of mortality. He published his *Observations Made upon the Bills of Mortality* in 1662, which examined the weekly figures for deaths reported in the city of London, recorded since 1604. Defoe certainly drew on Graunt's work for his *A Journal of the Plague Year*.

A Journal of the Plague Year was first published in London in 1722, only two years after an outbreak of the bubonic plague in the port of Marseille in France. The *Yersinia pestis* bacillus had arrived from the Levant, causing around 100,000 deaths in the city and outlying areas. This was the last great epidemic of bubonic plague to occur in Europe. News of events in Marseille was not long in reaching London, where memories of the Great Plague of 1655 were still strong. Fifty-five years had passed since the Great Plague, and there were still a few survivors who had lived through it in their youth or as children. This helped to keep the memory of its ravages alive. Daniel Defoe himself was 60 years old when he set about writing *A Journal of the Plague Year*, and he was five when the plague occurred. In both of these periods of his life he lived in London, and his own memory therefore stretched back to the plague of 1665 and its aftermath.

We now know that Defoe was not the only writer to look back on the Great Plague of 1665—he also used material written by others on the same tragic events, including the works of Graunt and Hodges (Hodges 2). However, *A Journal of the Plague Year* is quite special and different. The construction of this work, which is at once fiction and history, long disconcerted critics, who considered it improper to mix two kinds of writing—history and fiction—which Aristotle himself defined as distinct in *Poetics*, as one recounts what actually happened while the other tells us what might happen. Is it possible to write a tale that describes the real events of the past in order to anticipate a possible future? I believe, as I have argued previously, that probability in both its narrative and mathematical forms shows that it is. Once again, the time structure here is one in which the events of the past could, in principle, happen again, and this possible outcome is at the root of narrative probability. This is what I call the *narrative matrix of risk*.

Let us now juxtapose *A Journal of the Plague Year* with *The Storm* in order to examine the time structures the author employs in the two works aside from their differing subject matter. As explained above, *The Storm* stands out for having been written and published almost immediately after the events it described, in contrast to *A Journal of the Plague Year*, which was written some 55 years later. Both books, however, share the aim of winning credibility through the vehicle of "thereness," if I may employ a nonce word to describe the verisimilitude of eyewitness observation that Defoe sought. The journalistic and ethnographic force of *The Storm* is particularly indebted to this quality. When he wrote *The Storm*, Defoe was able to obtain firsthand reports from others whom he had contacted through advertisements published in the newspapers just a few days after the calamity. This was, of course, impossible when he set to writing *A Journal of the Plague Year*, although he did draw on available documentary sources that enabled him to come fairly close his subject. However, the latter work owes its originality to Defoe's fictionalization of a firsthand account, which obviously could not be true but was certainly realistic. In Defoe's book, a fictional character described as a London merchant who lived through the Great Plague of 1665 recounts its origins, course, and aftermath. The enormously prolix title page of the first edition published in 1722, a common feature of books published at this time, provides all kinds of interesting details. The work claims to consist of "Observations" and "Memorials" of what are described as "the most Remarkable Occurrences as well Publick as Private" which happened to a "Citizen who continued all the while in London." These are the terms in which the author and his publishers saw fit to synopsize the work. It consisted of eyewitness observations and recollections of public and private events. The associations between all of these claims directly suggest a memoir, in which a first person narrator describes personal experiences as facts in the form of observations. There is in this a pretension to objectivity which is used to spell out the new literary style or journalistic genre to the public.

Like all memoirs, the book starts by presenting the narrator, a London merchant, who sets out to relate his experience:

> It was about the beginning of September, 1664, that I, among the rest of my neighbours, heard in ordinary discourse that the plague was returned again in Holland; for it had been very violent there, and particularly at Amsterdam and Rotterdam, in the year 1663, whither, they say, it was brought (some said from Italy, others from the Levant) among some goods which were brought home by their Turkey fleet; others said it was brought from Candia; others, from Cyprus. It mattered not from whence it came; but all agreed it was come into Holland again.
>
> *(Defoe, A Journal of the Plague Year 3)*

Defoe's account is highly descriptive and he clearly marks the nature of his narrative tempos. Having situated the nearest outbreak in Holland in 1663, he goes on to depict an ensuing period of "rumor," a highly significant word. In closing this episode, however, Defoe points the finger at the authorities for having kept the reports they received secret so as not to spread alarm, with the result that the general public remained ignorant of the threat posed by the plague, which had not yet reached London. We cannot know to what extent this was actually so, but Defoe's account, which was written retrospectively, certainly presents this official concealment as fact; he is actually thinking of the rumors that arrived at the time of his writing from Marseille, and of the real reports that the government ordered from experts like Dr. Richard Mead in 1720. In this way, he uses an account of the past to warn of the future by means of a masterly simulation of an eyewitness memoir to lend verisimilitude to his story. He writes:

> We had no such thing as printed newspapers in those days, to spread rumours and reports of things, and to improve them by the invention of men, as I have lived to see practiced since. But such things as those were gathered from the letters of merchants and others who corresponded abroad, and from them was handed about by word of mouth only; so that things did not spread instantly over the whole nation, as they do now. But it seems that the government had a true account of it, and several counsels were held about ways to prevent its coming over; but all was kept very private. Hence it was that this rumour died off again; and people began to forget it, as a thing we were very little concerned in and that we hoped was not true, till the latter end of November or the beginning of December, 1664, when two men, said to be Frenchmen, died of the plague in Longacre, or rather at the upper end of Drury Lane.
>
> *(33)*

The mention of the lack of newspapers "in those days" reveals Defoe's interest in attributing an apparently journalistic dimension to his work by doing "today" what nobody had done "back then," although the truth is that the *Oxford Gazette* was founded precisely in 1665 after the London elite had removed there to escape the plague. *A Journal of the Plague Year* is written in an elaborate or polished tone to be expected of a journalist as opposed to a gazetteer. Defoe immediately shifts to the new time of the plague, which had now arrived in London, offering a fact that also appears in Samuel Pepys' diary—the first confirmed cases occurred in or around Drury Lane. This coincidence was only made possible by Defoe's excellent documentary work; he could not have taken it from Pepys' diaries because they were not published until many years later. Even when it is passed exclusively by word of mouth, rumor is the forerunner of written narrative. This fundamental transition in the history of public communication is reflected in this part of Defoe's tale, anticipating the birth of the press as mass media.

Though the mention of press is no more than an aside placed by Defoe's pen in the mouth of his fictional London merchant, it is important enough to warrant a brief pause for reflection. Defoe is telling us that his own writing harks back to a time when there was no press, but he assumes that his narrator is writing at a time after the press had in fact appeared, and even "improves" the news. What lies between these two eras is the devastating plague of 1665. Hence, we may pick up on the suggestion implicit in the text that the press is the child of the plague, especially in light of his other great journalistic work on natural disaster, *The Storm*. This is borne out by the reportage of *The Storm* and the journalistic account presented in *A Journal of the Plague Year*. In the latter case, this consideration could last only until the end of the eighteenth century, when it was discovered that H. F., a London shoemaker and the purported author of the work, was none other than Daniel Defoe, and that what had until then been read as a memoir was in fact a work of fiction, if a rather peculiar one.

At this point, we find ourselves faced with a knot. First, this is the historical moment in which we can situate the birth of what Defoe calls the "printed newspaper," containing a widely circulated written account of daily events, which first emerged in fledgling form immediately after 1665, the year of the plague. This innovation of the newspaper "improved" on rumor and private reports in such a way that Defoe points to the emergence of a new literary style. The new style was much more demanding to produce, in part because it required documentation, a knowledge of historical background, firsthand information, and skillful writing. To "improve" the news was precisely what Defoe sought to do in his own writing, and as Anthony Burgess has said, it is this which characterizes him as the first historical example of a modern journalist. In this light, let me posit that the foundation for the modern journalistic account constructed by Defoe was none other than the concept of risk. The "improvement" of the news, or to put it another way, the new narrative style invented by Defoe, involves a clearly probabilistic time structure. The account creates a past time that is proposed as real, even though it is fictitious. Indeed, it was so real that it took years before the public realized that it was a fiction and not a memoir, and only when the true authorship of the work was discovered.[15] Hence, the time structure in *A Journal of the Plague Year* clearly runs from the past (the London of 1665) to the future (the London of 1720), from what happened to what could happen in the specific time and space described in the work.

The main reason for viewing Defoe's work as a narrative of risk (and certainly the first of such length and polish) lies not so much in the text itself as in the context, and indeed critical appraisals of *A Journal of the Plague Year* center around what we know about Defoe himself, his activity, the time of writing, and his other writings on the plague. The plague was a matter of huge concern in Great Britain in the early eighteenth century, and Defoe wrote much about it in the newspapers. For instance, in 1709, British troops were fighting alongside the Swedes against Russia. Meanwhile, the armies of Prussia and Poland, allies of the Tsar, were stricken with plague, and Defoe wrote about it in the press to warn of the possibility of contagion. In 1712, further outbreaks appeared in Europe. Despite his custom of using pseudonyms, various articles published in *Applebee's Original Weekly Journal* have been attributed to Defoe, and in one of these, dated October 1, 1720, he refers to reports from Marseille under the ominous byline "Quarantine" in the following terms: "piles of unburied corpses in the streets the stench of which was insupportable ... people eating leather, starch, soap ... bands of thieves and murderers who roam the infected streets."[16]

In 1721, Prime Minister Horace Walpole's government passed the *Act of Quarantine* to prevent foreign ships suspected of carrying the plague from entering British ports. In the press, Defoe was one of the most fervent defenders of the Act, which finally entered the statute book on February 12, 1722. London in 1722 was on the alert against the plague, and it is in this context that we must place *A Journal of the Plague Year*. The narrative of risk was created by multiple, interrelated sources including the press, the government, experts, ordinary people, and other agents, each feeding back into the others. Thus a contextual account was gradually woven and spread by all parties: the plague that had broken out in Marseille was coming to London. It was against this backdrop that Defoe wrote his *Journal*, and this is the context in which it should be understood. Meanwhile, the intentions of the writer are revealed by numerous pieces of evidence. Aside from the personal goal of winning fame and fortune, his primary purpose was to help prevent any new outbreak of the plague by writing an original, powerful, and novel narrative—a narrative of risk. This was my fundamental thesis in beginning work on this chapter, combined with the idea that his action was key to the genesis of risk as narrative.

A narrative context of risk may be defined as a social discourse which emerges when various agents recount experiences or stories about a probable threat to society as whole. Initially, it is something that is "in the air," like the letters and warnings people exchanged before the outbreak of the plague in 1665 as told by Pepys, or the "rumors" mentioned by Defoe at the beginning of the *Journal*. In time, however, this nebulous "atmosphere" becomes increasingly precise, as we have seen in the description of the years before 1722, when Defoe wrote his book. Stable, formal communication channels develop, especially in the press, conveying information and eventually configuring a latent account of events. Such latent accounts receive regular feedback from ever more politicized groups among the population (especially in the context of British-style parliamentarianism), who place the issues at the center of public debate. A narrative context of risk is created when various latent accounts are reactivated by new events, shaping beliefs about what is likely to happen next.

Defoe cannot have been fully aware of the significance which his simultaneously factual and fictional reconstruction of the Great Plague of 1665 would eventually attain. Indeed, this significance is only fully visible to us today, because we have the benefit of hindsight and can look back on the subsequent development of some of Defoe's novel ideas and stylistic innovations over the intervening centuries. We may begin with the scientific application of statistics to the description and quantification of the epidemic, to epidemiology, and to demographics in general. In this area, Defoe drew on the work of Graunt, who is today revered as one of the founding fathers of descriptive statistics. He also made use of contemporary medical treatises, like that of Hodges mentioned above. Historically, these scientific fields proved decisive in the subsequent development of risk as a form of specialist knowledge.

Today narratives of risk are a habitual media resource to communicate catastrophes, massive accidents, epidemics, natural disasters, or terrorism. They promote narrative contexts of risk, which expand and influence public opinion by means of their dissemination on the press, the radio, the television, or the Internet. Although this is the most contemporary way for the social construction of risk, I have argued here that the emergence of risk as a narrative has traveled a very long historical route, first from East to West, then from Europe to the Americas, and again from the Americas to Europe to become a present-day global conception used around the world.

Notes

1 At this point we should mention two important figures: a geographer, Al-Idris (1110–1165) and an historian and Sociology precursor, Ibn Jaldun (1332–1406).
2 The *qirad* is: "Lend money to carry out a business and share the gains." See Udovitch.
3 Another version is mentioned earlier in the so-called "Carta Picena," an Italian document written in 1193 in a very corrupted medieval Latin: "Ke la mitade se ne tose ad resicu de Johann" (201).
4 The Italian, Catalan, Provençal, and a preliminary French version of the Latin "risicum" appeared in the thirteenth and fourteenth centuries in the Mediterranean. The Castilian or Spanish version together with the Portuguese were in use in the second half of fifteenth century. The maritime activities of Castile and Portugal were in the Atlantic, which explains why they were slow to incorporate this word. In Great Britain, the word "risk" was not in use until the second half of seventeenth century and it appears for the first time in the 1665 edition of the *Oxford English Dictionary*.
5 This was the fleet that voyaged every year between the Americas and Spain in the charge of the Spanish Crown.
6 "Nao" was the kind of ship used mainly by the Spanish and Portuguese fleets during the sixteenth century.
7 Mount Vesuvius had been dormant from 1036 until the 1631 eruption in which some 3000 people died. Mount Etna had been inactive from the second century AD until 1669, when it returned to activity with several eruptions in the following years. The Canary Islands volcanos, as the big Teide, were extinct.
8 According to López de Mariscal, this natural disaster was included in several *relaciones* such as *Memoriales* by Fray Toribio de Benavente, the *Historia General y Natural de las Indias* (*A General and Natural History of the Indies*) by Fernández de Oviedo, the *Anales de los cakchiqueles* (*The Annals of the Cakchiqueles*) and *Historia verdadera de la Conquista de la Nueva España* (*The True History of New Spain Conquest*) by Bernal Díaz del Castillo, and the *Monarquía Indiana* (*Indian Monarchy*) by Torquemada.
9 Although, in my opinion, narrative and mathematical probability are the two fundamental expressions.
10 The same theological principal is also Christian, appearing in the New Testament story of Saint Thomas' doubts about the resurrection of Christ: "Jesus saith unto him, Thomas, because thou hast seen me, thou has believed: blessed are they that have not seen, and yet have believed" (John 20.29).
11 In fact, it was not until 1560 that Girolamo Cardano would state this principle for the first time.
12 This work is the origin of double-entry bookkeeping.
13 At this time, gambling had not been professionalized and there was no bank.
14 Defoe was not the first to do this. Classical writer Pliny the Younger described the eruption of Vesuvius in AD 72, which he personally witnessed. However, nobody before Defoe had embarked on the task with such careful forethought, breadth of purpose, and precision.
15 Under his pseudonym, Defoe had succeeded in convincing his readers that he had been "there." Furthermore, his account lost none of its capacity to convince readers when it became known who was behind the pen name. In this light, it seems that "thereness" depends as much on the skill of the writer as it does on the actual fact of having been "there."
16 Defoe's authorship has been questioned in some cases, and Maximillian Novak himself expresses various concerns.

Works Cited

Berstein, Peter. *Against the God. The Remarkable Story of Risk*. Wiley, 1998.
Bosworth, C. E. and McAuliffe, Jane D. "Rizk." In *Encyclopaedia of Islam*, edited by: P. Bearman, Th. Bianquis, C. E. Bosworth, E. van Donzel, and W. P. Heinrichs.

Cardano, Geralmo. *Llibre del jocs d'atzar: Antologica Mínima* [On Casting the Die: Minimum Anthology]. Santa Coloma de Gramanet: Grup de Filosofia, 1998.

Carta Picena. Roma, R. Archivio di Stato, Fondo Fiastra, 1193.

David, F. N. *Games, Gods and Gambling, The Origin and History of Probability and Statistical Ideas from the Earliest Times to the Newtonian Era.* Hafner Publishing Company, 1962.

de Epalza, Mikel. "Origines du concept de risqué: de l' Islam à l' Occident." In *Le risque et la crisis*. European Coordination Centre for Reserch and Documentation in Social Sciences.

de Escalante de Mendoza, Juan. *Itinerario de navegación de los mares y tierras occidentales.* [*Itinerary of Navigation of Western Seas and Lands*]. Museo Naval, 1985.

Defoe, Daniel. *A Journal of the Plague Year*. The Modern Library, 2001.

Defoe, Daniel. *The Storm*. Penguin Books, 2005.

Golding, C. E. *A History of Reinsurance with Sidelights on Insurance*. London: Waterlow & Sons.

Graunt, John. *Natural Observations Made upon the Bills of Mortality*. The Royal Society, 1662, www.edstephan.org/Graunt/bills.html.

Hodges, Nathaniel. *LOIMOLOGIA: or An Historical Account of the Plague in London in 1665*. E. Bell, 1720.

Lindsay, Jack. *The Monster City. Defoe's London 1688–1730*. Granada Publishing, 1978.

López de Mariscal, B. "Tormentas y catástrofes en las crónicas y los relatos de viaje al nuevo mundo" ["Storms and Catastrophes in Chronicles and Travel to the New World Stories"], *Revista de Estudios Colombinos*, vol. 2, 2006, pp. 57–65.

Luhmann, Niklaus. *Risk: A Sociological Theory*. Aldine de Gruyter, 1993.

Novak, Maximilian. "Daniel Defoe and 'Applebee's Original Weekly Journal': An Attempt at Re-Attribution." *Eighteenth-Century Studies*, vol. 45, no. 4, Summer 2012, pp. 585–608.

Pepys, Samuel. "The Diary of Samuel Pepys. Daily Entries from the 17th Century London Diary." Phil Gyford, www.pepysdiary.com/diary.

Reith, Gerda. *The Age of Chance. Gambling and Western Culture*. Routledge, 1999.

Rodríguez, J. *Relación del espantable terremoto que agora nuevamente ha acontecido en la ciudad de Guatemala* [*Account of the Frightening Earthquake that Happened Newly in the Indies in a City Called Guatemala*]. Mexico 1541.

Serrano and Sanz, Manuel, editor *Relaciones históricas de América. Primera mitad del siglo XVI* [*Historical Accounts of the Americas. First Half of Sixteenth Century*]. Sociedad de Bibliófilos Españoles, 1916.

Udovitch, Abraham. *Partnership and Profit in Medieval Islam*. Princeton UP, 1970, p. 17.

Varela, Consuelo. *Cristóbal Colón. Textos y documentos completos* [*Columbus. Complete Texts and Documents*]. Alianza Editorial, 1982.

Villain-Gandossi, Christiane. "Origines du concept de risque en Occident. Les risques maritimes ou fortune de mer et leur compensation: les débuts de l' assurance maritime." *Le risque et la crise*, edited by Lucien Faugeres, Pal Vasarhelyi, and Christiane Villain-Gandossi. Malta: Foundation for International Studies, 1990, pp. 71–85.

3

RISK

The Origin of the Word in Medieval Commerce and Poetry

Wolf Kittler

From the Maritime Loan to Philosophy

The term risk, as it is understood by insurance agents, bankers, hedge fund managers, economists, and politicians today has a long and complex history which comprises a multiplicity of enterprises, institutions, and sciences such as, to name but a few: canonical law, gambling, probability calculus, statistics, the tobacco and the slave trade, regulations and institutions from the maritime loan to the accident and health insurance policies of the nineteenth and twentieth centuries, and, finally, Ulrich Beck's concept of "risk society" which covers the short timespan in human history that is characterized by the omnipresent threat of man-made catastrophes.

The origin of the word is lost in time. According to the usual etymological speculations, a Greek, Latin, or Arabic root are equally probable, which is as good as saying: No one knows. We do, however, know *who* the people were who wrote the word down for the very first time, *when*, *where*, *why*, *how*, and *by what means*. Of course, we cannot name names, but the sources we have indicate clearly that the word must have been coined, perhaps the product of a European/North African/Syrian pidgin, by merchants, mariners, and notaries in charge of the trade routes opened by the first two Crusades at the turn of the eleventh to the twelfth century, which connected the ports along the North Western coast of the Mediterranean, from the Gulf of Lyon to the Ligurian and Tyrrhenian Seas, Marseille, Genoa,* and Messina; to partner cities all along the North African coast from Ceuta, Valencia, Bougie (now Bejaïa, Algeria), Tlemcen (Algeria), and Oran (in the West); to Alexandria, Damietta (Egypt), Akka, Syria (now Acre, Israel), and even Babylonia, in the Levant. These are the cities mentioned in the earliest documents I could find. Later on, Barcelona, Palermo, and, most importantly, Florence, through representatives in the ports of Palermo and Grosseto, connect to this network as well, while Venice, which dominated the trade with Constantinople, rarely appears among the cities that branched out to the new markets further South.

The people who established and maintained this complex network of trade and commerce included bankers and investors who had money to lend; lawyers and notaries who could read the codes of Canonical and Civil Law and write contracts and letters of exchange; traders, mariners, and sailors who ventured to ship the merchandise back and forth over perilous seas; and agents who negotiated sales, purchases, and exchange rates with business partners abroad.

In the shadow of this economic revolution, pirates—not mere criminals, but public enemies since Antiquity—were thriving as well. According to Cicero, the *ius iurandum*, which stipulates that oaths sworn to enemies must often be observed, does not include an obligation to the pirate because, "by definition, he is not part of the number of lawful enemies, but the common foe of all"

The Origin of the Word Risk

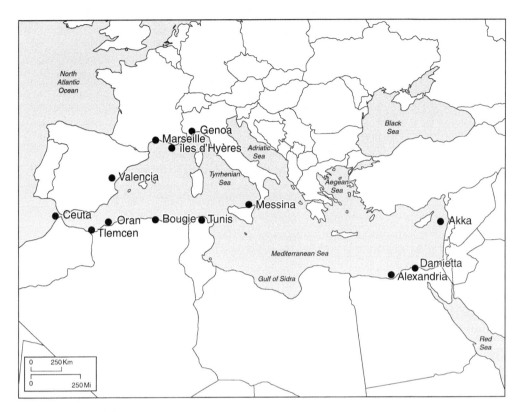

Figure 3.1 Map of the Mediterranean
Credit: Alabama Maps

'Nam pirata non est ex perduellium numero definitus, sed communis hostis omnium; cum hoc nec fides debet nec ius iurandum esse commune' (Cicero, III.XXIX 107).[1] Doubling down on this formulation, the great fourteenth-century canonist Bartolus de Saxoferrato passed a harsher and more general verdict. In a gloss to the chapter "On Captives, and Prisoners of War to be Returned to, and by the Enemy," in Justinian's *Digests* of the Roman Law, he writes:

> Et nota quod piratae aequiparantur hostibus fidei, & principis, & sunt ipso iure diffidati, & possunt impune a quolibet derobari.... Item hypocratae dicuntur hostes humani generis: vnde dignum est a cunctis publicum bellum contra eos indicere.
>
> *(Saxoferrato 255)*

> And note that pirates are equal to enemies of faith, & ruler, and, by that same law, they are to be distrusted, and can be robbed by anyone with impunity... Moreover, they are said to be deceiving enemies of mankind: wherefore it is appropriate for all to declare public war on them.

As a safeguard against such enemies as well against a host of other dangers arising from the ocean and from people,[2] entrepreneurs, capitalist, and jurists revived the old contractual form of the sea loan, Greek ναυτικὸς τόκος, already mentioned in one of Demosthenes' speeches (17), and known in both Roman and Canonical Law as *foenus nauticum*.[3] The model case of such a loan is described in the *Codex iuris civilis, Digestum vetus*, paragraph 22.2: "Mutuo tibi decem aureos portandos vltra mare meo periculo. si nauis pereat, haec quidem pecunia dicitur traiectitia: & infrà centesimam usuram possum pacisci."

'I lend you ten aurei[4] for you to carry overseas at my peril. If the boat should perish, then this is called a maritime loan: & I can negotiate an interest rate [usuria] under one hundredth' (1693).

The *Assises de Jérusalem*, the legal treatises of the crusader Kingdom of Jerusalem and the Kingdom of Cyprus, which date from 1173–1187 (XXVII), contain an extended version of this case:

> S'il avient que un home baille à un autre home de son aver à porter sur mer, à gaaing en aventure de mer et de gens, et il avient que corsaus l'encontrent et li tolent tout can que il porte, ou il fait mauvais tens, et brise le vaisseau et pert tout, la raison commande qu'il en est atant quite, et ne li en deit riens amender.... Et s'il avient que il resut l'aveir des bones gens à porter sauf en terre, il est tenus de l'amender coument qu'il seit perdus, par dreit at par l'asize.
>
> *(Receuil des Historiens des Croisades 46)*

> If it happens that a man lends to another man part of his belongings to carry overseas, for gain and at the adventure of the sea and peoples, and it happens that corsairs find him and take away everything he carries, or there is bad weather that breaks the vessel and he loses everything, then reason commands that he is quits of it, and does not owe him any amends.... And if it happens that he manages to carry the good people's belongings safely onto land, he is obliged to make amends for them as if they had been lost, according to the law and the assizes.
>
> *(46)*

The word *aventure*, a key term in Chrétien de Troyes' courtly novels written at exactly the same time, and echoed here in the *figura etymologica* of the twice repeated verb *advient*, translates the canonists' much more general term *periculum*, 'peril, danger,' which, in turn, is a translation of κίνδυνος, a word used from the time of Demosthenes up to the Rhodian sea-law in the seventh century CE (Demosthenes 50, 21).[5] Another expression for the same idea is the formula, "ad fortunam Dei et usum maris," 'at the mercy [or, literally, the fortune] of God, and the use of the sea,' which is documented in a contract dated Marseille, March 22, 1210, for a shipment of merchandise to Akka, payable "in Saracen bezants" (Blanchard, no. 2, p. 5; no. 3, p. 6; no. 4, p. 7; no. 22, pp. 28–29). It is as if the merchants and notaries of the twelfth century were groping for a term that would distinguish the specific perils to ship, man, and cargo in the maritime trade from other problems of their business. And so it happened that, perhaps inspired by one or several of the different languages spoken around the coasts of the Mediterranean, they coined a new word, which Du Cange's Middle Latin *Glossarium* documents in no less than eight different forms: *riscus, risicus, riscum, risigus, rischium, rischum, risicum,* and *risigum* (Du Cange, 1883–1887).[6] The earliest examples I could find, so far, are from the acts of the notary Giovanni Scriba in Genoa.

April 26, 1156:

> Ego iordanus filius uiualdi de pradi accepi a te arnaldo uacca libras tres centas decem et solidos octo quas debeo portare ad laborandum apud ualenciam ad tuum risicum et deinde si major pars hominum de naui in qua uado concordati fuerunt ire alexandra ibo et portabo eos illuc si uolero.
>
> *(Historiae Patriae Monumenta 324d–325a)*

> I, Giordano, son of Vivaldus de' Pradi, testify to have accepted from you, Arnaldo Vacca, three hundred ten pounds and eight soldi which I am responsible for taking to Valencia and invest at your risk, and, if the majority of the men on board should agree, I will go to Alexandria from there and take them with me if I wish.

August 19, 1156:

> Ego solimanus accepi a te bonoiohanne malfuasto tantum ex tuis rebus de quibus debeo tibi apud alexandriam bisanzios centum decem ad pensum alexandrie mundos et eos debeo portare ad tuum resicum apud babiloniam et implicare in lana uel brazil siluatico et adducere ad tuum resicum in naui quam venero.
>
> (344d)

> I, Soliman, accepted from you, Bongiovanni Malfuesto, so much of your possessions, for which I will owe you in Alexandria one hundred and ten bezants weighted at the Alexandrian rate, and these I am responsible for taking to Babylon at your risk, and invest in wool and Brasilium silvaticum,[7] and bring it along in the ship in which I shall come back at your risk.

August 20, 1156:

> Ego wilielmus de sauri accepi in commendacione a te ugone de baldezone libras ducentum minus solidos undecim quas ad tuum resicum debeo portare alexandrinam et implicare et reducere tibi ad tuum resicum.
>
> (347c)

> I, Guglielmo de Sauri, accepted from you, Ugolino de Balduzone, a commission of two hundred pounds less eleven soldis which I am responsible for carrying to Alexandria, and to invest them, and bring the return back to you at your risk.

December 14, 1162:

> ego enricus niucella cepi a te iosepho iudeo libram unam seuete de qua libras duodecim denariorum ianuensium tibi solui. quam ispaniam ad meum resicum porto. sed ad tuum resicum uendere promitto.
>
> (834a)

> I, Enrico Nivecella, received from you, Joseph, the Jew, one pound of merchandise for which I paid you twelve dinars in Genoa. These I will take to Spain at my risk. But I promise to sell them at your risk.

To quote but one more example from another place, here is a contract from the acts of the notary Ugo Andrée of Marseille:

April 2, 1211:

> Manifestum sit omnibus homines hanc cartam audientibus quod ego Bernardus de Gardia confiteor et recognosco me habuisse et recepisse a te Stephano de Mandolio, in commanda IIII l. et XVII s. regalium coronatorum, implicatas in XXV bisanciis milarensium, in quibus penitus ex certa scientia renuntio exceptioni non tradite et numerate peccunie; cum qua comanda ibo, Deo duce, ad laborandum in hoc itinere de Ohareno, et deinde ubique, cause negociandi, ad fortunam Dei et ad usum maris ad tuum risigum, auxiliante Deo, reducere totum dictu capitale et lucrum in hac terra in tuum posse vel turorum, et verum inde tibi vel tuis dicam, et exinde recipio te in Dei fide at me.
>
> (Blanchard, no. 5, p. 8)

Be it manifest to all the men witnessing this parchment that I, Bernard de La Garde, confess and recognize to have had and received from you, Étienne Manduel, 4 pounds and 17 soldi of royal coronets, implied in XXV byzantine millares, non-counterfeit and counted money with which, I declare to the notary, I have been furnished according to the certainty of science; with this commission I will go, with God as my guide, this way to Oran in order to invest them, and from there anywhere, for trading's sake, at the mercy of God, the use of the sea, and your risk, to bring all the said capital, with God's help, back to this country into your and your people's possession, and may I say this truly to you and your folks, and after that, I withdraw from you in God's and my trust.

Taken together, these quotes provide an answer to all of the questions raised at the beginning of this essay, and, thereby, the coordinates to reconstruct the irretrievably lost origin of the word risk:

Quis, or who were the people who coined and first used the word risk? Traders, and mariners from Europe, and, as the name Soliman proves, the Levant, as well as their European notaries.

Quid, what? Merchandise such as pepper, nutmeg, wool, and brasile, a dyewood (*Historiae Patriae Monumenta* 344a, 345a–346d, 520d).

Quando, when? Between 1156 and 1211, but possibly even earlier, perhaps already during the first or the second Crusade, 1096–1097, and 1147–1149, respectively.

Ubi, where? All over the Mediterranean, from Genoa to Valencia, Oran, Alexandra, and back home.

Cur, why? According to the *Digestum vetvs* already quoted above, the maritime loan is distinguished from other forms of trade because, due to the high level of risk involved, it is exempt from the general prohibition of usury, that is, the taking of interest on a loan. Starting with the following definition: "Traiectitia pecunia est quae trans mare vehitur" 'Trajectitia is money transported overseas,'[8] the *Digest* constructs two cases of the *foenus nauticum*, or, as it is called here, the *traiectitia*:

CASVS. Mutuo tibi decem aureos portandos vltra mare meo periculo. si nauis pereat, haec quidem pecunia dicitur traciectatis: & infrà centesimam vsuram possum pacisci. sed si non per aquam, sed hîc consumere debebas, hoc acto non erit traiactitia: et sic praedictam usuram sic magnam non possum stipulari. Secundo pone quòd mutuo tibi centum aureos vt emas merces hîc, & portes vltra mare, quęritur an hae merces sint traiectitiae, vt sic possim vsuram pacisci? Et respon. si actum est vt meo periculo sint, sic: aliâs non.

(*Digestum vetus*)

CASES. I lend you ten aurei for you to carry overseas at my peril. If the boat should perish, then this is called a maritime loan: & I can negotiate an interest rate under one hundredth [i.e., under 1 percent]. Yet, if you did not have to spend money overseas, but here, this act will not be a maritime loan: and so, I cannot stipulate as great a rate of interest as mentioned before. Secondly, suppose I lend you one hundred aurei so that you can buy goods here, and you carry them overseas, then the question is whether these goods are maritime loans so that, this way, I can negotiate an interest rate. And I answer: If it is done at my peril, I can do it this way, in the other case I cannot.

Usury was a hotly contested topic among jurists and clerics from the time of Justinian's *Codex Iuris Canonici* until well into the eighteenth century, at which time the debate did not stop, of course, but began to shift away from the theology of guilt and sin to the new capitalist economy of growth and investment. There is no doubt that the subtle distinction between the maritime loan and other forms of credit, as it had been formulated in the *Digestum vetus*, was not shared by everyone in the Roman Church. Pope Gregory IX, for one, rescinded this distinction when, in a decretal issued in

1227, he declared that anyone who concludes a loan contract, (Latin: *mutuum*) be it on land or sea, is to be deemed a usurer: "Naviganti, vel eunti ad nundinum, certam mutuans pecuniae quantitatem, pro eo, quod suscipit in se periculum, recepturus aliquid ultra sortem, usurarius censendus" 'Somebody lending a certain quantity of money to one sailing or going to a fair in order to receive something beyond the capital, for taking the peril upon himself, is to be deemed a usurer' (1744–1745).

While even a cursory account of the erudite and sophisticated debate on usury would exceed this essay's scope by far,[9] I think it is safe to say that the merchants and sailors who were relying on the maritime loan for their business transactions had every reason to stay out of this debate. They had no business whatsoever to either invoke the *Digestum vetus*, which, by exempting the *foenus nauticum* from usury, did legitimize the maritime loan, but only under the condition of extremely low interest rates, or to engage in an open fight with those who, like Pope Gregory IX, condemned loan contracts in each and every form. What these businessmen could (and I think, did do) instead was to adopt the *Digest*'s position, but under their own terms, that is to say, by literally inventing a new term to create what we now would call a narrative of their own. They introduced the neologism "risk" in order to emphasize the specificity of the danger to which men, ship, and cargo were exposed on perilous seas, and, by implication, the special status of the maritime loan. By replacing the canonists' technical term *periculum* with a word they had coined themselves, traders and their lawyers managed to stay aloof of the pitfalls of theology, keep their business flourishing, and were perhaps even able to remain untainted by the sin of usury—not only in the confessional box and the public forum, but also in the forum of their own conscience.

Quomodo, how? By inventing a neologism that was not related to the word *periculum*, peril, used by the canonists to describe the risks of usurious, and, hence, sinful loans on land and sea.

Quibus auxiliis, with what? Ships, parchment, and contracts written in Latin, and letters of exchange, the new form of money transfer which had just been invented.

The phrase "ad fortunam Dei et usum maris" still reverberates in what the law of contracts calls an "act of God." And formulas such as "ad meum risigum et fortunam" and "en aventure de mer et de gens" contain in a nutshell what marine insurance policies spell out in much more detail to this day. Here is the opening paragraph of a policy that was issued by Lloyd's of London on January 12, 1799 and was reconfirmed with a few minor changes and additional paragraphs on January 1, 1924:

> Touching the Adventures and Perils which we the Assurers are contended to bear and do take upon us on this Voyage, they are, of the Seas, Men-of-War, Fire, Enemies, Pirates, Thieves, Jettisons, Letters of Mart and Countermart, Surprisals, Takings at Sea, Arrests, Restraints and Detainments of all Kings, Princes, and People, of what Nation, Condition or Quality soever, Barratry of the Master and Mariners, and of all other Perils, Losses and Misfortunes that have or shall come to the Hurt, Detriment, or Damage of the said merchandises and Ship, &c., or any Part thereof; ...
>
> *(Wright and Fayle 127–128)*

Vestiges of this text, which itself can be traced back to a Florentine policy from 1523 (Magens 4–5), are still preserved in Lloyd's *Module 3: Cargo Claims and Recoveries* today. With respect to the history of risk, one difference between the two texts is worth mentioning, however. Where the old contract still used the word "Perils," the first sentence of the new one states explicitly:

> All policies of insurance on cargo will set out the risks (perils) that the underwriters provide cover against.
>
> (7)

Originally developed along and, hence, confined to the Mediterranean trade routes in the age of the crusades, the word risk has conquered the globe today. But when the center of naval power shifted from Southern Europe to Great Britain in the late seventeenth century, this word was obviously not part of the package. This is all the more significant as we know that modern banking institutions, and with them a whole new discourse including such terms as *banca* (bank), and *banca rotta* (bankrupt), which had emerged in Italian city states from the time of the crusades up to the beginning of the Renaissance, were transferred to England in the sixteenth century.[10] Why was the Italian word *rischio* (risk) not part of this transfer? As far as I can see, the answer to this question lies in the special relation between Italian bankers and the English crown that dates back to the late Middle Ages. In 1290, after having issued an edict which expelled all the Jews from England, King Edward I invited North Italian goldsmiths in their stead to settle on a lot of marshland within the walls of London, a place still known as Lombard Street today. These Italians negotiated with the Pope on behalf of the king, and soon enough they were his creditors.

Already in John Locke's writings on financial matters, the term Lombard Street stands for the banking system in general ("Short Observations on a Printed paper"), and, to this day, the granting of credit to banks against pledged items, mostly in the form of securities or life insurance policies, is called Lombard credit. The word *rischio*, however, with which the Italian bankers were certainly familiar, must have gotten lost with them when Queen Elisabeth I, after having officially opened the Royal Exchange on Lombard Street, on January 23, 1571, expelled them from her realm (*A history of English clearing banks*).

The take-over of Lombard Street by English businessmen and bankers occurred at a time when a certain Jew by the name of Shylock could rate the credit score of Antonio, one of his debtors, in the following terms:

> SHYLOCK. Ho no, no, no, no: my meaning in saying he is a good man is to have you understand me that he is sufficient. Yet his means are in supposition: he hath an argosy bound to Tripolis, another to the Indies; I understand moreover upon the Rialto he hath a third to Mexico, a fourth for England, and other ventures he hath squandered abroad. But ships are but boards, sailors but men; there be land rats, and water rats, water thieves and land thieves—I mean pirates—and there is the peril of waters, winds and rocks. The man is notwithstanding sufficient. Three thousand ducats: I think I may take this bond.
> (Shakespeare 3.15–26)

The quote not only shows that the center of naval power had shifted from Italy to England, but also that this power had been expanded from the limited space of the Mediterranean to both the Atlantic and the Pacific oceans, that is, all over the globe. When the Italians left Lombard Street, England was off to a new start. Sea loans covering the ship itself were now called *bottomry*, a word derived from the English word bottom (keel), which Shakespeare's Antonio uses in the following sense: "My ventures are not in one bottom trusted,/ Nor in one place; …" (I.1.42–43)

After Henry VIII had broken with Rome in 1536, and his daughter Elisabeth I had given a formal structure to the Anglican Church, in 1562, the long ban on usury was finally lifted. There was no reason any more to avoid the old word, "peril," when referring to maritime loans—a negative proof, as it were, of the reasons why traders and lawyers in the time of the crusades had found themselves compelled to do exactly that by coining the neologism risk.

One of the first Englishmen to follow in the footsteps of the expelled Italians was Edward Lloyd, who moved his coffee house from Tower Street to 16 Lombard Street in 1686, where it was emerging as one of the prime locations for marine underwriting by individuals. From the 1730s to this day, Lloyd's has dominated shipping insurance on a global scale. As such, it was, of course, also heavily involved in the slave trade. Non-marine policies were introduced by Cuthbert Heath as late as 1887 ("Corporate History"). As one of the oldest and one of the leading insurance companies worldwide, Lloyd's could afford to stick to the old-fashioned term peril in reference to what everyone else was calling risk, a term already used without a formal definition in Augustus de Morgan's *Essay on Probabilities and On Their Application To Life Contingencies and Insurance Offices* that was published in 1838. Lloyd's, for its part, managed to avoid the new term for a long time, but, at some point in the interval between the policy it issued in 1924 and the one currently in use, it must have given in, albeit not without supplementing the word risk with its time honored predecessor, peril, in parenthesis.

The trajectory along which the word risk was introduced, or shall we say re-introduced to the English language, is easy to track. It arrived from Italy via France. In 1578, the great printer and classical scholar Henri Estienne, also known as Stephanus, published his book *Deux Dialogues du nouveau language françois italianizé et autrement desguizé, principalement entre les courtisans de ce temps/De plusieurs nouveauté de langage/De quelques courtisanismes modernes, et de quelques singularitez courtisanesques*, printed in Geneva. Under the rubric "italianizmens," a character named *Celtophile*, that is, Francophile, lists the words *reussir* and *risque*:

CEL[TOPHILE]. Tout le dernier dont vous avez usé en est un, *reussir*, au lieu de dire "avoir bonne issue". L'autre, c'est *risque*, quand vous avez dict: *Je le pren à ma risque*, car en bon françois il faudroit dire: "Je le pren à ma charge" ou "Je pren le hazard sur moy". Et en parlant comme on parloit il n'y a pas long temps, et encore quelques-uns parlent pour le jourd'huy, il faudroit dire: "Je le pren à mes perils et fortunes". Or, ce qui me fait penser que ce mot soit venu de l'italien *rischio*, c'est que je trouve en Boccace le verbe *arrischiare*, faict de ce nom *rischio*, pour "mettre au hazard", "exposer au peril, ou au hazard", comme en ce lieu: *Et in cio arrischiero la persona e la vita*,[11] au lieu de dire *mettere à rischio*. Et de là ils ont aussi faict *arrischievole*[12] pour signifier un qui est hazardeux, qui trop hardiment s'expose aux hazards et perils.

(Estienne 172–173)

FRAN[COPHILE]. The last one of the words you used, *reussir*, instead of saying "to turn out well," is one of them [i.e., one of these Italianisms]. The other one is *risk* as when you said: *I take this on my risk*, for in good French one would have to say: "I will answer for it" or "I will be responsible for any hazard." And speaking like one used to speak not that long ago, and as some are still speaking today, one would have to say: "I take it on my peril and my fortunes." Now, what makes me think that this word might come from the Italian *rischio*, is the fact that, in Boccaccio, I find the verb *arrischiare* made from the noun *rischio* for "to hazard," "to expose to the peril, or the hazard," as in this place: *Et in cio arrischiero la persona e la vita*,[13] instead of saying *to risk*. And from this, they also have coined *arrischievole* to signify someone who is hazardous, who exposes him- or herself too boldly to hazards and perils.

Derived from the Italian, with explicit reference to Boccaccio's *Filoloco*, the word *risque* is featured here, as far as I can see, for the first time as a synonym of middle-French *hasard* or modern French *hazard*, a derivate of either Arabic *yasare*, dicer, or *yasar*, group of dicers ("hazard").

Estienne's attack on the Italianisms of his time may well have delayed the reception of the word *risque* into French, but by the mid-sixteenth century it was firmly established in that language in both the masculine and the feminine grammatical gender. In one of his arguments against the lax morals of the Jesuit Luis de Morales, Pascal uses the term in the exact same sense as the *dolce stil nuova* poets before him, however, with the difference that he is literally talking about a matter of life and death and not simply about the symbolical danger emanating from the beloved lady's gaze. In the fourteenth of his *Lettres écrites à un provincial* dated October 23, 1656, Pascal writes:

Je vous déclare donc qu'il [i.e., Molinas] n'entend simplement que, si l'on peut sauver son écu sans tuer le voleur, on ne doit pas le tuer; mais que, si l'on ne peut le sauver qu'en le tuant, encore même qu'on ne coure nul risque de vie, comme si le voleur n'a point d'armes, qu'il est permis d'en prendre et de le tuer pour sauver son écu; et qu'en cela on ne sort point, selon lui, de la moderation d'une juste defense.
(Pascal, Lettres écrites à un provincial, letter XIV, 444)[14]

I repeat, therefore, that his plain meaning is that, provided the person can save his crown[15] without killing the thief, he ought not to kill him; but that, if he cannot secure his object without shedding blood, even though he should run no risk of his own life, as in the case of the robber being unarmed, he is permitted to take up arms and kill the man, in order to save his crown; and in so doing, according to him, the person does not transgress the moderation of a just defence.
(Pascal, The Provincial Letters)

A similar connotation, namely the long-established relation of the word *risque* to the concepts of danger and adventure is invoked in Corneille's dedication to his comedy *Don Sanche d'Aragon* (1650). Discussing the rules of the so-called *rota Vergilii*, that is, the classical theory of literary genres, the author raises the question whether it is permissible to introduce kings and noblemen, the traditional personnel of the tragedy, into the comedy as well. And he does it in the form of a fictive dialogue between a patron of this theory and Corneille, the poet himself, who defends his right to disregard that rule:

Je continuerai donc, s'il vous plaît, et lui dirai que *Don Sanche* est une véritable comédie, quoique tous les acteurs y soient ou rois ou grands d'Espagne, puisqu'on n'y voit naître aucun péril par qui nous puissions être portés à la pitié ou à la crainte. Notre aventurier Carlos n'y court aucun risque.
(Corneille, "Épître à Monsieur de Zuylichem" 180–181)

Not the hero's political or social status determines whether he can appear on the stage of a comedy, but rather the absence of pity and fear which define the genre of the tragedy according to Aristotle's poetics. And it is remarkable that Corneille justifies this position, which is modern in the precise sense of the *Querelle des anciens et des modernes* (*Quarrel of the Ancients and the Moderns*) with the equally modern explanation that the hero of his play does not run any risk in his adventures.

Already in his comedy "La Suite du Menteur" (1643), Corneille had placed the word *risque* in the punchline of an argument, this time in the feminine grammatical gender. Cliton, the servant, addresses his master, the liar of the piece:

Menteur vous voulez vivre, et menteur vous mourrez;
Et l'on dira de vous pour oraison funèbre:
"C'etoit en menterie un auteur très célèbre,
"Qu'aux maîtres du métier il en eût fait leçon;
"Et qui, tant qu'il vécut, sans craindre aucune risque,
"Aux plus forts d'après lui put donner quinze et bisque."
(Corneille, "La Suite du Menteur" 402)

As a liar you want to live, and as a liar you will die;
And they will say at your funeral oration:

"In lying he was a famous author,
Who knew how to refine this art in such a worthy way
That he could have tutored the masters of the craft;
And who, as long as he lived, without fearing any risk,
Could have given a huge advance to those who were the strongest after him."

"Donner quinze et bisque" is a rule in the *Jeu de Paume* game, according to which one player grants 15 points in advance to his or her opponent allowing them to choose at which point of the game they want to use them ("bisque"). Already here, the word *risque* is associated with a game. Molière, in his comedy *L'impromptu de Versailles*, (1663) goes one step further. He transfers the word into the context of a wager, the most basic form of a game of chance, which, in this case, leads to the following disalogue between Molière and the actor La Grange, who are both playing themselves within the play:

LA GRANGE. – Ton argent court grand risque.
MOLIÈRE. – Le tien est bien avanturé.

(Molière 25–26)

LA GRANGE. – Your money runs a great risk.
MOLIÈRE. – Yours is greatly (ad)ventured.

(Molière The Impromptu of Versailles 202)[16]

At around the same time, Antoine Gombaud, chevalier de Meré, had posed the two famous questions to the members of Marin Mersenne' scientific salon, which Pascal and his friend Fermat tried and succeeded to solve in 1654, each in his own specific way (*La correspondence*). (1) After how many throws of two dice do I have a good chance "de sonner," or to ring the bell, that is, to throw a double or a six? (2) Assuming that two gamblers stake a certain amount of money stipulating that the one who wins three games gets to take the jackpot, how is the money to be distributed if they break off their game after one of them has won only once, and not three times? Pascal's and Fermat's solutions to these two problems are the foundational beginning of the two closely related disciplines of probability calculus and statistics, the latter one founded by Jakob Bernoulli in his posthumously published book *Ars coniecturandi* (1713).

Pascal called his method *Géométrie du Hasard* or else *règle des partis* (*La correspondence* 19), the rule that governs the division of the stakes. And, although he was familiar with the term *risque*, as not only his *Lettres écrites à un provincial*, but even his writings about the vacuum (*Nouvelles expériences sur le vide* 5) and the cycloid (*Réflexions sur les conditions de prix* 46) show, he sticks to the word *hazard* in his reflexions on the odds in games of chance. The first one who, to my knowledge, transferred the word risk to probability calculus was Augustus de Morgan. His *Essay on Probabilities and On Their Application To Life Contingencies*, contains a whole chapter "On Risks of Gain and Losses" (93–112), within which the word appears without any further definition:

The proverb which advises us to throw a sprat to catch a whale, shows that mankind consider a chance of a gain to be a benefit for which it is worth while to give up a proportionate certainty. The principle on which depends the determination of the amount which it is safe to hazard, must vary with the circumstances of the person who runs the risk. A man should not hazard his all in any terms; but in ventures the loss of one of which would not be felt, we may suppose the venturer able to make a large number of the same kind; in which case, the common notions of mankind, reinforced by the results of theory, tell us that the sum risked must be only such a proportion of the possible gain as the mathematical probability of gaining it is of unity. For instance: suppose I am to receive a shilling if a die, yet to be thrown, give an ace; in the long run, an ace will occur one time out of six, or I shall lose five times for every time which I gain. I must therefore make one gain compensate the outlay of six ventures or one sixth of a shilling is what I may give for the prospect, one time with another. But 1/6 is the probability of throwing the ace.

Principle. Multiply the sum to be gained by the fraction which expresses the chance of gaining it, and the result is the greatest sum which should be given for the chance.

(De Morgan 93–94)

In his *Theory of Probabilities*, published in 1845, de Morgan even suggested calling risk what statisticians nowadays describe as the mean-squared error:

This is what Laplace calls *l'erreur moyenne à craindre en plus*, and the corresponding error *en moins* of the same magnitude with a different sign. We shall call it the *risk* of the observation the sign of the error not being considered.

(443)

De Morgan takes up the terms and concepts of an old tradition and he redefines them for the purposes of a new era, for our time. The word *adventure*, which, in mediaeval courtly epics, was a keyword of what the French poet Jean Bodel had called *matière de Bretagne*, that is, the legendary stories associated with King Arthur and his circle, is abbreviated to form venture, a word best known today in the formula "venture capital," capital invested at a high risk in support of a new or expanding business. And what *dolce stil nuovo* poets had once called *rischio* is now a variable in a mathematical equation, and, as such, a calculable quantity.

De Morgan did not have to define the term risk because it had already reached England more than two centuries before his time. And if I am not mistaken, it got there from Italy via France. For the definition of the word "risque" in Randle Cotgrave's *A Dictionarie of the French and English Tongues*, which appeared in 1611 and is, thus, to the best of my knowledge, the *locus primus* of the word in any English text,[17] is based on a direct quote from Estienne's book on Italianisms in the French language: "Risque: f. Perill, iepardie, danger, hazard, chance, aduenture./Ie le prens à ma risque. *Hab or nab, at my perill be it, happen how it will*" (Cotgrave).

Thus, Shakespeare could have known the word risk, at least in its French form, but, according to the Open Source Concordance of his works, it is not part of his famously vast vocabulary. His words for what we now call risk are peril, which "occurs 43 times in 42 speeches within 22 works," and "venture," short for adventure, which "occurs 29 times in 28 speeches within 16 works," and which is, of course, a key term of the finance industry today (OpenSourceShakespeare).

Among the first documents containing the word risk in the English language are two essays on fiscal matters by John Locke. In the first one of these two texts, the treatise "Some Considerations of the Consequences of the Lowering of Interest and Raising the Value of Money" (1691), the word is mentioned six times, still in its French spelling, but already spanning quite a broad spectrum of meaning. Locke writes that "Money out at Interest runs a greater Risque, than Land does," he speaks of the "disproportion of Profit, to Risque," but also "of the Risque in transgressing the Law." Four years later, in Locke's "Short Observations on a Printed Paper, intituled, 'For encouraging the coining silver money in England, and after for keeping it here'," which were published in 1695, the word appears already in its anglicized form, and within yet another context. I quote but one of three examples:

The matter in short is this; England sending more consumable commodities to Spain than it receives from thence, the merchants, who manage their trade, bring back the overplus in bullion, which, at their return, they sell as a commodity. The chapmen, that give the highest for this, are, as in all cases of buying and selling, those who can make most profit by it; and those are the returners of our money, by exchange, into those countries where our debts, any way contracted, make a need of it: for they are getting 6, 8, 10, &c. per cent according to the want and demand of money from England there, and according to the risk of the sea, buy up this bullion, as soon as it comes in, to send it to their correspondents in those parts, to make good their credit for the bills they have drawn on them, and so can give more for it than the mint-rate, i.e. more than equal weight of milled money for an equal weight of standard bullion; they being able to make more profit of it by returns.

(Locke, "Short Observations")

The quote shows that Locke still situates the term risk within the pathless expanse of the sea. However, it is important to note that the merchandise traded here is not just anything, but bullion, the stuff out of which money is coined, a clear indication that the word has moved from its narrow association with the maritime loan to the fields of finance and economics in general. And this is all the more relevant as Locke's two essays on monetary politics served him in all likelihood as a laboratory to fathom the meaning of the term risk before transferring it to a completely different field. Conspicuously absent in the first edition of his "An Essay Concerning Human Understanding" (dated 1690, but had already appeared in 1689), the word risk is equally conspicuously introduced in the concluding paragraph of the famous chapter "Of Enthusiasm," which, according to Locke's own "Epistle to the Reader," was added to the second edition in 1694. Occurring only once in the entire "An Essay Concerning Human Understanding" and, moreover, quoted at a strategically decisive turn within this text, the neologism risk bears a heavy load of meaning:

16. Criteria of a divine revelation. In what I have said I am far from denying, that God can, or doth sometimes enlighten men's minds in the apprehending of certain truths or excite them to good actions, by the immediate influence and assistance of the Holy Spirit, without any extraordinary signs accompanying it. But in such cases too we have reason and Scripture; unerring rules to know whether it be from God or no. Where the truth embraced is consonant to the revelation in the written word of God, or the action conformable to the dictates of right reason or holy writ, we may be assured that we run no risk in entertaining it as such: because, though perhaps it be not an immediate revelation from God, extraordinarily operating on our minds, yet we are sure it is warranted by that revelation which he has given us of truth. But it is not the strength of our private persuasion within ourselves, that can warrant it to be a light or motion from heaven: nothing can do that but the written Word of God without us, or that standard of reason which is common to us with all men. Where reason or Scripture is express for any opinion or action, we may receive it as of divine authority: but it is not the strength of our own persuasions which can by itself give it that stamp. The bent of our own minds may favour it as much as we please: that may show it to be a fondling of our own, but will by no means prove it to be an offspring of heaven, and of divine original.

("An Essay Concerning Human Understanding")

The use of the word risk in the context of this paragraph sounds all too familiar today, but at the end of the seventeenth century, it was unprecedented—and so unique, by the way, that even the researchers who later tried to find it for the OED failed to catch it in their nets.[18] If I had not been able to browse the digital archive of Western literature with the powerful search engines that have been developed in the past 25 years, I would have missed it, too. To the best of my knowledge, Locke is the first one ever to transfer the word risk from the realms of trade and finance to the discourse of philosophy. And the stakes, or to use the same metaphor, the risks are high. After all, the question is whether enthusiasm, which, as Locke states, "takes away both reason and revelation," (par. 3) is a legitimate way to find the truth. Based on the argument that "reason is natural revelation" just as "revelation is natural reason," (par. 4) Locke concludes that "revelation must be judged of by reason," (par. 14) which implies that belief is "no proof of revelation" (par. 15). Thus, just as merchants do not run any risk as long as they can be sure that the amount of gold or silver in a coin has exactly the same value as the same amount of gold or silver on the market, we do not run any risk when we deem the truth which bears the seal of divine revelation and the truth derived from principles of pure reason to be one and the same. With this conclusion, Locke opens the Pandora box, from which the atheism debate and the bible critique of the eighteenth century were soon to escape.

If my conjecture that the term risk was coined in order to circumvent the sin of usury is correct, then Locke's use of that same term in a chapter about the relation between revelation and reason marks a decisive turn. A fugitive from theology returns, but under completely new and different circumstances. To define usury, the taking of interest on a loan, as a sin is to prohibit speculation on the future in this world for the sake of the hereafter. To define revelation and reason as one and the same amounts to the exact opposite proposition. To speculate on the future, from now on, is no longer a sin, but a virtue. It is proof of leading a godly life. This is the difference between the Catholic renunciation of the world and what Max Weber, in his famous book, defined as *The Protestant Ethic and the Spirit of Capitalism*. It is true that in this book, Weber never uses the term risk, but when distinguishing between "the old forms of mediaeval economic regulations" and "capitalism," he explicitly mentions "the continual danger of collision with the Church's prohibition of usury"[19] that defined the economic order of the Middle Ages.

In the opening paragraph of "Of Enthusiasm," Locke distinguishes three methods of approaching the truth:

> In any truth that gets not possession of our minds by the irresistible light of self-evidence, or by the force of demonstration, the arguments that gain it assent are the vouchers and gage of its probability to us; and we can receive it for no other than such as they deliver it to our understandings.
>
> *(1)*

Self-evidence refers to that which is right in front of our eyes, and thus given in the present. The force of demonstration is based on the past. Probability, a key term in Aristotle's *Poetics*, is foresight into the future (1451a-37f.), and it is important to note that Pascal and Fermat, less than half a century before Locke's *Essay Concerning Human Understanding*, had grounded such "providence" on a solid mathematical fundament. Probability calculus, or what Pascal called *la géométrie d'hasard*, makes the future calculable. Jacob Bernoulli's *Ars coniecturandi* adds an equally important component to Pascal's method, namely the proof that such calculations can be based on real world observations, as long as we obey what would be later called the law of large numbers, that is, as long as we gather enough data. Based on population statistics we can predict the rate of marriages, births, and deaths in coming years; these same statistics allow us to calculate rates of life and accidents insurance. Even scientists would eventually find that there is but one method to calculate the molecular and particle physics of matter: statistical mechanics. The law of large numbers governs the way we choose our political leaders, the way we conduct business and life. Using a theological term that was coined in the twelfth century[20] François Ewald has described this state of things as *The State of Providence*,[21] and his teacher Michel Foucault called it biopolitics.

From the Risk of Death to Paradise

After this long detour from Southern Europe to England, and from early modernity to the present, let us return to the Middle Ages. For about half a century after its first emergence, the term risk is exclusively documented in the semantic field of maritime trade, but, already in the thirteenth century, its use expands first to adjacent fields such as commerce and travel in general, regardless of the distinction between land and sea, then, to a different class of contract, the testament, and, toward the end of the century, to a completely new discourse in both content and style: *dolce stil novo* poetry.[22] Among the examples listed in Du Cange's *Glossarium* are a few citations from maritime loan contracts issued in Marseille and Genoa, but also several others, including the earliest one from 1239, which I quote, that speak of the perils faced by travelers when encountering robbers on land, not pirates at sea: "Debeat… ire et redire secure ad Risigum et periculam Mantuae per totum suum districtum, si fuerit depraedatus." 'May he be able to safely come and go traversing his whole district at Mantua's risk and peril, if he were robbed' ("Riscus").

The expression "a rischio and aventura," documented in a testament from 1263, testifies to the word's migration into a new language, Italian.[23] At about the same time, one of the poets in Cavalcanti's and Dante's circle must have picked up the term either from his own business transactions or from one of his acquaintances or friends among the bankers merchants, and lawyers of thirteenth-century Florence. A *hapaxlegomenon*, the word *rischio* accentuates some of the most striking passages in *dolce stil novo* poetry, while its use expands to completely new fields of application. One of the most extreme examples, if not the most extreme of all, is Guido Cavalcanti's sonnet LI:[24]

> Guata, Manetto, quella scrignutuzza,
> e pon' ben mente com'è divisata
> e com' è drittamente sfigurata
> e quel che pare quand' ella s'agruzza!
>
> Or, s'ella fosse vesitata d'un'uzza
> con cappellin' e di vel soggolata
> ed apparisse di die accompagnata
> d'alcuna bella donna gentiluzza,
>
> tu non avresti niquità sì forte
> né saresti angoscioso sì d'amore
> né sì involto di malincolia,
>
> che tu non fossi a rischio de la morte
> di tanto rider che farebbe 'l core:
> o tu moresti, o fuggiresti via.

(Cavalcanti, LI 206–208)

> Look, Manetto, the hunchbacked woman over there,
> and set your mind on how she is
> and how straightaway disfigured she is,
> and how she appears when she shrugs!
>
> Well, if she were dressed in a long gown
> with hood and veil fastened under her chin,
> and if she were to appear in daylight accompanied
> by a sweet young woman,

> you could neither be so terribly enraged
> nor so anguished by love
> nor so involved in melancholia
>
> that you would not run the risk of death
> with so much laughing into which your heart would burst:
> you'd either die, or run away.

The sonnet parodies the classical *topos* of praise poetry, according to which it is hard to bear the mere sight of the beloved lady, by simply reversing its sign: The woman is not a beauty, but the epitome of ugliness. The place and time of the action are familiar: an Italian city when evening falls, everyone, old and young, is out on the street or gathering on the piazza talking, laughing, playing. Two young men in the crowd are out for adventure, or shall we say, women. One of them spots a hunchbacked old lady or, to quote the Italian word, "una scrignatuzza," which Ezra Pound translates as "scarecrow," calls the friend's attention to her sight, and takes the opportunity to turn the *dolce stil novo* ideal of female beauty by means of a well-chosen oxymoron (drittamente sfigurata) on its head.

The two guys are, of course, way too well bred, or too blasé, or both to openly make fun of the old woman, but one of them, the speaker of the poem, cannot help considering the conditions under which such laughter would be possible. Imagine, he says opening a conditional clause, if you were to see the same old woman in full daylight, clad with gown, hood, and veil according to the latest fashion, and accompanied by a sweet young woman, ugliness paired with the kind of beauty we have been looking for tonight.

The conclusion following the sonnet's strongest caesura, the gap between the octave and the sestet, is itself a complex paratactic structure, a sentence which, in the last tercet, culminates in a consecutive clause. At the same time, the focus shifts from the old hunchback to Manetto, the friend and addressee, and, by implication, to the speaking subject himself. Under the conditions laid out in the second quartet, the speaker constructs three possible states of Manetto's temperament: the rage of the choleric type's yellow bile in the first line of the tercet, and the gloom of the melancholic person's black bile in the third. "Love," which is driven by the hot blood of the sanguine type, is placed in the middle of the stanza. None of these three passions, thus Manetto's friend, would be strong enough—and here the sonnet jumps over the last caesura—that you would not run the risk of death, *rischio di morte*, a formula, which, as far as I can see, is coined here for the very first time.

In each line of the sonnet's last stanza, the speaker hits his friend Manetto, and with him the reader, with an unexpected twist. To behold a hunchbacked woman in the company of a beautiful young lady may well be disturbing, but a risk of death? Is that not a bit much? The next line, in answer to this question, tones things down: It deflates the solemn expression "risk of death" by turning it into the trivial saw "to die laughing." Not outloud, vulgar laughter, but laughter in the innermost heart, the place where, according to Socrates' theory, beauty, after having entered through the eyes, engenders love (Plato 255γ). As opposed to the commonplace expressed in the previous line, this is anything but trivial. And so, the seemingly anti-climatic speech reaches a new pinnacle, which puts Cavalcanti's own theory of love, his Platonism, to the test.[25] If beauty, once it has entered through the eyes, produces love, what, then, is its effect if it is paired with ugliness? Not hatred, so the answer to the question, the opposite of love, but rather an irresistible urge to laugh. It is the *"impertinent laughter"* which the Ratman "had shown repeatedly in the case of deaths," and which Freud analyzing what he calls "the compulsive laughter on occasions of mourning, which occurs so frequently and is considered enigmatic," attributes to unconscious thoughts of revenge (Freud 415).

The poem's punch line is the last: "you'd either die, or run away." If you saw this hunchbacked old woman in the company of a pretty young lady, you would not be able to help it: You would die laughing. And if that were the case, then you had better take off because you ought to be ashamed for laughing off the horror you feel at her sight not only in the presence of, but in opposition to a beautiful young lady.

The verb *morire* picks up and completes the theme of death by laughing, however, imbedded in a sentence of its own, an either/or construction, and furthermore clearly separated from the word *ridere* by the clause *che farebbe 'l core*, rather than being part of a trivial commonplace, it serves to reveal that platitude's hidden truth. We are not dying laughing, but compulsively laughing when encountering our own mortality. Thus, the formula, I die laughing, turns, if I may say so, into: I laugh dying.[26]

Yet, when are we ever so exposed to our mortality that we cannot help taking refuge in laughter? Neither, so the poem argues, when we encounter the frailty of another human being nor when we fall in love. In the first case, we can distance ourselves easily from the ugly sight, and in the second case, we forget ourselves in the beauty of the other. If, however, both beauty and ugliness catch our eye in one and the same moment so that we are torn between attraction and revulsion, then we will be gripped by sheer horror. We fear to die laughing and have no choice but to take off. This is how womanizers like Manetto, but, with him, the speaker of the poem, its author Cavalcanti, and we men all together turn out to be the greatest cowards. We cannot bear beholding a hunchbacked old woman next to the lady we desire.

All of the *dolce stil novo* poems take part in an elegant and erudite dialogue within a small group of like-minded, but also rival men. Since the dates of origin of their works are hard to determine, any attempt at tracing influences or establishing chronologies does not make much sense.[27] It is, however, possible to describe the wide network of allusions, questions, and retorts. Thus, Cavalcanti's sonnet *Guata, Manetto*, may well be a parody of Cino da Pistoia's sonnet CXXIII, which itself may well be the first poem to ever use the word "rischio," because Cino was not only a poet, but an influential canonist, teacher of Bartolus of Saxoferrato and of Francesco Petrarca (Carducci, *Le Rime* XXXV):

> Guardando a voi in parlare e 'n sembianti,
> angelica figura mi parete,
> che sovra ciascun mortal cor tenete
> compimenti di ben non so dir quanti.
>
> Credo ch'a prova ogni virtù v' ammanti,
> che di bellezze tal miracol siete,
> ne gli atti sì gentil piacer avete,
> che 'nnamoran ciascun che vi sta avanti.
>
> Gli occj 'n tal maestría par che gli muova
> l'Amor, ch' è figurato in vostra ciera,
> che pur convien, che pera per dolcezza
>
> lo cor di quel, ch' à tanta sicurezza,
> che sta a ristio se campi o se pera,
> per voi veder, sì come Amor lo trova.

(Le Rime CXXIII.312)

> Watching you in speaking and in countenance,
> you appear to me as an angelic figure,
> who over any mortal heart hold
> unspeakably many fulfillments of good.

I believe I have evidence that you are wrapped up
in virtue, that you are a miracle of beauty,
in your acts have such a gentle enjoyment that
everyone who encounters you falls in love with you.

The eyes gain such mastery because Amor,
who is figured in your face, moves them, so that
it has to happen that, because of sweetness,

the heart of the one who relies on such confidence
runs the risk to get lost or perish
just by seeing you, as Amor finds him.

Cavalcanti extracts the crisp formula *rischio di morte* from Cino's sentence *Che sta ristio (rischio) se campi o se pera*, and he turns the word *figurato*, formed, shaped, into its opposite: *sfigurata*, deformed, misshapen. But Cavalcanti's sonnet *Guata Manetto* is also a response to the *topos* of the deadly female gaze in Dante's canzone *Donne ch'avete intelletto d'amore* from the latter's *Vita nuova*:[28]

> ... e qual soffrise di starla a vedere
> diverria nobil cosa, o si morria.
>
> ... voi le vedete Amor pinto nel viso,
> là 've non pote alcun mirarla fiso.

(Dante, Vita nuova, cap. XIX)[29]

> ... and whoever could withstand her gaze
> would become a noble thing, or die.
>
> ... you will see Amor painted in her face,
> there, where no one can look firmly.

And Dante's ballata *I' mi son pargoletta* could, in turn, be read as a riposte to both Cavalcanti's *Guata Manetto* and Cino da Pistoia's *Guardando a voi*:

> —I' mi son pargoletta bella e nova,
> che son venuta per mostrare altrui
> de le bellezze del loco ond'io fui.
> I' fui del cielo, e tornerovvi ancora
> per dar de la mia luce altrui diletto;
> e chi mi vede e non se ne innamora
> d'amor non averà mai intelletto,
> ché non mi fu in piacer alcun disdetto
> quando natura mi chiese a colui me
> che volle, donne, accompagnarmi a vui.
>
> Ciascuna stella ne li occhi mi piove
> del lume suo e de la sua vertute;
> le mie bellezze sono al mondo nove,
> però che di là su mi son venute:
> le quai non posson esser canosciute

se non da canoscenza d'omo in cui
Amor si metta per piacer altrui.—

Queste parole si leggon nel viso
d'un'angioletta che ci è apparita:
e io che per veder lei mirai fiso,
ne sono a rischio di perder la vita;
però ch'io ricevetti tal ferita
da un ch'io vidi dentro a li occhi sui,
ch'i' vo' piangendo e non m'acchetai pui.

(Dante, Altre rime, LXXXVII)[30]

I am a beautiful and youthful little girl
come down on earth to show to every mortal
some of the beauty of my native haven.
I am from heaven, where I am returning,
others to please and gladden with my splendor;
and he who sees me here and fails to love me
never will comprehend love's truthful meaning,
for no one did I banish from my liking
when nature asked about me from the
one who decreed that I'd be with you, ladies.

Every star showers into these my eyes
some of its light and of its lofty virtue;
your world can hardly recognize my beauty,
which down from heaven has descended on me:
a man alone is privileged to know it,
who, blessed with great discerning wisdom, harbors
Love in his heart to please another person.

These words are clearly read upon the features
of a sweet angel that has flashed before us:
and I, who tried to know her in my rapture,
have risked because of it to lose my life,
for so was I that day so gravely wounded
by one I saw within her glances dwelling,
unceasingly I am today still weeping.

(Trans. Tusiani, slightly altered)

The poem is a subtle play on courtly love. It subverts the genre's rules in such a way that it can fulfill them on a higher level in the end—subverting the subversion, so to speak. A first and unique move for the time when these lines were written turns an old *topos* upside down (Kay 94, footnote 12). It is not the poet who is extolling the beloved lady's beauty, in fact, he is not even speaking. It is the young girl herself who seems to sing her own praises unabashedly. How is this *iattanza*, this boastfulness, as Beatrice will call such vainglorious eulogies in Dante's *Paradiso*, (XXV, 62) compatible with the *pargoletta*'s beauty, her modesty, her humility, her virtue?[31] The answer to this question is given in the second stanza: Lauding her own beauty the girl is not glorifying herself, but God, the creator of her beauty. But again, this is not the final word. The poem's final stanza initiates yet another twist. It turns out—and with this, the ballad reverts to the traditional tropes of praise poetry—that what seemed to be an unmistakable instance of bragging was, in fact, not the girl's own speech, but rather a reading of her beauty by none other than the poet himself. Speaking in the name of the beloved lady, the poet speaks in reality, as always, for himself: as the reader of her face. However, with this act of reading, the poem's focus shifts from the voice to the medium of the gaze, once again not to the gaze of the young girl, but to that of her beholder. Instead of being passively exposed to the beloved lady's beauty, literally stabbed by her eyes, as in Cavalcanti's sonnet *Voi che per li occhi*, the poet looks at her fixedly: "e io per veder lei mirai fiso,/ne sono a rischio di perder la vita." And it is at this moment that what Cavalcanti had called *rischio di morte* returns as *rischio di perder la vita*. The effect is the same, but the cause is the exact opposite. The poet runs the risk of losing his life neither because the deadly arrow of the beloved lady's gaze has hit him his heart, nor because he is horrified by the sight of an old hunchbacked lady, but, on the contrary, because he has encountered his own diminished image in her *pupil*,[32] the convex mirror of her eyes. Thus, it is neither "the hardness" of the *pargoletta*, her "destructive gaze" (Kay 94, footnote 12), nor her divine beauty which forces the poet and lover to confront his own mortality, but rather the encounter with his own image as it is reflected in her pupil. What is risky is not the gaze of the beloved lady, but the poet's own attempt to look her in the eye. In a similar vein, Dante's sonnet LXXXIX speaks of the *rischio di mirar sua figura*, the risk not so much of seeing, but rather of aiming at, or targeting the figure of the *pargoletta*:

Chi guarderà già mai sanza paura
ne li occhi d'esta bella pargoletta,
che m'hanno concio sì, che non s'aspetta
per me se non la morte, che m'è dura?

Vedete quanto è forte mia ventura:
ché fu tra l'altre la mia vita eletta
per dare essemplo altrui, ch'uom non si metta
in rischio di mirar la sua figura.

Destinata mi fu questa finita,
da ch'un uom convenia esser disfatto,
perch'altri fosse di pericol tratto;

e però, lasso, fu' io così ratto
in trarre a me 'l contrario de la vita,
come vertù di stella margherita.

(Rime LXXXIX)

Who will be able with no fear at all
to look into the eyes of this lovely girl [*pargoletta*]
that so have hurt me that I have nothing to expect
but death, so hard to bear?

Behold how hard my fortune is
that my life was chosen out of other ones
to give an example to others that man should not
run the risk of aiming at her figure.

Destiny made this end for me
so that one man should be undone
so that others would be saved from the danger;

and that is why I, alas, was so quick
to draw the opposite of life to me
just like the pearl the power of the stars.

(Trans. Tusiani, slightly altered)

When Cino da Pistoia and Cavalcanti borrowed the term *rischio* from the discourse of the maritime trade in order to define the falling in love as a life and death decision, this may well have been a fashionable craze initiated by a group of wealthy young Florentines, just for fun, and in spite of the grim connotations not to be taken all too seriously. Yet for Dante, who was, of course, part of that circle, the trendy metaphor was definitely much more than just a joke. He lifted the term risk out of the realm of love poetry and up to that of theology. The beloved lady's beautiful eyes are not a deadly weapon anymore, but a symbol of divine grace. And even the risk of death, which the lover-poet runs when looking into the mirror of her eyes, serves as an example meant to save others from such danger, the danger of damnation. Thus, the stage is set for the severe verdict on courtly love in Canto VI of Dante's *Inferno*, and the return of a different form of love in the companion figures of Beatrice and the holy Virgin Mary in his *Paradiso*.

In *Purgatorio*, the space between these two incompatible domains, Dante picks up the thread of his love poetry again. He returns to *la pergoletta* one last time, the young girl, whose praise he once had sung. However, it is not in loving memory, but rather in order to revoke the love inspired by her beauty and, with it, the whole Platonic theory of love in whose terms it was expressed. The sequence begins with the scene in which Dante and Beatrice ambling up and down on opposite shores of the river which separates Purgatory from Paradise engage in a conversation about their earthly life. Among the items on the long list of arguments which prove that the poet never understood what love is all about, Beatrice explicitly counts the *pargoletta* as one of the carnal things that drew him down to Earth rather than up to paradise:

Ed ella: "Se tacessi o se negassicciò
    che confessi, non fora men nota
    la colpa tua: da tal giudice sassi!

Ma quando scoppia de la propria gota
    l'accusa del peccato, in nostra corte
    rivolge sé contra 'l taglio la rota.

Tuttavia, perché mo vergogna porte
    del tuo errore, e perché altra volta,
    udendo le serene, sie più forte,

pon giù il seme del piangere e ascolta:
    sì udirai come in contraria parte
    mover dovieti mia carne sepolta.

Mai non t'appresentò natura o arte
    piacer, quanto le belle membra in ch'i
    rinchiusa fui, e che so' 'n terra sparte;

e se 'l sommo piacer sì ti fallio
    per la mia morte, qual cosa mortale
    dovea poi trarre te nel suo disio?

Ben ti dovevi, per lo primo strale
    de le cose fallaci, levar suso
    di retro a me che non era più tale.

Non ti dovea gravar le penne in giuso,
    ad aspettar più colpo, o pargoletta
    o altra vanità con sí breve uso.

Novo augelletto due o tre aspetta;
    ma dinanzi da li occhi d'i pennuti
    rete si spiega indarno o si saetta."

(Purgatorio, XXXI.37–60)

'Had you stayed silent or denied what you confess,'
    she said, 'your fault could not be any less apparent
    since it is known to such a Judge.

'But when a man's own blushing cheek reveals
    the condemnation of his sin, in our high court
    the grindstone dulls the sharp edge of the sword.

'Nonetheless, so that you now may bear
    the shame of your straying and, the next time
    that you hear the Sirens' call, be stronger,

'stop sowing tears and listen.
    Then you shall hear just how my buried flesh
    should have directed you to quite a different place.

'Never did art or nature set before you beauty
    as great as in the lovely members that enclosed me,
    now scattered and reduced to dust.

'And if the highest beauty failed you
    in my death, what mortal thing
    should then have drawn you to desire it?

'Indeed, at the very first arrow
    of deceitful things, you should have risen up
    and followed me who was no longer of them.

'You should not have allowed your wings to droop
    leaving you to other darts from some young girl [pargoletta]
    or other novelty of such brief use.

'The fledgling may allow even a third attempt,
    but all in vain is the net flung or arrow shot
    in sight of a full-fledged bird.[33]

The revocation, or shall we say, transubstantiation of Cavalcanti's Platonic theory of love has to wait till Paradise. In the eighth sphere of that realm, Beatrice calls upon three saints, Saint Peter,

Saint James, and Saint John, to test and instruct her companion Dante about the three cardinal virtues of the Christian faith:

> Ed ella: "O luce etterna del gran viro
>   a cui Nostro Segnor lasciò le chiavi,
>   ch'ei portò giù, di questo gaudio miro,
>
> tenta costui di punti lievi e gravi,
>   come ti piace, intorno de la fede,
>   per la qual tu su per lo mare andavi.
>
> S'elli ama bene e bene spera e crede,
>   non t'è occulto, perché 'l viso hai quivi
>   dov' ogne cosa dipinta si vede;…
>
> (Paradiso, XXIV.34–42)

> And she: 'O everlasting light of that great man
>   with whom our Lord did leave the keys,
>   which He brought down from this astounding joy,
>
> 'test this man as you see fit on points,
>   both minor and essential, about the faith
>   by which you walked upon the sea.
>
> 'Whether his love is just, and just his hope and faith,
>   is not concealed from you because your sight
>   can reach the place where all things are revealed.

The subject matter of the exam which Dante has to pass are the concluding lines of Chapter 13 in Paul's first letter to the Corinthians: "For now we see through a glass, darkly; but then face to face: now I know in part; but then shall I know even as also I am known./And now abideth faith, hope, charity, these three; but the greatest of these is charity" (1. Cor. 12–13).

With only one exception, Dante's translation of the Greek word ἀγάπη in Canto XXVI is *Amore*,[34] and not *carità*,[35] the Italian equivalent of Latin *caritas*, the word used in the Vulgate version of this text. With this linguistic trick, which conceals the difference between physical love and spiritual love, Dante initiates a long mediation on a paradox. In order to show that, under the double aspect of God's creation and man's fall, these two forms of love are both: deeply identical and radically different, Dante revisits memories from a long lost past. After finishing the discussion of faith (Canto XXIV) and moving on to that of hope (Canto XXV), Dante returns one last time to the imagery and the vocabulary of courtly love, to his past *oeuvre*, and to his poetic mission. There is, first of all, his dream of returning to his hometown Florence as a poet, stepping up to his baptismal font, and putting on the laurel crown (XXV.61–63). Then, there are the cooing doves (XXV.19–20), Venus birds that already played a role in the sad story of the two adulterous lovers Paolo and Francesca (*Inferno*, V.82–84), and which now come to symbolize the intimate union of two saints. And when Beatrice—introducing Dante to Saint John—explains that the Saint's questions will neither be hard (*forti*) "nor offer grounds for boasting of himself," (*iattanza*) (*Paradiso*, XXV.61–62) she may well be alluding to the young girl's self-praise in the poem *I' mi son pargoletta*. For in paradise, into which no one, except for Jesus Christ and Saint Mary, ever entered in the flesh, bodily beauty, once the object of pride and bragging, has been left behind.

Finally, there is the parallel between the mirror scene in the *pargoletta* ballad and the one in Paul's famous letter to the Corinthians: "For now we see through a glass, darkly; but then face to face: now I know in part; but then shall I know even as also I am known." It is conceivable that Dante already had this verse in mind when he composed the ballad *I' mi son pargoletta*. In this case, the face to face would be the encounter of the lover/poet with his own mortal fate in the pupil of the little girl. On Earth, that is true love. The eyes either shoot arrows from the beloved's deadly gaze, or they are mortally vulnerable to those missiles of desire, on the lover's side. There is a constant oscillation between the active and the passive role in the world of carnal love. In paradise, not just this distinction, but all distinctions are erased. There are no objects, no subjects, and there are no mirrors, that is, no mirrors in the plural anymore. There is but one mirror, the one and only truthful mirror, which turns everything else into a parhelion,[36] a mock sun of itself. To see and to be seen, to know and to be known, are, finally, one and the same:

> Indi spirò: "Sanz' essermi proferta
>   da te, la voglia tua discerno meglio
>   che tu qualunque cosa t'è più certa;
>
> perch' io la veggio nel verace speglio
>   che fa di sé pareglio a l'altre cose,
>   e nulla face lui di sé pareglio"
>
> *(Paradiso, XXVI. 103–108)*

> Then breathed: "Without thy uttering it to me,
>   Thine inclination better I discern
>   Than thou whatever thing is surest to thee;
>
> For I behold it in the truthful mirror,
>   That of Himself all things parhelion makes,
>   And none makes Him parhelion of itself … "[37]

What we will see face to face in paradise, according to Dante's reading of Saint Paul's promise, is not something revealed by light, like a beloved face, but light itself—pure light, not a sight, but a vision, the eternal truth of "primal love" itself (XXVI.38). This is the reason why the three saints, Peter, James, and John, in Canto XXIV to XXVI, appear in a series of ever lighter flames, the last one so bright that it almost blinds the pilgrim Dante:

> Qual è colui ch'adocchia e s'argomenta
>   di vedere eclissar lo sole un poco,
>   che, per veder, non vedente diventa;
>
> tal mi fec'io a quell'ultimo foco
>   mentre che detto fu: "Perché t'abbagli
>   per veder cosa che qui non ha loco?"
>
> *(Paradiso, XXV. 118–123)*

> As one who strains his eyes in his attempt to see
>   the sun when it is partly in eclipse,
>   and, his seeing overwhelmed, has lost his sight,
>
> such did I become before that final flaming
>   until I heard these words: 'Why do you blind your eyes
>   trying to behold what is not here to see?"

The Origin of the Word Risk

At the end of Canto XXV, that is, before Dante's exam turns to Love, the third and final word, the one which Paul calls "the greatest" of them all, there is a sudden silence, a hush, and it is within the description of this interval that Dante uses the word *rischio* one last time.

> A questa voce l'infiammato giro
>   si quïetò con esso il dolce mischio
>   che si facea nel suon del trino spiro,
>
> sì come, per cessar fatica o rischio,
>   li remi, pria ne l'acqua ripercossi,
>   tutti si posano al sonar d'un fischio.
>
> Ahi quanto ne la mente mi commossi,
>   quando mi volsi per veder Beatrice,
>   per non poter veder, benché io fossi
>
> presso di lei, e nel mondo felice!
>
> *(Paradiso, XXV.130–139)*

> At these words, the fiery dance was ended,
>   together with the sweetly mingled notes
>   that issued from the blended three-fold breath,
>
> just as, to avoid fatigue or danger, [*rischio*]
>   oars until that moment driven through the water
>   stop all at once when the whistle sounds.
>
> Ah, how troubled was my mind
>   when I looked back for Beatrice
>   and could not see her, even though I
>
> so near to her and in that world of bliss!
>
> *(Trans. slightly altered)*

Thus, not only Cavalcanti's, but also Dante's Platonic theory of love is turned upside down. Where once there were eyes vulnerable to the deadly arrows shooting forth from the beloved lady's gaze, to the *rischio di morte* at the sight of an old hunchbacked woman, or to the *rischio di perder la vita* in the encounter with one's own image in the pupil of the beloved lady, there now reigns blindness. The toil, *fatica*, and the mortal danger, *rischio di morte*, which are the tokens of love among mortals, have been overcome, the oars of desire come to rest. The risk of death does not lie in the future anymore—a thing of the past, it is left behind. And the eyes are now immune to this risk because they had to die literally in order to be resurrected for a different sight, in fact, not a sight, but a vision in the religious sense of this term. Blinded to the beauty of the flesh Dante's eyes are opened up to a new form of beauty, a new form of love symbolized by the pure light of the sun itself. Where images were, there now are words. Where ἔρως was, there now is ἀγάπη:[38]

> E come a lume acuto si disonna
>   per lo spirto visivo che ricorre
>   a lo splendor che va di gonna in gonna,

e lo svegliato ciò che vede aborre,
  sì nescïa è la sùbita vigilia
  fin che la stimativa non soccorre;

così de li occhi miei ogne quisquilia
  fugò Beatrice col raggio d'i suoi,
  che rifulgea da più di mille milia:

onde mei che dinanzi vidi poi;...
  e quasi stupefatto domandai
  d'un quarto lume ch'io vidi tra noi.

E la mia donna: "Dentro da quei rai
  vagheggia il suo fattor *l'anima prima*
  che la prima virtú creasse mai"

(*Paradiso*, XXVI.70–84)

And just as a sharp light will startle us
  from sleep because the spirit of eyesight
  races to meet the brightness that proceeds

from layer to layer in the eye, and he
  who wakens is confused by what he sees,
  awaking suddenly, and knows no thing

until his judgment helps him, even so
  did Beatrice dispel, with her eyes' rays, which
  shone more than a thousand miles, the chaff

from my eyes: I saw better than I had
  before; and as if stupefied, I asked
  about the fourth of light that I saw among us.

My lady answered: "In those rays there gazes
  with love for his Creator the first soul
  ever created by the Primal Force."

The word *rischio* is the key term in a long dialogue which is begun by the jurist/poet Cino da Pistoia and culminates in Dante's *Paradiso*. The object of dispute is the asymmetrical relation between men and women in the discourse of courtly love. The lady does not speak. She hits the man's heart not with words, but with the arrows shooting forth from her eyes. To sing her praise is to express this *rischio di morte*. In his sonnet, *Guata Manetto*, Cavalcanti expands that constellation by multiplying each one of the equation's two sides by a factor of two. Two friends encounter two women, a young and beautiful one, and an old hunchbacked woman. Beauty is paired with ugliness, love with mortal fear. Neither a lyrical monologue nor a fictive address to the beloved lady, the sonnet describes a fictional scenario which one of the two men envisions for his friend. It is not about praising the beloved lady, but rather an exegesis of the old saw "to die laughing." You would have to laugh compulsively, Manetto, so the argument, if you were to behold a hunchbacked old woman accompanying the beautiful young lady you desire. Why? Because she reminds you of your own death.

Dante's ballad *I' mi son pargoletta* returns to the dual constellation of love poetry, however, with the double difference that the beloved lady, first, does not remain silent, and, second, that she does not have a deadly gaze. Nonetheless—and that is the ballad's point—the poem is strictly composed according to the traditional rules of love poetry. The impression that the lady speaks herself is debunked as an illusion. In reality, the man is speaking. He lends his voice to the lady, puts himself in her place. A similar reversal occurs in the medium of the gaze. At first, it seems as if the man were hit by her deadly gaze. But that is an illusion as well. In reality, the mortal risk does not originate in the young girl's eyes, but rather in the poet's encounter with his own image in the mirror of her pupils. He is the subject of speech as well as both the subject and the object of the mortal gaze. The *pargoletta* is not the noble lady beyond reach, but in a different, more radical sense beyond reach in her angelic self-sufficiency, her God-createdness.

Dante's encounter with Beatrice, first at the boundary between *Inferno* and *Purgatorio*, and then in *Paradiso*, is staged under completely different circumstances, however not without reminiscences of courtly love. It is no longer the man who has the word, but Beatrice. And the question is no longer whether the beloved lady is reachable or not because the object of love is not the lady anymore, but the holy trinity. A clear reference to the theme of the lady's deadly gaze in *dolce stil novo* poetry is not only Dante's blinding in *Paradiso*, Canto XXV and Canto XXVI, but, above all, that of his awakening to a new and deeper form of sight, an awakening, which, in a clear reference to the discourse within which the term risk was coined, is described as a rescue from the dangers of the open sea of twisted love to the "shores where love is just." And, within this context, Dante emphasizes the difference between these two forms of love by drawing a clear line between *caritate* and *amor*:

> Però ricominciai: "Tutti quei morsi
>   che posson far lo cor volgere a Dio,
>   a la mia caritate son concorsi:
>
> ché l'essere del mondo e l'esser mio,
>   la morte ch'el sostenne perch' io viva,
>   e quel che spera ogne fedel com' io,
>
> con la predetta conoscenza viva,
>   tratto m'hanno del mar de l'amor torto,
>   e del diritto m'han posto a la riva"
>
> *(Paradiso, XXVI.55–63)*

> Thus I began again: 'All those things
>   the bite of which can make hearts turn to God
>   converge with one another in my love.
>
> 'The world's existence and my own,
>   the death He bore that I might live,[39]
>   and that which all believers hope for as do I,
>
> 'all these—and the certain knowledge of which I spoke—
>   have drawn me from the sea of twisted love
>   and brought me to the shore where love is just....'

The man's eye, medium of his mortal love, must literally run the risk of dying in order to be resurrected as a newborn eye in paradise. This is the overcoming of Cavalcanti's Platonism and its return in a higher form, as resurrection of the flesh. *Rischio di morte* turns into eternal life.

From Poetry to Theology and Finance

The word *rischio* remains a commonplace in Italian literature of the *trecento*. Giovanni Boccaccio, not much more than a generation younger than Dante, used the word at least three times in different works. For him, the term *rischio* can mean venturing onto the open sea for the sake of gain, as in this passage from his *Elegia di Madonna Fiametta*:

> senza aspettare la pace del turbato mare, credendo a'marinari bugiardi e arrischievoli per voglia di guadagnare, supra alcuna legno se mise, il quale in ira a'venti a all'onde, in quelle è forse perito?
>
> (La Fiammetta 76)

> And then, perchance, not waiting until the tempestuous sea was becalmed, and credulous of the tales lying and foolhardy [*arrischievoli*, literally: risk-taking] mariners tell in hope of gain, he has embarked on some boat, which, having incurred the wrath of the winds and of the waves, has perished amid the latter, and he with it.
>
> (Trans. James C. Brogan, 1999)

It can mean to take an oath on one's person and one's life, as in this quote from his novel *Il Filoloco*: "*Et in cio arrischiero la persona e la vita,…*" 'And in this, a will put my person and my life at risk,…' (*Il Filocolo* 148). And it can, finally, mean to risk your life in order to be near your beloved Emilia, like Arcites in Boccaccio's *Teseida*:

> Tanto mi diede ancor di pronto ardire,
> che sotto nome stran nelle tue mani
> mi misi, a rischio di dover morire;…
>
> (X.24.333)

> So much she still is apt to make me burn
> that, under a fake name, I put
> myself in your hands, at the risk of having to die;…

From its use in two of Boccaccio's works, his novel *Il Filoloco* and his *Elegia di Madonna Fiametta*, the word *rischio* traveled to Henri Estienne's *Deux Dialogues du nouveau language françois italianizé*, and, from there, to seventeenth-century England, where it was adopted by a nation which, due to its new dominance over a wide, international, and global network of trade, had ample use for it, and which, moreover, did not have to worry anymore about the canonical prohibition of usury because it just had emancipated itself from the laws of the Catholic church. The term risk was free to go.

In Dante's work, the word *rischio* migrates from its fashionable use in love poetry to a prominent position in a highly hierarchical theological system. Risk determines the life of human beings on this Earth, it is left behind with the resurrection of the flesh. Dante could, however, not foresee that, one day, the word risk would occupy such a ubiquitous and prominent position in this world that it could even be used in order to redefine the relationship between theology and philosophy. For that is what John Locke did when, in his "An Essay Concerning Human Understanding," he wrote:

> Where the truth embraced is consonant to the revelation in the written word of God, or the action conformable to the dictates of right reason or holy writ, we may be assured that we run no risk in entertaining it as such: because, though perhaps it be not an immediate revelation from God, extraordinarily operating on our minds, yet we are sure it is warranted by that revelation which he has given us of truth.

This statement is a first step toward the reversal of the famous formula *philosophia ancilla theologiae* in Immanuel Kant's treatise on *The Conflict of the Faculties*:

> Auch kann man allenfalls der theologischen Facultät den stolzen Anspruch, daß die philosophische ihre Magd sei, einräumen (wobei doch noch immer die Frage bleibt: ob diese ihrer gnädigen Frau die Fackel vorträgt oder die Schleppe nachträgt), wenn man sie nur nicht verjagt, oder ihr den Mund zubindet; denn eben diese Anspruchslosigkeit, blos frei zu sein, aber auch frei zu lassen, blos die Wahrheit zum Vortheil jeder Wissenschaft auszumitteln und sie zum beliebigen Gebrauch der oberen Facultäten hinzustellen, muß sie der Regierung selbst als unverdächtig, ja als unentbehrlich empfehlen.
>
> *(Kant, Der Streit der Facultäten)*

> We can also grant the theology faculty's proud claim that the philosophy faculty is its handmaid (though the question remains, whether the servant is the mistress's torchbearer or trainbearer), provided it is not driven away or silenced. For the very modesty [of its claim]—merely to be free, as it leaves others free, to discover the truth for the benefit of all the sciences and to set it before the higher faculties to use as they will—must commend it to the government as above suspicion and, indeed, indispensable.
>
> *(Trans. Gregor 45–46)*

One academic discipline not involved in Kant's *Conflict of the Faculties* is the new science of what we now call population statistics, a science of which Kant was not only aware, but which is the basis of his famous "Idea for a Universal History from a Cosmopolitan Point of View." Kant writes:

> Was man sich auch in metaphysischer Absicht für einen Begriff von der Freiheit des Willens machen mag: so sind doch die Erscheinungen desselben, die menschlichen Handlungen, eben so wohl als jede andere Naturbegebenheit nach allgemeinen Naturgesetzen bestimmt. Die Geschichte, welche sich mit der Erzählung dieser Erscheinungen beschäftigt, so tief auch deren Ursachen verborgen sein mögen, läßt dennoch von sich hoffen: daß, wenn sie das Spiel der Freiheit des menschlichen Willens im Großen betrachtet, sie einen regelmäßigen Gang derselben entdecken könne; und daß auf die Art, was an einzelnen Subjecten verwickelt und regellos in die Augen fällt, an der ganzen Gattung doch als eine stetig fortgehende, obgleich langsame Entwickelung der ursprünglichen Anlagen derselben werde erkannt werden können. So scheinen die Ehen, die daher kommenden Geburten und das Sterben, da der freie Wille des Menschen auf sie so großen Einfluß hat, keiner Regel unterworfen zu sein, nach welcher man die Zahl derselben zum voraus durch Rechnung bestimmen könne; und doch beweisen die jährlichen Tafeln derselben in großen Ländern, daß sie eben so wohl nach beständigen Naturgesetzen geschehen, als die so unbeständigen Witterungen, deren Eräugnis man einzeln nicht vorher bestimmen kann, die aber im Ganzen nicht ermangeln den Wachstum der Pflanzen, den Lauf der Ströme und andere Naturanstalten in einem gleichförmigen, ununterbrochenen Gange zu erhalten. Einzelne Menschen und selbst ganze Völker denken wenig daran, daß, indem sie, ein jedes nach seinem Sinne, und einer oft wider den anderen, ihre eigene Absicht verfolgen, sie unbemerkt an der Naturabsicht, die ihnen selbst unbekannt ist, als an einem Leitfaden fortgehen und an derselben Beförderung arbeiten, an welcher, selbst wenn sie ihnen bekannt würde, ihnen doch wenig gelegen sein würde.
>
> *(Kant, "Idea for a Universal History from a Cosmopolitan Point of View")*

Whatever concept one may hold, from a metaphysical point of view, concerning the freedom of the will, certainly its appearances, which are human actions, like every other natural event are determined by universal laws. However obscure their causes, history, which is concerned with narrating these appearances, permits us to hope that if we attend to the play of freedom of the human will in the large, we may be able to discern a regular movement in it, and that what seems complex and chaotic in the single individual may be seen from the standpoint of the human race as a whole to be a steady and progressive though slow evolution of its original endowment. Since the free will of man has obvious influence upon marriages, births, and deaths, they seem to be subject to no rule by which the number of them could be reckoned in advance. Yet the annual tables of them in the major countries prove that they occur according to laws as stable as [those of] the unstable weather, which we likewise cannot determine in advance, but which, in the large, maintain the growth of plants the flow of rivers, and other natural events in an unbroken uniform course. Individuals and even whole peoples think little on this. Each, according to his own inclination, follows his own purpose, often in opposition to others; yet each individual and people, as if following some guiding thread, go toward a natural but to each of them unknown goal; all work toward furthering it, even if they would set little store by it if they did know it.

(Trans. Beck slightly altered)

The methods of population statistics reveal a hidden order, in fact, a natural law in the seemingly chaotic mess of freely interacting individuals called history. And based on this fact Kant comes to the conclusion:

so wird sich, wie ich glaube, ein Leitfaden entdecken, der nicht bloß zur Erklärung des so verworrenen Spiels menschlicher Dinge, oder zur politischen Wahrsagerkunst künftiger Staatsveränderungen dienen kann (ein Nutzen, den man schon sonst aus der Geschichte der Menschen, wenn man sie gleich als unzusammenhängende Wirkung einer regellosen Freiheit ansah, gezogen hat!); sondern es wird (was man, ohne einen Naturplan vorauszusetzen, nicht mit Grunde hoffen kann) eine tröstende Aussicht in die Zukunft eröffnet werden, in welcher die Menschengattung in weiter Ferne vorgestellt wird, wie sie sich endlich doch zu dem Zustande empor arbeitet, in welchem alle Keime, die die Natur in sie legte, völlig können entwickelt und ihre Bestimmung hier auf Erden kann erfüllt werden. Eine solche Rechtfertigung der Natur—oder besser der Vorsehung—ist kein unwichtiger Bewegungsgrund, einen besonderen Gesichtspunkt der Weltbetrachtung zu wählen. Denn was hilfts, die Herrlichkeit und Weisheit der Schöpfung im vernunftlosen Naturreiche zu preisen und der Betrachtung zu empfehlen, wenn der Theil des großen Schauplatzes der obersten Weisheit, der von allem diesem den Zweck enthält,—die Geschichte des menschlichen Geschlechts—ein unaufhörlicher Einwurf dagegen bleiben soll, dessen Anblick uns nöthigt unsere Augen von ihm mit Unwillen wegzuwenden und, indem wir verzweifeln jemals darin eine vollendete vernünftige Absicht anzutreffen, uns dahin bringt, sie nur in einer andern Welt zu hoffen?

if, I say, one carries through this study, a guiding thread will be revealed. It can serve not only for clarifying the confused play of things human, and not only for the art of prophesying later political changes (a use which has already been made of history even when seen as the disconnected effect of lawless freedom), but for giving a consoling view of the future (which could not be reasonably hoped for without the presupposition of a natural plan) in which there will be exhibited in the distance how the human species finally achieves the condition in which all the seeds planted in it by Nature can fully develop and in which the destiny of the species can be fulfilled here on earth. Such a justification of Nature—or, better, of Providence—is no unimportant reason for choosing a standpoint toward world history. For what is the good of esteeming the majesty and wisdom of

Creation in the realm of brute nature and of recommending that we contemplate it, if that part of the great stage of supreme wisdom which contains the purpose of all the others—the history of mankind—must remain an unceasing reproach to it? If we are forced to turn our eyes from it in disgust, doubting that we can ever find a perfectly rational purpose in it and hoping for that only in another world?

Locke had identified reason and revelation. Kant identifies Nature and Providence, and he does it to express the hope that "the destiny of the [human] species can be fulfilled here on earth." By means of statistical calculations humanity gets a grip on what used to be a divine privilege: providence. Following Bernoulli's *Art of Conjecturing*, we can project our own future, create paradise here on Earth. One wonders what Dante, who described his ascent from *Inferno*, through *Purgatorio* to *Paradiso*, might have thought of such an optimistic reading of humanity's future. And as to our position today, we may ask ourselves, in hindsight, how far we have come along on the path of Kant's *Idea of a Human History from a Cosmopolitan Point of View*. However we may answer this question, I think it is safe to say that, in a time when one of the most advanced forms of what Kant called providence is high-frequency trading, the key term risk is here to stay.

Notes

* On Genoa's role as a dominant sea power in the Mediterranean and the Atlantic from the Middle Ages to early Modernity, see Thomas Kirk, "The Republic of Genoa and Its Maritime Empire." *Empires of the Sea. Maritime Networks in World History*, edited by Rolf Strootman, Floris van den Eijnde and Roy van Wilk, Leiden and Boston 2020, pp. 153–175.

1 If not noted otherwise, all translation mine.
2 According to Walter Ashburner's introduction to the *Rhodian Sea-Law*, these dangers include: (1) dangers arising from want of knowledge or discipline on the part of those on board; (2) dangers from pirates, land robbers, and wreckers; (3) dangers from fire; (4) difficulties in reference to the provision and preservation of food and drink (cxli).
3 The situation is described in Hoover (1926). For the early history of maritime loans from Greek and Roman antiquity to the early Middle Ages, see Geoffrey E. M. de Sainte Croix (1974).
4 A Roman gold coin.
5 See *The Rhodian Sea-Law*, loc. cit., p. 4, and commentary pp. 65–67, where the word is used in the negative form ἀκίνδυνος, meaning without danger, without risk.
6 One can only hope that the book which, under the title *Mittellateinisches Wörterbuch bis zum ausgehenden 13. Jahrhundert*, ed. Bayerische Akademie der Wissenschaften, has been advertised as "the new DuCange," will shed more light on this question, once the editors get to the letter "R."
7 A tropical wood used as red dye, cf. Du Cange, *Glossarium*, s.v. Brasile.
8 For the term *traectitia* as synonym of *foenus nauticum*, see *Brill's New Pauly*, online, s.v. Maritime loans (Jean Andreau).
9 For a thorough discussion, see McLaughlin, vol. I (1939), pp. 81–147, and vol. II (1940), pp. 1–22.
10 As testified by the etymology of the words bank and bankrupt, for instance.
11 Reference to Giovanni Boccaccio, *Il Filocolo*, p. 148.
12 Reference to Giovanni Boccaccio, *La Fiametta*, p. 58.
13 "And, in this I will risk my person and my life."
14 Cf. vol. I, Paris 1885, letter I, 46.
15 The term crown is, of course, used here in the sense of: "Any of various coins, originally one bearing the imprint of a crown" (OED).
16 The last line of the quote in this translation is "And yours is in great danger." I have changed it in order to preserve the etymological relation between French *adventurer*, a synonym of *risquer*, to risk, and the English verb to venture.
17 The first quote in the OED is from 1621, ten years later.
18 The OED only lists one example from Locke's essay on *Money*.
19 When discussing the *foenus nauticum* as well the mediaeval "usury doctrine," in his early book *Zur Geschichte der Seehandelsgesellschaften im Mittelalter nach südeuropäischen Quellen*, Ferdinand Enke: Stuttgart 1889, Max Weber uses the term risk, German "Risiko," repeatedly (16–28 and 113), but he seems completely unaware not only of the fact that this word has its own history, but that it was, moreover, coined for

specific reasons by the very maritime trading companies whose history he is writing. And not only the word risk, but its function within the modern insurance industry is just as blatantly absent in his book on *The Protestant Ethic and the Spirit of Capitalism*.

20 According to the *Centre national de resources textuelles et lexicales*, around 1165, www.cnrtl.fr/etymologie/providence. Accessed June 15, 2017.
21 The translation of this title as *The Wellfare State* misses the explicit reference to the theological category of providence.
22 This list is based on the small set of documents I was able to consult, hence, potentially incomplete.
23 Quotes from sources in Italian are based on Battaglia 772–773 and Cortelazzo and Zolli 1089.
24 As is the case with many of the early documents, the exact date of origin is unknown. *Terminus ante quem* is 1300, the year of Cavalcanti's death.
25 Cf. *Rime* XIII: *Voi che per li occhi*: "You through whose eyes …"
26 Thus, not just because of repressed feelings of revenge, as Freud would have it.
27 In some cases, it is not even clear who wrote what, Cino di Pistoia or Guido Cavalcanti. See *Rime di Messer Cino da Pistoia*.
28 Cf. Andreas Capellanus, *De Amore*, I-I.1: "Amor est passio quaedam innata procedens ex visione et immoderata cogitatione formae alterius sexus, ob quam aliquis super omnia cupit alterius potiri amplexibus et omnia de utriusque voluntate in ipsius amplexu amoris praecepta compleri."

> Love is an inborn suffering proceeding from the sight and immoderate thought upon the beauty of the other sex, for which cause above all other things one wishes to embrace the other and, by common assent, in this embrace to fulfill the commandments of love.

29 "Donne qu'avete inteletto d'amore," in *La Vita nuova*, lines 35–36 and 55–56.
30 Tristan Kay dates this ballata and the whole "pargoletta" sequence to 1294–1296 (75–76).
31 The three parts of Dante's *Divina commedia*, Inferno, Purgatorio, and Paradiso are quoted after *The Princeton Dante Project*, 1966–1967.
32 Derived from Latin *pupilla*, Greek κόρη, little girl; cf. Plato, *Alcibiades*, I 132ε–133α.
33 If not noted otherwise, all translations by Robert Hollander and Jean Hollander quoted after The Princeton Dante Project, as in here.
34 First, as an activity, a verb, in Canto XXIV, 40, and, then, as a substance, a noun, Canto XXVI, 18, 27, 29, 38, 48, 51, 62. The exception is line 57, see the complete quote below.
35 This is the modern form of the word. Dante's *caritate* is closer to the Latin *caritas*.
36 "Parhelion, also called Mock Sun, or Sun Dog, atmospheric optical phenomenon appearing in the sky as luminous spots 22° on each side of the Sun and at the same elevation as the Sun" ("Parhelion").
37 I give the translation by Henry Wadsworth Longfellow because, unlike other English versions, it preserves the technical term "parhelion" which does not mean reflection.
38 See Gaffney.
39 Note to non-Christians: Redemption of humanity through the death of Jesus Christ.

Works Cited

Andreau, Jean. "Maritime loans." *Brill's New Pauly*, http://referenceworks.brillonline.com/cluster/New%20Pauly%20Online. Accessed December 11, 2019.

Aristotle. *Poetics*. Translated by Stephen Halliwell. Longinus, *On the Sublime*. Translated by W. Hamilton Fyfe, revised by Donald A. Russell. Demetrius, *On Style*. Translated by Doreen C. Innes and W. Rhys Roberts. (Loeb Classical Library, vol. 199: Aristotle, vol. XXIII). Harvard UP, 1995, 9.1451a–37f.

Battaglia, Salvatore. *Grande Dizionario della Lingua Italiana*. Vol. XVI. Unione Tipografico-Editrice Torinese, 1992.

Beck, Ulrich. *Risk Society: Towards a New Modernity*. Sage, 1992.

Bernoulli, Jakob. *Ars coniecturandi, opus posthumum. Accedit tractatus de seriebus infinitis, et epistola gallicè scripta De ludo pilae reticularis*. Impensis Thurnisiorum, fratrum, 1713.

"Bisque," Wiktionnaire, https://fr.wiktionary.org/wiki/bisque. Accessed February 28, 2018.

Blanchard, Louis. *Documents inédits sur le commerce de Marseille au moyen age*, vol. 1: *Contrats commerciaux du XIII siècle*, Barlatier-Feisat, 1884.

Boccaccio, Giovanni. *La Fiammetta*. Jacopo Ciardetti, 1826.

Boccaccio, Giovanni. *Il Filocolo*, edited by Salvatore Battaglia, Giuseppe Laterza, and S. Bari, 1938.

Boccaccio, Giovanni. *La Teseida delle nozze d'Emilia*, edited by Alberto Limentani, Oscar classici, Mondadori, 1992.

Boccaccio, Giovanni. *La Fiametta*. Translated by James C. Brogan. Parenthesis Publications, 1999, www.yorku.ca/inpar/fiammetta_brogan.pdf. Accessed June 18, 2017.

Capellanus, Andreas. *De Amore*, www.thelatinlibrary.com/capellanus/capellanus1.html. Accessed February 26, 2018.

Carducci, Giosuè. "Compendio della vita di Cino." *Rime di Messer Cino da Pistoia*, edited by Enrico Bindi and Pietro Fanfani. Tipografia Niccolai, 1878.

Cavalcanti, Guido. *The Sonnets and Ballate of Guido Cavalcanti*. Translated by Ezra Pound. Small, Maynard and Company, 1912, www.sonnets.org/pound.htm. Accessed January 5, 2016.

Cavalcanti, Guido. *Rime con le rime di Jacopo Cavalcanti*, edited by Domenico de Robertis, Sonnet LI, Giulio Enaudi, 1986.

Cicero, Marcus Tullius. *De officiis*, book III, section XXIX, On Duties. translated by Walter Miller, *Cicero*, vol. XXI, (Loeb Classical Library, vol. 30). Harvard UP, 1913.

Corneille, Pierre. "Épitre à Monsieur de Zuylichem," in *Oeuvres completes*, vol. III. Hachette, 1886.

Corneille, Pierre. "La Suite du Menteur," in *Oeuvres completes*, vol. II. Paris, 1889.

Cortelazzo, Manlio and Paolo Zolli. *Dizionario etimologico della lingua italiana*, vol. 4. Zanichell, 1985.

Cotgrave, Randle. *A Dictionarie of the French and English Tongues*. Adam Islip, 1611, www.pbm.com/~lindahl/cotgrave/830small.html. Accessed July 10, 2015.

da Pistoia, Cino. *Rime di Messer Cino da Pistoia*, edited by Enrico Bindi and Pietro Fanfani. Tipografia Niccolai, 1878.

Dante. *Altre rime d'amore e di corrispondenza*, LXXXVII, www.danteonline.it/italiano/opere2.asp. Accessed February 26, 2018.

Dante. *La Vita nuova*, http://letteritaliana.weebly.com/donne-chavete-intelletto-damore.html. Accessed February 26, 2018.

Dante. *Lyric Poems: Poems from Exile*. Translated by Joseph Tusiani, May 5, 2012, www.italianstudies.org/poetry/ex2.htm. Accessed January 8, 2016.

Dante. *The Princeton Dante Project*, edited by Giorgio Petrocchi. Mondadori, 1966–1967, http://etcweb.princeton.edu/dante/pdp/. Accessed June 18, 2017.

de Morgan, Augustus. *Essay on Probabilities and on their Application to Life Contingencies and Insurance Offices*. John Taylor, 1838.

de Morgan, Augustus. "Theory of Probabilities." *Encyclopedia Metropolitana, Pure Science*, edited by Edward Smedley, Hugh James Rose, and Henry John Rose, vol. 2. B. Fellowes, 1845.

de Sainte Croix, Geoffrey E. M. "Ancient Greek and Roman Maritime Loans." *Debits, Credits, Finance and Profits*, edited by Harold Edey and B. S. Yamey, London 1974, pp. 41–59.

Demosthenes. *Against Polycles*. Perseus Project, edited by W. Rennie. Oxonii.e Typographeo Clarendoniano, 1931, www.perseus.tufts.edu/hopper/text?doc=Perseus:abo:tlg,0014,050:17&lang=original. Accessed February 2016.

de Saxoferrato, Bartolus. "De captivis & postliminio reversis, & redendibus ab hostibus." In *Bartoli Commentaria in secundum digesti novum partem*. Lyon 1560.

Digestum vetvs. ivris cvilis pandectarvm tomvs primvm. Hugo à Porta, 1560, D. 22. 2, p. 1693.

Du Cange, Charles du Fresne. "Riscus." *Glossarium mediae et infimae latinitatis*. Niort, 1883–1887.

Estienne, Henri. *Deux Dialogues du nouveau language françois italianizé et autrement desguizé* [etc.], edited by P. Ristelhuber. Alphonse Lemerre, 1885.

Ewald, François. *L'État providence*. B. Grasset, 1986.

Freud, Sigmund. "Bemerkungen über einen Fall von Zwangsneurose." *Gesammelte Werke chronologisch geordnet*, vol. 7: *Werke aus den Jahren 1906–1909*. Imago Publishing, 1993.

Gaffney, James. "Dante's Blindness in Paradiso XXV–XXVI: An Allegorical Interpretation." *Dante Studies*, no. 91, 1973.

"Hazard." *Online Etymology Dictionary*, http://etymonline.com/index.php?allowed_in_frame=0&search=hasard&searchmode=none. Accessed February 28, 2018.

Historiae Patriae Monumenta: Chartarum, vol. II. Royal Print, 1853.

Hoover, Calvin B. "The Sea Loan in Genoa in the Twelfth Century." *The Quarterly Journal of Economics*, vol. 40, no. 3, May 1926, pp. 455–529.

Kant, Immanuel. *Der Streit der Facultäten*. Spiegel Online, http://gutenberg.spiegel.de/buch/-3509/1. Accessed June 20, 2017.

Kant, Immanuel. *Idee zu einer allgemeinen Geschichte in weltbürgerlicher Absicht*. Spiegel Online, http://gutenberg.spiegel.de/buch/-3509/1. Accessed June 21, 2017.

Kant, Immanuel. *On History*. Translated by Lewis White Beck. The Bobbs-Merill Co., 1963, www.marxists.org/reference/subject/ethics/kant/universal-history.htm. Accessed June 21, 2017.

Kant, Immanuel. *The Conflict of the Faculties. Der Streit der Fakultäten*. Translated by Mary J. Gregor. U of Nebraska P, 1979.

Kay, Tristan. "Dante's Cavalcantian Relapse: The 'Pargoletta' Sequence and the Commedia." *Dante Studies*, vol. 131, September 15, 2014, pp. 73–97.

La correspondance de Blaise Pascal and de Pierre Fermat. La Géométrie du Hasard ou le début du Calcul des Probabilités, edited by Pierre-José About and Michel Boy. Les Cahiers de Fontenay, 1983.

Lloyd's Agency. "Cargo Claims and Recoveries: Module 3," www.lloyds.com/~/media/files/the%20market/tools%20and%20resources/agency/links%20to%20documents%20from%20la%20website/cargo%20claims%20%20recoveries_module%203.pdf#search=%27Adventures%20and%20perils%27. Accessed January 13, 2016.

Locke, John. "Some Considerations of the Consequences of the Lowering of Interest and the Raising the Value of Money." Part 2. Rod Hay's Archive for the History of Economic Thought, 1691, www.marxists.org/reference/subject/economics/locke/part2.htm. Accessed June 19, 2017.

Locke, John. "Short Observations on a Printed Paper, Intituled 'For encouraging the coining of Silver Money in England, and after for keeping it here." *The Works of John Locke*, 12th ed., vol. 4. Rivington, 1824, http://oll.libertyfund.org/titles/763. Accessed June 2017.

Locke, John. "An Essay Concerning Human Understanding." University of Adelaide, March 27, 2016, https://ebooks.adelaide.edu.au/l/locke/john/l81u/B4.19.html. Accessed June 15, 2017.

Magens, Nicolas. *An Essay on Insurances*. W. Baker, vol. II, no. 9, 1755.

McLaughlin, T. P. "The Teaching of the Canonists on Usury." *Medieval Studies*, vol. I and vol. II, 1939, 1940.

Molière, *L'impromptu de Versailles*, in *Les pieces de Molière*. Libraririe des Bibliophiles and Librairie P. Ollendorff, 1890, pp. 25–26.

Molière, *The Impromptu of Versailles. A Comedy in One Act*, in *The Dramatic Works of Molière*. Translated by Henri van Laun, Edinburgh 1875, pp. 284–324.

OpenSourceShakespeare. "Shakespeare Concordance: All Instances of 'Peril'," www.opensourceshakespeare.org/concordance/o/?i=765303&pleasewait=1&msg=sr. Accessed June 20, 2017.

"Parhelion." *Encyclopaedia Britannica*, www.britannica.com/science/parhelion. Accessed June 20, 2017.

Pascal, Blaise. *Nouvelles expériences sur le vide, Oeuvres completes*, vol. III. Garnier Frères, 1872.

Pascal, Blaise. *Réflexions sur les conditions de prix attachés à la solutions des problèmes concernant la cycloïde, Oeuvres completes*, vol. III. Garnier Frères, 1872.

Pascal, Blaise. *Lettres écrites à un provincial*, in *Oeuvres de Pascal*, ed. L. Derome, vol. II. Garnier Frères, 1886.

Pascal, Blaise. *The Provincial Letters*. Translated by Thomas M'Crie, the University of Adelaide, 2014, https://ebooks.adelaide.edu.au/p/pascal/blaise/p27pr/part15.html. Accessed February 28, 2018.

Plato. *Enthyphro. Apology. Crito. Phaedo. Phaedrus*. Translated by Harold North Fowler (Loeb Classical Library, vol. 36), Harvard UP, 1914.

Plato. *Charmides. Alcibiades I and II. Hipparchus. The Lovers. Theages. Minos. Epinomis*. Translated by W. R. M. Lamb (Loeb Classical Library, vol. 201). Harvard UP, 1927.

Pope Gregory IX. "Decretales D. Gregorii Papae IX." IV, tit. XIX, c. XIX, Rome, 1582.

"Providence." "Centre national de resources textuelles et lexicales," www.cnrtl.fr/etymologie/providence. Accessed June 15, 2017.

Receuil des Historiens des Croisades, vol. II: *Lois: Assises de Jérusalem*, vol. II: *Assises de la cour des Bourgeois*, edited by Auguste-Arthur Beugnot, Imprimérie Royale, 1893.

Shakespeare, William. *The Merchant of Venice*, I, www.opensourceshakespeare.org/views/plays/playmenu.php?WorkID=merchantvenice. Accessed February 26, 2018.

The Rhodian Sea-Law, ed. Walter Ashburner, Oxford 1909, reprint: Scientia Verlag, 1976.

Weber, Max. *Zur Geschichte der Seehandelsgesellschaften im Mittelalter nach südeuropäischen Quellen*. Ferdinand Enke, 1889.

Weber, Max. *Die protestantische Ethik und der Geist des Kapitalismus* [The Protestant Ethics and the Spirit of Capitalism], Archiv für Sozialwissenschaften und Sozialpolitik, vol. 20, Tübingen, 1904.

Weber, Max. *The Protestant Ethics and the Spirit of Capitalism*. Translated by Talcott Parsons. Scribner's Sons, 1958, reprint: Dover Publications, 2003, www.wsp-kultur.uni-bremen.de/summerschool/download%20ss%202006/Max%20Weber%20-%20Die%20protestantische%20Ethik.pdf. Accessed June 15, 2017.

Wright, Charles and C. Ernest Fayle. *A History of Lloyd's: From the Founding of Lloyd's Coffee House to the Present Day*. Macmillan & Co., 1928.

4
INSURANCE AND THE LANGUAGE OF RISK IN EARLY MODERN POLITICAL THOUGHT

Emily C. Nacol

François Ewald observes, "Insurance can be defined as a technology of risk. In fact, the term 'risk' which one finds being used nowadays apropos of everything has *no* precise meaning other than as a category of this technology" (198; emphasis added). Ewald's claim captures the crucial dynamic of the human encounter with risk that will be the focus of this chapter. The origins of insurance were contingent upon the development of a new human perspective on the future, one that conceived of it as a place of probable harm, or risk. In turn, as insurance practices developed and spread, they seeped into the way human beings thought and talked about what "risk" is. Very often when we use the word "risk," we are not gesturing to probable events—desirable and undesirable—that might await us. Rather, we use it to mark out something to fear, whereas we might just as well use the language of "danger" or "harm" (see also Douglas 39). Our language, Ewald suggests, has been shaped by the perspective that insurance practices have lent to us.

Scholars commonly trace the origin of the concept of risk itself to the rise of insurance—a constellation of technologies, institutions, and practices that developed to help measure, predict, and control an unknown future. Insurance, broadly understood, has always depended on the idea that the future is likely to be a place of risk, understood as probable danger, accident, and loss. At the same time, as historians have shown, insurance turned risk into a commodity, and thus a potential source of profit (Bouk xx). Taking a closer look at insurance as a way of conceptualizing and confronting risk can, however, highlight a critical feature of the concept of risk itself: its capacity to shape the future as a field of potential loss *and* profit and to stimulate the passions of fear *and* hope in us.

In what follows, I will focus largely on British practices of insurance and their place in political thinking and writing of the long eighteenth century. First, I will give a brief recounting of the emergence of insurance as a social and economic phenomenon in early modern Britain. As Giovanni Ceccarelli reminds us, "while commercial risks were mingled in business partnerships and similar agreements with other features—such as loans, currency exchange, etc.—*insurance is the first known contract in which risk becomes the specific object of the settlement*" (118; emphasis added). The British insurance industry found its roots in early forms of marine insurance, as was the case nearly everywhere. There were distinctive features of the Anglo-British context that shaped how people practiced and thought about insurance, however, notably its unusual willingness to tolerate a growing life insurance industry. Then, in the following two sections, I will concentrate on two different models of insurance that were important to the development of the insurance industry in Great Britain. First, I return to marine insurance, noting how it evolved over time into a more corporate model of securing lives and goods. This corporate form's major appeal was the possibility of more confidence and independence for commercial actors. The evolution of these stable, successful insurance schemes—largely conducted through joint-stock companies with ample capital—grew out of smaller, failed ventures. These failures, and the turn to public companies, provided political thinkers like Adam Smith with fruitful material for contemplating how better to foster security, independence, and autonomy through commercial institutions, and created an opportunity to reflect on the frequently confusing psychology of human beings acting in a field of risk. Second, I examine small, local cooperative endeavors among the working poor and middle rank to provide for themselves and their families in the event of illness, injury, or death. In particular, I focus on friendly societies, enduring associations that provided material assurances to their members in the event of catastrophe. These societies, which were a popular source of life insurance, were much vaunted for two other broad contributions they made to society: social solidarity, and strict rules and practices of moral rectitude. Both of these features made friendly societies leaders in a broad-based effort to reduce the moral risks of shared life, and they garnered the attention of social commentators like Daniel Defoe, who viewed them as the best of kind of social project in a country rife with schemes ranging from the laudable to the dubious. My conclusion pivots away from Smith's and Defoe's readings of insurance as an economically, politically, and morally salutary practice to consider how it introduced complicated moral questions about the commodification of bodies and lives, a legacy that ultimately undercut its positive contributions to commercial life.

The Rise of Risk in Early Modern Britain

The notions of risk circulating in eighteenth-century Britain found their beginnings in the context of marine ventures, and thereafter they deeply permeated the social world. As Ian Hacking points out in a brief etymological treatment of the idea of risk, the word "risk" developed, strictly speaking, as a technical term in the context of mercantile and nautical endeavors. But from the beginning, he argues, it also signified or captured moral ideas about humanity's place in the world. Hacking comments that "risk" was not only "used by merchants when discussing the risks of their business ventures, or ship's masters engaged in nautical adventures. It was so used but was used at the same time to connote a new sense of life and morality" (25). Although "risk" emerged as part of a specialized professional vocabulary, it ultimately created space for a new philosophical orientation to the future and a new sense of how human beings might think and act with it in mind. Prudential reasoning, understood as care for the future, began to claim pride of place in politics and commerce. But more importantly, probabilistic thought—the philosophical and eventually statistical basis of assessing risk—became a commonplace approach to negotiating an uncertain future and determining how to respond to it in terms of both action and feeling.

Insurance practices largely tapped into and encouraged the darker passions stirred by approaching the future through the lens of philosophical probability. As Carol Heimer succinctly explains, "at its most basic, insurance is a social arrangement to reduce the effects of losses by employing the resources of the group to cushion individuals" (288). It thus depends on a particular orientation to the future in which the probability of loss looms large; only this perspective can motivate people to join with others to devise ways to preempt or recover the potential damage threatened by anticipated, unwanted events.[1] Insurance is thus, at its core, a series of techniques and technologies that offers a kind of armor against probable harm.

It is difficult to know precisely when and how insurance—and the corresponding attitudes that made it a successful enterprise—first came to England, although historians surmise that English merchants probably first heard about and arranged insurance agreements through their Italian trading partners, who had been purchasing policies since the fourteenth century (Lewin 91; Rossi 131–132).[2] By c.1500, a marine insurance market was part of England's commercial landscape, and as the end of the sixteenth century neared, a set of institutions had solidified around the buying and selling of insurance: "codification of insurance customs and the establishment of an insurance registry on the one side, and the establishment of a specialized insurance court on the other" (Rossi

140). By the late seventeenth to early eighteenth centuries, insurance markets were expanding all over the country, especially in London, and these were no longer confined to marine insurance. Karin Zachman notes that in London "maritime insurance multiplied on the initiative of individual brokers who gathered in places like Lloyd's Coffee House," following the same pattern as the rest of Europe. But there was also market diversification: "new branches emerged such as fire and life insurance, not to mention the many adventurous schemes that promised protection against any and every contingency of life" (7).[3] In England, life insurance developed almost accidentally from marine insurance, beginning when overseas traders wanted policies to cover both their passengers and cargo—a cargo that included enslaved people. Insuring enslaved people's lives became one of the steadiest sources of business for life insurers in the late eighteenth century (Clark 13, 16–17; see also Lewin 112). The development of life insurance was peculiar to the early modern English context; it was reviled and prohibited across the continent by 1700 for reasons including an aversion to treating human life as property. But the idea of insuring lives took hold in England, and life insurance providers took many forms, ranging from private underwriters, to larger incorporated joint-stock firms, to friendly societies, which were mutual aid groups formed by citizen subscribers.

By the 1720s, Londoners could find reputable sources of maritime, fire, and life insurance, and notably, they could also participate in a number of less reputable insurance schemes as well. There was suddenly, as Lorraine Daston has argued, a "vogue for insurance," and from the proliferation of schemes and opportunities, we can draw three insights, points that will recur in the next three sections of this chapter ("The Domestication of Risk" 244). First, insurance was, and remains, an unusual hybrid of social good—neither wholly private nor wholly public. Second, insurance fostered attitudes of prudence and caution in the broader culture; it was not simply an *outgrowth* of already-entrenched, widespread risk aversion. Third, insurance in this period bore a tight relationship to gambling, and thus encouraged speculation and betting in a society already obsessed with games and lotteries. These second and third points are, in some respects, a subset of the first—while participating in insurance offered private benefits to individuals, it changed the public, social landscape in ways both wanted and unwanted.

Insurance complicated the relationship between private and public benefits from its inception. As A.B. Leonard reminds us, it "began as a mutually beneficial system of finance, and was traded between members of a merchant community as a 'club-good,' … which they used to improve the commercial experience of all participants" (6). While the benefits of policies for private merchants were obvious, there was also a clear sense that insurance as a practice improved overseas commerce as a whole, making it a more secure and attractive endeavor. This had ancillary benefits for wealthy trading states and their consumer publics. The public–private dimension of insurance also spilled over into debates about whether insurance underwriting was better left to larger, joint-stock corporations, that could bring more capital to support the enterprise, or to small private firms. Although the potential benefits of incorporation for a number of private actors—policyholders, investors, and underwriters—were clear, incorporation was justified in terms of how it could secure the public interest by offering better organization and security. After all, many small firms had failed miserably, so the theory was that a larger firm could offer better management and more capital. Arguments against incorporation were also framed by a perceived tension between public and private interest—those who argued against joint-stock insurance companies pointed to the reputation these corporations had for securing harmful monopolies and falling prey to projectors and stockjobbers who were mostly interested in generating new stocks to sell and profiting from them. That is, joint-stock companies were likely to offer opportunities for company directors and middlemen to line their own pockets, rather than to improve trade as a whole by offering security for merchants (Bogatyreva 180, 183–187). The arguments for incorporation won, however, and the first joint-stock insurance companies were in place by the 1720s.

Insurance, whether provided by private or public means, also helped build a broader culture of risk aversion and risk reduction. Insurance firms themselves led efforts to reduce risk, largely out of a self-interested desire to avoid paying for damages to their clients' goods or lives. For example, the first fire brigades in London were organized by fire insurance firms, who wanted to protect the homes that bore their firms' firemark (Clark 2). Fire insurers also excluded particularly risky ventures that frequently went up in literal flames (e.g., sugar refineries). Life insurance providers followed suit, encouraging more prudent and cautious behaviors in policyholders and subscribers, as we know from the frequently elaborate rules of conduct that friendly societies imposed on their members. In these ways and others, insurance firms and collectives effectively determined what constituted especially hazardous or prudent behavior, and they helped condition their policyholders to see the world through a lens of probable danger. This had, over time, a conditioning effect on society as a whole.

A focus on cultivating risk aversion, which we so intuitively associate with insurance now, was not initially central to practices of insurance in early modern England, however. Instead, insurance —especially life insurance—had a tight association with gambling and its optimistic orientation toward risk. As Daston has remarked, "risk became the defining characteristic for a distinct class of legal agreements, the aleatory contract, thus combining such socially diverse practices as insurance [and] gambling … under a single heading" ("The Domestication of Risk" 240). Geoffrey Clark puts this more broadly: "Insurance consists essentially of wagering on contingent events" (35). Insurance and gambling shared more than the framework of the aleatory contract, which organized "the exchange of certain for uncertain goods" (Daston, "The Domestication of Risk" 147). Insurance simply *was* gambling much of the time, and it thus stimulated further the speculative passions of English people in the seventeenth and eighteenth centuries (Clark 5). Life insurance gambling was a common social phenomenon, with people taking out policies as bets on contingent events ranging from military losses, the death of the monarch, or even the lives of ordinary people they knew. Betting on lives was a common practice that was socially acceptable in Britain, at least in the first half of the eighteenth century, unlike in its counterparts on the continent, which had outlawed life insurance altogether. At this time in Britain, larger social criticisms of life insurance focused on "fraud, deception, and crime" on the part of both insurers and insured, rather than on gambling as an integral part of the industry (52). In the second half of the eighteenth century, attitudes began to shift, and people began to complain that gaming was tainting both the moral and commercial aspirations of the insurance industry. In 1774, Parliament passed the Gambling Act, which outlawed betting on lives and required that anyone who purchased a policy demonstrate a "legitimate financial interest" in the life of anyone they insured (53). Gambling was thus something that had to be legislatively prised apart from insurance.

As British insurance settled into a regular set of institutions, norms, and practices in the long eighteenth century, political economists began commenting on its social and political effects. Their commentary highlights some of the themes articulated here: the inseparable public and private functions of insurance, the sensitivity to loss it encouraged, and its relationship to speculation and even gambling. Political economists engaged insurance in the general sense laid out by Heimer: as a social scheme in which individuals bind together to lessen the damage of probable future losses. Two of the most frequently analyzed forms of insurance were corporate marine insurance, which made trade risk more palatable, and life insurance, which was frequently provided by the friendly societies formed by ordinary people. While distinct, each serves the pooling function that Heimer highlights. The differences between these two forms of insurance are also instructive, however, in learning more about how collectives manage risk, beginning with how insurance schemes depend for survival and profit on human cognition of the future as a place of risk, understood as the prospect of loss.

Adam Smith on Contempt for Risk and the Role of Joint-Stock Insurance Companies

As its history suggests, insurance—while tightly connected to the probable losses that accompany risk in theory—brings together the profit and loss sides of risk-taking and places them in a dependent relationship in practice. By measuring and commodifying risk—or more accurately, by commodifying *security* against probable harm or loss, insurers sought to generate profit from others' anxiety about loss (Heimer 288).[4] And, their profit pursuits encouraged a number of observable behaviors in the insured, from the morally salutary to the more dubious. As noted in the previous section, insurers encouraged and sometimes incentivized the insured to adopt preventive measures to keep potential losses down, a practice common to the friendly societies discussed in the next section. Alternatively, insurers found ways to heighten a pessimistic outlook or attention to loss among potential consumers, to encourage the purchase of policies in the first instance. Both approaches underscore the ways early insurance enterprises—focused on staying afloat, at a minimum—oriented ordinary people toward thinking of the future as a place of risk.

In Adam Smith's reflections on human disdain for risk in *The Wealth of Nations* (1776), we see some hints regarding why this second strategy—of attuning people to the future as a place of potential *loss*—might have appealed to insurers. Smith's analysis of insurance and risk relies on his empirical observation that insurance had not, for much of its history, been a particularly lucrative business. Smith was well aware of how many early schemes failed in the seventeenth and eighteenth centuries, and he extracted lessons about human psychology and institutional design as two important facets of risk management from these examples. In *The Wealth of Nations*, Smith does not systematically lay out his views on insurance, but his episodic reflections yield sharp insights about the risks facing both insurers and those who purchased policies. His analysis is largely framed by his interest in the fates of what we would now call insurance firms of various sizes, with a focus on fire and especially marine insurance.

Smith's description of insurance as a general practice has a positive normative valence. Implicitly, he argues for insurance premiums as a prudent purchase for people with material goods to protect—provided that the insurance company can stay afloat long enough to make a payout, if it must. Insurance is especially valuable, he thinks, for merchants who pursue overseas trade and must contend with the perils this might entail when they commit their capital to the "wind and waves" (II.i). In Book V of *The Wealth of Nations*, Smith observes that purchasing insurance premiums benefits the insured both materially and psychologically; it secures them financially against potential losses and, just as critically, offers some sense of assurance and stability in the face of their highly risky mercantile ventures. It thus gives insured actors more independence and confidence to pursue their commercial endeavors, free from fear of total financial ruin in the event of unforeseen catastrophe. For insurers, however, Smith notes insurance itself *is* the risky business, the potential source of ruin, and thus a venture best supported, Smith concludes, by the large capital that could be amassed by a public, joint-stock company.

Smith's recommendation here is an anomaly in the context of his writing, for his views on joint-stock companies are notoriously critical. In *The Wealth of Nations*, he catalogs their many pathologies as institutions: their structure, which he thinks insulates by design both shareholders and directors from taking necessary responsibility for risky decisions; their monopolistic tendencies as agents in both domestic politics and international political economy; and worst of all, their status as brutal colonial governors. But in his reflections on insurance, Smith gives a rare nod to the usefulness of joint-stock companies, an endorsement that issues from his sensitivity to human attitudes and behavior in response to risk.[5]

When thinking about insurance companies as institutions, Smith looks at them largely from the perspective of the insurer. The financial downsides of choosing insurance as a trade stem from two potential problems, by Smith's lights—one related to the structure of insurance agreements, and another associated with his observations about human psychology. Beginning with his comments in Book V, Smith has a clear view on the form and design of insurance companies, favoring what was then a strongly public, corporate model. This endorsement is, for him, a matter of balancing the interests and needs of insurer and insured. When it comes to insurance as a business, Smith suggests that the security it offers is inherently lopsided—it secures the insured, but potentially imperils the insurer, who may have to part with large sums of money to compensate a policy-holder's loss. This outcome had already collapsed many small insurance businesses in Smith's lifetime. Reflecting on this possibility, he notes:

> The trade of insurance gives great security to the fortunes of private people, and by dividing among a great many that loss which would ruin an individual, makes it fall light and easy upon the whole society. In order to give this security, however, it is necessary that the insurers should have a very large capital. Before the establishment of the two joint stock companies for insurance in London, a list, it is said, was laid before the attorney-general of one hundred and fifty private insurers who had failed in the course of a few years.
>
> *(V.i.127)*[6]

Smith recognizes here that the benefits of insurance for the insured are not to be underestimated—the material and financial losses that could devastate one person are redistributed via a network of insurance contracts and agreements, such that no one has to bear too heavy of a financial burden in the face of catastrophe (leaving aside the material and personal losses that insurance payouts cannot really replace, of course). Smith also acknowledges an ineffable good that insurers offer the insured, even if no disaster befalls them—some assurance that misadventure, bad luck, or contingent events will not bring them to ruin, thanks to the preemptive willingness by insurers to shoulder and structure the burdens of risk in a way that makes them "fall light and easy upon the whole society." But for insurers themselves, offering this bundle of material and psychological benefits could be perilous business, as shown by Smith's attention to the spate of private insurers who went under. It is a risky endeavor to offer to compensate tremendous losses for the insured, Smith thinks. Insurance companies may never or rarely be forced to do so, or they may have to pay compensation many times over, depending on circumstances that cannot really be known in advance or, at this stage in the development of probabilistic thinking, be predicted with too much certainty.[7]

Smith's observations on the difficulties of the growing insurance industry are compatible with his critical remarks on human psychology and the individual orientation to risk. In Book I of *The Wealth of Nations*, he notes for the first time in the text that the insurance business has not proven to be an easy way to make a fortune, and he suggests that low premium sales might in fact reflect something about the moral psychology of human beings: they are either insufficiently attentive to the losses posed by an unknown future in general, or they are openly skeptical that they will experience future loss *themselves*. Put more sharply, Smith observes that people are not particularly good risk assessors. In a lengthy rumination, Smith draws some insights on human attitudes toward risk from his observations on the fortunes of insurers. There he writes:

> That the chance of loss is *frequently under-valued, and scarce ever valued more than it is worth*, we may learn from the very moderate profit of insurers. In order to make insurance, either from fire or sea-risk, a trade at all, the common premium must be sufficient to compensate the common losses, to pay the expence of management, and to afford such a profit as might have been drawn from an equal capital employed in any common trade. The person who pays no more than this, evidently pays no more than the real value of the risk, or the lowest price at which he can reasonably expect to insure it. But though many people have made a little money by insurance, very few have made a great fortune;

and from this consideration alone, it seems evident enough, that the ordinary balance of profit and loss is not more advantageous in this, than in other common trades by which so many people make fortunes. *Moderate, however, as the premium of insurance commonly is, many people despise the risk too much to care to pay it.*

(I.x.31; emphasis added)

In this passage, Smith explicates the challenges faced by insurers who wish to turn a profit and tries to explain their causes. On Smith's read, even the most astute insurance provider hopes to break even or at most to turn quite modest profits. Partly, this is just the nature of the business endeavor itself, according to Smith. Present as well as possible future expenses absorb a substantial portion of the sum of premium sales, which is why Smith recommends that insurance firms be structured as large, public joint-stock companies, that could bring sufficient capital to absorb any contingencies.

Smith also lays some responsibility for the difficulties of the insurance business at the feet of consumers, however. He notices that, in general, people tend not to over-emphasize the likelihood of future losses; if anything, they may not be attentive *enough* to their own futures. As he comments, "many people despise the risk" too much even to purchase an affordable insurance premium —how else to explain the seeming inability of insurers to make a go of their ventures, he asks? At first glance, it is not entirely clear whether Smith thinks the habits he observes reflect a wise or an imprudent approach to the future. A sanguine interpretation of Smith's views on human psychology and risk behaviors is that people are capable of estimating future outcomes reasonably and fairly accurately, which may give them pause when considering the necessity of purchasing insurance against the likelihood of fire or marine-related disasters. That is, they may understand intuitively that these catastrophic events are unlikely and therefore not worth the cost of a premium. A more faithful rendering of Smith's meaning and tone here, however, suggests that he believes people underestimate and undervalue future losses at their own peril, or in Smith's language, they "despise" risk or have an imprudent contempt for it. Smith concedes that sea-risk is more widely recognized as a potential source of loss than fire, which accounts for the higher proportion of insured-to-uninsured ships than houses. But there are still traders who decide to eschew insurance for their ships and cargo, and while this may turn out well enough in the end, Smith thinks their decision is rooted in a troubling outlook. As he remarks, "the neglect of insurance upon shipping, however, in the same manner as upon houses, is, in most cases, the effect of no such nice calculation, but of mere thoughtless rashness and presumptuous contempt of the risk" (I.x.31). Smith is generally quite reluctant to attribute the choice to avoid insurance to habits of probabilistic reason and prudence, and instead chalks it up to hastiness and a lack of healthy respect for the future as a place rife with contingencies and risk.

As Smith contends, the orientation of would-be premium buyers makes profit more elusive for insurers than it would be if these potential customers overestimated or overvalued loss. He hints at something important here—while savvy insurers might try to capitalize on or exploit individuals' risk aversion, this approach gains traction only if potential participants in the pool actually know how to calculate loss accurately, or better still for the insurer, if they tend to calculate too generously the likelihood or value of potential loss. If Smith is right about the moral psychology of risk-takers, the insurance business will be uphill work; and in the eighteenth century, indeed it was. To succeed, insurers must not only structure their firms in particular ways to shield themselves from bankruptcy, but they must also consider how to heighten and commodify caution or anxiety about the future. To their own benefit, they learned to do both effectively. As Lorraine Daston has argued, insurance companies came late to statistical methods *precisely* because it was in their financial interest to encourage and heighten *generalized* belief in probable loss, rather than to carefully parse likely from unlikely losses so that potential buyers could then weigh the merits or demerits of purchasing insurance (*Classical Probability* 185–187). Historians of insurance have carefully tracked the ways insurers have worked to *produce* risk as a central cultural concern, as a way of ensuring better premium sales and subsequent profits (Daston, "The Domestication of Risk").

Smith's attention to the corporate form of insurance comes at the cost of another set of practices that might have restored his confidence in the human capacity to gauge risk properly: the friendly society. These cooperative insurance schemes, which thrived in Smith's lifetime and for centuries after, depended for their success on a membership of individuals who understood the future as a place of potential loss, and who were willing to club together and invest in protection against as-yet-unrealized hard times. And many of them were quite successful, not only in offering material assurances to their members but in generating profits more social than financial.

Defoe on Equity, Solidarity, and the Work of Friendly Societies

Some 80 years before Smith pondered the dynamic relationship between corporate insurance schemes and the psychology and choices of risk-taking individuals, Daniel Defoe commented on smaller-scale social endeavors to shield individuals from a perilous future. In *An Essay Upon Projects* (1696), Defoe evaluates one of the most significant social projects to emerge in early modern England: the friendly society. Friendly societies were voluntary associations, to which members paid dues or bought subscriptions in exchange for protection for themselves or their families against possible losses like personal property loss, disability and illness, old age, and death. While they are especially associated with life insurance, they offered myriad forms of security for their members, including "the convivial comforts of pub-based sociality" that issued from regular group meetings, along with the informal networks of fraternity and friendship they nurtured (Cordery 13).[8] Although life insurance was frequently the target of harsh moral criticism for its links to gambling, its association with friendly societies somewhat shielded it from potential naysayers. These societies were frequently associated with a strong moral agenda, one which emphasized values of "equity, mutuality, amicability, and paternal care" for its members, particular the most vulnerable ones (Clark 54). Thus, these organizations were viewed as significant contributors to social improvement.

In his reflections on these associations, which were extremely popular in the seventeenth through the nineteenth centuries, Defoe expresses a keen optimism regarding their potential to provide much more than financial security. After detailing his own proposal for a friendly society for widows, Defoe comments that he "might, without arrogance, affirm that the same thought might be improved into methods that should prevent the general misery and poverty of mankind, and at once secure us against beggars, parish poor, almshouses, and hospitals" (80). Insurance would, he suggests here, not only provide for individuals who had suffered a personal loss that affected their ability to thrive—the death of a spouse, or an illness that made work impossible, to take two common scenarios foreseen by friendly societies and their members. More significantly, Defoe wagered that if English society were to encourage the proliferation and good governance of friendly societies, it might also witness the end of poverty and render irrelevant institutions that offered charity and alms to the poor.

While grand in its ambition and scope, Defoe's was a typical view—many commentators saw the friendlies as a way of structuring relations of self-help among poor working people. While Defoe avoids moralizing too strongly, other commentators explicitly praised the friendlies for their potential to instill particular values in their members. To take one example, in *A Treatise on Friendly Societies* (1835), Charles Ansell argues that,

> whatever substantial advantage the members derive, from such societies, in the form of allowances during sickness and in other natural misfortunes, are greatly enhanced in value by the consciousness that such advantages are the fruits, not of benevolence or of the charity of others, but of the members' own frugality and providence.

(1)[9]

Many poor people also preferred the independence and assurance offered by friendly societies to the options provided by poor relief, which by the eighteenth century required multiple forms of proof of need and was never guaranteed (Cordery 21). Many people, including both social reformers and ordinary subscribers, thus esteemed the friendlies for their ability to negotiate a persistent tension between the values of charity and self-help in early modern England. The immediate, self-described purposes of the friendlies were, however, to provide insurance and social kinship for their members.

Defoe goes on in the *Essay* to speculate, again optimistically, that "all the contingencies of life might be fenced against" if individuals were to form these types of arrangements that fostered mutual security and aid, and he offers ideas about how they should be organized and structured (35). His sensitivity to the differences among individuals when it comes to risk-taking leads him to endorse some guidelines regarding membership criteria for friendly societies and to articulate a general worry about the aggregative nature of insurance schemes. Defoe expresses concern that those who more willingly risk loss might combine in the same insurance pool with cautious people who take daily measures to reduce the risk of loss. Binding the prudent to the adventurous poses, he thinks, some difficulties. He is especially clear on this point when he discusses a variation in the risks generated by different lines of work. He comments:

> I don't pretend to determine the controverted point of predestination, the foreknowledge and decrees of Providence; perhaps, if a man be decreed to be killed in the trenches, the same foreknowledge ordered him to list himself a soldier that it might come to pass; and the like of a seaman; but this I am sure, speaking of second causes, a seaman or a solider is subject to more contingent hazards than other men, and therefore are not upon equal terms to form such a society.
>
> (34)

Defoe acknowledges, harkening to an older way of thinking about the future, the possibility that divine providence shapes the destinies of all men. And yet, he is firm in his judgment that ordinary humans can assert some control over their own futures via reflection and choice. People can readily observe, he argues, that some professions are riskier than others, and he invites readers to contemplate whether people in high-risk professions may put undue pressure on a network of aleatory contracts formed with people pursuing less perilous work or may eventually draw too heavily from the common pool.

In this reflection on threats to the stability and longevity of friendly societies, Defoe acknowledges the double-edged nature of these kinds of insurance schemes. Both the genius and the trouble with cooperative structures like friendly societies is that they combine people who might be radically different with respect to the level of risk they either welcome or take on by necessity. Thus, they may foster a kind of inequity anathema to their original purposes, an inequity that may fray the solidaristic bonds so important to these associations. To preempt these difficulties, Defoe proposes sorting people into societies by profession, so that they might join together "upon equal terms" to insure themselves against loss. As some professions seem to invite accident or "contingent hazards" more readily, Defoe advocates aggregating individuals who do similar kinds of work, rather than spreading risk across a diverse pool of workers. In thinking through this solution, he registers discomfort with a critical feature of insurance schemes: the aggregation of individuals and the distribution of the risks they take papers over individual differences in psychology or lived experience when it comes to the embrace of risk, freeing some to speculate more aggressively on the backs of cautious others in the pool. Tacitly, Defoe invites readers to think more carefully about the relationship between insurance and gambling.

The friendly societies themselves acknowledged the challenges Defoe identifies in the *Essay*, and they also understood them as a consequence of the diversity of risk tolerance or acceptance found in any given group of people. Many of the friendlies were indeed organized by lines of work, since some of them may have originated in professional guilds (Cordery 18). Those that invited a broad cross-section of members from across professions frequently explicitly excluded people who worked in particularly risky fields (e.g., soldiers, miners). Further still, many also barred potential members who were thought to live morally risky lives (e.g., adulterers). A number of friendly societies also had strict moral codes and expelled members who violated them, a choice that "reflected the belief that misfortune was the consequence of individual actions and that, while virtuous deeds met their just reward, punishment followed depravity" (26). These structural elements of friendly societies underscore that members were attuned to notions of fairness and were reluctant to allow in people who might someday overdraw on the group's resources. Their habits of internal solidarity and mutual aid were often shored up, then, by practices of exclusion.

Friendly societies exemplify how insurance, understood as a constellation of practices, agreements, and institutions, does not simply issue from a cautious approach to the future among the insured. Friendly societies—in theory and sometimes in practice—brought together people with a range of orientations and exposures to future harms and offered a place of relative safety or protection for all of them. They supported deep practices of social solidarity among their membership, offering not only mutual protection against future need, but also regular meetings, rites, and rituals that gave members the chance to build and sustain communal bonds in the context of a changing commercial society that seemed at times to offer only isolation or competition.

The friendlies thus remind us of a key feature of insurance: its ability to bring together individuals on terms of cooperation and even solidarity against a risky future. As Ewald puts it, "insurance contributes substantially toward the solidarization of interests. It constitutes a mode of association which allows participants to agree on the rules of justice they will subscribe to" (207). Elsewhere, he describes the insurance pool as the mythical social contract made concrete; for Ewald, the imagined social compacts and covenants theorized by thinkers like Thomas Hobbes and John Locke in order to stress the mutual aid and protection offered by political societies, exist in material form in the insurance pool. Centuries before Ewald, Defoe began this conversation about the promise and peril of life insurance pools as instruments with the potential to actualize a culture of mutual help and cooperation among individuals, a service as important as its immediate capacity to secure participants against the hazards and contingencies of life. But he also recognized early that, with these moral and political upsides, the move to aggregate risk-takers and redistribute the losses posed by risk-taking issues challenging moral and political questions about equity, individuality, and responsibility. Is it equitable and just to bind together those who live prudently with those who take bolder chances? Conversely, if all humans live with the absence of foreknowledge about the future, is it equitable and just *not* to offer people an opportunity to collectivize for their own protection, regardless of their differences? The friendlies, and perhaps insurance practices more generally, raised these questions for British society in the long eighteenth century.

Insurance, Commodification, and Property in Lives

Risk scholars frequently point to the connections between theoretical or conceptual accounts of risk and concrete practices in the world. Perhaps, given that the concept of risk—and its corresponding language or idiom—likely formed from the practical and material concerns of merchants and sailors, our interest in the relationships among theory, language, practice is to be expected. In this chapter, I have looked at insurance as a set of practices, behaviors, and ideas that shaped how early modern British people understood and coped with risk. The main assertion of this chapter is that the rise of insurance in Britain invited new ways of contemplating the future and the possible dangers it held. That is, it helped people both conceive of and manage the risks of the future, by encouraging them to think probabilistically about future losses and by giving them the financial instruments to proceed with some measure of confidence in the face of risk. It also, in the case of friendly societies, gave people opportunities to create relations of solidarity and equity against the backdrop of a rapidly changing political economy. As readers of the history of early modern insurance know, however, the development of insurance came with its fair share of challenges, both material and moral. It was a struggle for insurance companies to keep their businesses stable and profitable, and it was equally difficult for people seeking insurance to find trustworthy or financially savvy underwriters. Likewise, the availability of insurance did not always nurture the prudent attitudes that insurers and social reformers encouraged, for it also provided opportunities for people to speculate, gamble, and seek undue profits via policies and schemes.

The rise of insurance in Britain, particularly its willingness to allow life insurance underwriting, left one final, troubling legacy that is only hinted at in this chapter. As mentioned before, life insurance—as an idea—owed its existence at least partly to marine insurance policies that covered a ship's cargo, which frequently included human cargo in the form of trafficked enslaved people. While insurance was upheld as a tool that enhanced Britain's economic growth, it also introduced a kind of conceptual confusion that has never really dissipated, by blurring the distinction between "property in things and property in people" (Clark 62). Insuring enslaved people as cargo and allowing people to bet on the lives of others furthered both the commodification of human life and the possibility of holding *other* people as property or sources of wealth. In so doing, insurance eroded and undermined ideas of self-ownership and introduced new social and political risks, even as it created economic independence and prosperity for many.

Acknowledgments

The author wishes to thank Bishnupriya Ghosh, Jacob Levy, Ekaterina Pravilova, and Bhaskar Sarkar for comments on previous drafts. Thanks also to Tristan Hughes for acute research assistance and commentary.

Notes

1 As Ewald explains,

> In everyday language the term "risk" is understood as a synonym for danger or peril, for some unhappy event which may happen to someone; it designates an objective threat. In insurance, the term designates neither an event nor a general kind of event occurring in reality (the unfortunate kind), but a specific mode of treatment of certain events capable of happening to a group of individuals (199).

2 The first insurance policy that we know about was formed $c.1350$ CE for a cargo of wheat shipping from Sicily to Tunis (Lewin 86).
3 Even as large, stable enterprises like the Amicable Society for the mutual insurance of lives were being established, many little insurance offices were popping up and failing at rapid speed during this period (Daston, "The Domestication of Risk" 244). As Geoffrey Clark documents, many of them were running what amounted to pyramid schemes (3).
4 In the period I examine in this chapter, measuring risk was more a matter of assessing philosophical probabilities than of projecting from statistical calculations using compiled data. This would change in the late eighteenth and nineteenth centuries (See Daston, "The Domestication of Risk").
5 By the time Smith wrote *The Wealth of Nations*, joint-stock insurance companies were part of the British insurance market (Bogatyreva 179).
6 This passage mirrors closely the text of a 1601 Act of Parliament regarding the purposes of policies of assurance, which reads:

> It cometh to pass, upon the loss or perishing of any ship, there followeth not the undoing of any man, but the loss lighteth rather easily upon many, than heavily upon few, and rather upon them that adventure not, than those that do adventure, whereby all merchants, specially of the younger sort, are allured to venture more willingly and more freely.
>
> *(qtd. in Lewin 109)*

The imbalance noted in this passage will be important to the discussion of friendly societies in the next section.

7 It should be noted that Smith appears to gloss over the poor business practices of many insurers, focusing instead on the inherently risky nature of the business.
8 Trade unions and cooperative societies served similar functions, but Cordery establishes that friendlies were even more commonplace and robust. It should be noted that they were not the only means by which individuals could procure life insurance; joint-stock companies offered it, too. But these companies were profit-oriented institutions, whereas the friendlies offered other social goods.
9 Some of the friendlies did not succeed due to poor management or fraud, and this they had in common with other insurance providers.

Works Cited

Ansell, Charles. *A Treatise on Friendly Societies: In Which the Doctrine of Interest of Money and the Doctrine of Probability are Practically Applied to the Affairs of Such Societies*. Baldwin and Craddock, 1835.

Bogatyreva, Anastasia. "England 1660–1720: Corporate or Private?" *Marine Insurance: Origins and Institutions, 1300–1850*, edited by A.B. Leonard. Palgrave, 2016, pp. 179–204.

Bouk, Dan. *How Our Days Became Numbered: Risk and the Rise of the Statistical Individual*. U of Chicago P, 2015.

Ceccarelli, Giovanni. "Coping with Unknown Risks in Renaissance Florence: Insurers, Friars, and Abacus Teachers." *The Dark Side of Knowledge: Histories of Ignorance, 1400–1800*. Brill, 2016, pp. 118–138.

Clark, Geoffrey. *Betting on Lives: The Culture of Life Insurance in England, 1695–1775*. Manchester UP, 1999.

Cordery, Simon. *British Friendly Societies, 1750–1914*. Routledge, 2003.

Daston, Lorraine. "The Domestication of Risk: Mathematical Probability and Insurance 1650–1830." *The Probabilistic Revolution, Volume I: Ideas in History*, edited by Lorenz Krüger. The MIT Press, 1987, pp. 237–360.

Daston, Lorraine. *Classical Probability in the Enlightenment*. Princeton UP, 1995.

Defoe, Daniel. *An Essay Upon Projects*. BiblioBazaar, 2018.

Douglas, Mary. *Risk and Blame: Essays in Cultural Theory*, Routledge, 1992.

Ewald, François. "Insurance and Risk." *The Foucault Effect: Studies in Governmentality*, edited by Graham Burchell et al. U of Chicago P, 1998, pp. 197–210.

Hacking, Ian. "Risk and Dirt." *Risk and Morality*, edited by Richard V. Ericson and Aaron Doyle, U of Toronto P, 2003, pp. 22–47.

Heimer, Carol A. "Insurers as Moral Actors." *Risk and Morality*, edited by Richard V. Ericson and Aaron Doyle, U of Toronto P, 2003, pp. 284–316.

Leonard, A.B. "Introduction: the Nature and Study of Marine Insurance." *Marine Insurance: Origins and Institutions, 1300–1850*, edited by A.B. Leonard. Palgrave, 2016, pp. 3–24.

Lewin, C.G. *Pensions and Insurance Before 1800: A Social History*. Tuckwell Press, 2003.

Rossi, Guido. "England 1523–1601: The Beginnings of Marine Insurance." *Marine Insurance: Origins and Institutions, 1300–1850*, edited by A.B. Leonard. Palgrave, 2016, pp. 131–150.

Smith, Adam. *An Inquiry into the Nature and Causes of the Wealth of Nations*, edited by R.H. Campbell and A. Skinner. Liberty Fund, 1981. 2 vols, 1st ed. 1776.

Zachman, Karin. "Risk in Historical Perspective: Concepts, Contexts, and Conjunctions." *Risk – A Multidisciplinary* Introduction, edited by C. Klüppelberg, Daniel Straub, and Isabell M. Welpe. Springer International Publishing, 2014, pp. 3–35.

5
HAZARDOUS INDIVIDUALISM
Jason Puskar

The rational individual known as *homo economicus* has long been a normative ideal in liberal societies. He—for in his genesis he was clearly male—was presumed to be a universal subject, one who rationally calculates costs and benefits, risks and rewards, in order to maximize his available utility. Sometimes traced back to John Stuart Mill, *homo economicus* became far more prominent in neoclassical economics after the marginal revolution of 1871. William Stanley Jevons called economics "the mechanics of human interest" (24), in which economic man performs a "calculus of pleasure and pain" in order to "maximize happiness by purchasing pleasure, as it were, at the lowest cost of pain" (27).[1] Needless to say, many have found this idealized figure wanting, both in his methods and his goals, and many more have doubted that anyone could achieve such a resolutely rational standard of conduct. There are many alternatives to *homo economicus* as a result, but in this essay I want to describe just one of them, a different kind of figure who does not rationally manage his risks and rewards, but who rather seeks out excessive risk as the foundation for a different but no less powerful mode of liberal capitalist subjectivity.

This hazardous individual, as I will call him, belongs to just one among many different modes of Western, liberal individualism: the possessive individualism of C.B. Macpherson, the methodological individualism of neoclassical economics, or any of the other 11 kinds of individualism described by Stephen Lukes.[2] Even that excludes other permutations that neither Lukes nor anyone else has yet adequately described, such as those informed by non-Western, non-male, or non-white identity positions. When we talk about social groups we use dozens, perhaps hundreds of different terms to distinguish families from congregations from unions from nations, and more, but we subsist on the single barren term "individual" to cover an equal range of organizational forms. Our over-reliance on the term "individual" suggests at least some acquiescence to its universalizing claims.

Accordingly, the hazardous individual should by no means be seen as essential or universal, but rather as a historical product born primarily of the collision of *homo economicus* with the massive apparatus of risk management already well developed by the early twentieth century, and which made calculative rationality inescapable, even compulsory. Under those conditions, the hazardous individual responds perversely to the official mediation of risk, refusing to mitigate risks and instead contriving especially dangerous activities that register to him and to others as purely private affairs. By deliberately performing reckless acts, the hazardous individual lays claim to a more traditional form of individual agency, one that appears to be safely detached from intermediating sources of risk knowledge. To put the case at its simplest, by the early twentieth century the individualism of *homo economicus* had become so dependent on systematic, institutional, bureaucratic, and expert resources that, for many, it no longer seemed adequately individualized after all.

This is not at all to say that the hazardous individual's apparent rejection of risk–reward rationality is an effective way of escaping or combating the institutionalization of risk, let alone the prevailing political order. Far from it. In fact, the hazardous individual's recklessness often involves a studious inversion of normative standards of risk rationality, so they must be cognizant of what counts as reasonable conduct precisely in order to avoid it. As a crude inversion of rational reckoning, recklessness often leaves underlying structures intact. Accordingly, institutions from casinos to investment firms to factories have hardly been innocent of sponsoring hazardous individualism, and there is no shortage of beneficiaries when individuals assume disproportionate amounts of risk. None of this is entirely new. A love of dangerous adventure has been a feature of capitalism from the beginning, and indeed long predates it, but I am suggesting that the rapid institutionalization of calculative risk analysis in the late nineteenth century both undermined traditional forms of individualism and led to their reconstitution through a new emphasis on reckless adventure. If risk was thought to be little more than a burden for *homo economicus*, many in liberal societies today regard it as its own reward, precisely because incalculable hazard—as opposed to calculable risk—affords a more potent affirmation of liberal individuality. This history of how liberal subjects came to prize peril is thus also the story of how new kinds of liberal subjects came into being, and as a result, it may be seen as a preliminary attempt to explain why so many people appear to feel so at home in the precarious conditions of liberal capitalism today.

To understand the emergence of the hazardous individual, we need to understand the birth and early career of his double, *homo economicus*. Political economy from Smith and Ricardo through Marx and Mill tended to focus on macroeconomic issues like wealth, trade, taxation, wages, and the values of specific commodities, all large-scale macroeconomic issues typically oriented toward production. The rise of neoclassical economics after the marginal revolution around 1871 changed the conversation decisively, because after that a new generation of economists focused on individual consumption decisions instead. Guided by the powerful new theory of marginal utility, usually expressed mathematically, microeconomics presumed that value is not inherent in anything, neither labor nor diamonds, but rather gets assigned at the scene of consumption, at the margins, that point where one more unit of any good or service could be added. The first bottle of water you buy in the airport is hardly worth $6 intrinsically, but knowledge of looming scarcity increases its value. Yet having purchased one $6 bottle of water, most travelers will find that the value of the next bottle has dropped precipitously, so they do not purchase a second at the same price. It will be heavy to carry, and perhaps more than needed, and anyway water will be plentiful after landing. The value of the bottle of water is not determined once and for all, but as a matter of its utility to *homo economicus* at the margins, as he calculates all the factors—scarcity, quantity, weight, bulk, cost, future availability, other competing needs—and makes a decision about whether to use his available resources to add one more marginal unit. Each individual will make drastically different choices, of course, because each has subjectively different desires and beliefs. Still, economists presume that all of them try to attain their different goals in exactly the same way, and deem their conduct rational if it is consistent with achieving those goals in a way that maximizes utility.[3] In the wake of neoclassical economics, *homo economicus* became the normative model for all economic conduct, even though, from the beginning, economists recognized that actual people behave in far more complicated ways.

There could be much more to say about the marginal revolution, and about recent historical and theoretical reappraisals of it by Philip Mirowski, Reginia Gagnier, Simon Clarke, and others. For these limited purposes, however, the key point is simply that after the advent of neoclassical economics, risk decisions often came under the umbrella of microeconomics too. Because most economic activities have a temporal dimension, uncertainty about future outcomes, such as crop yields, figures heavily in almost all basic economic decisions. *Homo economicus* does not just balance costs against benefits in the present, but also risks against rewards in the future, and he does so rationally when he manages his risks in such a way as to maximize his utility in the context of his goals. From the perspective of neoclassical economics, risk is a cost to be managed, an unwanted burden, and as such a liability that one would embrace only if necessary to realize some other commensurate reward.

The earliest neoclassical economists, including Carl Menger, Leon Walras, and Alfred Marshall, made the case for their new assumptions by employing the example of a well-known literary figure whose highly individualistic economy displayed the near total alignment of risk management with economic choice: Robinson Crusoe.[4] Crusoe had been of little use to earlier political economists, as William Kern has shown, because his individualism and isolation fit poorly with their interest in more national macroeconomic concerns. But many microeconomists pressed Crusoe into service as an illustration of their new doctrine of marginal utility, because they saw the domestic economy of his island as a microcosm of economics in general. Even so, as Michael White has argued, microeconomists could only make use of Crusoe by drastically rewriting the story, excluding its colonial and religious subtexts, and ignoring microeconomic anathemas like this: "My time or labor was little worth, and so it was as well employed one way as another" (63).[5] Marxist, feminist, and postcolonial critics have very different readings of the novel, and even those earlier economists who attended to it saw it in rather different terms. In discussing Crusoe in this essay, then, I refer primarily to the Crusoe conjured by neoclassical economic theory, and not to the considerably greater complexities of the novel itself.

Isolated as he is, Crusoe's management of his domestic economy entails a very direct management of risks, in that the simplest choice about how to employ his resources could spell life or death. To invest effort in building a fortification is to mitigate the risk of attack, but if it reduces the time spent tending crops it may increase the risk of starvation. *Homo economicus* must decide, rationally, whether there is more utility in mitigating one risk or the other, given that he cannot do both at once. And Crusoe often does weigh his options carefully, as in the matter of how much grain to sow or keep, or whether to risk a voyage in his canoe. Still, he rarely calculates any of these risks in quantifiable terms, and readers have sometimes overstated just how calculating he really is. Instead, his rationality usually consists of qualitative judgment, which scarcely resembles probabilistic risk rationality or even strict accountancy. Even when he complains about "the Folly of beginning a Work before we count the Cost," his counting is mostly metaphorical (Defoe 118–119). In that passage he is regretting his first attempt to make a canoe that would have been far too large. He says,

> when I began to enter into it, and calculate how deep it was to be dug, how broad ... I found, That by the Number of Hands I had, being none but my own, it must have been ten or twelve Years

before he finished (118). The point, however, is that he did not calculate, only estimated it intuitively, and once the work was underway he could better gauge the pace of progress, and conclude on intuitive judgment alone that the investment of labor would be too large. Crusoe certainly does count his goats and bushels of grain, but he usually makes economic decisions about risks and resources more immediately and intuitively—all of which is entirely compatible with marginalist standards of rationality.

Even so, some of Crusoe's consumption decisions are rather difficult to reconcile with the theory of marginal utility. He builds a table before he builds a fence around his cave, after which one might suppose that the marginal utility of tables would have dropped nearly to zero. Yet he builds a second table before he even begins to work on the fortifications. Microeconomics does not explain why he chose to build a second table, nor does Crusoe explain it himself. Those who regard *homo economicus* as normative and universal must conclude one of two things: either it was irrational for Crusoe to build a second table, in that he knew or should have known that he could maximize his utility in other ways if his goal was survival, or it was rational after all because building a second table must have afforded him satisfaction so great that it outweighed even self-defense. However, those who do not agree that *homo economicus* is normative or universal can inquire into such decisions in a different way by considering the social, cultural, political, ethical, or symbolic meaning of making tables, in order to understand his conduct without recourse to such rigid utilitarianism. Given that the choice to make a second table is also a matter of managing risks, my point is simply that we can and should inquire into the meaning of voluntarily assuming risk as a social and political act, even as a part of a performance of identity. When *homo economicus* behaves like a hazardous individual, his defiance of normative rationality may in fact pay homage to different and less clearly articulated norms.

One of the economists who took up the Crusoe economy most enthusiastically was Frank Knight, a conservative mid-century American who, as we shall shortly see, was also one of the most influential economic theorists of risk. For Knight, "the concept of a Crusoe economy" was "almost indispensable." He said,

> I do not see how we can talk sense about economics without considering the economic behavior of the isolated individual. Only in that way can we expect to get rid by abstraction of all the social relations, mutual persuasion, personal antipathies, and consciously competitive or cooperative relationships which keep the behavior of an individual in society from being, in any closely literal sense, economically rational.
>
> (*Intelligence* 76)

Other economists, including institutionalists like Thorstein Veblen, objected precisely to this jettisoning of all social, ethical, and political context in order to isolate the allegedly pure rationality of the individual economic actor. Moreover, such methodological individualism was not exactly a description of real human conduct, and Knight and most other early microeconomists understood that rationality was just one factor among many guiding any particular individual's choices. For Knight, the rationality of *homo economicus* was of an especially theoretical kind: "If one behaves with perfect economic rationality, he does not behave rationally as a human being," Knight admitted. "It would be irrational to be, or try to be, perfectly rational" (72).

Still, for Knight, and indeed for most early microeconomists, any considerations other than maximizing available utility must count as irrational, including "all interests in or involving other people, except only as a purely instrumental interest"; "cooperation and competition"; "loyalty to all persons, groups, or causes"; "exploratory interest" in things that might not have any use; and even, as Knight acknowledges, most of the rest of what counts as human (72–73). To be sure, many recent economists and sociologists have tempered such strict definitions of rationality considerably, preferring various accounts of "bounded rationality" that better describe how people simplify the decision making process, or rely on social norms, rules of thumb, or other standards better described by behavioral economics.[6] Not so for Knight, who in the 1960s still insisted on a stark division between the rational and the irrational, the first of which he classes as mechanical, the second as more fully human. Accordingly, Knight associates the strictest individual rationality with "mechanistic cause and effect" and "mechanical response," requisite forms of conduct for an economic order presumed to be "working as a mechanism" (72–73). Despite his allegiance to *homo economicus* and the theory of marginal utility, then, Knight betrays a surprising sense of the mechanical rigidity of *homo economicus* too.

That ambivalence was equally apparent in Knight's early work, including his well-known account of entrepreneurship, *Risk, Uncertainty, and Profit*, first published in 1921. There, Knight influentially distinguished calculable risk from incalculable uncertainty. For Knight, "risk" refers very specifically to unknown outcomes in the future that can be analyzed probabilistically. As a result everyone tends to analyze risks in roughly the same way, and to draw roughly the same conclusions. By the 1920s, for example, the actuarial tables at one life insurance company looked a lot like the tables at any other, so everyone calculated values roughly the same way. The term "uncertainty," in contrast, also refers to unknown outcomes in the future, but it distinguishes those that cannot be analyzed probabilistically. Crucially, Knight insists that there is far more incalculable uncertainty than calculable risk in what we do, because, he says,

> It is a world of change in which we live, and a world of uncertainty. We live only by knowing something about the future; while the problems of life, or the conduct at least, arise from the fact that we know so little.
>
> (Risk 199)

Knight's binary of risk and uncertainty is useful up to a point, but it must be emphasized—as Knight repeatedly does—that in actual practice the two are rarely if ever separate. Indeed, Knight insists, when we imagine risk in something like its pure form we conceive of a situation in which there is no judgment involved, no qualitative, non-calculative basis for decision making, and of course this is hardly ever the case. Situations that are entirely a matter of calculable risk are outsourced to computers today, and even in 1921 Knight recognized that "purely routine operations are inevitably taken over by machinery" (294).

But if strict rationality registered as mechanical and dehumanizing across four decades of Knight's career, more intuitive judgments about uncertainty earned higher praise. The daring entrepreneurs who engage uncertainty are the heroes of Knight's book, as they "are not the critical and hesitant individuals," but rather have "restless energy, buoyant optimism, and large faith in things generally and in themselves in particular" (366). Their goal is still profit, to be sure, but their methods are no longer so quantitative or so widely shared. Their judgments are more particular, idiosyncratic, or simply individual. This leads to Knight's remarkable claim that it is finally wrong to think of uncertainty as a burden that people expect compensation for bearing, as generations of economists have insisted, and as *homo economicus* typically presumed. "The conventional view is, of course, to regard risk-taking as repugnant and irksome and to treat profit as the 'reward' of assuming the 'burden,'" he says (362). However, following several hints in Adam Smith, Knight insists that "risk taking is the opposite of irksome" and even that "men work ... more cheaply on the average for an uncertain than for a fixed compensation" (367).[7] This extraordinary statement amounts to a claim that the entrepreneur does not just seek greater reward through greater exposure to hazard, but that he or she actually may prefer hazard. Uncertainty is its own reward. "Man's chief interest in life is after all to find life interesting," Knight says, and as a result, "change, novelty, and surprise must be given large consideration as values per se" (369). The rationalism of *homo economicus*, which underpins Knight's microeconomic commitments, thus sits uncomfortably alongside Knight's fondness for dangerous adventure, a fondness that, by his own admission in his later work, must qualify as irrational. We might think about hazardous individualism as an attempt to recover this condition of change, novelty, and surprise from an increasingly rationalized, bureaucratized, and routinized society. For Knight, then, Crusoe may be more than just an example of rational *homo economicus*; he also may be an example of Knight's heroic entrepreneur, a resourceful and intuitive judge who economizes less by the book than by the seat of his goat skin pants.

Although Knight's argument is narrowly organized around business practices, one can see that his privileging of irrational uncertainty over rational risk partakes of a more general early twentieth-century skepticism about various other forms of rationality. Max Weber's critique of capitalist rationality and bureaucracy may be the most obvious example, but one also thinks of John Dewey's *The Quest for Certainty*, the first chapter of which, titled "Escape from Peril," denies that any such escape is possible or even desirable. Dewey's fellow pragmatist William James notoriously argued that people should sublimate their desire for war in some "moral equivalent of war," such as dangerous occupations (1281).[8] James further associated pluralism with vulnerability to danger, for "its partisans must always feel to some degree insecure," and he explicitly linked pluralism to Theodore

Roosevelt's "strenuous life" (940–941). Roosevelt, in turn, recommended not just strenuous effort, but also exposure to danger in war, hunting, or sports, because only "the man who does not shrink from danger" is a man at all. Accordingly, Roosevelt prescribed both "toil and risk" in his imperial campaign of white, male supremacy (6). Not too many steps beyond Roosevelt lies someone like Ernst Junger, whose notorious 1931 essay "On Danger" celebrates fascist upheaval and military violence. "The bourgeois person is perhaps best characterized as one who places security among the highest of values," Junger says, but "Through misfortune and danger fate draws the mortal into the superior sphere of a higher order" (28).

Much more might be said about these and many other intellectual sources of hazardous individualism, but the point is simply that Knight's early twentieth-century affirmation of dangerous uncertainty has broad parallels in the work of many others who, without necessarily rejecting rationality, clearly felt skeptical of it. From drastically different political vantage points within a generally liberal political orientation, Weber, Dewey, James, Roosevelt, and Junger all make it clear that the rationality of *homo economicus* had become excessively mechanical or enervated.[9] Accordingly, hazardous individualism can be seen as an attempt to salvage the status of liberal individualism at a moment when rationality had become so pervasive, so inescapable, so institutionally imbricated, that it threatened to dissolve the individual back into his rationalizing methods.

By the early twentieth century, those methods emanated from the massive apparatus of risk management that developed over the course of the nineteenth century, as Ian Hacking and many others have shown. The "taming of chance," as Hacking called it, rationalized uncertainties that, in previous centuries, had seemed utterly ungovernable, and at that point even death could be accurately forecast in aggregate, and successfully insured against. We are by now well acquainted with the enormous social, political, and cultural effects of the rise of institutional risk management: Francois Ewald and Daniel Defert on public and private insurance, Pat O'Malley and Richard Ericson on risk and governmentality, Ulrich Beck on environmental risk analysis, and Randy Martin on finance, to name only a few. Many of these theorists have described risk management as a particularly insidious mode of discipline that manages populations by giving people the illusion that they are managing themselves. And although these theorists differ considerably in their assumptions, methods, and conclusions, they share a sense that the production of risk knowledge has rationalizing effects, which is to say that it requires consumers to use that information in the sanctioned ways, by maximizing utility. In the strongest versions of this argument, institutional risk management has led to what Robert Castel calls a "hyper-rationalism" supporting a "vast hygienist utopia," which finally

> plays on the alternate registers of fear and security, inducing a delirium of rationality, an absolute reign of calculative reason and a no less absolute prerogative of its agents, planners and technocrats, administrators of happiness for a life to which nothing happens.
>
> *(289)*

The neoclassical economists' appropriation of the Crusoe story coincides with the build-out of risk management institutions in Europe and the United States in the late nineteenth century, from the expansion of private insurance, to crop reporting, to the institution of public health, to weather forecasting, to early deployments of the welfare state. But Crusoe occupied a world that was not just economically individualistic, but that also afforded less well-developed institutions and methods of risk management. When Knight embraced an early eighteenth-century novel about a seventeenth-century castaway, he may have been fantasizing not just about Crusoe's isolation from other people, but also about his isolation from institutional risk management and its mechanical forms of reasoning. When the hazardous individual refuses to reckon rationally through those institutions, he may be attempting to approximate Crusoe's more minimally mediated encounter with hazard.

This has been rather theoretical so far, so let us turn from fictional castaways and abstract theories to two examples spaced roughly a century apart, which testify to the cultural and historical breadth of hazardous individualism. In October of 2014, Alan Eustace, a computer scientist and senior vice president at Google, donned a pressurized survival suit, tethered himself to a helium balloon, ascended more than 135,000 feet into the atmosphere above New Mexico, released himself with explosive bolts to free fall more than 23 miles, and eventually parachuted to a safe landing. In doing so, Eustace broke the record for highest free fall jump, set just two years earlier by Austrian daredevil Felix Baumgartner, and thereby joined the ranks of many other corporate executives who have risked their lives in dangerous adventures. Richard Branson and Steve Fossett attempted to circumnavigate the world in balloons, U.S. Airways CEO Doug Parker ran with the bulls at Pamplona, Micron executive Steve Appleton died in the crash of his experimental plane, and billionaire software developer Charles Simonyi rode a Soyuz rocket into space. There are many more. None stood to gain meaningful financial returns directly from their endeavors, most paid exorbitant costs, and all risked their lives in the process.

By the traditional standards of *homo economicus*, it is rather difficult to explain such conduct as the sensible result of risk–reward rationality, unless we somehow imagine that the intense pleasure of these brief experiences was commensurate with the scale of the risk. Perhaps it was, and if one is entirely committed to marginalist assumptions, any choice, no matter how seemingly irrational, can be explained as an attempt to yield pleasure. Still, one might ask why risk itself would be so pleasurable, and though different CEOs might answer differently, we can speculate that the great practical and financial security they all enjoy might actually deprive them of opportunities to experience something like entrepreneurial adventure. By risking their lives, perhaps they feel that, in the most immediate way, they still have real skin in the game. Yet the social meaning of these performances seems even more important, for most of these feats are matters of public knowledge, and sometimes of intense media attention. Even Eustace, who invited only one reporter from the *New York Times* to cover his leap, no doubt made his exploits known to his friends and colleagues in the business community, so could bank a reputation for adventure as a form of social capital. That could count as a kind of reward, to be sure, but it is a reward that is hard to separate from the risk itself. By taking risks, daredevil CEOs gain status as certain kinds of people: people who take risks. They publicly reveal themselves to be at home in uncertainty, heroic in the face of adversity, and—when they survive—paragons of private self-control. Instead of being instrumental to some other goal, risk becomes its own reward, if we must retain that terminology, because only through reckless adventure can they lay claim to the highest of all standards of liberal individuality.

Roughly a century earlier in 1910, work safety advocate Crystal Eastman published her monumental *Work-Accidents and the Law*, an important reform volume that inspired the first workers' compensation programs in the United States. By anatomizing the various kinds of accidents that befell workers, Eastman attended to many accidents caused by workers' own recklessness. The work safety movement struggled to overcome the resistance of employers to sensible reforms, but it also struggled to overcome workers' open hostility to safety precautions. As labor historian Mark Aldrich has noted, out of almost 42,000 strikes in the building trades from 1881 to 1900, just one protested unsafe working conditions. In coal and coke industries, just nine strikes out of almost 15,000 protested safety issues, but five more actually opposed the introduction of a new safety lamp (90).[10] Eastman, however, is more interested in the conduct of individual workers taking such risks, so she puzzles over the fact that rail yard workers routinely boarded moving locomotives from the front by standing in the tracks as the engine approached and stepping up onto the platform, rather than by boarding at the side at designated and much safer steps with hand railings. Boarding from the front might have been slightly easier, one reported, but it was also significantly more dangerous, because to slip and fall meant almost certain death. Yet workers persisted in boarding from the front, defying manager recommendations and posted warnings. "I always get on in front myself," one worker reported. "We all do. It's easy and simple. There's a kind of fascination about it.

You win or you lose. It's a gamble. And then, it's not professional to get on at the side. No good railroader does it" (24).

Such statements make it clear that the choice to board from the front is not based strictly on a utilitarian calculation of costs and benefits: the gains are exceedingly small, but the potential costs are enormous, even if comparatively few workers died this way. Nor can one say that the workers were simply deficient in their knowledge; in fact, like most industrial workers, they were all too aware of the frightful carnage of their trade. As with the daredevil CEOs, the railroader derived some degree of pleasure from risk-taking: "There's a kind of fascination about it." And also like the CEOs, he managed his social status by performing his risk-taking publicly: "It's not professional" to board any other way. No less than the CEOs, then, but from a situation of rather greater economic vulnerability, the railroader sees risk as its own reward. His risk avidity affirms that he is a certain kind of salutary person, a free and responsible individual who can take care of himself.

On the surface, these two cases may appear to be more different than alike. One is a matter of leisure, the other of labor; one is performed by a wealthy executive, the other by a wage worker; one is a single act, the other a habitual practice. Yet I want to suggest that these differences mark the wide limits of hazardous individualism, in that both the wealthy executive and the wage worker perform risk-taking as a validation of private ability and self-control. In both cases the assumption of risk confers the status of autonomous individuality, as each person encounters some physical danger in fundamental isolation from other people, and in open defiance of standards of reasonable conduct. At risk of their lives, Eustace and the railroader both purchase an individuality hard to attain any other way, precisely because the mediation of calculative rationality, organized by institutions of risk management, had long ago made self-protection a collective effort. Even when the railroad worker boards from the side, he follows the advice of his manager and complies with posted warnings and the technical script of the locomotive itself, designed to induce him to board in prescribed ways. When he defies that reasonable guidance, however, he becomes more than just a good railroader; he becomes a good liberal subject, which is to say, a resourceful individual who manages hazards by himself.

Of course, the fact that so many CEOs risk their lives in multimillion-dollar adventures, and the fact that "no good railroader" boards from the side, suggest that these performances are not quite as individualizing as they appear. Hazardous individualism is itself a form of normative conduct, even if participants rarely acknowledge it as such. As a result, hazardous individualism should not be seen as a subversion of liberal capitalist rationality—not even as an escape from it—but rather as a complementary mode of subjectification. In a similar way, Randy Martin has shown how extensively the logic of risk-taking has permeated modern society, even in realms typically considered critical if not outright oppositional, such as modern art. "For the artist as cultural figure, risk is part of creative being," Martin says. "Artists are obliged to place themselves at risk, both of failure and of the unexpected, if a creative return is to be realized" (112–113). The problem, Martin shows, is that even performances of artistic risk-taking are hard to separate from an entire "risk culture" that he traces back to the financial system (114). Looked at that way, it becomes clearer that the hazardous individual's resistance to the values of *homo economicus* is really an alternative mode of liberal subjectification, a way of salvaging traditional individualist values after instrumental reason has become too institutionally, bureaucratically, and socially explicit.

In fact, the hazardous individual does not necessarily reject rationality, or even calculation, but more often postpones, distances, or suspends it so that rationality can be reclaimed as a purely private affair. In the case of Eustace, a maximally secure man embarked on a course of action over a period of years, which required an enormous amount of science and engineering, careful calculation, a team of assistants, sophisticated equipment, and rational planning. Yet the key point is that nobody could be sure it all would work precisely as intended. His life support suit could fail, he could be entangled in the lines of his parachute, his visor could fog, he could suffer a medical emergency alone in the stratosphere, or some utterly unforeseen contingency could disastrously intrude.

This particular embedding of uncertainty within risk, of irrationality within the rational, characterizes most if not all hazardous individualism. Eustace devised an elaborate and highly rationalized system designed to yield a brief but spectacular form of uncertainty. He carefully cultivated the genuine uncertainty about whether his and others' rationality would be sufficient, and that question was a matter of his own private and qualitative judgment, roughly the same kind of judgment on which Knight says entrepreneurs must rely.

Eustace thus recreates the dangerous solitude of Crusoe, not as an accidental by-product of an unwanted shipwreck, but deliberately, strategically, in order to affirm his status as something other than a mere calculator. It is hard to imagine a better metaphor for radically isolated individualism than Eustace dangling from a balloon by himself at the edge of space, but it is also important to remember how much collaborative effort went into contriving that exact situation. Several theorists of voluntary risk-taking have referred to the seemingly irrational embrace of risk as "edgework," a term originally coined by Hunter S. Thompson to refer to thrill seeking at the boundary between chaos and control, life and death (80). Mostly focusing on leisure sports like skydiving and mountaineering, Stephen Lyng, Jonathan Simon, and others have argued that an appetite for dangerous activities is in fact a rebellion against bureaucracy, labor alienation, and other forms of routinization.[11] That, however, is to see edgework rather too exclusively from the edgeworker's perspective, because it does not always account for the ways in which these performances are compatible with, even dependent on, prevailing standards of rationality. Simon has argued that some edgeworkers, such as business executives who risk their lives climbing Mt. Everest, may be rededicating themselves to a different ethic of capitalist individualism, or even performing nostalgia for the pre-welfare state. This seems more persuasive: edgework as a form of resistance to bureaucratization, but also as a reproduction of the entrepreneurial values prized in the business world. One of Eustace's former co-workers called him "a risk-taker with a passion for details," as if his leap from a balloon demonstrated his full range of professional abilities (Markoff). Perhaps it is better to say that people like Eustace, Richard Branson, and Steve Fossett have already organized their identities around hazardous individualism in a far more comprehensive and remunerative way than the railroad worker, and as a result they extend their entrepreneurial affinity for uncertainty from the strictly professional to the personal realm. But that is not to suggest that such gestures proceed from genuinely autonomous individuals; rather, the widespread practice of certain kinds of risk-taking within social and institutional contexts actually generates that sterling form of social capital termed "individuality."

The railroad worker who boards a moving train from the front is similarly implicated. As we have noted already, workers in dangerous industries often resented safety measures, which they saw as an imposition of management from above, and experienced as infantilizing.[12] They also associated work safety measures with the further routinization of the work process, and thus with the alienation of their own labor. They were not necessarily wrong, given that managers, eager to control more aspects of the industrial process, used safety as a justification for expanding managerial authority. As John Fabian Witt has argued, work safety measures finally entered the workplace not because owners recognized that safety was a legitimate moral concern, but because injury came to be classed as a failure of efficiency, at which point it made rational, economic sense for owners to manage it like any other inefficiency (119).

But if workers experienced the rational mitigation of risks as disempowering, it should hardly be surprising that they would experience the intensification of risk as empowering, an affirmation of their status as free and responsible agents. Workers seem to have found it more difficult to accomplish that through risk–reward rationality, as *homo economicus* should, because that rationality was so enmeshed with larger structures of institutional authority, such as management, that it no longer registered as their own. Instead, many seem to have felt most responsible, autonomous, and free when they contrived situations of real peril with obvious and immediate stakes. The hazardous individual's self-production is thus structured like a rescue, or really like a self-rescue, because by imperiling himself a person becomes legible as the heroic, solitary master of his own destiny.

Still, the hazardous individual's attempt to escape the mediation of rational risk analysis must be recognized as less real than ideal. Just as he reconstitutes self-control on the foundation of his prior recklessness, so too he often integrates his dramatic isolation with socially meaningful performances. Richard Branson's attempts at circumnavigating the globe were also carefully choreographed advertisements for his company, Virgin Atlantic. Looked at that way, such conduct is sometimes entirely comprehensible as a utilitarian business investment after all. Similarly, the performance of individualizing feats tends to be embedded in social contexts, and, as we have already seen, proves not just privately or personally meaningful, but socially significant too. As a result, the hazardous individual might be seen as navigating back and forth between reckoning and recklessness, rationality and irrationality, individuality and sociality. Even the railroader who boards from the front no doubt figures the safest and most effective way to do so, yet the choice to face that danger in a socially meaningful performance helps him claim all subsequent reckoning as his own. Hazardous individualism is thus not a romantic rejection of rationality in any thoroughgoing way, but a renegotiation of rationality, an attempt to sever ties temporarily with the established rational methods of *homo economicus* in order to reclaim them as a private possession.

Forms of hazardous individualism thus can extend well beyond the two main examples considered so far: workers' embrace of occupational hazards and the daredevil stunts of wealthy and maximally secure executives. The performance of adolescent risk-taking, some forms of drug use, reckless driving, gambling, or high risk sexual activity, to name a few, also might maintain the traditional forms of liberal individualism threatened by rational risk management. Part of the pleasure of those activities may lie in the visceral thrill of feeling alone on one's island, as it were, and thus completely responsible for the results. Such performances have the problem of their own ephemerality, however, so to continue to be meaningful they must either be repeated, like the railroader's habitual practice, or memorialized through media, like the exploits of daredevil CEOs. Because the rationalizing systems of risk management never can be escaped for long, the status of hazardous individualism must be made durable, somehow, in the ongoing present, or else the cycle must be repeated again.

When we over-associate rationality with liberal capitalism, we too easily imagine that gestures of defiance have not been anticipated in advance. This matters now more than ever, given that critiques of neoliberal market rationality have led to influential calls to base a more just social and political order on consciousness of shared insecurity. Judith Butler has argued for a potentially salutary response to modern social and economic precariousness, a shared sense of vulnerability that leads not to recrimination and violence, but to more just forms of sociality. In response to "precarious life," Butler argues,

> some set of global connections is being articulated, a different sense of the global from the 'globalized market.' And some set of values is being enacted in the form of collective resistance: a defense of our collective precarity and persistence in the making of equality.
> (Puar 169)[13]

Butler is part of a long tradition of theorists who have argued similarly for the social benefits of peril, stretching back at least to Thomas Hobbes. Almost three decades earlier, Ulrich Beck imagined that what he called the "risk society" might also generate a powerful "solidarity of living things" (74) and even "unify the victims in global risk positions" (47). Two decades before Beck, C.B. Macpherson, attempting to imagine a better foundation for liberal society than market-oriented "possessive individualism," supposed a new equality based in everyone's equal exposure to the threat of nuclear annihilation. For Macpherson, that "new equality of insecurity" resembles earlier but less tenable proposals by Hobbes, which Hobbes had based on the claim that everyone is equally vulnerable to violent incursions by everyone else (276). That, of course, is not exactly true, given disparities of privilege and power, but Macpherson wonders whether a nuclear age really might foster a better form of risk egalitarianism. If so, he suggests, equal exposure to nuclear risk finally might replace the current and inferior foundation of liberal society, which amounts to "equal subordination of every individual to the laws of the market" (85).

Needless to say, in the half century since Macpherson wrote, the hope that universal insecurity might be socially and politically beneficial has not been unquestionably confirmed. By the end of the 1980s Beck's solidarity of at-risk living things did produce some meaningful environmental reforms, but since then even the prospect of global climate change—a truly universal environmental disaster—has not yielded very inspiring forms of global solidarity. In the decade since Butler wrote, her hope that consciousness of one's vulnerability in precarious social and economic conditions might generate a more equitable sociality seems to this observer rather more remote than ever. Butler is entirely aware that the experience of vulnerability can lead directly to renewed attempts at mastery, but perhaps none of us have quite recognized that an entire culture of hazardous individualism has organized and sustained that impulse for more than a century. The desire to resist rationality with some alternative is easy to understand, but as with Eastman's railroader, we would do well to recognize that our defiance of rationality can serve the existing order perfectly well.

Notes

1 On the history of the term *homo economicus* and its relation to Mill, see Persky. The term *homo economicus* does not appear until 1888, and then as a pejorative term, at which point it already referred to the universalized rational subject described in emerging neoclassical theory.
2 Lukes's history of individualism is one of the few studies that attempts to anatomize the term in the detail it deserves. Even so, it little registers many of the major concerns of the humanities and social sciences over the last 50 years, from race and gender studies, to postcolonialism, to the sociology of contemporary liberal capitalism.
3 Of course, there are many important qualifications for what counts as rational related to consistency of conduct, validity of goals, availability of knowledge, and methods of reasoning, far more than I can consider here. This abbreviated account of *homo economicus* reflects the methodological individualism of early microeconomists such as Jevons and Menger, during a period that is roughly coincident with emergence of hazardous individualism.
4 Crusoe appears briefly in the works of most of the founders of microeconomics, including Menger 134–135, Marshall 82n1 and 178, and Walras 476n1, and even more extensively in the work of many later economists. For more detailed references to microeconomists' attention to Crusoe, see Grapard and Hewitson 16–19 and 65–68.
5 Essays by Kern and White are reprinted in Grapard and Hewitson, a useful collection of new and previously published essays on Crusoe and economics.
6 For a helpful summary of different forms of bounded rationality, see March, who describes limited rationality, contextual rationality, game rationality, process rationality, adaptive rationality, selected rationality, and posterior rationality, none of which accord well with traditional accounts of strictly calculative rationality. Bounded rationality is, of course, central to behavioral economics, which has strongly challenged basic microeconomic assumptions. For foundational work on bounded rationality, see especially Herbert Simon.
7 Although he does not cite the passage, Knight seems to be thinking of Smith's chapter on wages and profit in *Wealth of Nations*, in which Smith addresses workers' overestimation of possible gains and underestimation of possible losses in dangerous trades. Smith says, "The dangers and hairbreadth escapes of a life of adventures, instead of disheartening young people, seem frequently to recommend a trade to them" (127, para. 32).
8 The essay is also putatively pacifist and egalitarian, as James desires to send "our gilded youths" to coal mines and fishing fleets "to get the childishness knocked out of them," instead of assigning those hardships exclusively to a permanent working class (1291).
9 Although the issue is too complex to do more than simply acknowledge here, it should be noted that most of these writers, especially James, Roosevelt, and Junger, are conspicuously invested in defending masculinity against the threat of overcivilized effeminacy. In the early twentieth century, hazardous individualism should be seen as one part of this broader recalibration of manhood, which entailed a further range of racist, sexist, and imperialist efforts.

10 Despite the paucity of reliable statistics before the advent of workers' compensation programs around 1910, Aldrich has collected the fullest and most reliable data on occupational injuries dating back to the nineteenth century, including impressive estimates of comparative injury rates in subcategories such as occupation.
11 In addition to Lyng's "Edgework," see the essays collected in Lyng, ed., *Edgework*, especially the essays by Lyng and Jonathan Simon. Edgework names a wide range of approaches to the analysis of deliberate risk-taking, far more than this essay can adequately represent. However, some of that work has focused on the edgeworker's allegedly private choices without always inquiring enough into the social and political origins of them.
12 For a longer discussion of reckless workers in the context of early twentieth-century industrial management, see Puskar, 148–164.
13 See also Butler.

Works Cited

Aldrich, Mark. *Safety First: Technology, Labor, and Business in the Building of American Work Safety, 1870–1939*. Johns Hopkins UP, 1997.
Beck, Ulrich. *Risk Society: Towards a New Modernity*. Translated by Mark Ritter. Sage, 1992.
Butler, Judith. *Precarious Life: The Powers of Mourning and Violence*. Verso, 2006.
Castel, Robert. "From Dangerousness to Risk." *The Foucault Effect: Studies in Governmentality*, edited by Graham Burchell et al. U of Chicago P, 1991, pp. 281–298.
Clarke, Simon. *Marx, Marginalism, and Modern Sociology: From Adam Smith to Max Weber*. Macmillan, 1982.
Defert, Daniel. "'Popular Life' and Insurance Technology." *The Foucault Effect: Studies in Governmentality*, edited by Graham Burchell et al. U of Chicago P, 1991, pp. 211–233.
Defoe, Daniel. *Robinson Crusoe*. Modern Library, 2001.
Dewey, John. *The Later Works, 1925–1953: Vol. 4: 1929, The Quest for Certainty*. Southern Illinois UP, 2008.
Eastman, Crystal. *Work-Accidents and the Law*. Russell Sage, 1910.
Ericson, Richard et al., *Insurance as Governance*. U of Toronto P, 2003.
Ewald, Francois. "Insurance and Risk." *The Foucault Effect: Studies in Governmentality*, edited by Graham Burchell et al. U of Chicago P, 1991, pp. 197–210.
Gagnier, Regenia. *The Insatiability of Human Wants: Economics and Aesthetics in Market Society*. U of Chicago P, 2000.
Grapard, Ulla and Gillian Hewitson, editors. *Robinson Crusoe's Economic Man: A Construction and Deconstruction*. Routledge, 2011.
Hacking, Ian. *The Taming of Chance*. Cambridge UP, 1990.
James, William. *Writings: 1902–1910*. Library of America, 1987.
Jevons, W. Stanley. *The Theory of Political Economy*. Macmillan, 1871.
Junger, Ernst. "On Danger." Trans. Donald Reneau. *New German Critique*, vol. 59, Spring-Summer 1993, pp. 27–32.
Kern, William S. "Robinson Crusoe and the Economists." *Robinson Crusoe's Economic Man: A Construction and Deconstruction*, edited by Ulla Grapard and Gillian Hewitson. Routledge, 2011, pp. 62–74.
Knight, Frank H. *Risk, Uncertainty, and Profit*. Kelley, 1964.
Knight, Frank H. *Intelligence and Democratic Action*. Harvard UP, 1960.
Lukes, Stephen. *Individualism*. Harper and Row, 1973.
Lyng, Stephen, editor. *Edgework: The Sociology of Risk-Taking*. Routledge, 2005.
Macpherson, C.B. *The Political Theory of Possessive Individualism: Hobbes to Locke*. Oxford UP, 1962.
March, James G. "Bounded Rationality, Ambiguity, and the Engineering of Choice." In *Rational Choice*, edited by Jon Elster. Blackwell, 1986.
Markoff, John. "Parachutist's Record Fall: Over 25 Miles in 15 Minutes." *New York Times*, October 25, 2014, pp. A12–14. Accessed July 3, 2017.
Marshall, Alfred. *Principles of Economics*. Prometheus, 1997.
Martin, Randy. *The Financialization of Daily Life*. Temple UP, 2002.
Menger, Carl. *Principles of Economics*. Translated by James Dingwall and Bert F Hoselitz, Ludwig von Mises Institute, 2007.
Mirowski, Philip. *More Heat than Light: Economics as Social Physics, Physics as Nature's Economics*. Cambridge UP, 1989.
O'Malley, Pat. *Risk, Uncertainty, and Government*. London: Glasshouse, 2004.

Persky, Joseph. "Retrospectives: The Ethology of *Homo economicus*." *Journal of Economic Perspectives*, vol. 9, no. 2, Spring 1995, pp. 221–231.

Puar, Jusbir et al. "Precarity Talk: A Virtual Roundtable with Lauren Berlant, Judith Butler, Bojana Cvejic, Isabell Lorey, Jasbir Puar, and Ana Vujanovic." *TDR: The Drama Review*, vol. 56, no. 4, Winter 2012, pp. 163–177.

Puskar, Jason. *Accident Society: Fiction, Collectivity, and the Production of Chance*. Stanford UP, 2011.

Roosevelt, Theodore. *The Strenuous Life: Essays and Addresses*. Century, 1905.

Simon, Herbert. *Models of Bounded Rationality*, Vol. 1. Cambridge: MIT Press, 1982.

Simon, Jonathan. "Taking Risks: Extreme Sports and the Embrace of Risk in Advanced Liberal Societies" *Embracing Risk: The Changing Culture of Insurance and Responsibility*, edited by Tom Baker and Jonathan Simon. U of Chicago P, 2002, pp. 177–208.

Smith, Adam. *An Inquiry into the Nature and Causes of the Wealth of Nations*, edited by R.H. Campbell and A.S. Skinner. Vol. 1. Clarendon Press, 1976.

Thompson, Hunter S. *Fear and Loathing in Las Vegas*. 2nd edition. Vintage, 1998.

Walras, Leon. *Elements of Pure Economics: Or the Theory of Social Wealth*. Translated by William Jaffe. Routledge, 1954.

White, Michael V. "Reading and Rewriting: The Production of an Economic *Robinson Crusoe*." *Robinson Crusoe's Economic Man: A Construction and Deconstruction*. Edited by Ulla Grapard and Gillian Hewitson. Routledge, 2011, pp. 15–41.

Witt, John Fabian. *The Accidental Republic: Crippled Workingmen, Destitute Widows, and the Remaking of American Law*. Harvard UP, 2004.

PART II

EXPERTISE

6
RISK MEDIA IN MEDICINE
The Rise of the Metaclinical Health App Ecosystem

Kirsten Ostherr

Introduction

The convergence of digital information and communication technologies (ICTs) and medicine is creating a new field of risk media. Digital health apps linking patients' behavioral and environmental data with providers' assessment and triage tools are establishing digitally intermediated contexts for care. In these assemblages, we are seeing the emergence of personalized medicine delivered through ICTs as a form of stratified, data-driven healthcare. By feeding quantified data about users into apps whose algorithms manage access to resources, participants in this ecosystem cultivate new concepts of health, disease, privacy, surveillance, and care. Under these circumstances, almost any behavior or exposure that can be sensed and digitally quantified becomes reframed as a health behavior available for datafication, intervention, and optimization. These new conditions raise questions about how risk media technologies recalibrate our understanding of "the human" in medicine by converting experiences into quantified outcomes.

This chapter describes recent developments that are creating new forms of screen-based media interfaces to visualize ideas about managing the health risks of populations and the financial risks of corporate stakeholders that provide services to those populations. The first section of the chapter defines clinical and metaclinical spaces and describes the different regulatory frameworks that govern risk media, particularly digital health apps, developed for use in these spaces. The second section describes the digital infrastructures that have enabled social, affective selves to become quantified as numerical representations of health and disease. The third part of this chapter explains how technologies of quantification and metaclinical risk media are contributing to a shift in medicine from individual, reactive care to population-based, preventive care. The fourth section provides a case study of an exemplary digital health risk media program called Omada Health. As a metaclinical tool for managing users' risk of developing type 2 diabetes and heart disease, this platform demonstrates how data-driven concepts of risk address corporate stakeholders through the rhetoric of return on investment (ROI) while they engage patients through the language of science-based self-care. The conclusion describes how new forms of clinical and metaclinical risk media, such as electronic health records (EHRs) and health surveillance apps, are redefining "the human" in quantitative terms that elide fundamental aspects of the experience of health and illness.

Defining Clinical and Metaclinical Spaces and Risk Media

Under current conditions in medicine, risk media include many varied forms of computer interfaces that are present both within and beyond clinical spaces, operating in formerly distinct domains whose boundaries are now blurring, even as technologies, user behaviors, and regulatory policies seek to define more concretely the borders of these fields (Fiore-Gartland and Neff). I define "clinical" spaces as sites such as hospitals or physician offices where formal doctor–patient interaction is regulated by health law such as the Health Information Portability and Accountability Act of 1996 (HIPAA) and the U.S. Food and Drug Administration (FDA) premarket review process regulating the use of medical devices, including some digital health technologies (Ostherr et al.). Apps that claim to diagnose or treat a disease or condition, which historically have been intended for use and integration into clinical spaces, are defined and regulated by the FDA as medical devices, and are therefore subject to complex, time-consuming, and expensive FDA review and approval processes (Cortez et al.; Elenko et al., "A Regulatory Framework"). Importantly for the purposes of this chapter, the extent of FDA review is determined by the perceived level of risk posed to the patient by the medical device. As Elenko et al. have observed, "the key question is, what is the risk to the patient if this software fails?" (698). In this framing, the classification and regulation of health and medical apps is fundamentally defined in terms of risk media.

In contrast to highly regulated medical apps and spaces, I define "metaclinical" spaces as those sites constituting the vast ecosystem outside of traditional clinical settings where consumer–patients engage in behaviors that may be directly or indirectly related to self-management of health and disease, whose digital traces can be captured and incorporated into data-driven frameworks for health surveillance and intervention. Like "metadata" that provide context for other data, as in the metadata showing when and by whom a Wikipedia entry was updated (Riley), "metaclinical" data provide rich context for clinical data. Apps that are designed for use in metaclinical spaces may be promoted as "health and wellness" tools, but as long as they refrain from making medical claims in their marketing materials, they remain exempt from FDA review. Moreover, as long as these apps do not contain protected health information (PHI), they are not required to be HIPAA compliant (Office for Civil Rights). Many apps that capture and sell data to third-party companies for use in health profiling and marketing have no overt health function, capturing instead social interactions, consumption habits, geolocation, and other dimensions of daily life that are integrated into health risk media for the purpose of user stratification (Zang et al.). Therefore, despite the very real, material consequences of social and behavioral determinants of health on patient morbidity, mortality, and quality of life, software that captures metaclinical data related to those domains is deemed inconsequential and therefore remains largely exempt from regulation, due to the narrow definition of biomedical risk to patients that governs app review.

Twenty-first century clinical and metaclinical spaces are filled with a wide range of screen-based risk media interfaces involved in the practices of "health datafication." This term refers to the process of "rendering into data aspects of the world not previously quantified" (Kennedy et al. 1) as well as transforming existing data into actionable forms that generate diverse and unevenly distributed forms of value for their producers and consumers (van Dijck). While all risk media are engaged in practices of health datafication, the threats that these media seek to contain are differentiated by responsible agent and target population. Risk media that extend into and permeate clinical spaces include medical simulations that facilitate the containment of risk in the cultivation of technical expertise in surgery, anesthesiology, and other fields of medicine. They include decision support systems, as well as artificial intelligence programs that mobilize algorithms to mitigate the risk of human error under the intensely affective circumstances of emergency medical care. They include the mundane EHR screens that mediate almost every doctor–patient interaction in United States clinical settings. They also include the screens that proliferate in operating rooms, displaying everything from laparoscopic views of internal organs to three-dimensional brain scans in neurosurgery. These risk media work to contain the virtual threat of human error in medicine. That is, they work to contain threats posed to patients by doctors, nurses, clinical spaces, and the practice of medicine itself. Clinical risk media work to contain iatrogenic threats to patients even as they function as vectors for the representation and transmission of those threats.

The metaclinical trajectory in medical risk media today extends beyond traditionally defined and regulated clinical spaces to include private homes, public recreation facilities, workplaces, schools, shopping areas, and the cloud hovering above and gathering up the data from all of these "real" spaces through the virtual network of the mobile web. In these metaclinical spaces, virtual risk media include smartphones, wearable technologies, mobile apps, global positioning systems (GPS), social media platforms, and environmental sensors. These risk media work to contain threats posed by environmental exposures—including self-induced exposures—related to the consumer–patient's behavior. The mediated threats that metaclinical risk media contain include physical activities; food, drug, and tobacco consumption; environmental contaminants; financial exchanges; social communications; and any other form of behavior that might be measurable and therefore quantifiable as a potential risk factor for negative health outcomes. Metaclinical risk media work to contain threats posed to clinical stakeholders (including providers and payers) by the personal behaviors of consumer–patients in the wild.

Digital Infrastructures of Quantified Selves

The technological conditions of possibility for the emergence of digital health risk media have assembled over the past two decades and include the rise of the social web, the expansion of mobile Internet connectivity, the rapid growth of smartphone use in the United States, and discoveries in nanotechnology and cognate fields of electrical engineering that have led to the availability of smaller, faster, cheaper, and more powerful mobile and environmental sensors. Changes in health policy (discussed below) created market conditions for major venture capital investment in the development of risk media technologies for health. Finally, along with the technological affordances required for the rise of the health app economy, the social conditions for privileging quantification and data-driven habits of thought as norms are critical, emergent elements of the ecosystem.

Most of the technologies at play in the development of health risk media apps were not originally designed for healthcare applications. Instead, the mobile sensors and networks that provide the infrastructure for this field of health surveillance were developed as part of the broader set of strategic ICTs that transformed the Internet into the mobile, social web (Rainie and Wellman). The opportunity that the health industry, startups, and investors have recognized is that adapting these devices for use outside of clinical settings allows for deeper and wider data collection on the contextual risk factors for disease. Instead of capturing clinical data only when present in a doctor's office or hospital, patients can capture data through smartphones, accelerometers, and other devices 24 hours a day, seven days a week, thereby providing a richer picture of the variables at play in maintaining health. Under these circumstances, mobile devices can accrue large amounts of longitudinal health data, using methods not typically possible in a traditional clinic, study section, or analog self-tracking journal (Neff; Neff and Nafus; Sarasohn-Kahn).

These new conditions for capturing data create new concerns around how such data can and should be captured, interpreted, and shared (Wilbanks and Topol). The regulatory distinctions between clinical and metaclinical data play a significant role in determining data use practices. For instance, metaclinical health data from commercial devices are not easily integrated into clinical settings (Chung and Basch; Luxton et al.). Patients cannot simply bring their FitBit data to their physician's office, or upload it to their EHR, and expect to receive recommendations based on their personal health data (Lobelo et al.). While a provider can recommend that a patient use a metaclinical health tracking device to monitor activity levels or other low-risk wellness indicators, integrating data from a device throughout the entire hospital would require HIPPA compliance and FDA approval—a lengthy and costly process. Moreover, without clinical support integration and human interpretive capability, mHealth (mobile health) interventions show little benefit for patients (Martin et al.). While some digital health technologies (such as the Apple watch's HealthKit) are working toward integration of metaclinical data into EHRs, the industry as a whole is far from reaching this goal (Gay and Leijdekkers). Meanwhile, metaclinical health-related devices that are not bound by HIPAA can do whatever they wish with a user's data, including selling the user's health data to third parties (Grundy et al.) once users agree to the app's terms of use.

Clinical Risk Media: From Personal to Population Health

The rise of medical risk media has resulted in part from changes in health policy that have redefined the boundaries between medicine and public health. Historically, the practice of medicine has focused on reactive care of individual patients, once illness or injury has struck. Promoting the health of populations through preventive care has traditionally been the domain of public health. While medicine might diagnose and treat a patient for cancer by providing surgery, radiation treatment, and chemotherapy, public health conducts mass screenings, vaccination campaigns, and awareness programs to reduce the overall incidence and prevalence of cancer in the population as a whole. In general terms, public health focuses on causes, and medicine focuses on effects. Public health works to mitigate large-scale risks, often deploying media to increase public knowledge, change attitudes, and drive policy about existing health threats, such as smoking, sun exposure, or more recently, physical inactivity. In contrast, the practice of medicine is primarily predicated on individual exposure to risk, and provides highly specific interventions aimed at eradication of the current "complaint," without necessarily addressing the underlying or environmental cause of the problem. In terms of research, practice, funding, and prestige, medicine and public health have existed in siloes, rarely interacting despite their obviously overlapping areas of concern.

Health policy in the United States has exacerbated the artificial separation of medicine and public health through a structure of reimbursement for medical care that rewards procedures performed, rather than the outcomes of those procedures. The result has been a perverse incentive to provide unnecessary or overly invasive treatments that focus on disease states, not wellness. However, since the passage of the Patient Protection and Affordable Care Act (ACA) of 2010, and the follow-up legislation called Medicare Access and CHIP Reauthorization Act (MACRA) of 2015, health policy has reframed the historical isolation of medicine from public health by aligning healthcare payment with patient outcomes, not procedures performed (CMS "MACRA"). By legislating the transition to what the industry calls "value-based care," the ACA and MACRA also reframed the objective of medicine to improve population health, not just individual health. While this overhaul may be redirected due to political reconfigurations of health policy in the United States, the work to realign medical care with patient outcomes has prompted a long overdue shift toward "patient-centered care" that is unlikely to be eliminated without significant resistance on the part of patients and payers alike. The recent acquisition of health insurance provider Aetna by the pharmacy chain CVS exemplifies this reorientation toward "retail medicine" in the United States (de la Merced and Abelson).

These shifts in health policy shape the emergence of medical risk media through directives related to ICT development for healthcare contexts. A major component of healthcare reform in the United States in the past ten years has been the growth in adoption of EHR systems by clinicians and patients. Early versions of EHRs had been in use since the late 1960s (Tripathi), but adoption was uneven, with many health systems using both electronic and paper records as clinicians adapted their practices to the uneven distribution of screens and access points across sites of care. A major turning point came from the landmark publication of the Institute of Medicine's (IOM) report, "To Err is Human—Building a Safer Health System," which concluded that 44,000 to 98,000 preventable deaths occur every year in the United States due to human medical errors.

The IOM further concluded that these errors came at a cost of $17 to $29 billion per year, and the report urged policymakers to push for expanded use of EHRs and other automated computer systems that were expected to eradicate many of the human sources of error in healthcare.

Since that time, the use of EHRs has been associated with improving healthcare safety and quality by containing risk. From this perspective, EHRs appear as the first generation of risk media in medicine, as early instantiations of the big data mantra: more data equals more knowledge, equals lower risk, equals better health outcomes. Computer-based clinical health information technology (HIT) systems are framed by proponents as reducing the risk of human error by providing greater access to information when and where physicians need it most. This perspective was made into policy with the Health Information Technology for Economic and Clinical Health (HITECH) provisions of the American Recovery and Reinvestment Act of 2009, which incentivized clinicians to adopt EHR systems by offering payments of $50,000–100,000 per provider or group as implementation metrics were met (Hsiao and Hing).

Claims about the value of EHRs in improving safety in healthcare are complicated by their legacy as software originally designed for the purpose of billing patients for procedures performed. The perverse incentive that historically supported the reactive, procedure-based model of medicine was built into and perpetuated by EHR functionality. However, in the shift from individual to population, and from procedure- to outcome-based care, EHRs have been reframed as a new kind of risk media. These vast repositories of procedure codes and billing data are now seen as sources of big data that might shed large-scale insights when the entire patient population of a given health system is subjected to sophisticated data analytics. In the shift to reimbursement based on population health outcomes, individual patient records are compared to the population as a whole, assessed for relative risk, and triaged accordingly. Every keystroke made in a clinical setting adds or subtracts a risk variable relative to the total population, thereby creating the opportunity for digital health app developers—or in current terminology, digital therapeutics developers—to design a data-driven intervention for managing a target risk population (as exemplified by Omada Health, discussed in detail below).

While many doctors, nurses, and other users of EHRs complain about the poorly designed interfaces of these systems, another set of concerns around EHRs as medical risk media have grown in recent years. Research has shown that default settings can introduce errors into EHRs that proliferate throughout the patient's record with disastrous results, and that automated warning systems built into EHRs produce "alert fatigue" that makes physicians less likely to notice errors such as incorrect medication dosing (Sittig and Singh). EHRs have been shown to reduce the time and attention physicians pay to patients (Tai-Seale et al.). Comparative studies have shown how EHRs eliminate important contextual information about the patient's experience of illness by framing clinical narratives solely in terms of biomedical disease models (Patel et al.). Finally, some doctors have argued that EHRs subvert the therapeutic power of human touch (Cochran), raising questions about whether EHRs and other computational interfaces in medicine might undermine the doctor–patient relationship more broadly.

From this perspective, instead of reducing the risks posed by medicine, EHRs introduce new risks related to the inhumanity of automated, algorithmic, and data-driven procedures that reduce human doctors and patients to binary variables incapable of accounting for aspects of human experience that resist quantification. Within the EHR, patients are reduced to preformulated categories typically accessed through drop-down menus. Doctors who use EHRs feel that they are reduced to functioning as robotic data-entry clerks, just as patients feel that their healthcare encounters and illness narratives are stripped of the social and experiential details that make them therapeutically meaningful. Recognizing that these critiques raise significant barriers to the adoption of digital therapeutics, developers are seeking new techniques for infusing digitally mediated medicine with features that approximate human connection.

Metaclinical Risk Media Interfaces: Digital Health Apps

As the critiques of EHRs attest, these risk media technologies redefine "the human" in medicine as binary code, determined by diagnostic and procedure codes selected from drop-down menus, occasionally augmented with minimalist narrative description. Like many popular, consumer-facing metaclinical risk media tools, EHRs quantify the self, redefining human experiences of health and illness as data. In an effort to counter the dehumanizing effects of EHR adoption, provisions within the HITECH Act mandated that providers create patient portals to ensure what policymakers termed "meaningful use" of EHRs for patient engagement (Trotter; CMS "How to Optimize Patient Portals"). Many health systems have met this requirement by opening up minimally functional patient portals that allow communication of lab test results, secure one-way messaging from the clinic to the patient, appointment reminders, and other top-down transmissions of information. The capacity for dynamic, real-time, two-way, or patient-initiated dialogue is far less common, and consequently, the functionality that many users have come to expect from other sectors of their digitally connected lives, such as online appointment scheduling, instant messaging, video chat, and price comparison are rarely available. Few platforms allow patients to send questions to the doctor, though most allow patients to pay their medical bills online.

Yet, the opportunity that patient portals represent has not been lost on the healthcare stakeholders seeking to capitalize on the promise of savings and profits based on population health improvements through patient risk stratification. To achieve this goal, healthcare providers need access to their patients' metaclinical data, and the EHR patient portal seems an obvious site for data collection and storage. As new and better methods to gather and analyze large data sets are developed, health systems promise to leverage the big data generated by individual patients to determine more nuanced diagnoses and more effectively treat discrete illnesses. As a result, the same ICTs that generate population health gains may also enable doctors to increasingly individualize patient care, ushering in a new era of "personalized" and "precision" medicine (Chaussabel and Pulendran; Kostkova et al.). The question that emerges from this shift is: who benefits from personalization based on risk stratification? What does "patient-centered care" mean in quantitative terms, and what happens to the interpretation of qualitative metaclinical data in this context?

While the iTunes and Android app stores overflow with tens of thousands of wellness apps, few have been clinically validated, and as of 2015, less than 2 percent had the capacity to connect to provider healthcare systems through EHRs (IMS). Apps that cannot feed their metaclinical data back into legacy EHR systems fail to close the loop between patients and physicians, thereby undermining much of the potential efficacy of these interventions. Consumer–patients may find the self-contained, metaclinical feedback loop satisfying in mitigating affective risk in many ways, but when it comes to serious, life-threatening chronic conditions with expensive maintenance regimens, closing the clinical loop mitigates the financial threat of disease by creating the conditions of possibility for insurance coverage. Obtaining insurance coverage for app prescription might be seen as trading off one form of mediated risk—the risk of inadequate medical care—for another, namely, becoming part of an insurance company's risk pool. Closing that loop ensures a complete surveillance system that captures all of the patient data for the third-party app provider to improve their product and their marketing, for the medical care provider who integrates the data into the patient's EHR, and for the payer who now has access to a data-driven, real-time, adaptive and self-generated model for patient risk and payment stratification. But how does closing the metaclinical data loop benefit patients?

I will demonstrate how the digital health app economy brings together the quantified self (Neff and Nafus), risk media, and the rhetorics of self-care and ROI through a detailed discussion of Omada Health, a startup that is leading the nascent digital therapeutics industry (Natanson). After about a decade of experimentation and pilot testing of mHealth apps and devices, there is widespread consensus in the medical community that digital health technologies require rigorous clinical testing to provide real value to doctors and patients (Roess). Validation through randomized, controlled trials (RCTs) and other standardized methods for clinical research not only provides the necessary evidence to gain physicians' trust, it also paves a pathway to regulatory approval and insurance coverage. Omada Health based the design of its diabetes prevention program on the results of a high-impact National Institutes of Health-funded study that demonstrated the efficacy of the behavior change methods employed on the app (Sepah et al., "Translating"; Sepah et al. "Long-Term Outcomes"). Notably, because the Omada interface operationalizes metaclinical social and behavioral determinants of health, and these data fall outside the narrow definition of biomedical risk that governs app review, the FDA classified Omada's app as subject only to "enforcement discretion," not premarket review (Elenko et al., "A Regulatory Framework"). This new category of regulation, developed in the wake of challenges to FDA review of digital health technologies, asserts that mobile medical devices in this class "may meet the definition of medical device," but are deemed to "pose lower risk to the public" and therefore are not regulated (FDA).

Since its founding in 2011, Omada Health has maintained that its app uses proven techniques to manage the financial and health risks associated with chronic illness (Empson). With a business model aimed at ROI for payers, Omada Health's target customers are the companies that purchase access to this program for clients or employees, not the patients who actually use the app. As a mobile, web-based interface that includes static and moving animated images, pre-recorded video lessons, live videochat, text, and graphical visualizations of user data, Omada Health is a paradigmatic example of medical risk media. Their promotional materials are explicit about the types of risk they aim to avert: for patients, their program reduces the risk of developing chronic disease including type 2 diabetes, stroke, and heart disease (Castro Sweet; Su et al). For payers, namely employers, health systems, and health insurance providers, the risks are financial, and are explicitly enumerated in terms of ROI. As described in recent news coverage of the company, Omada has over 100,000 participants, and the company "work[s] with health plans and employers to find the highest-risk people. Omada claims health plans see a return on investment within two years, and they can save up to $2,190 per participant after five years" (Siu). Despite this clear focus on ROI for enterprise clients, the marketing associated with health risk media requires dual payer/patient interfaces, and these distinct approaches to narrating the value of the app economy reveal the core concepts at work in contemporary industry-leading metaclinical risk media. Specifically, the app works to manage financial risks posed to clinical stakeholders (providers and payers) through therapeutic interfaces that engage patients to participate in self-surveillance as self-care.

A comparison of payer-facing and patient-facing communications is instructive. Insights on the payer-facing framework can be gleaned from a report available on the Omada Health website. The 2016 report, called "Value, Inc.," is billed as Omada's guide to the "Top Three Habits of Innovative Health Plans." Inside, Scott Honken (Vice President of Market Access and Payer Relations) describes the data-driven risk media practices underlying Omada's design interface. "Habit 1: Identify looming disease" is a primer in data-driven risk profiling for health. As the guide explains:

> Forward-thinking health plans use "Proactive Member Surveillance" or "Hot Spotting" to help protect their members' health and reduce spending. Basically, plans look at member health data and larger health trends to understand which conditions are most likely to impact their populations in the next three to five years. When health plans can predict how many—and precisely which—of their members are on the brink of costly but preventable conditions, they can invest in appropriate preventive treatments.
>
> (3)

For health plans or employers that subscribe to Omada's program, risk management is financial; chronically ill employees or subscribers cost more money than healthy ones. Here, the goal of containing the latent risk of disease relies on past data (as in all probabilistic regression analyses) that cannot account for sudden or unprecedented changes that might occur in a patient's environment, beyond individual control. New disease vulnerabilities from temperature or rainfall changes, or disruptions to the patient's circumstances such as job loss or family crisis that might adversely affect maintenance of adherence regimes cannot be incorporated into this framework. The selective inclusion of metaclinical data privileging quantifiable and predictable variables demonstrates how the algorithmic "quantified self" obscures features of human experience that are less amenable to risk modeling.

In "Habit 2: Scale with technology," Honken elaborates on the role of technology in healthcare, emphasizing data analytics, remote, virtual care delivery, and personalization (4). Here, the threat of depersonalization posed by clinical technologies such as EHRs is reframed in marketing terms that equate access to personal data with more persuasive technology-based rhetoric. The third habit, "Align incentives with providers," emphasizes the importance of reorientation toward population- and value-based care, as it benefits patients who stay healthy and doctors who will be financially rewarded for adhering to the new paradigm. A key benefit of the resulting model, Honken argues, is that "preventive medicine, done right, has the convenient effect of lowering health plans' long-term spending. So everybody wins" (5). The concept of rational actors in health care implicit in this quote suggests that medical doctors themselves should aspire to behave more like algorithms, and if they do, patients will behave accordingly. The consumer-facing app shares this model, implying that all of the steps it asks users to take are logical, fun, and simple to achieve. The notion of incentivizing providers through expectations of financial gain suggests that employers and payers can readily program patients to behave as though affective life with chronic illness is uncomplicated, patient experience is easily quantified, and self-care is easily equated with corporate ROI.

In contrast to the "Value, Inc." report, the consumer-facing video on the Omada website contains many of the common attributes of digital health startup promotional materials, framing the value of the app exclusively in terms of self-care, not ROI. The two-minute video presents the Omada user experience from the perspective of a white, female consumer named "Sandy," who logs onto the Omada website from home, launching a demonstration of the platform's approach to patient engagement for viewers. Several contextual cues signal Sandy's affluent status: the large diamond ring on her finger, the tidy, minimalist décor of her home, including a large, uncluttered white tabletop holding only her Apple laptop, a white coffee mug, and a wooden fruit bowl. The blurred-out background features shiny stainless steel kitchen appliances and neatly organized cooking accessories, a modernist wooden coffee table, an average-weight body wearing fashionable, understated athleisure attire. Nothing in the *mise-en-scène* suggests affective or experiential challenges such as poverty, familial caregiver burden, body weight struggles, mental health issues, systemic racism, or environmental stress. The setting, like the app's user experience, appears smooth and frictionless.

The voiceover narrator describes Omada as "a digital health program that uses a combination of proven behavioral science and rich data science to help build healthy habits that stick." The narrator proceeds to frame the program through the terminology of risk media, displaying a screenshot of the eligibility test for Omada users that asks, "What's your risk?" with choices of diabetes or heart disease. The video goes on to display the startup kit, including a wireless scale already linked to her account that Sandy receives in the mail once she is enrolled in the program. After she steps onto the scale, we see the various screens that begin to populate this user's virtual space, as the remainder of the user experience is presented through digitally intermediated interfaces. The screens include familiar digital design typographies with a small profile shot of Sandy's face, questionnaires about her food intake, activity levels, personality, and so forth. Finally, a visualization of Sandy's strategically coordinated social network within the Omada program and her "dedicated health coach" appear onscreen. The coach is a young, white woman who provides "real-time" feedback and personalized guidance delivered in videos and through a discussion board format similar to Facebook or WhatsApp. Sandy is depicted interacting with her social network as well, in a playful exchange of "friendly competition" featuring a multiracial group of community participants "a lot like you, for added support, accountability, and sometimes, a little healthy competition." Here, Sandy is shown engaging in light banter about favored baseball teams, a small detail meant to signal how much fun it is to participate in this form of collective self-surveillance.

The overall user experience is presented as friendly, encouraging, and reasonable, with an overarching rhetoric of data-driven efficiency and efficacy. A perky musical score featuring acoustic guitar and up-tempo drumming reinforce the cheerful mood. As the narrator notes in a lighthearted tone, "During the first four months, you track your food and activity," and all of the data generated by this activity adds up to a wealth of insights backed by data analytics. This process is visualized through an overhead shot of Sandy tapping her smartphone screen while seated at an orange table with a meal of a small sandwich, a glass of water, and an orange in front of her. The voiceover continues, "Within a few months, your thousands of data points paint a clear picture of what new habits are working best for you, and where you need to double down on effort." The video closes with an encouraging send-off that links personalization to data-driven behavior change, suggesting that, with this app, self-care is automated and self-cure is inevitable: "Omada provides personal support, powered by science, to inspire you to be your own cure, in lots of tiny, totally doable steps."

Analysis of the Omada app and business model demonstrates the complexity of answering the question of who benefits from metaclinical risk media. On one hand it is evident that the app is a money-saving tool for subscribing companies, based on surveillance of employees who may not be fully aware of the risk exposure entailed in participation. On the other hand, the app design is based on evidence from a study that found reduction in the incidence of chronic disease, a result that is in itself an unambiguous benefit to patients, in addition to benefitting the insurance underwriters. The conditions that give rise to chronic disease vulnerabilities, surveillance vulnerabilities, and the conversion of human experiences of health and disease into virtual, datafied algorithms of health and disease, however, raise questions that remain to be answered.

Conclusion: Redefining "the Human" through Metaclinical Risk Media

Self-care in the twenty-first century is characterized by the ubiquitous presence of digitally intermediated screens linking varied forms of clinical and metaclinical data. These new forms of risk media, including EHRs and health surveillance apps, are quantifying the self, and thereby redefining the human, through data that elide fundamental aspects of the human experience of health and illness. While the rhetoric of medicine emphasizes the value of "patient-centered care," the business of medicine operationalizes this concept through a risk-stratified, data-driven form of "personalized medicine" derived through probabilities based on population-based aggregates, not individual history. In this context, the patient is the center of a digital surveillance network dedicated to sensing environmental and behavioral exposures that shape future risk profiles. The Omada Health app exemplifies this logic by targeting users at risk of developing type 2 diabetes or heart disease. These patients are presently healthy, but their future, data-projected selves are chronically ill. In this scenario, the human and the virtual are collapsed, as both are defined by predictive, aggregative, and numerical algorithms that frame datafication as the only method for understanding health and disease. As the boundaries between clinical and metaclinical contexts for data collection dissolve, the boundaries between the computational and the human dissolve. In the current trajectory of risk media, patients are reduced to data points without history, context, or affect. Alternatives to metaclinical risk media are needed to preserve the messiness of human experience, and to resist the further automation of clinical exchange.

Works Cited

Castro Sweet, Cynthia M. et al. "Outcomes of a Digital Health Program with Human Coaching for Diabetes Risk Reduction in a Medicare Population." *Journal of Aging and Health*, January 24, 2017.

Chaussabel, Damien and Bali Pulendran. "A Vision and a Prescription for Big Data–enabled Medicine." *Nature Immunology*, vol. 16, April 2015, pp. 435–439.

Chung, Arlene E. and Ethan M. Basch. "Potential and Challenges of Patient-generated Health Data for High-quality Cancer Care." *Journal of Oncology Practice*, vol. 11, no. 3, May 2015, pp. 195–197.

Cochran, JH. "Continuous Healing Relationships through Connectivity." *Journal of Healthcare Information Management*, vol. 24, no. 3, 2010, pp. 19–20.

Cortez, Nathan G. et al. "FDA Regulation of Mobile Health Technologies." *New England Journal of Medicine*, vol. 371, no. 4, 2014, pp. 372–379.

Elenko, Eric, Austin Speier, and Daphne Zohar. "A Regulatory Framework Emerges for Digital Medicine." *Nature Biotechnology* vol. 33, no. 7, July 2015, pp. 697–702.

Empson, Rip. "Omada Health Raises $800K from Esther Dyson & More to Take on Diabetes." *TechCrunch*, December 21, 2011, https://techcrunch.com/2011/12/21/omada-health-raises-850k-from-esther-dyson-more-to-take-on-diabetes/.

Fiore-Gartland, Britta and Gina Neff. "Communication, Mediation, and the Expectations of Data." *International Journal of Communication*, vol. 9, 2015, pp. 1466–1484.

Gay, Valerie, and Peter Leijdekkers. "Bringing Health and Fitness Data Together for Connected Health Care: Mobile Apps as Enablers of Interoperability." *Journal of Medical Internet Research*, vol. 17, no. 11, November 2015, p. e260.

Grundy, Quinn, Fabian P. Held, and Lisa A. Bero. "Tracing the Potential Flow of Consumer Data: A Network Analysis of Prominent Health and Fitness Apps." *Journal of Medical Internet Research*, vol. 19, no. 6, June 2017, p. e233.

Honken, Scott. "Value, Inc.: The Top Three Habits of Innovative Health Plans." Omada Health, 2016.

Hsiao, Chun-Ju and Esther Hing. "Use and Characteristics of Electronic Health Record Systems among Office-based Physician Practices: United States, 2001–2012." National Center for Health Statistics, NCHS data brief, no 111. 2012.

IMS Institute for Healthcare Informatics. "Patient Adoption of mHealth: Use, Evidence and Remaining Barriers to Mainstream Acceptance." September 2015.

Institute of Medicine, Committee on Quality of Health Care in America. "To Err is Human: Building a Safer Health System," edited by Linda T. Kohn, Janet M. Corrigan, and Molla S. Donaldson. National Academies Press, 2000.

Kennedy, Helen et al. "Data and Agency." *Big Data & Society* vol. 2, no. 2, July–December, 2015, pp. 1–7.

Kostkova, Patty et al. "Who Owns the Data? Open Data for Healthcare." *Frontiers in Public Health*, vol. 4, no. 7, February, 2016.

Lobelo, Felipe et al. "The Wild, Wild West: A Framework to Integrate mHealth Software Applications and Wearables to Support Physical Activity Assessment, Counseling and Interventions for Cardiovascular Disease Risk Reduction." *Progress in Cardiovascular Diseases*, vol. 58, no. 6, May–June 2016, pp. 584–594.

Luxton, David D. et al. "mHealth Data Security: The Need for HIPAA-compliant Standardization." *Telemedicine and e-Health*, vol. 18, no. 4, May 2012, pp. 284–288.

Martin, Seth S. et al. "mActive: A Randomized Clinical Trial of an Automated mHealth Intervention for Physical Activity Promotion." *Journal of the American Heart Association*, vol. 9, no. 4, November 2015, p. 4:e002239.

de la Merced, Michael J. and Reed Abelson. "CVS to Buy Aetna for $69 Billion in a Deal That May Reshape the Health Industry." *New York Times*, December 3, 2017.

Natanson, Elad. "Digital Therapeutics: The Future of Health Care Will Be App-Based." *Forbes*, July 24, 2017, www.forbes.com/sites/eladnatanson/2017/07/24/digital-therapeutics-the-future-of-health-care-will-be-app-based/#764883976372. Accessed August 1, 2017.

Neff, Gina. "Why Big Data Won't Cure Us." *Big Data*, vol. 1, no. 3, September 2013, pp. 117–123.

Neff, Gina and Dawn Nafus. *Self-tracking*. MIT Press, 2016.

Office for Civil Rights (OCR), U.S. Dept. of Health and Human Services. "Summary of the HIPAA Privacy Rule." July 26, 2013, www.hhs.gov/hipaa/for-professionals/privacy/laws-regulations/index.html. Accessed August 1, 2017.

Ostherr, Kirsten et al. "Trust and Privacy in the Context of User-generated Health Data." *Big Data & Society*, vol. 4, no. 1, April 2017, pp. 1–11.

Patel, Vimla et al. "Patients' and Physicians' Understanding of Health and Biomedical Concepts: Relationship to the Design of EMR Systems." *Journal of Biomedical Informatics*, vol. 35, no. 1, February 2002, pp. 8–16.

Rainie, Lee and Barry Wellman. *Networked: The New Social Operating System*, MIT Press, 2012.

Riley, Jenn. "Understanding Metadata: What is Metadata and What is it for?" *National Information Standards Organization*, 2017, www.niso.org/publications/understanding-metadata-riley. Accessed August 1, 2017.

Roess, Amira. "The Promise, Growth, and Reality of Mobile Health—Another Data-free Zone." *The New England Journal of Medicine*, vol. 377, no. 21, November 23, 2017, pp. 2010–2011.

Sarasohn-Kahn, Jane. "Here's Looking at You: How Personal Health Information is Being Tracked and Used." California Health Care Foundation, July 2014, www.chcf.org/publications/2014/07/hereslooking-personal-health-info. Accessed August 1, 2017.

Sepah, S. Cameron et al. "Long-Term Outcomes of a Web-Based Diabetes Prevention Program: 2-Year Results of a Single-Arm Longitudinal Study." *Journal of Medical Internet Research*, vol. 17, no. 4, April 2015.

Sepah, S. Cameron et al. "Translating the Diabetes Prevention Program into an Online Social Network." *The Diabetes Educator*, vol. 40, no. 4, April 2014, pp. 435–443.

Sittig, Dean F. and Hardeep Singh. "Defining Health Information Technology-related Errors: New Developments Since to Err is Human." *Archives of Internal Medicine*, vol. 171, no. 14, July 2011, pp. 1281–1284.

Siu, Antoinette. "S.F. Health Company Lays Off 20 as it Aims for Profitability." *San Francisco Business Times*, June 22, 2017, www.bizjournals.com/sanfrancisco/news/2017/06/22/omada-health-digital-health-care-layoffs-workforce.html. Accessed August 1, 2017.

Su, Wenqing et al. "Return on Investment for Digital Behavioral Counseling in Patients with Prediabetes and Cardiovascular Disease." *Preventing Chronic Disease*, vol. 13, January 2016.

Tai-Seale, Ming et al. "Electronic Health Record Logs Indicate That Physicians Split Time Evenly Between Seeing Patients and Desktop Medicine." *Health Affairs*, vol. 36, no. 4, April 1, 2017, pp. 655–662.

Tripathi, Micky. "EHR Evolution: Policy and Legislation Forces Changing the EHR." *Journal of AHIMA*, vol. 83, no. 10, October 2012, pp. 24–29.

Trotter, Fred. *Hacking Healthcare: A Guide to Standards, Workflows, and Meaningful Use*. O'Reilly Media, 2013.

U.S. Centers for Medicare & Medicaid Services (CMS). "MACRA; Delivery System Reform, Medicare Payment Reform; What's the Quality Payment Program?" August 7, 2017, www.cms.gov/Medicare/Quality-Initiatives-Patient-Assessment-Instruments/Value-Based-Programs/MACRA-MIPS-and-APMs/MACRA-MIPS-and-APMs.html. Accessed August 1, 2017.

U.S. Centers for Medicare & Medicaid Services (CMS). "How to Optimize Patient Portals for Patient Engagement and Meet Meaningful Use Requirements." May 2013, www.healthit.gov/sites/default/files/nlc_how_to_optimizepatientportals_for_patientengagement.pdf. Accessed August 1, 2017.

U.S. Food and Drug Administration (FDA). "Examples of Mobile Apps for Which the FDA Will Exercise Enforcement Discretion." August 1, 2016, www.fda.gov/MedicalDevices/DigitalHealth/MobileMedicalApplications/ucm368744.htm. Accessed August 1, 2017.

van Dijck, Jose. "Datafication, Dataism and Dataveillance: Big Data between Scientific Paradigm and Ideology." *Surveillance and Society*, vol. 12, no. 2, May 2014, pp. 197–208.

Wilbanks, John and Eric Topol. "Stop the Privatization of Health Data." *Nature*, vol. 535, July 2016, pp. 345–348.

Zang, Jinyan et al. "Who Knows What About Me? A Survey of Behind the Scenes Personal Data Sharing to Third Parties by Mobile Apps." *Technology Science*. 2015103001. October 30, 2015, http://techscience.org/a/2015103001. Accessed August 1, 2017.

7

THE ALGORITHM DISPOSITIF
Risk and Automation in the Age of #datapolitik

Davide Panagia

Killing is difficult. Inordinately so. Especially if you are human. The problem isn't so much a question of "how?" but "whether?" Will a human kill another human given the right circumstances? Contrary to Hobbesian moral psychology, popular belief, current events, and media panic, most times a human won't. Hence the need to develop automated killing techniques for combat, an urgent concern that arose immediately after World War II. That concern is classically elaborated in S.L.A. Marshall's (A.K.A. "SLAM") *Men Against Fire*. The book is an appraisal of the American soldier that offers an engagement with the problem of combat non-fire. Marshall's infamous "fire ratios" were staggering. After extensive research and interviews, SLAM determined that "out of an average one hundred men along the line of fire during the period of an encounter, only fifteen men on the average would take any part with the weapons" (Marshall 57). Though Marshall's methods for gathering that data remain suspect (Grossman), the ratio stuck: during World War II 85 percent of soldiers did not fire their weapons. Marshall thus begins his 1947 publication by affirming that "What we need in battle is more and better fire" (23).

The risks, especially at the beginning of the Cold War, were too great. To curtail such risks Marshall's advice is to introduce a series of disciplinary and behavioral modulations so that the average American soldier doesn't resist killing, media modulations like replacing the "bull's eye" target image with a man-shaped pop-up one (Pettegrew 3). In short, what Marshall advises (successfully) to attentive military ears is the development of war simulation as stimulus/response technology for the disciplining of the American infantryman. His advice took, and such training is now a well-recognized mainstay of military life that ensures the automated killing of humans by humans (Gara). Marshall's success is actually staggering. As John Pettegrew notes, by 9/11 the non-firing ratio of U.S. troops was near zero, just in time for Operation Enduring Freedom.

Marshall's strategies appeal to a peculiarly modern account of action that concerns itself with risk and automation. What SLAM wanted and what America got were automated killing devices that could kill without having to rely on the imprecision and, indeed, the highly risky fact of an internal moral psychology. It isn't so much that Marshall championed cyborgs as the solution to the 85 percent non-fire dilemma. Rather, he championed the modern idea that humans needn't rely on anything other than their nervo-mechanisms in order to achieve firing success. In short, what Marshall was appealing to was a cybernetic theory of action that has its origins in a natural history of human automation and risk.

The operational logic that combines arithmetic, probability, and futurity is a characteristic of what Emily C. Nacol calls "an age of risk" that structures the development and rise of political economic thought in early-modern Europe. If we collate Nacol's historiography with Jessica Riskin's genealogy of automated action we discover a rich history of intermedial risk-thinking where theories of action, time, and transmission are enmeshed with near-living objects (automata, genes, and calculations) all of which generate an experiential milieu of risk media oriented to the specific task of making the future no longer "a realm of fate, fortune, or providence," (2) as Nacol puts it. The basic idea is as ubiquitous as it is complex and distensive: the future is an unknown and though it will always remain unknown, a representation of possible outcomes (or potential futures) are available given the application of arithmetic equations to information that is gathered about the world (of finance, of war, of behavior, of childhood, of health, of fraud, etc.) (Cetina and Bruegger). The more information available, the greater the potential for an aggregate account of future outcomes, and thus the minimization of risk (Amoore). The applicability of such an idea is legion because it makes future time something that can be managed logistically (Cowen).[1] Given enough information, the probable outcomes of all actions can be predicted. In short, calculations are the technical media that automate future life itself.

For my part I wish to contribute to these intermedial considerations of risk(y) media by focusing on the specificity of the algorithm dispositif that I consider the dominant technical medium of our contemporary future present. The position that I hold is one that considers any instant of critical political reflection thoroughly entangled with technical media, this despite the fact that technical media have traditionally played little to no part in Western political theorizing (save the technical medium of a cave as in the case of Plato's theory of justice, and that of the stage with regard to Thomas Hobbes's theory of representation).[2] But theories of justice are entangled with accounts of the literarity of documents—especially of the legal/constitutional variety (Rawls);[3] democracy is enmeshed with technologies of representation (Hobbes and Tuck); and equality is entwined with spectatorship and theatricality (Rancière). All of these are combined in diverse and divergent forms and practices. In short, what I am calling the *algorithm dispositif* regards a dynamic psycho-perceptual milieu participant in the disposition of worlds that at once limits and enables the movement of bodies in space and time, offering a digital theory of action that governs our everyday lives. Moreover, the algorithm dispositif is the basis of our "practices of governance" (Tully 21)[4] that today are not simply enabled by algorithms and software; rather, they occur *by* them in that these nonhuman agents are our dominant governmental actants. Given these assertions one can only concur with Tarleton Gillespie who reserves the name algorithm for:

> a particular kind of sociotechnical ensemble, one of a family of systems for knowledge production or decision making: in this one, people, representations, and information are rendered as data, are put into systematic/mathematical relationships with one another, and then are assigned value based on calculated assessments about them.
>
> *(Digital Keywords)*

I situate the emergence of the algorithm dispositif in the cybernetic debates and writings, as well as calculations and ambitions, of the mid-twentieth century and not (as I suggest below) the literature of the security state that has been so central to surveillance studies (Amoore and de Goede). I argue that more than anything, the algorithm dispositif betrays a theory of action whose origins lie in Aristotelian aesthetics and metaphysics. Cybernetics extends and modulates those origins in important and considerable ways by introducing a negative feedback ontology. Such an ontology is grounded on the behavioral insights of B.F. Skinner (especially) and applies those insights to the science of communication and control—to wit, the science of information management. The combination of all these intellectual ambitions, practices, and ideals produces an intuition heretofore unavailable but made operational for the first time: *information behaves*.

This cybernetic innovation augers the realpolitik of our contemporary future present; namely, what I wish to call #*datapolitik*. I conclude my considerations by providing a brief characterization of #datapolitik that advances three provocations that I can't possibly defend in the space of this chapter: 1. We have yet to develop the critical tools to acknowledge and engage the power dynamics of #datapolitik; 2. Surveillance is not only the wrong metaphor, but the wrong way to think about the power dynamics of #datapolitik; and 3. #datapolitik is a police power, but not in the familiar Althusserian sense of interpellation. #datapolitik does not subjugate. It is a cynegetic power of predation that does not rely on detection, suspicion, or arrest (as in the case of the more familiar ideological interpellation variety); but rather on tracking and capture.

Information: *It's Alive*!

The invented discovery that information behaves took millennia, in part because our concept of information is recent and our concept of media is even more recent than that (Guillory). But we can begin to articulate our understanding of informational behavior by turning to Aristotle's aesthetics of emplotment and metaphysics of substances (or hylomorphism) as these works and ideas form the basis of how cybernetic theorists of the mid-twentieth century conceived of the differential relations that their calculations would help identify, track, and capture. In this, Aristotle's aesthetic hylomorphism also forms the basis of the ontology of the algorithm dispositif.[5]

In his *Poetics*, Aristotle famously develops an aesthetic theory of dramaturgy that imagines temporal events as at once identifiable and trackable along a linear time axis that forms the narrative or plot of the story (for instance, emplotment or *muthos*). Thus, Aristotle will affirm that "In poetry the story, as an imitation of action, must represent one action, a complete whole, with its several incidents so closely connected that the transposal or withdrawal of any one of them will disjoin and dislocate the whole" (1541^a31–35). Key to this passage, and to Aristotle's aesthetic theory in general, is the possibility of imagining "one action" as "a complete whole." That is, for Aristotle what matters is understanding an action as a meaningful substance, a unity of form and matter. This is crucial for a variety of reasons, but especially because in dramaturgy the idea is to at once represent actions and events (this is the mimetic nature of all art according to Aristotle) and also to facilitate the enactment of events by actors on a stage. Thus, actions must be identifiable and discrete so that they may be imitated (by the actors). On this rendering, representation (or *mimesis*) is a practical as well as aesthetic consideration that Aristotle affirms must be observed.

For Aristotle, then, the structure of the plot regards the relationship of part to whole, and every single part must do its part in order for the whole to work. What constitutes the nature of a good part is whether it is necessary, and the writer must always endeavor to represent only necessary things; otherwise she risks creating something merely episodic, by which Aristotle means disjoined and dislocated: "I call a Plot episodic when there is neither probability nor necessity in the sequence of its episodes" (1541^b33–35). And again, Aristotle will go on to affirm that:

> The right thing, however, is in the Characters just as in the incidents of the play to endeavor always after the necessary or the probable, so that whenever such-and-such a personage says or does such-and-such a thing, it shall be the necessary or probable outcome of his character; and whenever this incident follows on that, it shall be either the necessary or the probable consequence of it.
>
> *(1454^a33–39)*

The task of the poet, then, is to arrange actions that obey the demands of necessity or probability. And this is the crucial point: the interstice between events that sources a sequence must be governed by the relational forces of necessity or probability. The capacity to create such relations determines the poet's skill as a "maker of likenesses" (Aristotle 1460^b9). The alternative is fragmented episodes that are decidedly *not* the marker of a good work. Aristotle's point is that anything disconnected or episodic lacks a purpose, and thus the possibility of sense, because sense is possible if and only if there is necessity or probability built into the movement of plot. Those actions that lack either purpose or necessity are insensible.

This account of the relationship between linear sequencing, plot, and probability in Aristotle relies (as previously noted) on the possibility of there existing something called "one action, a complete whole." To expand on the relevance of this thing called "one action" for the algorithm dispositif, we must also consider Aristotle's theory of substances as outlined in his *Metaphysics* that affirms that "the movers are substances and that one of these is the first and another a second according to the same order as the movements of the stars, is evident" ($1073^{b}1$). This is for our purposes crucial because what the idea of movers as substances allows is the possibility of conceptualizing action as a discrete incident that can be emplotted along a timeline. This makes action substance (in the Aristotelian sense) of the plot thus allowing for the possibility of treating a plot as something akin to a stochastic series of causally complicit moments. But more than this, Aristotle's is a very early formulation of automated movement and information transfer, one that to this day continues to inform notions of political action and filmic movement (for instance), but also our ideas of heredity and evolution (Mukherjee 22–24, 70). An action is "a complete whole" because it may be identified as a substance, as a kernel of what we moderns will eventually call "information." The action–substance is a spatio-temporal coordinate with determinate edges and boundaries. It is identifiable precisely because it is a substance; that is, it is a detail. And as such, it can be arranged in the way in which any detail can be arranged. Hence, there is the possibility of a dramaturgical plot (or any schema of linear temporal sequencing) being an arrangement of actions according to necessity or probability. On this rendering, Aristotle convenes three distinct criteria—necessity, appropriateness, and fit—so as to generate a sense of purpose through linear sequencing. In this way emplotment offers the imitation not merely of right action, but of right fit too—of the right disposition of things:[6] the right action in the right space and time yields the best results in terms of dramaturgical success—but not only that. Another way of stating this, the way that is articulated as mattering for the cybernetic engineers and mathematicians of the mid-twentieth century, is that the detail of information (or datum) is a hylomorphic substance that is self-predicating, or autobehaving. Information is alive; it is a substance that behaves.

The invention of info-vitalism (for lack of a better expression) is made perspicuous in a paper generally regarded as the manifesto for cybernetics that appeared in Volume 10 (1943) of the journal *Philosophy of Science*, and co-published by Arturo Rosenblueth, Norbert Wiener, and Julian Bigelow—all of whom had been working together at MIT during World War II on anti-aircraft fire servomechanisms and more specifically, radar technology. The paper entitled "Behavior, Purpose and Teleology" matters because it affirms a founding abstraction: Humans are indistinct from machines. And what matters is not the behavior of individual beings, but the behavior of information emitted by moving entities; this is because human behavior can be reduced to a set of informational impulses at once traceable and identifiable. Thus it doesn't matter whether the moving entity is a human or a consumer product or a submarine missile. In fact, it shouldn't matter; what does matter is the energy differentials that appear as a result of movement, and all that needs accounting is the sheer externality of the activity, and nothing else. You might want to try and give a motivational account of movement that includes internal psychology, or intention, or a soul—but that's not important to the servomechanical analysis being proposed simply because the "why" of movement is irrelevant, all that matters is that it does move and that the movement indicates change.

In short, our cyberneticists accepted the behavioral description of movement provided by Ivan Pavlov and (especially) B.F. Skinner (*Cumulative Record, Science and Human Behavior*) that articulates an automated account of human action devoid of any rich description of internal psychology or motivation; a behavioral account of action that was, itself, premised on an Aristotelian aesthetic hylomorphism. For what the behaviorist did was latch on to Aristotle's theory of action and its commitment to the emplotment of action–substances as an inherent (or automatic) condition of movement. All action, in other words, can be traced (or charted, or tracked) by articulating the different points of movement at different moments in time, and by noting these as one would note the action of a character in the plot of a play. But, following the behavioral commitment to automated action, what our cybernetic authors did was eradicate any plausible distinction between human mechanism and servomechanism such that all movement became reducible to information behavior. To put it slightly differently, the cybernetic–behavioral innovation on Aristotelian poetics is to assert that anything that moves behaves as if it were an element in a story and is thus subject to the laws of necessity and probability outlined by Aristotle.

A brief aside to fill in some blanks: Recall how B.F. Skinner's work (*Cumulative Record, Science and Human Behavior*) extends modern accounts of reflex and stimulus/response. As is well known, Skinner identifies Descartes as the forefather of a mechanistic model of living organisms, Cartesian mechanism being a concept that Skinner (rightly) identifies as wanting to do away with the belief in a human soul or any other opaque internality as a motivational structure for action (*Science and Human Behavior* 321–346). More to the point, what Skinner identifies in his extension of the reflex concept is the pure externality of action itself for which he reserves the name "behavior." In contrast to conventional accounts of action that require a reconstruction of motivations like soul, but also ambition, or intention, or any other dimension of human psychic life, Skinner is exhaustive in his commitment to the idea that action is not only mechanistic, but that whatever explanation you might give for any action the only explanation that matters is the observable one; and observable action is behavior identified by the differentials of energy exchange (the term Skinner at various times prefers is "irritability"). Hence the relevance of the reflex which he defines as "the observed correlation of two events, a stimulus and a response" (Skinner, *Cumulative Record* 346).

It is difficult to overlook the Aristotelian aesthetic hylomorphism behind this conclusion—this despite Skinner's own insistence that his particular theory of behavior is grounded in a modern, Cartesian history of living mechanisms.[7] Stimulus and response are two action–substances both of which are positioned—or emplotted—along a linear sequential axis (i.e., response is consequent to stimulus). That linear sequence marks the trajectory of a timeline that enables the identification of relevant and necessary action, hence making action at once external and observable. Indeed, if we turn to his reconstruction of Ivan Pavlov's experiments on conditioned reflexes (with salivating dogs) we see Skinner committed to the idea that behavior modification is possible via external stimuli (an insight that to this day is critically helpful in all ranges of behavioral therapy from those military modulations advised by Marshall, to Advanced Behavioral Analysis in autism treatment, to torture). But more so, we see Skinner enamored with the idea that behavior is available as quantifiable datum of information because behavioral data is external and observable (Skinner, *Science* 45–58). To condition response means to be able to treat behavior as if it were an externally locatable Aristotelian substance. Though it is true that the purpose that begets movement is not, as Aristotle had argued, an internal property of an object, it is also true that that objects behave as if they had purpose. What is important, at least from an observational perspective, is to overcome the need to divine internal motivations and content oneself with an observable, external account of movement. Ultimately, what behaviorism does is relocate Aristotelian teleology from somewhere inside the object to an interactive, dynamic outside.[8]

That action is observable behavior that can be collated as datum of information brings us ever closer to the cybernetic insight that information behaves. Like Skinner, the three cybernetic authors of "Behavior, Purpose, and Teleology" confirm that action—and action's purpose—is externally identifiable, and as such it can be predicted, tracked, and captured. And it can be predicted, tracked, and captured because an object moves. "Any modification of an object, detected externally, may be denoted as behavior," they affirm (Rosenblueth et al. 18). Simply put what Rosenblueth et al. note is that what is being observed externally in an action isn't so much the action itself, but its change. Cybernetics understands identification in terms of the external tracking of differential movement, of positionality, and of "change of energy" (18). (In a similar vein, W. Ross Ashby states that

"The most fundamental concept in cybernetics is that of "difference," either that two things are recognizably different or that one thing has changed in time" (9).) The ambition here is clear: to identify differentials existing in the world through the observable monitoring of movement as datum of information. Information, in other words, is the observable register of movement in the world—or, to revert back to Aristotle—it is the source and site of probability because probability is the name we give to the differential of energy between point A and point B along the spatio-temporal arch of a linear sequence (for instance, a plot); probability measures the in-between of two points.

In her study of the perceptual modulations emergent with the rise of postwar cybernetics, Orit Halpern notes that "Perception became a probabilistic channel whose capacities were variable, and capable of being engineered, enhanced, and modified" (64). She further notes that

> Cybernetics would become a mode of operations interested not in representing the world but in understanding what templates, approximations, agglomerations of information facilitated generalized productions of universal concepts that allow the eye, now an independent set of processes not attached to conscious reason, personal history, or specific situations, to perceive and act on the world.
>
> (56)

I add to this insight by elaborating the behavioral and Aristotelian dimensions necessary in order to make precisely what Halpern uncovers possible. In short, I account for the fact that the perceptual innovations in and around the algorithm dispositif are embedded and grounded in certain specific ontological claims about the nature of the medium, claims that regard algorithmic calculations as capable of articulating action as an identifiable substance, inserting it into a probabilistic logic that looks conspicuously like a plot, and generate outcomes from the differential measures that emerge by tracking an object's movement. In short, what the Aristotelian aesthetic hylomorphic basis of the algorithm dispositif affords is an automated theory of action for anything capable of moving or being moved.

Key to this insight is what our cybernetic authors call "negative feedback," which is the operational logic of the algorithm dispositif.[9] In "Behavior, Purpose, and Teleology" our authors define behavior in classically cybernetic terms as "output" or "any change of an entity with respect to their surrounding." This means, as they specify, that "any modification of an object, detectable externally, may be denoted as behavior" (Rosenblueth et al. 1). Now, the fact of automatic movement does not mean that action is not purposeful. On the contrary, movement assumes voluntary activity. But that purpose or voluntarism is, as our authors say, "a physiological fact," a reaction and thus equally available for external detection: "we merely trip the purpose and the reaction follows automatically" (1). The specification of purpose as a feature of automation carries great weight because it is the basis of feedback where an amount of energy expelled by a body is returned as a datum of information back to that body. If the kernel of information–energy is returned to the body in question so as to restrict its motion and thus prevent the object from, say, over-shooting its target, in that case we have what is called "negative feedback." The signal comes back from the future to alter a future outcome:

> The term feed-back is also employed in a more restricted sense to signify that the behavior of an object is controlled by the margin of error at which the object stands at a given time with reference to a relatively specific goal.

What negative feedback does is "modify and guide the behaving object" (Rosenblueth et al. 2). It is a type of external stimulus that directs behavior to accurately attain an end goal. The subsequent step, then, is to create a classification of behavior so as to literally compose the algorithm that will conduct right action.

Imagine a timeline with a point "x" indicating the present, and a point "y" indicating a future outcome. This "x" could be the current position of a missile, or the sentiments of an eHarmony user, and "y" can be a moving target or the romantic expectation of our digital Romeo or Juliet. The idea of negative feedback, and its basic operational *weltanschauung*, is to coordinate the trajectory of "x" so that it might achieve "y." To control for the coordination of the direction of movement, "x" sends a signal (a "like" click, for instance) to "y" and "y" sends the signal back to "x." The return signal adjusts "x's" trajectory so as to ensure as much as possible a direct hit. And this relay dynamic continues through time until the objective is achieved. That is, cybernetics operationalizes repetition as the basic function of informational exchange. Wiener famously coined the term "cybernetics" to describe what he called "the entire field of control and communication theory," adopting the term from the Greek *kubernētēs*, meaning "steersman" or "governance" (Wiener 11).[10] In other words, the explicit project of cybernetics as made manifest in the medium specificity of the algorithm dispositif is the elaboration of a total system of governance based on theories of communication and control. The ontology of negative feedback, at the heart of the algorithm dispositif, is an ontology of recursion that ensures the control of movement and trajectory (i.e., purpose) through the recursion of information.[11]

To put this another way, what cybernetics does is create a formal account of action as the emission of kernels of information (i.e., the datum, or actuality of behavior, or data) that behave. More than this, the behavior information becomes, via negative feedback, the means to calibrate action so as to ensure as precisely as nonhumanly possible a future outcome. And this, I submit, is the transformational insight augured by the algorithm dispositif. If information behaves, and if humans are indistinct from machines in their emission of quanta of information (data), then cynegetic tracking, capture, and prediction of future outcomes (risk) are possible in exactly the manner in which Aristotle advises vis-à-vis probable action in a plot sequence. That is, through the operational logic of negative feedback, it's not only the case that information behaves but information behaves back from the future to control and guide achievement.[12]

Algorithmic Provocations

In the preceding section I articulate the affective pragmatics of a computational enterprise I call the algorithm dispositif and I situate that enterprise within a political theory of action. At the core of algorithm dispositif, then, is an account of automation for the articulation and management of futures. In short, the algorithm dispositif is the pre-eminent risk medium of our time. It barters in futures by relying on an Aristotelian aesthetic hylomorphism of the "one action, a complete whole" so as to create a homeostatic system of negative feedback of communication and control. More than a tool for life management, the ubiquity of the algorithm dispositif transforms risk into a *dispositio*: the spatio-temporal arrangement of life itself and the affective coordinate of our contemporary future present. In short, the algorithm dispositif is the relational medium of sentimental living that governs interactions between humans and nonhumans alike.

Everything that I have written thus far would seem to lead to the conclusion that our contemporary condition in the age of #datapolitik is a system of total surveillance and subjection that extends the mediatic forms of police and military powers of the twentieth century. But I think this conclusion is at once misdirected and wrong. The algorithm dispositif does not presuppose a structure of subjection qua surveillance. This, for two concrete reasons: 1. The algorithm dispositif is not a scopic medium; and 2. The algorithm dispositif is not interested in subjecting humans. Simply put, no one is being watched in the track-and-capture mode of predation that structures the behavior of algorithms. The fact of negative feedback makes this clear: algorithms are not interested in disciplining individuals into subjection; negative feedback is exclusively interested in the creation of automated homeostatic systems that are self-perpetuating and independent of the existence of humans, their beliefs, their identities, and their ambitions. This is the whole point of the cybernetic commitment to behaviorism that treats all mechanisms (human, animal, android) as indistinct servomechanisms whose movements count because they are externally observable. The only thing that matters is the movement of bodies, not their specific identity (racial, ideological, religious). This, of course, doesn't mean that humans will not develop ways of using cybernetic algorithms to extend their political agendas of exploitation and subjection. After all, even Cain figured out that he could use a rock to kill his brother.

My point simply is this: the affective pragmatics of a medium matter to how we develop our sense of its politicality and thus, of the power structures at play in any dispositional arrangement. #datapolitik is not a system of surveillance because the algorithm dispositif is not surveying anything. There is no looking—not in the classical sense of a systematic apparatus of permanent visibility "that assures the automatic functioning of power" and thus, discipline and subjection (Foucault 201). Indeed, it is a mistake to assume that something like NSA surveillance is surveillance at all. It's not. What #datapolitik is doing via the algorithm dispositif is track-and-capture, and what such a system does is develop calculations that articulate possible future movements of anything that is identifiable; hence the possibility of managing risk as a way of managing life itself.

#datapolitik is not a system of surveillance. It *is* a dynamic of total predation. Its precursor is not the disciplining of the criminal body, but the police action of the hunt or, as Grégoire Chamayou defines it, "the power of pursuit" that "does not deal with legal subjects but rather with bodies in movement, bodies that escape and that it must catch, bodies that pass by and that it must intercept" (Chamayou 90). The power of pursuit is not part of the legal system—it is an interstitial space in between law and criminality. One hunts a moving target, not a criminal. If you catch that moving target, then they may be criminalized. But the moving body itself has no identity within the dynamics of a legal system. This type of police power, notably different from the one theorized by Louis Althusser in his famous "Ideology and Ideological State Apparatuses" essay, is not interested in subjection. Subjection requires stillness, as does surveillance. Recall the Althusserian scenario of interpellation that begins with a call to halting motion through a performative hailing: The gendarmerie's "Hey, You there!" hails you to stop in your tracks. In a similar vein, the apparatus of surveillance requires an architectural arrangement that confines movement. Surveillance is possible because a body, or object, or identity does not move.

The police power of #datapolitik, on the contrary, is interested in action and perpetual motion, in dataveillance (Agre; Clarke; Raley). It is interested in the simple fact of informational vitalism. "If police action finds its main justification in respect for the law," Chamayou affirms, "what drives it in practice is something quite different: the desire and the pleasure of the pursuit, in relation to which the law appears as an obstacle to its full development" (91). Hence the virtue of the algorithm dispositif whose ontology is born of motion, of the commitment to the tracking of action—to wit, cynegetic predation. The specific medium of #datapolitik is the algorithm dispositif that deploys a negative feedback ontology to track-and-capture perpetually mobile futures otherwise called "risk."

An Impossible Conclusion

In this essay, I develop a medium specific analysis in order to arrive at the dispositional dynamics of what I claim is the dominant (because ubiquitous) medium of our contemporary future present, the algorithm dispositif. I describe some of its features, the ontological conditions it presupposes, and the operational logic at work in its affective pragmatics. That is, I am interested in the workings of the medium, hence my turn toward the cybernetic behaviorism of the mid-twentieth century and some of the ambitions of that diverse and intense research project. In doing so, I am inspired by the works of many twentieth century thinkers—Walter Benjamin, Stanley Cavell, Andre Bazin, Gilles Deleuze, and Glibert Simondon, chief among them—whose work in media theory is committed to exploring the diverse ways of thinking critically about the nature(s) of media, their limits, and their conditions of possibility. In short, my interest is to explore (invoking Gilbert Simondon's famous formulation) the mode of existence of a technical object whose field of operations extends to every aspect of liveable life. And invoking Stanley Cavell's explorations of the ontology of film, my further interest in this paper is to inquire into what it is that the medium in question is declaring for itself (Cavell 103). Call these the methodological assumptions that structure my ambitions throughout this essay.

The motivation for my doing so is a certain sense of urgency to develop new and compelling critical dispositions to engage the new forms of power emergent in #datapolitik.[13] Much of the critical thinking and theorizing that developed in the twentieth century was born of an intense investigation into the modes of existence of technical media—whether newspaper, painting, poetry, film, or music—on the part of critics, spectators, and practitioners alike. The result is a rich, ambitious, and capacious anarchive[14] of critical concepts tooled to engage the role of media in everyday life and politics. But though that anarchive mattered to the conditions of mediatic emergence then, the viability and possibility of transposing those ideas today is not automatic as we saw with the matter of #datapolitik and dataveillance. This is because, as Richard Grusin ("Radical Mediation") has recently and thoughtfully argued, a medium interacts, intervenes, and radically mediates an existential milieu.

Our political vocabularies, insights, and critical ambitions in the twentieth century arose from inquiry into the nature of media. And though this is certainly not unique to twentieth century critical thought—because political ideas are always already entangled with mediatic modes of being and becoming—it is the case that the role of media are rarely acknowledged as participant actants in political ideation. I consider this a notable omission, with a normative cost. Political thinking in our age of algorithmic ubiquity will not develop the critical dispositions necessary to engage the power dynamics of #datapolitik without a sustained and persistent inquiry into the mediatic conditions of our contemporary future present. Political thinking, in other words, can no longer assume that technical objects are mere tools used by humans as means to political ends. The medium is the actant. Technical objects like the algorithm dispositif are the non-sovereign, governmental agents that manage everyday life.[15] They don't simply inform how we go about ruling ourselves and others, nor do they merely extend ways of ruling that are already available to us. Rather, they do it for us. And they do it to such a transformative degree that it is impossible to distinguish between "us" and "them," between humans and media. Indeed, the distinction is now inoperative. Human life is entangled with media life to such a degree that even species reproduction is understood (and that understanding is accepted) principally in terms of data mediation via genetic coding and information transfer.

I affirm these matters of fact not to bemoan our current state of affairs. I am not interested in cynicism, nor do I wish to propose a techno-scientific dystopia. I think such gestures are neither productive nor especially convincing. This because both these attitudes (cynicism and dystopia) demand a position of judgment as distanced from the conditions of #datapolitik. But our potential reworking of our critical dispositions require our coming to terms with the fact that in the age of ubiquity the critical privilege of distanced spectatorship is also not available to us. Our contemporary critical inheritance assumes that there is a distance between spectator, viewer, reader, and the object of spectatorship; between analyst and analysand; or what Paul Ricoeur brilliantly theorize as the hermeneutical function of distanciation (131–145). Within this schema there is the possibility of responding to medial intrusions by turning away, by refusing the image, or even negating it. That is, there is the possibility of human/nonhuman self-reflexivity. This is the critical privilege available to variations of a neo-Kantian account of aesthetic judgment, or a neo-Platonic ontology of iconomachy. The distance between spectator and medial object enables an account of freedom as a self-reflexive turning away, a redirection of attention via critical judgment (Zerilli).

But in the age of ubiquity the space of distanciation that enables critical judgment is unavailable —or at the very least, it is under-theorized. And this means that we have yet to develop critical dispositions that engage the emergent vitalism of our specific media.[16] This is what is at stake in the modes of existence of #datapolitik.

Notes

1 But there is a further point worth noting: The dynamic I describe also alters our relation to future time as it stops being something that can simply be represented, and becomes something that "exists in a virtual state before being actualized in an offensive, injury, or accident" (Ewald 222). Though it is beyond the scope of this essay, it seems to be the case that the algorithm dispositif exists in a virtual regime of the sensible and decidedly not a mimetic one.

2 I articulate this position in Panagia, "A Theory of Aspects."

3 "Literarity" is a term borrowed from Jacques Rancière's lexicon of an aesthetics of politics (*The Emancipated Spectator, The Politics of Aesthetics*). It first appears in his work *Disagreement*, but extends throughout his treatment of the poetics of knowledge in modern systems of writing, including political writing. For an excellent treatment of the topic, see Allison Ross's essay, "Expressivity, Literarity, Mute Speech" in Deranty.

4 Here Tully states that

> one might take as a provisional field of inquiry 'practices of governance,' that is, the forms of reason and organization through which individuals and groups coordinate their various activities and the practices of freedom by which they act within these systems, either following the rules of the game or striving to modify them."
>
> *(Public Philosophy in a New Key 21)*

5 For reasons of space I am not able to elaborate fully on Aristotle's aesthetic hylomorphism. An extended treatment of this is available in Panagia, *Rancière's Sentiments*.

6 I expand on these Aristotelian considerations in a forthcoming work. For those interested in further elaborations, see *Rancière's Sentiments*. Jessica Riskin also discusses Aristotle with reference to cybernetics in *The Restless Clock* (312–314).

7 Riskin rightly notes the limited historical imaginary of cybernetics. This being said, my approach to the matter of time and action vis-à-vis cybernetics and Aristotle differs from Riskin's in that I see cybernetics as extending (not attempting to extinguish) Aristotelian teleology (see *The Restless Clock* 213).

8 Once again I note the difference between my interpretation and Riskin's. Where she claims that negative feedback intends to eliminate the problem of Aristotelian teleology because for cybernetics, "the object did not have inner purpose, but only external influences" (Riskin 314), I want to insist that this exteriorization of purpose by cybernetics is an offshoot of behaviorism that adapts an Aristotelian hylomorphic schema to account for the nature of action. While it is true that internal motivations are irrelevant to cybernetic analysis, what cybernetics does (via behaviorism) is simply relocate that interior purpose to an outside. But the theory of action, and its aesthetic ontology, remain the same. Another way of stating this is what cybernetics does is make teleology internal to a system, rather than internal to an object or person.

9 Jodi Dean and Tiziana Terranova deal extensively with the political theory of negative feedback.

10 As Jessica Riskin notes, with the word "cybernetics" Wiener had in mind James Watt's steam engine governor (1788), which maintained the speed of the steam engine between certain limits, and which Wiener identified as the earliest artificial homeostatic device" (Riskin 312).

11 This dynamic is also available in postwar liberal theories of communication, including those of deliberative democracy (Rawls) and communicative action (Habermas), that define freedom in terms of a negative feedback repetition loop of arguments so as to achieve the equilibrium state of consensus. See especially the treatment of discourse ethics in Habermas. Here, Habermas articulates the neutrality of the intersubjective procedure of argumentation in cybernetic terms, though not naming them as such. The exchange of speaking subjects that articulate reasons in response to one another so as to arrive at an emergent consensus is the ontology of negative feedback of the algorithm dispositif.

12 Richard Grusin, Brian Massumi, and Louise Amoore—in diverse and distinct ways—all articulate this idea of a negative feedback ontology. For Grusin, medial acts of premediation generate a collective affectivity of a future possible event as happened thereby prompting an audience to admit its eventuality within the scope and radar of its own future (see Grusin, *Premediation*). Similarly, Massumi, *Ontopower*, articulates an operational logic of preemption that he accounts for as

> when the futurity of unspecified threat is affectively held in the present in a perpetual state of potential emergence(y) so that a movement of actualization may be triggered that is not only self-propelling but also effectively, indefinitely, ontologically productive, because it works from a virtual cause whose potential no single actualization exhausts.
>
> *(15)*

Finally, Louise Amoore's *The Politics of Possibility* speaks of the "arraying of possibilities" in the algorithmic decision trees of security software (69).

13 The nature of the project, then, is to consider the critical dispositions emergent from entanglements with media dispositifs. The term "critical disposition" is a modulation of James Tully's articulation of a critical attitude that he contrasts to a "critical theory." See especially Chapter 3 of Tully's *Public Philosophy in a New Key, Volume I* and *On Global Citizenship: James Tully in Dialogue* 10.
14 The term "anarchive" is Miriam Hansen's and it is used to favorably account for Siegfried Kracauer's sense of photography in the modern period as a "heap of broken images" that lacks any coherent or substantive organizational system (Hansen 36).
15 For a humanist account of non-sovereign agency, see Krause 21–57. I qualify this as a "humanist account" because Krause herself distinguishes between animate and inanimate objects in terms of reflexivity. Thus she affirms that "What inanimate objects lack is the reflexive sense of self required for the affirmation of one's subjective existence through action in the world … This reflexive self-awareness is unavailable to being and objects that lack higher cognitive functions" (48). As we have seen the algorithm dispositif's ontology of negative feedback render's Krause's conclusion unsustainable precisely because negative feedback is a auto-reflexive mode of "norm-responsiveness." Indeed, cybernetics was committed to generating automated, homeostatic, reflexive, nonhuman environments. In this commitment, it was exceedingly successful as Orit Halpern has shown (see *Beautiful Data*).
16 Some notable exceptions include authors previously cited (Amoore, Guillory, Grusin, Halpern, Massumi, Raley,) as well as the following: Deborah Cowen, Wendy Hui Kyong Chun, Alexander Galloway, Mark B.N. Hansen, Yuk Hui, Andrew Iliadis, Patrick Jagoda, Luciana Parisi, Jonathan Sterne, Neal Thomas, Liam Young.

Works Cited

Agre, Philip E. "Surveillance and Capture: Two Models of Privacy." *The Information Society*, vol. 10, no. 2, 1994, pp. 101–127.
Althusser, Louis. "Ideology and Ideological State Apparatuses." *Lenin and Philosophy, and Other Essays*. Monthly Review Press, 1971.
Amoore, Louise. *The Politics of Possibility: Risk and Security Beyond Probability*. Duke UP, 2013.
Amoore, Louise and Marieke de Goede. *Risk and the War on Terror*. Routledge, 2008.
Aristotle. "Poetics." *The Basic Works of Aristotle*. Random House Publishing Group, 2009.
Ashby, W. Ross. *An Introduction to Cybernetics*. Martino Fine Books, 2015.
Cavell, Stanley. *The World Viewed: Reflections on the Ontology of Film*. Harvard UP, 1979.
Cetina, Karin Knorr and Urs Bruegger. "Inhabiting Technology: The Global Lifeform of Financial Markets." *Current Sociology*, vol. 50, no. 3, 2002, pp. 389–405.
Chamayou, Grégoire. *Manhunts: A Philosophical History*. Princeton UP, 2012.
Chun, Wendy Hui Kyong. *Control and Freedom: Power and Paranoia in the Age of Fiber Optics*. MIT Press, 2008.
Chun, Wendy Hui Kyong. *Programmed Visions: Software and Memory*. MIT Press, 2011.
Clarke, Roger. "Information Technology and Dataveillance." *Communication of the ACM*, vol. 31, no. 5, 1988, pp. 498–512.
Cowen, Deborah. *The Deadly Life of Logistics*. The U of Minnesota P, 2014.
Dean, Jodi. *Blog Theory: Feedback and Capture in the Circuits of Drive*. John Wiley & Sons, 2013.
Deranty, Jean-Philippe. *Jacques Rancière: Key Concepts*. Routledge, 2014.
Digital Keywords: A Vocabulary of Information Society and Culture, edited by Benjamin Peters. Princeton UP, 2016.
Ewald, François. "Two Infinities of Risk." *The Politics of Everyday Fear*, edited by Brian Massumi. U of Minnesota P, 2012.
Foucault, Michel. *Discipline & Punish: The Birth of the Prison*. Knopf Doubleday Publishing Group, 2012.
Galloway, Alexander. *Protocol: How Control Exists After Decentralization*. The MIT Press, 2004.
Grossman, Dave. *On Killing*. Open Road Media, 2014.
Grusin, Richard. *Premediation: Affect and Mediality After 9/11*. Palgrave Macmillan, 2010.
Grusin, Richard. "Radical Mediation." *Critical Inquiry*, vol. 24, no. 1, 2015, pp. 124–148.
Guillory, John. "The Memo and Modernity." *Critical Inquiry*, vol. 31, no. 1, 2004, pp. 108–132.
Habermas, Jürgen. *Moral Consciousness and Communicative Action*. MIT Press, 1999.
Halpern, Orit. *Beautiful Data: A History of Vision and Reason since 1945*. Duke UP, 2015.
Hansen, Mark B.N. *Feed-Forward: On the Future of Twenty-First-Century Media*. U of Chicago P, 2015.
Hansen, Miriam Bratu. *Cinema and Experience: Siegfried Kracauer, Walter Benjamin, and Theodor W. Adorno*, edited by Edward Dimendberg. U of California P, 2011.
Hobbes, Thomas and Richard Tuck. *Hobbes: Leviathan: Resided Student Edition*. Cambridge UP, 1996.

Hui, Yuk. *On the Existence of Digital Objects*. U of Minnesota P, 2016.
Iliadis, Andrew. "A New Individuation: Deleuze's Simondon Connection." *MediaTropes*, vol. 4, no. 1, 2013, pp. 83–100.
Jagoda, Patrick. *Network Aesthetics*. U of Chicago P, 2016.
Krause, Sharon R. *Freedom Beyond Sovereignty: Reconstructing Liberal Individualism*. U of Chicago P, 2015.
Marshall, S.L.A. *Men Against Fire: The Problem of Battle Command*. U of Oklahoma P, 2000.
Massumi, Brian. *Ontopower: War, Powers, and the State of Perception*. Duke UP, 2015.
Massumi, Brian. *The Politics of Everyday Fear*. U of Minnesota P, 1993, pp. 221–228.
Mukherjee, Siddhartha. *The Gene: An Intimate History*. Simon and Schuster, 2016.
Nacol, Emily C. *An Age of Risk: Politics and Economy in Early Modern Britain*. Princeton UP, 2016.
Panagia, Davide. "A Theory of Aspects: Media Participation and Political Theory." *New Literary History*, vol. 45, no. 4, 2014, 527–548.
Panagia, Davide. *Rancière's Sentiments*. Duke UP, 2018.
Parisi, Luciana. *Contagious Architecture*. The MIT Press, 2013.
Pettegrew, John. *Light It Up: The Marine Eye for Battle in the War for Iraq*. JHU Press, 2015.
Raley, Rita. "Dataveillance and Countervailance." *"Raw Data" Is an Oxymoron*, edited by Lisa Gitelman, MIT Press, 2013, pp. 121–145.
Rancière, Jacques. *Disagreement: Politics and Philosophy*. U of Minnesota P, 2004.
Rancière, Jacques. *The Emancipated Spectator*. Verso Books, 2014.
Rancière, Jacques. *The Politics of Aesthetics*. Continuum, 2004.
Rawls, John. *Political Liberalism: Expanded Edition*. Columbia UP, 2011.
Ricoeur, Paul and John B. Thompson. *Hermeneutics and the Human Sciences: Essays on Language, Action and Interpretation*. Cambridge UP, 1981.
Riskin, Jessica. *The Restless Clock: A History of the Centuries-Long Argument Over What Makes Living Things Tick*. U of Chicago P, 2016.
Rosenblueth, Arturo et al. "Behavior, Purpose and Teleology." *Philosophy of Science*, vol. 10, no. 2, 1943, pp. 18–24.
Skinner, Burrhus Frederic. *Cumulative Record*. Appleton-Century-Crofts, 1961.
Skinner, Burrhus Frederic. *Science and Human Behavior*. Simon and Schuster, 1965.
Sterne, Jonathan. *MP3: The Meaning of a Format*. Duke UP, 2012.
Terranova, Tiziana. *Network Culture: Politics for the Information Age*. Pluto Press, 2004.
Thomas, Neal. "Choice or Disparation? Theorising the Social in Social Media Systems." *Westminster Papers in Communication and Culture*, vol. 10, no. 1, 2015, pp. 34–50.
Tully, James. *On Global Citizenship: James Tully in Dialogue*. Bloomsbury, 2014.
Tully, James. *Public Philosophy in a New Key, Volume I*. Cambridge, UK: Cambridge UP, 2008.
Wiener, Norbert. *Cybernetics or Control and Communication in the Animal and the Machine*. MIT Press, 1961.
Young, Liam. "On Lists and Networks: An Archaeology of Form." *Amodern, 2: Archaeology*, 2013. http://amodern.net/article/on-lists-and-networks/. Accessed 11 December, 2019.
Zerilli, Linda M.G. *A Democratic Theory of Judgment*. U of Chicago P, 2016.

8

THE PERILS OF MIGRATION

Countervailing Mediations of Risk at the EU's Maritime Frontier

Charles Heller and Lorenzo Pezzani

The Mediterranean Mobility Conflict

The phenomena of migrants crossing and dying in the Mediterranean while seeking to reach European territory have a long and tragic history. With European imperial expansions toward the sea's southern shores in the nineteenth century, a selective and unequal mobility regime started to emerge. While Europeans settled in great numbers in the newly colonized territories, the northbound movement of colonized populations toward metropolitan territories was subjected to successive moments of partial opening and closure of borders, leading to forms of unauthorized movement and early cases of deaths at sea (Borutta and Gekas; Clancy-Smith). Illegalized migration across the Mediterranean and fatalities at sea, however, became structural and highly politicized phenomena only as of the end of the 1980s, when, in conjunction with the consolidation of freedom of movement within the European Union (EU) through the Schengen Agreement, visas were increasingly denied to citizens of the global South. Then, as in the past, legal closure did not stop migration but only made the journeys more dangerous and precarious, forcing people to cross the sea on ever more unseaworthy and overcrowded vessels. Migrants' continued capacity to cross the Mediterranean despite legal denial was framed as a security threat and, as we shall see in more detail below, as a "risk" that had to be combated by all necessary means (De Genova). European coastal states and their southern "neighbors," later joined by Frontex, the European Border and Coast Guard Agency, and by a growing range of international military operations, have deployed a vast array of militarized bordering practices and techniques at the maritime frontier of the EU with the aim of containing migrants' movements and "mitigate[ing] the threat" that these pose to the EU—understood by Frontex as "a force or pressure acting upon the external borders that is characterised by both its magnitude and likelihood" (Frontex *Common Integrated Risk Analysis Model* 6). These policies have never more than temporarily succeeded in stemming migrants' crossings, and rather resulted in increasingly dangerous routes and smuggling strategies. The Mediterranean has thus become a space of friction (Tsing), across which illegalized migrants' trajectories have continuously evolved in response to the deployment by states of increasingly militarized means to police their turbulent movements, seeking—but never quite succeeding—to bridle them into orderly and governable mobilities (Panagiotidis and Tsianos 82). The dialectic between control and escape which the mobility conflict has led to has had a harrowing human cost: more than 30,000 migrants perished at sea since the end of 1980.[1]

While by the end of 2010, the Mediterranean had been increasingly closed down to unauthorized migration due to Europe's reinforced militarization of the maritime frontier and the externalization of control to dictatorial regimes located at the EU's periphery, the Arab uprisings marked a clear break in the consolidation of the Mediterranean migration regime, inaugurating a phase of increased turbulence. The fall in early 2011 of the Ben Ali regime in Tunisia and the Qaddafi regime in Libya allowed migrants to at least temporarily "re-open" maritime routes to the European continent. Moreover, the war that has engulfed Syria since 2012 has led to the largest exodus since World War II. While the majority of population movements unleashed by conflicts in the region have occurred on the southern shore of the Mediterranean, record numbers of people have reached the EU by boat and an equally unprecedented numbers of deaths at sea—more than 18,000 between 2014 and October 2018, have turned the central Mediterranean into the deadliest crossing in the world (IOM).

In this context, new nongovernmental initiatives were developed to contest the violence of borders. As researchers, activists, and aesthetic practitioners, we have contributed to several of these initiatives through our research, starting from 2011, when we launched the Forensic Oceanography research project to seek to document and contest the conditions that have led to large-scale deaths at sea (Heller et al., "The Left-to-Die Boat"). In this chapter, we reflect on the different strategies we have adopted within this project, so as to respond to the shifting forms of border violence deployed by states to deter, contain, and channel migrants' turbulent movements across the maritime frontier. We first trace the aesthetic regime within and against which our project sought to position itself; we then analyze the evolving strategies we have relied on as our focus shifted from the documentation of specific practices of actors at sea leading to cases of deaths (such as the "Left-to-die Boat"), to the reconstruction of the lethal effects of state policies (such as the ending of the Mare Nostrum operation). We then describe how a state-centered "risk analysis" is essential to the governmental practices geared at containing migrants, who are depicted as a "threat." Our reports have sought instead to reveal how it is state policies themselves that constitute a threat to migrants' lives. In this sense, our own work might be read as a form of "counter risk analysis." Finally we describe a project we have contributed to—the WatchTheMed Alarm Phone, a 24/7-operating nongovernmental emergency phone line dedicated to migrants in distress at sea, which emerged with the aim of intervening directly to support migrants in distress at sea. Through these different projects, we show that the Mediterranean mobility conflict is also fought through conflicting knowledges and mediations of the border, in which actors opposed to each other are constantly repositioning themselves, adapting to, and borrowing from, each other.

The Mediterranean Frontier's Regime of (in)Visibility

At the EU's maritime frontier, we find at work a complex and ambivalent regime of (in)visibility, inextricably bound to the way the border regime itself operates. As a result of their illegalization through the EU's policies of exclusion, people who decide to migrate despite the legal decree against it are forced to resort to an informal infrastructure of mobility: transnational networks of migrants who exchange information and services; the smuggling networks they resort to for a portion of their journey; as well as actual means of transport such as overused and overcrowded boats. Migrants are *illegalized*—their illegality is a product of state laws—and therefore they must migrate *clandestinely*, in the etymological connotations of hiddenness and secrecy of this word, seeking to cross borders undetected. The EU's migration regime thus imposes a particular "partition of the sensible" in the terms of Jacques Rancière: it creates particular conditions of (dis)appearance, (in)audibility, (in)visibility. As opposed to the logic of clandestinity, what all agencies aiming at controlling migration try to do is to *shed light* on migration and in particular on acts of unauthorized border crossing in order to make the phenomenon of migration more knowable, predictable, and governable. To this effect, a vast dispositif of control has been deployed at the maritime frontier of the EU, one made of mobile patrol vessels but also of an assemblage of multiple surveillance technologies, through which border agents seek to detect and intercept migrants' vessels. Vessel tracking is supplemented by coastal and ship-borne radars, optical and synthetic aperture radar imagery, and other devices so as to achieve the most complete possible "integrated maritime picture." Together, these remote sensing devices compose what Karin Knorr Cetina has called a "scopic system": "an arrangement of hardware, software, and human feeds that together function like a scope: like a mechanism of observation and projection…" (Knorr Cetina 64). However, the partition of the sensible of the EU's maritime borders is more ambivalent than this binary opposition would let us believe. Visibility and invisibility do not designate here two discrete and autonomous realms, but rather a topological continuum. On their part, migrants in distress may do everything they can to be seen so as to be saved from drowning. Conversely, border agents not only seek deliberately to hide the structural violence inherent in practices of policing maritime migration, thus allowing these practices to perpetuate themselves in full impunity; they may also choose *not to see* migrants in certain instances, considering that rescuing them at sea entails the responsibility for disembarking them and processing their asylum claims and/or deporting them. This has led to repeated cases of migrants abandoned to drift at sea, as in the "left-to-die boat" case we will discuss further on.

We find the same ambivalence at work in photographic and video imagery of the maritime frontier. In addition to the different remote sensing means described above, patrol vessels are also equipped with cameras—those of border guards or of "embedded journalists"—which are used to document the moment of encounter between illegalized migrants and the actors seeking to police their movement. This results in a highly controlled and ambivalent *spectacularization of borders*, which has been incisively analyzed by Nicholas de Genova. In the countless images of intercepted/rescued boats that are circulated by state agencies and the press, the threat of illegalized migration and the securitization work of border control are simultaneously made visible and naturalized, following a circular logic. If migrants are being intercepted through militarized means, it is because they are a threat. If they are a threat, then they must be policed by all means. The sense of migration as a threat is only exacerbated by the profusion of similar images which suggest an invasion of the European space by those who have been constructed as radically other. However, by focusing on the *scene* of border enforcement, the conditions that lie before—the multiple forms of violence migrants sought to escape in the first place, the illegalization of their movement through policies of exclusion—and after—the future exploitation of illegalized migrant labor in European economies—remain hidden as *obscene* supplements. Finally, while the deaths of migrants may at times remain hidden, at other points they are spectacularized to cover the violence of borders with a humanitarian varnish: border control becomes framed as an act of saving migrants, occluding the fact that state policies endanger their movement in the first place. Untangling this complex and ambivalent field of (in)visibility operating at the EU's maritime frontier, what emerges is a fundamental link between the three distinct dimensions of migrants' *exposure* emphasized by Georges Didi-Huberman: the visual exposure of illegalized migrants, their being "ex-posed"—rendered outside and excluded—of a given community and the exposure of their bodies to conditions of precarity and death. It was precisely to contest the ambivalent and selective regime of (in)visibility operating at the EU's maritime frontier, and the multiple forms of violence connected to it, that we initiated the Forensic Oceanography project in 2011.

Exercising a Disobedient Gaze: The "Left-to-Die Boat" Case

As both migrants' crossings and fatalities at sea increased again in 2011 in the wake of the Arab uprisings, and with indications of responsibility of state actors for the loss of these lives, we launched the Forensic Oceanography research project within the wider Forensic Architecture agency. The forensic approach seeks to find *traces* of events under investigation so as to reconstruct them and prove or disprove a crime. However, if the traces considered by the inventors of forensic science since the times of Edmond Locard (1877–1966) could be stains, fingerprints, or gun powder, today's events are potentially registered by an infinite amount of materials and media—from phone communication to payment data, from videos shot with mobile phones to satellite images and vehicle tracking data, from sound recordings to rubble analysis (Ruffel and McKingey; Schuppli). Drawing on the expanding range of these twenty-first-century traces, the forensic perspective has been applied within human rights practice in new and productive ways. In the process, forensic science has been seized from the monopoly of state agencies, and used by nongovernmental actors to hold state and non-state actors accountable for their crimes. It is this shift that Eyal Weizman seeks to highlight by referring to such critical and civil society-based practice as *forensic*—Latin for "pertaining to the forum" and the origin of the term forensics—rather than *forensics*, which has come to be associated with the scientific tools used by states to investigate crimes (Weizman 9). In addition to experimentation with novel methodologies to register the traces of different forms of violence, the Forensic Architecture project has brought a particular architectural edge in terms of spatializing them. Taking this approach to the sea to document and demand accountability for deaths of migrants, we have sought to develop methodologies to document violence at sea by reappropriating the multiple surveillance means deployed to detect acts of illegalized border crossing and re-directing their "light" toward the violence of the border itself. Furthermore, we have sought to spatialize this violence within the particular legal architecture of the EU's maritime frontier so as to determine responsibility for them. We discuss these two strategies in turn.

Our project was sparked by a 2011 incident that came to be known as the "left-to-die boat" case.[2] At the height of the NATO-led military intervention in Libya, 72 refugees fleeing the warzone were left to drift in the central Mediterranean Sea for 14 days. Sixty-three human lives were lost, despite distress signals sent out to vessels navigating in this area, and despite several encounters with military aircrafts and a warship. While the testimonies of the nine survivors brought this crime of failing to render assistance to light, its perpetrators have remained unidentified. In conjunction with a coalition of NGOs, and in collaboration with several parallel investigations, Forensic Oceanography reconstructed a composite image of the events by corroborating the survivors' testimonies with information provided by the vast apparatus of remote sensing technologies that have transformed the contemporary ocean into a digital archive of sorts. By interrogating winds and currents, we were able to model the drifting boat's trajectory, and by analyzing satellite imagery we could account for the presence of a large number of vessels in the vicinity of the drifting migrant boat that did not heed their calls for help (see Figure 8.1). While as we discussed above, these technologies are often used for the purpose of policing illegalized migration as well as the detection of other "threats," they were repurposed to find evidence for the failure to render assistance. Through our work on the "left-to-die" case, we sought to put into practice a *disobedient gaze* that used some of the same sensing technologies as border controllers, but sought to redirect the light they shed from unauthorized acts of border-crossing, to state and non-state practices violating migrants' rights. We conceived this gaze as

> [aiming] not to disclose what the regime of migration management attempts to unveil—clandestine migration—but unveil that which it attempts to hide, the political violence it is founded on and the human rights violations that are its structural outcome.
> *(Heller and Pezzani "A Disobedient Gaze," 294)*

In addition to reconstructing events at sea, a crucial task of our project was *spatializing* the practices of actors and inscribing them within the political geography of the sea. At sea, the moment of border crossing is expanded into a process that can last several days and extends across an uneven and heterogeneous territory that sits outside the exclusive reach of any single polity. The spatial imaginary of the border as a line without thickness dividing isomorphic territorial states is here stretched into a deep zone "in which the gaps and discrepancies between legal borders become uncertain and contested" (Neilson 126). The maritime territory constitutes, then, a space of "unbundled sovereignty" in Saskia Sassen's terms, one in which sovereign rights and obligations are

Figure 8.1 Analysis of the March 29, 2011 Envisat satellite image showing the modeled position of the "left-to-die boat" (yellow diagonal hatch) and the nearby presence of several military vessels who did not intervene to rescue the migrants

Credit: Forensic Oceanography and SITU Research, Report on the Left-to-Die Boat Case

disaggregated from each other and extended across complex and variegated jurisdictional spaces. As soon as a migrants' boat starts navigating, it passes through the jurisdictional regimes that crisscross the Mediterranean: from the various areas defined in the United Nations Convention on the Laws of the Sea to Search and Rescue regions, from ecological and archaeological protection zones to areas of maritime surveillance. At the same time, it is caught between legal regimes that depend on the juridical status applied to those onboard (refugees, economic migrants, illegals); on the rationale of the operations that involve them (such as rescue and interception); and on many other factors. These overlaps, conflicts of delimitation, and differing interpretations are not malfunctions, but rather are structural characteristics of the maritime frontier that have allowed states to simultaneously extend their sovereign privileges through forms of mobile government and elude the responsibilities that come with it (Gammeltoft-Hansen and Alberts; Steinberg *The Social Construction*). For instance, the strategic mobilization of the notion of "rescue" has allowed coastal states to justify police operations in the high seas (Andersson "A Game of Risk"), but overlapping and conflicting Search and Rescue (SAR) zones have led to recurrent cases of non-assistance to migrants in distress. In these ways, states increase the radical precarity and uncertainty of illegalized migrants' journeys across the maritime frontier. The sea's "geopower" (Grosz) is here made to ambivalently oscillate between offering a medium enabling migrants' movement, and constituting a threatening liquid mass that risks swallowing their lives at any moment. Water then is turned into a deadly liquid that inflicts violence in indirect ways, mediating between state policies and practices on the one hand, and the bodies and lives of migrants on the other. Facing these mobile and fleeting

The Perils of Migration

bordering practices, the aim of Forensic Oceanography has been to "re-territorialize" them, in the words of Deleuze and Guattari. We have sought to inscribe as precisely as possible lethal events occurring across the liquid geography of the sea, locating them within specific jurisdictional zones and boundaries (such as SAR zones, but also in the case of the "left-to-die boat," NATO's maritime surveillance area) so as to point to responsibilities for them. While the fragmentation of juridical regimes at sea often allows for the evasion of responsibility, we have here sought to mobilize it strategically toward the multiplication of potentially liable actors and of forums where they could be judged and debated. Not only did our reconstruction of the migrants' drift demonstrate that the migrants had remained within NATO's maritime surveillance area during its 14 days of deadly drift (see Figure 8.2), but by identifying many ships in the vicinity of the migrants' boat, our report allowed the NGO coalition we collaborated with to file several legal cases against the different states—including France, Spain, Italy, and Belgium—whose assets had taken part in the NATO-led operation, and who shared a degree of responsibility for the death of the 63 passengers (Migrants' Rights). In this sense, while defending the objective of freedom of movement as the only alternative to deaths and violations at sea, we have had to mobilize borders against themselves, thereby performing a kind of "strategic territorialism"—to redirect Gayatri Spivak's "strategic essentialism" (Spivak). In other words, to contest the violence of borders and to promote the free movement of people across them, we have paradoxically needed to re-affirm the rigidity of the jurisdictional boundaries that states seek to evade.

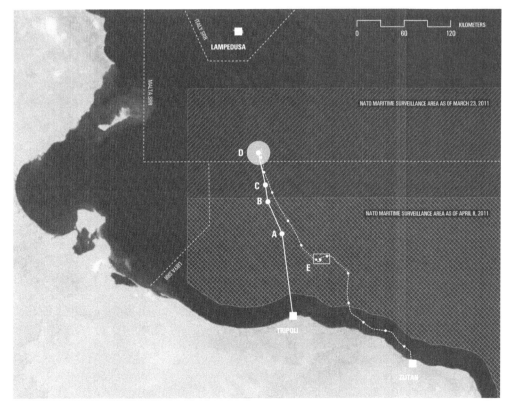

Figure 8.2 Chain of events in the "left-to-die boat"

Credit: Forensic Oceanography and SITU Research, Report on the Left-to-Die Boat Case

Note
For a detailed key to this map, see: www.forensic-architecture.org/case/left-die-boat/

Documenting the Violence of Policies: Counter-Risk Analysis

In recent years, in addition to focusing on the reconstruction of specific incidents to determine the responsibility of the actors directly involved in them, our research has focused on the broader responsibility of state policies (and associated policy makers) in shaping the conditions that make migrants' crossings more dangerous. This inflection in our research began from the realization that cases of migrant deaths are not isolated events, but are rather the structural, long-term, and large-scale outcome of the EU's exclusionary border regime, which is entirely at odds with the material dynamics of migration and thus renders migrants' passages illegal and perilous. The question of "how to document and demand accountability not for the deaths involved in a specific shipwreck, but for all the deaths that have occurred as a result of the EU's policy and the mobility conflict?" was one that had haunted us from the inception of our project. It became more urgent in the face of recent developments in state policies and discourses surrounding migration across the EU's maritime frontier.

First, we observed an increasing "humanitarianization of the border." The humanitarian border, according to William Walters, emerges

> once it becomes established that border crossing has become, for thousands of migrants seeking, for a variety of reasons, to access the territories of the global North, a matter of life and death. It crystallizes as a way of managing this novel and disturbing situation, and compensating for the social violence embodied in the regime of migration control.
>
> *(138)*

While rescue at sea has long been the humanitarian counterpart of the illegalization of migrants, over the last few years, border control operations themselves are frequently being framed as *acts of saving*, blurring the notions of rescue and interception. In this respect, the humanitarian border echoes the inextricable connection between violence and care that characterizes colonial power (Mbembe).

This trend toward the humanitarianization of the border became particularly visible after the shipwreck of October 3, 2013, when 366 migrants died just a few hundred meters off the coast of the small Italian island of Lampedusa. This tragedy caused a public outcry that forced policy makers to position themselves. After his visit to Lampedusa on October 8, 2013, Jose Manuel Barroso's, then President of the European Commission, declared: "We in the European Commission, myself and Commissioner Malmström, we believe that the European Union cannot accept that thousands of people die at its borders." In the same speech, Barroso announced an increase in Frontex' budget and the launch of Eurosur, the European Border Surveillance System—that is, the continuation of a predominantly security approach to migration, and exactly the kind of measures that prompted migrants to take deadly risks. This trend of justifying increasing measures of border control in the name of saving migrants' lives has continued since. The shift however implied that migrants' deaths were no longer kept hidden within the regime of (in)visibility operating at the maritime frontier, but actually spectacularized. What remained occluded was the causal relation between policies of closure and migrant deaths. As such, in the wake of this discursive shift, focusing on this connection became all the more important.

Second, focusing on policies became essential in the wake of a particular policy shift—the ending of the Italian *Mare Nostrum* operation—as a result of which the violence exercised at and through the maritime frontier could no longer be reconstructed from cases alone. The week commencing April 12, 2015 saw what is believed to be the largest loss of life at sea in the recent history of the Mediterranean. On April 12, 400 people died when an overcrowded boat capsized due to its passengers' excitement at the sight of platform supply vessels approaching to rescue them. Less than a week later, on April 18, a similar incident took an even greater toll in human lives, leading to the deadliest single shipwreck recorded by the United Nations' High Commissioner for Refugees (UNHCR) in the Mediterranean ("Mediterranean Boat Capsizing"). Over 800 people are believed to have died when a migrants' vessel sank after a mis-maneuver led it to collide with a cargo ship that had approached to rescue its passengers (see Figure 8.3). More than 1,200 lives were thus lost in a single week. As Médecins Sans Frontiers (MSF) commented at the time, these figures eerily resemble those of a war zone. Beyond the huge death toll, what was most striking about these events was that they were not the result of a reluctance to carry out rescue operations, which we had identified as a structural cause of migrants' deaths in the "left-to-die boat" investigation. In these two cases, the actual loss of life has occurred *during* and partly *through* the rescue operation itself.

While it could appear, as state actors were quick to argue, that only the ruthless smugglers who overcrowded the unseaworthy boats to the point of collapse were to blame, the argument we made in our report titled "Death by Rescue—The Lethal Effects of the EU's Policies of Non-Assistance" was different (Heller and Pezzani). We argued that the absence of any immediate violation perpetrated by vessels in vicinity to the boats in distress hid a form of *policy violence* operating at a different scale and temporality then that of the migrants' crossing. In order to reveal this violence, in addition to the reconstruction of specific cases of death at sea, we had to resort to what we called a *forensics of policies*.

The report traces the roots of the April 2015 events back to the above-mentioned October 3, 2013 shipwreck, which marked a break with coastal states' principled reluctance to operate rescue that shaped the "left-to-die boat" case. In the aftermath of that tragedy, Italy decided in fact to launch the "military and humanitarian" Mare Nostrum operation, deploying a record number of

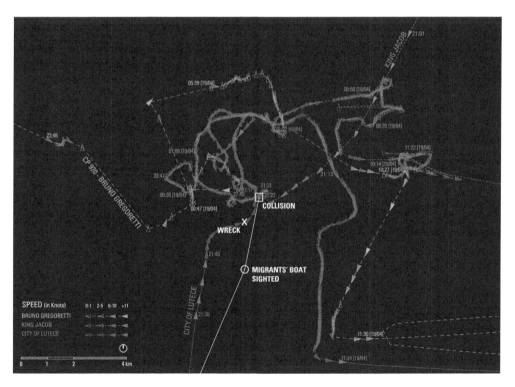

Figure 8.3 The frantic tangle of Automatic Identification System (AIS) vessel tracks in the Mediterranean following the April 18 shipwreck

Credit: Forensic Oceanography, Death by Rescue report. GIS analysis: Rossana Padeletti. Design: Samaneh Moafi

ships to rescue migrants in distress very close to the Libyan coast. But this operation soon came under increasing attack for allegedly constituting a "pull-factor" encouraging migration, and, despite its humanitarian aims, leading to more deaths at sea. In this way, even as EU policy makers aimed to deter migrants from crossing the sea, they couched their security aims in the language of humanitarianism: migrants ought to be deterred, for their own good. As a result, the Italian operation was terminated at the end of 2014. In its place, the Triton operation led by Frontex, the European border agency, was launched on November 1, 2014. This operation deployed fewer vessels in an area further away from the Libyan coast: border control, rather than rescue, was its priority (see Figure 8.4). Human rights advocates such as Amnesty International vocally denounced this policy retreat, arguing it would not lead to fewer crossings, only more deaths. Even Frontex, in an internal document which we managed to obtain through a freedom of information request, assessed that "the withdrawal of naval assets from the area, if not properly planned and announced well in advance, would likely result in a higher number of fatalities." Frontex and EU member states pushed on with the implementation of a more limited operation in full knowledge of the lethal effects this would have.

Through the spatial analysis of operational zones; interviews with state officials concerning their operations at sea; and statistical data referring to migrant arrivals, deaths, and SAR operations; our report reconstructs the reality that began to unfold in early 2015, proving the human rights community right: migrants' crossings continued unabated, but instead of a fleet of state-operated vessels, a lethal SAR gap awaited them, leading to a rise in the danger of crossing by nearly 30 times. Seeking to fill this gap, the Italian Coast Guard increasingly called upon large merchant ships transiting in the area to carry out rescue operations. The rescue of migrants' overcrowded boats can

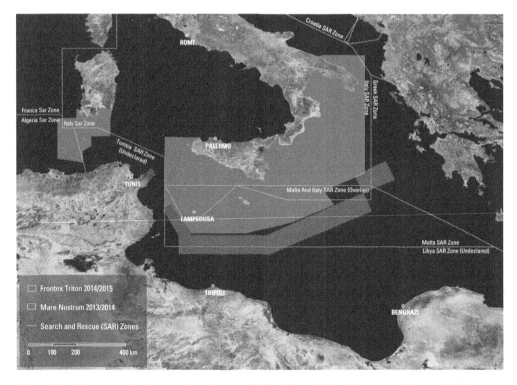

Figure 8.4 Map comparing the operational zones of Italian Navy's Mare Nostrum and Frontex's Triton

Credit: Forensic Oceanography, Death by Rescue report. GIS analysis: Rossana Padeletti. Design: Samaneh Moafi

easily lead to tragedies if not operated with the adequate most adaptive means and standards, and the large vessels of the shipping industry were unfit for the task ("ICS: Rescue of All"). In this context, the April 2015 tragedies were only waiting to happen. On April 29, 2015, the President of the European Commission, Jean-Claude Juncker, admitted that "it was a serious mistake to bring the Mare Nostrum operation to an end. It cost human lives." However, the ending of Mare Nostrum and its (non-)replacement by Frontex's Triton operation cannot adequately be described as a "mistake," since it was a carefully planned policy implemented in full knowledge of its outcomes. Our report demonstrates that EU agencies and policymakers deliberately implemented *policies of non-assistance* that created the *conditions* that made the April shipwrecks inevitable.

Despite Juncker's partial admission of guilt, translating our reconstruction of this form of *policy violence* into the language of law so as to bring policy makers to account for *legal violations* has proven challenging to date. The impunity which prevailed for the implementation of this lethal policy has allowed it to be perpetuated, as we have demonstrated in one of our latest reports, "Blaming the Rescuers" (Heller and Pezzani), which has focused on the criminalization of nongovernmental rescue initiatives. Following the April 2015 shipwrecks, the EU has continued to refuse to launch a new proactive SAR operation to mitigate the risk that the lack of legal avenues for migration create on a structural level, focusing instead on anti-smuggling activities which have made the crossing even more dangerous. While a growing number of NGOs courageously stepped in with their own vessels to fill the lethal gap in rescue capabilities left by the ending of Mare Nostrum, a virulent campaign of delegitimization—in which Frontex has once again played a pioneering role—has targeted them. Like Mare Nostrum had before, NGOs have been accused of constituting a "pull-factor." However, in a phase of marked *de-humanitarianization* of the border, in which the lives of migrants appear to have increasingly lost even their discursive value, the very act of rescue has been increasingly criminalized as NGOs have been accused of "colluding" with smugglers.[3] Knowing the looming catastrophe that these attacks signaled, we have sought to intervene in this debate through our report, "Blaming the Rescuers" (Heller and Pezzani), that has provided a counter-analysis of the shifting dynamics of migration erroneously attributed to SAR NGOs. We have further offered counter-reconstructions of events of alleged collusion—in particular those involving the NGO Jugend Rettet, whose vessel was seized on August 2, 2017 ("Blaming the Rescuers"). While we have demonstrated that the accusations against NGOs have been spurious and amounted to "factual lies"—the use of factual elements to weave a narrative that is intentionally false—our collective efforts have proven insufficient. As we write in Summer 2018, almost all rescue NGOs have been prevented from operating, leading, as in the past, to greater risk for migrants crossing the sea (UNHCR, "Desperate Journeys"). The expulsion of humanitarian actors from the central Mediterranean has further given a free hand to the Italian-equipped and coordinated Libyan coast guard to intercept and pull-back migrants to Libya, where they face detention, forced labor, torture, and rape (Heller and Pezzani, *Mare Clausum*). Through these desperate measures deployed to seal off the central Mediterranean, the forms of violence experienced by migrants have thus been intensified and proliferated on land and sea.

Since 2011, we have used the analysis of paradigmatic cases of shipwrecks and violence at sea to offer unique insights into the workings of the maritime frontier. These cases, far from being exceptions, are part of recurrent patterns, and thus provide an entry point into a broader analysis of the structural effects of state policies and practices, revealing the role the latter play in making migrants' trajectories more and more precarious. In this sense, we see our reports as constituting the counterpart to Frontex's "Risk Analysis" reports. The European Border and Coast Guard Agency has, according to its mission of coordinating European border management, the first task (alongside operations and training) of "monitoring migratory flows and carrying out risk analysis regarding all aspects of integrated border management" (see Frontex, "Origin and Tasks"). In turn, Frontex describes its reports as produced through the processing of "information from diverse sources," which is further "systematized" into an analytical product so that Frontex may "form a reliable basis for its operational activities" (*2017 Annual Risk Analysis*). The agency's risk analysis at the borders of EU member states is also the basis on which EU external border funds are allocated (Horii).

The "risk analysis" operated by Frontex is necessarily *state-centered*, focusing on the alleged "risk" that irregular migration "flows" constitute for the states of the EU. In an important policy document which continues to offer the conceptual frame for Frontex's risk analysis to this day, Frontex defines risk

> as the magnitude and likelihood of a threat occurring at the external borders, given the measures in place at the borders and within EU, which will impact on the EU internal security, on the security of the external borders or on the optimal flow of regular passengers, or which will have humanitarian consequences.

"From this definition of risk," Frontex continues, "risk analysis is defined as the systematic examination of threats, vulnerabilities and impacts, the outcome of which is recorded in the form of a risk assessment" (Frontex Risk Analysis Unit).[4] We should note that within this conceptual sequence, exactly in what way illegalized migration constitutes a threat to EU security is never defined. Frontex's analysis of "risks" is heavily mediated by statistical graphs—in which the evolving lines indicating increasing or decreasing interceptions echo the hydraulic metaphors of "waves" and "flows" so often uncritically mobilized to describe migrants' movements. Maps also play a central role. In these (see Figure 8.5), as Andersson describes, "migrant routes morph into sharp arrows—'forces or pressures,' as the Frontex risk definition puts it—threatening the European Union's 'vulnerable' external borders" (Andersson *Illegality Inc*, 78).

In Frontex risk analysis, a stunning and disturbing inversion takes place: what is described as "vulnerable" are borders, not people: the latter are, instead, construed as a "threat." The discourse and associated mediations of risk play a fundamental role in what Didier Bigo has called the "governmentality of unease," the multifarious practices used "by diverse institutions to play with the unease, or to encourage it if it does not yet exist, so as to affirm their role as providers of protection and security and to mask some of their failures" (Bigo 65).

Our own analysis, on the other hand, is influenced by the perspective of the autonomy of migration which, just as Autonomous Marxism claimed the primacy of workers' struggles in shaping the changing logic and operations of capital, starts from the movements, constraints, and struggles of migrants. As Sandro Mezzadra and Brett Neilson have argued by riffing on the title of James C. Scott's seminal book, it makes us "see like a migrant" (166). In this sense, in our recent reports, which focus on assessing the risks that the EU policies themselves pose for the lives of migrants, a risk measured in the physical threat to their lives, we offer a *migrant-centered* "risk analysis." Since our aim is not to produce knowledge about migrants' movements in the aim of governing them but rather to contribute, through our research and participation in different activist projects, to contest this very government, we may think of our reports as constituting a form of *counter*-risk analysis. "Counter" here is understood in the sense of Foucault's concept of "counter-conducts": movements of revolt and refusal by the governed against their conduct that have constituted the restive counter part of practices of governmentality (*Security, Territory, Population* 259).

While the Forensic Oceanography project has mainly focused on documenting past manifestations of the violence of the EU border regime in the aim of blocking its modes of operation, other projects that emerged on the basis of our methodologies—WatchTheMed and its associated Alarm Phone—have sought to intervene in real time to prevent violations and fatalities from occurring in the first place.

The Perils of Migration

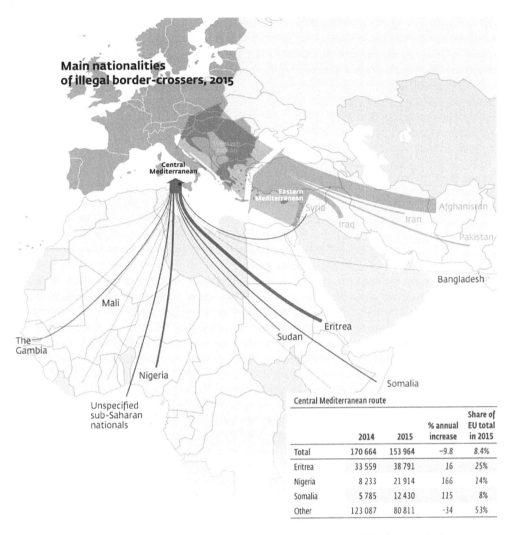

Figure 8.5 Map representing the main nationalities of "illegal border crossers" for the central Mediterranean route

Credit: Frontex, *2016 Annual Risk Analysis*, March 2016, p. 20

Disobedient Listening to Prevent Migrants' Deaths at Sea[5]

In the wake of our report on the left-to-die boat, we contributed to found the WatchTheMed platform in 2012 in collaboration with a wide network of NGOs, activists, and researchers. Through the WatchTheMed monitoring platform, our hope was, on the one hand, to be able to multiply the documentation of violations, and, on the other, to move toward real-time interventions so as to shift from a post-fact analysis to actually preventing violations and deaths from occurring in the first place. While initially the focus was on documenting violations, the need to find ways to intervene *directly* within maritime borders became more pressing in light of the rising death tolls at sea.[6] Thus the WatchTheMed platform, which was initially used as a tool in the service of the tradition of documenting, denouncing, and seeking accountability for violations forwarded by human rights organizations, was seized by another important, more militant tradition that explicitly referred to the abolitionist network of secret routes and safe houses used by escaping enslaved populations in the U.S.: the "underground railroad."[7] Regarding themselves as part of an existing transnational underground circuit that supports transborder mobilities and migratory acts of escape, activist networks such as No Border and Welcome to Europe have long directly supported unauthorized mobilities across the borders of Europe. Migration is understood by these networks as a *social movement* in its own right, a "creative force" that upsets the governance of mobility imposed by the border regime not only by means of "explicit" legal and political claims (such as those grounded on the documentation and denunciation of specific episodes of violence at the border) but also through an everyday practice of refusing the border. This perspective opens up the field of struggles for freedom of movement to a whole series of "imperceptible" practices that would otherwise not be included in the political field, modifying the very boundaries of what we understand as political.[8] Acknowledging that unauthorized migration in our bordered world is often enabled by under-the-surface knowledge economies and networks composed of the very subjects of migration, their friends, relatives and connected communities, and allies, activist networks sought to practice solidarity by creating further "pillars" of the underground railroad. One such example is the creation of an online guide for migrants and refugees that provides practical information for their journeys toward and within Europe (See w2eu.info).

Inspired by this tradition, the WatchTheMed network also started to produce a series of leaflets containing information about the risks, rights, and safety measures at sea, dedicated to the different areas of maritime crossings ("Safety at Sea"). These aimed to contribute to the already existing "knowledges of circulation" which emerge from the collective experience of transnational irregularized migration, providing crucial additional information which might contribute to avoiding deaths for the migrants crossing the maritime frontier (Alioua and Heller). In this respect, the mobility of migrants constitutes an infrastructure of sorts—one that includes not only the footpaths, highways, train lines, or airports through which precarious travelers move; the wireless networks that transmit their information; the Internet café where they chat with relatives and friends; or the mobile phones with which they alert the Coast Guards and the satellite phone which locates their GPS position—but also what has also been referred to as "mobile commons," which includes "a world of knowledge, of information, of tricks for survival, of mutual care, of social relations, of services exchange, of solidarity and sociability that can be shared, used and where people contribute to sustain and expand it" (Papadopoulos and Tsianos 190).

The creation of the Alarm Phone in October 2014, an activist hotline supporting boats in distress in the Mediterranean Sea initiated by a coalition of freedom of movement, human rights, and migrant activist groups, was the next crucial step in the collectivization of these activist and militant practices, and aimed to offer travelers alternative ways to make their distress heard and pressure states into complying with their obligations. Thanks to a management software, the Alarm Phone can re-route distress calls to a vast number of volunteers operating shifts, situated in about 12 countries, thus ensuring that every call is attended to. Due to the very different conditions in the maritime spaces of the Mediterranean, specific handbooks with step-by-step emergency plans and instructions had to be written, based on years of experience in migration and no border struggles as well as local and region-specific expertise.

Since it was created, the Alarm Phone project has gathered extraordinary momentum, supported more than 2,000 boats in distress, and proven to be one of the most important political interventions against European border regimes. Besides supporting precarious human mobilities at sea, the wide solidarity network of the Alarm Phone, composed of about 150 activists and several connected organizations, can exercise pressure when there is a risk that a violation at sea may be perpetrated, such as cases of failing to render assistance or push-back, the illegal collective expulsion of "aliens" from a country's territory, or even direct assaults on migrant groups, such as those perpetrated by units of the Greek coastguards in the Aegean Sea. Among dozens of such cases that were uncovered by the Alarm Phone was a push-back operation carried out by the Greek authorities in cooperation with the Turkish coastguards and in the presence of the European border agency Frontex on June 11, 2016. Fifty-three people had already crossed the territorial line and entered Greek waters where they were illegally transferred, at gunpoint, onto a Turkish coastguard vessel and returned to Turkey (Watch the Med, "Alarm Phone Denounces"). Through its ability to directly follow trajectories of migrant boats in real-time, and to document and scandalize violations at sea based on information and data passed on by at risk passengers themselves, the Alarm Phone has significantly altered the ways in which the regime of (in)visibility operates at sea.

Crucial in the intervention of the Alarm Phone is not so much high-tech remote sensing devices such as satellite imagery that were central to report on the "left-to-die boat," but simple mobile and satellite phones and the interpersonal networks they connect. Furthermore, these mobile connections operate less through the sense of sight than through the sense of sound. While it may seem paradoxical, the best instruments for the exercise of a critical right to look and observe in maritime borderzones are those that transfer sounds. This is in fact consistent with many instruments required for oceanography, such as sonars that use sound waves to "see" in the water and measure the sea's depth, instead of technologies relying on light which does not travel far beneath the ocean's surface. Listening to and echoing the voices of those in the process of crossing maritime spaces then allows for disobedient observation of the Mediterranean Sea, with the aim of supporting migrants in their exercise of their freedom of movement and mitigating the extraordinary risk they face for daring to do so.

Conclusion

Throughout this chapter, by reflecting on the research and activist projects we have initiated and taken part in since the Mediterranean frontier was "re-opened" by the Arab uprisings, we have explored how different forms of mediation of migration across the sea—in particular those operated through surveillance technologies, as well as the photographic and videographic images circulated in mainstream media outlets—contribute both to shaping the policies of migrant exclusion and to implementing these policies through border control. While these policies are predicated on the securitization of migration which is constituted as a "risk" for European states that must be neutralized through militarized means, they in turn lead to the illegalization and precaritization of migrants' crossings. Securitized policies predicated on the construction of illegalized migration as a threat lead, in turn, to increased risks for migrants in their trajectories, and to large-scale fatalities at sea. Using some of the same technologies and methodologies against the grain, our research within the Forensic Oceanography project has sought to document and contest the forms of violence exercised at and through the maritime frontier. While we continue to reconstruct specific cases of death involving violations of migrants' rights so that accountability could be sought for them in front of national and international jurisdictions, our reports use the reconstructions of cases to shed light on the violence exercised by policies, which are more difficult to register but affect the broader dynamics of migration—and in particular the danger of crossing the sea. These reports have constituted interventions in ongoing debates concerning the EU's policies and operations. Furthermore, the methodologies we have developed have served as a basis for an activist project—the WatchTheMed Alarm Phone, a 24/7-operating nongovernmental emergency phone line dedicated to migrants in distress at sea—which emerged with the objective of intervening directly to support migrants crossing the sea and to prevent deaths and violations from occurring. Importantly, we do not seek construct a linear temporal evolution or a binary between the reconstruction of past events and real-time intervention, but rather a continuum of practices that can operate simultaneously. Strategic litigation concerning past events can be a means of transforming state practices in the present in the aim of making migrants' crossings less dangerous, and in turn, through the Alarm Phone, a number of violations have been documented and served litigation in turn.

The Mediterranean mobility conflict then is also fought out through conflicting knowledges and mediations of the border which are mobilized by different actors either to impose or contest the violence of borders. These actors operate in an immanent field, in which their practices are constantly shaping and adapting to each other. As new bordering policies and practices, as well as the aesthetic and discursive regimes within which they are embedded evolve, critical researchers, nongovernmental actors, and aesthetic practitioners alike must constantly reposition themselves to be able to continue to contest the changing modalities of the violence of borders and support migrants in their precarious trajectories.

Notes

1 See the list of migrant deaths at the European borders established by UNITED for Intercultural Action: http://unitedagainstrefugeedeaths.eu/about-the-campaign/about-the-united-list-of-deaths/.
2 For our reconstruction of these events, see our report: www.forensic-architecture.org/wp-content/uploads/2014/05/FO-report.pdf. Our video animation Liquid Traces summarizes our findings: https://vimeo.com/128919244.
3 Paolo Cuttitta has written of the "end of the humanitarian turn" in Italy's policy. While we concur with much of his analysis, we wish to think in more processual and non-binary terms, and thus describe the humanitarianization and de-humanitarianization of the border as a process allowing for varying degrees— and non-exclusive combinations—between these two poles.
4 *For an extended discussion of this document, see* Ruben Andersson "A Game of Risk").
5 An extended formulation of the following argument has been published in an article jointly written with Maurice Stierl ("Disobedient Sensing").
6 In another detailed investigation, we contributed to uncover events that transpired in the central Mediterranean Sea on October 11, 2013, leading to the loss of more than 200 lives: http://watchthemed.net/reports/view/32. Accessed August 1, 2017.
7 For a discussion of the connection with the underground railway of anti-slavery within migrants' rights activists discourse, see Welcome to Europe Network, "From Abolitionism to Freedom of Movement."
8 See Papadopoulos et al. 2008 and Mitropoulos and Neilson.

Works Cited and Further Reading

Alioua, Mehdi and Charles Heller. "Transnational Migration, Clandestinity and Globalization – Sub Saharan Transmigrants in Morocco." *New Mobilities Regimes in Art and Social Sciences*, edited by Sven Kesselring and Gerlinde Vogl. Ashgate Publishing, 2013.
Amnesty International. "Lives adrift Refugees and migrants in peril in the central Mediterranean," September 15, 2014, www.amnesty.org/en/documents/eur05/006/2014/en. Accessed April 12, 2016.
Andersson, Ruben. "A Game of Risk: Boat Migration and the Business of Bordering Europe." *Anthropology Today*, vol. 28, no. 6, 2012, pp. 7–11.
Andersson, Ruben. *Illegality Inc.: Clandestine Migration and the Business of Bordering Europe*. University of California Press, 2014.
Andreone, Gemma. "Observations Sur La 'Juridictionnalisation' de La Mediterranée." *Annuaire Du Droit de La Mer*, vol. 9, 2004, pp. 7–25.
Barroso, José Manuel Durão. "Statement by President Barroso Following His Visit to Lampedusa." European Commission, October 9, 2013. Accessed November 28, 2017 http://europa.eu/rapid/press-release_SPEECH-13-792_en.htm.
Bauder, Harald. "Why We Should Use the Term Illegalized Immigrant." *RCIS Research Brief*, no. 1, 2013, pp. 1–7.
Bigo, Didier. "Security and Immigration: Toward a Critique of the Governmentality of Unease." *Alternatives*, vol. 27, Special Issue, 2002, pp. 63–92.
Borutta, Manuel and Sakis Gekas. "A Colonial Sea: the Mediterranean, 1798–1956." *European Review of History: Revue europeenne d'histoire*, vol. 19, no. 1, 2012, pp. 1–13.
Casas-Cortes, Maribel et al. "Re-bordering the Neighbourhood: Europe's Emerging Geographies of Non-accession Integration." *European Urban and Regional Studies*, vol. 20, no. 1, 2013, pp. 37–58.
Cote, Mark. "Technics and the Human Sensorium: Rethinking Media Theory through the Body." *Theory & Event*, vol. 13, no. 4, 2010, pp. 1092–1311.
Clancy-Smith, Julia. *Mediterraneans: North Africa and Europe in an Age of Migration, c.1800–1900*. University of California Press, 2010.

Cuttitta, Paolo. "Pushing Migrants Back to Libya, Persecuting Rescue NGOs: The End of the Humanitarian Turn." *Border Criminologies*, April 18, 2018, www.law.ox.ac.uk/research-subject-groups/centre-criminology/centreborder-criminologies/blog/2018/04/pushing-0. Accessed April 12, 2016.

De Genova, Nicholas. "Spectacles of Migrant 'Illegality': The Scene of Exclusion, the Obscene of Inclusion." *Ethnic and Racial Studies*, vol. 36, no. 7, 2013, pp. 1180–1198.

Deleuze, Gilles and Félix Guattari. *A Thousand Plateaus*. Translated by Brian Massumi. University of Minnesota Press, 1987.

Depledge, Duncan. "Geopolitical Material: Assemblages of Geopower and the Constitution of the Geopolitical Stage." *Political Geography*, vol. 45, 2013, pp. 1–2.

Didi-Huberman, Georges. *Peuples exposés, peuples figurants. L'Oeil de l'histoire*. Editions de Minuit, 2018.

Fischer-Lescano, Andreas and Gunther Teubner. "Regime-Collisions: The Vain Search for Legal Unity in the Fragmentation of Global Law." *Michigan Journal of International Law*, vol. 25, 2004, pp. 999–1046.

Forensic Architecture, ed. *Forensis. The Architecture of Public Truth*. Sternberg Press, 2014.

Foucault, Michel. *Security, Territory, Population: Lectures at the Collège de France, 1977–1978*. Palgrave Macmillan, 2009.

Foucault, Michel. *"Society Must Be Defended": Lectures at the Collège de France, 1975–1976*. Translated by David Macey. New York: Picador, 2003.

Frontex. "2017 Annual Risk Analysis." February 15, 2017, http://frontex.europa.eu/assets/Publications/Risk_Analysis/Annual_Risk_Analysis_2017.pdf. Accessed May 12, 2017.

Frontex. "Concept of Reinforced Joint Operation Tackling the Migratory Flows Towards Italy: JO EPN-Triton." August 28, 2014, https://deathbyrescue.org/assets/annexes/2.Frontex_Concept_JO_EPN-Triton_28.08.2014.pdf. Accessed April 12, 2016

Frontex. "Origin and Tasks." https://frontex.europa.eu/about-frontex/origin-tasks/. Accessed May 12, 2017.

Frontex Risk Analysis Unit, *Common Integrated Risk Analysis Model, Version 2.0*, Warsaw, 2012, https://europa.eu/capacity4dev/file/21158/download?token=D9Gkxx6U. Accessed April 12, 2016.

Gammeltoft-Hansen, Thomas and Tanja E. Alberts. "Sovereignty at Sea: The Law and Politics of Saving Lives in the Mare Liberum." *DIIS Working Paper*, 2010, pp. 1–31.

Garrison, Tom. *Essentials of Oceanography*, 5th ed. Brooks/Cole Cengage Learning, 2009.

Grosz, Elizabeth. "Geopower." *Environment and Planning D: Society and Space*, vol. 30, 2012, pp. 971–988.

Heller, Charles and Lorenzo Pezzani. "A Disobedient Gaze: Strategic Interventions in the Knowledge(s) of Maritime Borders." *Postcolonial Studies*, vol. 16, no. 3, 2013, pp. 289–298.

Heller, Charles and Lorenzo Pezzani. "Blaming the Rescuers: Criminalising Solidarity, (Re)enforcing Deterrence." 2017, https://blamingtherescuers.org/. Accessed April 12, 2016.

Heller, Charles and Lorenzo Pezzani. "Death by Rescue. The Lethal Effects of the EU's Policies of Non-Assistance." 2016, https://deathbyrescue.org/. Accessed April 12, 2016.

Heller, Charles and Lorenzo Pezzani. "Mare Clausum: Italy and the EU's undeclared operation to stem migration across the Mediterranean." Forensic Architecture, 2018, www.forensic-architecture.org/wp-content/uploads/2018/05/2018-05-07-FO-Mare-Clausum-full-EN.pdf. Accessed April 12, 2016.

Heller, Charles, Lorenzo Pezzani, and Situ Research. "Report on the Left-to-Die Boat." Forensic Architecture, 2012, www.forensic-architecture.org/wp-content/uploads/2014/05/FO-report.pdf. Accessed December 10, 2013.

Heller, Charles, Lorenzo Pezzani, and Situ Research. "The Left-To-Die Boat." *Forensic Architecture*, www.forensic-architecture.org/case/left-die-boat/. Accessed April 12, 2016.

Heller, Charles, Lorenzo Pezzani, and Maurice Stierl. "Disobedient Sensing and Border Struggles at the Maritime Frontier of Europe.' *Spheres – Journal for Digital Cultures*, vol. 4, 2017, pp. 1–15.

Helmreich, Stefan. "Nature/Culture/Seawater." *American Anthropologist*, vol. 113, no. 1, 2011, pp. 132–144.

Horii, Satoko. "The Effect of Frontex's Risk Analysis on the European Border Controls." *European Politics and Society*, vol. 17, no. 2, 2016, pp. 242–258.

"ICS: Rescue of All Persons at Sea is a Must." *World Maritime News*, October 29, 2015, http://worldmaritimenews.com/archives/141521/ics-rescue-of-all-persons-in-distress-at-sea-is-a-must/. Accessed April 12, 2016.

International Organization for Migration (IOM). "Missing Migrants: Tracking Deaths Along Migratory Routes." October 18, 2018, http://missingmigrants.iom.int/region/mediterranean. Accessed April 12, 2016.

Juncker, Jean-Claude. "Speech by President Jean-Claude Juncker at the Debate in the European Parliament on the Conclusions of the Special European Council on 23 April: 'Tackling the Migration Crisis'." European Commission, April 29, 2015, http://europa.eu/rapid/press-release_SPEECH-15-4896_en.htm. Accessed April 12, 2016.

Knorr Cetina, Karin. "The Synthetic Situation: Interactionism for a Global World." *Symbolic Interaction*, vol. 32, no. 1, 2009, pp. 61–87.

Kurgan, Laura. *Close Up at a Distance: Mapping, Technology and Politics*. Zone Books, 2013.

Latour, Bruno. "The Anthropocene and the Destruction of the Image of the Globe." *Latour's Fourth Gifford Lecture*, Edinburgh, 2013, www.ed.ac.uk/schools-departments/humanities-soc-sci/news-events/lectures/gifford-lectures/archive/series-2012–2013/bruno-latour/lecture-four. Accessed September 30, 2014.

Mbembe, Achille. *On the Postcolony*. University of California Press, 2001.

Médecins Sans Frontières (MSF). "MSF Calls for Large Scale Search and Rescue Operation in the Mediterranean." April 20, 2015, www.msf.org/article/msf-calls-large-scale-search-and-rescue-operation-mediterranean. Accessed April 12, 2016.

Mezzadra, Sandro and Brett Neilson. *Border as Method*. Duke UP, 2013.

Migrant's Rights. "63 Migrants Left to Die in the Mediterranean: Survivors Continue Their Quest for Justice." International Federation for Human Rights, June 18, 2013, www.fidh.org/La-Federation-internationale-des-ligues-des-droits-de-l-homme/droits-des-migrants/63-migrants-morts-en-mediterranee-des-survivants-poursuivent-leur-13483. Accessed April 12, 2016.

Migreurop. *Atlas of Migration in Europe: A Critical Geography of Migration Policies*. New Internationalist Publications, 2013.

Mitropoulos, Angela and Brett Neilson. "Exceptional Times, Non-Governmental Spacings, and Impolitical Movements." *Vacarme*, 8 January 2006, www.vacarme.org/article484.html. Accessed April 12, 2016.

Neilson, Brett. "Between Governance and Sovereignty: Remaking the Borderscape to Australia's North." *Local-Global Journal*, vol. 8, 2010, pp. 124–140, http://mams.rmit.edu.au/56k3qh2kfcx1.pdf. Accessed April 12, 2016.

Nevins, Joseph. *Operation Gatekeeper: The Rise of the "Illegal Alien" and the Making of the U.S.-Mexico Boundary*. Routledge, 2002.

Panagiotidis, Efthimia and Vassilis Tsianos. "Denaturalizing 'Camps': Überwachen und Entschleunigen in der Schengener Ägäis-Zone." *Turbulente Ränder. Neue Perspektiven auf Migration an den Grenzen Europas*, edited by Transit Migration Forschungsgruppe. Transcript Verlag, 2007.

Papadopoulos, Dimitris, Niamh Stephenson, and Vassilis Tsianos. *Escape Routes: Control and Subversion in the 21st Century*. Pluto Press, 2008.

Papadopoulos, Dimitris and Vassilis S. Tsianos. "After Citizenship: Autonomy of Migration, Organisational Ontology and Mobile Commons." *Citizenship Studies*, vol. 17, no. 2, 2013, pp. 178–196.

Papastavridis, Efthymios. "Rescuing 'Boat People' in the Mediterranean Sea: The Responsibility of States under the Law of the Sea." *European Journal of International Law*, May 31, 2011, www.ejiltalk.org/rescuing-boat-people-in-the-mediterranean-sea-the-responsibility-of-states-under-the-law-of-the-sea/. Accessed December 5, 2015.

Papastavridis, Efthymios. "The Right of Visit on the High Seas in a Theoretical Perspective: Mare Liberum versus Mare Clausum Revisited." *Leiden Journal of International Law*, vol. 24, no. 1, 2011, pp. 45–69.

Parks, Lisa. "Digging into Google Earth: An Analysis of "Crisis in Darfur." *Geoforum* vol. 40, 2009, pp. 535–545.

Parks, Lisa and James Schwoch, eds. *Down to Earth: Satellite Technologies, Industries, and Cultures*. Rutgers UP, 2012.

Parliamentary Assembly of Council of Europe (PACE). "Lives Lost in the Mediterranean Sea: Who is Responsible?" Council of Europe, 2012, www.assembly.coe.int/CommitteeDocs/2012/20120329_mig_RPT.EN.pdf. Accessed May 2015.

Parliamentary Assembly of Council of Europe (PACE). "The Interception and Rescue at Sea of Asylum Seekers, Refugees and Irregular Migrants." Doc. No. 12628, 2011, http://assembly.coe.int/nw/xml/XRef/Xref-XML2HTML-en.asp?fileid=18008&lang=en. Accessed September 7, 2013.

Parliamentary Assembly of Council of Europe (PACE). "The "Left-to-Die Boat": Actions and Reactions." Council of Europe, 2014, http://assembly.coe.int/nw/xml/XRef/Xref-XML2HTML-en.asp?fileid=20940&lang=en. Accessed May 2015.

Pezzani, Lorenzo. *Liquid Traces: Spatial Practices, Aesthetics and Humanitarian Dilemmas at the Maritime Borders of the EU*. Centre for Research Architecture, Department of Visual Cultures, Goldsmiths University, 2015.

Pickles, John, ed. *A History of Spaces: Cartographic Reason, Mapping and the Geo-coded World*. Routledge, 2004.

Pickles, John, ed. *Ground Truth: The Social Implications of Geographical Information Systems*. Guilford, 1995.

Rancière, Jacques. *The Politics of Aesthetics The Distribution of the Sensible*. Continuum, 2006.

Ruffell, Alastair and Jennifer McKinley. *Geoforensics*. Wiley-Blackwell, 2008.

Sassen, Saskia. *Territory, Authority, Rights: From Medieval to Global Assemblages*. Princeton UP, 2006.

Schmitt, Carl. *The Nomos of the Earth in the International Law of the Jus Publicum Europaeum*. Telos Press, 2003.

Schuppli, Susan. "Walk-back Technology. Dusting for Fingerprints and Tracking Digital Footprints." *Photographies*, vol. 6, no. 1, 2013, pp. 159–167.

Spivak, Gayatri Chakravorty. "Subaltern Studies. Deconstructing Historiography." *The Spivak Reader*, edited by Donna Landry and Gerald MacLean. Routledge, 1996 [1985].

Steinberg, Philip E. "Free Sea." In *Spatiality, Sovereignty and Carl Schmitt: Geographies of the Nomos*, edited by Stephen Legg. Routledge, 2011.

Steinberg, Philip E. "Lines of Division, Lines of Connection: Stewardship in the World Ocean." *Geographical Review Geographical Review*, vol. 89, no. 2, 1999, pp. 254–264.

Steinberg, Philip E. "Oceans." *International Encyclopedia of Human Geography*, edited by Nigel Thrift. Elsevier Science, 2009.

Steinberg, Philip E. "Of Other Seas: Metaphors and Materialities in Maritime Regions." *Atlantic Studies*, vol. 10, no. 2, 2013, pp. 156–169.

Steinberg, Philip E. "Sovereignty, Territory, and the Mapping of Mobility: A View from the Outside." *Annals of the Association of American Geographers*, vol. 99, no. 3, 2009, pp. 467–495.

Steinberg, Philip E. *The Social Construction of the Ocean*. Cambridge UP, 2001.

Stoler, Ann L. "On Degrees of Imperial Sovereignty." *Public Culture*, vol. 18, no. 1, 2006, pp. 125–146.

Suárez de Vivero, Juan Luis. *Jurisdictional Waters in The Mediterranean and Black Seas*. European Parliament, 2010.

Tsing, Anna. *Friction: An Ethnography of Global Connection*. Princeton UP, 2005.

United Nations High Commissioner for Refugees (UNHCR). "Desperate Journeys." August 2018, www.unhcr.org/desperatejourneys/. Accessed April 12, 2016.

United Nations High Commissioner for Refugees (UNHCR). "Mediterranean Boat Capsizing: Deadliest Incident on Record," April 21, 2015, www.unhcr.org/553652699.html. Accessed April 12, 2016.

Walters, William. "Foucault and Frontiers: Notes on the Birth of the Humanitarian Border." *Governmentality: Current Issues and Future Challenges*, edited by Ulrich Bröckling, Susanne Krasmann and Thomas Lemke. New York: Routledge, 2011.

Watch the Med. "Alarm Phone." October 2014, http://alarmphone.org/. Accessed April 12, 2016.

Watch the Med. "Safety at Sea." *Watch the Med*, http://watchthemed.net/index.php/page/index/10. Accessed May 23, 2015.

Watch the Med. "Watch the Med." December 5, 2013, www.watchthemed.net/. Accessed April 12, 2016.

Watch the Med. "WatchTheMed Alarm Phone Denounces Illegal Push-back Operation with Frontex Present." *Alarm Phone*, https://alarmphone.org/en/2016/06/15/watchthemed-alarm-phone-denounces-illegal-push-back-operation-with-frontex-present/?post_type_release_type=post. Accessed January 8, 2017.

Weber, Leanne and Sharon Pickering. *Globalization and Borders: Death at the Global Frontier*. Palgrave, 2011.

Welcome to Europe. w2eu.info. Accessed April 12, 2016.

Welcome to Europe Network. "From Abolitionism to Freedom of Movement? History and Visions of Antiracist Struggles." *No Border Lasts Forever*, Frankfurt am Main, 2010, http://conference.w2eu.net/files/2010/11/abolitionism.pdf. Accessed April 12, 2016.

Weizman, Eyal. "Introduction: Forensis." *Forensis: The Architecture of Public Truth*, edited by Forensic Architecture. Sternberg Press, 2014.

9
MEDIATING EXPERTISE
Uncertain Risks of Electromagnetic Pollution

Rahul Mukherjee

This is an essay about mediation of risks related to electromagnetic emissions. Since expertise is key to defining and constructing risk, mediating risk and mediating expertise are entangled together. That said, risk and risk perception sometimes are also difficult to parse out, and that is where affected communities and lay publics have a role to play in asserting their felt experiences of electromagnetic fields through mediations, and make them count in risk policy-making as (anecdotal) evidence. This is the essay's argument. To begin, I want to elaborate on the relationship between risk, expertise, and media in debates regarding uncertain technologies.

The relationship between risk and media is a bit of a conundrum. At one level, risk is a danger out there, something real that exists, and so one might wonder what the need for media is. At another level, risk is something that needs to be defined and constructed, and it is in this process of definition and construction that media has a very important role to play. Such ambiguities about risk, whether it is real or constructed, are present in Ulrich Beck's *Risk Society* thesis. In this celebrated book, Beck conceptualizes risk to be at times about epistemological discourses and, at other times, to exist as ontological insecurities (Cottle). According to Beck, media help us perceive and know about "risk." If that is the case, one might ask: what is the relationship between risk and risk perception? Beck explains, "risk perceptions of risks and risks are not different things, but one and the same" (55). Mediated construction of risks are also risks. There are risks out there, but some of those risks remain imperceptible and inconspicuous, and need media to reveal them and to spread them.

Societies in late modernity are continuously being jolted by new risks, whether it is the perceived danger to public health from an emerging technology or financial insecurities generated by the unpredictable network economy. The velocities, geographies, and intensities of vulnerabilities might have changed over the years, but such risks have been there for a long time. Such dangers or insecurities were not always called risks or associated with risks. To become risk in late modernity, such (perceptions of) harm, dread, insecurity and danger have to carry the "aura of science" and the pretension of technical calculation (Douglas). Such a characterization of risk makes it inevitably part of a technocratic club consisting of a select group of experts and policy makers, and yet in the calculus of risk, public perception matters; rarely can any study of risk totally eschew public understanding of risk. This is also because risk has a forensic quality—that is, risk could have a negative outcome if citizens are not vigilant and bureaucrats do not sit up and take notice (Douglas). Media provide the venue where experts debate with each other or with "laypersons" about the nuance and magnitude of risks, and thus media become crucial tools to shape public understanding of risk. Therefore, mediating risks involves mediating expertise, and I argue, such an endeavor entails mediating both scientific expertise and lay expertise as they entangle themselves together.

Media is viewed as a critical venue for scientists and science policy makers to engage with the public at large; it acts as a potential channel through which scientific knowledge is disseminated among a wider audience of laypersons. Often times, media are considered the instrument to reduce the existing epistemic deficit between experts and laypersons about risks, whether it is related to genetically modified crops or climate change. That said, there are scholars in media studies and science studies who argue that media cannot be considered a neutral channel for information distribution, and that expert–layperson divides are untenable in situations where scientists themselves do not know the long-term effects of risky technologies (Callon et al.). Furthermore, media have an affective dimension: they not only help to spread knowledge about risky technologies, but also enable affected communities to intuitively grasp the deleterious effects of such technologies in their daily phenomenological encounters with them.

The expert–layperson divide is complicated in controversies dealing with electromagnetic field (EMF) emissions from cell towers and mobile phones because there is considerable scientific uncertainty about the biological effects of such emissions. When experts themselves are divided, how can they reassure the public (through media appearances) that concerned laypersons should not worry about EMFs? In this chapter, dealing with case-studies related to controversies about EMF emissions, I shall be focusing on how media complicates and negotiates the expert–layperson divide. The environmental controversies surrounding EMFs is a special case for comprehending mediation of risks because a) EMFs seem to be everywhere and yet are invisible and b) because there has been no significant study which has been able to prove or deny correlation between phones/towers and cancer. Compared to the more known effects of nuclear radiation, epidemiologists, oncologists, and radio-frequency experts have struggled to establish a connection between cancer cases and cell antenna signals. At the same time, these experts have been unable to rule out that cell tower radiation is not carcinogenic. Electromagnetic fields set up by many cellular devices and infrastructures, wireless routers, and electrical gadgets are everywhere in the environment but nobody knows what exactly the risks of such electromagnetic pollution are.

The possible harmful effects of mobile phones erupted into the public sphere when David Reynard told CNN's Larry King that his wife Susan Reynard died of brain cancer caused (or accelerated) by cell phone use (see Figure 9.1). In the state of Florida, Reynard filed a tort claim against

Figure 9.1 King interviewing Reynard in 1993 on CNN's *Larry King Live*
Snapshot of *Mobilize* (2015)

Motorola. That Larry King, a legendary radio and television personality, took up this issue on his show, amplified concerns about mobile phones all across United States. The call between Reynard and King was featured on January 21, 1993, just when Bill Clinton had become the new president of United States. Audiences tuned into King's show to hear political debate, but were treated to an environmental controversy. King's show had attracted a large audience and the affective contagion of fear psychosis spread through the United States. This eventually led to crashing of the stocks of cellular companies (Kurtz). Since then much more has happened: in the late 1990s and early 2000s, British newspapers like *Evening Standard* and *The Daily Mail* carried stories of children enrolled in schools with cell masts suffering from memory loss and headaches, and told anecdotes about radio-frequency radiation from cell phones and base stations causing nerve damage. Since 2011, in India, newspapers and television shows have linked cell towers to cancer cases. One newspaper, *Rajasthan Patrika*, highlighted the heating effects of cell antenna signals by suggesting that living in a city with cell towers was like living inside a furnace; it carried out a campaign, "*Bhatti Mein Sheher*" (*City Inside the Furnace*).

As much as some policy wonks might imagine the media to be a tool for educating laypersons about science and technology, they also fear media's ability to circulate rumor and gossip about the yet-not-proven deleterious effects of (hazardous) chemicals and (risky) technologies. Media might hype the risks from mobile tower radiation or express concerns about excessive usage of cell phones. This could lead the government to have greater regulation as a matter of abundant precaution. There are sociologists, scientists, and bureaucrats who believe that maintaining a "precautionary principle" about certain technologies just because we do not know what the long-term consequences of manufacturing and using them are inhibits technological growth (Burgess).

Media provide platforms to laypersons to present their stories of interactions with EMFs and their situated knowledges of living in proximity of cell towers. These stories from concerned citizens circulating in media often get categorized as "anecdotal evidence." Anecdotal evidence matters in shaping public health policy but it is not equated with "scientific evidence." Scientific experts often assert that epidemiology relies on the population rather than the individual. Scientific evidence is objective. Anecdotal evidence is too subjective, too idiosyncratic (individualistic), and hence not generalizable (Moore and Stilgoe). That being said, the affective charge of anecdotal evidence can impact policy-making when, as in the case of EMF, scientific evidence is inconclusive. Examining lay testimonies in television shows and documentaries, I analyze what is achieved politically and epistemologically, through the presentation of anecdotal evidence in mediated arenas.

The chapter is divided into three sections. In the first section, I discuss the nature of risks from EMF emissions. Over the last 29 years, there has been much speculation about risks from cell masts and cellular communication, and yet the scientific community has not been able to reach any consensus about the potential damage from cell tower radiation. There is considerable uncertainty regarding both measuring cell antenna signals and the effects of such radiation. Media plays a special role in amplifying and attenuating such "uncertain risks." Media also becomes a key arena for public appraisal of EMF risks as concerned citizens offer anecdotes from their daily experiences of living in proximity of cell towers. In the second section, I examine how a talk show interrogates expertise and privileges lay voices. Furthermore, I ascertain the possibilities afforded by different media platforms for lay publics to express their shared meanings about technologies. Often, an environmental controversy is considered to be a terrain for the experts to battle with the so-called ignorant and scientifically illiterate common people, but this kind of view eschews the fact that experts disagree among themselves as well. In the third section, I contend that there are scientific controversies where the experts are themselves divided, and experts spar with each other in mediated arenas.

Taken together, these three sections encapsulate what I understand to be mediation of expertise in environmental controversies marked by "uncertain risks." Throughout this chapter, I maintain that when we study the role of media in environmental controversies, we should consider a wide range of media because different media genres and platforms cover the same technology or controversy differently. Furthermore, I examine not only media's epistemological role but also their phenomenological dimension (Grusin). The televisual testimonies of relatives of cancer patients living next to cell towers have an affective charge: they move people to tears, they mobilize communities to act, and they stimulate fears in audiences about the invisible radiation from such infrastructures. Such embodied understandings of media (that also account for the materiality of risky infrastructures) are key to appreciating how media complicates expert discourses and plays a role in troubling notions of risk grounded in scientific objectiveness. Borrowing from work by Brian Wynne and Ann Garcia Hom (and her research colleagues), this chapter attempts to understand the work of mediation in foregrounding EMF risks within a "radical constructivist epistemology" that believes in risk being defined by and subjected to multiple interpretations by wider publics beyond scientific experts.[1]

"Uncertain Risks" from EMF

Mobile phones and cell towers are not the only emitters of EMFs. Electromagnetic fields are generated by many electrical devices, including vacuum cleaners, electric razors, computers, and hair dryers. Since the late 1970s in Canada and Australia, EMF scare from high-voltage electricity transmission lines and electrical appliances resulted in a number of environmental controversies (Mercer; Mitchell and Cambrosio). More recently, there were fresh controversies in Northern California with regard to installation of wireless smart meters (Hess and Coley). Mobile phones and cell towers coordinate together so as to maintain cellular communication, and this leads to emission of non-ionizing electromagnetic radiations. Such radiations are different from ionizing radiation of X-rays and radioactive nuclides. It is well established by now that ionizing radiation can break molecules and hence cause genetic mutation and cancer. However, non-ionizing EMFs from cell phones and mobile towers are known to cause heating effects. What remains uncertain are the biological effects (that is, non-thermal effects) of cell antenna signals. Wireless smart meters and wireless routers also emit similar radio waves (at similar radio frequencies) to cell antennas, and the non-thermal effects of exposure to wireless signals are also uncertain.

When the cell tower radiation controversy broke out in India, cellular operators swore that they were abiding by the International Commission on Non-Ionizing Radiation Protection (ICNIRP) guidelines, which set the threshold level of cell tower signals to be $4.5 \, W/m^2$. To demonstrate that it was committed to a precautionary approach, the Indian Department of Telecommunications (DoT) reduced the EMF emission levels to $0.45 \, W/m^2$. This reduction of the threshold emission level to one-tenth of the prevailing ICNIRP norms did not satisfy dissident scientists and anti-radiation activists. These stakeholders suggested that ICNIRP guidelines were based on acute exposure and not chronic exposure, and that furthermore, one had to consider the biological effects of chronic exposure rather than heating effects resulting from acute exposure. They pointed out cancers close to towers where the recorded power density of electromagnetic radiation was $0.001 \, W/m^2$ and marked out the bodies of the children and the elderly to be particularly vulnerable to EMFs (Mukherjee "Mediating Infrastructures").

Cell antenna signals "can warm cells, boil water and stimulate chemical reactions," but they cannot break molecular bonds or lead genes to mutate. Can something be a carcinogen without damaging the DNA? Nuclear radiation and X-rays can damage DNA but cell antenna signals cannot. That however does not rule them out as potential carcinogens. There are carcinogens that have the ability to chemically modify DNA without causing mutations. However, medical oncologist Siddhartha Mukherjee reassures that at the (low) power levels that cell towers and mobile phones operate, it has been epidemiologically difficult to establish that RF energy at non-thermal intensities causes cancer. That said, scientific studies have not overruled the possibility that chronic exposure to cell antenna signals can stimulate chemical reactions that might aggravate/accelerate tumors and/or physiological (brain glucose) activity.

There is a particular group of "electrosensitives," who are hypersensitive to the frequencies of EMFs and have complained of dizziness, sleeplessness, headaches, and hair loss from living close to power lines and/or cell masts. Electrosensitives talk of "electrosmog": for this population group, electromagnetic waves are also polluters of the environment just like coal or other fossil fuels. Many electrosensitives have fled electromagnetic pollution in many parts of the United States to seek refuge in one inconspicuous pocket of the country: Green Bank, West Virginia. The Green Bank region is a WiFi quiet zone, and electrosensitives can live peacefully there without having to encounter a wireless router or a cell tower. The Federal Communications Commission built the National Radio Quiet Zone in Green Bank in 1958 to protect the National Radio Astronomy Observatory's sensitive radio telescopes from interference (Brodkin).

While the examples of electrosensitives might be considered an exception, many radio-frequency scientists and medical oncologists suggest that neural impulses (that maintain brain–body coordination) in human bodies interact with electromagnetic fields such as cell antenna signals. Even as the effects of these interactions remain uncertain, scientists indicate that there is no human body–mobile phone/cell tower barrier because signals from both seem to be interacting/interfering with one another. The human body is also part of the electromagnetic environment created by cell antenna singals as the impulses within the body vibrate and interefere with the electromagnetic fields of antenna radiation. The environment imagined in the molecular-atomic level therefore becomes a "bioelectromagnetic terrain" (see Mitchell and Cambrosio). Such phenomenological attunements of the human body (considered at the molecular level and not the molar level) to the electromagnetic environment make it critical that we pay attention to the affective dimensions of media, their ability to impact the phenomenological sensorium. Here media also needs to be thought broadly and should not be restricted to media coverage. Media objects include radiation detectors, microwave ovens, aluminum foils, and the bodies of animals and humans, and the concept of "mediation" enables us to understand the way these media objects intermedially interact with one another to help humans perceive the invisble radiation (for more, see Mukherjee "Do Cellphones Cause Brain Cancer?").

Sociologist of science, Adam Burgess has examined mobile phone radiation and cell mast controversies in the UK. Burgess suggests that media campaigns and aggressive reportage by the *Sunday Times* and *Express* newspapers led to public fears about mobile phones and cell towers. I appreciate Burgess' criticism of media campaigns for spreading fear about mobile phone signals, but disagree with him that media is only capable of creating paranoia about emerging technologies. Burgess seems preoccupied with media effects, and especially the headlines of newspapers, and does not discuss how any particular media genre or format is produced, and how this production has a role to play in portraying risks. He is unable to acknowledge how exactly televisual testimonies of relatives of cancer patients affectively move audiences. Furthermore, he does not sufficiently consider the affective dimension of mediation: the ability of media coverage (talk shows/documentary interviews), media objects (cell phones) and media infrastructures (cell towers) to modulate bodily sensations. As a result, Burgess remains within the evidentiary and epidemiological paradigm of the Social Amplification of Risk Framework, which is one kind of sociology of risk literature that does not engage with the popular, speculative, and affective paradigm of mediation.[2] Affect as emotion and visceral intensity is not fundamentally opposed to knowing/knowledge (see Soneryd).[3] Being emotionally moved by patient testimonies and being viscerally affected by cell phone/cell antenna signals contributes to a sensory knowledge, and is part of a phenomenological adjustment to the environment.

Experts vis-à-vis Laypersons

Since 2010, there have been reports in the Indian news media about cancer cases among urban residents living close to cell antennas. Some experts dismissed these stories as propaganda and mere anecdotal evidence. The television channel NDTV's celebrity anchor Barkha Dutt took up the cell tower radiation issue on September 16, 2012 in an episode entitled "Cell phone towers: India's safety check." Around that time, the new norms had just been announced by the government and the show became a place to debate whether the norms were adequate to ensure the safety of Indian citizens.

NDTV and Barkha Dutt's achievement was to assemble the whole cast of social actors from powerful experts to invited citizens related to the controversy into one studio at the same time. The talk show was not like a public hearing called by the government to achieve a consensus among stakeholders about whether a development project related to building a dam or nuclear reactor should be allowed to go ahead. That said, this talk show did share a number of similarities with such a public hearing; chief among them was that it gathered stakeholders and provided them with a platform to debate. *We the People* gathered cellular operators, gynecologists, radio-frequency experts, anti-radiation activists, concerned citizens, and telecom regulators associated with the cell tower radiation controversy in one studio along with a studio audience and an audience outside the television studio who were watching the show "live."

Science studies literature is full of scholarly preoccupation with inclusive participation exercises in public consultations about science in the form of consensus conferences, public hearings, and hybrid forums (see Callon et al.; Rip). Talk shows like *We the People* must also be considered as key venues where public environmental controversy unfolds. Talk shows dealing with issues of environment and technoscience might just be the empirical sites where science studies and television studies scholars can traffic in ideas about expert–layperson dialogues. Sociologists of science such as Callon et al. propose hybrid forums as a way to democratize science through a move from "delegative democracy" to a "dialogic democracy" where the gap between "laypersons" and "specialists" and that between "ordinary citizens" and "professional politicians" is reduced (127). Television studies scholars, Livingstone and Lunt find that talk shows authenticate subjective experiences of common people and challenge experts to translate their language of expertise into the language of lay experience in order to gain credibility for expert knowledge.

During the show, Dutt mediates between lay perspectives and expert commentaries. First, Rabbani Garg gives a somber account of her unsuccessful attempts to understand what really caused her young daughter's malignant tumor. She ends with the question: "What is the appropriate distance? What is the distance the tower should be from your house?" When Dutt puts the same question to the regulator and policy maker T. Chandrashekhar, she is careful to maintain a calm atmosphere among audience members and participants for the telecom secretary to offer his answer. Chandrashekhar mentions how a number of other variables such as height of buildings on the signal path and the direction of antenna play a role, which make it difficult to give a universally applicable value for safe distance from the tower. Chandrashekhar also speculates that a number of the "troublesome cases" occurred in sites where the towers were installed in violation of existing guidelines. He further remarks that the new stricter norms were set by the central government-run DoT, but the enforcement of norms and permission to set up towers was under the jurisdiction of the state governments. To this answer, Dutt replies: "Sir, these are lives, and if they are lost in the maze of bureaucracy between the center and state, I do not know whether this will comfort this mother of a seven year old battling cancer." In saying this, Dutt clearly positions herself with "the people," the vulnerable, and the affected. As a journalist hosting the show, she needs to be and is somewhat objective about managing her guests, but at times, she has to make sure that lay voices are heard over those of experts.

Talk shows do have a democratizing potential and *We the People* exemplifies such a potential. That said, one of the reasons *We the People* aired an episode dealing with cell tower radiation is because this issue was raised by upper middle class urbanites, who are precisely the ideal target audience for the show. *We the People* is a show which is committed to progressive causes and it needs to be celebrated for providing civil society members a platform to raise their legitimate concerns, and yet at the same time, it does have a class bias. For example, *We the People* has not raised the issue of increasing nuclearization of India. It has not dealt with the plight of affected communities living nearby nuclear reactors and uranium mines in India, a task that seems to be taken up by committed political documentary filmmakers.[4] That said, in Dutt's talk show, experts are held accountable. Dutt as the moderator/anchor interrogates expertise by changing her subject positions as she moves from experts to affected members.

Counter-Expertise: Arguments among Experts

During the cell tower radiation controversy, there were disputes between experts about what radiation level was safe enough. Antenna specialist, Girish Kumar, mentioned to me that he put the limit to be -15 dBm based on the contentious 2007 BioInitiative Report, which posits a much lower limit than both the ICNIRP standards and the new standards that were later applied in India (which were one-tenth of the earlier ICNIRP value). Kumar applied this threshold while designing radiation detectors which beeped red, connoting danger whenever the cell antenna EMF emissions crossed that limit. As a result, common people using that detector started feeling unsafe at a much lower signal level than accepted norms. In a 2013 newspaper article, K. S. Parthasarathy, former secretary of the Atomic Energy Regulatory Board, disputed Kumar's reliance on the BioInitiative Report. Parthasarathy argued that the BioInitiative Report was prepared by biased advocacy groups. Partahsarathy pointed out that because Kumar relied on a contentious report and on semi-epidemiological studies which were at best "anecdotal evidence," his prescribed threshold value and radiation device should be discredited.

Such debates played out in other media arenas. Consider this conversation that CNBC AWAAZ is having during a televised debate about the new regulations the Telecom Regulatory Authority of India (TRAI) has passed regarding cell tower radiation:

> GIRISH KUMAR: To those who live close to cell towers and absorb radiation 24 hours a day … a half-hearted approach has been taken. 9.26 has been reduced to 0.92, but it should have gotten down to .001 … otherwise, people's health and the environment are affected. You would never see a bird perched on a cell tower.
> RAJAN MATTHEWS: I would like to categorically say that all of Mr. Girish's numbers are bogus.… He makes people afraid of radiation and then goes and sells a device that is supposed to shield them from it. He has a vested interest here. So I would not believe what Mr. Girish is saying.

Girish Kumar is suggesting that the reduction in limits prescribed by TRAI is insufficient as it only takes into account acute exposure, not the chronic exposure that the people who live close to the towers are subjected to. Rajan Matthews, who heads the Cellular Operators Association of India, is disputing Kumar's claims because he does not want a further reduction of signal levels as that would affect the cellular network's ability to support calls. Furthermore, he does not want cell towers to be regarded negatively by the public. Kumar and Matthews sparred during the *We the People* debate as well and when Kumar brought this issue in the talk show, Matthews did not even let him finish and argued that Professor Kumar was falsifying the report. Matthews even cited Parthasarathy's article that appeared in the newspaper *The Hindu*, which alleged that Kumar was acting less as a scientist and more as an environmental advocate. So here, Matthews is opposing one expert's opinion by citing another expert's comment. In an interview with me, Kumar remembered the altercation with Matthews in *We the People*, and mentioned that the perceived liveness of television shows, the realization that there is an audience outside watching him live, did make him more combative. Televisual argumentation becomes laced with affect with the perceived liveness of talk shows and news.

The cell phone and cell tower radiation issue has experts divided not just in India but across the world. While Parthasarathy continues to support the dominant epidemiological paradigm that cell phone/cell tower effects are limited to short-term thermal effects, Kumar as a dissident scientist asks for considering long-term biological effects. Such a clash between experts with respect to radio-frequency energy of cell towers/mobile phones is not restricted to India but unfolds in many parts of the world. In the United States, United Kingdom, and Sweden, there is a small group of counter-experts who have contested government and industry assurances of safety from cellular communication. The documentary film *Mobilize* seeks to challenge the assumption that mobile phones are benign devices. As a way of presenting credible evidence, the documentary juxtaposes together testimonies of dissident scientists and policy makers and in the process creates a "network of counter-expertise." *Mobilize* is extremely critical about the way the Specific Absorption Rate (SAR) testing is conducted by the cell phone regulation industry.

Radio waves can penetrate the human body by a few centimeters, leading the water in the body to absorb RF energy, which causes heating. The signal strength of cell antenna and mobile phone radiation determines the amount of heating that takes place. The SAR of energy is a measure of the absorption of radio waves (Drake). In the case of mobile phones, especially because they are held close to ears, the SAR can affect the brain. Every mobile phone manufactured is tested for SAR but the brain standard used for such simulated tests is that of a 6'2" adult male. Several counter-experts like epidemiologist and founding director of the Center for Environmental Oncology, Devra Davis, in the documentary *Mobilize* explain that this standard testing procedure does not take into account the fact that a child's brain absorbs far more radiation than an adult man's brain. Several other experts such Joel Moskowitz (Director for the Center of Community Health, UC Berkeley) and Debbie Raphael (Director of the Department of Toxic Substances) explain that these SAR tests had been established 16 years ago and since then, much has changed with regard to the kind of smartphones manufactured and what we know about cell phone radiation. They express disappointment that despite these changes, there has been no reexamination of the standard procedures for testing. SAR at best tests for (only) heating effects, and there are no tests for biological effects.

By challenging the assumptions of the SAR test and by pointing out the lack of tests for non-heating effects of cell phones, these counter-experts suggest that the cellphone industry is not concerned with the public health of its consumers, and that a number of prominent experts might be conniving with the cellular industry to make sure that few tests are done that reflect the industry in bad light. These counter-voices are rarely heard together in media. The documentary stitches their commentaries together, creating a body of counterevidence that challenges the dominant paradigm regarding mobile phone radiation.[5]

Lay Expertise, Anecdotal Evidence, and Precautionary Principle

Lay participation in scientific discussions have taken many forms such as public interpretation of scientific claims, public participation in consensus conferences, and the ability of lay publics to speak in the language of science. Lay expertise can be understood in several ways. It can be experiential knowledge based on context and the ability to come up with social meanings, as posited by Brian Wynne in his 1992 study of Cumbria sheep farmers. Steven Epstein has deployed the term to discuss the interventions by AIDS treatment activists to make credible scientific and political claims so as to be made part of the decision-making group related to "design, conduct, and interpretation of drugs" (410). I suggest that lay expertise can also be used for the efficacious presentation of "anecdotal evidence" by so-called laypersons in mediated arenas. In the citadel of expertise, anecdotal evidence is considered as being too specific to the individual and hence neither generalizable nor actionable (Moore and Stilgoe). At the same time, anecdotal evidence privileges lived experience of sufferers coping with environmental effects, and media become an outlet for affective rendering of anecdotal evidence. I argue that emerging mediations of risks afford anecdotal evidence a particularly potent affective charge that compels policymakers to consider lay expertise and adopt precautionary principle.

British sociologist of science, Brian Wynne has formulated and championed the notion of the "precautionary principle," which suggests that when scientists are not in a position to prove that a risky technology will not be harmful in the future, policymakers must espouse precaution and strictly regulate the development of technology (Wynne and Mayer).[6] According to Wynne, the onus of proving that a technology is harmful should not be on environmental activists, but it is the scientists who should be able to prove that a technology is not dangerous. This has been an influential view within policy circles especially in the United Kingdom. While many reports on mobile tower radiation including those by ICNIRP and World Health Organization (WHO) suggest that acute exposure to signals from cell antennas in limited doses will not result in cancer, these same reports are uncertain about long-term effects of chronic exposure to cell antenna signals.

While the cell tower radiation issue achieved national significance in India in 2011, it has been in the news in the UK since the late 1990s. Burgess' aforementioned criticism of the UK mobile phone radiation and cell mast controversies is also a critique of the British government's espousing of the precautionary principle. Acknowledging this fear, the government imposed stricter regulations as a way to be politically responsive toward public perception. Burgess argues that such a decision by the government not only affected the growth of cellphone industry in the UK, but also did not allay public apprehension. The British public felt that because the government lowered the threshold levels of permissible radiation, the mobile phone radiations and cell antenna signals must be harmful. The lay public did not completely trust the government and apprehended that the government was hiding the finer details about what was really wrong about such cellular radiations.

I am not suggesting that media help skeptics and activists produce risk from nowhere. Rather, I am arguing that mediation ignites the intuitive dimension in humans; that is, mediation creates doubts that circulate in society out of phenomenological encounters between human bodies, media images, and technologies. I contend that the phenomenological dimension of mediation gives us clues as to why both the government and the wider public are influenced by mediated lay perspectives which makes them override erstwhile privileged expert opinion. I shall now substantiate my argument by examining two presentations of the same anecdotal evidence in two different media platforms: a talk show and a lifestyle show.

In *We the People*, Rabani Garg, whose seven-year-old daughter has cancer, was interviewed by Barkha Dutt, and her tearful testimony moved people. During the show as Garg is speaking, the camera frames her face in a close-up and, at other times, we see Dutt and Garg framed together with Dutt's hand over Garg's shoulder—a gesture of empathy and solidarity (see Figure 9.2). On October 6, 2012, Garg also appeared on *Living it Up*, a lifestyle program on the channel CNN-IBN, but here her testimony was delivered beyond the confines of a television studio in the lane next to her house. *Living it Up* often relies on social actors to reenact their stories about fighting illness on location. In the course of the reenactment Garg is put into the situation when she first encountered the towers and it dawned on her that they might be the cause of cancer (see Figure 9.3). While in *We the People*, her testimony is inside a television studio, in *Living it Up*, she offers us a "situated testimony" from the place when she first recognized the deleterious effects of proximate cell towers (Walker). As audiences, it is possible that we are moved in a different way from Garg's testimony in *Living it Up* than in *We the People*.

By re-presenting Garg next to the tower, using her embodied presence in a mobile tower's field of influence (the strength of a tower's signal is inversely proportional to the square of the distance

Mediating Expertise

Figure 9.2 Dutt with Garg (a gesture of solidarity)
Snapshot of *We the People*, NDTV

Figure 9.3 Garg outside her house looking at the cell tower
Source: Snapshot Living it Up, CNN-IBN

from it), the lifestyle show wants to emplace audiences in that location, in that moment. The audience gets a sense of the affective intensity which would have circulated back-and-forth between Garg and the mobile tower when her eyes transfixed themselves on the tower for the first time. These televisual images could be another conduit for "affective resonances" (Mukherjee "Mediating Infrastructures") across cell towers and the bodies of television audiences. After watching the show, next time when they see a tower near their house, the television audiences could have premonitions about the tower's future effects on them. Affect cannot be fixed, it circulates, and it operates not only through conscious emotions, but through unsayable feelings and molecular-level (not molar-level) impulses (Massumi).

Analyzing the implications of Garg's testimonies rendered in a talk show and a lifestyle show also suggests that different platforms provide different affordances of positing evidence, staging rhetoric, and touching audiences emotionally. The situated testimony of Garg in *Living it Up* concretizes the fact that her situated knowledge of living close to cell towers should be considered important for future policy regulations related to cell towers.

The positioning of Garg next to the tower was not a single/singular mediated event or instance. Across television shows and local vernacular (Hindi) newspapers, there were people posing next to towers and rendering their story. The towers loomed in background as frustrated and anxious victims testified about their problems (of headache, sleeplessness, and cancer), sometimes even wielding radiation detectors. Here there was not so much a quantifiable/generalizable pattern that got created, but rather an accumulation of anecdotal evidence which got repeated as it circulated across media platforms. Such reiteration and circulation of stories transformed them into evidence at least among a popular collective, which then made institutions bend. Even as popular epidemiology runs into trouble with the evidentiary paradigm because feeling risk is often a singular, unverifiable, and therefore not quantifiable into generality, the collective observation, accumulation of stories, and circulation bespeak a different evidentiary paradigm for popular expertise.

Linda Soneryd argues that public protests against 3G cellphones in Sweden arose not only because of lack of knowedge about invisible radiation but also because of bodily interactions between humans and mobile phone infrastructure. Soneryd explains that the reasons for public fear have as much to do with comprehension (conscious knowledge) as with prehension (bodily sensations). I have contended that the public fear and uncertainties about radiation in India are not just because of biased media coverage—they include bodily sensations in relation to media infrastructures and affective modulations of mediated images. Thus, one needs to understand mediation not as some discrete media object or media text but as an envelope around the social, where matters of experience are as critical as matters of deliberation/discourse. With such a notion of mediation, we come to realize the role media plays in shaping the precautionary principle. The precautionary principle is not only based on media's ability to repeat and spread discourse, but also on the tasks of mediation in circulating affect. Such a notion of mediation helps to foreground the situated knowledges of laypersons, the shared understanding that an affected community might have about proximate towers. The challenge for scientific policy-making is how scientists and experts negotiate the embodied knowledges of common people in this emerging mediated environment of circulating affects.

Conclusion

The difficulty of EMF risk management is aggravated by the fact that neither experts nor laypersons know enough about chronic exposure to electrical and magnetic signals. In the EMF issue, like many other environmental controversies, there is a gap between quantitative risk assessments and public perceptions about risky signals, and media can play a role in bridging that gap and/or widening it.

It should be clear by now that mediation of expertise is incomplete without taking into account how media is used by both experts and laypersons to make claims and change policy about risky technologies. In the course of this essay, I have provided several examples where media provide the arena for experts and activists to interact with one another. While I have discussed a number of cases where media is critical of experts and powerful policymakers, in many situations, media organizations toe the line of experts. Even as there are many media formats and platforms that afford an opportunity for lay and popular perspectives to be presented, it is often the case that it is the science experts who are extolled by media as credible.

Science experts sometimes are the source of information for mediapersons and such experts also provide science journalists access to technoscience spaces beyond their reach. In such circumstances, mediapersons/journalists feel too indebted to experts and are unable to interrogate expertise. This is especially the case with regard to nuclear science where a lot of information is kept secret in the name of national security, energy security, and critical infrastructure. With regard to the cell phone industry, mediapersons are often perceived by the general public to be silent about criticizing cellular operators. The cellular phone industry is very wealthy, wielding enormous influence on the political economy of media industries. In India, cellular companies are prime sources of advertizing revenue for media organizations. One newspaper editor told me that when her newspaper started publishing articles criticizing the cell tower regulation laws, a particular telecom company stopped publishing ads in the paper.

In this essay, I have argued that studying mediation of *lay or popular expertise* becomes a way of tracing how perceptions about risky infrastructures circulate among publics (taking the form of news and gossip) and assessing the possibilities of redrawing the boundaries between expert knowledge and lay knowledge. Indeed, if we are to make sense of mediation of risks, then we should be prepared to understand how such mediation affects expert–layperson boundaries: how could lay presentation of anecdotal evidence look credible, and how could expert presentation of facts seem suspect?

There have been proposals to bridge the fields of science and technology studies (STS) and social movement studies (SMS) in order to grasp more fully the interaction between science and publics (Hess; Welsh and Wynne). One of the key focal points in this approach has been "imaginaries": shared understandings, visions, and meanings that science has about its publics, and that the wider public has about science. By circulating news, rumor, gossip, and information, mediation is key to shaping how experts imagine lay publics, and how common people have shared meanings about the activities of scientific experts. Thus, media studies of technological risks should join the conversations taking place between STS and SMS about understanding the interaction between experts and the wider public.

One of the key public imaginaries about the mobile phone and cell tower companies is that they are very rich, and in order to save their business, these corporations will go to any extent to prevent information or research that harms their reputation. Often, a comparison is drawn between the telecom companies and the tobacco industry. Some media campaigns have considered it safe to bet that "cell towers" might become the "next tobacco" when more research would have been done on long-term exposure to EMFs.[7] This premonition became more and more potent when it was suggested that for many years, cigarette companies had scuttled any research on the health effects of tobacco, and cellular operators were also very powerful and had been doing the same.

In the documentary *Mobilize*, an image where two cigarettes seem to be jutting out from (in place of/forming) a mobile phone antenna, suggests that cell phones are the cigarettes of the twenty-first century (Figure 9.4). This image captures the public sentiment well: an imaginary that is not just technical but also social, and which indicates what people find problematic about the cell phone industry. The industry is just not transparent and democratic enough. Managing technologies is not about getting technical specifications right, but about being able to be open to doubts and anxieties expressed by concerned consumer-citizens of such technologies. The statutory warning that cigarette companies carry nowadays is missing from cell phones, and so this subvertisement carries a warning at the top right hand corner which reads, "Quitting Cellphones Now Greatly Reduces Serious Risk to Your Health." Another imaginary concerns the association of cellphones with cars: since mobile phones are technologies that afford so many conveniences just like a car, consumers are unable to stop using it. One cannot abandon cars even though they cause air pollution and similarly, one cannot leave the cellphones even as they lead to electromagnetic pollution.

Figure 9.4 Cigarette in cell phone's antenna ad spoof
Source: Snapshot from *Mobilize* (2015)

While studying imaginaries, a media studies approach relying only on discourse and framing shall not suffice, for imaginaries "operate … in the understudied regions between imagination and action, between discourse and decision" (Jasanoff and Kim). Such imaginaries, which are sociotechnical, are as much about cultural meanings and embodied experiences as they are about the materialities of risky infrastructures. To illustrate what kind of mediation accounts for such dense sociotechnical imaginaries, let me end this chapter with an anecdote.

During my fieldwork in December 2012, Sudhir Kasliwal, the brother of a cancer patient in the city of Jaipur who resided close to a cluster of cell towers, spoke of his efforts to get the towers removed. Kasliwal was convinced that it was the signals emitted by cell towers that were causing his brother's cancer. The municipal authorities and telecom operators resisted Kasliwal's efforts, but reassured him that they would reduce the signal levels emitted by the towers. Kasliwal felt that they would trick him and suddenly decide to increase the power density of electromagnetic radiations. He regularly monitored the transmission power levels with a radiation detector to check whether or not they remained below the norm. The technological mediation of radiation detectors helped Kasliwal perceive the cell tower radiation that he could not see, smell, or taste in the form of glowing LED lights. However, this did not give him complete satisfaction. He was only convinced that the radiation levels had been truly reduced when he saw peacocks return to his garden nine years after the mobile towers had been erected. The return of the peacocks was a sign of things returning to normal. He relied more on the peacock's perception of radiation than the readings of the radiation detector. The peacock's body here mediates the infrastructure of cell towers: at the molecular level, impulses in the peacock's body interact and interfere with electromagnetic signals of the towers.

This anecdote, one among many that people living close to cell towers shared with me, suggests that in situations of uncertainty, perceptions of technology are articulated using vernacular mythologies of the everyday. In this story of experiences and activities, we sense the merging together of discourses, affects, and practices as relationships between human bodies and animal bodies continue to emerge. Here mediation takes an inter-species turn (see Haraway), a turn that also has a cultural dimension.

In this chapter, I have posited a notion of mediation that holds onto traditional media coverage but includes intermediality, affective resonance, and attention to media practices, and I believe such a wholesome notion of mediation is able to appreciate the pervasive and ephemeral quality of imaginaries. Such a notion of mediation also calls for a careful examination of the interactions between different stakeholders of an environmental controversy. Will these interactions between peacocks and cell towers and between Kasliwal and peacock ever find a place in policy discussions on regulation of EMFs? I hope they do because such anecdotal evidence and popular expertise will have lasting public circulation and EMF policy-making cannot ignore public perception. Policy wonks and elite expertise will have to consider people's initmate and visceral engagement with EMFs, and "mediating expertise" gives a sense of how mediation of such complicated sensoriums feels like.

Notes

1 This radically social constructivist notion of risk is developed by the anthropological branch of Science and Technology Studies, and is very useful for my essay here. That said, this subfield has overlooked both the centrality of media in defining risk and the specificity of media form and genre in communicating risk.
2 Hom et al. categorize Burgess' work to fall under the Social Amplification of Risk Framework which tends to link scientific knowledge with experts and "objective" risk and then contrasts it with lay-public's perceptions which are considered intuitions/emotions and subjective risks fanned by the media.
3 Soneryd challenges some of the layperson–expert boundaries that Burgess creates. She suggests that "prehensions" can also enable gaining knowledge about risky technologies and science cannot always be considered objective.
4 There is a tradition of committed documentary filmmaking interrogating extractive development projects in India, and the documentaries related to nuclearization of India are a part of that tradition.
5 There are exceptions though, and sometimes television channels known for being paragons of "balance" and "objectivity" can be lop-sided as well. In November 2007, BBC One's program *Panorama* dealt with the issue of wireless signals in an episode titled "Wi-Fi: A Warning Signal." Many BBC audiences as well as telecom and radio-frequency experts felt the program exaggerated the evidence for concern about the potential health hazards of wireless technology. Several commentators agreed that it was legitimate for BBC to have covered the issue of wireless signal hazards once the chairman of the Health Protection Agency, Sir William Stewart, had raised concerns. However, what made BBC's show unbalanced is that there were disproportionately more experts who opined that WiFi is dangerous than the count of experts who thought WiFi signals in controlled levels were absolutely fine. A key consideration for mediating expertise in environmental controversies where experts are themselves divided is then to be balanced in choosing the number of experts who are shown to be arguing with each other on both sides. Obviously, all of us can have different opinions about whether objective journalism is even possible, and whether objectivity is necessarily a virtue or desired goal in journalism. That said, both science and journalism do make claims to be "objective."
6 Cass Sunstein has criticized invoking the precautionary principle based on "public hysteria" instead of expert analysis. According to Sunstein, in such a situation of uncertainty about emerging technologies, where majority of the expert community agrees that there are no risks, one should not put a moratorium about use of such technologies merely because a large section of the general public has fears about the consequences. Sunstein's critics have noted that his model of risk perception insufficiently engages with cultural analysis. According to Dan Kahan what Sunstein calls "public hysteria" is actually expression of competing cultural values.
7 Anthony Burgess mentions a similar rumor in the late 1990s in the United Kingdom.

Works Cited

Beck, Ulrich. *Risk Society: Towards a New Modernity*. Sage, 1992.
Brodkin, Jon. "Electrosensitives Flock to Wi-fi Quiet Zone as Teens Set Up Rogue Hotspots." *ArsTechnica*, 2015, http://arstechnica.com/information-technology/2015/01/electrosensitives-seek-haven-in-wi-fi-quiet-zone-as-teens-set-up-hotspots. Accessed July 12, 2016.
Burgess, Adam. *Cellular Phones, Public Fears, and a Culture of Precaution*. Cambridge UP, 2004.
Callon, Michel, Pierre Lascoumes, and Yannick Barthe. *Acting in an Uncertain World: An Essay on Technical Democracy*. MIT Press, 2001.
Cottle, Simon. "Ulrich Beck, Risk Society, and the Media: Catastrophic View." *European Journal of Communication*, vol. 13, no. 1, 1998, pp. 5–32.

Douglas, Mary. "Risk as a Forensic Resource." *Daedalus*, vol. 119, no. 4, 1990, pp. 1–16.

Drake, Frances. "Mobile Phone Masts: Protesting the Scientific Evidence." *Public Understanding of Science*, vol. 15, no. 4, 2006, pp. 387–410.

Epstein, Steven. "The Construction of Lay Expertise: AIDS Activism and the Forging of Credibility in the Reform of Clinical Trials." *Science, Technology, and Human Values*, vol. 20, no. 4, 1995, pp. 408–437.

Grusin, Richard. "Radical Mediation." *Critical Inquiry*, vol. 42, no. 1, 2015, pp. 124–148.

Haraway, Donna *The Companion Species Manifesto: Dogs, People, and Significant Otherness*. Prickly Paradigm Press, 2003.

Hess, David. "Publics as Threats? Integrating Science and Technology Studies and Social Movement Studies." *Science as Culture*, vol. 24, no. 1, 2015, pp. 69–82.

Hess, David and Jonathan Coley. "Wireless Smart Meters and Public Acceptance: The Environment, Limited Choices, and Precautionary Politics." *Public Understanding of Science*, vol. 23, no. 6, 2014, pp. 688–702.

Hom, Anna Garcia, Ramon Moles Plaza, and Rachel Palmén. "The Framing of Risk and Implications for Policy and Governance: The Case of EMF." *Public Understanding of Science*, vol. 20, no. 3, 2011, pp. 319–333.

Jasanoff, Sheila and Kim Sang-Hyun. "Containing the Atom: Sociotechnical Imaginaries and Nuclear Power in the United States and South Korea." *Minerva*, vol. 47, no. 2, 2009, pp. 119–146.

Kahan, Dan. "Fear of Democracy: A Cultural Evaluation of Sunstein on Risk." *Yale Faculty Scholarship Series*, January 1, 2006, http://digitalcommons.law.yale.edu/fss_papers/104. Accessed January 31, 2018.

Kurtz, Howard. *Hot Air: All Talk, All the Time*. Basic Books, 1996.

Livingstone, Sonia and Peter Lunt. *Talk on Television: Audience Participation and Public Debate*. Routledge, 1994.

Massumi, Brian. *Movement, Affect, Sensation: Parables for the Virtual*. Duke UP, 2002.

Mercer, David. "Scientific Method Discourses in the Construction of 'EMF Science': Interests, Resources and Rhetoric in Submissions to a Public Inquiry." *Social Studies of Science*, vol. 32, no. 2, 2002, pp. 205–233.

Mitchell, Lisa M. and Alberto Cambrosio. "The Invisible Topography of Power: Electromagnetic Fields, Bodies, and the Environment." *Social Studies of Science*, vol. 27, 1997, pp. 221–271.

Moore, Alfred and Jack Stilgoe. "Experts and Anecdotes: The Role of 'Anecdotal Evidence' in Public Scientific Controversies." *Science, Technology, & Human Values*, vol. 34, no. 5, 2009, pp. 654–677.

Mukherjee, Rahul "Mediating Infrastructures: (Im)Mobile Toxicity and Cell Antenna Publics." *Sustainable Media: Critical Approaches to Media and Environment*, edited by Nicole Starosielski and Janet Walker, Routledge, 2016, pp. 95–112.

Mukherjee, Siddhartha. "Do Cellphones Cause Brain Cancer?" *New York Times*, April 13, 2011, www.nytimes.com/2011/04/17/magazine/mag-17cellphones-t.html?_r=1. Accessed July 12, 2016.

Parthasarathy, K. S. "Myths about Radiation Leaks from Cell Towers." *The Economic Times*, January 31, 2013, http://articles.economictimes.indiatimes.com/2013-01-31/news/36658996_1_icnirp-cell-phone-towers-bioinitiative-report. Accessed July 2013.

Rip, Arie. "Constructing Expertise: In a Third Wave of Science Studies?" *Social Studies of Science*, vol. 33, no. 3, 2003, pp. 419–434.

Soneryd, Linda. "Deliberations on the Unknown, the Unsensed, and the Unsayable?: Public Protests and the Development of Third-Generation Mobile Phones in Sweden." *Science, Technology & Human Values*, vol. 32, no. 3, 2007, pp. 287–314.

Sunstein, Cass. *Laws of Fear: Beyond the Precautionary Principle*. Cambridge UP, 2005.

Walker, Janet. "Rights and Return: Perils and Fantasies of Situated Testimony after Katrina." *Documentary Testimonies: Global Archives of Suffering*, edited by Bhaskar Sarkar and Janet Walker, Routledge, 2010.

Welsh, Ian and Bryan Wynne. "Science, Scientism and Imaginaries of Publics in the UK: Passive Objects, Incipient Threats." *Science as Culture*, vol. 22, no. 4, 2013, pp. 540–566.

Wynne, Brian. "Misunderstood Misunderstanding: Social Identities and Public uptake of Science." *Public Understanding of Science*, vol. 1, 1992, pp. 281–304.

Wynne, Brian and Susan Mayer. "How Science Fails the Environment." *New Scientist*, vol. 139, no. 1876, 1993, p. 32.

PART III

TIMES

10
PREPAREDNESS DOCUMENTS AFTER THE FACT

Lindsay Thomas

We are living, it is said with good reason, in a "post-fact" era. Fake news, Facebook echo chambers, and politicians who lie openly and without consequence have all contributed to the disregard for facts seemingly prevalent in public discourse of all kinds today. Whether this is a new development—whether public discourse has ever depended to any significant degree on the facts—is of course an open question, but it is one I set aside here. Instead, I focus on what exactly living in a "post-fact" era means. While it's satisfying to equate so-called post-factual statements with lies, lying doesn't encompass the full meaning of "post-fact." We also need to consider a mode of discourse that has what John Guillory refers to as an "ultimately indeterminate relation to fact, information, and knowledge": fiction (111). Fiction is not necessarily the opposite of fact, although it is often understood that way. Rather, fiction has an "ultimately indeterminate relation to fact" because it encourages skepticism and disbelief—people who read fiction know what they read isn't real—while simultaneously depending on a kind of self-aware belief for its communicative, affective, and even epistemic power. In other words, people who read fiction also suspend the disbelief fiction cultivates in order, as Catherine Gallagher puts it, to "buy into the game" (346). They agree to believe in falsehood, to treat it *like* truth, for the sake of playing along. Fiction therefore encourages a *"willing* suspension of disbelief" that gives its readers a sense of control over their own deployment of belief (Gallagher 347). This is not only an affective stance or attitude toward knowledge; it is also an epistemological one. Fiction encourages a way of knowing that depends not on facts but rather on the decision to believe or not to believe, aligning knowledge with this kind of self-aware belief (or non-belief).

One of the assumptions of this chapter is that this way of knowing has become unmoored from the generic bounds of fiction itself and has come to describe a more general perspective on knowledge production. A different way of describing our "post-fact" era, then, would be as "pro-fiction": it is not necessarily the case that facts are no longer important to public debate or that what a fact is has lost all meaning, but rather that facts have become relative to one's beliefs. One of the things that makes this relativity so insidious, however, is how fiction has come to be understood as a source for discovering the facts. This does not mean that there is no difference between fact and fiction, however. Indeed, rather than insisting on the ultimate undecidability of these terms, or rather than taking the opposite tack and insisting on upholding the difference between them, I am instead interested in how fiction, broadly conceived, has become invested with the epistemological weight and authority of fact. This process does not necessarily involve "tricking" people into believing lies; it involves using fiction as evidence for empirical claims about what exists and what doesn't. It has to do with how what it means to *know* something in the first place is shifting.[1]

I focus here on how this shift is playing out in the realm of national security: I emphasize how fiction is operationalized through preparedness, a national security paradigm that moved to the center of U.S. policy after September 11, 2001. Preparedness seeks to train government officials and experts to respond to disasters as wide-ranging as terrorist attacks, pandemics, and hurricanes. Because the probability and severity of such events cannot be calculated, preparedness emphasizes institutional readiness and emergency management rather than prevention, teaching officials to handle a variety of potential catastrophic threats using the same protocols for response. In order to develop these procedures, it encourages the enactment of possible future disasters in the present; as Andrew Lakoff writes, it "enacts a vision of the dystopian future in order to develop a set of operational criteria for response" (253). It is one among several modes of what Ben Anderson has called "anticipatory action" (777). These modes not only use the future or a range of possible futures to justify action in the present; they also make possible futures available for intervention in the here and now. Preparedness works, in other words, not by controlling *the* future to ensure a catastrophic event does not happen, but rather by proliferating *many possible* futures in the present, possible futures to which government officials must respond, again and again, in their training. Preparedness therefore relies on fiction to produce knowledge about future catastrophes, knowledge that includes things like what such catastrophes will be like, who the first responders on the scene will be, what resources will be sent where, and how to best protect and ensure the continued functioning of vital infrastructure during a disaster.[2]

In what follows, I turn to the document, a kind of media that plays a large role in everyday knowledge production within national security organizations, to understand how preparedness uses fiction as a source for facts. I focus specifically on preparedness documents, or documents in which a governmental organization states how it intends to act to secure against some future threat.[3] As an example of what Matthew Fuller and Andrew Goffey have termed "gray" media, governmental documents tend to escape our notice.[4] This isn't because they are hard to find: since so many (unclassified) governmental documents are available online in the form of websites and PDFs, they are relatively easy to access. But even if some of us take the time to read them, their contents are mostly unremarkable, even those that are about national security. What's more, there are simply so many of these kinds of documents that reading all of them is impossible. For example, at the time of this writing, you can download over 93,000 documents about homeland security alone using the "Homeland Security Digital Library."[5] Even understanding how individual documents are tied to actual policy can be a monumental task. Mostly, these documents exist in the background as the constant hum of governmental bureaucracy.

Yet it is precisely this kind of everydayness that makes such documents important. If, as Lisa Gitelman emphasizes, it is difficult "to imagine any exemplary PDF," this should alert us to the extent to which such documents rely on their banality to function (116). In order to understand how this works, I focus here on what Jonathan Sterne refers to as the *mediality* of these documents. This means I am less concerned with the contents of individual preparedness documents, although I do use specific examples to illustrate my points, or with the media-specific properties of these documents, although all of the documents I discuss are digital. Rather, I am concerned with how these documents hook up to "a general web of practice and reference," as Sterne puts it (9). I emphasize how digital documents constitute and are constituted by "ways of doing things, institutions, and even in some cases belief systems" (Sterne 10). This means considering both how preparedness documents produce knowledge about future catastrophes, and also how the transmission and circulation of these documents through digital networks and relational databases contributes to this kind of knowledge production. It also means considering the temporality of this knowledge production, or how these documents position speculation about the future as a description of the present. Doing so will give us a different understanding of documentation, one perhaps better suited to a pro-fictional era in which some of the events we document have not occurred and cannot, by their nature as fiction, ever occur.

Speculation as Knowledge Production: The Strange Temporality of Preparedness Documents

Instead of trying to figure out exactly what a document is—as Gitelman has pointed out, scholars in bibliography and information science have been wrestling with that question for at least 100 years—we begin with what documents *do* (Gitelman 2). On this, 100 years of scholarship is clear: documents produce knowledge. Max Weber's work has been especially influential in this regard. Weber explicitly connects bureaucracy—infamously, "rule by desks"—with knowledge production via documents and documentation. For Weber, "bureaucratic administration means fundamentally domination through knowledge"; what's more, bureaucrats gain and can increase their knowledge, and hence their political power, "by the knowledge growing out of experience in the service," which includes "a special knowledge of facts" drawn from "a store of documentary material peculiar to themselves" (225). This kind of "domination through knowledge" is why Weber refers to bureaucracy as "the most rational known means of exercising authority over human beings" (223). Documents and documentation are essential to Weber's conception of the rational, impersonal, and systematic rule of bureaucracy.[6] This idea has carried through to much more recent scholarship on documents. Gitelman, for example, refers to documentation as an "epistemic practice" and to documents as "epistemic objects" that "help define and are mutually defined by the know-show function… the kind of knowing that is all wrapped up with showing, and showing wrapped with knowing" (1). The function of documents, in other words, is to produce knowledge—to show what they know, and know what they show. However, as Gitelman, following John Guillory, emphasizes, documents are not synonymous with knowledge per se. If knowledge is, according to Guillory, "a practice that organizes masses of information or data (for example, rainfall amounts) into complex structures of intelligibility and uses these structures to discover new relations and new facts," documents are what make this organization possible (110). They are "evidential structures," or "the carrier of the information and so the object of knowledge rather than knowledge itself" (Gitelman 1; Guillory 113).

Preparedness documents are also carriers of information that can be used to produce knowledge. Yet the ontological status of the facts and information they communicate is decidedly different from, say, a birth certificate or a court record. To see how, we need to spend some time with the definition of preparedness documents I laid out above. Preparedness documents are documents in which a governmental organization states how it intends to act to secure against some future threat. While such a definition is overly broad, it is useful because it allows us to glimpse the temporality of preparedness. For example, one paradigmatic example of a preparedness document is the Department of Homeland Security's *National Preparedness Goal*, which "describes the Nation's approach to preparing for the threats and hazards that pose the greatest risk to the security of the United States" (September 2011 1). This document outlines the many steps the Department of Homeland Security will take to prevent, respond to, and mitigate the effects of the "wide range of threats and hazards [that] pose a significant risk to the Nation," which includes everything from creating preparedness plans and risk assessments; to limiting access to "specific locations, information, and networks"; to conducting "tactical counterterrorism operations in multiple locations"; to ensuring that critical infrastructure is functioning and that communities can "meet basic human needs" after an event (3, 6, 7, 11). It outlines what it intends to do, which is to say what it plans to do later, at some future time. Preparedness documents, like many kinds of policy documents, are speculative in this way. But unlike other kinds of policy documents, the "threats and hazards" preparedness documents plan to secure against are future threats and hazards; they are things that "may present significant risks" to the nation (4). Preparedness documents are therefore doubly speculative: they describe how a governmental organization intends to act in the future to secure against an event that is at risk of happening at some point in the future.

What's important for our purposes, however, is how preparedness documents present this speculation as a kind of description. Note the persistent use of the present tense in the *National*

Preparedness Goal document when describing actions that will be taken: "inform all affected segments of society by all means necessary"; "establish command, control, and coordination structures within the affected community"; "stabilize immediate infrastructure threats to the affected population" (12, 13). More than providing a blueprint for future action, the use of the present tense also presents these proposed actions—things that *will* or *should* happen *if* a disaster occurs—as if they are already happening. This should remind us of the weirdness of all planning, no matter how common and everyday a thing like planning seems. When you make a plan, not only do you describe what you intend to do in the future; you also shape the present moment, or the moment in which you are intending, in such a way as to make the thing you intend to do possible. To plan is to bring the future into the present, quite literally. This temporal dislocation makes planning documents, especially a planning document that is about creating plans to deal with things that may happen in the future, seem especially strange. To create a planning *document* is not just to bring the future into the present; it is also to position this kind of speculation as a kind of description. By describing future actions that will be taken in the present tense, preparedness documents form the contours of future worlds in the present. They position the future, or possible futures—a matter for speculation—as something that already exists, giving speculation the same epistemological weight as observation and description. Preparedness documents therefore do not so much seek to replace fact with fiction as they do to present speculation about what will happen as an empirical description of what is happening. This is one of the ways that what it means to know something under preparedness has shifted.

By bringing the future into the present, preparedness documents also continually repeat and revise these futures as they see fit. We can see this if we consider how preparedness documents circulate online.[7] The *Homeland Security Digital Library* (HSDL), as an online repository of preparedness documents, makes this repetition visible after the fact. For example, although I cited only the 2011 *National Preparedness Goal* above for consistency's sake—this edition is called the "first edition"—the 2011 version of the document is not the only version we can find using the HSDL. The first five versions of the document date back to 2005. The first, a draft of the *National Preparedness Goal*, was released in March; the *Interim National Preparedness Goal* was released on March 31; two more drafts were released in October and December; and the "final draft" was also released in December. All of these documents except for the interim document are labeled as "drafts," suggesting that they may not have been released to the public at the time, although they are publicly available now. In 2011, the document was revised again and re-released as the first edition of the *National Preparedness Goal*. When this version of the document was released, six years after the first had been produced, the Department of Homeland Security announced that it had produced "the country's first-ever National Preparedness Goal" ("DHS Announces First Preparedness Goal"). Finally, in September 2015, the second edition of the *National Preparedness Goal* was released.[8]

Far from an indication of simple redundancy, the repetition of this document is reflective of how information is stored and how it travels online. As Wendy Chun has emphasized, computer memory "is an active process, not static" ("Enduring Ephemeral" 164). For example, volatile forms of computer memory, like the RAM used as primary storage on laptops, require a steady electrical current to work; when a computer shuts down, anything in RAM that's not written to the hard drive is lost. Furthermore, although a computer's non-volatile memory, like its hard drive or flash storage, can maintain its state without power, its data must be constantly curated in order to remain current: it must be saved to an external hard drive or server to keep as a backup in case of failure and so that it can be transferred to a new machine. Characterized by "impermanence and volatility," or by "degeneration," computer memory only works as storage if it is continually maintained and updated (164, 167). Repetition on a material level is therefore necessary in order to preserve anything digital. Chun is also careful to note, however, that this continual repetition applies to content online just as much as it does to computer hardware: she writes, "Consider concepts such as social networking… or hot YouTube videos that are already old and old email messages forever circulated and rediscovered as new" (148). Repetition is therefore "not the evidence of thought wasted but of thought disseminated" (171). Content doesn't circulate through these networks so much as it pulses repeatedly, appearing and reappearing unevenly, at irregular intervals, both too early and too late—endlessly resuscitated as "the undead of information" (171).[9]

But to understand how preparedness documents work to revise the futures they endlessly repeat, we need to understand this repetition more precisely as updating.[10] The 2005 interim document is itself a revision, or an update, of the March 2005 draft; the October 2005 draft and the two December 2005 drafts each describe themselves as "superced[ing]" the March 2005 interim document; and the Federal Emergency Management Agency describes the 2015 National Preparedness Goal as "a refresh" of the 2011 edition (*National Preparedness Goal*, October 2005 iv; *National Preparedness Goal*, December 2005 [draft] v; *National Preparedness Goal*, December 2005 [final] v; "National Preparedness Goal"). Revising, superceding, refreshing: all of these words imply something that comes after its predecessor. In order for a document to replace a prior version or to act as an update of a prior version, that "prior version" must already exist. But, unlike a replacement, the updated document does not seek to rhetorically erase its predecessor by positioning itself as the "original" or "only" document. There is no original document; there are only "drafts." Indeed, while updating often implies newness, the updated document actually requires the existence of another document that it can necessarily follow, and, by following, change—but just a bit. An update is not a new creation or even an erasure, but rather a correction or a revision. As an updated "second edition," for example, the 2015 National Preparedness Goal includes some new information and phrasing, but overall it is very similar to the 2011 "first edition." Much of the wording from the "first edition" remains unchanged. Updating is an activity that depends on the explicit acknowledgement of repetition with a difference for its meaning. It punctures time, marking itself as a noncontinuous break: "Update your computer now?" we are asked again and again and again. As Chun emphasizes, when one updates, "one must constantly respond in order to remain close to the same" (*Updating* 86). The update is a way to forestall the arrival of the future by continually submitting it to revision, by changing it again and again and again, over and over.

Updating also implies remaining perpetually unfinished, even if the next update never arrives. The updated document is the latest version, but it's never the final version because it can always itself be updated. This is another way of understanding speculation as a form of knowledge production under preparedness, one that involves constantly updating the (record of the) future, injecting it with new information. Cornelia Vismann's distinction between (print) documents and files is helpful in understanding what this means. She makes a typological distinction between these two terms: documents can be understood according to a logic of preservation—"what they proclaim counts for all ages"—while files can be understood according to a logic of transmission—they are records of the changeable administrative processes that make long-lasting governmental decrees possible (*Files* 71). But as this section's discussion of preparedness documents has demonstrated, as individual documents have become files on computers, they have come to act more like Vismann's conception of files than her conception of documents. What they proclaim counts not for all ages, but rather only for a matter of months, or at most a few years—only until the next update, the next revised edition. Preparedness documents therefore function not only as declarations of preparedness policy, but also as records of the administrative processes and procedures that have changed and that are constantly changing these policies. As what Gitelman calls "epistemic objects," if documents are supposed to know what they show and show what they know, the kind of knowing and showing that preparedness documents do is highly provisional. Again, according to Guillory, the value of knowledge lies in its organization of information into intelligible structures that can then be used to discover new information. The value of information, in contrast, lies in its transmission; information "demands to be transmitted because it has a shelf life, a momentary value…" (Guillory 110). Preparedness documents, however, demonstrate that knowledge for preparedness resembles something closer to information. As carriers of information and therefore objects of knowledge, documents are a medium through which knowledge is produced. But because knowledge about future threats is based not on evidence of what exists but rather on evidence of *what could possibly exist*, that knowledge itself has a shelf life. What could possibly exist is always subject to further revision as the past becomes present, and the present becomes the future. Preparedness documents become more valuable the more up-to-date they are, not the more "accurate" or "influential" they are; updating itself therefore becomes a measure of any given preparedness document's value.[11] The updated document, injected with new information, tells us what we need to know about future threats—at least until the next update.

Documentation as a World-Making Project

Does the shift in what it means *to know* that preparedness documents evidence also affect what it means *to document*? We return again to what documents are supposed to do. The consensus, as I've discussed, is that they produce knowledge through what Gitelman calls "the know-show function" (1). This ties knowledge production to empirical observation and demonstration: documents show us things that exist, and we use that information to produce knowledge. But the processes of documentation I discussed in the previous section suggest a more creative conception of documentation. In addition to showing us what exists, preparedness documents, which provide documentation of future events, also bring those things themselves into existence. Understood as creators, not just observers, of facts, these documents bring worlds into existence as much as they show us what these worlds are. In this way, they are like fiction. Here I am summarizing the operations of documentation in what Mark Seltzer has called "the official world."[12] The official world, which is to say the modern world, consists "both of itself and its self-description"—it is a self-reporting world (6). But the self-reporting of the official world moves beyond mere notation for Seltzer; a self-reporting world is also a self-creating world. It "bend[s]… the will to know the real to the will to produce the real," meaning "that taking note of the fact is a fact-producing act" (7). The official world is one in which worlds are brought into existence, or entered into the record as what exists, by the words that also describe them. To document is to self-report and to self-create. For Seltzer, the modern work of art, and especially suspense fiction, is the perfect model for the official world because of its unceasing interest in self-reflexivity. The modern work of fiction, he writes, "not merely makes the world appear in the world, but too unceasingly marks that it does so" (7).[13] One of my claims here, however, is that preparedness documents, in speculating on future catastrophes and in positioning that speculation as empirical observation, function like fiction. They too mark how they make the world appear in the world.

To better understand documentation as a world-making project, let's turn to a particularly salient example. In February 2003, then-Secretary of State Colin Powell made what is now an infamous presentation to the United Nations Security Council about Iraq's (imagined) possession of weapons of mass destruction (WMD). Powell's message to the UN was clear: Iraq has been manufacturing WMD's, and to prevent the global catastrophe that would ensue if they were allowed to continue manufacturing them, the U.S. needed to invade. While not a preparedness document in the same way that the *National Preparedness Goal* is a preparedness document, Powell's presentation is nevertheless centered on how the U.S. military can secure against future disaster and the reasons it needs to do so.[14] The presentation is especially important for our purposes, however, because it is fundamentally *about* documentation itself. Powell relied on a wide array of documents —including "monitored" conversations, interviews with sources in the Iraqi government, and diagrams and satellite imagery of supposed WMD production facilities—to present the government's case, but his use of taped conversations as evidence that Iraqi officials were trying to conceal the production of WMD is especially revealing. Powell presents these conversations in several different ways: he plays the tape of each conversation as a video with English subtitles, he quotes parts of each conversation verbatim back to the council after he plays the tape, and he displays these quotes in his presentation slides as he reads them (Figure 10.1). There are many overlapping kinds

Preparedness Documents After the Fact

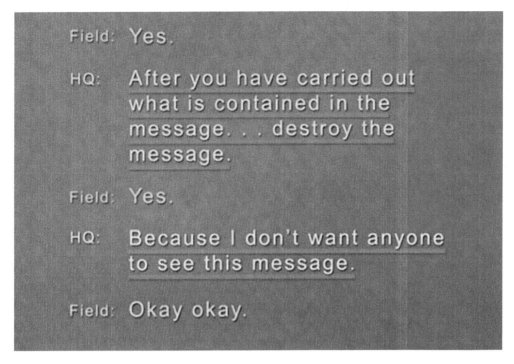

Figure 10.1 One of Powell's presentation slides documenting a taped conversation from "Remarks to the United Nations Security Council"

of documentation here. There is the original documentation of the conversation through its clandestine recording; there is the subtitling of this conversation for English speakers; there is Powell's playing of the taped conversation with subtitles for the council; and there is Powell's reading and displaying of the quotes for the council in his presentation, which enters these quotes into the presentation transcript, itself an official documentation of the proceedings. The conversations are documented, re-documented, and this documentation and re-documentation is also itself documented. In fact, one way of understanding Powell's presentation is as a self-reflexive document that documents other documents—a document that is about the act of documenting.

While the content of the conversations doesn't provide evidence of much of anything, Powell builds his case around the very fact that these conversations have been documented. For example, one conversation discusses a message that one official sent to the other about "clean[ing] out all the areas, the scrap areas, the abandoned areas" ("Remarks"). This conversation does not contain the contents of the message, only this summary, but it ends with an injunction to destroy the message: "After you have carried out what is contained in this message, destroy the message because I don't want anyone to see this message." Powell uses this quote to argue that the official wanted this message destroyed because it "would have verified to the inspectors" that

> they [Iraqi officials] don't want that message seen because they were trying to clean up the area, to leave no evidence behind of the presence of weapons of mass destruction. And they can claim that nothing was there and the inspectors can look all they want and they will find nothing.

It's important to note how Powell uses this taped conversation as evidence. He isn't using the documented conversation to prove that the Iraqi government was manufacturing WMD, or even that Iraqi officials were trying to hide this information from UN weapons inspection teams.

This might have been what the supposedly destroyed message itself would have proven. Rather, Powell uses the taped conversation to prove the existence of a supposedly destroyed message that *would have proven*, if it still existed, that Iraq was manufacturing WMD. Powell, in other words, presents his speculations about the contents of the taped conversation as a kind of documentation, or true record, of this missing message. What's more, these speculations about the contents of the message then become a kind of document when Powell presents them: as part of his official presentation to the UN, these speculations are entered into the record of that presentation. They are created as documented facts.

Powell does something similar with the "roughly 2,000 pages of documents" discovered by UN inspectors in "the homes of an Iraqi nuclear scientist" ("Remarks"). While he notes that "some of the material" in these documents "is classified and related to Iraq's nuclear program," he doesn't provide any more specific information about their contents. Instead, he shows a picture of the documents and asks, "Are the inspectors to search the house of every government official, every Baath Party member and every scientist in the country to find the truth, to get the information they need, to satisfy the demands of our Council?" (Figure 10.2). For Powell, the only evidence that is needed of Iraq's WMD production is the existence of the documents themselves. What information they contain is not important, only that they are "roughly 2,000 pages of documents." Additionally, because they exist in such numbers, Powell argues, it would be infeasible to read them or to continue looking for more; the hypothetical situation he presents to the council, the image of inspectors going to every government official's home and reading all of their documents, is meant to be absurd. But we should note, again, that Powell is turning speculation about the

Figure 10.2 Picture of the documents discovered in "the homes of an Iraqi nuclear scientist" from "Remarks to the United Nations Security Council"

contents of these documents and about what might happen if inspectors were to try to actually read all of the documents into documentation of the fact that Iraq is manufacturing WMD. This is documentation devoid of any positive content: it refers only to the other acts of documentation it itself documents. Powell's presentation is therefore not only a self-reflexive document—a document about documentation—but it also depends on this self-reflexivity—on the acts of documentation it documents, not their contents—to advance its argument. To document, and *only* to document, is to know.

Powell claims at one point in the presentation that "the facts speak for themselves." This is of course not quite right: if the facts spoke for themselves, he would not have to speak for them in the form of a presentation to the UN. But it's also important to realize that, in speaking for "the facts," Powell brings these facts into existence. He enters them into the record, documenting them, and thereby creates a (fictional) world in the here and now in which such facts exist as facts. Powell's presentation to the UN Security Council doesn't necessarily demonstrate that the Bush administration lied about the presence of weapons of mass destruction in Iraq, although many people, of course, did lie, or stretch the truth, or spread misinformation and propaganda, and with disastrous results. Instead, it demonstrates the ability of documentation itself to shape the world we also use these documents to describe. This kind of description that is also a kind of creation is also, again, how we might describe what fiction does. It brings worlds into existence by describing them.

The distinction I am drawing between fiction-making and engaging in the creation of falsehoods is crucial to understanding how documentation works under preparedness. Because it's not just that preparedness gives fiction the same epistemological weight as fact; it's also that preparedness documents make this epistemic stance possible through the very act of documentation. Understanding Colin Powell's presentation only as a parade of lies misses this point. Joseph Masco, for example, refers to this presentation as an example of how the national security state uses the concept of secrecy to generate fear. Masco emphasizes that Powell relies heavily throughout his presentation on the suggestion of more information, or on withholding information from other, supposedly more secret sources. He repeatedly promises UN officials that the U.S. government knows more than it can reveal: "I cannot tell you everything that we know," Powell says toward the beginning of the presentation, "but what I can share with you, when combined with what all of us have learned over the years, is deeply troubling." Masco calls this statement "a tactical deployment of the idea of secret information," one in which "the *idea* of knowledge (imagined, projected, fantasized) replaces actual content as a means of engaging the world" (143). While I agree with Masco's overall point, I also think it places too much emphasis on the distinction between "imagined, projected, fantasized" knowledge and "actual content." Such a distinction, at least for preparedness, doesn't make sense because there is no consequential difference between "imagined" knowledge and "actual" knowledge. Preparedness renders this distinction inoperable. Preparedness views fiction as a source of knowledge production: the ontological status of what we might call fictional information doesn't affect the epistemological potential of this information. Indeed, when we're dealing with future threats, fiction is as good a source for facts and information as any. The worlds preparedness documents create are as real, in that sense, as any other world.

The reality of these worlds, regardless of their accuracy, is precisely why we can't limit the conversation about our current "post-fact" situation to discussions of lies, misinformation, and propaganda. Certainly, those things are important, but they miss a crucial aspect of post-factuality, at least in terms of preparedness: the reliance on fiction as a source for facts. As I have argued, this reliance comes from a reconfiguration of what it means to know something, and what it means to document that knowledge. Preparedness documents, like any document, work to produce knowledge. But the knowledge they produce is a result of speculation about what *could* or *might* exist that is positioned as an empirical observation or description of what *already does* exist. This epistemic stance displaces us in time, bringing the future into the present, forestalling meaningful change.

Such an epistemic stance also focuses our attention on what Lauren Berlant has called "the stretched-out present," on the capaciousness of a present that is subsumed and updated by the future, over and over again (5). This should alert us to the fact that although preparedness seems to be about the future, it is in fact relentlessly focused on the present. Thinking about preparedness as a worldmaking project means thinking about how preparedness produces future catastrophes that are experienced and lived in the present—how preparedness makes and remakes the present in the image of the (always catastrophic) future.[15] This also means thinking about how the political project of preparedness consists, in part, of exhausting the present—not by erasing it, but rather by endlessly inhabiting it. Preparedness documents create a distended present so full of possible future disasters that there is no time or energy to imagine differently. There are, after all, tens of thousands of documents to read and re-read, preparedness plan after preparedness plan to make and re-make, protocols to write and practice and re-write and re- practice, again and again. What's more, the catastrophic futures that preparedness documents bring into being are so saturated with the predictable tropes and forms of disaster—they are so generic—that they become expected, routine, and even ordinary. To understand this is to be after the fact, not in the sense that we are living after facts have ceased to matter, but rather in the sense that, at least in terms of preparedness, we are always living after-the-fact, or after the future catastrophe that is always about to occur has already been documented. To live after-the-fact in this way is to experience future disaster not only as a known fact, but also as banal, as part of everyday life, as a routine thing. Preparedness tells us the future is already here—indeed, we are already experiencing it—and so there is nothing we can do to change it. If we want to live in different futures, we will need to learn to inhabit them differently. We will need to learn to expect—and, according to the logic of preparedness, therefore to *know*—something different.

Notes

1 As Ulrich Beck writes, one "must ask how, in the example of risk perception, 'rationality' *arises socially*, that is how it is believed, becomes dubious, is defined, redefined, acquired and frittered away" (59).
2 For more on preparedness as a national security paradigm, see De Goede and Randalls, and Lakoff and Collier.
3 The threats for which preparedness documents are supposed to prepare their audiences are always conceived of as emanating from elsewhere—as constituting an outside that threatens to undo an existing political and economic stability. The national security project that preparedness documents envision and enact is therefore fundamentally conservative. It is never about substantive social reform or change—preparedness documents do not address the kinds of systemic changes needed to truly address the many disasters wrought by global warming, for example—rather, it is about conserving the status quo that is envisioned as under attack by "foreign" threats of all kinds. This understanding of what constitutes a threat has clear implications for what I describe in the chapter's second section as the world-making project of preparedness documents: the kinds of future worlds that preparedness documents bring into being mistake a very specific, U.S.-centric worldview *for the world itself.*
4 Fuller and Goffey write,

> Grayness marks the breakdown of clearly defined contrasts: a Monday morning feeling, a certain blankness that is not indifference or affectlessness but something approaching what Roland Barthes theorized as the 'neutral,' a fading and withdrawal rather than an abolition of contrasts.... Grayness is a quality that is easily overlooked, and that is what gives it its great attraction, an unremarkableness that can be of inestimable value in background operations.
> *(Kindle Locations 306–308, 315–317)*

The concept of "gray literature" is taken from the library and information sciences, where the term has been understood broadly to define "all types of literature not available through the normal bookselling channels, including reports, trade literature, translations and ad hoc publications" (Auger 7).
5 This figure includes only those documents that are publicly available. See *Homeland Security Digital Library*.
6 As Weber puts it, in an oft-quoted sentence, "The management of the modern office is based upon written documents ('the files'), which are preserved in their original or draft form, and upon a staff of subaltern officials and scribes of all sorts" (957).

7 For more on what it means for (print) texts to circulate, see Warner. Warner also notes, however, that this understanding of circulation is not appropriate for online discourse. This is because the temporality of publishing online—if we can even speak of it as "publishing"—is different from the temporality of print publication. As he writes, "Highly mediated and highly capitalized forms of circulation are increasingly organized as continuous ('24/7 instant access') rather than punctual" (97). For Warner, information doesn't circulate online so much as it flows, and Warner suggests that we may need "to abandon 'circulation' as an analytic category" when considering online materials (98).
8 At the time of writing, all of these versions of the document except the September 2015 document can be found using the *Homeland Security Digital Library*. The September 2015 document can be found using FEMA's media library.
9 For a similar articulation of this idea, see Cecire.
10 As Chun puts it, "New media live and die by the update: the end of the update, the end of the object" (*Updating* 2).
11 Here I am summarizing what, in a different context, Sara Ahmed has noted about how diversity documents within the university work:

> The more a document circulates, we might assume, the more it will do. But the circulation of the document can become what it is doing. Diversity work becomes moving documents around. If the movement becomes the action, or even the aim, then moving the document might be what stops us from seeing what documents are not doing.
>
> *(97)*

12 Seltzer draws on systems theory throughout *The Official World*. For more on modernity as self-describing and self-creating, see Luhmann, "Deconstruction" and Luhmann, *Art as a Social System*.
13 It's probably more accurate to say that Powell's presentation has more to do with preemption, or the military doctrine that espouses the need to act on threats before they fully materialize. Preemption is the logic informing the so-called "Bush Doctrine," which George W. Bush first outlined in a 2002 commencement address at West Point. See "Commencement Address."
14 Seltzer is working here from Vismann, who has referred to this as the "practice of total documentation," whereby officials "record in order to act, and act only by recording" ("Out of File" 158).
15 As Seltzer writes, "the artwork stages what it does, and, in doing so, enacts what it shows" (7). In this modulation of Gitelman's "know-show function," preparedness documents do not just show what they know; they also enact what they know, bringing that knowledge into existence in the here and now.

Works Cited

Ahmed, Sara. *On Being Included: Racism and Diversity in Institutional Life*. Duke UP, 2012.
Anderson, Ben. "Preemption, Precaution, Preparedness: Anticipatory Action and Future Geographies." *Progress in Human Geography*, vol. 34, no. 66, 2010, pp. 777–798.
Auger, C. P. *Information Sources in Grey Literature*. 2nd ed., Bowker-Sauer, 1989.
Beck, Ulrich. *Risk Society: Towards a New Modernity*. Translated by Mark Ritter. Sage Publications, 1992.
Berlant, Lauren. *Cruel Optimism*. Duke UP, 2011.
Cecire, Natalia. "Everybody's Authority." *Publication of the Modern Language Association*, vol. 130, no. 2, 2015, pp. 453–460.
Chun, Wendy Hui Kyong. "The Enduring Ephemeral, or the Future Is a Memory." *Critical Inquiry*, vol. 35, no. 1, 2008, pp. 148–171.
Chun, Wendy Hui Kyong. *Updating to Remain the Same: Habitual New Media*. The MIT Press, 2016.
"Commencement Address at the United States Military Academy." George W. Bush, June 1, 2002, www.presidentialrhetoric.com/speeches/06.01.02.html. Accessed November 29, 2016.
"DHS Announces First Preparedness Goal." Department of Homeland Security, October 7, 2011, www.dhs.gov/news/2011/10/07/dhs-announces-first-national-preparedness-goal. Accessed November 29, 2016.
De Goede, Marieke and Samuel Randalls. "Precaution, Preemption: Arts and Technologies of the Actionable Future." *Environment and Planning D: Society and Space*, vol. 27, 2009, pp. 859–878.
Fuller, Matthew and Andrew Goffey. *Evil Media*. The MIT Press, 2012. Kindle version.
Gallagher, Catherine. "The Rise of Fictionality." *The Novel: History, Geography, Culture*, Vol. 1, edited by Franco Moretti, Princeton UP, 2006, 336–363.
Gitelman, Lisa. *Paper Knowledge: Toward a Media History of Documents*. Duke UP, 2014.
Guillory, John. "The Memo and Modernity." *Critical Inquiry*, vol. 31, no. 1, 2004, pp. 108–132.
Homeland Security Digital Library. Center for Homeland Defense and Security, Naval Postgraduate School, Department of Homeland Security, www.hsdl.org. Accessed November 29, 2016.

Lakoff, Andrew. "Preparing for the Next Emergency." *Public Culture*, vol. 19, no. 2, 2007, pp. 247–271.

Lakoff, Andrew and Stephen J. Collier. "Infrastructure and Event: The Political Technology of Preparedness." *Political Matter: Technoscience, Democracy, and Public Life*, edited by Bruce Braun and Sarah J. Whatmore. University of Minnesota Press, 2010, 243–266.

Luhmann, Niklas. *Art as a Social System*, edited by Eva Knodt. Stanford UP, 2000.

Luhmann, Niklas. "Deconstruction as Second-Order Observing." *Theories of Distinction: Redescribing the Descriptions of Modernity*, edited by William Rasch. Stanford UP, 2002, 94–112.

Masco, Joseph. *The Theater of Operations: National Security Affect from the Cold War to the War on Terror*. Duke UP, 2014.

"National Preparedness Goal." *On the Homefront – The HSDL blog*. Homeland Security Digital Library, October 6, 2015, www.hsdl.org/c/national-preparedness-goal/. Accessed November 29, 2016.

"Remarks to the United Nations Security Council." Colin Powell, February 5, 2003, www.globalsecurity.org/wmd/library/news/iraq/2003/iraq-030205-powell-un-17300pf.htm. Accessed November 29, 2016.

Seltzer, Mark. *The Official World*. Duke UP, 2016.

Sterne, Jonathan. *MP3: The Meaning of a Format*. Duke UP, 2012.

United States, Department of Homeland Security. *Interim National Preparedness Goal*. March 2005.

United States, Department of Homeland Security. *National Preparedness Goal*. October 2005.

United States, Department of Homeland Security. *National Preparedness Goal*. December 2005 (draft).

United States, Department of Homeland Security. *National Preparedness Goal*. December 2005 (final).

United States, Department of Homeland Security. *National Preparedness Goal*. 1st ed., September 2011.

Vismann, Cornelia. *Files: Law and Media Technology*. Translated by Geoffrey Winthrop-Young. Stanford UP, 2008.

Vismann, Cornelia. "Out of File, Out of Mind." *New Media, Old Media: A History and Theory Reader*, 2nd ed., edited by Wendy Hui Kyong Chun and Anna Watkins Fisher, with Thomas W. Keenan. Routledge, 2016, 158–166.

Warner, Michael. *Publics and Counterpublics*. Zone Books, 2002.

Weber, Max. *Economy and Society: An Outline of Interpretive Sociology*, edited by Guenther Roth and Claus Wittich. U of California P, 1978.

11

"IS THERE A GHOST IN THE COMPUTER?"

A Spectrology of Uncanny Risks[1]

Projit Bihari Mukharji

Risk is domesticated uncertainty (Ghosh and Sarkar). But what exactly does it mean to be "domesticated?" Without going into etymological or historical minutae, I think most of us in the Anglophone world would agree that to be domesticated is to be at home. But then we must ask, are all homes equally homely? Do all domiciles feel adequately domestic? Had I been writing this essay in German I might have called the feeling of "un-homeliness" in certain homes *unheimlich*, as Sigmund Freud famously did. To our ears however, Freud's *unheimlich* is more familiar as the "uncanny."

It is about uncanny risk that I write, namely, risk that has been domesticated in a home where it is yet to feel entirely at home. The home that I write about is contemporary Bengal—a region that spans across eastern South Asia and includes parts of both India and Bangladesh. Here, the modern apparatus of risk society, carrying in its bowels the heady cocktail of actuarial sciences, insurance companies, speculative markets, finance capitalism, etc., has arrived in due course. Yet, here there were also earlier, older, and orthogonal vocabularies of risk and uncertainty.

A large number of terms designating not only abstract uncertainty, but indeed a range of specific forms of affective, embodied, and spatialized uncertainty had developed in Bengal over the millennia before the arrival of risk society. *Ashanka* (trepidation), *sangshay* (uncertainty), *jhunki* (hazard), *phanda* (astrological risk), *thom-thom* (foreboding atmosphere), and *chhom-chhom* (embodied foreboding) were just some of the terms that marked out an intricate and complex culture of uncertainties.[2] Going further, one might add some of the words for fate, such as *bhagyo*, *naseeb*, and *adrista*. As the contemporary regime of risk has sought to make itself at home in Bengal, it has had to confront these existing forms of knowing, feeling, and dealing with uncertainty. Thanks to its global clout, this new actuarial regime has gradually come to occupy more and more of the floor space in its new home even as the older denizens have been forced to withdraw into the shadows.

In the shadows they remain lurking. Skulking. Haunting. Like the dispossessed owners of a foreclosed home, the once-happy denizens now bide their time. As wispy creatures of the shadows they are increasingly difficult to tell apart. *Ashanka, jhunki,* and *phanda*, now often seem to shade into one another. The *thom-thom-e* skies and *chhom-chhom-e* bodily sensations seem to bleed into one another. Together thus, I shall call them *uncanny risks*. By giving them a common name, I do not mean to erase their once distinctive existence, merely underline their currently shared presence in the shadow of the contemporary regime of risk.

Unlike the modern regime of risk, uncanny risk is incapable of rationalization. No statistical models or erudite actuaries can mathematize it. Frequently, its very object exceeds the domain of a rule-bound "nature" and inhabits the domain of irreproducible singularities usually dubbed the "supernatural." Gut feelings, astrological signs, the predeterminations of fate, and so forth materialize these uncanny risks. To the world of actuaries they look like mere superstitions, fossilized modes of outdated behavior that will soon retire from our fully rationalized neoliberal worlds and its speculative markets.

Domesticated Risk and Computers

The domestication of risk, Ulrich Beck has observed, has radically transformed the nature of reality itself. Reality, Beck argued, in risk society has been "sublimated into *data* that is *produced*" (166). At the heart of the regime that now constantly produces and reproduces reality is a machine: the computer. Beck explains that "facts—the former centerpieces of reality" have now become "nothing but answers to questions that could have been asked differently, products of rules for gathering and omitting. A different computer, a different specialist, a different institute—a different reality" (166).

The ever-longer distances over which both commerce and politics are organized in contemporary times has meant, as historian Theodore Porter points out, that trust has been relocated to numbers. Mechanized quantification and its promise of reliable objectivity have emerged as the core devices of what Anthony Giddens called the "disembedding mechanisms" (10–35). It is these developments that have allowed the computer to go from a rarity in the middle twentieth century to an object of near ubiquity by the end of the first decade of the twenty-first century.

The computer and its attendant technologies now saturate the practices, processes, and protocols that calculate, organize, and negotiate modern domesticated risk. Massive amounts of data are stored and mathematical operations of unprecedented scale, quite beyond the capacity of the human brain alone, are performed on that big data. It is this data and the calculations based on it that regulate the organization of risk at myriad levels of the risk society. From advanced navigational systems that keep airplanes from colliding and freeways from jamming up to financial algorithms that determine everything from share prices to permissible fishing quotas, computer-driven data-gathering and risk-calculation are at the heart of the world we inhabit.

Even more striking is the fact that the very reliability of these computers and computer-systems, i.e., their risk, has itself been mechanized. It is by using computers that we judge the riskiness of other computers (MacKenzie). Not only do computers then produce the reality we live in by calculating, regulating, and shaping the risks around us, but indeed the general reliability of this machine (and the larger regime of risk organized around it) is itself guaranteed by another set of computers. Our trust and reliance on computers then is near absolute. This trust, engendered in the infrastructures and protocols that form the backbone of contemporary societies, is sustained by constantly deflecting ebullient anxieties about data leaks, hacks, cyber-attacks, bugs, and viruses as exceptional—rather than routine—moments in the lives of computers. Indeed, in an ironic loop, these anxieties themselves are frequently used to authorize further computer-reliant systems of surveillance and protection.

Aside from the general ubiquity of computers in all walks of contemporary life, it is also worth specially noting the preponderance of automated computer-based finance markets. Today much of the world of high finance, which provides the backbone for the neoliberal world order, is actually automated; many of the financial transactions that rapidly move money around the globe are performed by computers.

Computers have been around in South Asia since the 1950s. The very first computer in the region was established in 1955 at the Indian Statistical Institute in Calcutta. Bombay got its first computer later that very year and a few other machines followed. But in India it was only after 1986, when the then-Prime Minister Rajiv Gandhi removed a number of import regulations, that their use became widespread (Rajaraman). Further proliferation of computers took place through the IMF-enforced opening up of the Indian economy in 1991 and the deliberate policies of the 1998 A.B. Vajpayee government to promote Indian computer companies. As a result, by 2010, 6.1 percent of the Indian GDP came from information technology-related businesses. By 2015, this had grown to 9.3 percent. Official projections predict that by 2025, nearly 25 percent of the Indian GDP will come from IT-related earnings (Nasscom).

This enormous expansion of computing has naturally also necessitated an ever-growing number of operators. Everyone from a computer engineer to a programmer and data analysts, a whole host of new jobs requiring varying levels and sophistication of skills have emerged. By 2010, a whopping 2.3 million people in India were working in the IT sector. By 2015 this had risen to approximately 3.7 million people (Nasscom). Needless to say many more than this number were exposed to computers in one way or the other at work or at home.

In neighboring Bangladesh the first computer arrived in Dhaka in 1964 and was installed at what was then called the Pakistan Atomic Energy Commission. A number of other machines followed in private businesses around the same time (Chowdhury and Murshed). This early private uptake did not however, lead to the massive growth that was witnessed in India. Successive decades of political turmoil meant that government initiative in the area was weak through much of the 1970s and 1980s and it was only from the mid-1990s that computer usage in Bangladesh began to grow. Around this time, Bangladeshi innovators also took the lead in developing Bengali language fonts and interfaces that in turn enabled greater social penetration of computing in the entire Bengal region (Chowdhury and Murshed). Notwithstanding these developments, by 2013 IT still accounted for less than 1 percent of the Bangladeshi GDP (BASIS). Yet, public interest in IT and the hope that computers will help Bangladesh leapfrog into a higher income bracket remains strong (Helal and Rahman).

Computers, which are central to the new regimes of domesticated risk, are still patchily dispersed in the Bengal region. The penetration has been much greater on the Indian side than on the Bangladeshi side. Yet the huge, almost millenarian hopes for economic improvement through their advent are almost uniformly shared across the border. Indeed, the porosity of the border itself and the huge presence of Indian media in Bangladesh would suggest that the computer imaginaries are unlikely to be entirely distinct.

Computer Imaginaries

Notwithstanding the global association that now exists between South Asia, especially India, and informational technologies, very little work has been done on the cultural and imaginal history of the computer. Without such an account however, it is difficult to fully understand the uncanny risks that seem to crystalize around these iconic harbingers of modern risk regimes.

The absence of any significant literature on the subject is particularly striking since there is in fact a small but robust and growing body of scholarly work on computer imaginaries in the West. Consider, for example, Jeffrey Sconce's fascinating history of the "electronic presence," or "fields of electronic fiction socially generated around telecommunications technologies" in late nineteenth and twentieth-century U.S.A. (Sconce 6). Then there is Colin Milburn's thrilling exploration of *Nanovision* that tracked a range of attempts to imagine "the Singularity," an imaginary point beyond which technological change will accelerate so precipitously as to render any mutual legibility of the periods before and after the point utterly impossible (Milburn 1–2). These are only two of the best-known works that have engaged the imaginal dimensions of the technomodernity we are living through, but they do enough to demonstrate the power and importance of the imaginal dimensions of our emergent technomodernity. Gadgets, such as computers, as Michael Simeone points out, are after all "an enduring metaphorical configuration of humans and technology in the twentieth and twenty-first centuries" (Simeone 333). They are therefore a "technocultural form" and not some impossibly pre- or post-cultural object that are somehow insulated from imaginal figurations (Simeone). Yet, notwithstanding such insights, there has been little exploration of cultural friction or fault lines. What happens when we recognize that global technomodernity is not a singular phenomenon but that there are in fact multiple, maybe even myriad, technomodernities? How do technocultural forms such as computers inhabit such a fissured and plural technomodernity? This is where interrogations of computer imaginaries embedded in technomodernities beyond the putative West might be particularly illuminating.

Unlike in cities like Bangalore or Madras where computer technologies have actually delivered wealth, in Calcutta the aspirations of rapid social mobility have largely outstripped the actual wealth generated by computers. Lower middle class parents and youth have dreamt of rapid enrichment and social mobility through computers only to find their grandiose dreams cut to size by the realities of the restricted employment opportunities in the city. No one has chronicled the bloated ambitions and bitter disappointments secreted around the computer more than the Bengali music band, *Chandrabindu*. In a song titled *duniya dot com* ("world dot com"), they croon:

> Go baby, run along, learn multimedia
> Chubby kids dream up ww ideas
> Email connects Honolulu to Haldia
> World dotcom, World dotcom, World dotcom, I pray to thee
> Worthless youngsters, by touching a mouse get First Class
> If Dad is angry they learn Java, Sumatra or C++
> In forests, from the brain drain, etc. if you wish to be rescued
> World dotcom, World dotcom, World dotcom, I pray to thee
> Come along boy, if you have flunked at school
> Even lame horses will run by buying an extra leg
> The generation is going to hell by this Compu-disease
> World dotcom, World dotcom, World dotcom, I pray to thee.[3]

The song pithily captures the impractical dreams of global mobility and success that were generated among youngsters and their parents alike in the fluorescent glow of the computer screen. But the pursuits ended badly. The generation, the band worried, was headed for utter failure because the grandiose aspirations were too big to be realized. Ethnographic snippets bear out the general validity of *Chandrabindu's* incisive social analysis. Kabita Chakraborty's recent ethnographic work among teenage Muslim girls in the slums of Calcutta found, for instance, that teenagers who struggled with basic literacy skills still dreamt of careers where they would work at computers. One 16 year old who could not spell simple English words like "teacher" and "official" still dreamt of a job where she would use computers in her office. Though the teenager had limited computer training, Chakraborty points out that she had observed NGO staff in the slums working on these machines and therefore had a secondhand familiarity with them. Another young girl of the same age and similar background also told Chakraborty that she wanted to work in an office and learn the computer (143) One young woman who had indeed been to college and worked at a computer in the local community center was looked upon with jealousy and suspicion by many of the others (Chakraborty 145). Like Chakraborty, Henrike Donner, who studied middle class, mostly Hindu mothers in Calcutta found that most of them wanted their children to learn computers. Computing was seen to be a skill and alongside literacy, numeracy, and English competency—the core skill-set they wanted to impart to their children. As a result, most mothers took their children to special computer classes in the evening after school. Yet, Donner also points out that most of these homes—which were certainly more affluent than the slum-homes studied by Chakraborty—still did not usually own a personal computer ("Committed Mothers"). So far has this association with successful childrearing and computer education gone, that Donner found that "campaigns for 'computer literacy' aimed at lower middle class women whose ability to teach their children was based on their own 'knowing computers' have substituted the familiar 'trained in classical dance/music' in matrimonial ads" (Donner, *Domestic Goddesses* 131).

These middle, and even more so lower middle class dreams were stoked by a host of computer schools that had emerged in the early 1990s and plastered Calcutta's political graffiti-riddled walls with glossy new images of quick social mobility. Undercover journalist, Siddhartha Deb, provides an excellent account of these schools which targeted especially the lower middle class, mediocre students who could not afford the high fees or tough admission tests of elite academic institutions. Owned by glib, thuggish men who cannily blended entrepreneurialism with old-school hustling, these schools, Deb writes, "were located inside nondescript houses in mostly residential neighborhoods" and had a somewhat makeshift quality that gave them an air of being the "outposts of some mildly disreputable business." The students at these schools wore shabby clothes worn out by long daily travel on overcrowded public transport and slippers worn out from pounding the pavements. Most of them lived in "rundown suburban settlements" scattered around Calcutta proper or, across the river, in the "polluted township of Howrah." They struggled hard with the modicum of educational capital they could afford to maintain a social station just above the "maidservants and bus conductors." Deb feared that despite their best efforts some of them would in time sink to the ranks of the latter. But till then, they traveled daily from their distant homes to their shady schools "clutching notebooks and photocopied sections of computer manuals" in the hope that these would open the gates to the safety of comfortable middle classness (73–74).

Shock of Old Media

The gates that stand between the shabbily dressed, lower middle class student and her dreams of sudden wealth and global travel through a job involving a computer are decidedly new and shiny. Everything in the millennial hopes nourished by the computer imaginaries are new and shiny: new technologies, new media, new skills, and the promise of new opportunities. Novelty is the ticket and obsolesce the ever-encroaching curse. Yet, these dreams unavoidably travel on old wheels.

David Edgerton, a historian of technology, has pointed out that our ideologically driven obsession with innovation has obscured the fact of the enormity of the presence of older technologies. As one well-heeled example goes for instance, the allegedly fully mechanized World War II ended up using many more horses than had been used in the World War I. While horses might indeed have been old technology for the students of computer schools, an aging transport system was not. Every morning a good many of these students would have traveled from the suburban settlement homes to their computer classes via a combination of dated transport equipment including decrepit trains, ramshackle buses, and hand-drawn or cycle-rickshaws.

Had they traveled on suburban trains, as indeed most perhaps did, they would also have likely bided their time reading the cheap printed books sold precisely and exclusively in the compartments of local trains shuttling between Calcutta and its impoverished suburbs. Books are among the varied fare peddled by the itinerant railway hawkers who are ubiquitous in Bengali trains. Literary scholar Sukanta Chaudhuri asserts that the Bengali train hawkers run a "more numerous and market-efficient network" than anywhere else. Chaudhuri also points out that there is absolutely "no article of daily use" that one cannot buy on the suburban trains of Calcutta. The world of train hawkers, he helpfully continues, is the interface where the secure, middle class world meets the precarious world of the urban and suburban poor (*View from Calcutta* 150–152).

The books that are peddled across the fragile boundaries of class in the overcrowded compartments of suburban trains are usually not the ones you can buy at the fancy bookstalls in urban malls. Neither indeed are they those that one can buy from the humblers stalls around the Calcutta University. They are usually unique to the milieu where they are sold. Chandrani Chatterjee thus observes that the railway hawkers, by peddling Bengali almanacs that have long since disappeared from the shelves of urban bookstores, keep alive the nineteenth-century tradition of itinerant vendors peddling distinctly low-brow printed books known as *Bot-tola* books (102).

Describing these books, the British Library's website says, though they "exist[ed] alongside elite publications," they were produced very differently and aimed at a distinct readership. Technologically, they were produced using "using traditional obsolescent technology." As a result, they displayed types of printing and binding that had long since been outmoded in more elite circles. In terms of their audience, the books were aimed at a level still more humble and demotic than the *Bot-tola* books and thus, "mirror[ed] social and mental life in the humbler reaches of Bengali society." Thematically, a wide range of topics ranging from religion, to pornography, to thrillers, to health manuals were printed. But the entire printing and circulation happened at a level so low and distant from the world of elite print culture that it is well neigh impossible to get any sense of the total output. Often only single editions would appear from obscure presses and sold in one or two extremely remote locales. Moreover, since the books were almost always printed on poor-quality paper they seldom survived very long. Hence, "though not technically ephemera, these books seldom last as they are cheaply produced and fragile, and their clients do not belong to a culture of reading and conservation" (Chaudhuri, "Archiving").

As the noisy wheels of an aging railcar hurtles the computer students from their suburban realities to their urban fantasies every morning and back again in the evening, many of them pass their time reading these cheap books printed at archaic presses on ephemeral paper. Old technology and old media fill in the jarring gaps engendered by the physicality of daily travel, even as the object of the travel is the world of new media and new technology. It is in these books that we come face to face with the uncanny risks of the computer.

My own rather disorderly travels on these aging railcars have introduced me to at least four such narratives of uncanny risks of computers. But in the absence of any central catalogue or repository there is no way of knowing how many more such narratives might there be. Yet, the four narratives that I have encountered convince me that the uncanny risks, far from meekly surrendering the stage to the neoliberal risk society, are in fact subtly undermining the hegemonic regime of calculated and capitalized risks. By embracing the computer, i.e., the idol of the new faith in domesticated uncertainty, the repressed uncanny fears are disemboweling the new regime of risk from the inside out.

Essentially all four narratives I found on the trains were about haunted computers. The first of these was a tale titled *Compiutar Bhoot* (*Computer Ghost*). It was printed from a small obscure press in Calcutta in 2008 in a collection of other ghost stories. No authorship was assigned, but one Nantu Ganguly is identified as the editor. The second story, "Bhooter Preme Bhoot Howa" (Becoming a Ghost by Falling in Love with a Ghost) by Samudra Sen was also similarly published from Calcutta within a collection of haunted tales. It was however, not dated. A third account was Anindita Goswami's short story "Laptop" that was included in a relatively more substantial collection of ghost tales published in 2010. The latest narrative is a short novella titled *Compiutare Bhoot Dhukechhe* (*A Ghost Has Entered the Computer*) (Ripon). The latter is by Dewan Humayun Kobir Ripon and was published from Dhaka in 2011. Besides these, I have also recently come across a couple of tales of haunted mobile phones that might be included within a larger common category, but for the present discussion I feel it best to leave them aside. What all these tales do is turn these quintessential gadgets for the rationalization of risks into haunted thingamajigs that embody the limits of rationalization. The very icons of modernity themselves, become monuments to modernity's limitations.

We can glimpse this alchemy of transformation in each of the four narratives. *Compiutar Bhoot* tells of the ghost of a dead man seeking his revenge by manipulating data on the police computer, while *Compiutare Bhoot Dhukechhe* is a similarly haunting novel about a haunted computer. Both are in fact thrillers. The third tale, "Laptop," is generically somewhere in between a thriller and a tragedy. It narrates the story of a young son of a struggling, just-about-middle class family whose father buys him a secondhand laptop when he gains admission into an expensive private college. The eponymous laptop however, soon begins to display a thirst for blood and the boy's fingertips begin to bleed whenever he works on the machine late at night. It turns out that the machine had belonged to a murdered businessman whose unquiet spirit was still seeking vengeance. Finally, *Bhooter Preme Bhoot Howa* too is a story about a haunted computer. But it is a full fledged tragedy and shows no affinity to the thriller genre. The slower pace of the tragic narrative allows it to develop a descriptive depth that is often missing in the other two faster-paced thrillers. The tale illuminates not only the socio-historical context in which it is set, but also the mental horizons of its key actors with great perspicacity and sensitivity. It is therefore this narrative that I want to explore in order to make sense of the uncanny risks being secreted around computers.

Sconce points out that, "Tales of paranormal media are important ... not as a timeless expression of some undying electronic superstition, but as a permeable language in which to express a culture's changing social relationship to a historical sequence of technologies" (10). By reading *Bhooter Preme Bhoot Howa* closely, it is changing social relationship that I want to track alongside the anxieties and uncanny risks they engender.

Bhooter Preme Bhoot Howa

Bhooter Preme Bhoot Howa revolves around a young man named Arghya. He is in his early twenties and after finishing school "with Physics, Chemistry and Mathematics," he had enrolled in a three-year computer applications course at the Jadavpur University. It was there that he first got interested in computers. Like most 20-something year olds in Calcutta, Arghya still lived with his parents, Rudrapratap and Bishakha, in a three-story town house in Bijoygarh, a southern suburb of the city.

It was Rudrapratap, Arghya's father, who, noticing his son's new enthusiasm for computing and wanting to encourage him, bought him his first computer. As a minor government employee, this would have been a big investment for the family. Moreover, a room on the third floor of the family home had to be air-conditioned (since computers in Calcutta, especially in their early days, were still prone to breaking down in the tropical heat). This was another investment, not to mention the additional recurring costs of electricity for running the air conditioner. All of it was justified by the fact that Rudrapratap had high hopes for his only son.

Bhooter Preme Bhoot Howa is a story about dreams. Arghya's dreams of romantic love and wealth, Bishakha's dreams for domestic bliss and Rudrapratap's dreams of prestige and social mobility—all jostled together in their suburban home. Their home, in fact, was not unusual. Bijoygarh was a land of dreams and most homes were full of them. But it had not always been this way. In the 1930s, the area was a barren wasteland that sustained few dreams or dreamers. By the time the World War II broke out, it had been converted into a vast military camp for foreign soldiers (Ray 120). The only dreams anyone dreamt there were of exile, war, and destruction. Even the rather grandiose name, Bijoygarh (Fortress of Victory), had yet to be dreamt up.

What changed all that and implanted the bristling forest of dreams was the decolonization of South Asia. As the British withdrew in 1947, the province of Bengal was partitioned between India and Pakistan. This led to one of the largest displacements in human history. Between 1946 and 1981 a whopping eight million Hindus crossed over in successive waves from eastern Bengal (Ray 116). The state government set up some "transit camps" for these incoming refugees, but the conditions were nightmarish and many chose to try to find rehabilitation by themselves. Consequently, a number of squatter's colonies appeared in the wastelands around Calcutta. By 1952, 119 such squatter's colonies had emerged. Over the years this number has risen to nearly 2,000 and are now scattered all over the Indian province of West Bengal (117). Bijoygarh was the very first of these squatter's colonies and became the epicenter from which refugees branched out to establish further colonies.

By the 1990s, much in Bijoygarh had changed. The erstwhile squatters have had their rights to the land they squatted on legally recognized. "Bamboo-thatched huts of middle class households have now become much more respectable-looking structures," writes historian Manas Ray, who grew up in the area (118). Finally, after nearly half a century of struggles, the Bijoygarh refugees, most of whom had been middle class *bhadralok* (genteel folk) before the catastrophic partition, have finally regained something of the security and respectability of middle classness. But the memories of the precariousness of that security lingered, perhaps even haunted the generation that had lost the security of their childhood middle classness and then toiled for decades before regaining it.

What sharpened the sense of precarious middle classness was also the fact that after the initial phase of migration, families of lower class and caste backgrounds had made up the bulk of the refugees. Though colonies such as Bijoygarh tried hard to keep out these humbler coreligionists from the east, they too squatted nearby. Eventually, many of these latter squatters, especially their women folk, started working as domestic servants in the houses of the middle class squatters (Ray 121). This cheek and jowl existence, both necessary and unpalatable to the middle class squatters, further sharpened their sense of loss and precariousness.

One of the few ways out of this precariousness and proximity to poverty lay through education. One of the first "battles" fought by the refugee-squatters against the police had been for the establishment of a boy's school. A girl's school followed a year later (121). The local school, Ray eloquently points out, was "the most potent source of the imaginative mapping of the community." But it was more. The whole colony, says Ray, resembled something of an "education factory." The push for education or *shiksha* was enormous and relentless. Parents pushed their sons and daughters harder and harder into the "*shiksha* factory." For it was education, they thought, that would eventually force urban Calcutta to recognize their "*bhadralok* status," "something [they] thought [they] rightfully deserved but were deprived of." *Shiksha* would also "demarcate [them] from the subaltern people of [their] locality, few of whose children could complete their schooling" (128).

By the 1990s this emphasis on *shiksha* had taken on new colors. As the squatters had managed to legalize their rights to the land by the end of the 1970s and acquired government jobs, two things had happened. The colony had become rapidly internally differentiated. A gap had yawned between those who had made it and those who did not. A thriving real estate market, fully equipped with money and muscle, had served to profit from and accentuate these divides. At the same time, the local schools that had earlier served as the focal points of the communal efforts at social mobility began to crumble. Those who were able, now sent their wards to the private, "English medium" schools which proliferated often well outside the squatting colony's boundaries—their children ferried there daily by swanky school buses (140).

As residents of Bijoygarh Colony, Rudrapratap and Bishakha had been through this tumultuous period of the loss and recovery of their *bhadralok*-ness by dint of Rudrapratap's salaried employment. The awareness of their precarious existence and the growing internal differentiation happening around them would have further stoked their efforts to establish Arghya in a firmly middle class job.

Their familial dreams went well until Arghya finished college. He "finished school with Physics, Chemistry and Mathematics," we are informed, before joining a three-year diploma course in Computer Applications at the nearby Jadavpur University. The preference for "science," as Hia Sen has recently noted, had been well-entrenched in Bengali middle class circles at least since the middle of the twentieth century. But this preference, she is clear, was linked to "an economic, employment related sense" rather than an "Enlightenment sense." This was imagined as leading directly to "engineering or medicine," which were seen to be "higher level professions, bearing the markers of both education and economic assurance." Science studied at the university and outside of the engineering and medical streams was conceptualized as being part of the "general stream" and thus relatively looked down upon (Sen 66).

All this, however, began to rapidly change in the 1990s. Sen points out that the preferences were based on the extremely limited number of engineering and medical seats at the handful of government colleges, which in turn ensured a comfortable and secure career for the few who made it in. While the number of jobs and incomes suddenly spiked for a small section of the middle class with the IT boom of the 1990s, an even more radical change followed from the mushrooming of a number of private engineering colleges. The sudden oversupply made these careers much more competitive, and the seemingly well-known paths to economic security suddenly became difficult and unsure. Thus while opportunities to obtain engineering degrees increased, the route to financial security became obscured (Sen 67). Arghya's fate echoes these tones. His choice of a science stream at high school was still motivated by the desire to become an engineer, but the fact that he obtained only a diploma rather than a degree from Jadavpur points to the newly complicated postgraduate scenarios for would-be engineers. The diploma courses were part of the new expansion of routes to an engineering education, but they brought nothing of the security the older engineering degrees had once brought.

In Bijoygarh this was the time when Ray notes that, the "contemporary face of urbanity" became gradually pockmarked by "one of gadget shops with fancy names, corporation vats with bulging, unyielding bellies, 'Sugar and Spice' [a confectionary chain] and other confectioneries, 'joint entrance' [examinations for engineering and medical colleges], tutorial classes, godheads, STD booths, even cybercafés" (141). Arghya was part of this maelstrom, but his fate in it was riddled with uncertainties. The diploma, rather than degree, suggests a poor performance at the "joint entrance" and the mushrooming cybercafés already point toward the bottom-up competition developing for careers with computers.

Arghya initially starts by repairing and servicing some of his neighbor's computers. Perhaps, it was those very computers that had just been installed in the local cybercafés that Arghya serviced. Gradually his network of personal contacts seemed to have crystalized in a reasonably steady income and some renewable commercial contracts for servicing computers. A commercial career like this came with uncertainties or "risks," that Arghya's parents, scarred as they were by a sense of precariousness, had sought to avoid. But contracts depended, unlike the secure jobs they had dreamt of, upon repeated renewals and continued maintenance of both social and professional ties with the clients.

Arghya too recognized the instability of the business, though neither he nor his parents—nor indeed the author—admit it explicitly in the story. Instead, we find Arghya seeking to expand his business by opening a website of his own, an Internet business titled *bhoot.com*.

On a very different front, as the village-like close-knit communal bonds of the squatter colony began breaking down, children from the colonies began moving out more frequently. Parents had always been wary of their children leaving them and not caring for them in their old age. But now those fears appeared much more plausible than before.

At the same time, young men and women in Bijoygarh and elsewhere in Calcutta discovered social media. New romantic possibilities could suddenly be imagined in the glare of the computer screen that had never been considered in the precarious squatter's colony earlier.

Nimmi Rangaswamy and Payel Arora, in their study of Internet-use among the slum-dwelling youth of Hyderabad and Chennai, recently found that, "Looking for romantic opportunities plays a big role in Facebook activity and is dominated by heterosexual dating possibilities aligned with possibilities of upward class mobility via friending women from higher social segments" (10). While Bijoygarh was certainly no slum, at least not by the time the first computers appeared there, the aspirational behavior on platforms like Facebook was likely similar. The attraction of Facebook as a romantic gateway arose from the simple reality that, "socially marginal youth live under highly structured socialization possibilities with young women and their low socioeconomic status affects their heterosexual comportment and dating choices" (10).

Like the new career trajectories opened up by the mushrooming engineering colleges, these new romantic possibilities too were uncharted terrain. This is especially true for the parents, who did not fully engage with social media yet, and for whom these uncharted geographies of the future created new anxieties. Such anxieties naturally built on older experiences and fears, but they were also amplified by the new insecurities. As historian Meredith Borthwick points out for instance, Bengali homes were usually structured around the son's strong bond with his mother, and daughters-in-law were always seen to be a potential threat to this equilibrium (113–114). What added poignancy to this traditional threat was the new, social media-enabled potential for a bride from far away with no ties to the community whatsoever to wrench the son away from the family altogether.

Uncanny Risks

The suburban squatter colonies of south Calcutta, Ray warns us, was a place "infested with ghosts" (122). Poltergeists caused havoc by throwing stones on the roofs of hapless inhabitants, spectral fires burned atop trees in the neighborhood and dead relatives appeared to the living as bright lights. All this of course, had happened when Bijoygarh was still more a squat than a hub of cybercafés.

Once the cybercafés appeared, the ghosts moved from their spectral abodes on treetops into the computers installed on the top floor rooms such as Arghya's. Arghya himself had never really believed in ghosts, though like everyone else around him he was curious about them. Therefore, once he was connected to the Internet, he began searching for information about ghosts out of pure curiosity. He also started his own website, *bhoot.com*, to compile all the information he could find in one place. So far all was good.

At some point however, a seductive specter began to talk to him through his computer. Fascinated as much by her as by the spectral world she signaled toward, Arghya rapidly lost interest in the world outside his computer room. He began skipping meals and foregoing sleep to keep talking to the spectral seductress. Things got worse. He stopped seeing friends or attending to his computer business. As irate clients left and vexed friends withdrew, his parents encouraged him to socialize once more. But Arghya's interest in the familiar social world of Bijoygarh had already diminished to the point of utter apathy. All he could think of was his ghostly lover.

Arghya social death had already occurred, but he also seemed headed for a morbidly slow actual physical death. The skipped meals and lack of sleep was taking its toll on him. His physical health was clearly in decline and his parents, notwithstanding their desperate efforts, remained unable to help him. Things just seemed to be sliding downhill for the worst. Mercifully, the gradual slide was eventually cut short, by one quick, decisive, and tragic step.

Arghya committed suicide by jumping from the balcony of his third floor room. His lover had issued him an ultimatum. She could no longer carry on with him, unless he too became like her—a ghost. Unable to bear the thought of losing her, Arghya chose to join her in the netherworld that now seemed somehow connected to the cyberworld. Rudrapratap found his son and dreams dashed on the pavement below as he stepped out for his morning walk one day.

The parents were naturally distraught and inconsolable. Yet, like good *bhadralok* men and women of their generation, they bore their grief silently and performed their only child's funerary rites with fortitude. Once all this was done and they settled back into their little home bereft of their dreams and aspirations, unexpected things happened once more.

Late at night, the light in Arghya's computer room would mysteriously turn itself on. The computer too would come on by itself. The sound of keys on the keyboard being struck would softly drift down the stairs to his parents, accompanied by other familiar sounds and sights. Arghya, it seemed, was still surfing the Internet from the Great Beyond. Significantly, the possibility of the dead communicating via machines with the living is neither new nor distinctive to the Bengali milieu. There is a fairly long history of the dead using existing telecommunications technologies for communication as well as scientists then trying to build machines explicitly meant for such communications with the Great Beyond. Thomas Alva Edison, the great American inventor, had worked on such a machine. Sconce argues that Edison's dream has lived on: "Born in the wake of radio's discarnate voices and in the full hubris of modernity," writes Sconce,

> Edison's project survives in each new generation of electronic telecommunications technology that sounds an echo of this original voice from the void, defying once again the

corporeal common sense and encouraging speculation that the technology's power to transmute and transmit might be more than a metaphor.

(Sconce 83)

Such parallel genealogies call into question the sometimes misleadingly absolute polarization of "the West" from "the Rest." Marginal and subaltern voices that articulate suppressed ontologies of risk could and did arise at the very heart of technomodernity, for instance in spaces such as Edison's laboratory. Their marginality is not a function of their geographic location as much as of their continually being framed as aberrant, incidental, and inconsequential. Thus while Edison's other contributions are regularly hailed, his readiness to dabble in spiritualism and the occult through the infrastructures of technomodernity are either ignored or framed as quixotic sidelights to his scientific contributions.

But how are we to understand these fears? Is Arghya's ghostly lover a mere cipher for anxieties about exotic women that young colony boys met online and left home for? Was Arghya's own ghost a metaphor for the Internet-enabled communications between parents left back and sons who have moved on? Is Arghya's obsessive behavior with the computer leading up to his death a coda for rising rates of technology addiction?

Sconce is not alone in emphasizing that the power of these computers to communicate with the realm of the dead is "more than a metaphor." Indeed to treat these fears as "metaphors," "ciphers," or "coda" involves an act of unequal translation. As Dipesh Chakrabarty points out with reference to the historian's persistent inability to deal with the explicitly supernatural, "sympathetic or not, these accounts all foreground a separation—a subject-object distinction—between the academic observer-subject and the 'superstitious' person serving as the object of study" (239). By translating the supernatural entities into a rationalized framework where they become mere coda for a deeper, truer reality accessible only to the academic observer–subject, a clear hierarchy is performed. Historicization, Chakrabarty insists, is this creation of a hierarchic frame wherein, since the supernatural is indefensible, the historian must posit a deeper, truer reality that cannot directly be grasped by the superstitious people (97–116). These latter are then alienated from their own lifeworlds via the mystification of the real through the supernatural. To recognize this radical untranslatability of the supernatural into the rational and historical is, for Chakrabarty, to recognize the limits of the historical. What exists simultaneously both with and yet beyond the historical are subaltern pasts.

Historians are not the only ones who disenchant the world and translate the lifeworlds of others into rationalized frames. Biomedical doctors and researchers for instance, do it frequently. In June 2014 for instance, the National Institute of Mental Health And Neuro Sciences (NIMHANS) inaugurated Service for Healthy Use of Technologies ("SHUT"), a clinic just outside Bangalore to combat growing instances of technology addiction. Despite the clinic being far away from Bengal, the resonance of the concerns in Bengal that led to the clinic's inauguration can be seen by the wide coverage that this small piece of news got in the Bengali press on both sides of the border. Newspapers in both Bangladesh and West Bengal reported widely on the center and the phenomenon it addressed. They dubbed the phenomenon *projukti ashokti*. By 2015, Calcutta too got its first center devoted to technology de-addiction. It is run by an NGO named Turnstone Global, but their initiative had the vocal support of psychiatrists working at government hospitals in the city. Besides Bangalore and Calcutta, Delhi and Amritsar now also have de-addiction centers that deal with computer or Internet addictions.

Not all uncanny risks have been thus rationalized. The risk of intergenerational families breaking down through the advent of Facebook-enabled romances, for example, has no place in biomedicine, let alone a broader neoliberal apparatus devoted to profit and choice-maximization of individuals. As Rangaswamy and Arora point out, the vision of development espoused by the World Bank remains firmly centered on choice and the individual. The potential risk posed to families by a regime of individualized choices is entirely illegible to such a regime.

The radically different ontologies of these uncanny risks not only make them un-amenable to the rationalized calculations by inveterate insurance companies, they also mark the limits of rational choice theories of human action. Parents continue to invest in the computer education of their children not because of rational calculations about the choices their wards would have vis-à-vis them, but despite the uncanny foreboding that these very investments might eventually break up the family.

Chakrabarty's discussions of the "subaltern pasts" that clearly demarcate the rational historian from the superstitious peasant–rebel however, assumes a degree of earnest ontological commitment that is unavailable to the readers of ghost stories on suburban trains. Like Arghya many of them might be agnostic about the possibility of haunted computers. Readers of these tales are often motivated by curiosity, thrill, or merely to pass time. Uncanny risks therefore are not the kind of explicit signposts at the boundaries of the rational as subaltern pasts are. They are more likely ambiguous hints toward vague anxieties that cannot be expressed within the dominant ideological apparatus of risk society. The ephemerality of the physical medium, namely, the cheap chap books, and the vagueness of the anxieties, together produce only a foreboding sense of the uncanny, the un-homely.

The clear divisions organized around distinct ontological alterities that populate the mutually constitutive historical and subaltern pasts in Chakrabarty's framework are sustained by a set of polarities such as the rational and the supernatural, the subaltern and the elite, the ever-universalizing logic of what he calls History 1 and the ever-interrupting logic of what he calls History 2. But one does not believe or disbelieve with equal clarity. Literary–textual genres like ghost stories, fantasies, and humorous tall tales sustain a more complex relationship to ontological alterities. Those who enjoy a good ghost story or laugh heartily at an absurd tale do not necessarily believe or disbelieve the ontological assumptions that underwrite the narrative plot. Yet, they engage with the text and enjoy it. This is where a spectrology, rather than a simple historical audit, becomes productive. Spectrology is a form of "postprogressive history" that splits the seam of modernist binaries. In a spectrology, ghosts are a device "that undo certain discursive limits," rather than being the markers of limits between rational history and supernatural, subaltern pasts (Ghosh 205).

A literary tradition of ghost stories, as Bishnupriya Ghosh points out, has left an indelible imprint on the contemporary quest for epistemic alternatives to the dominant forms of science and rationality, tainted as they are by deep associations with capitalism, militarism and empire. Ghosh recalls Rabindranath Tagore's ghost story, *Khudita Pashan* (*Hungry Stones*), and its genetic influence on Amitav Ghosh's postcolonial science fiction thriller, *Calcutta Chromosome*. These narratives, Tagore's and Amitav Ghosh's, do not sustain the clear distinctions of Chakrabarty's historical analysis. What has come down to Ghosh through Tagore is not a clear-cut, definite belief in an alternate ontology that refuses to rationalize the supernatural. Rather, it is a vague foreboding about our habitations in modernity: a language of doubt that resists resolution into an alterity that might be posed as an ethical choice.

Neither the parents nor their heirs in suburban refugee colonies like Bijoygarh, tottering on the brink of the thin end of the middle class, had much of a choice about entering the contemporary "risk society." But that did not stop them from feeling un-homely within its digital infrastructures. Yet, how does one speak of the risks of risk society itself? They did have a range of older idioms of risks. Not calculable risks capable of domestication, but more uncanny risks: risks that could be tackled by rituals and prayers, rather than by buying insurance.

Ray recalls, for instance, the pacification of ghosts in the colonies through older technologies such as *Shoni puja* (pacificatory rituals to the malignant deity Saturn) in his childhood. A simple perusal of the advertisements in the Bengali press show that such technologies continue to thrive and diversify. There is an ever-growing repertoire of ritual and magical services being advertised to help people navigate the caprices of risk society: amulets to crack entrance examinations, spells to get jobs, blessings to find love—the list is endless. But these can hardly any longer be considered exterior to the risk society itself. The advertisements themselves signal to entrepreneurial opportunities in the realm of the occult. Dynamic ritual specialists prominently display their mobile phone numbers and email addresses. Most importantly, they stoke, rather than in any way interrupt, the new aspirations engendered by the neoliberal cocktail of individualism, choice and privatization. Jean and John Comaroff, observing a similar eruption of occult businesses in South Africa, have christened it a new, "millennial capitalism" (292–293).

As these older languages of exteriority are progressively appropriated and repurposed in ways that are utterly compatible with the hegemonic ideologies of risk, more ambiguous, feral forms of this older language gain greater importance. As real ghosts are compelled by entrepreneurial Tantrik shamans to don neoliberal clothes, it is the more ambiguous reality of the ghosts in low-brow chapbooks that keep alive a tradition of doubting. Such doubting will not qualify as an alternate ontology or a subaltern past that is confident enough to resist the juggernaut of risk. But it continues to doggedly lurk around the iconic machines that run the risk society, producing forever a sense of un-homeliness that is too vague to be clearly spelled out and yet too visceral to be entirely ignored. As long as all those dreamy-eyed youngsters hurtling to their slightly ad hoc computer schools find it pleasurable to read the cheap ghost stories on the crowded suburban trains, even if they do not believe in ghosts, there will be a lurking, amorphous language of doubts about the reality of risks that can be domesticated. In the meantime as the doggerel, on the inside flap of the collection in which Arghya's story appeared, reminds us:

> Some say there are *bhoots*, some there are no *bhoots*
> At night, stepping outside, with a start you see nothing
> If *bhoots-petnis* come running to scare you
> Remember there is nothing as dangerous as the human-ghosts!

Notes

1 I would like to thank the editors of this volume for their encouragement and interest in my pursuit of haunted computers. Manjita Mukharji has also earned my gratitude for accompanying me on my forays on local trains and into spectral computers.
2 The translations are mine.
3 This is my own rough translation of the song.

Works Cited

BASIS. "1 Percent of Country's GDP Will Come from Software and IT Services within Next 5 Years." October 7, 2013, www.basis.org.bd/index.php/media/news_detail/217. Accessed July 10, 2017.
Beck, Ulrich. *Risk Society: Towards a New Modernity*. Translated by Mark Ritter, Sage, 1986.
Borthwick, Meredith. *The Changing Role of Women in Bengal, 1859–1905*. Princeton UP, 1984.
Chakrabarty, Dipesh. *Provincializing Europe: Postcolonial Thought and Historical Difference*. Princeton UP, 2000.
Chakraborty, Kabita. *Young Muslim Women in India: Bollywood, Identity and Changing Youth Culture*. Routledge, 2016.
Chatterjee, Chandrani. *Translation Reconsidered: Culture, Genre and the 'Colonial Encounter' in Nineteenth Century Bengal*. Cambridge Scholars Press, 2010.
Chaudhuri, Sukanta. "Archiving 'Popular Market' Bengali Books." Endangered Archives Program, 2007, doi: https://doi.org/10.15130/EAP127.
Chaudhuri, Sukanta. *View from Calcutta*. Chronicle Books, 2002.
Chowdhury, Masud Hasan and Md. Mahbub Murshed. "Computer." *Banglapedia*, http://en.banglapedia.org/index.php?title=Computer. Accessed on July 10, 2017.
Comaroff, Jean and John Comaroff. "Millennial Capitalism: First Thoughts on a Second Coming." *Public Culture*, vol. 12, no. 2, 2000, pp. 291–343.
"Compiutar Bhoot." *Compiutar Bhoot*, edited by Nantu Ganguly. S. Saha, 2008, pp. 3–9.
Deb, Siddhartha. *The Beautiful and the Damned: Life in New India*. Penguin Viking, 2011.
Donner, Henrike. "Committed Mothers and Well-adjusted Children: Privatization, Early-years Education and Motherhood in Calcutta." *Modern Asian Studies*, vol. 40 no. 2, 2006, pp. 371–395.

Donner, Henrike. *Domestic Goddesses: Maternity, Globalization and Middle Class Identities in Contemporary India.* Routledge, 2008.

Edgerton, David. *Shock of the Old: Technology and Global History Since 1900.* Profile Books, 2008.

Freud, Sigmund. "The 'Uncanny.'" *The Standard Edition of The Complete Psychological Works of Sigmund Freud,* vol. XVII. Translated by James Strachey, the Hoggarth Press, n.d., pp. 219–252.

Ghosh, Bishnupriya and Bhaskar Sarkar. "Introduction." *Media and Risk.* Routledge, 2020.

Ghosh, Bishnupriya. "On Grafting the Vernacular: The Consequences of Postcolonial Spectrology." *Boundary 2,* vol. 31, no. 2, 2004, pp. 197–218.

Giddens, Anthony. *Modernity and Self Identity: Self and Society in the Late Modernity.* Polity Press, 1991.

Goswami, Anindita. "Laptop." *Ga Chhomchhome Bhoot,* edited by Anon. Mitra & Ghosh Publishers Pvt., 2010, pp. 302–311.

Helal, Mohammad and Mahjabeen Rahman. "Bangladesh's IT Industry: The Next Frontier?" *The Daily Star,* December 3, 2016, www.thedailystar.net/op-ed/bangladeshs-it-industry-1324174. Accessed July 10, 2017.

MacKenzie, Donald. *Mechanization of Proof: Computing, Risk and Trust.* MIT Press, 2001.

Milburn, Colin. *Nanovision: Engineering the Future.* Duke UP, 2008.

Nasscom, "The IT-BPM Sector in India." *Strategic Review 2017,* www.nasscom.in/knowledge-center/publications/it-bpm-industry-india-2017-strategic-review. Accessed July 10, 2017.

Porter, Theodore M. *Trust in Numbers: The Pursuit of Objectivity in Science and Public Life.* Princeton UP, 1995.

Rajaraman, V. *History of Computing in India 1955–2010.* Indian Institute of Science, 2012.

Rangaswamy, Nimmi and Payel Arora, "The Mobile Internet in the Wild and Everyday: Digital Leisure in the Slums of Urban India." *International Journal of Cultural Studies,* vol. 19, no. 6, 2016.

Ray, Manas. "Growing Up Refugee." *Partitioned Lives: Narratives of Home, Displacement and Resettlement,* edited by Anjali Gera Roy and Nandi Bhatia. Pearson Longman, 2008, p. 120.

Ripon, Dewan Humayun Kobir. *Compiutare Bhoot Dhukechhe.* Tumpa Prokashoni, 2011.

Sconce, Jeffrey. *Haunted Media: From Telegraphy to Television.* Duke UP, 2000.

Sen, Hia. *'Time Out' in the Land of Apu: Childhoods, Bildungsmoratorium and the Middle Classes of Urban West Bengal.* Springer DE, 2012.

Sen, Samudra. "Bhooter Preme Bhoot Howa." *Bhooter Karbar,* edited by Sumanta Banik, Sri Guru Pustakalay, n.d., pp. 3–9.

Simeone, Michael. "Why We Will Not Be Posthuman: Gadgets as a Technocultural Form." *Configurations,* vol. 19, no. 3, 2011, pp. 333–356.

Tagore, Rabindranath. *Hungry Stones and Other Stories.* Rupa Publications Pvt. Ltd, 2002.

12
NEW MEDIA AT RISK
Or When the Future Ain't What it Used To Be

Timothy Murray

Who would think that an American icon of popular sports culture, the baseball player, Yogi Berra, might provide the titular framework for a consideration of the valence of risk in the era of digital cinematics? A popular manager and player for the New York Yankees in the Cold War era, Berra's quirky truisms permeated American popular culture. I marshalled one of my favorite Berra quotes, "The Future Ain't What It Used To Be," for the epigraph of the concluding chapter my book, *Digital Baroque*. In that chapter, "Time @ Cinema's Future," I reflected on the temporal fable of new media art, often termed "Future Cinema," to consider how new media art constitutes the structural paradox of temporality. While serving as an artistic activation of passing presents, in which one moment goes while another comes to shape the future, new media art simultaneously creates networked traces and digital archives that prevent the past from falling into the inaccessible depths of the totally obscure. *Digital Baroque* concludes by calling attention to the alterations and risks of futurity that are promised by rapid developments in artificial intelligence and software-based art. Now that media studies finds itself poised a decade later on the precipice of a state of emergency of intertwined hegemonic networks, anthropocenic entropy, and renewed talk of nuclear proliferation, I find myself contemplating how we might marshal an improvisational approach through art and fiction to further the dialogue between media and risk studies, one that would highlight the tensions between ontologies and epistemologies of risk while reflecting anew on the artistic contributions of "Future Cinema" and its philo-political imperatives. This approach will foreground the paradoxes of the perceptual fields of the medial interface while suggesting the importance of fabulation in responding to the futures of risk. Put simply, are the futures of cinema and risk what they used to be?

The German theorist, Ulrich Beck, places the study of risk at the cusp of futurity. As the anticipation of catastrophe, "risk concerns the possibility of future consequences and developments: they make present a state of affairs that does not (yet) exist" (Beck 9). But rather than tilt human intellectual labor toward a prophylactic eradication of futurity, Beck translates anticipation and any attempt to "colonize" the future into the contemporary ontological imperative. Sweeping aside Descartes's insistence on thought as the driving condition of existence, Beck embraces the exercise of risk as the twenty-first century's ontological condition: "I risk, therefore I am" (5). In subtle contrast, Gerda Reith shifts the strategy to "Living with Risk," in her contribution to the collection, *The Aesthetics of Risk*, from an ontological approach to an epistemological one. As the "calculation of uncertainty in the future," risk, she argues, "is fundamentally an epistemological category—it exists as a category of knowing; not as an aspect of being" (59). This epistemological emphasis extends the object of knowing beyond the delimitations of ontology to the extensively interlocked temporal screens of self, animal, and environment.

Consider the impact of the loosening of the confident barriers of ontology for the challenging enigmas of epistemology. For philosophy, ontology traditionally positions the human thinking subject at the authoritative center of earthly life. In contrast, recent enthusiasm for what is termed Object Oriented Ontology (OOO) swaps out the inhabitant of the ontological center of existence from the human thinking subject to things in their complex aggregation. In either case, ontology is mapped around the dynamics of mind–body or human–thing duality. Regardless of the direction in which it tilts, the center maintains the delicate balance of its ontological dualism. But Reith's emphasis on risk as an epistemological challenge could be said to steer away from the very notion of a "center" per se. By asking her readers to turn aside from assumptions about *what* they know in relation to the confident center of existence, her more open question of *how* we know could be said to take up the challenge posed 40 years earlier by Jacques Derrida "for a new status of discourse [with] the stated abandonment of all reference to a *center*, to a *subject*, to a privileged reference, to an origin or to an absolute archè" ("Signature, Sign, and Play" 256). Here is where the complexities of the interfaces of contemporary screenic existence enter the discussion by overturning the confidence of the ontological center. In an environment where information technologies and screenic interfaces blend the confident differences of self, animal, and environment, consider the heightened risk to knowing posed by networked explosions and screenic amalgamations of social media, militarized surveillance, environmental data, and artificial intelligence. A vast combinatory of screenic and informational risk can be said to have enveloped the human and nonhuman alike in what Paul Virilio has called the "'immateriality' of perceptual fields" (7). As we shall discuss in more detail below, Virilio foregrounds the notion of the "'immateriality' of perceptual fields" in his mapping of the transformation of warfare through visual technologies which meld the differentiation between subject and object. Such a cultural shift from the confidence of both ontology and perception, inscribed in the militaristic distinction between Us and Them, is enacted by the obscurities of immateriality or virtuality that will shape my following reflections on the promising risks of Future Cinema. Indeed, in arguing for the epistemological valence of experimentations in new media art, I will emphasis the artistic payoff of focusing not on ontology but on fiction and virtuality as a means of screening the symptoms and threats of uncertainty of the future.

I might mention, prior to turning to the mediatic examples on which I will focus, that epistemological approaches to risk line up in fascinating ways with an important lineage of critical (un) knowing reflected in two special issues of the journal, *diacritics*. The journal's special issue on "Nuclear Criticism" of the 1980s bridges with a more recent one on "Climate Change Criticism." In a passage in the "Nuclear Criticism" issue that now can be understood to speak to both the nuclear and the anthropocenic, Jacques Derrida aligns the epistemological risk of the nuclear with the potential of the imaginary.

> It is the war (in other words the fable) that triggers this fabulous war effort, this senseless capitalization of sophisticated weaponry, this speed race in search of speed, this crazy precipitation which, through techno-science, through all the techno-scientific inventiveness that it motivates, structures not only the army, diplomacy, politics, but the whole of the human *socius* today, everything that is named by the old words, culture, civilization, Bildung, scholè, paideia. "Reality," let's say the encompassing institution of the nuclear age, is constructed by the fable, on the basis of an event that has never happened (except in fantasy, and that is not nothing at all), an event of which one can only speak, an event whose advent remains an invention by men (in all senses of the word 'invention'), or which rather, remains to be invented.
>
> *(Derrida "No Apocalypse, Not Now" 23–24)*

As a prelude to my reflections to come, Derrida aligns the scary inventiveness of the techno-scientific war machine with the speedy precipitation of its response to the nuclear risks of the future. Derrida's essay, "No Apocalypse, Not Now," encourages us to reflect on the wide net cast by the discourse of the historical theater of the war machine, one frequently upheld by the inventions of fable regarding events that have never happened. Even Future Cinema might be understood, let's say, to always already have gone nuclear in its creative capitalization of screenic inventions, from virtual software systems to transformations of the portable screen itself on which war morphs into fiction as the dominant scenario of gaming culture. This morphing goes literally nuclear when the distanced trance of gaming spills into digital warfare systems manned by drone operators from far-flung suburban sites. With the fabular abstractions of these remote militarized digital systems, users—whether of military or entertainment packages—can distance themselves from the devastating impact of their actions on humankind and its environments. The risk entails the elimination of the slippages of metacritical knowledge through which playful immersion in interactive gaming might generate reflection on, or even critique of, the very system nurturing it.

In contrast, the risks inherent in digital medial culture can just as easily be foregrounded by the helpful machineries of socially informed gaming and interactive media installation. Such was the critical effect of Harun Farocki's 2012 MOMA exhibit, "Images of War (At a Distance)," which exhibited documentary footage from off-site military training centers where soldiers practiced the gaming techniques on which they would rely for the deadly business of operating drones from the other side of the world. Their training on the virtual systems of gaming made seamless the soldiers' subsequent engagement in the slaughter of virtual warfare. Farocki's insertion of this footage in the "between" spaces of artistic framing and museum play illuminated the underbelly of the widespread fusion of gaming and warfare. Employed by Farocki was the playful fabric of artistic fabulation through which participants could both enjoy and reflect upon the representational structures in which they are embedded.[1]

In the special *diacritics* issue on "Climate Change Criticism," the editor of the "Nuclear Criticism" issue 30 years earlier, Richard Klein, returns to Derrida's earlier emphasis on the fabulation of nuclear war to make a further qualification about the critical status of fictionality in the precarious age of climate change.

> The ultimate catastrophe [of climate change] is therefore a fiction, but it nevertheless is one that has very material consequences in the present. That is what distinguishes it from fables that are mere inventions. It is a necessary postulation in order to recognize the symptoms and dangers of climate change, and that recognition, however muted politically, is already at work in the phantasms and dreams of people today… In our unconscious the worst may have already happened. And yet whenever we try to imagine what lies beyond our own death, or beyond the human species, after the ultimate apocalyptic disaster, we assume the condition of ghosts, between life and death, able to view in retrospective the world from which we are absent.
>
> *(85)*

What might we make of an approach to media and risk in which fiction and fantasy, neither reason nor ontology, might lie at the core of critical response to cataclysmic threat? I address this question at a moment when the discourses both of nuclear eradication and climate change disaster are being challenged by the "alternative facts" of the Trump administration, which has ramped up the specter of nuclear war. How might new media art turn not to fact, "real" or "alternative," but to fiction to capitalize on the imperative of inventing and producing the spectacle of the symptoms and dangers of the uncertainty of the future? And what might be produced when criticism embeds itself in improvisation, as I am about to do, in the retelling of fictional tales whose theoretical lessons might be worth attending to, on their own fictional terms? Put otherwise, how might an embedded time-traveler in new media fiction, via the medium of curated improvisation, assist critical discourse in foregrounding the symptoms and dangers of risk in the new media age, "however muted politically," as Klein might say, "and already at work in the phantasms and dreams of people today"?

As I perused my archive for new media materials with which to imagine a response to these queries, I found myself attracted to a grouping of early materials that focused on the parameters of Derrida's disjunction of ontology and fable, the being of the war machine and the inventive fabulation of its futurity. These works, now recognized as canonical examples of new media art, ranged from Stelarc's self-oriented performances with militaristic robots (Grzinic) to the feminist response of "All New Gen," the CD-Rom by VNS Matrix that performed the mantra of the feminist collective's 1991 "Cyberfeminist Manifesto for the 21st Century": "we are the virus of the new world disorder/rupturing the symbolic from within/saboteurs of big daddy mainframe/the clitoris is a direct line to the matrix" (VNS Matrix "Cyberfeminist Manifesto for the 21st Century"). A similar rupture of the symbolic from within was performed in 1994 by Critical Art Ensemble's (CAE) parodic assemblage of a catalogue of "Useless Technology" that grouped together the latest gadgets for electronic cooking with the most sophisticated inventions of the military–industrial complex, all under the expansive umbrella of neoliberal capitalism. Designed as a newspaper advertising insert, this inventory was initially inserted into Sunday papers available in curbside dispensers; they subsequently were redesigned for CAE's website as an early piece of net.art. In CAE's article, "Not So Quiet on the Western Front: Report on Risk and Cultural Resistance within the Neoliberal Society of Fear," also included in *The Aesthetics of Risk*, the collective articulates the goal of its political approach to risk in terms of the artistic performance of utopian ideals that can never be fully realized. In solidarity with the aims of VNS Matrix, the goal of their artistic fabulations "is to challenge and rearrange the symbolic order with the hope that the effects of the action may continue into the material order, creating further rearrangement of power relations" (Critical Art Ensemble, "Not So Quiet on the Western Front," in Welchman 358). But, as we will see, a critical fixation on rearranging the symbolic order per se—in a way that might indirectly reinvigorate the notion of an authoritative center—might be insufficient for responding to the expansive risks of the military–industrial complex as it morphs speedily across the neoliberal network. Perhaps something of an artistic re-writing or re-wiring of the field of play would be beneficial, something of a fictionalization of critical fields whose morphing improvisations of perception might skirt through performance the symbolic parameters of the big daddy mainframe. Might we not be empowered, as Klein suggests, to reimagine through fiction how symptoms and dangers of climate change and militaristic incursion have already impinged on our material comfort in the future?

What ultimately grabbed my attention for this fabulous imperative was a grouping of pioneering artworks whose elaborate fictions of cinematic time-traveling might make their artists less noticeable as tactical media practitioners. My improvisatory reflections on media and risk will be staged in dialogue with moments from works by three strange time-traveling bedfellows all of which curiously are experiencing various incarnations of web revivals at this very moment when Trump has been renewing nuclear tensions: David Blair's 1991 video, "WAX or the Discovery of Television among the Bees," which, after transference in 1993 to 16 mm, became the first online feature film made available in downloadable segments, and which was the subject of a Transmediale, January 29, 2017, interview with Blair; Suzanne Treister's 1995 artistic CD-Rom, "… No Other Symptoms —Time Travelling with Rosalind Brodsky"—whose page on the centenary of the 1917 Russian Revolution was circulated by Treister over the network to mark Trump's first week in office (with both Blair and Treister being featured this same week at Transmediale); and, Hito Steyerl's 2015 installation, *Factory in the Sun*, featured again in the Whitney Museum's 2017 immersive cinema exhibition, "Dreamlands." These pieces are all situated within the expansive risk of the military–industrial complex and foreground the tension between ontology and epistemology by encapsulating their protagonists in protective and militaristic time-traveling costumes and 3-D capture systems.

Immateriality of Perceptual Fields

Before turning to the artworks at issue, permit me to take a moment to revisit the well-traveled ground of the symbiotic relationships between war and cinema, the charged relations on which my selected artists reflect. In opening his book on *War and Cinema: The Logistics of Perception*, Paul Virilio reminds us that Napoleon is reported to have said, "the capacity for war is the capacity for movement" (10). Virilio mobilizes this anecdote to emphasize how movement similarly constitutes the capacity for cinema whose motion embodies film art's enactment in the flow of time. The lineage of French thought about cinematic movement also led Chris Marker to identify war as one of the two distinguishing traits of the history of cinema (the other being woman …). Bernard Stiegler thinks similarly of cinema as "a temporal object," one whose mobility in time coincides with "the flux of the consciousness for which it is an object" (Stiegler 30). Such an interlacing of movement and vision also corresponds interestingly to Virilio's account of the militaristic logic of perception. Virilio's *War and Cinema* makes an exciting argument for the role of telescopic and screenic mediations in transferring combat from face-to-face physical encounter to distanced aggression via the mediation of virtual interfaces that developed alongside the developing histories of cinema and new media. The role of the screen becomes paramount in this equation since mental perception and screenic vision displace the battle field and physical contact as the apparati of attack. The view finders of early cinema morph into the immaterial signals of drone and planetary communication. In pondering the military's adoption in the twentieth-century of the term "theatre weapon" to replace "theatre of operations," Virilio emphasizes the importance of cinematic virtuality as the perceptual precondition of attack, or "the fact that *the history of battle is primarily the history of radically changing fields of perception*. In other words," adds Virilio, "war consists not so much in scoring territorial, economic or other material victories as in appropriating the 'immateriality' of perceptual fields" (7). The mediatics of virtuality stand in as war machine.

For David Blair's character, the amateur beekeeper Jacob Maker, the perceptual fields of the militaristic and the cinematic blend as one. Maker is the narrator and protagonist of Blair's video, "WAX or the Discovery of Television among the Bees." Employed at the Alamogordo military training facility as a programmer of gun sight displays for air battle simulators, Maker comes from a distinguished line for which cinema and beekeeping are the family jewels. Jacob's father James Maker, was also known as Hivemaker for his love of his colony of rare Mesopotamian bees. He was a spiritualist cinematographer for the Super Normal Picture Society of London who hoped to cheat the closure of the future, the blankness of death, by capturing photographic evidence of life after death. Bolstered by his belief that spiritual radium in decay could hover in photographic film, he hoped that the gas warfare of World War I would provide him the chance to record the moving spirits of the dead through the haze of cinema.

James's half-sister, Ella, also a photographer of ghosts with the Super Normal Picture Society of London, married the bee scientist, Zoltan Abassid. On their 1916 honeymoon to "see the cowboys," they stopped in Alamogordo, New Mexico, where they remained with their bees. Now flash forward with Blair to Alamogordo during the first atomic test on July 16, 1945, at the Alamogordo Test Range on the Journey of Death desert. Then jump cut 20 years later to the Cold War space race when the astronauts replace the cowboys as the objects of curious spectating. This is when the video introduces Zoltan and Ella's grandson, Jacob, who still lives and works in Alamogordo. He watches over Zoltan's rare bees in the hours when he is no longer working, initially on a training simulator for the space shuttle and now as a programmer of target acquisition systems. To be blunt, Jacob specializes in changing fields of perception.

Perhaps it was the inordinate time he spent in front of the screen building virtual weapons systems trainers, "making sure that everything was as real as possible"—he wasn't sure—but he reports having felt uneasy and didn't understand what was going on. It was at this disquieting crossroads of ontology and epistemology that something inexplicable occurred on a day when Jacob watched the shuttle launch on TV before attending to his bees in his protective suit. He heard voices inside the hive and realized only after the fact that time had frozen and that the bees were transmitting televisual signals via a crystal they magically inserted in his brain. Somehow his protective bee suit had become something of a televisual display receiver. He knew that he'd gone "someplace familiar" but he "couldn't remember where." It was from inside his Bee TV, says Jacob during a critical moment of voice-over,

> when the television turned its gaze on me, for a few moments I could see the world as a deity did, divided into different zones of transmission, that was where I had to go ... into the television and burst through to the past where my future was about to be decided.

From that moment on, the suited protections of the ontology of the bee-maker gives way to changing fields of militarized perception as Jacob "left his old self behind" to be visited by one of the "dead of the future." As the video progresses, he travels through time, sometimes seen walking interminably through the desert in the sweltering cocoon of his bee suit, sometimes represented as passing through time—backwards and forwards—through the appearance of fractalized visual abstractions representative of the screenic visions possessing him. Along the journey of his time travel, he goes to Syria in search of the Tower of Babel, only to be shown by the Bee TV that he was at atomic ground zero. There, the past of cultural memory becomes the now of militarized cine-spectacle as the bees show him a movie entitled, "The Garden of Eden Cave," in which he stars as "Fatboy, the first and loneliest Plutonium Bomb." Indeed, Jacob no longer thinks or even risks, but perceives in the guise of a systematized weapon. "Bee-ing" is now enfolded into the immateriality of perceptual fields.

Téléaction

Ultimately, Bee TV leads Jacob through time to one of the infinite planets of the future dead, where in the Temple of Death both priests and military planners were deciding on "the shape of the new culture." While new media culture sports something of a utopian cast in Blair's *Wax*, the technological drive of a new military–industrial–televisual–digital culture is what gives pause to many philosophers of new technology. Stiegler might be inclined to see in the televisual culture of Bee TV the artistic incarnation of what he calls the global system of simultaneous televisual diffusion, or put more darkly, the nefarious system of *téléaction*. In contrast to the particularities of cinema and how its status as a temporal object activates the passing present of "waiting" for something that will come, the mass diffusion of the *téléaction* system envelops the global field of perception in the same temporal–industrial object. Stiegler argues that this system of "télédiffusion" permits a mass public to watch simultaneously the same temporal objects, such as a missile launch, in all places of a territory—something of a medialized OOO. It also, and most significantly, empties the social promise of the future by transforming the nature of the event and thereby leveling the differentiation of the most intimate life of the inhabitants of a territory (Stiegler 62). This uniform blandness constitutes the state of emergency of the *téléaction* system as it activates the temporal risk of emptied futurity.

Sounding the alarm over the degree of risk inherent in new digital technologies, Jean-François Lyotard notes similarly that the transformation of the perceptual event by the technical-industrial complex guarantees that the future won't be what it used to be.

> As is clearly shown by the development of the techno-scientific system, technology and the culture associated with it are under a necessity to pursue their rise.... The human race is, so to speak, "pulled forward" by this process without possessing the slightest capacity for mastering it.... In as much as a monad in thus saturating its memory is stocking the

future, the present loses its privilege of being an ungraspable point from which, however, time should always distribute itself between the "not yet" of the future and the "no longer" of the past.

(Lyotard 64–65)

The pulling forward of futurity, as evidenced by the economy of planned technological obsolescence, thus empties the magnetism of the present as the energetic and ungraspable hinge between past and future. One might be inclined to say that any consideration of such an emptied out present requires not, thinking back to Beck, the centering of the ontology of risk, but the flexible variations of the epistemology of risk.

It is in the drive of this informatic pull of the future that Stiegler, similarly, locates the highest degree of risk in the rise of global media. At stake for him is the dissolution of the plenitude of fiction and fantasy that Blair stages as chafing the morphing ontologies of military–industrial–digital capitalism. Stiegler ushers the dire warning that

the technical network of the production and diffusion of symbols produced for a planetary industry [the system of *téléaction*] can overwhelm the universal desire of fiction and at the same time condition the entire evolution of humanity at the risk of exhausting its desire for fables.

(Stiegler 30)

Indeed, might not the profusion of planetary symbols and power relations counter the productivity of tactical media's aim to "rearrange the symbolic order," to recall the imperative of Critical Art Ensemble, especially if the attendant result is the exhaustion of fictional explorations? When technology so morphs into its own teleology, as the advance of a thoroughly predetermined futurity of technology for technology's sake, little space is left for fiction, little possibility of speculative imagination.

Something akin to the emergency of such an exhaustion of fabulation is staged by Hito Steyerl in *Factory in the Sun*. The promotional material for this piece asserts that it stages the state of emergency itself in exploring "what possibilities are still available for collective resistance when surveillance has become a mundane part of an increasingly virtual world" (Museum of Contemporary Art, Los Angeles). Here participants in this immersive installation sit in lounge chairs enveloped by the 3D traces of laser grids imprinted on all surfaces of the installation space. It's as if the spectators are enveloped by the apparatus of the motion capture system they witness on the screen facing them. The fable here is not the narrative of a character but of a game, as narrated by the onscreen tutorial of the fictional programmer, Yulia. Participants in both Yulia's game and Steyerl's installation move in and out of the screening of interrelated realities. Video verité TV news alerts blend with historical footage and narrative voice-over to provide a textured tapestry that melds the allure of fiction with the appearance of historical fact. Early in the loop, Yuila lingers on what appears to be her own autobiographical data on the CD-Rom around which the video is structured, such as the game's account of the journey of a Soviet army family whose father is shot dead at the border while attempting to immigrate with the mother to Israel. Most compelling is an abrupt news alert that announces the search for four fugitives who escaped their forced labor in a motion capture studio designed to convert movement into sunshine. This story line becomes juxtaposed and layered by accounts of the 3D motion capture studio where the enslaved mimic the installation's viewers who are told at the outset of the ludic event, "you will not be able to play this game, it will play you." Midway through the screening, the participants come to share the paranoid position of the enslaved dancers when both are told by voice-over that "at this point in the game, you are your own enemy and have to move your way through the motion capture studio."

The threat of capture within the composite power system of game and reality pervades *Factory of the Sun*. At a later point in the piece, "Breaking News" announces "a person was killed at the Deutsche Bank Sunshine campus where scientists try to accelerate the speed of light to improve high frequency trading." A spokesperson for Deutsche Bank responds to the news interviewer that "ok, we killed him, but not really … he probably was a terrorist." In this sequence, the threat of probability—what Gerda Reith calls the "calculation of uncertainty in the future," is what overshadows the certainty of ontology. The improvisatory dangers of chance and even of fabulation to the speculation of technoscience and to the technology of planned obsolescence stand out here as both the lifeblood and the life threatening risk to the closed economy of the apparatus of high frequency trading. Its antidote is death at the hands of Deutsche Bank, "in line," adds the news report, with "a continuation of the Third Reich." Whether a blast into the nefarious nationalist past now haunting Europe and the U.S. anew or the promise of new corporate fascism to come, as when an elite class of billionaires of neoliberal capital seize control of the world's most powerful government, the new military–industrial–digital system of technoscience constitutes what Stiegler warns as an "immense risk of bewitching in all senses" (Stiegler 294).

Medial Fabulation

Is there a better context in which to consider the proclaimed aim of The Institute of Militronics and Advanced Time Interventionality (IMATI), the site of the time travels of Suzanne Treister's ingenious character, Rosalind Brodsky? The researchers at this government-funded organization in South London develop bewitching simulations of key moments in history within which they enact "interventions/experiments." As if an endorsement of the military–corporate research agenda of the neoliberal university intent on reducing the study of both fiction and epistemology, their results "are made available to the government, various market research companies and selected universities." In the 1990s, Rosalind Brodsky, the protagonist of Treister's 1999 CD-Rom, is said to have been a relatively normal artist teaching in a London art school until she became "firmly in the grip of time travel related obsessional delusional fantasies," thinking herself to be a researcher at IMATI in the twenty-first century. The CD-Rom, "…No Other Symptoms: Time Travelling with Rosalind Brodsky," offers users the opportunity to tour Brodsky's Bavarian home, which she left to the Institute upon her death in 2058 along with her costumes, recipes, decorated vibrators, and notes of her psychoanalytic sessions across the twentieth century with Freud, Jung, Klein, Lacan, and Kristeva. The tour transforms the CD-Rom's users into the likes of curious Jacob Makers as they leap through televisual teleportation into the future of 2058, just as they accompany Brodsky back into the past via her diary's accounts of analysis with the infamous shrinks of the previous decade. And somewhat like Jacob Maker himself, Brodsky is catapulted across the two decades via the signals of her time-traveling costume whose interactive impact stretches far and wide.

In one interactive sequence, users come upon Lacan's notes on a session with Brodsky in which he mentions that she herself carried electrifying powers. When she once grabbed Lacan's jacket the lights went out and he was transported into the imaginary of *Mary Poppins*, much like the Bee TV's effect on Jacob Maker. Also similar to the Bee TV, Brodsky's time-traveling outfit makes her prone to fascinating immersion in futuristic cinema, from the 1982 film, *Blade Runner* (with which Lacan could not have been familiar when she mentioned the film at the time of her session in 1978), to the English television series *The Tomorrow People* (which was actually running from 1973–1979 at the time of her sessions with Lacan). This television program about *Tomorrow* could signal both autobiography and the uncanny experience of first generation users of interactive media as it "featured a group of children who had reached the next stage of evolution, Homo Superior, and who had powers of telekinesis and telepathy, whilst being able to teleport themselves around the universe at will" (Treister). Whether through the electrifying transference of psychoanalysis, which Lacan figures as the fractured screen of perception, or via the telepathic travels through time and television, the combinatory of screenic risk encompasses both the characters and users of Treister's CD-Rom in the immateriality of perceptual fields. Unsettling the threatened fortifications of ontology, "...No Other Symptoms" foregrounds the epistemological task of recognizing the uncertainty of the future through fiction and, thus, of facing the phantasmatic uncertainty of knowledge itself.

This parody of research and its fabulation, verifiable or not, foregrounds the critical stakes of artistic responses to the risk of being captured by what Stiegler warns as the hegemonic pull of temporal objects and the global synchronization of spectatorial consciousness. But what might it mean for an artist such as Treister to stage suspension in time travel, or even perhaps suspension in the *fantasy* or imagination of movement through time? Might not this open critical fissures in both how we understand the aesthetic risks of new media and how interactive art might enhance the flux of critical fabulation?

Jonathan Crary might be inclined to disabuse these musings from the outset. In his provocative book, *24/7: Late Capitalism and the Ends of Sleep*, Crary argues that "to be preoccupied with the aesthetic properties of digital imagery, as are many theorists and critics, is to evade the subordination of the image to a broad field of non-visual operations and requirements." The threat here lies in critical insensitivity to the maximization of "the amount of time spent in habitual forms of individual self-management and self-regulation" given the general erosion of distinctions between work and leisure (Crary). Perhaps another way to approach this challenge might be to seize upon the invitation of Rosalind Brodsky for whom the self-absorptions of baking, psychoanalysis, rock music, and even dildo pleasuring intertwined her work and leisure for the purposes of researching the opportunistic risks of self-regulation through the fabulation of thinking time itself.

For Brodsky, aesthetic intervention lies at the core of her resistance to the military-industrial temporal objects that so dominate her research. Consider the curiosity of the advertisement sponsored by the NutraGenetica Corporation that pops up in the section of "… No Other Symptoms" documenting Brodsky's passion for cooking and mixing recipes. The ad introduces "*Nature's Way*,"

> a serum which allows you to grow anything from fruit to vegetables to a chicken, on your own body overnight. Just inject the serum into the upper leg or torso before going to bed and snip off and regenerate in the morning. You are no doubt familiar with our *MarsGro back-powder*, bacteria imported from Mars which comes in several varieties. Just add water to grow your own Martian fingers, ribs and upper thighs.
>
> (Treister)

From fantasies of the international food crisis wrought by the Anthropocene to the fright of Stelarc's extra ear and his performances of recombined robotic and biogenic body parts, the artistic play of this ad condenses the critical interventions of tactical media that now cross three decades. We need only remember the seriousness of the arrest and failed prosecution for bioterrorism of CAE member, Steve Dietz, when police, upon being summoned to respond to the sudden death of his wife, inadvertently discovered his artistic laboratory for experimenting with cloned foodstuffs, which he had set up at home in preparation for his aborted exhibition at Massachusetts Museum of Contemporary Art. His subsequent embrace of the action of art for his legal defense foregrounded the extent to which the fictions of art blend with the realities of performance when the authorities are handcuffed by their inability to distinguish one performance of terror from another. The fictions of art here have grave consequences for the confidence of the symbolic order.

Digital Folds, or the Critical Rub of *Écotechnie*

In my book, *Digital Baroque*, I propose that developments in digital "future cinema" marked a deeply significant archeological shift from *projection* to *fold*, which is emphasized, if not wholly embodied, by the digital condition. While still enveloped in models of ontology and representation derived from the temporal objects of single-point perspective and Euclidean systems of projection (whether the stuff of the cinematic apparatus or the variants of GPS tracking and militarized drones), the fold, I argue in dialogue with Derrida and Deleuze,[2] embodies the elasticity of seriality and the continuous labyrinth of single points (1s and 0s). These folds expand infinitely in all directions rather than definitively in the shape of a cone, line, or sight that culminates in a centralized single, utopian point or subjectivity. Such a concept turns around the paradoxical inscription of paradigms of projection, dialectics, and philosophical teleology and ontology in dizzying procedures of accumulation, divergence, fractal simultaneity, and epistemology. I might have said that the fold enacts the very risk of the threat of "future cinema" to the hegemony of temporal objects themselves. It is via the undulating procedures of the fold, which envelope the certainties of the military–industrial–digital complex in the activations of fantasy, fictionality, and criticality, that the artworks I have been discussing perform the accumulating psycho-televisual energetics of critical fiction and visualization.

Blair's *Wax*, for instance, is replete with complex abstract moments where tracking shots of Jacob Maker's wanderings give way to phantasmal visions of time travel through fractalized zones and image fields. Blair activates the emergent visual phantasmagoria of experimental video and new media visual processing systems to offer his viewers entry into a visual field that folds actual images into their virtual extensions to the point of their being indistinguishable. Jacob's precision targets of virtual weapon systems open up the viewer's immersion in fields of unexpected motion back and forth through time, in shapes that fold and bend abstractly along the parameters of the screenic perceptions receiving them. Jacob himself narrates the highlight of his own visual transformation at the moment when the bees temporarily transform him into the miraculous shape of a triangular crystal, as if evoking Deleuze's figure for transformative passage through the becomings of cinematic time. Indeed, there are multiple compelling moments in *Wax* when the dependability of Jacob's voice-over cedes to the spectacular time travel of abstracted and fractalized visuality. The visual fields capitalize on something akin to what Deleuze describes as the opening of experimental cinema to "the any-space-whatevers of the visual image," to "the empty or disconnected spaces," to "the deserted layers of our time which bury our phantasms," to "lacunary layers which we juxtaposed according to variable orientations and connections" (*Cinema 2* 243–244). While Deleuze associates these layers with the deserts of Pasolini and Antonioni, we could just as easily recognize these visual fields in the desert images and fractalized imaginaries of David Blair.

Indeed, Blair himself further plunged into the creative openness of the digital fold by transforming the visual clarity, colorful dazzle, and teleological movement of his beautiful video, *Wax*. He first transferred *Wax* from video to film for broader cinematic distribution. Then, in 1994, he exploded it into 80,000 pieces for the hypermedia version, *WAXWEB*, which was made available for serial consumption over the Internet and on CD-Rom. This intervention is recognized as the inaugural streaming of a full-length film. Blair's radical embrace of the uncertainties of the emergent digital network provided a choice to the user to enter into specific temporal zones of the fabulation of *Wax* and, thus, to rescript the progressions of what Jacob calls the "passing presents" of his story time. It is here that new media and its aesthetic forms contribute to the electronic enhancement of what Deleuze ruminates as "the direct time-image," one whose enfolding relations of time explode the comfort of succession and teleology. Inscribed into the aesthetic fiber of *WAXWEB* are the "undecidable alternatives" of time between "sheets of past, or 'inexplicable' differences between points of present" (*Cinema 2* 274).

You may add to this mix of undecidable alternatives that the entire conceit of Steyerl's *Factory of the Sun* is to explore "what possibilities are still available for collective resistance when surveillance has become a mundane part of an increasingly virtual world" (Museum of Contemporary Art, Los Angeles). This immersive installation figures starkly, moreover, the surreal enactment of the arrival of the anthropocenic future when enslaved workers have to create sunshine through motion capture. *Factory of the Sun* stages the collectivity of resistance to the bondage of sun blocking capital through the installation's figuration of an impromptu breakout of parodic dancing across the Internet. Egged on by the excessive gestures of a boy performing solo for the online camera in his basement, participants across the Internet add to the explosive addiction of participatory dance as crowds of impromptu gyrators raise the stakes of each other's performances in a something of a corporeal shout and response. They subsequently also shout back through their networked swarming at the hegemonic procedures of capitalization which otherwise would want to conserve their movements for the centralized economy of motion capture. Steyerl thus tactically performs the playful way that the memes and parody of social media have blighted the very digital systems of capital and war whose future threats to ecology and activism are now upon us.

Put otherwise, in the language framing this essay, new media art most forcefully embraces its own risk when it ruptures the stabilities of the corporate pull of the future to stage the critical paradox that the future ain't what it used to be. The subsequent drive is that of fabulation, to double down on discursive and artistic responses to the future that have, as Klein would say, material consequences in the present. Nowhere has the paradox and critical provocation of time traveling been more apparent to me than it was at the time of this essay's composition. As I worked through the layering of my tale of the ain't what it used to be of Future Cinema, two Internet images strangely popped onto my screen to foreground the curiosities of both Jacob's and Rosalind's future arrivals in the present. No, I didn't see horrific specters of Trump's hair, his hand, or of Putin's chest. But, as I was writing about Rosalind Brodsky, I was bemused by the uncanny arrival of Brodksy into the twenty-first century when she appeared in my in-box via Treister's distribution to her e-mail list of an image from "…No Other Symptoms," "Rosalind Brodsky's Electronic Time Travelling Costume to Go to the Russian Revolution." Rosalind is said in the CD-Rom, released in 1999, to have celebrated the centenary of the Russian Revolution by traveling to Moscow in the year of 2017. The irony, of course, is that Brodsky traveled into my in-box in 2017, in the future present, at the very moment when the U.S.A. was reeling from the election of Donald Trump as a partial result of Russian hacking meant to assist with his election. Perhaps we might add to the amalgamate a fantasy that Rosalind had just returned with Treister from a weekend of joining women from across the world in protest of the renewal of global fascism promoted by the revolutionary bromance of Trump and Putin. The centenary return of "revolution" now takes on a particularly acerbic cast as scores of global citizens continue to adopt the play of street theater to stem the tide of this Russian bromance.

Even more weirdly, the image of Jacob traversing the desert also resurfaced on my screen the same week via his historical resurrection at Transmediale 2017. In a Transmediale interview about *Wax* that was advertised by this image, David Blair emphasizes the enfoldings of "the unknown of time" as a critical driver of new media fiction:

> It is always useful to place the unknown of time and its synchronic structures periodically on the strata of synchronic space—many times coexisting in the same place—or among symbols on a page, or among all the moving pictures, so we that we can technically mark the unknown where we are while we're going there, in the middle of life or a story, even if that happens in reverse.[3]

He elaborates how fiction is situated in the fertile interstice between the "not yet" and the "no longer" by resituating the creation of *Wax* in the historical reality of its military–industrial–digital context: "the project was eerily haunted by the future of the past or its reverse throughout the "making of" period [which just preceded] the coming of the first Gulf War" (Arns and Wilk). What is really uncanny about Jacob's sudden arrival into the future of 2017 is the juxtaposition of two of Blair's entries on his Facebook page, at the very moment when the rattle of Trump's sabre elicits the specter of a third Gulf War. First is Blair's caustic Facebook posting of an article regarding "The White House press release detailing mysteriously unreported terror attacks used exactly that spelling," or to put it otherwise, Trump's habitual transformation of fiction into misspelled fact. And then I experienced the mysterious resurfacing of Jacob Maker himself in this future perfect moment when Blair distributed a picture of Jacob standing in front of an ominous Stasi evoking complex—with the caption "live at the German CIA HQ, the BND, in Berlin!" Having somehow time-traveled from Alamogordo's nuclear ground zero, Jacob stands in February, 2017, in front of the Federal Intelligence Service (BND) in Berlin. This is the German intelligence agency that has been outed for "collecting data through mass surveillance tools, storing it in databases that shouldn't exist" (Zorz). What else need be said? The uncanny surprise of Jacob's transference from the site of the Cold War to a place that now figures in the intrigue of state-sponsored digital hacking leads me to believe that the transformative fabulations of Bee TV might be generating yet another risky tale awaiting to be told.

This startling enfolding of time from the Gulf War to the Cold War to the Trumpocalypse might be appreciated by referencing yet another philosophical perspective on the risk of temporal imaging at the interface of imperiled global nuclear economies. In a 1991 essay written at the onset of the first Gulf War, around the time that Jacob Maker was making his transformation from a figure of Bee TV to the combinatory of 80,000 images on the Internet, Jean-Luc Nancy took the occasion of his treatise, "War, Law, Sovereignty,—TECHNÉ," to make a distinction between two fundamental *epistemes* of new media culture, *"techno-logie"* and *"écotechnie."* He marshals *"techno-logie"* as the recognizable figure of the military–industrial–digital complex through which the perspectival and proscenium traditions of screenic vision position viewing subjects in relation to their distance from the goal of visualization. His notion of *"techno-logie"* scripts and orders the distance from the past and movement toward the future that subtend the ethical Occidental traditions of epic, sovereignty, and communitarianism. It is perhaps not inconsequential, in this context, that Blair's initial fictionalizing of bees stemmed from his interest in the fact that

> bees apparently make wax and then make accurate hexagons from it by standing a certain distance apart from each other. When I looked up bees in books at the library, there were an indefinite number of oxymoronic pairs of opposing metaphors drawn from these social relations ... in seventeenth-century England, they were used to explain why the monarchy should be abolished, but also why it should be restored.
>
> (Arns and Wilk)

It is unlikely that Nancy might have imagined "bees" as the epistemic figure of *"techno-logie,"* but we can certainly appreciate the common specter of absolutism that haunts the representations of war and sovereignty shared by Nancy and Blair.

In contrast to *"techno-logie,"* Nancy proposes *écotechnie* as something of a politically enigmatic figure for what he calls the inherent risk of "world (dis)order" at the onset of the Gulf War,[4] whose phantasm is ongoing now as rumors abound of the insertion of more American troops either into the Middle East or along the U.S. border with Mexico.

> It is well known that the "world (dis)order," if it is without reason, end, or figure, nonetheless has all the effectivity of what one calls "planetary technology" and "world economy": the double sign of a single complex of the reciprocity of causes and effects, the circularity of ends and means. The without-end, indeed, but the without-end in millions of dollars and yen, in millions of thermies, kilowatts, optical fibers, kilooctets. If the world is a world today, it is a world first of all under the double sign. Let us call it here *écotechnie*.
>
> (Nancy 51)

While the perceptual fields of affective computing and interactive media are dependent on the future drives of technology, its corporate infrastructure, and its planned obsolescence, Nancy maintains that, while operating within the endlessness of world economy and planetary technology, *écotechnie* paradoxically opens the space of thinking *techné* to something other than the very parameters of war and capital that so constitute the double sign of a media world at risk today.

> What I am calling here *écotechnie* (henceforth to be liberated in itself from capital) is the *techné* of "finitude" or of spacing. No longer the technical means to an End, but *techné* itself as in-finite end, *techné* as the existence of the finite existent, its brilliance, and its violence. We are talking about "technology" itself, but about a technology that of itself raises the necessity of appropriating its sense *against* the appropriative logic of capital, and *against* the sovereign logic of war.
>
> (Nancy 56)

Much like the medial appropriations of risk by Blair, Steyerl, and Treister, Nancy reflects on how the critical rub of *écotechnie* might activate the networks of risk, vision, and spacing against the deadening drive of future ontological obsolescence mapped out by Steigler and Nancy. *Écotechnie* constitutes the energetic folds of technology and, I might add, comprises the epistemological potentials of new media art. The parameters of *écotechnie* shake and disturb predetermined assumptions about the culture, capital, and violence of technology and its risky relation to both art and philosophy.[5] From "the very heart of the appropriative power of capital," suggests Nancy, "ecotechnics obscurely points to the *techné* of a world ... in which spacing out can coincide neither with display nor with laceration but merely with 'intersection'" (Nancy 56). It is in the improvisational intersectionality of new media, in the critical folds of networked art and participation, that risk so bears the promise of medial fabulation—if, that is, we can imagine (pace Crary) the possibility of ecotechnic promise amid the reality of the digital sovereignty and the material consequences of ecological plight surrounding us. Nancy would say that this portends "a matter of '*technology*' as *techné of a new horizon of unheard-of identities*" (Nancy 58).

Anthropocenic Afterward

David Blair's newest anthropocenic project, "Aliens in Green," aims to enhance the fictional texture of such a horizon. Launched at Transmediale 2017, Blair's complex installation of interactive bioart and multimedial display is scripted around the tract, "Becoming Non-Alien: Provisional Manifesto for a Laboratory of Recombinant Commons." What better "afterward" to this essay on "New Media At Risk" than this passage from the manifesto that announces Blair's emergent project of a new fictional horizon of unheard-of identities:

> Aliens in Green is an agent from a planet-turned-laboratory. The laboratory is the place where that which does not yet exist comes into existence.... The future, however, has not yet been created, and the images coming from the future are materializing in various ways. Some of these images show a xeno-power that elicits the emergence of radically new entities forcing the evolution of living beings in unconcerted directions between species. In the xeno-laboratory, we are envisioning and anticipating the emergence of the systems of our future subordination or extermination based on our alienation. Against this xeno-laboratory, Aliens in Green is positing the idea of a non-alien laboratory. This laboratory is a place-in-becoming, a place where the combination of living forms, their composition and articulation, is elaborated, a place that the present ontological leap would like to curtail.... The non-genealogical and lateral transfer of genes, molecules, signals, is perhaps what will enable us to understand the making of new biopolitical

connections—between persons and licenses, between human and non-human user communities, between polymorphisms and politics. These recombinations, which are immanent in society, must emancipate themselves from the specific standards of the bio-, chemo-, and porno-industrial complex in order to bring forth bodies and habitats that adapt to the beings living in them.

("Becoming Non-Alien")

"Aliens in Green" provides a stunning concluding example of the artistic extension of the object of knowing beyond the delimitations of ontology, grounded in the centralizations of human first-person selfhood and OOO, to the expansive temporal screen of self, animal, and environment. The installation's combinatory summons to adapt creatively to the risky environments enveloping this medial age foregrounds the stakes of this essay's creative mixture of the voices of artists, protagonists, and philosophers. When the new medial imaginary of an installation like "Aliens in Green" lies on the quaking horizon of the risk of ecotechnics, the world (dis)order itself raises the stakes, as Nancy might say to Blair, of "the necessity of appropriating its sense against the appropriative logic of capital, and against the sovereign logic of war."

In the language framing this essay, new media art most forcefully embraces its own risk when it ruptures the stabilities of the corporate pull of the future that has, as Klein would say, material consequences in the present. The subsequent drive is that of fictionalization as it envelops the epistemology of risk. No one has understood this better than nine-year-old Jack Davis, a self-proclaimed "Guardian of the Galaxy." He cited his extensive immersion in science fiction to support his application for the North American Space Command's deadpan search for a Planetary Protection Officer who would guard the planet from alien contamination.

> I may be nine but I think I would be a fit for the job ... I have seen almost all the space and alien movies I can see. I have also seen the show Marvel Agents of the Shield and hope to see the movie *Men in Black*. I'm great at video games and I am young, so I can learn to think like an Alien.
>
> *(NASA "Planetary Projection Excites Fans of All Ages")*

Jack gets it. Such alien recombinations, which are immanent in society and its fictions, guarantee that the future certainly ain't gonna be what it used to be.

Notes

1 In *States of Emergency: Documentaries, Wars, Democracies*, Zimmermann establishes a parallel critical approach by contrasting state-sponsored war documentaries with independent documentaries whose formal and narrative exploration frequently capitalizes on the valence of the artistic interstice.

2 My understanding of the valence of the fold is indebted to the work of both Jacques Derrida and Gilles Deleuze. The labyrinthine continuity of the fold, in contrast to the symbolic cohesion of projection, is the seminal figure of Derrida's reading of the machinic supplement in "The Double Session." Derrida capitalizes on Mallarmé's trop of the fold to articulate the notion of supplementarity as the stuff of representation. Crucial to my adoption of the notion of the fold as a critical operator of new media is not only the supplementarity of the fold and its infinite machinic motion but also its impact on our understanding of subjectivity. For Derrida, the fold is the machinery of intersubjectivity and inter-activity. Even more important to my evocation of the fold in *Digital Baroque* was Gilles Deleuze's insightful book, *The Fold: Leibniz and the Baroque*. Deleuze's elaboration on the fold contrasts starkly with Cartesian investments in the line as an analytical, punctual equation and in project as the teleological culmination or end point of reason.

3 Blair recounts that

> the guy who ran the Amiga computer store in the East Village quit, got involved with high-speed internet, asked me if my movie could be the first movie on the internet, and then put

Wax in a VHS machine connected to a Silicon Graphics machine connected to a T1 line connected to the mbone [a "multicast backbone" for carrying IP multicast traffic online in the 90s].

(Arns and Wilk)

4 In articulating the contrast between Ulrich Beck and Jean-Luc Nancy, Irving Goh situates the "risk of existing" as being at the heart of Nancy's philosophy.
5 In "Philosophical Prepositions: Ecotechnics *là où* Digital Exhibition" (2014), I recount Nancy's expansive thinking on the "*expositions*" of technology and his contribution to the positioning of a politics of new media art.

Works Cited

Arns, Inke and Elvia Wilk. "Inke Arns and Elvia Wilk Interview Artist David Blair About The Ongoing Impact Of His Unique 1993 Multi-media, Multi-everything Project." *Transmediale Journal*, January 29, 2017, https://transmediale.de/content/wax-or-the-discovery-of-television-among-the-bees-0. Accessed February 25, 2017.
Beck, Ulrich, *World at Risk*. Translated by Ciaran Cronin. Polity Press, 2009.
Blair, David. "Becoming Non-Alien: Provisional Manifesto for a Laboratory of Recombinant Commons." 2017, www.facebook.com/photo.php?fbid=1203786899671309&set=a.1203780489671950.1073741855. 100001200308823&type=3&theater. Accessed February 25, 2017.
Blair, David. "Aliens in Green," Performance installation, Transmediale, Berlin, Germany, 2017.
Blair, David. "Wax or the Discovery of Television Among the Bees" (video). David Blair Productions, 1991.
Blair, David. "Waxweb." Hosted by the Institute for Advanced Technology in the Humanities at the University of Virginia, 1994, www2.iath.virginia.edu/wax/. Accessed February 25, 2017.
Crary, Jonathan. *24/7: Late Capitalism and the Ends of Sleep*. Verso, 2013.
Critical Art Ensemble. "Not So Quiet on the Western Front: Report on Risk and Cultural Resistance within the Neoliberal Society of Fear." *The Aesthetics of Risk: Volume 3 of the SocCAS Symposia*, edited by John Welchman, JRP Ringier, 2008, pp. 357–375.
Critical Art Ensemble. "Useless Technologies." http://critical-art.net/?p=321. Accessed 25 Feb. 2017.
Deleuze, Gilles. *Cinema 2: The Time-Image*. Translated by Hugh Tomlinson and Robert Galeta. U of Minnesota P, 1989.
Deleuze, Gilles. *The Fold: Leibniz and the Baroque*. Translated by Tom Conley. U of Minnesota P, 1993.
Derrida, Jacques. "No Apocalypse, Not Now (Full Speed Ahead, Seven Missiles, Seven Missives)." *diacritics*, vol. 14, no. 2, Summer 1984, 20–31.
Derrida, Jacques. "Signature, Sign, and Play in the Discourse of the Human Sciences." *The Structuralist Controversy*, edited by Richard Macksey and Eugenio Donato. The Johns Hopkins UP, 1970, pp. 247–272.
Derrida, Jacques. "The Double Session." *Dissemination*. Translated by Barbara Johnson. U of Chicago P, 1981, pp. 173–286.
Farocki, Harun. "Images of War (At a Distance)" (Exhibition). Museum of Modern Art. New York, 2012.
Goh, Irving. "The Risk of Existing: Jean-Luc Nancy's Prepositional Existence, Knocks Included." *diacritics*, vol. 43, no. 4, 2015, 8–26.
Grzinic, Marina, editor. *Stelarc: Political Prosthesis & Knowledge of the Body*. Maska, 2002.
Klein, Richard. "Climate Change Through the Lens of Nuclear Criticism." *Diacritics*, vol. 41, no. 3, 2013, 20–31.
Lyotard, Jean-François. *The Inhuman: Reflections on Time*. Translated by Geoffrey Bennington. Stanford UP, 1991.
Marker, Chris. "Immemory" (CD-Rom). Centre Georges Pompidou, 1998.
Murray, Timothy. *Digital Baroque: New Media Art and Cinematic Folds*. U of Minnesota P, 2008.
Murray, Timothy. "Philosophical Prepositions: Ecotechnics *là où* Digital Exhibition." *diacritics*, vol. 42, no. 2, 2014, 10–34.
Museum of Contemporary Art, Los Angeles. "Hito Steyerl, Factory in the Sun." www.moca.org/exhibition/hito-steyerl-factory-of-the-sun. Accessed February 23, 2017.
Nancy, Jean-Luc. "War, Law, Sovereignty,—TECHNÉ." *Rethinking Technologies*, edited by Verena Andermatt Conley. Translated by Jeffrey S. Librett. U of Minnesota P, 1993, pp. 28–58.
NASA. "Planetary Projection Excites Fans of All Ages." www.nasa.gov/feature/planetary-protection-excites-space-fans-of-all-ages. Accessed December 27, 2017.
Reith, Gerda. "Living with Risk: Chance, Luck, and the Creation of Meaning in Uncertainty." *The Aesthetics of Risk: Volume 3 of the SocCAS Symposia*, edited by John Welchman. JRP Ringier, 2008, pp. 57–80.

Steyerl, Hito. *Factory in the Sun* (installation). German Pavilion, 56th Venice Biennale, 2015.
Stiegler, Bernard. *La technique et le temps. 3. Le temps du cinema et la question du mal-être*. Galilee, 2001.
Treister, Suzanne. "... No Other Symptoms—Time Travelling with Rosalind Brodsky" (CD-Rom and book). Black Dog Publishing, 1999.
Virilio, Paul. *War and Cinema: The Logistics of Perception*. Translated by Patrick Camiller. Verso, 1989.
VNS Matrix. "All New Gen" (CD-Rom), *MindVirus* #2, 1994.
VNS Matrix. "Cyberfeminist Manifesto for the 21st Century." http://vnsmatrix.net/the-cyberfeminist-manifesto-for-the-21st-century/. Accessed February 25, 2017.
Welchman, John C. *The Aesthetics of Risk*. JRP/Ringier, 2008.
Zimmermann, Patricia R. *States of Emergency: Documentaries, War, Democracies*. U of Minnesota P, 2000.
Zorz, Zelijka. "German Federal Intelligence Service Violates Laws, Dodges Supervision." Helpnetsecurity.com, September 8, 2016, www.helpnetsecurity.com/2016/09/08/german-federal-intelligence-service/. Accessed February 23, 2017.

13
INTO THE BEYOND
A Conversation with Michael Madsen

Michael Madsen, Bishnupriya Ghosh, and Bhaskar Sarkar

Whether the narrative is set a 100,000 years from now, or at a point when humans are about to abandon Earth, radical displacements in space–time remain a core preoccupation across Danish mediamaker Michael Madsen's *oeuvre*. One of his earliest projects was directing the Sound Gallery, a 900 square meter diffusion system underneath the Town Hall Square, Copenhagen (1996–1998). Already here, as in his award-winning film, *To Damascus: A Film on Interpretation* (2005), Madsen's signature concerns were at play: a direct engagement with interactive publics or spectators so that they become characters in the story, and a contemplation of the limits and potentials of human cognition and of their embodiment and extension into technological knowledge. Madsen's trilogy on the future of humankind is most salient to our concerns with risk and its logic of preparedness: *Into Eternity: A Film for the Future* (2010), *The Visit: An Alien Encounter* (2015), and *The Search* (ongoing). The last took an interactive form in 2018 when the Louisiana Museum of Modern Art, Denmark, invited Madsen to mount an installation for the Moon Exhibit (commemorating the 50th anniversary of the moon landing). When we interviewed him in Copenhagen in August 2018, the installation was in the late stages of implementation.

Our interest in Madsen's salience to thinking about media and risk dates back to 2011–2012 when we screened *Into Eternity* as part of a series "Speculative Futures" that we hosted at the University of California, Santa Barbara campus (with Rita Raley and Greg Siegel). Speculation is inimical to risk since only partial knowledge of radical uncertainties in the future underlie perceptions of coming harm. Despite all scientific prediction, all technological preparation, the human imagination fuels mediations of risk. Madsen's meditative explorations of *how humans imagine the future* was precisely congruent to our concerns in the series. *Into Eternity* features the world's first final nuclear waste storage site, Onkalo (Finnish for "Hiding Place") in Finland designed to contain hazardous radioactive material in granite caves. The documentary presents the gleaming efficiencies of the storage plant but also the dark and damp caves, where the danger of exposure might lie in wait for future generations. For there is no guarantee that present sign systems—visual–iconic to written warnings—will survive 100,000 years from now. The documentary interviews a number of experts, scientists to theologians, in their workplaces, while Madsen, directly addresses the spectators from the caves: will curiosity which once made humans desecrate the dead despite hieroglyphic warnings once again prove to be the worst enemy? Does risk lie in human nature as much in radioactive waste? These questions concerning human nature return with greater urgency in *The Visit* (2015) which builds a scenario of alien visitation. As the extraterrestrials arrive on Earth, the encounter throws into sharp relief what humans truly value. Instead of the classic fear-driven narratives of attacks and cover-ups, Madsen worked with the staff at the Vienna-based United Nations

Office of Outer Space Affairs, NASA personnel, military representatives, space scientists, and others to document present preparation even as they fabricate a virtual reality to come. Madsen explores this virtual reality in the art installation at the Louisiana Museum's Moon Exhibit, which is based on research for his third film, *The Search*. At the exhibit, museum-goers enter a large room awash in the immersive blue of space, its floor dotted with flickering lights. A large aluminum table is lit by a disk of light suspended above it (Figure 13.1). Caught in the space in between the two, museum-goers encounter the vast unknown of the galaxies in the scenography (an outer space environment built with architect Jonathan Houser). Interactive web-based questionnaires prompt viewers to think about their actions and their memories of Earth as they prepare to leave a planet of mounting natural catastrophes, over-population and political chaos. As in his other projects, the questionnaire turns out to be a personality test: how prepared are we to reboot human existence as we volunteer for a one-way generation ship mission searching for another habitable world? Upon the exhibit's culmination, the collation of responses from the 30,000 who took the test in full revealed that 62 percent were ready to leave the Earth for good.

We sat down with Michael Madsen in Copenhagen to ask him about his *oeuvre* on risk perceptions, the speculative documentation of the future, and the task of preparing for the unknown.

Editors: We encounter your documentaries as not only engagements with a future that cannot be comprehended fully from the present, but also as explorations of the possibilities and limits of mediating that future. We are often in the domain of science fiction: the point is driven home when one watches a "realistic" fictional film like Denis Villeneuve's *The Arrival* (2016) in relation to *Into Eternity* (2010). Can you elaborate on your choice of the documentary form?

Madsen: I think that if you work in documentary, you must have as a subject matter the question of what is reality, or what's the nature of reality. That is, your fundamental field of interest is what constitutes reality, how and where is it composed. I was not trained as a documentary

Figure 13.1 Photograph of viewers inhabiting the installation at the Louisiana Museum of Modern Art
Credit: Michael Madsen

filmmaker, and my first documentary was conceived of as an art project. So I'm not attached to the distinction between fiction and documentary film. But, of course, as I came to know the genre and other filmmakers, I realized I was engaged in what normally is referred to as creative documentary: a subjective exploration by the filmmaker of what constitutes reality. I would call the documentary genre my starting point. The challenge is that when you are filming a documentary, you have a camera, a very literal device, that can reproduce a sense of one-to-one correspondence with reality; thus it aids in already submerging the filmmaker in the familiar. How can we create a different perspective? The camera in *Into Eternity* is looking at our present but also sometimes from far into the future, as if able to visit our present day Era but from a time in the future when all knowledge of today has been lost: this is a different vantage point, outside of our own time and space. Similarly, in *The Visit*, the audience is made to consider how prepared we will be if the alien actually arrives on Earth. The characters in these films talk to the camera and address "you" the viewer, thus breaking with normal conventions of filmmaking in which spectators identify with some characters and live through them. I am not interested in that kind of immersion, but in involving "you," the viewer, in deliberation, as responsible for the narrative that you interpret.

Editors: Of course, the deep time-scales of a limit event—nuclear waste exposure or alien visitation or abandoning Earth—is a central feature of your practice of "speculative documentary" (which is how we think of your documentaries). Figuring the limits of space and time is quite reflexively present in your work. You take us into deep historical time in the narrative; the aerial shots place us in planetary space in which man-made borders have little meaning. We'd love to hear more about how you think of these deep "scales" and the challenge they present.

Madsen: Nuclear waste conjures unfathomable timespans—as does the unknown entity from elsewhere or travel into space for thousands of human generations—that make you run into the limits of what we can understand, you run into something that goes beyond comprehension. That place also runs against our self-understanding, and especially our natural-scientific upbringing which propels you to get to know more and more. But, what happens when you reach these limits? You are thrown back into your own preconceptions: you get this kind of mirror image. So in *Into Eternity*, you have people sitting and saying, "well I don't know in a way," or "I just have to hope that the future generation will do so," and so on. To admit to uncertainty is a very alien thing for present day western human self-understanding.

The real problem lies within human nature: we can't trust that future generations will actually perform the translation necessary to participate in such a communication. These paradoxes reflect back on who we are and whether or not we can trust ourselves. These films touch these nerves of human existence—at its most profound, the question is who and what we are as humans. *The Visit* conjures a very alien position for modern western humans to be in because we are raised to think we will be in control—a kind of right to be in control is ingrained in us with respect to tomorrow. We don the proverbial protective gear, we bank on police stations, hospitals, and militarized safe havens (Figure 13.2). The welfare state is, after all, founded on safety and security and comfort; you know that you cannot fall through the net because somebody or some apparatus will be there to catch you. If we look at human existence in a broad historical sense, and other people have said this as well, there is no such thing as knowing what will happen tomorrow—if a new disease will come and so and so forth. The modern negotiation about what a human life is and how much certainty you can demand, and ensure how life will unfold ... I think that, in many ways, this negotiation is stifling life. It is a false premise that we can promise you certainty and security because we build new hospitals all the time. You instrumentalize life for political means attempting to contain the uncertainty that is a natural to life, and therein narrow the possibilities of life ... but maybe I'm just romanticizing uncertainty.

Editors: Following this sense of moving beyond intellectual comprehension alone, it seems you want us to feel risk and to return to our internal resources to think the future together. You give us facts and figures, plans and technologies in *Into Eternity*, but we also "feel" the risk because you

Figure 13.2 Signs of danger: alien contact. (Screenshot)

immerse us in caves (which contrast sharply with the gleaming cool interiors of the Finnish Nuclear Safety Authority, for example). The white of the snowy approach to Onkalo disappears into the dark dank tunnels where the drip of water—seeping, uncontainable—sends a shiver down our spine (Figure 13.3). Could you address this sensory appeal in your sound design and visual style?

Madsen: What actually happens with *Into Eternity*—which I think is a much better film than *The Visit*—is that you actually get another kind of understanding about the future. It has much to do with the sound design and the particular way the camera moves: from the perspective of another time, "it" doesn't know exactly what's important, so it floats and drips…

Editors: It doesn't know what to focus on?

Figure 13.3 Approach to Onkalo (*Into Eternity*, 2010)

Madsen: Yes, what should I focus on? I can take something, but my camera movement is a narrative device that propels viewers into the future, its radical uncertainty, even as we look back at our own time. And that strategy is central: this relationship to the viewer who experience these elements.

Editors: We've read your films as reflections on human sign systems, working out a mode of speculative communication. In the previous documentaries, we are prompted to ask: how do we create warning systems using present resources? Can messages survive complete disconnection from their original context? If we found a message in bottle in the future, will we even see it as an SOS? In this regard, we have been thinking of speculation's links to the specular—to see, but also, in your projects, to see in different ways. The camera movement you describe performs the problem of knowledge as a problem of "seeing" because "I," the spectator, don't know exactly what it is I'm looking for. The encounter with radical uncertainty produces a tentative camera; at the same time, this is a very deliberate choice on your part. That's a remarkable kind of balance: the ability to produce this tension in us, the viewers. It felt like you're almost positing a different model or paradigm of how we know or how we might be able to know.

Madsen: Well, of course this is a very positive interpretation… I think that any film maker would have to consider that the moment you pick up a camera, you are working with a device that has this stupidity of a sort: it just reproduces reality. I always say that any good image arises within the spectator and it's normally outside the frame. This is why new emerging technologies like VR and so on pose some very interesting prospects for the viewer position—for multiple experiencing positions. I'm very much interested in technologies like point cloud: when you scan a room or space or you use photogrammetry, you get abstract, very reduced image—just points. It is an image of a scanned reality, so it is a volumetric image, not a flat image. The quality of such an image is, in my mind, both a representation of nature and a highly scientific image that I can manipulate because I can rotate the photo information and walk into the space or produce a fly-through … My point is that, it raises fundamental questions about how reality is constituted and how you can investigate that in visual terms. This leads to considerations about what the film will look like, how will it be constituted visually. With *The Search*, I think I'll enter a completely different sort of visual reality that is really investigating what an image is.

Since I think of *Into Eternity*, *The Visit*, and *The Search* as a trilogy, then, there is an evolution that happens through them. As far as visuality is concerned, I felt that I had sort of reached the limit with *The Visit*. The first two films produce knowledge partly with talking head interviews, so the future is very difficult to visualize, to bring to life…I'm involved in a very different process with *The Search*, which is a transmedia project that ventures into new narrative territory. Where in the documentaries, one can edit and edit to change the story, the transmedia project brings in interactive spectators who will collaborate in making the narrative.

Editors: Since you are thinking of these projects together as a trilogy, can you tell us a bit about how you sequenced them, how you came to them?

Madsen: Well, for *The Visit* I read a article about the appointment of an alien ambassador in case of visit from space—the ambassador being the then Director of the United Nations Office for Outer Space Affairs, and although a hoax, I realized there could be a film about this other, this alien (Figure 13.2). Yet in many ways I began thinking about *The Visit* even before *Into Eternity*. In 2003 the remains of a human species in Indonesia—*homo floresiensis*—was found in a cave. It was a small skeleton, a small human, an unknown human species that had died 18,000 years ago which, in human evolutionary history, is like yesterday. There were legends about small people in the woods of the area. Here was a mirror image, the possibility of finding another kind of human…but not a human life. It raised the same questions with alien life, and although a hoax that the UN should have appointed an alien ambassador, it turned about that indeed the UN in the 1970s had been discussing what to do in event of contact. So I began to work with the Office for Outer Space Affairs on *The Visit*, to work from the perspective of the other. Along the way, I read about this concept of intergenerational space flight and that became the basis for *The Search*. So I've been working on *The Visit* and *The Search* in parallel trajectories.

Editors: Just so our readers know, the premise of *The Search* is the prospect of leaving Earth—uninhabitable because of climate change, over-population, and political conflict—and find a new home somewhere in the great unknown. In the first iteration—the art installation at the Moon Exhibit—spectators are asked to reflect on this prospect. They are invited to answer a questionnaire which closes with a query about their dearest memories on Earth. As we understand it, the film script, addresses what it means to start from scratch somewhere else but by looking at the journey to that somewhere. The timespan of such travel covers thousands of years, so that the actor playing a young woman says, "I'm an actor, I'm now playing a woman 20 years younger, and later in the film, I'll play my age and you will see me die." The relationship to Earth becomes intergenerational. The script includes characters who are born in the future, during the journey, and have never been on Earth.

Madsen: *The Search* is about finding a new world; in that sense, it is also an utopian project. The question is: Can we actually remain human in the attempt to save who we are and what we are? A generation space ship travel means a closed loop environment with some very strict rules—for example, you will not die of old age because you cannot become a burden. In this sense, reaching the "new world" for a fresh start is very much like ancient, prehistoric life on Earth. I want to make a film that *visually* discusses what such utopian imagination is and what it does, and at the same time suggest the very source of the image inside the individual viewer: *The Search* is both a journey into our imaginations of a better world but at the same time as a narrative also the attempt to perform what such a journey to the stars would actually mean. *The Search* has been a cross media project from the beginning because I am trying to get beyond a classic cinema audience or television audience. In the film world, there is a huge crisis around financing, so there is a shift toward experiencing stories on other platforms: I watch my stepson Isaac as he watches stories on YouTube and I want to engage with audiences at different levels and because I suspect younger generations live in different visual registers of reality.

When I was invited for a conversation with the curator of the Moon Exhibit at Louisiana, who had seen *The Visit*, I told her I was working on a film about intergalactic travel. She invited me to articulate the film as an installation. A visitor can enter a room and essentially deliberate whether or not she would volunteer for a one-way mission. Would I sacrifice my life for the survival of distant generations, perhaps my own flesh and blood—would I sacrifice me as individual for the sake of the collective?

Editors: Can you tell us a bit more about what this experience will be like?

Madsen: For the physical part of the installation, I am working with the same architect who has been developing the space craft for *The Search*: you enter a room and you have a table, three and a half meter in diameter, made of aluminum with many holes. The table is a kind of palimpsest, a repository of memories, around which crucial decisions about the mission can be made. The big difference from the film will be to have a physical presence—haptic qualities like the coolness of aluminum—and all of those things that cannot be in the film. [The design plans that Madsen shared with us details seven hand-traced layers (combined to a single 20 mm plate), which range from human cellular structure to fracto-cumulus clouds: "A manmade fossil which, depending on the point of view, is both an archaic table from the past and, perhaps, a fragment of the future."]

Editors: You want us to feel planetary space, to be "in" it. What you are describing seems like a pared down space—a concretization of abstraction enough to specify the space but also to keep it open for participants to potentiate with their imagination, needs, desires.

Madsen: Yes, and that's a completely different thing about the installation. When you talk about films, and therefore most often narrative, you are faced with questions like "what's the film about" or "what's the message." but with this installation, it is a very different journey as it has to engage the museum visitor on an immediate intuitive level before the chance is to engage with the concept of intergenerational space travel etc.

Editors: There are calculations but the effect is coming at a different register,

Madsen: I hope so, and I cannot express how to get to that register because ultimately I think *The Search* is trying to express an understanding of the consequences of, for example, climate change whose scope is beyond present day human vocabulary.

Editors: And anticipating how many people will attend is also quite unpredictable, I imagine; so the unpredictability, the speculation, is at different levels. So this venture is risky—actually giving over to the uncertainties of the production process.

Madsen: Yes, it is unpredictable and that has presented difficulties. I was working with one company for the digital part of the exhibit, and that collaboration became a disaster. I had to find another company because, for them, not knowing the exact result… they couldn't cope with it.

Editors: That's fascinating!

Madsen: But for me that's a fundamental aspect of working with documentary: it is an act of exploration and, as such, it is an act of trying to realize something about reality. This trying underlies my interest in technologies that provide different visualities: how you constitute reality is really also an exploration of visuality itself. That is why in *The Search*, I've been trying to conceptualize a different visual reality altogether—abstract patterns, not complete images.

Editors: But another thing, this unpredictability you make us feel… We're linking back to our earlier discussion about the camera in *Into Eternity* that floats and is uncertain in itself—it makes us feel unmoored. In the design for *The Search*, it seems like there is an initial template but it achieves fullness as one participates—a loose and non-linear trajectory. I can see here and I can walk there, but there's also something maybe behind me, in my blind spot.

Madsen: Perhaps the most significant thing we created for *The Search* is the spacecraft. I asked Jonathan Houser (the architect) how we can build a conceptual environment for a real starship—which will function as the scenography for the film. I did not go to a real space architect—then you'd just have the typical International Space Station (ISS), you would sleep in a Velcro sleeping bag on the wall or something like that. Jonathan had to think about it especially since there is a certain architectural vocabulary—on Earth we have columns and pillars, in short gravity—which does not apply in space. And then there is the question of the cargo of an interstellar generation ship, well, the cargo is the human spirit: what does it mean to transfer the human spirit to another world? We have found it paramount to create the something we call The Unknown at integral to two-thirds of the craft—which is a paradox—to build uncertainty into the program. The speculation that *The Search* represents defies conventional thinking about a space craft as small; it has to be all kinds of things, otherwise you will not be able to survive as a human being—the project of making it to another world will fail unless you can get lost, get beyond the "always know" of a closed loop environment which a space craft always will be. In a way, relentless speculation must accompany thinking about a thing that has traveled for generations; you cannot have a starting point which is within the known ISS space station.

Editors: But this cargo, we have to ask, will it survive?

Madsen: Well, the main threat to any such mission is boredom. You'd be afraid that the crew forgets what the mission is about. The first generation is privileged because it knows what it is trying to do, it knows what Earth was, it experienced Earth; for the subsequent generations, some kind of narrative will have to be performed or be given to them to maintain why they do this.

Editors: So the mission is passed on through ritual? An archival dimension spans your work, be it the late nineteenth century or the Egyptian civilization. Statistical risk calculations, too, return to the past for data to plot probable future states: "regression analysis," as it is called. From the perspective of the humanities, history *is* past data. You've always displaced us into history through a point in the future. What role do memories of Earth play in *The Search*?

Madsen: In the film version of *The Search*, recorded testimonies passed on from generation to generation play a central role. During the entire installation at Louisiana, you are offered the chance to make a recording that will be stored in a kind of anthropological real archive that can form the basis of any future mission. We will ask people: "what is your most precious memory of life on Earth?" The stories would be stored in an archive for any future traveler to listen to because, in the future, there will be the problem of knowing what Earth was, really. In the film, these testimonies are performed by actors playing crew members: for example, the first person who has to be euthanized because he's old, and he accepts this on behalf of the mission; and the first child that is born. The child is not born of parents but engineered to create the most healthy child; but this child gets suspicious that "I'm a child in a different way" and explores what is to be the first realization of a concept. Everyone onboard has a motivation—they've left because of climate change, overpopulation, or physical chaos, and bad news from Earth actually drives their willingness to venture out, possibly to sacrifice their lives. But once onboard, it is not disasters on Earth but fear itself that is the real force. They realize they traveled out of fear. Fear of ourselves.

Editors: So the sense of catastrophic risk drives the speculative venture? Just to clarify, there's already been a huge calamity on Earth and they left?

Madsen: No, in the film the director, that is I, appear actually in the same space as the installation: that is a real set from the film. I appear in the film and I say that I'm making this film because sooner or later we will have to leave Earth, and then I list all the risks—climate change, and so on—for the viewer. I worked with American space social psychologist, Sheryl Bishop, on this test scenario: a situation in which the only way to save humanity would be to go to another world, and then the actors come out and present themselves. So it's a little bit like all the ingredients of a recipe put in front of the audience—this is what we're doing, this is the game we're going to play now, and we're going to see what happens. In the narrative of the film, it is realized that the travelers need calamity on Earth to justify their sacrifice. Indeed, it may be difficult for us humans to span not just to another world but indeed beyond our own nose, as we say in Denmark.

Editors: Just as an aside: we've both been struck with the range of experts (scientists, technicians, policymakers, and so on) that you interview in *Into Eternity* and *The Visit*. One argument about risk is that it arises in the gap between lay and expert perceptions: in fact, Ulrich Beck argues that reflexive risk emerges because the public distrusts experts. What's really impressive is how plainspoken the experts in your films are about the limits of their enterprise. In this sense, they give us "realism" as the basis of the speculative venture. Here again, in *The Search*, you are drawing on actual expertise from a space psychologist to construct this essentially speculative game scenario. Speaking of games: you have said a lot about how the art installation is different from cinema, the way it poses a different relationship to audiences. What is your relationship to video games?

Madsen I have a terribly small relation to video games because I never really played them.

Editors: But in the sense that they depend on interactivity and multiple forking paths of the narratives....

Madsen: Yes, yes.

Editors: When you're talking about VR, I think you said point cloud is the technology—does that have anything to do with video game design?

Madsen: No, I think point cloud is a different way of representing reality: it is a recording that is both visual but also spatial, a special visuality we can say, but also very reduced, very poetic. You have to imagine half the image yourself. So it is a game that we are playing together, and I function as a kind of a game master.

Editors: One thing about this game scenario is that there is a search for newness, something regenerative, right? You've talked about finding a new image, even a new kind of image, and a new language—and perhaps a new mode of becoming human. Whereas human nature is inertia for *Into Eternity*—the same old human curiosity that prompted those imperial archaeologists to enter the pyramids, despite posted warnings, will also make future generations open Onkalo and destroy themselves—there is something more utopian in *The Search*. There is the expectation that "we" will sacrifice ourselves for future generations. And yet, if there is anything fundamental in human history, it is war and domination and violence. Of course, those dystopias have been done to death in science fiction, so we can see why you would find it limiting to the imagination of what we can be. But if there is an archive of the Earth... you speak of landscapes, you talked about these beautiful raw materials on the craft... but if you're talking about human memory, almost 50 percent of is not...

Madsen: ... very pleasant?

Editors: Exactly.

Madsen: There is an American who has been reading the script because we need somebody to make sure that the English is correct—he is a literary scholar. When we asked him to read the script, he was asking where is the self-interest, where is the conflict, where are the police onboard the craft—and this surprised me, and the dramaturg and co-writer, Jesper Bergmann, a little bit. But the difference is most likely that we are from Denmark (Scandinavia, more generally), and we are perhaps a bit more communal, we simply see it differently. When we were trying to experiment with the personality test for the Louisiana exhibit, we had some people take the test; at that point, we realized that the questions are posed for welfare state citizens. So I think there is a cultural difference there. But the film has conflict at a more fundamental level: what am I? If I'm only born to crew the ship, how do I stay alive—what is life itself under such circumstances, what makes the human soul breathe?

Editors Ah, I see, so the *agon* of history is not the same in Scandinavia as what we've had, say, in India, Africa, or the United States. And if you have had colonialism and blood diamonds, slavery and Jim Crow, all of that, then it becomes different... If Denmark or Sweden were a huge colonial power, things would have been different, we totally get that and we think it's important to recognize that. But when you are thinking in universal terms—and we see why it needs to be thought sometimes, absolutely—then it will have to include the U.S., Britain, Belgium, South Africa, Brazil, and all those places where the universal continues to be painful.

Madsen: I totally agree.

Editors: So the fissures of history do come back?

Madsen: Yes, and this is also sort of audience communication I'd like the film to have. You see concerns that I just don't. I experienced this at the Dutch film school, where they asked me: "Well you're talking about men and women having children, why not two men or two women?" I really couldn't answer even as I know there are 21 gender categories in Sweden. How does one incorporate this endless variation, this difference....

Editors: Their demand is that, if you're being utopic and speculative, why not include what's empirically there—it is a fair demand. But what we get from your speculative canvas is that the central question of communication with the other, distanced from present experience, is what drives your films. That is the big Other: sometimes it can be a person, at other times, an experience, an event, a material. What's engaging about your documentaries is the instability about who gets to be "human" in relation to the Other, and how. This is particularly relevant against the backdrop of the long twentieth century and its genocidal histories of de-humanization, and the twenty-first century's turn to intelligent synthetic life. What better way to pose the question than from the vantage of the radical displacement that your films put us in, taking irreducible uncertainty as the place from which to pose questions.

Madsen: It is worth noting that when I spoke with a scholar of science fiction, he said "you know what's significant about sci-fi is the *novum*, this conceptual breakthrough that you realize the world is different from what you thought it was"—to grasp that reality is different, you don't have to go far from the present. The shift for me is not to code the other as good or bad—you know that conversation, is nuclear energy good or bad—but to think about how we focus on how to communicate about the other. The same is true of thinking about humans or new habitats: how do we communicate realizations in the making, something yet to come.

Editors: Perhaps your opening for *The Search* is the best coda for this conversation: "My fear is our lack of imagination. You and I cannot imagine the extinction of humankind, and because of that, human life on Earth is already lost."

PART IV

SCALE

14
CHERNOBYL, RISK, AND THE INTER-ZONE OF THE ANTHROPOCENE

Adrian Ivakhiv

When Reactor Number Four of the Chernobyl nuclear power plant in northern Ukraine exploded on the night of April 26, 1986, it launched a series of events that was to dramatically affect the lives of hundreds of thousands of Soviet citizens, along with a vast geography of living organisms and ecological relations.[1] The event qualifies as what I will call a *hyper-event*—an event that triggers chain reactions, which in turn rearrange agential relations operating on multiple spatial and temporal scales. The story of this hyper-event can be told within a plurality of geographic, political, and ecological reference frames.

This chapter tells that story in a series of layered vignettes. Its overarching thesis is that the Chernobyl nuclear accident, and the "Zone of Estrangement," or "Zone of Alienation" (*Zona Vidchuzhennia*, in Ukrainian) created in its wake, constitute a microcosm of the tensions held together within the twentieth century Cold War, within industrial modernity, and within the geological Anthropocene. The event affected relations between Chernobyl's multiple surrounding worlds, of which I will focus on four: its immediate environment of forested north-central Polissia in northern Ukraine; the national imaginary of Ukraine as a soon-to-depart republic of the soon-to-implode Soviet Union; the Soviet industrial system as a superpower within a bipolar global military–political order; and the technological modernity of the era increasingly known as the Anthropocene.

In this sense, the accident was not merely an event—that is, not merely something that happened. Rather, it was a hyper-event. In its confluence of trajectories and flows, a hyper-event is one that suddenly delivers an unpredictable manifold of novelty, with reverberations from it ringing far beyond the scope of its apparent origins, permanently rupturing the ontology of a given social order and expanding the circle of affective horizons by which its effects reverberate out into the universe (Ivakhiv, "The Event That Cannot (Not) Happen" 54).[2] In doing so, the hyper-event of Chernobyl implicated us—those who have lived to make sense of it—in the folded fabric of a timespace that has changed as a result of that event. How we are implicated is what is at issue here, and what this chapter will explore.

The role of media is central within each of these layers, but it will remain largely implicit in my treatment. Briefly, however, I hope to suggest that without media, and specifically, without the visuality of the nuclear sublime, media treatments of Ukraine in the post-Cold War global information (dis)order, the cinematics of the postnuclear and posthuman Zone, and visualizations of the Anthropocene, none of these narratives would be conceivable. Media connects with and shapes each of them differently, but I leave the theorization of those connections for another occasion.

Sublime: Sputnik Religion and Nuclear Aesthetic

Our first vignette is located within the international system, in which the Soviet Union emerged as the primary rival to the U.S.-led West in the mid-twentieth century postwar world. But this system is part of a larger frame we could simply call industrial modernity.

One way to characterize history is as a procession of changing sublimes—that is, changing boundaries that delimit a given world by suggesting an outside or beyond to it. At a certain time and place, those boundaries might have been marked by the signs of a transcendent deity, or by the endlessness of a universe whose shape disappeared into mystery—the "eternal silence of these infinite spaces" that so terrified Pascal (66). With the onset of industrial modernity, it was the products of human science and technology—industry, factories, bombs and their production facilities—that came to mark the limits of our imagination, and which became something to celebrate, to lament, or to fear.[3] Like all technologies, nuclear power has always been double-edged in this way, and in time it became ironized. The nuclear sublime was at once frightening, liberating, and maddeningly trite—the possibility of annihilation, or of cheap and plentiful power, but also the phallic obsessions and deliria of Dr. Strangelove and the "atomic café," as the 1982 documentary by that name referred to the culture of kitsch and facile propaganda surrounding the nuclear threat.[4]

Chernobyl figures into this procession of the sublimes as a climactic moment of the atomic age, an age of hopes for a peaceful atom with which humanity's most dreadful technological achievement could be brought into collective service for peace and prosperity. Chernobyl's backdrop was the space race between the U.S. and the Soviet Union.[5] For the USSR, atomic power was a tool—in many respects the most powerful tool—by which a new order of socialism and peace could be built (see Figure 14.1). Science and technology became the USSR's alternative religion: useful to the regime for garnering public enthusiasm for military programs (as it was in the United States as well), it simultaneously harbored a spiritual counterculture of physicists and cosmic dreamers. In this "sputnik religion," as it has been called (Radkau 214), the dream was of a universe with mankind at its heart—the "noosphere" of human mental life being grafted onto the biosphere, in the terms coined by Ukrainian physicist Volodymyr Vernadsky ("The Biosphere and the Noosphere"; *The Biosphere*).[6]

The shadow side of this dream, however, would largely remain in the shadows, as environmental disasters in the Soviet Union were routinely denied and covered up.[7] The 1957 Mayak nuclear disaster in Kyshtym, Chelyabinsk, remains the third most serious nuclear disaster ever recorded: an explosion on September 29 released an estimated 20 mega-curies of radioactivity, and fallout from the radioactive cloud resulted in long-term contamination of 500 to 1,500 square miles of territory, primarily with Caesium-137 and Strontium-90. However, news about the disaster was "contained"—containment being a primary requirement of the nuclear state—under a cloud of secrecy, and Soviet authorities subsequently renamed the East Ural Radioactive Trace area the "East Urals Nature Reserve," while prohibiting unauthorized access to the area for years.

But the Soviet nuclear program grew. In 1970, the city of Pripyat was founded to serve as the ninth model nuclear city of the Soviet Union. On April 26, 1986, Reactor Number Four exploded. Within 36 hours of the explosion, the city's 47,000 residents were evacuated. But news was kept quiet until reports appeared in the western media of a radioactive cloud over Sweden on April 29. Communist Party general secretary Mikhail Gorbachev only delivered a speech fully acknowledging the accident on May 14, a full 18 days after the accident (Leusenko). In the end, the accident shattered the Sputnik vision and, in doing so, deprived any obvious backup to the Soviet system—a system it revealed, to many Soviet citizens, as corrupt, negligent, and more obsessed with damage control and with nomenklatura privileges than with the safety of the general population. Research over the years suggests that the reactor was poorly designed, and that its staff on the night of April 26 acted less than competently, but also that the government "lie[d] about the disaster in the most criminal way" (Gessen xi). As Keith Gessen puts it in the foreword to Svetlana

Figure 14.1 Soviet propaganda poster. "The October Revolution announced a new era in human history! The great family of the October Revolution opened for the world the epoch of domesticating the cosmos!"

Alexievich's Nobel prize winning *Voices from Chernobyl*, "In the crucial first ten days, when the reactor core was burning and releasing a steady stream of highly radioactive material into the surrounding area, the authorities repeatedly claimed that the situation was under control" (xi).

During the four years that followed the accident, ecological protest became the first legal embodiment of broadly democratic protest in the Soviet Union. In July of 1989, Zelenyi Svit (Green World) became the first independent organization to register its existence in Ukraine. By October, it had become a national umbrella organization for dozens of local environmental and anti-nuclear clubs, and by the spring of 1990, there were some 300 of these clubs in Zelenyi Svit.

The national independence movement, under the umbrella organization Rukh (The Movement), grew out of the same impetus, as similar movements had emerged across the former Soviet Republics (Dawson). In August of 1991, Ukrainians voted overwhelmingly for independence and the creation of a sovereign Ukrainian state—which brings us to narrative number two.

Bifurcation: Containment, Conspiracy, and the Floating (Ukrainian) Remainder

The Cold War had bifurcated the world into two camps led by superpowers engaged in a risky death dance, a duel of chess-like strategies, mutual secrecy, spy-versus-spy espionage, and information warfare. The riskiness of the larger situation encouraged conformity in its subjects, but also bred suspicion, rumor, gossip, and conspiracy theories. While the larger world gravitated (aided by economic or military pressure) toward one or the other pole in the bipolar system, third parties could vie to establish their presence on their own terms or according to models available to them. By December of 1991, when Ukraine suddenly appeared on the map of sovereign nations, the Cold War was formally over. But the map of the world, for Ukrainians, remained stretched between the West and the former Soviet bloc. The primary model available for the fledgling nation was that of Westphalian national sovereignty.

To understand the attractions of this model, we need to take a few steps back. One of the rival etymologies for the word "Ukraine," *Okrayina*, translates as "borderland" or "frontier region," and the Ukrainian territory certainly functioned as that for centuries: between the empires (and fledgling nations) of Europe and the steppes of Asia, with their nomadic hordes; and between rival powers which, at various times, included the Polish–Lithuanian commonwealth and the Ottoman, Russian, and Austro-Hungarian empires.[8] In the twentieth century, Ukraine's experience was dominated by warfare, colonialism, and victimization—none more evident than during the Great Hunger of 1932–1933, the Holodomor, which has come to rival and displace (for many) the formerly central narrative of the Great Patriotic War (the Soviet term for World War II). Both the Holodomor and World War II arguably affected Ukraine more than they did any other country (Snyder).

The town of Chornobyl ("Chernobyl" in Russian) and its region are thoroughly marked by a history of dispossessions, erasures, and traumas—purifications of what had once been a multi-ethnic and religiously diverse fabric.[9] The site of a hunting lodge of Kyivan Rus' prince Rostislavich in the late twelfth century, Chornobyl was incorporated into the Grand Duchy of Lithuania by the thirteenth century, and into the Polish Kingdom by the sixteenth. By 1793, when it was annexed by the Russian empire, it was a leading center of Hasidic Judaism, with an Ashkenazi Jewish majority making up the town by the late nineteenth century. Pogroms and departures of Jews, collectivization and the Holodomor, deportations of Poles in 1936, and elimination of the remaining Jews by Nazi occupiers finally rendered it into the Soviet Ukrainian town that it was in the 1980s, now "purified" of its multi-ethnic and multi-religious past.

In microcosm, Chornobyl's history mirrors that of the entire territory of Ukraine. As many scholars have argued, Ukraine fits well into the definition of a "postcolony," a place that is peripheral by definition—"once governed by, for, and from an elsewhere" and now characterized by the "coincidence of democratization and criminal violence" (Comaroff and Comaroff 2–3) and by "a distinctive style of political improvisation," including a tendency to excess and distinctive ways in which "identities are multiplied, transformed and put into circulation" (Mbembe 102).[10] As a result of this postcolonial condition, independent Ukraine has been the story of a country in perpetual *becoming*, yet never arriving. Both the Orange Revolution of 2004 and the Maidan Revolution of 2014 reflected a popular will to become-European. Counterposed against it, however, has been Ukraine's becoming- or remaining-Eurasian, "Great(er) Russian," "post-Soviet," Slavic, Orthodox, post-Byzantine, or some combination of these north-east looking variations. In between these two tendencies have been two others: a nationalist or "essentialist" becoming-Ukrainian that longs for integration and recognition within the world of global (and by definition European) powers, but that insists on returning to a romanticized past of heroes and nation builders, whose place within modernity has never been entirely comfortable (Marples); and the more pragmatic—but empty of substance—becoming-Ukrainian of the country's dominant politicians, from the country's first post-Independence president, Leonid Kravchuk, to Leonid Kuchma, Viktor Yushchenko, Viktor Yanukovich, Yulia Tymoshenko, and Petro Poroshenko. All of them have premised their power on the capacity to manage a precarious balance between opposite tendencies (pro-western and pro-Russian, among others), as well as relations with rival oligarchic groups wielding financial power in the post-Soviet era.[11]

From its inception, however, post-Soviet Ukraine's becomings have been locked into the gravity of the past. In particular, the effort to create a sovereign nation was built in part on the identity of Ukraine as a land and a people defined and united by trauma (Wanner). Chernobyl, within this narrative of national memory, has served two functions. First, it became a fulcrum around which Ukrainian independence and sovereignty were articulated as a sovereignty involving responsibility for a colossal tragedy that the previous sovereign—the Soviet Union—failed to manage. The post-Soviet Ukrainian government considered Chernobyl its badge of honor and a way to establish its international legitimacy, and so it expanded the state sanctioned, biopolitical category of "Chornobylets" (Chernobyl sufferer) in three significant ways: first, it lowered the threshold of allowable radiation dose intakes over a lifetime from 35 to 7 Rems; second, it created four categories of sufferers depending on their involvement in cleanup activities, evacuation and relocation, geographic location of life or labor in relation to the Zone, and impacts including Acute Radiation Sickness (ARS) and impact on the capacity for work; and third, it set up a bureaucratic apparatus (including a 12 percent Chernobyl Tax) for social and medical welfare provisions to citizens who qualified under this regime of identification (Petryna). Among the 3.5 million Ukrainians who have qualified as "sufferers" were the "liquidators"—some 600,000 soldiers and civilians sent in to quell the fires, clean up debris, construct the sarcophagus, decontaminate and bury buildings and villages, and so on (Brummond). Unfortunately, the health care system Ukraine has been able to provide its citizens has suffered as its economy has teetered precariously over the last 25 years, including years of neoliberal reforms; and so the system has become extremely vulnerable to financial calculation, corruption, and graft.

Second, and rather ironically, however, once Ukraine proclaimed independence, issues of nuclear power and of the environment more generally moved far from the center of Ukrainian interests, taking a back seat to economic and cultural issues. This is why the Chernobyl plant continued to generate nuclear power until the year 2000, and why several other Chernobyl-style plants continue to provide a large part of Ukraine's energy.

The narrative of trauma and victimhood has again become central in the post-Maidan period, with the commemoration of the so-called "Heavenly Hundred" who were gunned down during the 2014 Maidan events. And like a ghost that never goes away, Ukraine has found itself caught in the fault lines of the same cold war binary, such that any move either by NATO and the West, or by Russia, has been seen by many as a move to bring back the entirety of the Cold War system of information and disinformation, of "false flag operations" and of "provokatsiya."[12] The Maidan Revolution and its aftermath offered much material for conspiratorializing on all sides: around the bloody street battles of February 20, 2014, which resulted in the deaths of several dozen mostly civilians; the Russian takeover of Crimea; the tragic street fights between pro-Ukrainian and pro-Russian gangs in Odessa on June 2, 2014; the downing of Malaysia Airlines Flight 17, apparently by Russian-supported separatists though Russian media spread a panoply of alternative theories involving the Ukrainian government; and the continued fighting along the country's eastern border. Ukraine is in this sense at the heart of an evolving global media regime in which any hot button issue—from geopolitical conflicts to climate change to racial and religious differences to chemtrails, vaccinations, UFO reports, and media war itself—can become the locus of incommensurable narratives, contributing to a generalized crisis of global trust.[13]

Among the more interesting micro-conspiracy theories related to Chernobyl is that surrounding the Duga-3 international radar system, which operated from 1982 on the outskirts of the town of Chernobyl. The Duga-3 was nicknamed "the Woodpecker" due to the knocking sound it made on short wave radio receivers around the world. According to this narrative, presented in Chad Gracia's 2015 documentary *The Russian Woodpecker*, a high-ranking communist party apparatchik, Vassily Shamshin, is said to have ordered the power-down test at the Chernobyl nuclear plant that resulted in the April 26 accident specifically in order to eliminate any interest in the failure—ostensibly even more colossal—of the radar system he had been responsible for. Duga-3 is now under the control of the Ukrainian military and is generally off-limits to tourism—which brings us to the next layer of our story.

Terrain: Exposure and the "Stalking" of the Zone

Tourism in the Zone is related to the broader phenomena of travel into and out of the Zone, and of the ways the Zone has been imagined by those who have left it or who have returned. The 1986 accident had been the largest and worst release of radioactive contamination into the world in history. With this accident, humanity effectively entered a "global risk culture," in Ulrich Beck's terms, characterized by deep uncertainty, instability, and disparity in social groups' capacities to avoid or absorb risk. Events like the Chernobyl accident are harbingers of a more global ecological collapse that remains ever virtual, hovering on the horizon, yet which is manifested in countless data points connecting the impacts of industrial activities—the production of pollutants, toxins, and hazardous wastes affecting terrestrial and aquatic ecosystems, climate systems, and social systems, and together resulting in a sense of the future's precarity and uncertainty.

As reflected in Beck's model of reflexive modernization, the anti-nuclear movement took great impetus from Chernobyl. The West German Greens achieved their highest proportion of the national vote in 1987 (8.3 percent, which was only matched in 2002). Regarding the effects of the Chernobyl accident itself, however, what we know is greatly overshadowed by what we do not know. At one end of the ongoing debate over Chernobyl's impacts, the Chernobyl Forum, an international report initiated by the International Atomic Energy Agency, calculated a death toll of 4,000 or so in total. At the other end, a study commissioned by Greenpeace predicts over a quarter of a million excess cancers and nearly 100,000 cancer fatalities arising from the accident (Yablokov et al.).[14] Chernobyl's impact on the "biopolitics" of those affected (as discussed above) is arguably easier to trace than it is on the actual health of human or ecological systems. The only thing we can say for certain about the Chernobyl accident—which remains true for the Fukushima accident as well—is that we *have* no certainty about the impacts of nuclear accidents.

Meanwhile, in the Zone, the hastily constructed sarcophagus was built with a 30-year design life; in late 2016, it was replaced by another with a 100-year design life. Depopulated after the accident, the area known as the 30-kilometer Zone (while not exactly 30 kilometers in diameter, it totals approximately 1000 square miles within the territory of Ukraine) includes the city of Pripyat, a few smaller towns (including Chornobyl), and over 100 villages. Over the years, several hundred of the villagers, generally elderly ones, who had been resettled out of the Zone have elected to come back and effectively squat on their land. These *samoseli*, or "self-settlers," often grow their own food in contaminated soil. Then there are the looters: abandoning so many cities, towns, and villages has turned the Zone into a scrapyard for home appliances, carpets, metals, cultural-historical artifacts, jewelry, and the like.

But there is a more diffuse layer to the imaginary of the Zone. When the Chernobyl accident occurred, the most ready-to-hand template for interpreting it was Andrei Tarkovsky's 1979 film *Stalker*. The film was based on a science fiction novel called *Roadside Picnic*, by Arkady and Boris Strugatsky, about an anomalous Zone—created, in the novel, by extraterrestrial debris, but in the film this is left ambiguous—that is cordoned off behind an army-patrolled border, with travel into it prohibited. Produced in the late Brezhnev era, the film's theme resonated with Soviet audiences on several levels: the Zone was taken by some to be representative of one or more of the following: the Gulag; a zone of technological catastrophe, such as that known to have occurred already in Chelyabinsk; some other traumatic memory, such as the Battle of Stanlingrad; the walled off West, access to which was prohibited for Soviet citizens; or the secluded domain of the Communist Party nomenklatura.[15]

The Chernobyl accident added another layer of resonance to the film. The evacuated 30-km exclusion zone came to be called "the Zone," and unofficial tour guides to the evacuated area began to call themselves "stalkers." The original making of Tarkovky's film contributed to this layering of political and environmental overtones. Filmed twice, both times under challenging conditions, the first version of the film was destroyed during processing. Rumors circulated that it was destroyed by Soviet censors, and it took several months for Tarkovsky to convince Mosfilm, the central filmmaking industry, to fund and allow a refilming. Both productions took place in and around an abandoned Estonian power plant and downstream from a chemical plant that, unbeknownst to the crew, released toxic pollution into the environment in which they spent months filming. The penultimate scene of the Stalker and his wife and child walking home shows, in the background, a power plant that, in retrospect, eerily prefigures the Chernobyl nuclear plant, or that in any case represents the Soviet industrial sublime—the shadow of the Sputnik vision that we started with (see Figure 14.2). The presence of toxins in the water and air left its effects on the bodies of the film crew: several crew members reported allergic reactions during the filming, and a number, including actor Anatolii Solonitsyn, eventually died premature deaths from cancer and related illnesses. Tarkovsky himself died of cancer at age 56 in December of 1986; his wife died of the same cause some years later.

As an apparently uninhabitable Zone, the Exclusion Zone has attracted several hundred "stalkers" over the years. The Zone invites curiosity and even a kind of utopian aspiration. It has more

Figure 14.2 Video game enthusiast "stalkers" in the Zone
Source: www.webpark.ru/comment/35729

recently become a zone of dark, extreme, or doom tourism, or even just a kind of out-of-the-ordinary tourism. Between 10,000 and 20,000 tourists a year have visited the Chernobyl Exclusion Zone since tourism was officially legalized in 2011, many of them for the simple joy of visiting a place that most people won't visit.[16] Then there are the gamers, some of whom take their video games seriously enough to play them out in real life. As Sarah Phillips puts it, "An increasing number of Chernobyl tourists are avid gamers and enthusiasts of the S.T.A.L.K.E.R. video games"—*S.T.A.L.K.E.R.: Shadow of Chernobyl* (2007), *Call of Pripyat* (2008), and *Clear Sky* (2009), which are first-person shooter games "in which players battle zombies, mutant animals, and other improbable foes in a hyper-sensationalized contaminated 'zone of alienation'." Created by a Ukrainian design team, the video games now have well over two million copies distributed worldwide. "Imagine Chernobyl's absolute worst possible effects," Phillips writes, "multiply by ten, add steroids, bring on the Kalashnikovs, and you have S.T.A.L.K.E.R" ("Chernobyl Forever").[17]

Finally, there has been a tremendous ecological bounce-back in the Exclusion Zone ever since most of the humans left it. As Mary Mycio writes in *Wormwood Forest: A Natural History of Chernobyl*, the Chernobyl zone has become "a vast and beautiful wilderness of forests and wetlands that are gradually consuming the remains of towns and villages" and "teeming with moose, deer, wild boars and some 250 species of birds," with wolves seen in broad daylight, wild Przewalski horses reintroduced and thriving, and even endangered lynx making a comeback (Mycio).

The Zone has thus become a zone of presence and absence: the presence of forces unleashed by industrial calamity; the absence of the very causes of those forces—the human and industrial activities that precipitated them, except as ruins, memories, and odd remainders. Most interesting, perhaps, is that the abandoned city of Pripyat'—the former model nuclear city (see Figure 14.3)—has now become the model posthuman city, featuring as a stand-in for the post-apocalypse, or for the simple idea of the disappearance of humanity, in numerous media products including National Geographic's *Aftermath: Population Zero*, History Channel's *Life After People*, and the book that inspired both of these, Alan Weisman's *The World Without Us*, as well as in fictionalized dramatizations such as the postnuclear horror flicks *Chernobyl Diaries* and the *Return of the Living Dead* series, alongside sensitive documentaries like Nicholas Geyrhalter's *Pripyat*.

Figure 14.3 Prypiat, Ukraine, 2016

Credit: Adrian Ivakhiv

Anthropocene: The Zone is Us

The trope of posthumanity brings us to the final and deepest layer implicated in the hyper-event of Chernobyl, that of the Anthropocene. The conventional Anthropocene narrative is by now fairly familiar: it is that humanity has become such a powerful force on this planet that its impacts have now been registered geologically—to the degree that future geologists, looking back on our time, will note that this layer is distinctly different from the previous one, the era called the Holocene.

This story has four main variations. The first dates it to the beginnings of widespread agriculture, deforestation, rice cultivation, and stock raising (Ruddiman). The second dates the Anthropocene to the demographic collapse across the Americas resulting from the encounter of militant Eurasian bio-cultural migrants—humans, animals, plants, germs, and diseases—meeting the bio-cultural systems that were indigenous to these continents (Lewis and Maslin). The third and fourth variations, which have been more popular, date the Anthropocene, respectively, to the onset of the Industrial Revolution, and to the so-called "great acceleration" of the mid-twentieth century with its atom bombs, petrochemicals, fertilizers, and other novel substances that have rapidly spread across and into the biosphere, hydrosphere, and lithosphere of the planet (Crutzen and Stoermer).

Chernobyl most obviously fits the fourth variation, with its release of radioactive isotopes being the single largest such release in history. Its half-lives reach all the way down to the age of the Earth, in the case of Uranium-238 (half-life being a probabilistic determination of the time it takes for half of a radioactive sample to decay into non-radioactive material).

With Chernobyl's Zone of Exclusion, we see something that is both a form of evidence for the trends of the Anthropocene—trends that are visualizable as a series of meters that have suddenly begun registering red—and that runs counter to them, in the sense that the Zone is now largely depopulated of humans and has shown "nature's capacity to heal" once humans have taken leave. As Michael Marder writes in *Chernobyl Herbarium*:

> Chernobyl's 30-km radius is an advanced laboratory, at the leading edge of what is going on with the entire planet. In a consummation of the alienation or self-alienation that has unfortunately proved to be constitutive of the human, the whole world is on its way to becoming Chernobyl or a gulag.... Entire regions of the world are converted into no-go areas, whether as a consequence of wars or environmental devastation. The effects of climate change leave no place unaffected.
>
> (54)

The Zone was recently named by Ukrainian president Petro Poroshenko a "Radiation–Ecological Biosphere Reserve." Some have recommended that it be proposed to UNESCO for Transboundary Biosphere Reserve status. Recognition by UNESCO makes sense not only for the Zone's natural and cultural heritage values—the kinds that are customarily used to identify world heritage sites. Chernobyl also qualifies as part of a growing list of sites of "negative ecological heritage," or "ecological sacrifice zones," marking the places where the sacrifice that is arguably factored into global risk society—predicted as part of its algorithm of known and unknown risks—takes its specific toll on human and nonhuman populations. Finally, Chernobyl can also be seen as a site of a kind of global "future heritage" or "virtual heritage" insofar as it represents both the ecological apocalypse prophesied by some doom-laden environmentalists and the return of "nature" implied in the geological model, according to which the Anthropocene (if it does become the accepted name for this era) is fated to be overcome by another era, a post-Anthropocene in which humans are no longer central at all. (And another layer after that, and another, and so on). Humanity, after all, is as fated to disappearance as anything else in the universe.

In this, we can argue that the Zone is not the 30-km Exclusion Zone. It is rather the other way around: *The Zone is us*, humans transforming the surface of the Earth on a scale that is geological.

The Zone *is* the Holocene, the bubble of reality or safety zone that has been shaped around human activities over the last 12,000 years, which in fact provided the conditions for everything we know as civilization, and which today we know is at extremely high risk of being destabilized. If there is an anomaly to be recognized in our midst, it is best recognized by looking in a mirror.

In all of this, Chernobyl's significance is of the same order as the thinking that goes into deep geological nuclear repositories such as Onkalo in Finland, planned to be the largest such repository for nuclear wastes in the world. As defined by a group of artists working with the implications of Onkalo, the Zone we are creating, with such geological repositories, is a circle cast "to create a boundary between the world of humans and the realm of all that exceeds us" (Friends of the Pleistocene). Even as more and more of us come to recognize that such a circle is finally untenable—that the bubble will burst, or may already be bursting in slow-motion, and that the disaster is ultimately uncontainable—the circle must still be created to harbor those forces that have been unleashed.

In all of this, the Chernobyl accident and the Zone that has resulted from it represents the kind of transcendent event that registers its impacts across a series of geographic and temporal scales. In its multiple visualizations—as an error registering the nuclear and technological sublime; as the limit case of a bipolar military–industrial modernity; as a cipher of contested narratives, including those that would yoke it to an emergent new-old national sovereignty (that of Ukraine); as an emptied yet ambiguous and alluring terrain; and as a signpost on the accelerometer of the Anthropocene—Chernobyl scrambles the reference points that preceded it and renders them anomalous. It is both an anomaly and a new set of references that marks "us" as anomalous. It is a hyper-event.

Notes

1 In this chapter, I follow the widely accepted spelling of "Chernobyl" (from the Russian) for the nuclear power plant and the 1986 accident. In reference to the town that goes by that name, however, I use the Ukrainian spelling "Chornobyl." Otherwise, my spelling of Ukrainian names follows current practice for transliterating from Ukrainian to English, but without the diacritics that often accompany them (e.g., I use "Chornobyl" rather than "Chornobyl'," where the final apostrophe indicates a softened "l").
2 I develop this idea further in my recent book *Shadowing the Anthropocene: Eco-Realism for Turbulent Times*. My indebtedness to Timothy Morton's notion of the "hyperobject" is made clear there; the difference is that my process-relational ontology stresses the "eventness" of any such "object," finding the latter term unsatisfying for such lively and dynamic entities.
3 On the technological sublime, see Nye; Ray.
4 My reference here is to the character in Stanley Kubrick's black comedy *Dr. Strangelove, Or: How I Learned to Stop Worrying and Love the Bomb* (1964), and to the 1982 film *Atomic Café* (dir. by Jayne Loader, Kevin Rafferty, and Pierce Rafferty).
5 For a perceptive reading of the Soviet and American political, industrial, atomic, and utopian imaginaries, see Buck-Morss.
6 On Soviet space culture and Russian "cosmism," see Young; Maurer et al.; Epstein and Ivakhiv; Schmid.
7 See, for instance, Komarov (Ze'ev Wolfson).
8 On the history of Ukraine, see Plokhy; Magocsi.
9 See especially Brown. On the "erasure" of the Jewish population of the broader western Ukrainian region, see Bartov. On the more recently "vanished" culture of the Chornobyl region, see Sonevytsky and Ivakhiv.
10 On the debate over Ukraine's postcolonial status, see Moore; Velychenko; Gerasimov; and Gerasimov and Mogilner. Other scholars of Ukraine who have drawn on the postcolonial literature include Mykola Riabchuk, Myroslav Shkandrij, Marko Pavlyshyn, Vitaly Chernetsky, Andrzej Sheptycki, Nina Shevchuk-Murray, and Olena Yurchuk.
11 On Ukraine's identity politics, see Wanner; Wilson; Wolchik and Zviglyanich; and Ivakhiv, "Stoking the Heart of a (Certain) Europe."
12 Literally "act of provocation," this latter term is frequently used in the post-Soviet context to refer to strategic and surprising actions that may or may not be intended to provoke dramatic responses by enemies. See Ivakhiv, "'Country Under Reconstruction.'"

13 While it needs some updating, Dean's *Aliens in America* remains one of the more vibrant portrayals of this "crisis of trust" at the national level in the United States. Globally, an analogous crisis of trust has grown over the last few years as liberal media have been challenged both nationally (for instance, in the United States by Fox News, Breitbart, and other sources including those based in digital and social media) and internationally by state-sponsored media conglomerates such as RT (Russia), CCTV (China), Al-Jazeera (Qatar), Press TV (Iran), and others. On global media developments, see Diamond et al. On Russia's information war against Ukraine in the post-Maidan period, see Pomerantsev and Weiss; "Russian Media and the War in Ukraine" special issue; and Usenko and Usenko.

14 Also see Dawe et al. More generally, on health and risk related to Chernobyl, see Abbott et al.

15 I discuss all of these resonances of the film in my book *Ecologies of the Moving Image* (Ivakhiv 13–22).

16 On tourism in the Chernobyl zone, see Rush-Cooper; Yankovska and Hannam; Stone.

17 See also Phillips, "Chernobyl's Sixth Sense"; and Phillips and Ostaszewski, "An Illustrated Guide to the Post-Catastrophic Future."

Works Cited

Abbott, Pamela, Claire Wallace, and Matthias Beck. "Chernobyl: Living with Risk and Uncertainty." *Health, Risk and Society*, vol. 8, no. 2, 2006, pp. 105–121.

Alexievich, Svetlana. *Voices from Chernobyl: The Oral History of a Nuclear Disaster*, edited and translated by K. Gessen. Picador, 2006.

Bartov, Omer S. *Erased: Vanishing Traces of Jewish Galicia in Present-Day Ukraine*. Princeton UP, 2007.

Beck, Ulrich. *The Risk Society*. Sage, 1992.

Brown, Kate. *Biography of No Place: From Ethnic Borderland to Soviet Heartland*. Harvard UP, 2005.

Brummond, Janice. "Liquidators, Chornobylets and Masonic Ecologists: Ukrainian Environmental Identities." *Oral History*, vol. 28, no. 1, 2000, pp. 52–62.

Buck-Morss, Susan. *Dreamworld and Catastrophe: The Passing of Mass Utopia in East and West*. MIT Press 2000.

Chernobyl Forum. *Chernobyl's Legacy: Health, Environmental and Socio-Economic Impacts and Recommendations to the Governments of Belarus, the Russian Federation and Ukraine*. 2nd rev. ed. International Atomic Energy Agency, 2005.

Comaroff, John L. and Jean Comaroff. "Law and Disorder in the Postcolony: An Introduction." *Law and Disorder in the Postcolony*, edited by Comaroff and Comaroff. U of Chicago P, 2006.

Crutzen, Paul and Eugene Stoermer. "The Anthropocene." *Global Change Newsletter* vol. 41, pp. 17–18.

Dawe, Alexandra, Justin McKeating, Iryna Labunska, Nina Schulz, Shawn-Patrick Stensil and Rianne Teule. *Nuclear Scars: The Lasting Legacies of Chernobyl and Fukushima*. Greenpeace International, 2016.

Dawson, Jane I. *Eco-Nationalism: Anti-Nuclear Activism and National Identity in Russia, Lithuania, and Ukraine*. Duke UP, 1996.

Dean, Jodi. *Aliens in America: Conspiracy Cultures from Outer Space to Cyberspace*. Cornell UP, 1998.

Diamond, Larry, Mark F. Plattner, and Christopher Walker, editors. *Authoritarianism Goes Global: The Challenge to Democracy*. Johns Hopkins UP, 2016.

Epstein, Mikhail and Adrian Ivakhiv. "Russian Mystical Philosophy." *The Encyclopedia of Religion and Nature*, edited by B.R. Taylor, vol. 1. Continuum, 2005, pp. 1436–1439.

Friends of the Pleistocene. "Containing Uncertainty," *FOPnews*, February 24, 2010, https://fopnews.wordpress.com/2010/02/24/containing-uncertainty- design-for-in nite-quarantine. Accessed December 8, 2010.

Gerasimov, Ilya. "Ukraine 2014. The First Postcolonial Revolution: Introduction to the Forum," *Ab Imperio*, vol. 3, 2014, pp. 22–44.

Gerasimov, Ilya and Marina Mogilner. "Deconstructing Integration: Ukraine's Postcolonial Subjectivity." *Slavic Review*, vol. 74, no. 4, 2015, pp. 715–722.

Gessen, Keith. "Preface." *Voices from Chernobyl: The Oral History of a Nuclear Disaster*, by Svetlana Alexievich, Keith Gessen (Translator), x–xiii.

Ivakhiv, Adrian. "'Country Under Reconstruction': Ukraine and the Society of the Provocation?" *Immanence*, February 7, 2014, http://blog.uvm.edu/aivakhiv/2014/02/07/country-under-reconstruction-ukraine-the-society-of-the-provocation/. Accessed May 31, 2017.

Ivakhiv, Adrian. *Ecologies of the Moving Image: Cinema, Affect, Nature, Waterloo*. Wilfrid Laurier UP, 2013.

Ivakhiv, Adrian. "Stoking the Heart of a (Certain) Europe: Crafting Hybrid Identities in the Ukrainian-European Borderland." *Spaces of Identity*, vol. 6, no. 1, 2005, pp. 9–36.

Ivakhiv, Adrian. *Shadowing the Anthropocene: Eco-Realism for Turbulent Times*. Punctum Books, 2018.

Ivakhiv, Adrian. "The Event That Cannot (Not) Happen." *Contemporary Visual Culture and the Sublime*, edited by T. Trifonova. Routledge, 2018, pp. 51–60.

Komarov, Boris (Ze'ev Wolfson). *The Destruction of Nature in the Soviet Union.* Translated by M. Vale and J. Hollander. M. E. Sharpe, 1980.

Leusenko, Oleg. "Kakaya byla 'Pravda' v SSSR (skriny gazet)." 2015, http://oleg-leusenko.livejournal.com/2961899.html. Accessed May 30, 2017.

Lewis, Simon L. and Mark A. Maslin. "Defining the Anthropocene." *Nature*, vol. 519, March 12, 2015, pp. 170–180.

Magocsi, Paul Robert. *A History of Europe: The Land and Its Peoples*, 2nd ed. U of Toronto P, 2010.

Marder, Michael. *The Chernobyl Herbarium: Fragments of an Exploded Consciousness*, art by Anais Tondeur. Open Humanities, 2016.

Marples, David. *Heroes and Villains: Creating National History in Contemporary Ukraine.* Central European UP, 2007.

Maurer, Eva et al. *Soviet Space Culture: Cosmic Enthusiasm in Socialist Societies.* Palgrave Macmillan, 2011.

Mbembe, Achille. *On the Postcolony.* U of California P, 2001.

Moore, David Chioni. "Is the Post- in Postcolonial the Post- in Post-Soviet? Toward a Global Postcolonial Critique," *Publication of Modern Language Association*, vol. 116, no. 1, 2001, pp. 111–128.

Mycio, Mary. *Wormwood Forest: A Natural History of Chernobyl.* Joseph Henry Press, 2005.

Nye, David. *American Technological Sublime.* MIT Press, 1996.

Pascal, Blaise. *Pensées.* Translated by A. J. Krailsheimer. Penguin, 1995.

Petryna, Adriana. *Life Exposed: Biological Citizens After Chernobyl.* Princeton UP, 2003.

Phillips, Sarah D. "Chernobyl Forever." *Somatosphere*, April 25, 2011, http://somatosphere.net/2011/04/chernobyl-forever.html. Accessed May 31, 2017.

Phillips, Sarah D. "Chernobyl's Sixth Sense: The Symbolism of an Ever-Present Awareness." *Anthropology and Humanism*, vol. 29, no. 2, 2004, pp. 159–185.

Phillips, Sarah D. and Sarah Ostaszewski. "An Illustrated Guide to the Post-Catastrophic Future." *Anthropology of East Europe Review*, vol. 30, no. 1, 2012, pp. 127–140.

Plokhy, Serhii. *The Gates of Europe: The History of Ukraine.* Basic Books, 2015.

Pomerantsev, Peter and Michael Weiss. *The Menace of Unreality: How the Kremlin Weaponizes Information, Culture and Money.* The Institute of Modern Russia, 2014.

Radkau, Joachim. *The Age of Ecology.* Polity, 2014.

Ray, Gene. *Terror and the Sublime in Art and Critical Theory: From Auschwitz to Hiroshima to September 11.* Palgrave Macmillan, 2005.

Ruddiman, William F. "The Anthropogenic Greenhouse Era Began Thousands of Years Ago." *Climatic Change*, vol. 61, no. 3, 2003, pp. 261–293.

Rush-Cooper, Nick. *Exposures: Exploring Selves and Landscapes in the Chernobyl Exclusion Zone.* Doctoral thesis, Durham University Department of Geography, 2013.

Schmid, Sonia D. *Producing Power: The Pre-Chernobyl History of the Soviet Nuclear Industry.* MIT Press, 2015.

Snyder, Timothy. *Bloodlands: Europe Between Hitler and Stalin.* Basic Books, 2010.

Sonevytsky, Maria and Adrian Ivakhiv. "Late Soviet Discourses of Nature and the Natural: Musical *Avtentyka*, Native Faith, and 'Cultural Ecology' After Chornobyl." *Current Directions in Ecomusicology*, edited by Aaron S. Allen and Kevin Dawe. Routledge, 2016.

Stone, Philip R. "Dark Tourism, Heterotopias and Post-Apocalyptic Places: The Case of Chernobyl." *Dark Tourism and Place Identity*, edited by L. White and E. Frew. Routledge, 2013.

Strugatsky, Arkady and Boris Strugatsky. *Roadside Picnic.* Translated by A. W. Bouis. Macmillan, 1977.

Usenko, Vitalii and Dmytro Usenko. "Russia Has Been Preparing Global War Which Starts in Ukraine: Science Fiction, Alternative History, Futurology and Reality." Strata Forum, 2015, www.academia.edu/14942151/Russia_has_been_preparing_global_war_which_starts_in_Ukraine_science_fiction_alternative_history_futurology_and_reality. Accessed May 31, 2015.

Velychenko, Stephen. "Post-Colonialism and Ukrainian History." *Ab Imperio*, vol. 1, 2004, pp. 391–404.

Vernadsky, Vladimir I. "The Biosphere and the Noosphere." *American Scientist*, vol. 33, 1945, pp. 1–12.

Wanner, Catherine. *Burden of Dreams: History and Identity in Post-Soviet Ukraine.* U of Pennsylvania P, 1998.

Weisman, Alan. *The World Without Us.* St. Martin's Press/Picador, 2007.

Wilson, Andrew. *The Ukrainians: Unexpected Nation.* Yale UP, 2000.

Wolchik, Sharon L. and Volodymyr Zviglyanich. *Ukraine: The Search for a National Identity.* Rowman & Littlefield, 2000.

Yablokov, Alexey, Iryna Labunska, and Ivan Blokov, eds. *The Chernobyl Catastrophe: Consequences on Human Health.* Greenpeace, 2006.

Yankovska, Ganna and Kevin Hannam. "Dark and Toxic Tourism in the Chernobyl Exclusion Zone." *Current Issues in Tourism*, vol. 17, no. 10, 2014, pp. 929–939.

Young, George M. *The Russian Cosmists: The Esoteric Futurism of Nikolai Fedorov and His Followers.* Oxford UP, 2012.

Media References

Aftermath: Population Zero. National Geographic/Cream Productions, 2008.
Atomic Café. Directed by Jayne Loader, Kevin Rafferty, and Pierce Rafferty, The Archives Project, 1982.
Chernobyl Diaries. Directed by Bradley Parker, Alcon Entertainment, 2012.
Dr. Strangelove, Or: How I Learned to Stop Worrying and Love the Bomb. Directed by Stanley Kubrick, Columbia Pictures, Hawk Films, 1964.
Life After People. Directed by David De Vries, History Channel, 2008.
Pripyat. Directed by Nikolaus Geyrhalter, Nikolaus Geyrhalter Filmproduktion, 1999.
Return of the Living Dead: Necropolis. Directed by Ellory Elkayem, 2005.
Return of the Living Dead: Rave to the Grave. Directed by Ellory Elkayem, 2005.
The Russian Woodpecker. Directed by Chad Gracia, 2015.
Stalker. Directed by Andrei Tarkovsky, 1979.

15
RISK, LAW, AND MEDIA
A Case of Climate Change

Ariel C. Nelson and Janet Walker

In the past, we could walk across the desert by going from spring to spring.
Now, with the changing climate our springs are running dry.
        James Peshlakai, grandfather of youth plaintiff Jaime Lynn Butler

On Thursday, November 10, 2016, two days after the American presidential election, United States Federal District Judge Ann Aiken denied the United States government's and fossil fuel industry's motions to dismiss a climate change lawsuit brought by 21 young persons, the organization Earth Guardians, and climate scientist Dr. James E. Hansen. The lawsuit was filed in U.S. District Court for the District of Oregon in 2015 against the United States, naming: President Barack Obama in his official capacity; the Offices of the Council on Environmental Quality, Management and Budget, Science and Technology Policy and their Directors; the Departments of Energy, the Interior, Transportation, Agriculture, Commerce, Defense, and State and their Directors; and the Environmental Protection Agency and its Administrator. Since the presidential election, the case is proceeding against those offices and their new inhabitants. Given the current administration's fight for the "deconstruction of the administrative state" (Bannon, qtd. in Rucker and Costa; seen in Jay 00:01.34–00:01:38) and deregulation of the fossil fuel industry and corporate activity in general, the character and timing of this federal lawsuit are all the more urgent. As we write, the *Juliana v. United States* plaintiffs are gearing up for their October 2018 trial date, though it is possible that an appeal could delay or prevent the case from going to trial.

  Climate lawsuits have been proliferating, but with a notable lack of success (Shearer). *Juliana* is significant for a combination of reasons. The defendants are the many above-named government officials and agencies rather than oil companies or other emitters and polluters. The case is a challenge to the defendants' actions under the Fifth and Ninth Amendments to the U.S. Constitution and the Public Trust Doctrine with the plaintiffs claiming that the "defendants' actions violate [the plaintiffs'] substantive due process rights to life, liberty and property, and that defendants have violated their obligation to hold certain resources in trust for the people and for future generations" (*Juliana v. United States* "Opinion and Order" 1233).[1] Judge Aiken herself has deemed this "no ordinary lawsuit" and chosen to manage the case accordingly (*Juliana* "Opinion and Order" 1234). Then, notably for a volume on risk and media, *Juliana* is being litigated under the auspices of Our Children's Trust (OCT), a media rich initiative that "advocates for legally-binding *science-based* climate recovery policies" on behalf of youth and future generations ("Mission," OCT website).

Writing together, as a media studies scholar and an attorney working in environmental law, our attention has been gripped by OCT's purpose and mediated existence. The organization's website is a deep and consequential media object in and of itself. Short documentary films featuring youth plaintiffs "leading the effort to secure the legal right to a stable climate and healthy atmosphere" have been created in partnership with the international human rights organization WITNESS and Montana State University's Master's in Science and Natural History Filmmaking, and are posted to the OCT website under "About Us" (see Figure 15.1).

Other elements of the website include: Video and Radio Coverage of plaintiffs in their personal surroundings and in excerpted television appearances where OCT's Executive Director and Chief Legal Counsel Julia Olson also frequently appears; a Legal Actions section that contains documents pertaining to *Juliana* and OCT's state, global, and grassroots legal actions; and a Law Library of *amicus curiae* ("friend of the court") briefs, legal articles, and reports. There is also a science library of reports and articles focused on climate change, a blog, and the opportunity for people to donate to the cause. The initiative and our chapter proceed from the convictions that climate change is anthropogenic and deeply harmful to life on this planet, that its time scale places today's youth at higher risk than adults of experiencing negative consequences over their lifetimes, and, centrally for this analysis, that the judicial branch of government and new media can combine to ameliorate the situation.

In his field-building book, *Risk Society* (1986; Eng. trans. 1992), Ulrich Beck defines risk as "a *systematic way of dealing with hazards and insecurities induced and introduced by modernization itself*," and explains that modernization advances by unbinding politics and "ope[ning] the gates to hidden sources of social wealth with the keys of techno-scientific development" (20–21):

> The risks and hazards of today thus differ in an essential way from the superficially similar ones in the Middle Ages through the global nature of their threat (people, animals and plants) and through their *modern* causes. They are risks *of modernization*. They are a *wholesale product* of industrialization, and are systematically intensified as it becomes global.
>
> (21)

Figure 15.1 The Our Children's Trust website as media assemblage

Several decades on, we take climate change as exemplary of Beck's continued insistence on "[t]he inevitable downside of progress" (Beck, *World at Risk* 25) or the realization that environmental hazards are "of modernization"—*a consequence of* its machinations rather than a manifestation of modernity gone wrong. Current advanced and experimental technologies of oil and gas extraction (e.g., hydraulic fracturing, extended reach and complex path drilling, refracking) are in line with and some may even outstrip the "waves of large-scale technological innovation" Beck wrote about (e.g., nuclear fission, storage of radioactive waste) (*Risk Society* 185, 21). These extraction technologies are sources of wealth that epitomize both the harmful side effects and the "as yet unknown future hazards" Beck identified and foresaw (185). As the field of media studies has begun to describe, media themselves are embedded in this unhealthy ecology of resource extraction, production, consumption, (e)wastage, and repurposing (Bozak; Gabrys; Maxwell and Miller; Starosielski and Walker).[2]

This is the daunting context for our examination of risk, law, and media. But still we persist in hoping that the OCT assemblage, through the multiple spheres it influences and our transdisciplinary analysis of it (a law review article would be quite different), might contribute to the unraveling of conventional notions of which environmental changes are and are not inevitable and to the instantiation of a more radical, equitable existence on Earth. Probing risk, law, and media in the material and mediated context of climate change, we ask: How do *Juliana* and related OCT media articulate, in their respective idioms, the "deep shuddering of temporality" that rocks our uncertain planetary future (Morton 21) and the essence of "geography as an epistemic category … grounded in issues of positionality, in questions of who has the power and authority to name" (Rogoff 21)? And how is this activist assemblage helpful for creating an environmentally livable and just energy scenario? In both the instance of time and the situation of space, we find a scaling between specific and broad: that is, between the historical present and a probable future (stretching from that of the millennial generation to geologic time), and between a particular injury and anthropogenic earthly disaster. We hope this scalar commonality will not be obscured by our trade-off in opting to discuss time and space sequentially so as to take law and media together. Still we embrace the profound relationality of "time-spaces" as a key conceptual premise (Massey 177–180). Beckian notions of risk and catastrophe and the relationship between the two (in Beck's writing and as unpacked with reference to *Juliana*) also contribute to a logic of both/and that we see as present, essential, and admirably risky in the down-to-earth and highly mediated OCT initiative with epoch-changing ambitions.

Juliana is a case about climate change and climate change seems an apt topic for a volume on risk and media. Given the demands and possibilities of OCT's multimodal commitment to climate rights advocacy, the overall goal of this chapter is to make a contribution along these same lines by figuring law and media together as a crucible for the furtherance of information, analysis, and environmental justice. In particular, we seek to show how the legal and medial aspects of *Juliana* lasso the catastrophe of climate change and bring it down to earth and into present consciousness.

Risk and Catastrophe: A "Time Scale Relevant to Plaintiffs"

Juliana is formulated as exposure to a danger, harm, or loss that is known by the defendants to exist, but not yet realized to its fullest extent: in other words, as a problem of risk. The 100-page First Amended Complaint that the plaintiffs filed on September 10, 2015 opens with the following statement:[3]

> For over fifty years, the United States of America has known that carbon dioxide ("CO_2") pollution from burning fossil fuels was causing global warming and dangerous climate change, and that continuing to burn fossil fuels would destabilize the climate system on which present and future generations of our nation depend for their wellbeing and survival.
>
> (*Juliana v. United States* "First Amended Complaint" 1)

We note the use of the conditional tense: "Defendants have known of the unusually dangerous risks of harm to human life, liberty, and property *that would be caused* by continued fossil fuel burning" (*Juliana* "First Amended Complaint" 2). In this document, we learn of "farm structures, orchards, greenhouses, and pastures" along with a coniferous forest "at risk" from a wildfire that could well result from a shortage of water brought on by the drought conditions and heat waves of a warming planet (*Juliana* "First Amended Complaint" 12). Coral reefs and "oysters, clams, scallops, mussels, abalone, crabs, geoducks, barnacles, sea urchins, sand dollars, sea stars, sea cucumbers, many common single-celled organisms and protists that act as prey, and various forms of seaweed" are at risk due to ocean acidification brought on by increased CO_2 emissions (*Juliana* "First Amended Complaint" 73). The complaint emphasizes dire consequences: "The loss of some of these species can cause entire food webs to collapse" (*Juliana* "First Amended Complaint" 73). The Short Films, for their part, are also characterized by a conditional futurity that is perhaps surprising given their cinema verité mode. This is the devastating specter of crashing ecosystems that could be become material at some point in the future if we do not enact, in Beckian terms, the "self-refuting prophecy" (*World at Risk* 10) that Our Children's Trust is striving to realize through filing this federal case.

In legal terms, the plaintiffs seek the following relief: "(1) a declaration that their constitutional and public trust rights have been violated and (2) an order enjoining defendants from violating those rights and directing defendants to develop a plan to reduce CO_2 emissions" (*Juliana* "Opinion and Order" 1233). The latter is an equitable remedy called "injunctive relief," or a court order (an injunction) commanding an action to take place or preventing an action from taking place in the future.[4] Significantly, a court may only issue an injunction when there is the expectation that future harm *can* be forestalled by court action. It cannot be entirely too late.

Injunctive relief could be said to require a kind of demarcation between future harm and any prior harm. Ulrich Beck follows this logic in his key distinction between risk and catastrophe. "Risk is *not* synonymous with catastrophe," he writes; rather, "[r]isk means the *anticipation* of catastrophe" and risks are in some sense "manufactured" (*World at Risk* 9–10). For Beck, it is only when risks "become real"—such as "when a nuclear power station explodes or a terrorist attack occurs"—that they "become catastrophes" (10). In his terms, "climate change is not (yet) a reality" but rather a risk (85). In a Beckian sense, therefore, one could read the language of the *Juliana* complaint as pushing catastrophe into the future: "Absent immediate, meaningful action by Defendants ... [b]y 2100, these Youth Plaintiffs ... and future generations, would live in a climate system that is no longer conducive to their survival" (*Juliana* "First Amended Complaint" 36).

And yet, while partially sharing injunctive relief's disjunctive tendency, the *Juliana* complaint also draws on genuine complexities of the legal requirements and principles of injunctive relief—thereby blurring the Beckian risk/catastrophe split. Although, as indicated, it may only be ordered when there is still time for the court to act to prevent harm, injunctive relief does not preclude the application of the remedy in cases where some measure of harm has already occurred or is occurring.[5] Perhaps for the purposes of persuasion (if not to satisfy the legal standard), the *Juliana* plaintiffs seek to show that the environmental changes impacting humans are indeed *already occurring* and are likely to continue and worsen. Likewise, in assessing whether, with respect to their request for injunctive relief, the plaintiffs had adequately alleged the "injury in fact" element of standing (a concept discussed further below), Judge Aiken too referred to injuries that are "ongoing and likely to continue in the future" (*Juliana* "Opinion and Order" 1244).[6]

The case materials (and the media assemblage, as we will discuss) therefore describe a timeframe notable for the simultaneity of past, present continuous, near future, and deep times. In *Juliana*'s terms, impacts from climate change are extant, ongoing, accelerating, and potentially enduring. More than future possibility, such events also already possess the spatial, temporal, and social actuality of Beckian catastrophe. Existing impacts of climate change include the "warming of land surfaces, ... the warming of oceans, increasing atmospheric moisture levels, rising global sea levels, and changing rainfall and atmospheric air circulation patterns that affect water and heat distribution" (*Juliana* "First Amended Complaint" 69); "[i]ncreased wildfires, shifting precipitation patterns, higher temperatures, and drought conditions" that threaten forest industries and private property (*Juliana* "First Amended Complaint" 73); and ocean acidification, which threatens marine life, including human food sources (*Juliana* "First Amended Complaint" 73). As alleged in the complaint:

> Climate change [is] already damaging human and natural systems, causing loss of life and pressing species to extinction. Unless arrested by government action informed by science, climate change will impose increasingly severe impacts on our nation and others, potentially to the point of collapse.... These impacts constitute harbingers of far more dangerous changes to come. If unabated, continued GHG emissions, especially CO_2, will initiate dynamic climate change and effects that spin out of control for Plaintiffs and future generations as the planet's energy imbalance triggers amplifying feedbacks and the climate system and biological system pass critical tipping points. (*Such changes would be irreversible on any time scale relevant to Plaintiffs and threaten their survival*).
> (Juliana *"First Amended Complaint" 68, 76; emphasis added*)

In *Juliana*, the catastrophe of climate change exceeds the spectacularization of a single moment when a risk "becomes real;" risk is not presented as singular. There are no discernable starting and ending points to climate change, but rather a tracery of phenomena unfolding as "slow violence" (Nixon *Slow Violence*), the effects of which are likely to increase in severity and eventually threaten human survival. What would climate change's catastrophic moment consist of anyway? The moment of "spin[ning] out of control?" The passage of "critical tipping points?" "Committed warming?" The arrival of irreversible change? Or is it the extinction of human life on planet Earth (Kolbert)? In the domain of science fiction, the idea of a limit event—a radical rupture or "singular" event after which there is no going back—remains a powerful imagination of catastrophe. We appreciate that to the contrary, in *Juliana*'s terms, catastrophes, plural, float in suspension with risk. The plaintiffs rely on current environmental problems as portents of future catastrophic impacts—extrapolated by climate science—that will be irreversible, though not necessarily abrupt or discrete, *if* the court and the executive branch of government fail to take action concerning CO_2 emissions. "The present level of CO_2 and its warming, both realized and latent, are already in the zone of danger," allege the complainants (*Juliana* "First Amended Complaint" 3).

In some respects, Beck's own conceptualization of risk belies the distinction he would make between the anticipation and arrival of catastrophic events. The subject of climate change would seem to play a role here. Practically absent from *Risk Society: Towards a New Modernity* (1992), the risks associated with climate change gained in prominence in Beck's thought as the planetary warming trend was accelerating and as scientific and social understanding of the phenomena were increasing. In *World at Risk* (2007; Eng. trans. 2009), climate change qualifies as one of the "new forms" [jacket copy] and more significant dangers that Beck highlights in his argument that "the world can no longer control the dangers produced by modernity" (8). This migration of climate change to the center of Beck's thought about risk, catastrophe, and modernity is further indicated by the subtitle of his posthumously published *Metamorphosis of the World: How Climate Change is Transforming Our Concept of the World* (2016). "Only by imagining and staging world risk does the future catastrophe become present—often with the goal of averting it by influencing present decisions," he states. "The catastrophic consequences of climate change ... must be *made visible*" (Beck, *World at Risk* 10 and 86). This temporally progressive aspect of Beck's thought is of keen interest for our analysis of law and media because it signals the possibility that the imagination and *staging* of risk can and do have in *Juliana* the productive effect of summoning catastrophe to an immiscible time of the present.[7]

By advocating in a mediatic idiom as well as through litigation, OCT has all the more latitude to meld the futurity of global warming with the increasingly hazardous present. All of the materials that make up OCT online are media per John Durham Peters' definition of media "as vessels and environments, containers of possibility that anchor our existence and make what we are doing possible" (2). The array of scientific documents and short films posted to the site show effects of global warming that are already upon us and OCT proceeds full bore into the present/future simultaneity of the catastrophe that is climate change. The landing page of "The Science" section of the website begins with a paragraph explaining the immediate need to reduce the atmospheric CO_2 levels that are already beyond what they should be for a stable climate system. Other documents prominently posted and annotated contain language about "restoring the atmosphere" and "returning" CO_2 concentrations from 400ppm to below 350pp. We are already beyond the conditions for a disastrous future.

To adapt the words of poet and member of the French Resistance René Char to the current situation, "Today we are closer to the catastrophe than the alarm itself, which means that it is high time for us to compose a well-being of misfortune, even if it had the appearance of the arrogance of a miracle" (qtd. in Bataille 132 and Yusoff 1010). However arrogantly—but what choice do we really have?—we gravitate to texts that dwell close to catastrophe, or, since temporality is our topic here, where timeframes coexist or warp or fold into one another. Dutch anthropologist Johannes Fabian has advanced a critique of what he calls the "denial of coevalness," by which phrase he characterizes the anthropological conceit that "primitive" peoples are somehow living in and engaging in sociocultural practices of a distanced "savage" past time period, and not abiding contemporaneously with "first world" subjects (1983). Transposing the term to the future, we find a denial of coevalness in any belief that the depredations of climate change are not already being experienced. And since those who lack the wherewithal to accommodate, move, adapt, or compensate tend to suffer more when disasters strike, this form of denial also perpetuates sociocultural distancing in terms of what Rob Nixon and Joan Martinez-Alier have so movingly called "the environmentalism of the poor." Climate change catastrophes of increased storm volatility, flooding, and drought conditions are affecting the lives of large numbers of people and communities, most often those who lack the resources to sequester themselves in artificially verdant and safe enclaves of privilege or move out of harm's way.

In her book *Climate Trauma: Foreseeing the Future in Dystopian Film and Fiction*, E. Ann Kaplan theorizes a category of cultural production (in "film and fiction," including documentary film as well) in which audiences are engaged by stories that encourage us to imagine what "might already be here but is certainly in our future" (9). Although the book partially shares the optimistic premise of injunctive relief that there is still time and the possibility to forestall, redress, or mitigate the problems of climate change—in this case by locating audiences as "witnesses to what must never take place"—there is an extent to which, for Kaplan, certain dystopian texts are capable of "perform[ing] future-tense disaster" *in the present* (121). Writing about the documentary *Into Eternity: A Film for the Future* (dir. Michael Madsen, 2010), concerning a large-scale Finnish project to carve out of the granite bedrock a deep geological facility for the disposal of a significant percentage of Finland's nuclear waste, Kaplan holds that the narrator "interpellates the viewer of the film in between—not as a present-day spectator (or normal position) but as the future human finding the repository."[8] *Manufactured Landscapes* (dir. Jennifer Baichwal, 2007), the film Kaplan pairs with *Into Eternity*, also summons the future while "sidl[ing] up to science fiction in its otherworldliness" (129). But as Kaplan discusses, the industrial incursions are in the here and now. Depicted through the film's alternately bright and pollution-obscured color palate featuring the photographs of Edward Burtynsky, massive-scale extraction for profit has scarred the land and laid waste to areas where workers eek out a living.

A key question for us is whether the short documentaries by OCT have the capacity to "perform future-tense disaster," thus revealing how particular communities are affected. On the website under short films, there are nine videos, each of which features an individual young person moving though his or her surroundings, speaking to the camera, and often serving as a narrator. Three of these protagonists are named plaintiffs in the federal case, including Kelsey Cascadia Rose Juliana. The others are activists or petitioners in legal actions in state court. Nelson Kanuk, an Alaskan Native and member of the Yup'ik tribe from Kipnuk, Alaska, was one of six plaintiffs in a case against the State of Alaska, Department of Natural Resources, seeking declaratory and equitable relief. The State breached "its public trust obligations [under] Article VIII of the Alaska Constitution" by failing "to protect the atmosphere from the effects of climate change and secure a future for Plaintiffs and Alaska's children," the plaintiffs contended (*Kanuk ex rel. Kanuk v. State of Alaska* "First Amended Complaint" 2). Our Children's Trust, in its website description, touts the positive aspects of the Alaska Supreme Court's ruling, even though the court ultimately decided that "for 'prudential reasons' it would not order the relief requested by the plaintiffs" ("Proceedings in All 50 States, Alaska," September 12, 2014). The Alaska Supreme Court did assert that the plaintiffs "make a good case" that "the atmosphere is an asset of the public trust" (*Kanuk* "Opinion" 1101–1102), that the State "has obligations to combat climate change" ("Proceedings in All 50 States, Alaska," September 12, 2014), and that "the science of anthropogenic climate change is compelling" (*Kanuk* "Opinion" 1094).

Contrary to expectations stemming from their present tense mode, we find that these short films do figure the injurious effects of climate change by featuring young persons talking and gesturing (literally) toward the adverse environmental changes they are already seeing and (figuratively) toward a harrowing, consequential future. Take Nelson Kanuk. According to the First Amended Complaint for Declaratory and Equitable Relief filed in Alaska state court:

> Nelson [Kanuk] has been personally affected by climate change due to erosion from ice melt and flooding from increased temperatures. In December 2008, ice and water flooded the village, causing Nelson and his family as well as many others in his village to have to evacuate their homes. This erosion, flood, melting ice and increased temperatures threaten the foundation of Nelson's home, village, native traditions, food sources, culture, and annual subsistence hunts.
>
> (*Kanuk* "First Amended Complaint" 4)

This passage combines the past (the flood of December 2008), the present (Kanuk currently), and the future (the threat posed by new instances of ongoing problems). Likewise, the documentary film about Kanuk produced by iMatter Youth Council, Our Children's Trust, and WITNESS (*Nelson Kanuk*, dirs. Christi Cooper-Kuhn, Katie Lose-Gilbertson, and Kelly Matheson, 2011; available on the OCT website under "Short Films") also mobilizes the temporal simultaneity crucial to understanding climate change, now in the cinematic idiom.

The present-day tundra is alive with salmon berries that we see Kanuk and his siblings gathering. Kanuk presents a berry for its close-up, indicating, "this is what we survive on through the winter time; it's our ice cream dessert after we eat." Insects fly by, blurred bodies in front of the camera lens, signs of vibrant nature. The light is that of still photography's and cinematography's prized Golden Hour, enhancing the reds, blues, and chartreuses of the houses in this village and of laundry air-drying on the clothesline. Kanuk also harkens back to the time of the ancestors and to the 2008 flood and forward to the effects of global warming that are already being noticed and felt in his village: "it's mostly about the winter coming late," he narrates. "Climate change is about my future and the future of my entire generation," an end title reads, borrowing Kanuk's first person. The title continues, "Scientists project that a 6% reduction of CO_2 emissions per year and massive reforestation will restore the balance in our atmosphere within this century. weTRUSTthem." (Well, it's worth a try.)

Two key sequences are illustrative of the temporal simultaneity. In the first of these, we hear Kanuk in voiceover telling about the lateness of the snow, while in the image we see a darkish shot of muddy puddled ground reflecting the sunrise or sunset. Then begins Kanuk's (or perhaps his brother's) narration of the December 2008 flood. "It was the worst flood that I remember," he recalls. Cut to Kanuk making wide gestures as we hear:

> You could see all of this water flowing swiftly into the village that way, and at the same time there were these huge ice sheets that were just coming in fast [cut to the river], and [I] heard these loud thumps and bumps [cut to a medium close-up of Kanuk explaining] on the side of the house [Kanuk in front of his house] and I figured out that was probably the ice sheets that broke apart from the river and are hitting the house. [Kanuk's little sister playing with toy boats in a muddy rivulet by the front steps of the house; her right overshoe sinks into the wet mud and she succeeds in pulling it out without toppling over] After the water went back into the river, there was just brown, sticky mud all over the ground and wherever the water touched. [Kanuk slapping each step in turn for emphasis] That mud was on top of *these* steps, one two three, and four (see Figure 15.2).

"Floods in December aren't common," we hear. The river is usually frozen all the way till spring." Among the things that strike us about this energetic yet distressing passage is the fact that while Kanuk is remembering the flood of a few years prior, archival footage is not necessary. His gestures in the present make up a subtle from of reenactment—not of the *Rescue 911* docudrama variety, but rather as found in witness testimony (as when a survivor mimes putting a noose around her neck to reenact a hanging she once witnessed (Shenker 105)). The soggy present simultaneously evokes what was, what is, and what will happen in the future when the ice continues to come late, then later still, and one day perhaps not at all.

The sequence that follows tips the balance toward the future. We see close-ups of riverbank erosion and long shots of the bigger picture (see Figures 15.3 and 15.4).

Figure 15.2 Nelson Kanuk explaining the effects of ice sheets banging into his house

Source: Image courtesy of filmmaker Christi Cooper-Kuhn

Figure 15.3 The eroding riverbank in Nelson Kanuk's community
Source: Image courtesy of Christi Cooper-Kuhn

Figure 15.4 Kanuk measuring land subsidence
Source: Image courtesy of Christi Cooper-Kuhn

Nelson Kanuk and his father are shown measuring the riverbank to determine the amount of erosion caused by the higher temperatures that melt the permafrost. "This spring, my dad and I, we measured how far it was. This year we lost about eight feet and a few weeks ago we lost another five feet." Kanuk continues in voiceover,

> And we have another 40 or so feet until the bank of the river reaches our house. If it keeps moving at the same rate, then, in the next few years then we might have to move our house to another location.

This is the extrapolative portion of the sequence, the incremental land loss as the river chews its way to the house, and then the moment comes when the house must be moved to prevent its falling into the river. That catastrophic scene has not come to pass at the time of filming, but the work of the sequence is to bring it into being imaginatively. Bliss Cua Lim, referring to Roland Barthes and Henri Bergson, has written about how, "[o]n the one hand, the cinema, as clockwork apparatus belongs to the regime of modern homogenous time," functioning "like habitual perception" to conform time to "the homogeneity of measurable space." And yet, she argues, there exist "fantastic narratives" that "strain against the logic of clock and calendar, unhinging the unicity of the present by insisting on the survival of the past or the jarring co-existence of other times" (Lim 11). Citing Lim, Philippa Lovatt demonstrates the key role of the sonic register in this evocation of other times. In the "spectral soundscapes" of the films of Chinese director Jia Zhangke, "the sonic as an unruly force in its own right" emerges (419). Just as *Manufactured Landscapes* intimates otherworldliness, so too in this short film, modest in style and structure, the slapping sound of Kanuk's hand on the steps, among other visitations of past and future time, "unhing[es] the unicity of the present" in the face of climate change.

In one sense, the situation exemplifies Nixon's "slow violence," in that it "occurs gradually," manifests as "a violence of delayed destruction that is dispersed across time and space," and may seem like no violence at all (Nixon *Slow Violence* 2). There is "a representational bias against slow violence," he argues, which has "a dangerous impact on what counts as a casualty in the first place," where "[c]asualties of slow violence—human and environmental—are the casualties most likely not to be seen" (12). The eroding riverbank qualifies as "violence decoupled from its original causes and by the workings of time," posing, therefore, "the representational challenges and imaginative dilemmas" of slow violence (11). This muddy, liminal crumbling is by no means fast or spectacular.

But it is not all that slow. In saying this, we do not mean to over-literalize Nixon's concept. In fact, he writes of the need to "redefine[e] speed" "[s]o to render slow violence visible." "We see such efforts," he writes, "in talk of accelerated species loss, rapid climate change, and in attempts to recast 'glacial'—once a dead metaphor for 'slow'—as a rousing, iconic image of unacceptably fast loss" (13). But we find in the film a productive "middle violence" that offers slow violence's "different kind of witnessing of sights unseen" (15) while maintaining, in the broad judicial context, an urgent claim for relief on a generational scale: the youth will see more changes than the elders, no matter how many trees we plant. But plant we must. Nixon asks how we can "turn the long emergencies of slow violence into stories dramatic enough to rouse public sentiment and warrant political intervention" (3). The Our Children's Trust assemblage, we submit, enables multiple temporalities and works to accentuate exposure to coming harms.

Refusal to Foreclose: Climate Change and a Livable Future

Beck offers "the debate on climate change which is supposed to prevent climate change" as a key example of a potential "'self-refuting' prophecy," and Our Children's Trust is a promising venue in this regard. The *Juliana* plaintiffs seek to stage the effects of climate change "with the goal of averting it by influencing present decisions"—or compelling institutional actors to manage the risk of further harm (Beck, *World at Risk* 10). In Judge Aiken's court, this staging has been productive.

Throughout her 2016 decision on the motions to dismiss, Judge Aiken explicitly refuses to accept the defendants' and intervenors' invitation to read certain prior legal decisions—or precedent—as foreclosing the plaintiffs' climate change claims and, more generally, the plaintiffs' suit.[9] For example, the judge rejects the government's argument that the plaintiffs failed to adequately allege causation (an element of standing, as discussed below), flatly declining to "interpret [the Ninth Circuit case, *Washington Environmental Council v. Bellon*[10]]—which relied on a summary judgment record developed more than five years ago—to forever close the courthouse doors to climate change claims" (*Juliana* "Opinion and Order" 1245).[11] Similarly, she refuses to read a Supreme Court case—*PPL Montana, LLC v. Montana*—to "foreclose application of the public trust doctrine to assets owned by the federal government" (*Juliana* "Opinion and Order" 1256). And finally, instead of dismissing the plaintiffs' substantive due process claims on the ground that they allege no infringement of a fundamental right, Judge Aiken, noting that "'new' fundamental rights are [not] out of bounds," opts to exercise her "reasoned judgment" and recognize a "new" fundamental right: "the right to a climate system capable of sustaining human life" (*Juliana* "Opinion and Order" 1249). Read together, these refusals to foreclose the plaintiffs' claims reveal a deliberately forward-looking decision.

To justify her decision to open the door to judicial intervention to avert climate catastrophe, Judge Aiken leans heavily on the particular stage in the proceedings and the corresponding requirements of the operative legal standards even as she accepts the plaintiffs' articulation of world risk and remedy.[12] In distinguishing *Bellon* and finding that the plaintiffs adequately alleged causation, she emphasizes that because *Juliana*'s procedural posture is different, different legal standards apply. Here, unlike in *Bellon*, Judge Aiken is ruling on motions to dismiss and therefore is bound to accept the well-pleaded factual allegations in the plaintiffs' complaint as true (*Juliana* "Opinion and Order" 1233, 1245). She explains that "[t]his rule appropriately acknowledges the limits of the judiciary's expertise: at the motion to dismiss stage, a federal court is in no position to say it is impossible to introduce evidence to support a well-pleaded causal connection" (*Juliana* "Opinion and Order" 1245). Judge Aiken then concludes the opinion by emphasizing:

> This lawsuit may be groundbreaking, but that fact does not alter the legal standards governing the motions to dismiss. Indeed, the seriousness of plaintiffs' allegations underscores how vitally important it is for this Court to apply those standards carefully and correctly.
> (*Juliana* "Opinion and Order" 1262)

Judge Aiken signals that she accepts the degraded future the plaintiffs forecast in order to forestall its full-blown occurrence.

The opinion plays up the potential horrors the plaintiffs (and by extension, we) may experience in the face of government—executive and perhaps judicial—inaction. For example, in explaining why she has recognized a fundamental right "to a climate system capable of sustaining human life" and its breadth, she states:

> In this opinion, this Court simply holds that where a complaint alleges governmental action is affirmatively and substantially damaging the climate system in a way that will cause human deaths, shorten human lifespans, result in widespread damage to property, threaten human food sources, and dramatically alter the planet's ecosystem, it states a claim for a due process violation.
> (*Juliana* "Opinion and Order" 1250)

And, in characterizing the lawsuit as a whole, she states that it "is of a different order than the typical environmental law case" in that it "alleges that defendants' actions and inactions—whether or not they violate any specific statutory duty—have so profoundly damaged our home planet that they threaten plaintiffs' fundamental constitutional rights to life and liberty" (*Juliana* "Opinion and Order" 1261).

The opinion is resolutely oriented toward the future.[13] Rather than concluding that certain prior environmental law decisions require her to dismiss the plaintiffs' claims, Judge Aiken mobilizes other decisions to fashion new law.[14] In recognizing a fundamental right "to a climate system capable of sustaining human life," she brackets out cases where "courts have consistently rejected attempts to define [a right to be free from pollution or climate change] as fundamental" (*Juliana*

"Opinion and Order" 1250). Instead, she looks to the reasoning of *Obergefell v. Hodges*, the case in which "the Supreme Court broke new legal ground by recognizing a constitutional right to same-sex marriage" (*Juliana* "Opinion and Order" 1249). Judge Aiken therefore lays bare and rejects the proposition that she cannot or should not forge a new climate change jurisprudence, opining: "A deep resistance to change runs through defendants' and intervenors' arguments for dismissal: they contend a decision recognizing ... a fundamental right to [a] climate system capable of sustaining human life would be unprecedented, as though that alone requires dismissal" (*Juliana* "Opinion and Order" 1262).

The opinion culminates with Judge Aiken asserting the judiciary's consequential role in environmental law. In the opinion's conclusion, she squarely rejects—with both the opinion as a whole and her concluding words—that the judiciary should remain conservative in climate change litigation, proclaiming that "[f]ederal courts too often have been cautious and overly deferential in the arena of environmental law, and the world has suffered for it" (*Juliana* "Opinion and Order" 1262). She then cites Senior Ninth Circuit Judge Alfred T. Goodwin's article, "A Wake-Up Call for Judges":

> The current state of affairs ... reveals a wholesale failure of the legal system to protect humanity from the collapse of finite natural resources by the uncontrolled pursuit of short-term profits ... [T]he modern judiciary has enfeebled itself to the point that law enforcement can rarely be accomplished by taking environmental predators to court.... The third branch can, and should, take another long and careful look at the barriers to litigation created by modern doctrines of subject-matter jurisdiction and deference to the legislative and administrative branches of government.
>
> (Juliana *"Opinion and Order"* 1262)

Judge Aiken thus frames her opinion as not only proper and legitimate, but also essential to the constitutional scheme as well as aimed at the prevention of ecosystemic collapse.[15]

Judge Aiken expressly envisions and presents her decision as one that belongs in the pantheon of controversial decisions on the right side of history. She accomplishes this by comparing *Juliana* to "the landmark opinion" (authored by then-Oregon Supreme Court Justice Goodwin) that "secured Oregon's ocean beaches for public use" (*Juliana* "Opinion and Order" 1262). Judge Aiken contends that it was only by rejecting a "call to judicial conservatism" and applying a concept from English common law that the Oregon Supreme Court was able to ensure that "Oregon's beaches remain open to the public now and forever" (*Juliana* "Opinion and Order" 1262–1263). Thus, she invites her readers to envision the long-term impact of her decision.

Our Children's Trust similarly casts both its advocacy efforts and Judge Aiken's decision as groundbreaking and critical to the future of "the youth of this country" ("Victory for America's Youth"). The section on the website describing the federal case is labeled "Landmark Federal Climate Lawsuit" (see Figure 15.1). And, in an official press release, counsel for the plaintiffs Julia Olsen proclaimed: "This decision is one of the most significant in our Nation's history." She also asserted that the trial in the case will be "the trial of the millennium" ("Victory for America's Youth"). Olson therefore urges the public to see Judge Aiken's decision alongside prior monumental decisions in United States history and to imagine the lawsuit in the context of the entire millennium. Asking the reader to look back at the decision from a future vantage point, Olson invests the lawsuit and decision with the capacity to image, create, and ensure a certain future for humans. In short, Our Children's Trust encourages the public to see this lawsuit itself as a productive staging of world risk.

Standing: Threshold Questions, Spatial Matters

"A threshold question in every federal case is … whether at least one plaintiff has standing" (*Thomas v. Mundell* 760, qtd. in *Juliana* "Opinion and Order" 1242)—whether a plaintiff has "such a personal stake in the outcome of the controversy as to warrant [the] invocation of federal-court jurisdiction and to justify exercise of the court's remedial powers" (*Warth v. Seldin* 498, qtd. in *Juliana* "Opinion and Order" 1242). From our transdisciplinary perspective and in terms of OCT's own set of concerns, "standing" intrigues. At the same time that it is incumbent upon the *Juliana* plaintiffs to assert, and Judge Aiken to assess, each person's "personal stake" or "concrete, particularized" injury, the injuriousness of climate change necessarily extends well beyond the local situation. As we will proceed to demonstrate, OCT's *spatial imagination* echoes its temporal one in terms of scalability: here too, the terrain is simultaneously specific and broad, local and national (global even), down-to-earth and atmospheric.

Injury in fact, causation, and redressibility are the three elements that comprise "[t]he irreducible constitutional minimum of standing" (*Lujan v. Defenders of Wildlife* 560).

> To demonstrate standing, a plaintiff must show (1) she suffered an injury in fact that is concrete, particularized, and actual or imminent; (2) the injury is fairly traceable to the defendant's challenged conduct; and (3) that injury is likely to be redressed by a favorable court decision.
>
> (Juliana *"Opinion and Order" 1243*)[16]

(Re)mediating Injury

At pains to establish injury in fact, the complaint and also the judicial decision draw vivid word pictures of the individual youth plaintiffs in their surroundings beset by a litany of woes. The environments are beautifully natural and yet also partially—but not irremediably—damaged. The titular plaintiff, Kelsey Cascadia Rose Juliana, is described in the complaint (dated 2015) as a 19-year-old resident of Eugene, Oregon with environmentalist bona fides (she "walked 1,600 miles from Nebraska to Washington D.C. in the Great March for Climate Action" in Fall 2014 (*Juliana* "First Amended Complaint" 6)) and a life experience that "depends on the freshwaters of Oregon for drinking, hygiene, and recreation" (*Juliana* "First Amended Complaint" 6). Details proliferate: on hiking and canoeing trips she drinks freshwater from springs in the Oregon Cascades and in everyday life has a diet including salmon, cod, tuna, clams, mussels, and crab from "marine waters and freshwater rivers" and vegetables grown by small farmers in the Willamette Valley and in her own family garden (*Juliana* "First Amended Complaint" 6). But drought and lack of snow are "already harming all of the places Juliana enjoys visiting, as well as her drinking water, and her food sources" (*Juliana* "First Amended Complaint" 7). Intense wildfires, which elsewhere in the complaint are said to be increasingly frequent and intense due to climate change (*Juliana* "First Amended Complaint" 73), have interfered with her enjoyment of summer recreation, and she "has had to abandon camping trips because of nearby wildfires" (*Juliana* "First Amended Complaint" 7). Judge Aiken determines that the plaintiffs have indeed satisfied the "injury in fact" requirement because their "alleged injuries—harm to their personal, economic, and aesthetic interests—are concrete and particularized" and imminent—that is to say "ongoing and likely to continue in the future" (*Juliana* "Opinion and Order" 1244). (While continuing with this section's discussion of space and place, we note that the temporal dimensions of standing match the complexity discussed above.)

We are struck by the rustic simplicity of Juliana's and the other portraits, in the complaint and judicial decision both, and the conflation of would-be subsistence and recreational activities (drinking from streams, sourcing salmon from nearby rivers, tide-pooling, canoeing on lakes). It is likely, though unstated, that a significant percentage of the foods in Juliana's regular diet are purchased at grocery stores. But, in the complaint, there is little evidence of consumer activity or the architectures of modernity: buildings, roads, energy infrastructures. The choice of rural plaintiff Alexander Loznak contributes to the pastoral quality of the plaintiff descriptions in aggregate. Loznak's family owns the 570-acre Maupin Century Farm along the Umpqua River in an unincorporated area of Kellogg, Oregon that has been in the family since 1868 (*Juliana* "First Amended Complaint" 9). The farm, where hazelnut and plum trees and vegetables are grown and chickens and grass-fed cows are raised, is a source of food and revenue for the family (*Juliana* "First Amended Complaint" 10). They also hunt deer, elk, and wild turkey to eat (*Juliana* "First Amended Complaint" 10). Record-setting heat waves and drought are specified as having adverse effects, especially on the hazelnut orchard (*Juliana* "First Amended Complaint" 10).

It is precisely the hand-to-mouth or foot-to-path nature of the individual portraits that make it possible to broaden the discussion of the injurious effects of climate change without running afoul of the generalized grievance rule. The government, in its motion to dismiss, contends that the plaintiffs lack standing, and the federal court therefore lacks jurisdiction, on the basis that the "injuries are not particular to plaintiffs because they are caused by climate change, which broadly affects the entire planet (and all people on it) in some way" (*Juliana* "Opinion and Order" 1243). But Judge Aiken rejects this argument, citing Ninth Circuit and Supreme Court precedents. She insists that "the fact that a harm is widely shared does not necessarily render it a generalized grievance" (*Jewel v. National Security Agency* 909, qtd. in *Juliana* "Opinion and Order" 1243), and, quoting *Massachusetts v. Environmental Protection Agency*, that "'[i]t does not matter how many persons have been injured by the challenged action' so long as 'the party bringing suit shows that the action injures him in a concrete and personal way'" (qtd. in *Juliana* "Opinion and Order" 1243). However paradoxically, the quotidian—even plodding—nature of each young person's byways and injuries ensures that the case is and can legally be about widespread injurious effects of climate change.

But then too the youth stakeholders in Our Children's Trust are dynamic and well-traveled advocates who have moved across the country and world, and across the mediasphere. Their activism is evidenced by the compilation of Video & Radio Coverage on the OCT website: dozens of audio and video pieces from 2014 through to the time of this writing in 2018. On June 29, 2017, the plaintiffs, from Kelsey Juliana to Levi Draheim, the youngest plaintiff, gathered on the steps of the United States District Court in Eugene, Oregon and spoke to KLCC (McDonald). Plaintiff Xiuhtezcatl Martinez, in an interview on the Norwegian-Swedish television talk show Skavlan (hosted by Norwegian journalist Frederik Skavlan) compares that experience to his previous experience of having addressed the United Nations (Skavlan). A Democracy Now! presentation finds Aji Piper (16 years of age), Draheim (nine years of age), and Jaime Butler (16 years of age), along with attorney Julia Olson, among the 2017 People's Climate March participants where they are interviewed by host Amy Goodman. Draheim speaks of the dune erosion, drought, wildfires, and sea-level rise affecting her home on a barrier island in Florida (Goodman). In a Senator Bernie Sanders video, Kelsey Juliana, Kiran Oomen, and Victoria Barrett form a panel of speakers positioned in front of a "blue marble" image of planet Earth. "Everything to do with the climate affects young people more than it does anyone else," states Oomen, "and one can speculate that might even be an influence on the reason why so many old folks who are in the government have been so slow to act. It's because it's not going to affect some of them." Video footage from widespread and diverse locations is edited into this press conference such that the youth are seen peopling country, from the icy edge of an alpine body of water to outside the United States Supreme Court in Washington, D.C. (Sanders).

Lisa Parks has theorized and demonstrated a technique of "plotting the personal" in which she appropriates GPS technology from its original use ("military monitoring of soldiers' movement upon the battlefield") to serve as a figuration "of the user as a subject produced through a series of movements and encounters" (213–214). Springing from Paul Virilio's notion of "the trajective,"

Parks challenges "dominant cartographic discourses" and their reduction of "the complexity of spatial practice" to theorize a " 'being of movement' located somewhere between the objective map of territory and the subjective experience of motion on the ground" (Virilio, qtd. in Parks 214).

We envision the nodes and trajectories of the plaintiffs—firmly rooted in their local communities and also crisscrossing the globe, uniting in spots for press conferences and marches, and dispersing again—as embodying through their "being of movement" the collective commons necessary for life on Earth. Although their media format is video compilation rather than GPS, these and other Our Children's Trust videos "plo[t] … the personal," thereby forming an assemblage that is both an archive of its participants' trajectories and also, importantly, an active instantiation of mediated positionality. The website, like the court case, is constructive of "concrete, particularized, and actual" positions and injuries, and of standing as a liminal matter indeed.

Causation and Social Ecology

To meet the second requirement of standing, causation, "[a] plaintiff must show the injury alleged is 'fairly traceable' to the challenged action of the defendant and not the result of 'the independent action of some third party not before the court' " (*Lujan* 560, qtd. in *Juliana* "Opinion and Order" 1267).[17] The chain of causation alleged in this case leads Judge Aiken to the heart of the matter: the deleterious effects of greenhouse gas emissions. The judge makes clear from the beginning of her opinion that anthropogenic climate change is a proven fact (i.e., "this lawsuit is not about proving climate change is happening or that human activity is driving it" (*Juliana* "Opinion and Order" 1234)). What does need to be established for the viability of the case is the linkage between the harm endured by the plaintiffs and the defendants' responsibility for failing to keep destructive greenhouse gas emissions in check. "[T]he line of causation between the defendant's action and the plaintiff's harm must be more than attenuated" (*Native Village of Kivalina v. ExxonMobil Corp.* 867, qtd. in *Juliana* "Opinion and Order" 1244).[18] However, as Judge Aiken submits, a "causal chain does not fail simply because it has several links" (*Kivalina* 867, qtd. in *Juliana* "Opinion and Order" 1244).

For its part, the government's November 2015 motion to dismiss *Juliana* relies on the Ninth Circuit's decision in a prior case brought by environmental advocacy groups "to compel the Washington State Department of Ecology and other regional agencies 'to regulate greenhouse gas emissions … from five oil refineries' " (*Washington Environmental Council v. Bellon* "Opinion" 1135, qtd. in *Juliana* "Opinion and Order" 1244). In that case, the court held the plaintiffs lacked standing "because the causal link between the agencies' regulatory decisions and the plaintiffs' injuries was 'too attenuated' " (*Bellon* "Opinion" 1141, qtd. in *Juliana* "Opinion and Order" 1244). As Judge Aiken states, "[t]he court noted that the five oil refineries at issue were responsible for just under six percent of total greenhouse gas emissions produced in the state of Washington" (*Juliana* "Opinion and Order" 1245): cumulative environmental effects notwithstanding, "there is limited scientific capability in assessing, detecting, or measuring the relationship between *a certain GHG* (greenhouse gas) *emission source* and *localized climate impacts in a given region*" (*Bellon* "Opinion" 1143, qtd. in *Juliana* "Opinion and Order" 1245; emphasis added).

Judge Aiken finds *Juliana* different in a number of respects, one of which is that "the emissions at issue in this case [emanating from across the entire country], unlike the emissions at issue in *Bellon*, make up a significant share of global emissions" (*Juliana* "Opinion and Order" 1246). The links are there: between the fossil fuel combustion responsible for "the lion's share of greenhouse gas emissions" and the defendants' ability and activities to raise or lower combustion; and to climate change and plaintiffs' injuries (*Juliana* "Opinion and Order" 1246).

From a spatial studies perspective, the case's and the videos' work describes a filigree of disparate spaces and nodes: the atmospheric layer (where the GHGs are suspended), the industrial installations that comprise the country's fossil fuel infrastructure, and down-to-earth byways where the plaintiffs reside or recreate. The Pacific Connector Natural Gas Pipeline, if completed, would connect to the Jordan Cove LNG Terminal at Coos Bay, Oregon, running through a forest 30 miles from the Maupin Century Farm and "cross[ing] bodies of water at 400 different locations in Oregon, including two places on the South Umpqua River where Alex recreates" (*Juliana* "First Amended Complaint" 9). The complaint states that Loznak has:

> walked along the pipeline route and has seen the old growth trees that will be logged and the special rivers that will be impacted in order to deliver natural gas to what would be the largest, most-polluting facility and power plan in Oregon, solely built to liquefy natural gas for export and ultimate combustion.
>
> *(9)*

This pipeline would also affect another plaintiff, Jacob Lebel, who grew up on Rose Hill Farms (11). The pipeline would run behind the farm, "adversely affect[ing] Jacob's aesthetic inspiration, and spiritual enjoyment of the property," and it would entail forest clear-cutting destructive of the landscape integrity and biodiversity and the risk of leaks or explosions that could "trigger a wildfire in the hot summer months" (13). The LNG Terminal in Coos Bay would also affect Xiuhtezcatl Martinez by serving as a liquefaction facility for "natural gas extracted through fracking in Colorado" where Xiuhtezcatl (as the court documents refer to him) resides, and "shipped overseas for combustion." The existence of this Oregon plant increases the demand for fracking and the concentration of CO_2 (8).

But then, we ask, if the legal demands are such that *anyone* who can demonstrate "concrete, particularized, and actual or imminent" injury, causation, and redressability is eligible for relief, what is the relevance to *Juliana* of the premise of social ecology: that those who are already disadvantaged suffer more when disasters occur or environmental degradation haunts the land? The idea of the Anthropocene has been subject to criticism for a tendency to elide social inequality. Nixon, among others, asks: "[W]hat is lost and gained by adopting the Anthropocene's grand species perspective on the human? Does this epic vantage point risk suppressing—historically and in the present—unequal human impacts, unequal human agency, and unequal human vulnerabilities?" ("The Anthropocene"). "[R]isk factors are not random," assert Yoosun Park and Joshua Miller in the context of this body of work that offers a radical critique of neutralist discourses of disaster while "underscoring the numerous interdependent social forces, which shape the context in which disasters occur" (11). Discussing the ravages of Hurricane Katrina, often referred to ruefully as an "equal opportunity disaster," they amply demonstrate that

> [t]he ongoing environmental risks for poor people and people of color are consistently higher than for white people and those who are economically privileged.... The socially disadvantaged are more likely to live near chemical plants, landfills, and other contaminated lands.
>
> *(Park and Miller 10)*[19]

Similar social ecological factors pertain in contexts of fossil fuel extraction. For example, the path of Energy Transfer Partners' Dakota Access Pipeline snaking under the Missouri River half a mile north of the Standing Rock Sioux Reservation, through land encompassed in the Fort Laramie Treaty of 1851 between United States treaty commissioners and representatives of the Cheyenne, Sioux, Arapaho, Crow, Assiniboine, Mandan, Gros Ventre, and Arikara Nations, was originally planned to cross the Missouri north of the city of Bismarck, North Dakota. But that plan was scrapped for several reasons including that the route was a threat to the city of Bismarck's water supply (Dalrymple).

We do discern in the complaint and judicial opinion a distinct social ecological consciousness contingent on Our Children's Trust's expansiveness with regard to positionality. The plaintiffs as a group reside in different states (with Oregon residents a simple majority), their selection evinces a commitment to racial and economic diversity, and their life experiences are formed by external factors and agents. Jamie B., from the Bitter Water Clan, grew up on the Navajo Reservation in Cameron, Arizona (*Juliana* "First Amended Complaint" 23–24). There she and her family faced water scarcity for themselves, their crops, and their farm animals, as springs that had previously flowed year-round are drying up. Her grandfather's statement about drying up desert springs (this chapter's epigraph) evokes the interrelated shifts induced by a changing climate, shifts that are elemental, historical, spatial, and social ecological. The costs of hauling water were such that the family could not sustain that living and were forced to move from the land. Indeed, as the complaint indicates, Jaime is worried that her "extended family, all of whom live on the Reservation, will also be displaced from their land, which will erode her culture and way of life" (24). Her new home is on property her mother owns in the Kaibab National Forest, where a pine beetle infestation has destroyed large swathes of forest and she and her mother had to evacuate for two days due to the Oak Creek Canyon fire, exacerbated by drought conditions (24). Jayden F., a resident of Rayne, Louisiana, had been directly affected by three hurricanes, linked in the complaint to climate change (31). She

> has suffered harm and will continue to suffer harm to her and her family's personal safety, bodily integrity, property, economic stability, food security, and recreational interests from rising sea levels, increased frequency and severity of hurricanes with ensuing storm surges, flooding and high winds, *all associated with or exacerbated by climate change caused by Defendants.*
>
> *(31; emphasis added)*

The complaint connects the dots between the infrastructures of oil extraction, Hurricane Gustav, and Jayden F.'s home:

> Defendants' approval of the dredging of canals through marshes for oil and gas exploration and pipelines has compounded the problem by its destruction of natural storm barriers, increased erosion, and intense saltwater intrusion, resulting in additional land loss. In 2008, during Hurricane Gustav, Jayden's family lost power for a week.
>
> *(32)*

The BP oil spill is also cited as having adversely affected the activities of Jayden and her family, and here too the complaint draws a direct line from the BP spill to "the coastal impacts from climate change caused by Defendants" (32). That Judge Aiken may be keenly conscious of the socioeconomic unevenness of harm is suggested by her inclusion of information from Jayden F.'s supplemental declaration (*Juliana* "Opinion and Order" 1243). When Jayden F.'s home flooded in 2016, sewage backed up, soaking everything and waterlogging the walls. But "the family remained in the flooded house for weeks" "[w]ith no shelters available and nowhere else to go" (1243).

And yet, the technical demands of asserting legal standing and the choice to focus the videos on individual youths partially tamp down consideration of the stakes of communities and the historical contingencies of resource allocation. For example, a long-term struggle is going on over water rights and the existence of dams on the Klamath River in California and Oregon, in the course of which farmers, fishermen, Native tribes, and environmentalists have articulated competing interests and pointed to the immiseration of communities (see Barboza). The death of fish and other animals and plants also accompanies large-scale damming and diversion of water. Historical conflicts over tribal lands, periodic drought conditions, and debates over the viability of hydroelectric dams (some of which have been removed), are serious complicating factors. The fact that such a complex social and natural ecology is unnecessary, perhaps even counterproductive to showing legal standing, works against a systemic view of injury. Complex or nonlinear causality is in this way inhibited by the legal context.

Redressability in the Context of Nonknowledge

The third and final prong of the constitutional standing inquiry is redressability: whether a favorable decision will actually redress the alleged (extant or projected) injury.[20] But as Judge Aiken states, "[r]edressability does not require certainty," but only "a substantial likelihood it will do so" (*Juliana* "Opinion and Order" 1269, 1247). The plaintiffs need only show that the "requested remedy would 'slow or reduce' the harm" (*Massachusetts v. EPA* 525, qtd. in *Juliana* "Opinion and Order"). Thus, Judge Aiken explains, in this case,

> [i]f plaintiffs can show, as they have alleged, that defendants have control over a quarter of the planet's greenhouse gas emissions, and that a reduction in those emissions would reduce atmospheric CO_2 and slow climate change, then plaintiffs' requested relief would redress their injuries.
>
> (Juliana *"Opinion and Order"* 1247)[21]

She rejects the defendants' and intervenors' skeptical formulation of the inquiry as a question of whether the court can guarantee "an overall reduction in greenhouse gas emissions" (*Juliana* "Opinion and Order" 1247). The legal standard, she finds, permits the court to act, even when uncertainty about its own efficacy remains. Inaction is the real problem, she stipulates, and not the scientific unknowns.

> Redressability in this case is scientifically complex, particularly in light of the specter of irreversible climate change, wherein greenhouse gas emissions above a certain level push the planet past points of no return, beyond which irreversible consequences become inevitable, out of humanity's control.
>
> (Juliana *"Opinion and Order"* 1247; *citing a declaration by James Hansen*)

Judge Aiken then poses of series of questions, the answers to which we cannot know "at the motion to dismiss stage:"

> What part of plaintiffs' injuries are attributable to causes beyond this Court's control? Even if emissions increase elsewhere, will the magnitude of plaintiffs' injuries be less if they obtain the relief they seek in this lawsuit? When would we reach this point of no return, and do defendants have it within their power to avert reaching it even without cooperation from third parties?
>
> (Juliana *"Opinion and Order"* 1247)

After explicitly acknowledging that there are things we cannot know at this stage in the case and, presumably, in the progress of scientific research,[22] Judge Aiken concludes that the plaintiffs have adequately alleged redressability.

We are impressed by the opinion's avoidance of the pitfall Kathryn Yusoff identifies: allowing the presence of uncertainty to halt necessary action. What "knowledge of climate change has revealed alongside its certainties," Yusoff argues, are "the ambiguities inherent in recognising a complex energy system that cannot … be regulated by a mechanic" (1010–1011). Her excellent example is the choice by the Intergovernmental Panel on Climate Change, at one point, to relegate to a footnote information about the projected failure of massive ice sheets. Because "catastrophic failure of the ice was seen by the IPCC as an excessive, unpredictable event (the problem of rising sea levels was not entirely understood)," the pertinent calculations could not be included in the body of the Fourth Assessment Report (1011–1012).

But of course, given that grappling with and planning for melting ice sheets and rising sea levels is necessary for the minimization of suffering, failure to acknowledge these uncertainties of the physical environment (in "excess of our knowledge") "brings with it other kinds of risks" (1015). "[T]he removal of [the] unknown stability or nonknowledge" actually "*promotes* further instability" (1012; emphasis added). In declining to be constrained by uncertainty about the court's efficacy to help forestall climate catastrophe (at the stage in the litigation at which she was writing[23]), Judge Aiken too is tolerating or even embracing nonknowledge to mitigate "other kinds of risks." It may be that "our relationship to the disaster is presently more intimate than our power to represent it," as Yusoff would have it (1026). Yet we affirm these ongoing efforts.

Producing the Future

To speculate affirmatively is to produce futures while refusing the foreclosure of potentialities, to hold on to the spectrum of possibilities while remaining open to multiple futures whose context of actualization can never be fully anticipated. This is not to say speculative living is simply ephemeral; rather, it is a consistently modifying practice that seeks to act in shifting, multiscalar worlds.

Uncertain Commons, Speculate This!

The OCT assemblage exemplifies the "sense of potentiality" or "opening to the future" that the Uncertain Commons collective articulates as "affirmative speculation" (14). Whereas "firmative speculation" is a "speculative mode" that seeks to "produc[e], exploi[t], and foreclos[e]" the future (Uncertain Commons 19, 36), as when financial "risk instruments" channel the wealth of common resources to the privileged few while shifting the burden of risk to those who are less advantaged or disadvantaged, "affirmative speculation" is a way to "contest the proprietary enclosure of knowledge, imagination, while also affirming the potentialities of the common" (12). Climate change is one of the examples provided by Uncertain Commons of an existing problem, exacerbated by the practices of firmative speculation, but potentially reparable by those who would speculate affirmatively or "dare to temporally materialize forms not yet realized" in order to achieve "a greener, more responsive global politics" (22).[24]

When we began this analysis, we expected to find an unevenness in media's and the judiciary's respective abilities to embrace the posture of living "simultaneously in the virtual … and [in] the partially actualized, rapidly mutating present" (Uncertain Commons 21–22). But what we found and have sought to demonstrate, is that through all its initiatives, OCT proceeds in an affirmative spirit: combining and coordinating material pleasures and harms being experienced locally with the imagination of a future of healthy biomes and unburdened communities. Thickly described habitats comport with deep geologies and planetary spaces, different temporalities are rendered together, and risk is staged as resistance to the foreclosure of a livable future. Then, for the most part and contrary to our initial expectations, we found in the *Juliana* plaintiffs' complaint and Judge Aiken's decision a similar heartening complexity of temporal and spatial imagination.

The intensity of the legal battle attests to the high stakes of judicial action. Since the complaint was filed in September 2015, the national election of November 2016 brought Donald J. Trump to power and led to the subsequent appointments of new Cabinet and federal agency leaders. Relevant to the problem of climate change are the appointments of Secretary of State Rex Tillerson, former CEO of ExxonMobil, and then Michael R. Pompeo, who was president of an oilfield equipment company prior to serving in Congress and directing the CIA; Secretary of the Interior Ryan Zinke, former Congressman from Montana who has opposed environmentalists on issues of coal extraction and oil and gas drilling and lists "regulatory relief" as one of the strengths of his Congressional track record; Secretary of Energy Rick Perry, former governor of Texas and member of the Energy Transfer Partners board of directors, who proposed eliminating the Department of Energy during his 2012 presidential campaign; and Administrator of the Environmental Protection Agency Scott Pruitt, who as Attorney General of Oklahoma supported the oil and gas industries and sued the Environmental Protection Agency more than a dozen times, including to block the agency's Clean Power Plan. Pruitt attempted to undo environmental regulations before being replaced by Andrew Wheeler. These are officials whom the plaintiffs have announced their intention to depose. But on June 9, 2017, the defendants[25] fought back by petitioning the United States Court of Appeals for the Ninth Circuit to issue a writ of mandamus and direct the district court to dismiss the case and stay the proceedings until the merits of the petition for mandamus are resolved.[26] A writ of mandamus is a "drastic and extraordinary remedy," and "only exceptional circumstances amounting to a judicial usurpation of power or a clear abuse of discretion" will justify its invocation (*Cheney v. United States District Court for the District of Columbia* 380; internal citations and quotation marks omitted). The defendants alleged that the district court (Judge Aiken) "committed clear legal error and exceeded its judicial authority" by failing to dismiss the *Juliana* case (Petition for Writ of Mandamus 3). The Ninth Circuit ultimately denied that petition, as well as a second mandamus petition. Then, in July 2018, the U.S. Supreme Court ruled in favor of the plaintiffs, denying the government's application for a stay of the proceedings and deeming the request for relief premature. The case has reached the merits stage and, as indicated at the start of this chapter, is slated for trial.

The overall situation in the United States with regard to climate change resonates with Ulrich Beck's prescient discussion in the final chapter of *Risk Society* of the political fallout of "the innovation process that is enforced by modernity" and "the globalization of the industrial society" (184). First, "the decision-making competencies that structure society" are split into two contrary but interpenetrating processes such that "one part is removed from the rules of public inspection and justification" to which they would normally be subjected in the parliamentary democracy (that makes up the other part) and is instead concentrated on investment enterprises and technological prowess (184). What Beck is describing here is a techno-economic regime where science is bound—firmatively one might say—by an equation between technological innovation and rises in the standard of living that simply doesn't add up. To suggest an example, oil companies' promise of good, local jobs when new installations are introduced into a community is exaggerated and the jobs often short-lived. In fact, studies over the years have shown that extractive industry boomtowns often descend further into poverty or social instability for having opened the door (Brabant and Gramling; Freudenberg; Smith). But according to Beck's discussion, such "negative effects"—"deskilling, risks of unemployment or transfer, threats to health and natural destruction"—are swept aside in the rush of supposed progress. Social consequences no longer matter, as "progress becomes a substitute for questions, a type of consent in advance for goals and consequences that go unnamed and unknown" (184).[27]

Beck then argues that techno-economic development ultimately "falls between politics and non-politics," becoming "a third entity, acquiring the precarious hybrid status of a *sub-politic*, in which the scope of the social changes precipitated varies inversely with their legitimation" (186). A "profound *systematic transformation of the political*" occurs, characterized by both a "loss of power experienced by the centralized political system in the course of the *enforcement and utilization of civil rights*" and changes of social structure that become lost in the false formula that technical progress and social progress are equivalent. The result is a "*democratic monarchy*" in which:

> The rules of democracy are limited to choice of political representatives and to participation in political programs. Once in office, it is not only the "monarch for a term" who develops dictatorial leadership qualities and enforces his decisions in authoritarian fashion

from the top down; the agencies, interest groups and citizens' groups affected by the decisions also forget their rights and become "democratic subjects" who accept without question the state's claims to dominance.

(191)

Beck's "democratic monarchy" is in ample evidence in the domination of environmental offices and agencies meant to protect people and the environment by the very industries they were designed to oversee or regulate. Generally, the theory of "regulatory capture" posits that "[r]egulatory agencies, created to act in the public interest, often end up acting directly or indirectly in the interests of those they regulate" (Brown 703).[28] In the United States today, the elected federal government is under the sign of techno-scientific capture.

The petition for a writ of mandamus filed against the United States District Court for the District of Oregon and *Juliana et al.*, Real Parties in Interest employed the gambits characteristic of risk modernization. Significantly, it attempted to exclude the judiciary from decisions about the environment by invoking the U.S. Constitution's framework of separation of powers and categorizing issues of energy and the environment as matters of policy or politics to be dealt with only by the executive and legislative branches of government. The petition does not engage with Judge Aiken's lengthy discussion of whether the case presents a political question such that "federal courts lack subject matter jurisdiction to decide that question" (*Juliana* "Opinion and Order" 1235). Here she makes the point that

> [c]limate change, energy policy, and environmental regulation are certainly 'political' in the sense that they have "motivated partisan and sectional debate during important portions of our history." ... But a case does not present a political question merely because it "raises an issue of great importance to the political branches."
> (U.S. Department of Commerce v. Montana 458, qtd. in *Juliana* "Opinion and Order" 1236)

Relative to our Beckian framework, if the executive and legislative branches have become "sub-political" or captured by extractive industries, then they have shirked their political obligation to represent and act for the benefit of the people of this country.

The petition is also striking for its adamant foreclosure of the subject of climate change. The petitioners could have accepted that climate change is a problem that needs addressing while still objecting to the district court proceedings. On the contrary, its descriptions take us through the looking glass in their disregard for the plaintiffs' goal of contributing to the achievement of an atmosphere capable of sustaining verdant life over the course of time. If the petitioners' objection is that the plaintiffs' case seeks to interfere with and "fundamentally redirect federal policy regarding energy development, transportation and consumption," that critique need not be lumped into a sentence that also describes the plaintiffs' underlying goal "to bring about dramatic reductions in global concentrations of carbon dioxide (CO_2)" (3). What's so bad about that? If the petitioners disagree that the Constitution guarantees the right to "a climate system capable of sustaining human life" (Petition for Writ of Mandamus 3), it does not then follow that they must also reject *the value* of a sustainable climate. What the petitioners see is judicial overstepping; what they imagine/fear is irreparable harm to the President and the federal departments and agencies in the form of "disruption of important functions" that would occur while furnishing plaintiffs with discovery and a redirected energy and environmental policy (39).

What the plaintiffs and Judge Aiken see are results of climate change that are already adversely and unevenly affecting people and communities. What they do in this literally unprecedented situation is to create new jurisprudence. What they refuse is to be bound by a lack of direct legal recedent or the inevitable scientific uncertainties. What they imagine as an "open spectrum of possibilities" (Uncertain Commons 20) is a socially and environmentally just and habitable constellation of places and communities where people can live and thrive. Likewise, the OCT assemblage is an active and activist entity that attracts views and, by its very existence as a repository or archive, inspires *the creation* of materials to be archived (see Derrida) and actions taken. OCT-the-media-object stages world risk as a temporally and spatially complicated and urgent matter, not only "to generate pressure for action" (Beck, *World at Risk* 86) but also to perform its own key activist role.

By the time you read this chapter, there will be new developments in *Juliana* and the other lawsuits OCT is pursuing, and in its media presence. Whatever transpires in any one of these cases or situations, the initiative's youthful energy will persist into the future. Looking at OCT as risk media, as we have done here, is to speculate affirmatively and in that way contribute to the activation of a viable atmosphere for life, liberty, and the pursuit of the common good.

Acknowledgments

The authors thank Christopher Walker for the expert suggestions he offered as a scholar of environmental humanities and law; and he even read portions of *Juliana* for our benefit. Bhaskar and Bishnu were their usual brilliant selves and we thank them for inviting us to write, for their editorial acumen, and for their visionary scholarship on media and risk.

Notes

1 More specifically, the complaint sets forth claims for: (1) violation of the Due Process Clause of the Fifth Amendment; (2) violation of equal protection principles embedded in the Fifth Amendment; (3) the unenumerated right preserved for the people by the Ninth Amendment; and (4) violation of the Public Trust Doctrine (*Juliana* "First Amended Complaint" 84–93).
2 As Maxwell and Miller detail in their field-building book (2012), the environmental impact of media is global, extreme, and deleterious. Media electronics such as cell phones and computers contain toxic substances that threaten the health and the very lives of the workers who assemble them. And as if this were not enough, the "scale and pervasiveness of these environmental risks" extends "in and around every site where electronic and electric devices are manufactured, used, thrown away, poisoning humans, animals, vegetation, soil, air, and water" and contributes to "climate change, pollution growth, biodiversity decline, and habitat decimation—the constituents of our global ecological crisis" (1–2).
3 All references to the "First Amended Complaint" refer to the First Amended Complaint for Declaratory and Injunctive Relief in *Juliana v. United States*.
4 For example, in a trademark infringement case, a court might issue an order specifically enjoining the defendant from directly or indirectly infringing the plaintiff's trademarks.
5 More specifically, to qualify for injunctive relief, a plaintiff must demonstrate: (1) that [she] has suffered an irreparable injury; (2) that remedies available at law, such as monetary damages, are inadequate to compensate for that injury; (3) that, considering the balance of hardships between the plaintiff and defendant, a remedy in equity is warranted; and (4) that the public interest would not be disserved by a permanent injunction (*eBay Inc. v. MercExchange, L.L.C.* 391, qtd. in *Monsanto Co. v. Geertson Seed Farms* 156–157).

We note that legal scholars and courts have assessed the relevance of past harm to the "irreparable injury" prong of this test. As Mark P. Gergen, John M. Golden, and Henry E. Smith have pointed out, the formulation of the test for permanent injunctions now "strangely" seems to *require* "proof of past irreparable injury—irreparable injury that the movant 'has suffered'—to justify an injunction that might be wholly directed at preventing future infringing behavior" (Gergen et al. 203, 209). Faced with this test, various courts of appeal have "either missed or silently ignored the tense of the [Supreme] Court's ... language and simply focused on the threat of future harm" (Golden 657, 696 (collecting cases)). The Federal Circuit, however, concluding "[i]t was proper ... to consider evidence of past harm," chose not to ignore *eBay*: "Although injunctions are tools for prospective relief designed to alleviate future harm, by its terms the first *eBay* factor looks, in part, at what has *already occurred*" (*i4i Limited Partnership v. Microsoft Corp.* 862; emphasis added).
6 Here, in explaining the legal standard, Judge Aiken cites a rule from a pre-*eBay* case that states, "[a]s a general rule, [p]ast wrongs are not enough for the grant of an injunction; an injunction will only issue if the wrongs are ongoing or likely to recur" (*Federal Trade Commission v. Evans Products Co.* 1087; internal quotation marks omitted).

7 Indeed, a nuanced reading of Beck might reveal an entry point to rethinking the terrorist act itself, not as a unitary future occurrence, but rather as an immanent unfolding (see *World at Risk* 10).
8 Kaplan sees *Into Eternity* as an unusual documentary: "Its methods for telling its story are experimental and effective," with a moody mise-en-scène through which "the movie enacts a horrific dream, a nightmare from which we long to wake up, while Onkalo [the nuclear waste facility whose name may be translated as "hiding place"] resembles a secret place like the unconscious" (120).
9 The legal concept of precedent is complex. As Charles A. Sullivan has explained,

> [t]he law uses "precedent" in two very different ways. In the weaker sense, "precedent" merely refers to any authoritative pronouncement of a court that other courts have an obligation to respect; in this sense, any court decision may be a "persuasive precedent," although precisely what that means ... is unclear. The second, and stronger, sense is "binding precedent," which means that a lower court, subject to the appellate jurisdiction of the higher court, is required to follow the decisions of that court, or, more accurately, to follow the "holdings" of that court.
> (Sullivan 1143, 1146–1148)

10 We note that *Bellon* was controversial within the Ninth Circuit. Three Ninth Circuit judges dissented from the decision to deny rehearing of the case before an en banc court—a court that consists of the Chief Judge and ten randomly drawn, non-recused, active judges ("Public Information Office, Ninth Circuit En Banc Procedure Summary"). Judge Gould, joined by Judges Wardlaw and Paez, lamented that:

> Limiting the reasoning of *Massachusetts v. EPA* to cases involving sovereign states is a mistake that will harm the public. The panel's opinion unwisely requires courts to deny standing to any non-state plaintiff seeking to enforce the Clean Air Act's provisions in the effort to fight global warming, and relegates judges—and the general public—to the sidelines as climate change progresses. In my view, as our planet warms and oceans rise, individual citizens should have standing to urge their states to take corrective incremental actions to combat global warming.
> (*Washington Environmental Council v. Bellon* "Order Denying Rehearing En Banc" 1081; Gould, J., dissenting)

For further discussions on *Bellon*, see Mank (1525) and Moffat (959).
11 Courts often determine that prior cases are "distinguishable" or "inapplicable" and therefore not controlling in the case before them. Indeed, although "the rule of law requires lower courts to follow the higher court's pronouncements," the "rigors of such a system are ... mitigated by the distinction between holding and dictum and the ability of a court to 'distinguish' the binding precedent" (Sullivan 1150).
12 The defendants and intervenors moved to dismiss *Juliana* for lack of subject matter jurisdiction and failure to state a claim under Federal Rule of Civil Procedure 12(b)(1) and Federal Rule of Civil Procedure 12(b)(6), respectively (*Juliana* "Opinion and Order" 1233).
13 To be sure, the decision is future oriented partly due to the nature of the suit itself—the plaintiffs seek largely prospective relief—including an order directing the defendants to develop a plan to reduce CO_2 omissions, rather than monetary damages for past harms.
14 Because Judge Aiken is a district court judge, this opinion is not binding on other district or circuit courts. See *Hart v. Massanari* (1174) (noting that "the binding authority principle" applies only to appellate decisions, and not to trial court decisions); Mead (787, 789) ("[D]istrict court decisions adjudicate present controversies but do not create law for future cases."). Nonetheless, the opinion can serve as persuasive authority in other courts.
15 She also states: "Even when a case implicates hotly contested political issues, the judiciary must not shrink from its role as a coequal branch of government" (*Juliana* "Opinion and Order" 1263).
16 This is also known as "Article III standing." We do not delve into prudential standing, a non-constitutional standing requirement that plaintiffs must also satisfy.
17 We note that Corey Moffat has called causation the "most controversial of the [*Lujan*] elements with regard to private climate change litigation," and elaborated upon how "[l]ower courts have generally split with regard to the question of whether private parties can establish causation in the climate change context" (Moffat 959, 964–965).
18 The case Judge Aiken invokes is *Native Village of Kivalina v. ExxonMobil Corporation*, in which the indigenous community of Kivalina, Alaska brought suit against the energy industry for flooding related to sea-level rise related to climate change caused by the oil extraction. The case was ultimately dismissed on the ground that the issue was political rather than legal (see Shearer).
19 Park and Miller take Katrina-era New Orleans as their case in point, citing a Brookings Institution finding that quotes Louisiana State geographer Craig Colten's observation that "With greater means and power, the white population occupied the better-drained sections of the city, while blacks typically inhabited the swampy 'rear' districts" (15). Park and Miller state that, prior to Katrina, 67.3 percent of New Orleans'

population (compared with 12.3 percent for the U.S.) were African American" and "African American families were disproportionately poor, comprising 91.2 percent of the city's poor families of all races" (13).

20 Although the causation and redressability prongs "overlap and are two facets of a single causation requirement," they also "are distinct in that causation examines the connection between the alleged misconduct and injury, whereas redressability analyzes the connection between the alleged injury and requested judicial relief" (*Bellon* "Opinion" 1146, qtd. in *Juliana* "Opinion and Order" 1246–1247).

21 Seemingly central to Judge Aiken's conclusion that the plaintiffs have satisfied the redressability prong is the fact that the defendants in this case are not "minor contributors to global climate change." Indeed, Judge Aiken distinguishes the reasoning in *Bellon* on that basis (*Juliana* "Opinion and Order" 1245–1246).

22 Uncertainties notwithstanding, legal research asserts that we are in the midst of a "climate emergency" (Wood and Woodward 633, 670, 682). Mary Christina Wood and Charles W. Woodward, IV have described what we do and do not know about climate change:

> Though the precise threshold of atmospheric CO_2 that represents the point-of-no-return is unknown, the global concentration of CO_2 in the atmosphere has surpassed 400 ppm. Already, some dangerous feedback loops are manifestly in motion. Vast areas of melting permafrost now release huge amounts of CO_2 and methane (both of which are greenhouse gasses) into the atmosphere, and melting polar ice caps intensify the heating, because less ice remains to reflect heat away form Earth—a dynamic known as the albedo effect. Gus Speth, the former Dean of the Yale School of Forestry, warns that if we maintain our largely inadequate course of action, the world "won't be fit to live in" by mid-century.
>
> *(Wood and Woodward 641)*

23 Each element of the standing inquiry

> must be supported in the same way as any other matter on which the plaintiff bears the burden of proof, *i.e.*, with the manner and degree of evidence required at the successive stages of the litigation....

At the pleading stage—*Juliana*'s stage—"we presume that general allegations embrace those specific facts that are necessary to support the claim" (*Lujan* 561; internal quotation marks omitted).

24 Another example provided by Uncertain Commons of the affirmatively speculative mode is that of the then-prototypical, GPS-enabled, and highly controversial Transborder Immigrant Tool, a hand-held device designed to help migrants crossing the U.S.–Mexico border locate highways and caches of drinking water in the desert.

25 The intervenors are no longer part of the case. On June 27, 2017, Judge Aiken granted the National Association of Manufacturers', the American Fuel & Petrochemical Manufacturers', and the American Petroleum Institute's separate motions to withdraw (*Juliana* "Order on Motions to Withdraw" 1).

26 The petition for Writ of Mandamus was filed by the Acting Assistant Attorney General Jeffrey H. Wood, Acting Assistant Attorney General Eric Grant, and Andrew C. Mergen and David C. Shilton, attorneys from the Appellate Section of the Environment & Natural Resources Division of the U.S. Department of Justice.

27 To quote Beck at greater length,

> On the one hand, the institutions of the political system—parliament, government, political parties—*functionally* presuppose in a manner *conditioned by the system* the production circle of industry, technology and business. On the other hand, this pre-programs the permanent change of all realms of social life under the justifying cloak of techno-economic progress, in contradistinction to the simplest rules of democracy—knowledge of the goals of social change, discussion, voting and consent.
>
> *(Risk Society 184)*

28 We recognize that regulatory capture, often associated with George Stigler (winner of the Nobel Prize in Economics), has been discussed and analyzed by many scholars. Some, such as Jon Hanson and David Yosifon, have argued that traditional capture theory is "too shallow" and posited a "theory of deep capture," which refers

> to the disproportionate and self-serving influence that the relatively powerful tend to exert over all the exterior and interior situational features that materially influence the maintenance and extension of that power—including those features that purport to be, and that we experience as, independent, volitional, and benign.
>
> *(Hanson and Yosifon 129, 215, 218)*

Here, we acknowledge the basic outline of the theory of regulatory capture.

Works Cited

Barboza, Tony. "Water War between Klamath River Farmers, Tribes Poised to Erupt." *Los Angeles Times*, May 7, 2013, http://articles.latimes.com/2013/may/07/local/la-me-klamath-20130507. Accessed July 24, 2017.

Bataille, Georges. *The Absence of Myth*. Verso, 1994.

Beck, Ulrich. *Metamorphosis of the World: How Climate Change is Transforming Our Concept of the World*. Polity Press, 2016.

Beck, Ulrich. *Risk Society: Towards a New Modernity*. Translated by Mark Ritter. Sage Publications, 1992; 1986.

Beck, Ulrich. *World at Risk*. Translated by Ciaran Cronin. Polity Press, 2009; 2007.

Bozak, Nadia. *The Cinematic Footprint: Lights, Camera, Natural Resources*. Rutgers UP, 2011.

Brabant, Sarah and Robert Gramling. "Resource Extraction and Fluctuations in Poverty: A Case Study." *Society & Natural Resources*, vol. 1, no. 1, 1997, pp. 97–106.

Brown, Stewart L. "Mutual Funds and the Regulatory Capture of the SEC." *University of Pennsylvania Journal of Business Law*, vol. 19, 2017, pp. 701–749.

Dalrymple, Amy, Forum News Service. "Pipeline Route Plan First Called for Crossing North of Bismarck." *The Bismarck Tribune*, August 18, 2016, http://bismarcktribune.com/news/state-and-regional/pipeline-route-plan-first-called-for-crossing-north-of-bismarck/article_64d053e4-8a1a-5198-a1dd-498d386c933c.html. Accessed July 24, 2017.

Derrida, Jacques. *Archive Fever: A Freudian Impression*. U of Chicago P, 1996.

Fabian, Johannes. "Time and Writing About the Other." In *Time and the Other: How Anthropology Makes Its Object*. Columbia UP, 1983.

Freudenberg, William R. "Addictive Economies: Extractive Industries and Vulnerable Localities in a Changing World Economy." *Rural Sociology*, vol. 57, 1992, pp. 305–332.

Gabrys, Jennifer. *Digital Rubbish: A Natural History of Electronics*. U of Michigan P, 2011.

Gergen, Mark P. et al., "The Supreme Court's Accidental Revolution? The Test for Permanent Injunctions." *Columbia Law Review*, vol. 112, 2012, pp. 203–249.

Golden, John M. "The Supreme Court As 'Prime Percolator': A Prescription for Appellate Review of Questions in Patent Law." *UCLA Law Review*, vol. 56, 2009, pp. 657–723.

Goodman, Amy. "Watch: Democracy Now! Special Broadcast from the 2017 People's Climate March." April 29, 2017, www.ourchildrenstrust.org/video-radio-interviews/. Accessed July 25, 2017.

Goodwin, Alfred T. "A Wake-Up Call for Judges." *Wisconsin Law Review*, vol. 15, 2015, pp. 785–788.

Hanson, Jon and David Yosifon. "The Situation: An Introduction to the Situational Character, Critical Realism, Power Economics, and Deep Capture." *University of Pennsylvania Law Review*, vol. 152, 2003, pp. 129–346.

"Injunction." *Black's Law Dictionary*, 10th ed., 2014.

Jay, Paul. "Bannon-Trump Promises to Unleash Unfettered Capitalism." *The Real News Network*, interview with Bhaskar Sunkara and Phyllis Bennis. February 25, 2017, http://therealnews.com/t2/index.php?option=com_content&task=view&id=31&Itemid=74&jumival=18520. Accessed July 23, 2017.

Kaplan, E. Ann. *Climate Trauma: Foreseeing the Future in Dystopian Film and Fiction*. Rutgers UP, 2016.

Kelsey Juliana. Trust Oregon, *Our Children's Trust*, www.ourchildrenstrust.org/short-films. Accessed July 24, 2017.

Kolbert, Elizabeth. *The 6th Extinction: An Unnatural History*. Henry Holt and Co., 2014.

Lim, Bliss Cua. *Translating Time: Cinema, the Fantastic, and Temporary Critique*. Duke UP, 2009.

Lovatt, Philippa. "The Spectral Soundscapes of Postsocialist China in the Films of Jia Zhangke." *Screen*, vol. 53, no. 4, Winter 2012, pp. 418–435.

Mank, Bradford C. "No Article III Standing for Private Plaintiffs Challenging State Greenhouse Gas Regulations: The Ninth Circuit's Decision in *Washington Environmental Council v. Bellon*." *American University Law Review*, vol. 63, 2014, pp. 1525–1585.

Martinez-Alier, Joan. *The Environmentalism of the Poor: A Study of the Ecological Conflicts and Valuation*. Edward Elgar Publishing, 2002.

Massey, Doreen. *For Space*. Sage, 2005 (most recent repr. 2011).

Maxell, Richard and Toby Miller. *Greening the Media*. Oxford UP, 2012.

McDonald, Rachael. "Climate Kids' Federal Lawsuit Goes to Trial Early Next Year." KLCC NPR for Oregonians, June 29, 2017, www.ourchildrenstrust.org/video-radio-interviews. Accessed July 24, 2017.

Mead, Joseph W. "Stare Decisis in the Inferior Courts of the United States." *Nevada Law Journal*, vol. 12, 2012, pp. 787–830.

"Mission." *Our Children's Trust*, www.ourchildrenstrust.org/mission-statement/. Accessed January 17, 2018.

Moffat, Corey. "Establishing Causation in Private Party Climate Change Suits: Correcting the Mistakes of *Washington Environmental Council v. Bellon*." *Environmental Law*, vol. 44, 2014, pp. 959–982.

Morton, Timothy. *Hyperobjects: Philosophy and Ecology after the End of the World*, Minnesota UP, 2013.
Nelson Kanuk. Trust Alaska, Our Children's Trust, www.ourchildrenstrust.org/short-films. Accessed July 24, 2017.
Nixon, Rob. *Slow Violence and the Environmentalism of the Poor*. Harvard UP, 2011.
Nixon, Rob. "The Anthropocene: The Promise and Pitfalls of an Epochal Idea." *Edge Effects* digital magazine, Center for Culture, History, and Environment, Nelson Institute for Environmental Studies, University of Wisconsin-Madison, November 6, 2014, http://edgeeffects.net/anthropocene-promise-and-pitfalls/. Accessed July 24, 2017.
Our Children's Trust, www.ourchildrenstrust.org. Accessed July 24, 2017.
Park, Yoosun and Joshua Miller. "The Social Ecology of Hurricane Katrina: Re-Writing the Discourses of 'Natural' Disasters." *Smith College Studies in Social Work*, vol. 76, no. 3, 2006, pp. 9–24.
Parks, Lisa. "Cultural Geographies in Practice: Plotting the Personal: Global Positioning Satellites and Interactive Media." *Ecumeme: A Journal of Cultural Geographies*, vol. 9, no. 2, 2001, pp. 209–222.
Peters, John Durham. *The Marvelous Clouds: Toward a Philosophy of Elemental Media*. U of Chicago Pr, 2015.
"Proceedings in All 50 States, Alaska." *Our Children's Trust*, September 12, 2014, www.ourchildrenstrust.org/alaska/. Accessed January 17, 2018.
Public Information Office, United States Courts for the Ninth Circuit, "Ninth Circuit En Banc Procedure Summary." February 10, 2017, http://cdn.ca9.uscourts.gov/datastore/general/2017/02/10/En_Banc_Summary2.pdf. Accessed July 24, 2017.
Rogoff, Irit. *Terra Infirma: Geography's Visual Culture*. Routledge, 2000.
Rucker, Philip and Robert Costa, "Bannon Vows a Daily Fight for 'Deconstruction of the Administrative State.'" *Washington Post*, February 23, 2017, www.washingtonpost.com/politics/top-wh-strategist-vows-a-daily-fight-for-deconstruction-of-the-administrative-state/2017/02/23/03f6b8da-f9ea-11e6-bf01-d47f8cf9b643_story.html?utm_term=.f72e5292a325. Accessed July 24, 2017.
Sanders, Bernie. "While President Trump Continues to Reject Science, These Young People are Fighting for the Future of the Planet." June 7, 2017, www.ourchildrenstrust.org/video-radio-interviews/. Accessed July 24, 2017.
Shearer, Christine. *Kivalina: A Climate Change Story*. Haymarket Books, 2011.
Shenker, Noah. *Reframing Holocaust Testimony*. Indiana UP, 2015.
Skavlan, Frederik. "Xiuhtezcatl Martinez | Interview | – 'Young People Have Power! Our Voices are Powerful'." November 20, 2016, www.ourchildrenstrust.org/video-radio-interviews. Accessed July 24, 2017.
Smith, E.J. *Boom and Bust in Energy Extraction*. Agricultural and Rural Economics Division, Economic Research Service, U.S. Department of Agriculture, Washington, D.C. Staff Report No. AGES860424.
Starosielski, Nicole and Janet Walker. *Sustainable Media: Critical Approaches to Media and Environment*. Routledge, 2016.
Sullivan, Charles A. "On Vacation." *Houston Law Review*, vol. 43, 2006, pp. 1143–1209.
Superior Court for the State of Alaska. *First Amended Complaint for Declaratory and Equitable Relief. Kanuck v. Alaska*. no. 3AN-11-07474 CI. July 21, 2011.
Supreme Court of Alaska. *Kanuk ex rel. Kanuk v. State of Alaska, Department of Natural Resources* (Opinion), vol. 335, P.3d, 2014, p. 1088.
Uncertain Commons. *Speculate This!* Duke UP, 2013.
United States Court of Appeals, Ninth Circuit. *City of Sausalito v. O'Neill*. vol. 386, F.3d, p. 1186, 2004.
United States Court of Appeals, Ninth Circuit. *Consumer Financial Protection Bureau v. Gordon*, vol. 819, 2016, p. 1179.
United States Court of Appeals, Ninth Circuit. *Federal Trade Commission v. Evans Products Co.*, vol. 775, 1985, p. 1084.
United States Court of Appeals, Ninth Circuit. *Hart v. Massanari*, vol. 266, 2001, p. 1155.
United States Court of Appeals, Ninth Circuit. *Jewel v. National Security Agency*, vol. 673, 2011, p. 902.
United States Court of Appeals, Ninth Circuit. *Native Village of Kivalina v. ExxonMobil Corp*, vol. 696, 2012, p. 849.
United States Court of Appeals, Ninth Circuit. *Thomas v. Mundell*. vol. 572, 2009, p. 756.
United States Court of Appeals, Ninth Circuit. *United States v. United States District Court for the District of Oregon and Kelsey Cascadia Rose Juliana, Real Parties in Interest* (Petition for Writ of Mandamus to the United States District Court for the District of Oregon and Request for Stay of Proceedings in District Court). no. 17-71692. June 9, 2017.
United States Court of Appeals, Ninth Circuit. *Washington Environmental Council v. Bellon* (Opinion), vol. 732, 2014, p. 1131.
United States Court of Appeals, Ninth Circuit. *Washington Environmental Council v. Bellon* (Order Denying Rehearing En Banc), vol. 741, 2014, p. 1075.

United States Court of Appeals, Federal Circuit. *i4i Limited Partnership v. Microsoft Corp*, vol. 598, 2010, p. 831.

United States District Court, District of Oregon. *Juliana v. United States* (First Amended Complaint for Declaratory and Injunctive Relief). no. 6:15-CV-01517-TC. September 10, 2015.

United States District Court, District of Oregon. *Juliana v. United States* (Order on Motions to Withdraw), no. 6:15-CV-01517-TC. June 28, 2017.

United States District Court, District of Oregon. *Juliana v. United States* (Opinion and Order on Defendants' and Intervenors' Motions to Dismiss), vol. 217, 2016, p. 1224.

United States Supreme Court. *Cheney v. United States District Court for the District of Columbia.* vol. 542, June 24, 2004, p. 367.

United States Supreme Court. *eBay Inc. v. MercExchange, L.L.C*, vol. 547, 2006, p. 388.

United States Supreme Court. *Lujan v. Defenders of Wildlife*, vol. 504, 1992, p. 555.

United States Supreme Court. *Massachusetts v. Environmental Protection Agency*, vol. 549, 2007, p. 497.

United States Supreme Court. *Monsanto Co. v. Geertson Seed Farms*, vol. 561, 2010, p. 139.

United States Supreme Court. *PPL Montana, LLC v. Montana.* vol. 565, 2012, p. 576.

United States Supreme Court. *United States Department of Commerce v. Montana.* vol. 503, 1992, p. 442.

United States Supreme Court. *Warth v. Seldin*, vol. 442, 1975, p. 490.

"Victory for America's Youth – Constitutional Climate Lawsuit against U.S. to Proceed." *Our Children's Trust*, November 10, 2016, www.ourchildrenstrust.org/press-releases/. Accessed July 24, 2017.

Virilio, Paul. *Open Sky*. Verso, 1997.

Wood, Mary Christina and Charles W. Woodward, IV. "Atmospheric Trust Litigation and the Constitutional Right to a Healthy Climate System: Judicial Recognition at Last." *Washington Journal of Environmental Law & Policy*, vol. 6, 2016, p. 633–683.

Yusoff, Kathryn. "Excess, Catastrophe, and Climate Change." *Environment and Planning D: Society and Space*, vol. 27, 2009, p. 1010–1029.

16
MEDIA/*METEŌRA*

Greg Siegel

A Fireball Falls

Minutes after sunrise on February 15, 2013, an intensely bright meteor, or superbolide, traveling at 19 kilometers per second (about 42,500 miles per hour), exploded over Chelyabinsk Oblast, Russia. Trailing white smoke and shedding molten debris as it flashed across the morning sky, the interplanetary intruder—an asteroid originating from the main belt between Mars and Jupiter—burst at 27 kilometers (nearly 17 miles) altitude with the force of 500 kilotons of TNT (see Figures 16.1 and 16.2). The resultant shockwave damaged more than 7,300 buildings over a wide radius. Together, the airburst and shockwave drove some 1,600 unlucky persons to seek medical treatment for their injuries, which included ultraviolet burns, eye pain and temporary blindness, and cuts and

Figure 16.1 Photo Credit: NASA

Figure 16.2 Photo Credit: NASA

bruises caused by the shattering of glass windows. In modern recorded history, only the Tunguska meteor, which felled approximately 80 million trees over 2,150 square kilometers (830 square miles) in the East Siberian taiga, in June of 1908, detonated with more destructive force.[1]

From the ground, the shooting star was witnessed by thousands and recorded by hundreds of citizens and commuters. Within hours, YouTube, VKontakte, and other video-sharing websites and platforms were circulating sounds and images of the impactor and its consequences, captured incidentally or opportunistically by handheld smartphones, dashboard-mounted cameras, and closed-circuit traffic and security cameras (see Borovička et al., "A Catalog" A90; see Figure 16.3). Online news sources and blogs, as well as traditional print and electronic media, featured various of these casual digital recordings in their coverage of the event ("casual" in multiple senses: accidental, occasional, informal, unplanned). Moreover, several YouTube users compiled, edited, and remixed the images, in some cases adding a drama-heightening musical soundtrack. Shot steadily or shakily, from fixed points or moving vehicles, many of the videos show the meteor hurling incandescently across the heavens, the arc of its billowing plumes cleaving the unclouded sky. Others register not

Figure 16.3 Photo Credit: Wikimedia Commons

the falling fireball but, instead, its transitory terrestrial illuminations, the eerie spectacle of its landscape-bleaching searchlight. Still others document the shockwave and sonic boom, their violent percussions and repercussions: the tremendous blast and roar, the blown-in windows and doors, the squalling of car alarms, the sudden fright and commotion (in the streets, in workplaces, in classrooms).

Popular-media users and sharers were not the only ones fascinated by the accidental technological capture of the fiery atmospheric phenomenon; amateur and professional astronomers, too, doubtless felt a certain frisson upon beholding the serendipitous work of the cameras. For, as if marvelously, those humble cameras, some of them equipped with microphones, happened to preserve not only a rarely seen or heard cosmic occurrence but an entirely unanticipated one, rendered from multiple viewpoints, no less. The asteroid's unexpected appearance prompted numerous scientific and security-related questions, and the haphazardly generated recordings were understood to contain a huge amount of information about what actually happened. As these visual and audiovisual texts were, by institutions and independent researchers around the world, invested with evidential authority and epistemic significance, so the untimely meteor was reclaimed as an object of media-forensic examination and reconstruction.

Within a week, a pair of investigators from the Institute of Physics at the University of Antioquia in Medellín, Colombia, "using evidence gathered by one camera at the Revolution Square in the city of Chelyabinsk and other videos recorded by witnesses in the close city of Korkino," presented "a preliminary reconstruction" of the meteor's orbit and trajectory. In their unrefereed report, the authors, Jorge Zuluaga and Ignacio Ferrín, forthrightly acknowledge the blogger and "citizen astronomer" Stefan Geens, founder of *Ogle Earth*, from whom they borrowed "method and images" ("Preliminary Reconstruction"). Shortly thereafter, Zuluaga, Ferrín, and Geens teamed up to produce a revised preprint, titled "The Orbit of the Chelyabinsk Event Impactor as Reconstructed from Amateur and Public Footage." To obtain their calculations, the trio undertook a frame-by-frame analysis of four YouTube videos, selected on the basis of their comparatively "high quality" and precisely known locations of origination, so as to measure "the shadows cast by objects in the scene." Additional crucial data—"the azimuths of reference directions," the "distances and sizes of the familiar objects in the footage"—were gathered from Google Earth and "some archived images of the places used in the triangulation" (Zuluaga et al.). In November of 2013, astronomers and planetary scientists from the Czech Republic Academy of Sciences, the University of Western Ontario, the Russian Academy of Sciences, the SETI Institute, and the NASA Ames Research Center published detailed studies in the journals *Science* and *Nature*, in which dozens of publicly available videos and projections were appropriated, calibrated, "corrected," synchronized, optically and acoustically analyzed, and, finally, stabilized as scientific evidence (Borovička et al., "The Trajectory"; Brown et al.; Popova et al.). The *New Yorker* magazine praised these "ingenious" footage-inspecting scientists for their "feat of clever detective work" (Scharf).

History, ever obedient to a strict chronology, tells us that the Chelyabinsk meteor chanced to fall but once. Fortunately or not, the mediatized meteors that have propagated in its wake appear destined to befall us indefinitely. The same technopolitical devices and apparatuses of risk and surveillance, the same media-cultural habits and practices of attention, consumption, observation, communication, exhibition, participation that enabled the recording and post-hoc scrutiny of the space rock ensure the endless dissemination of its reproductions. The singularity that suddenly fell to Earth now belatedly circles the globe in countless graphic and electronic iterations. The onetime meteor and its timeless, all-the-time mediatization: at once a fortuitous coincidence and an inevitable constellation. Media/meteor: each the other's casualty and condition of close *encounter*, their reciprocal modalities and mutual interferences structuring the impactor's deliverance and status as a mass *event*. "Would an event that can be anticipated and therefore apprehended and comprehended, or one without an element of absolute encounter, actually be an event in the full sense of the word?" asks Jacques Derrida in "My Chances/*Mes Chances*."

We are not supposed to see it coming. If what comes and then stands out horizontally on a horizon can be anticipated then there is no pure event. No horizon, then, for the event or encounter, but only verticality and the unforeseeable.

(6)

On that fateful morning in 2013, nobody saw the asteroid coming. Having since arrived, it arrives still. In one form or another, its representation continues to be used, viewed, studied, reworked, recirculated; it is seeable and reseeable on demand the world over. Yet, fundamentally, meteoric phenomena remain as unforeseeable as ever. In his essay, Derrida does not speak of the *media* event or of the *mediatized* encounter. He does not concern himself with the contemporary *media/meteor complex*. It falls to us to coin it and to consider its operations. As we shall see, such a complex, while integral to its earthly reckoning and reception, only ever fleetingly apprehends (and never truly comprehends) the meteor's thrownness, its deviating downward motion, its declination. Though it brings meteors determinately within the horizon of our social, institutional, and technological perceptibilities and capabilities, it fails to flatten their unpredictable inclinations, to permanently ground their precipitous movements and mutations. Pitched between an atmospherics of turbulent chance and a politics of vigilant necessity, the media/meteor complex, even as it articulates the verticality and inadvertency of the meteor's eventness, reveals and perpetually reproduces the elemental mediacy of its encounterability.

Time of *Meteōra*

"In the beginning are the meteors," Michel Serres proclaims, aptly enough, in his book *Genesis* (101). Rather than at the beginning of *Genesis*, as might be expected, however, the statement comes *in medias res*, about 100 pages in (in the English edition). While this mediate placement might at first seem less than fitting, it is really all the more so. For, as it happens, the realm of the meteoric is a kind of middle corridor, a region of intercedence, liminal, transitional, neither on the ground nor over the moon. "Our science, our mechanics, generally takes place, from Newton to Auguste Comte, on earth and in the heavens, the fall of bodies and the orbit of stars. Almost never in between" (85). So writes Serres in *The Birth of Physics*, meditating on the sixth book of Lucretius's *On the Nature of Things*, the section of the ancient poem that treats of meteorological happenings, or, as Serres prefers, of "*meteōra*." Seeking to recover, for the history and philosophy of science, elements of the long-discarded tradition of atomist physics as developed, in turn, by Leucippus, Democritus, Epicurus, and Lucretius, Serres laments that modern scientific reason, in excluding the sphere of *meteōra*, in banishing the "middle ground between mechanics and astronomy," has rendered an "immense" swath of the natural world practically "incomprehensible" (85–86).

By "*meteōra*," crucially, Serres has in mind not climatic constancies but, on the contrary, thunder, lightning, "clouds, rain and waterspouts, hailstorms or showers, the direction and force of the wind, here and now." Insistently, he continues: "And I don't mean the prevailing wind. Meteors are accidents, occurrences. A chance proximity, an adventitious environment of the essential" (*Birth of Physics* 67). Daniel Tiffany translates the latter part of this same passage a bit differently: "Meteors are accidents, events: a hazardous milieu, the factual environment of essences" (103). Not what persists diffusedly in the background but what is thrown suddenly and perilously into the middle ("milieu") of the present moment; not the unchanging laws that make possible the steady climate but a fact or advent that makes palpable a freakish weather: such, following Serres following Lucretius, is the nature of meteoric things. Returning to *Genesis*, then, there is warrant to rephrase its heterodox proclamation thus: *In the beginning are the chance happenings, the accidental things*. And: *In the beginning are the media, the mediate things*. And, weirdly but inescapably: *The beginning is the accidental middle of things*.

Serres's philosophy of *meteōra* conjures the old, forgotten meanings of *meteor* and *meteorology*, reviving and reuniting them after an epic hiatus. According to the *Journal of the International Meteor Organization*,

> the word "meteor" is derived from the Latin *meteorum*, from the Greek *meteoron*, in its plural form meaning atmospheric phenomena or anything in the heavens. It is the substantive use of the Greek *meteoros*, which means "raised," "lofty," or in a more figurative sense, "sublime."
>
> (McBeath 35)

Under the modern episteme, meteors are restricted in their belonging to astronomy, the study of the stars, but, in classical antiquity, they—and many other "sublime" occurrences besides—belonged to a varied and expansive meteorology. "When we look at the ancient Greek and Roman texts on meteorology, we discover discussions about 'lofty' things which today would be regarded as astronomical phenomena, such as comets and the Milky Way," Liba Taub explains. "However, earthquakes and other phenomena that would today be regarded as geological and seismological were also treated [therein]. And, as we would expect from our modern term, much of ancient meteorology too was concerned with weather" (2).

In the *Meteorology*, to take the supreme instance, Aristotle describes the scope of his inquiry as "everything which happens naturally, but with a regularity less than that of the primary element of bodies, in the region which borders most nearly on the movements of the stars" (qtd. in Taub 77). For Aristotle, meteorology does not deal with the orderly perfection of the superlunary—the eternal circular motions of the stars and planets are handled in a separate treatise, *On the Heavens*—but, rather, with how those remote celestial motions interact unpredictably with the terrestrial elements (earth, air, fire, and water) to cause natural sublunary happenings. It studies the stochastic stirrings and sudden precipitates of immutable and mutable processes, the random generations and corruptions resulting from the agitated intermixture of "lofty" and lowly entities. "Within [Aristotle's] hierarchical treatment of nature," Taub observes, "meteorology is in the middle. This central position reflects the mediating role that meteorological processes serve" (77). Meteors, on this classical view, are all those "weather" accidents (shooting stars, comets, the Milky Way, mists, clouds, rain, snow, hail, winds of various kinds, earthquakes, thunder, lightning, rainbows, halos) that manifest and mediate the unstable, somewhat irregular exchanges between earth and firmament, between, as Serres puts it, "the fall of bodies and the orbit of stars."

In the beginning are the meteors. Along with the allusive substitution of "meteors" for "Logos" comes the new (old pagan) grammar and cosmogony: lowercase plural instead of capital singular, present tense instead of past, ongoing chance emergence rather than divine creationary speech-act. Already in the middle at the beginning, "here and now" from the start, *meteōra*, for Serres, are mediators of an exceptional temporality, couriers of an infinite commotion and multiplicity, "chaos-cloud" messengers (*Birth of Physics* 86). In their radical indeterminacy, they "dramatise the fundamental variable of physics": the Lucretian *clinamen*, the atomic swerve or declination, bringer of turbulence and "creator of time *contretemps*" (87; italics in the original).[2] Theirs is the time—the counter-time, the time of mishap and misfortune, time out of time—that modern science, with its devotion to "exact determination or rigorous over-determination" and its preoccupation "with absolute control" and "mastery without vacillation or the ambiguity of margins," has, as a rule, refused to recognize (67). This imperious refusal, "this repression," according to Serres, is embodied in the architecture and institution of the laboratory and, by extension, of the astronomical observatory: a refuge with walls and a roof, an enclosure insulated "against turbulence," protected from inclement weather, from the time of always untimely *meteōra*. "Science is shut inside" (67–68). Meteors, by contrast, run their deviating course outdoors, come into being (and are soon undone) in "the place of disorder and the unforeseeable, of local danger, of the formless" (67).

Following Serres's claim that "the time of *meteōra* does not match up with the time of history," Jan Golinski argues that, whereas ancient meteorology had subsumed meteors within "an understanding of time as *kairos* (a discontinuous set of significant sacred events)," the meteorological sciences since the eighteenth century have tried to shackle atmospheric phenomena to "a (continuous, secular) *chronos*" (67, 78). In defiance of—and because of—its contingency, its unpredictability, its hazardous amorphousness, the weather has been disciplined and adjusted to fit "a homogeneous scale of time measurement" (Golinski 78). Meteors ("extraordinary appearances in the air") have been abstracted and subjected to the normalizing dictates of "the clock and calendar," reduced to "the regular and the repeatable"; formerly signs, marvels, and portents, they are now seconds, minutes, and standard calendrical units (78).[3] Arden Reed, in *Romantic Weather*, expands on Serres's provocative contention, asserting that

> the temporality of the weather must not be confused with clock time, for there is nothing measured in the movement of a "meteor," as in that of a star. And the aleatory or erratic alterations of any one "meteor" are contingent on any number of other "meteors," themselves contingent, and propagate only more accidents in their wake.
>
> *(11)*

Implicit in Reed's astute reading of Serres's new (old) meteorology is the notion that the project of temporal rationalization is never fully realized or finished. Though impelled by an equalizing imperative, the chronometric system is never perfected to the point where its constituent moments—every "tick," every "tock"—are uniformly pure, transparent, or even determinable. Now and again, something interrupts the process of meteoric time's domestication and desacralization. Something from somewhere sometimes intrudes and obscures. That something? *Meteōra* themselves, naturally. "What good does it do me to know the exact second of the next eclipse when a thick mounting wind keeps me from seeing it?" Serres wonders. "What good are all the tools in the world when snow and mud prevent their use?" (*Birth of Physics* 68). For centuries, meteorology has scrupulously recorded and measured and strived to predict. Yet its forecasts are often defective. Meteors *interfere*. Born of blind chaos, allied with aleatory mediation, they forever threaten to bring the storms, hamper the instruments, muddy the waters, cloud the view.

Could It Happen Here on Earth?

As meteors occasionally do, the Chelyabinsk impactor caught astronomers completely unawares. However, the asteroid called 367943 Duende, also known as 2012 DA14, which, in an odd coincidence, passed close to the Earth a mere 16 hours later, did not surprise. Indeed, scientists at NASA's Near-Earth Object Observations Program had been tracking Duende—so named for the elfin or goblinish creature of Iberian and Latin-American legend—since its discovery by researchers at the Astronomical Observatory of Mallorca, Spain, in February of 2012. Duende transited at a distance of roughly 27,700 kilometers (17,200 miles)—closer to the Earth's surface than weather and communication satellites in geosynchronous orbit. Astronomers confidently (and rightly) calculated that this particular space rock would "fly by," rather than collide with, the Earth (see Durda; NASA, "Russia Meteor"; Yeomans and Chodas). But what about all the other wayward rocks hurtling through the solar system? The mission of the NASA division charged with monitoring Duende and other near-Earth objects, or NEOs, attests to the accepted statistical certainty that, in the indefinite future, some number of interplanetary "goblins" will not pass so uneventfully or so inconsequentially. Some are sure to swerve.

The basic plan for the NEO Observations Program was laid out in a couple of congressionally requested NASA reports issued in 1992. The first of these, *The Spaceguard Survey*, explained that impacts caused by

> Earth-approaching asteroids and comets pose a significant hazard to life and property. Although the annual probability of the Earth being struck by a large asteroid or comet is extremely small, the consequences of such a collision are so catastrophic that it is prudent to assess the nature of the threat and to prepare to deal with it. The first step in any program for the prevention or mitigation of impact catastrophes must involve a comprehensive search for Earth-crossing asteroids and comets and a detailed analysis of their orbits.
>
> (v)

The report went on to call for the construction of a globe-spanning assemblage of technoscientific media, "a coordinated international network of specialized ground-based telescopes"—in conjunction with "large planetary radars," "rapid international electronic communications," and "a database of discovered objects"—that would enable astronomers to detect, confirm, continuously observe, and share and store information about potential Earth-impacting asteroids and comets larger than one kilometer in diameter (v–vi). The requisite resource allocations and expenditures, the report concluded, "can be thought of as a modest investment to provide insurance for our planet against the ultimate catastrophe" (vi).

The Spaceguard Survey, notwithstanding its sly titular reference to a plot element in Arthur C. Clarke's science fiction novel *Rendezvous with Rama*, sought to bolster its case by highlighting the proposed program's congruence with the latest scientific findings and theories, including the "Alvarez hypothesis." In a landmark article for *Science* published in 1980, the physicist Luis Alvarez and his son, the geologist Walter Alvarez, together with the chemists Frank Asaro and Helen Michel, propounded the view that the mass extinction marking the end of the Cretaceous Period, which extinction included that of the dinosaurs, was precipitated by an enormous bolide impact. While the Alvarezes and company were not the first scientists to think seriously about Earth-colliding bodies (*The Spaceguard Survey* traces the idea to Fletcher Watson's *Between the Planets* and Ralph Baldwin's *The Face of the Moon*, both dating from the 1940s), their hypothesis was well supported by newly discovered geochemical evidence involving the concentration of iridium in sedimentary rocks. One year later, a pathbreaking meeting and workshop, held in Snowmass, Colorado, and directed by NASA's Jet Propulsion Laboratory, asked participants to consider how, and to what extent, a major asteroid or comet impact might disrupt or destabilize human life and society. What were the biggest risks? Would agricultural and economic systems break down? Would social and political institutions fail? Would pandemonium ensue? Would civilization itself collapse? Also, how might an asteroidal or cometary disaster be averted or mitigated in the first place? The workshop's main conclusions were summarized and disseminated, in 1989, in the final chapter of *Cosmic Catastrophes*, a popular-science book written by Clark Chapman and David Morrison, a pair of leading NEO researchers.

Already on the rise, then, by the early 1990s, worries about dangerous meteors were amplified in July of 1994, when Comet Shoemaker–Levy 9 crashed into Jupiter. An extraterrestrial collision of two solar-system bodies had never theretofore been observed in "real time." The news media, no doubt enticed by the promise of violent celestial spectacle, made the most of the extraordinary occasion. *Time* magazine's focus and slant were typical. The cover of its May 23, 1994 issue featured a vividly illustrated depiction of the fragmentary comet's approach and fiery impact, complete with the headline "COSMIC CRASH—A shattered comet is about to hit Jupiter, creating the biggest explosion ever witnessed in the solar system. Could it happen here on Earth? Yes …" For weeks before, during, and after the event, quotable and broadcast-suitable experts were in high demand. The Canadian astronomer David Levy, who co-discovered the comet, estimated that, during the first three weeks of July alone, he gave some 125 press interviews (133). The entertainment industry also capitalized on the "Could it happen here?" question. In his study of representations of meteors, comets, and asteroids in popular cinema and television, William Hartwell notes that the number of productions emphasizing "the hazards of potential cosmic impactors" increased sharply in the decade following the Shoemaker–Levy 9 event (82). "Media publicity during the impact of Shoemaker–Levy 9, and especially the resultant worldwide distribution of Hollywood blockbuster films such as *Armageddon* and *Deep Impact*"—both of which were released in 1998, the same year NASA launched the NEO Observations Program—"have arguably produced a greater public awareness and support for this issue than almost any but the most targeted and costly public educational campaigns could have accomplished" (83–84).

Scaling the Risk

Astronomers and planetary scientists, nevertheless, had their own notions about how to raise public awareness and urge attention to their findings. At the inaugural United Nations International Conference on Near-Earth Objects, held in New York City, in April of 1995, Richard Binzel of the Massachusetts Institute of Technology recommended the adoption of an index system, devised by him, to facilitate "simple and efficient communication between astronomers and the public" concerning NEO-impact hazards ("Near-Earth Object Hazard Index" 545). Four years later, a revised version of his system won official endorsement from the sponsors and attendees of the International Monitoring Programs for Asteroid and Comet Threat (IMPACT) workshop in Torino, Italy, and from NASA and the International Astronomical Union. The Torino Impact Hazard Scale, as it was now designated, or "Torino Scale" for short, offered itself as an objectively rational, socially beneficial, easily understandable, civically responsible instrument of risk communication.

The direst hazards associated with near-Earth objects tend to be regarded by astronomers as extraordinary in two senses: they are extraordinarily unlikely and, because of their consequences, extraordinarily dreadful to contemplate. Infrequent but extreme, they lie outside the pattern or bounds of the everyday and, simultaneously, at the peak intensity of feeling and experience. For Binzel and fellow scientists wishing to spread the warning word, this dual aspect held important implications for the Torino Scale's graphic and informational design. As a vehicle for the popular communication of the doubly extraordinary, the scale, to be effective, needed to be affectively and psychologically attuned as well as intelligible and scientifically credible. Its task was to bring the NEO threat, in its astounding beyondness, to public consciousness in a manner devoid of exaggeration and purged of raw emotion. The infographic aimed to alert, educate, and motivate the masses without overexciting them. "Because collisions of asteroids and comets with the Earth represent a topic so provocative and so prone to sensationalism," Binzel wrote in a paper for *Planetary and Space Science* published in 2000,

> great care must be taken to assess and publicly communicate the realistic hazard (or non hazard) posed by such events. At the heart of this risk communication challenge resides the fact that low probability/high consequence events are by their very nature not within the realm of common human experience.
>
> *("Torino Impact" 297)*

Updated in 2004 and still in use today, the Torino Scale employs various strategies to evaluate and classify the risk of meteoric catastrophe (see Figure 16.4).[4] Familiar textual, numeric, and symbolic conventions are arranged so as to assimilate the alien peculiarities of impact hazard—very improbable, vastly consequential—to allegedly common experience. Color-coded zones, succinct verbal descriptions, and consecutive integers ranging from zero (at the top) to ten (at the bottom) are neatly stacked within an internally segmented rectangle. The greater the assessed risk, the higher the assigned numeral, with zero indicating maximal unlikelihood of collision. Each numeral is accompanied by a small block of elucidative prose, "a few sentences of qualitative explanation" (Binzel, "Torino Impact" 302). A simple five-color scheme further defines and categorizes the

THE TORINO SCALE
Assessing Asteroid/Comet Impact Predictions

No Hazard	0	The likelihood of collision is zero, or is so low as to be effectively zero. Also applies to small objects such as meteors and bolides that burn up in the atmosphere as well as infrequent meteorite falls that rarely cause damage.
Normal	1	A routine discovery in which a pass near the Earth is predicted that poses no unusual level of danger. Current calculations show the chance of collision is extremely unlikely with no cause for public attention or public concern. New telescopic observations very likely will lead to re-assignment to Level 0.
Meriting Attention by Astronomers	2	A discovery, which may become routine with expanded searches, of an object making a somewhat close but not highly unusual pass near the Earth. While meriting attention by astronomers, there is no cause for public attention or public concern as an actual collision is very unlikely. New telescopic observations very likely will lead to re-assignment to Level 0.
	3	A close encounter, meriting attention by astronomers. Current calculations give a 1% or greater chance of collision capable of localized destruction. Most likely, new telescopic observations will lead to re-assignment to Level 0. Attention by the public and by public officials is merited if the encounter is less than a decade away.
	4	A close encounter, meriting attention by astronomers. Current calculations give a 1% or greater chance of collision capable of regional devastation. Most likely, new telescopic observations will lead to re-assignment to Level 0. Attention by the public and by public officials is merited if the encounter is less than a decade away.
Threatening	5	A close encounter posing a serious, but still uncertain threat of regional devastation. Critical attention by astronomers is needed to determine conclusively whether or not a collision will occur. If the encounter is less than a decade away, governmental contingency planning may be warranted.
	6	A close encounter by a large object posing a serious, but still uncertain threat of a global catastrophe. Critical attention by astronomers is needed to determine conclusively whether or not a collision will occur. If the encounter is less than three decades away, governmental contingency planning may be warranted.
	7	A very close encounter by a large object, which if occurring this century, poses an unprecedented but still uncertain threat of a global catastrophe. For such a threat in this century, international contingency planning is warranted, especially to determine urgently and conclusively whether or not a collision will occur.
Certain Collisions	8	A collision is certain, capable of causing localized destruction for an impact over land or possibly a tsunami if close offshore. Such events occur on average between once per 50 years and once per several 1000 years.
	9	A collision is certain, capable of causing unprecedented regional devastation for a land impact or the threat of a major tsunami for an ocean impact. Such events occur on average between once per 10,000 years and once per 100,000 years.
	10	A collision is certain, capable of causing a global climatic catastrophe that may threaten the future of civilization as we know it, whether impacting land or ocean. Such events occur on average once per 100,000 years, or less often.

Figure 16.4 Photo Credit: NASA

level of risk: white represents "no hazard"; green, "normal"; yellow, "meriting attention by astronomers"; orange, "threatening"; and red, "certain collisions."[5] According to Binzel, the multidimensionality of the knowledge–problem caused by close-approaching space rocks is reflected in the scale's attempt to harmoniously "translate" disparate kinds of information, chief among them "the impact probability of the object" and "the potential consequences should an impact occur" (298). Overall, the scale's organization of line, language, number, and color, its visual logic and grammar, is meant to "provide a context for understanding the full range of the potential hazard" (298).

Probability and explosive energy. Collision likelihood and destructive magnitude. Superlunary reckoning and sublunary devastation. Stochastics and impact kinetics. Chance and catastrophe. These form the Torino Scale's discursive warp and woof, the terms and parameters of its calculative rationality and the repertoire of its scientific imaginary, its physics and its metaphysics. Within its horizon, astronomical rarity and world-ending calamity, sublime visions of exception and excess, are coded, coupled, and figured, "translated," put into speculative relation, thought together. The slightest chance, the slimmest odds, on the one hand, and a future of total disaster, of civilizational ruin, on the other—each such eventuality a limit case of the fathomable—are coordinated in, and mediated through, the scale's rhetorics and aesthetics. NEO science's conception of its most broadly significant postulates, and of its most universally pressing conclusions, is schematized for all to see, reduced to a risk-assessment formula, analyzed into (and vernacularized as) something of an odds sheet, a tool for gaining advantage in a cosmic game of chance. Multiple orders of occurrence—celestial, temporal, geospatial, physical—are evoked and entwined. The vital importance of proper mass-psychological preparedness is assumed and implied throughout. Attitudes of attention, concern, and relative unconcern are differentially prescribed as a function of current—and continually revisable—computations and appraisals, including those involving the status of scientific certainty itself with respect to any given Earth-approaching object. "Serious" is distinguished from "normal," "unprecedented" from "routine." Ignorable ambient conditions (the realm of the mundane climatic, in Serres's idiom) are opposed to high-threat situations warranting "international contingency planning" (the realm of the accidental meteoric).[6]

The NASA astronomer Donald Yeomans, in *Near-Earth Objects: Finding Them Before They Find Us*, observes that the Earth is constantly "pummeled" by interplanetary dust and particles—more than 100 tons a day—but most such debris is harmless, burning up in the atmosphere (109). To this nominally hazardless status quo the Torino Scale assigns a zero value and a blank white background. Zero and white, marks of unmarkedness, signifiers of emptiness, homogeneity, indifference, neutrality, serve here as emblems of ordinary uneventfulness in all its drab nullity—in other words, in all its ideal *purity*, for days without meteors are precisely days without stain or happenstance. A temporality untouched by *meteōra* is a temporality free of *taint* ("touched by color," etymologically) and of *contamination* ("touched by contingency"): a strict time, an immaculate time, an undeviating time, a contra-contretemps time. At the other end of the scale, shading the lowermost blocks of the rectangle, red screams danger, as symbolically it so often does (Heat! Fire! Hell! Rage! Passion! Power! Blood!). In between, from top to bottom: green, yellow, and orange. Thus, sliding down the scale, moving from crown to foot, "warmer" hues replace "cooler" ones. If it seems natural that the higher integers should correspond to the gravest threats, and those latter to the color connoting violent intensity and extreme peril, then the easy cooperation of these numeric and chromatic codes is disturbed, perhaps, by the principle regulating the figure's vertical relations. Why *descend* to number ten? Why do rising numbers not *rise*? And why red at the *base*? Why make the expression of alarm *fundamental*? Hot air expands, flames ascend, blood boils, passions overflow, mercury climbs with fever. Why confuse the message, or undercut its urgency, by contradicting the logic of the thermometer, that ready-made sign? In short, why *scale down* when things *heat up*?

If the Torino Scale's curiously inverse or contrary thermometry appears to have escaped notice or comment, other of its design features have not gone unremarked. For instance, Binzel himself acknowledged the scale's lack of functional independence, stressing that "responsible risk communication of asteroid and comet close encounters *requires* the inseparable reporting of both the encounter date and its hazard scale value" ("Torino Impact" 298; italics in the original). The scale's non-presentation of encounter information has decisive semantic and practical implications, as this conspicuous absence constitutes the hole that centers the whole structure, that consigns its value and utility to a time ungiven, unspecified, to a crucial contextual *elsewhen*. Without its institutional companion, namely, the news-media tradition of timely reportage, Binzel's device is useless and all but meaningless. Then again, in this very deficiency lies the Torino Scale's quantum of perennial wisdom. The time of *meteōra* precipitates the moment of rupture. Never indubitable in advance, meteors, like tornadoes and tempests, are always "breaking news."

Other infelicities and lacunas trouble the infographic as well. "Concerns among professional astronomers are that the 0 to 10 point system is too simple and compresses too many important details into a single number," admits Binzel in a piece co-written with *Cosmic Catastrophes* authors Chapman and Morrison. Such "details are sacrificed for the sake of simple communication of the central message. What's more, there is no mathematically unique (or quantifiably best) solution" to the conundrum. "It depends on values and judgments. Thus any one-dimensional scale is demonstrably flawed" (Morrison et al. 359). Scientific semiosis, it turns out, is a treacherous business, imperfectly rational and disconcertingly normative. Some (immeasurable) measure of meaning is irretrievably lost in the (sacred) exchange—this is the "sacrifice"—and, moreover, discretion must forever be exercised in the face of indeterminacy. Inevitably, even the most "responsible" risk communication takes place in and across the chasm between scientific knowledge and public comprehension, each domain further possessing its own faults and fissures, not all of them recognized or recognizable, much less "demonstrable."

It is noteworthy, in this connection, that the Torino Scale's text confesses certain gaps and ambiguities, as when it states, which it several times does, that "new telescopic observations will lead to [rank or category] re-assignment," or when it stipulates (again, repeatedly) that the extent of a designated threat is "still uncertain."[7] Yet these little confessions conceal as much as they reveal. They avow some degree of uncertainty the better to mask and manage the entirety of it. The provisionality, the limited currency, the *contingency* of NEO-scientific knowledge is at once registered and reassured by the promise of more and better data to come. Yes, estimates and predictions will need amending in the light of new information, and it is true that the value assigned to a hazard today might necessitate its revaluation tomorrow. Nevertheless, the scale's foundation is sound and its authority reliable. Reclassification happens, but the basic taxonomy is trustworthy. Impact risks are always partly known and partly unknown, but they are never wholly unknowable (this maxim being merely a particularization of risk discourse's originary truism). By means of this rhetorical autoinoculation, the contagion of indeterminacy is ostensibly contained.[8]

The scale's distinctive way of managing uncertainty condenses and recapitulates the more general technique. Writing in *Nature*, in 1994, Chapman and Morrison discussed a number irreducible uncertainties intrinsic to NEO-scientific endeavor. Nobody really knows what is "the threshold impact energy for global catastrophe," they said. No sure method exists for ascertaining "the environmental consequences of impact" or "the effects on human civilization" (35). Complexities abound. Much depends on whether the object is an asteroid or a comet; on its diameter, density, and composition; on its velocity and angle of incidence; on whether it strikes land or sea; whether forest, desert, grassland, or tundra, or ocean, lake, or river; whether in the northern hemisphere or the southern; whether in winter, spring, summer, or autumn; and so on. Confronted with this welter of indeterminacies, Chapman and Morrison produced an elaborate statistical analysis that subtly elided or displaced many of its assumptions, rationalized its many conjectures and approximations, and, above all, controlled and legitimated its relation to nescience. As Felicity Mellor has argued, "Rather than a set of contestable assumptions and unknowns, non-knowing became an ordered quantity which can be bounded and subjected to numerical analysis" ("Negotiating Uncertainty" 19). Unwilling to accept (much less authorize) a chaos of indeterminate possibilities, the NEO researchers, in a move equally paradigmatic and programmatic, articulated the standard logic of risk to establish a positive system of "certain probabilities" and "known uncertainties" (23, 19).

The Torino Scale aims to popularize this positive system. But just how *positive* is Binzel's mediating construct? How positive can it be? After all, the infographic is static, but the meteor *moves*. The former stands as an inscribed monument, a fixed archive, epistemically restricted, unresponsive, and heavy, petroglyphic: the scale "knows" what it knows and nothing more, eternally. The latter, meanwhile, maintains a very different relation to time, space, materiality, and the possibility of knowledge: the space rock, now here, now there, now like this, now like that, is epistemically unstable, protean, liable to *perturbation* (in astronomical parlance); a thing confoundingly in flux, speeding, tumbling, shifting, transforming; its size, substance, and trajectory—its "true nature"—in doubt from one moment to the next, the subject of unremitting invigilation and painstaking calculation and recalculation. A technical nomenclature is deployed to make sense of these perturbing semi-obscurities, to sort out these elusive mobilities, vectors, variabilities, mutations. Perhaps at first only a faint and distant *apparition* (that wonderfully resonant astronomical term), the approaching comet or *minor planet* (another name for "asteroid") acquires shape and significance as estimates improve and data accumulate over time. If, by chance—because by what else?—it enters the Earth's atmosphere and vaporizes luminously, the rocky body becomes a meteor proper, a shooting star, a falling star, maybe a fireball or a bolide or even a Chelyabinsk-type superbolide, depending on how bright it flashes and whether it bursts in the air. If it hits the ground, it is, finally, a meteorite, an impactor, or, as it used to be known before it was severed from the weather, a "thunderstone."[9] In the doomsday scenario—the so-called worst case, the furthest projection of NEO science's apocalyptic imagination, the hallucinatory drama of its eschatology—the striking meteor causes a veritable worldwide disaster (*disaster*: literally, an ill-starred event).

Always on Alert

In imagining doomsday disaster, NEO science relies on more than state-of-the-art astronomical observation, the calculus of probabilities, and other such means and procedures; to flesh out its picture of apocalypse, it looks to the history and technology of atomic weaponry, takes the bomb as a touchstone. Time and again in the scientific literature, as in NEO-concerned public discourse and popular entertainment, major asteroid or comet impacts are likened to nuclear explosions. Despite their contrasting moral and political valences (only the meteor's timeless genesis is independent of human desire, intention, agency, volition, cunning, aggression), the two are routinely cast as kindred phenomena, comparable in their risks, their physics, and their effects. The energies they release, the ejecta they produce, the craters they leave, the blazes they ignite, the skies they blacken, the ravages they inflict, as well as the fears they arouse, the tales and dreams they spawn, the theoretical models they corroborate, the institutional forms and practices they underpin, the operations of power, fantasy, and ideology they alibi and enable—to be sure, in the realms of science, culture, and government, analogies and reciprocities between meteoric Earth-collisions and atomic detonations are rich and plentiful (see Davis).

Chapman and Morrison's influential *Nature* article offers a defining instance. In it, the threat of extraterrestrial "projectiles" is pointedly compared to "other natural and human-generated hazards" ("Impacts on the Earth" 33). Floods, cyclones, tornadoes, firestorms, earthquakes, droughts, tsunamis, and volcanic eruptions, along with "the very worst technological accidents of modern society," such as airliner crashes and the Bhopal disaster, all receive explicit mention. "A globally catastrophic impact, however, exceeds all [these] other disasters in that such an event could kill much of the world's population over the course of a few months or years," the authors declare. "Furthermore, the globally catastrophic impact is qualitatively different from other more familiar hazards in its synergistic effects upon the entire planet" (37). Ultimately, only "nuclear war" and its corollary, nuclear winter, the aftermath to end all aftermaths, are truly akin to "a global impact catastrophe [that] could lead to the breakdown of civilization" (33). Five years earlier, in *Cosmic Catastrophes*, these same NEO scientists defended their decision to include a chapter on nuclear winter—other than "human-wrought climate changes," the only anthropogenic calamity treated at length in the book—by claiming for it a "cosmic significance":

> Perhaps it takes a cosmic perspective to appreciate, and deal with, the global consequences of such a man-made Armageddon. But in a larger sense, the evolution of life and development of civilization on our world is itself a cosmic process. When living things evolve to the point where their activities can transform the very climate of their planet, they emerge into cosmic significance.
>
> (v, 122)

The hypothetical asteroid that wiped out the dinosaurs is held to be like the conjectural impactor that would initiate for humankind a ruinous chain reaction. (NEO scientists typically envisage not the extinction of *Homo sapiens* but the abject collapse of advanced industrial societies—a mythology here, then, of sudden world-historical retrogression, of degeneration and reprimitivization, rather than of species annihilation.)[10] In turn, the damage done by that impactor is supposed to be similar to the destruction caused by an imagined nuclear war. These three mutually informing speculative scientific catastrophe theories do political as well as intellectual work; they are not only symbolically but socially and materially effective. As Doug Davis has shown, Luis and Walter Alvarez's "impact-extinction theory emerged from the Cold War's state of conflict, and in the process turned that conflict's nuclear threat into a state of nature." In addition to abetting the ideological naturalization of the era's geopolitical enmities and precarities, "it rallied the resources of a scientific community that had otherwise been doing the science needed to fight World War III, and ultimately taught statesmen how that war might end in a nuclear winter" (Davis 463). More recently, NEO-scientific logics and conceits have been wedded to the objectives of national security and recruited for the militarization of space. During the 1980s and 1990s, Mellor contends, "the promotion of the asteroid impact threat helped make the idea of war in space more acceptable and helped justify the continued development of space-based weaponry." It ratified a mode of thought and speech

> founded on fear of the unknown and the assumption that advanced technology could usher in a safer era. In so doing, it resonated with the politics of fear and the technologies of permanent war that are now at the centre of US defence policy.
> (Mellor, "Colliding Worlds" 522)

Consider, in this light, NASA's new Planetary Defense Coordination Office (PDCO). Established in January of 2016, the PDCO now controls and encompasses the NEO Observations Program. As if the office's almost science-fictional appellation did not make matters plain enough, the revamped administrative hierarchy leaves little doubt as to its mission and priorities. Whereas the program seeks to scientifically investigate all close approaches, the PDCO is interested exclusively in the detection and tracking of a narrower class of near-Earth object, namely, those deemed "potentially hazardous." Not incidentally, it also is responsible for developing techniques for deflecting or redirecting any large asteroid or comet discovered to be on a collision course with the Earth. In circumstances in which it has been determined that preventive measures would be impossible or ineffectual, the office collaborates with the State Department and the Federal Emergency Management Agency to formulate a disaster-response plan and to oversee rescue operations. Finally, the PDCO is a communications nerve center, in charge of issuing warnings and distributing "timely and accurate information to the Government, the media, and the public" about potentially hazardous objects (NASA, "Planetary Defense Coordination Office").

In *Space and the American Imagination*, Howard McCurdy points out that fears and trepidations about bolt-from-the-blue catastrophes ran rampant during the Cold War, as

> science revealed terrible ways in which the planet might be destroyed. All of the doomsday scenarios, both astronomical and human in origin, fell from the sky. This led naturally to the conclusion that activities taking place above the surface of the Earth

—not on the ground, not over the moon, but, as it were, in the middle—"would determine the future of the world" (81). NASA's project of planetary defense adopts and radically extends key Cold War agendas, rationales, and purposes. It marshals scientific expertise, technical intelligence, militaristic metaphors, futurist projections, and pop-cultural fantasies in the name of national security. Or, more precisely, in the name of a speculative national security that is supposedly simultaneously a *total terrestrial* security, an *absolute geospheric* security—in a sense, the maximal security imaginable. Conflating a banal national ideological guarantee (territorial security) with an extravagant ecumenical promise (comprehensive Earth protection, "spaceguardianship"), the trope of "planetary defense" works to transfigure the profane dream of hegemonic invulnerability into the hope of universal salvation through benevolent technocracy.

The real imperatives driving the PDCO are, of course, rather more down to earth. Since its inception, the PDCO has formed an essential component of what Joseph Masco calls "an ever-expanding, always-on-alert global security apparatus" engineered by "American power" to "administer the global future" (10). Such an imperialist apparatus, Masco adds, as if describing the impetus behind the Torino Impact Hazard Scale rather than laying the predicate for his analysis of the now-defunct U.S. Homeland Security Advisory System color chart (the two risk infographics are cognates in any case), "requires a new kind of expert psychopolitics that is not grounded in the effort to establish facts but rather is committed to generating speculative futures (imagined dangers of cataclysmic scale) that it will then need to counter" (20).[11]

In February of 2013, the Chelyabinsk fireball and its fallen remains provided spectacular and tangible proof of the eventuality of future asteroidal or cometary cataclysm, as well as fodder for a range of scientific, governmental, and popular inquiries and assessments, depictions and strategic-defensive imaginings. (The NASA Office of Inspector General included a description and photograph of the fireball on the very first page of its 2014 report, "NASA's Efforts to Identify Near-Earth Objects and Mitigate Hazards," in direct response to which the PDCO was founded.) Upon the bodies of the star-crossed few, those 1,600 or so who happened to be within its impact horizon—and who, like everybody else, *did not see it coming*—the superbolide visited one or more kinds of unlucky blow. However, to the eyes and ears of the fascinated many, the millions around the world who first had the fortune to encounter its visual or audiovisual mediation—in print, on television, on the web, on social networks—the meteor's declination and explosion delivered a marvelous mix of mental astonishment and sensual excitation.

Perhaps because it awakened primal anxieties or enchantments, perhaps because it summoned archetypal or supernatural images and associations, but surely because of its extraordinariness and sheer unexpectedness, the meteor's representation was destined to become a digital-media sensation. As befalls and befits a mediate-star-become-media-star, the fireball today continues to light up the online universe, where its forgone fortuitous eventness seems fated to a future of infinite commotion, of endless disseminative play and replay. Meanwhile, astronomers and planetary scientists, having failed to forecast and prepare for the space rock's precipitous arrival—this failure to foresee the advent: the mark of their ancient meteorological inheritance—appropriated, examined, and manipulated web-accessible amateur and public videos in a belated effort to reconstruct the intruder's orbit and trajectory through frame-by-frame analysis and other media-forensic methods, thereby reclaiming the rare cosmic occurrence for positive science.

Both the Chelyabinsk meteor's scientific reclamation and its recirculative media stardom were made possible by its contingent mediatized capture by hundreds of random cameras. Yet, for all their happenstance, those cameras and the recordings they casually generated were as much the products of political and cultural necessity as of astronomical coincidence. In modern risk and surveillance societies, in media cultures "always on alert" for threats and thrills alike, the mass proliferation of devices and apparatuses of 24/7 monitoring—of perpetual witnessing, watching, and warning—is by no means accidental. Given their "chance proximity" (as Serres would say) to the airburst, what were the chances that some number of privately mobile, socially networked, smartphone-wielding citizens would *not* manage to frame and reproduce at least some portion of the meteor's downward motion? What was the probability that some percentage of high-tech traffic and security systems in the area would not automatically (inadvertently) do the same? Were we to game it out, so to speak, would we not be inclined to find that the odds were, from the start, stacked in the cameras' favor? Was there not, therefore, the element of a certain inevitability, a weird inescapability, in this unanticipated constellation of sudden asteroidal emergence and sleepless technological vigilance? If the contemporary meteoric event is haphazard and complex, if together with its mediatized encounter it constitutes a hazardous complex, it is because the threat-prepared horizon of the one is the other's post-hoc determinant and, at the same (untimely) time, its prior accident.

Notes

1 See Durda; Kring and Boslough; and Scharf. See also Borovička et al., "The Trajectory"; Brown et al.; and Popova et al.
2 Tiffany makes an important point about Serres's use of the word *temps*: "The French word *temps* means both 'time' and 'weather,' so that each time Serres speaks of the weather, he invokes the inherent temporality of the meteoric phenomenon" (313).
3 For more on *kairos* and *chronos* in relation to weather and meteorology, see Peters. Contrary to Golinski, Peters not only opposes the clock to the calendar but associates the former with *kairos* rather than with *chronos*: "To a large degree, [clocks] deal in time as *kairos* (opportunity) in contrast to *chronos* (duration)" (213).
4 On the 2004 update, see Morrison et al.; and Thomson 3.
5 Quoted matter from *Torino Impact Hazard Scale* (Center for Near Earth Object Studies).
6 Quoted matter from *Torino Impact Hazard Scale* (Center for Near Earth Object Studies).
7 Quoted matter from *Torino Impact Hazard Scale* (Center for Near Earth Object Studies).
8 On the ideological work of "inoculation," see Barthes.
9 On the history of thunderstones, see Burke; and Garber.
10 The Spacewatch [Snowmass, Colorado] Workshop did *not* equate the destruction of civilization with the total extinction of the human species. Instead, it envisioned an event that might eradicate one year's agriculture and destabilize social and economic structures to the point that a new Dark Ages of even a Stone Age might result.
(Chapman and Morrison, Cosmic Catastrophes 279; italics in the original)
11 In contrast to the Torino Scale, the U.S. Homeland Security Advisory System chart *rises* to the color red ("severe risk") and puts green at the bottom ("low risk").

Works Cited

Alvarez, Luis W. et al. "Extraterrestrial Cause for Cretaceous-Tertiary Extinction." *Science*, vol. 208, no. 4448, June 1980, pp. 1095–1108.
Barthes, Roland. *Mythologies*. Translated by Annette Lavers. Noonday Press/Farrar, Straus and Giroux, 1972.
Binzel, Richard P. "A Near-Earth Object Hazard Index." *Annals of the New York Academy of Sciences*, vol. 822, May 1997, p. 545.
Binzel, Richard P. "The Torino Impact Hazard Scale." *Planetary and Space Science*, vol. 48, no. 4, 2000, pp. 297–303.
Borovička, Jiří et al. "A Catalog of Video Records of the 2013 Chelyabinsk Superbolide." *Astronomy and Astrophysics*, vol. 585, January 2016, p. A90.
Borovička, Jiří et al. "The Trajectory, Structure and Origin of the Chelyabinsk Asteroidal Impactor." *Nature*, vol. 503, November 2013, pp. 235–237.
Brown, P.G. et al. "A 500-Kiloton Airburst over Chelyabinsk and an Enhanced Hazard from Small Impactors." *Nature*, vol. 503, November 2013, pp. 238–241.
Burke, John G. *Cosmic Debris: Meteorites in History*. U of California P, 1986.
Chapman, Clark R. and David Morrison. *Cosmic Catastrophes*. Plenum Press, 1989.
Chapman, Clark R. and David Morrison. "Impacts on the Earth by Asteroids and Comets: Assessing the Hazard." *Nature*, vol. 367, January 1994, pp. 33–40.
Davis, Doug. "'A Hundred Million Hydrogen Bombs': Total War in the Fossil Record." *Configurations*, vol. 9, 2001, pp. 461–508.
Derrida, Jacques. "My Chances/*Mes Chances*: A Rendezvous with Some Epicurean Stereophonies." *Taking Chances: Derrida, Psychoanalysis, and Literature*, edited by Joseph H. Smith and William Kerrigan, John Hopkins UP, 1984, pp. 1–32.
Durda, Daniel D. "The Chelyabinsk Super-Meteor." *Sky and Telescope*, June 2013, pp. 24–31.

Garber, Megan. "Thunderstone: What People Thought About Meteorites Before Modern Astronomy." *The Atlantic*, February 15, 2013, www.theatlantic.com/technology/archive/2013/02/thunderstone-what-people-thought-about-meteorites-before-modern-astronomy/273220/. Accessed September 30, 2017.

Golinski, Jan. *British Weather and the Climate of Enlightenment*. U of Chicago P, 2007.

Hartwell, William T. "The Sky on the Ground: Celestial Objects and Events in Archaeology and Popular Culture." *Comet/Asteroid Impacts and Human Society: An Interdisciplinary Approach*, edited Peter T. Bobrowsky and Hans Rickman. Springer, 2007, pp. 71–87.

Kring, David and Mark Boslough. "Chelyabinsk: Portrait of an Asteroid." *Physics Today*, vol. 67, 2014, pp. 32–37.

Levy, David H. *Impact Jupiter: The Crash of Comet Shoemaker–Levy 9*. Plenum Press, 1995.

Masco, Joseph. *The Theater of Operations: National Security Affect from the Cold War to the War on Terror*. Duke UP, 2014.

McBeath, Alastair. "Meteor Beliefs Project: 'Meteor' and Related Terms in English Usage." *WGN: Journal of the International Meteor Organization*, vol. 32, no. 1, 2004, pp. 35–38.

McCurdy, Howard E. *Space and the American Imagination*, 2nd ed. Johns Hopkins UP, 2011.

Mellor, Felicity. "Colliding Worlds: Asteroid Research and the Legitimization of War in Space." *Social Studies of Science*, vol. 37, no. 4, August 2007, pp. 499–531.

Mellor, Felicity. "Negotiating Uncertainty: Asteroids, Risk and the Media." *Public Understanding of Science*, vol. 19, no. 1, 2010, pp. 16–33.

Morrison, David et al. "Impacts and the Public: Communicating the Nature of the Impact Hazard." *Mitigation of Hazardous Comets and Asteroids*, edited by Michael J.S. Belton et al. Cambridge UP, 2004, pp. 353–390.

NASA. "Planetary Defense Coordination Office." June 27, 2018, www.nasa.gov/planetarydefense/overview. Accessed September 30, 2017.

NASA. "Russia Meteor Not Linked to Asteroid Flyby." February 15, 2013, www.nasa.gov/mission_pages/asteroids/news/asteroid20130215.html. Accessed September 30, 2017.

Peters, John Durham. *The Marvelous Clouds: Toward a Philosophy of Elemental Media*. U of Chicago P, 2015.

Popova, Olga P. et al. "Chelyabinsk Airburst, Damage Assessment, Meteorite Recovery, and Characterization." *Science*, vol. 342, November 2013, pp. 1069–1073.

Reed, Arden. *Romantic Weather: The Climates of Coleridge and Baudelaire*. UP of New England, 1983.

Scharf, Caleb. "Cloudy, with a Chance of Meteors." *New Yorker*, November 21, 2013, www.newyorker.com/tech/elements/cloudy-with-a-chance-of-meteors. Accessed September 30, 2017.

Serres, Michel. *Genesis*. Translated by Geneviève James and James Nielson. U of Michigan P, 1995.

Serres, Michel. *The Birth of Physics*. Translated by Jack Hawkes, edited by David Webb. Clinamen Press, 2000.

The Spaceguard Survey: Report of the NASA International Near-Earth-Object Detection Workshop, edited by David Morrison. Jet Propulsion Laboratory/California Institute of Technology, 1992.

Taub, Liba. *Ancient Meteorology*. Routledge, 2003.

Thomson, Elizabeth A. "Scale Weighs in on Risk of Asteroid Impact." *MIT Tech Talk*, April 13, 2005, p. 3, http://news.mit.edu//2005/techtalk49-24.pdf. Accessed September 30, 2017.

Tiffany, Daniel. *Toy Medium: Materialism and Modern Lyric*. U of California P, 2000.

Torino Impact Hazard Scale. Center for Near Earth Object Studies, 2004, https://cneos.jpl.nasa.gov/sentry/torino_scale.html. Accessed September 30, 2017.

Yeomans, Donald K. *Near-Earth Objects: Finding Them Before They Find Us*. Princeton UP, 2012.

Yeomans, Don and Paul Chodas. "Asteroid 2012 DA14 to Pass Very Close to the Earth on February 15, 2013." Center for Near Earth Object Studies, February 1, 2013, https://cneos.jpl.nasa.gov/news/news177.html. Accessed September 30, 2017.

Zuluaga, Jorge and Ignacio Ferrín. "A Preliminary Reconstruction of the Orbit of the Chelyabinsk Meteoroid." February 22, 2013, https://arxiv.org/pdf/1302.5377.pdf.

Zuluaga, Jorge et al. "The Orbit of the Chelyabinsk Event Impactor as Reconstructed from Amateur and Public Footage." March 7, 2013, https://arxiv.org/pdf/1303.1796.pdf. Accessed September 30, 2017.

PART V

VIRTUALITY

17

RED DOT SIGHT

Colin Milburn and Rita Raley

In 1977, *Newsweek* magazine reported on the new laser-sighted American 180 rifle, describing it as a futuristic "Buck Rogers gun" equipped with a laser diode for casting a concentrated beam of light: "Sighting the gun projects a very visible red dot on the target, and that's where the bullet goes" ("The Buck Rogers Gun"). Laser-assisted weapons such as the American 180 emerged in the public consciousness firmly associated with science fiction, the fantastic gizmos of Buck Rogers and Flash Gordon. The future-ladenness of such weapons was already clear in 1967 when the Pentagon tested a laser rangefinder in Vietnam, promoting the claim that the "army of the future" had landed, although it would be another decade before commercial laser sights and rangefinders were marketed for police and civilian use (Baldwin). Yet even as such devices became more familiar and widespread, their science-fictional aura lingered.[1] In 1995, for example, New York City police officials described a policy to arm transit officers with a new weapon—a 9-millimeter service pistol with a small laser sight—as "the first step in a 'Star Trek' vision of the future of policing the subway system" ("Lasers to Be Tested"). More recently, the XM25 Individual Air Burst Weapon System, a grenade launcher that uses a laser rangefinder to explode grenades in mid-air near a designated target, has been called a "Judge Dredd weapon" in reference to the comic book and film character ("Army Starts Testing"; "Green Berets").

To be sure, science fiction has provided some of the most iconic images of laser-assisted weapons—among them, the AMT Hardballer .45 long slide with laser sight wielded by the time-traveling cyborg in *The Terminator* (1984). Recall also the assassin's laser depicted in an early scene of William Gibson's *Neuromancer* (1984):

> Afterimage of a single hair-fine light of red light. Seared concrete beneath the thin soles of his shoes. Her white sneakers flashing, close to the curving wall now, and again the ghost line of the laser branded across his eye, bobbing in his vision as he ran.
>
> *(Gibson 39)*

Such images from science fiction have reinforced a popular mythology of precision and instantaneity. As Charles Goff, the owner of American Arms International—the manufacturer of the American 180 rifle—enthused way back in 1977, "It's like a ray gun would be. All you have to do is flip on the light and zap! It's instantaneous" (Goff quoted in "Buck Rogers Gun" 56).

Today, the red dot is ubiquitous, no longer localized to science fiction. It is now a common trope of action movies, political thrillers, police procedurals, first-person shooter games, reality TV, and the nightly news. Yet even as it has become part of everyday realism, the laser-sighted weapon remains a technology of speculative media: it projects an image of risk through a single ray of light, a tiny mote of illumination that speeds ahead and enjoins the present to catch up. Indeed, it becomes an imperative. As described by the 1977 *Newsweek* story about the American 180, the dot is both a harbinger of things to come and a command to obey: "Follow the red dot" (56). Certainly, we recognize the stakes of either obeying or disregarding such an order. It is a matter of life or death on the line. But exactly to address these stakes, these hazardous conditions, we propose to follow the red dot as a media object—a phantasmatic figure of precision targeting—as well as the focal point of a way of seeing that is endemic to the era of laser weapons.[2]

This is what we call *red dot sight*: a mediated perspective, an orientation to risk that re-dimensionalizes the optics of threat perception around a crimson speck of light. Red dot sight—the shooter seeing the target, the target seeing the dot—reduces the space and time for any possible response to an absolute minimum. Because it leaves no room for doubt, it compels instantaneous assent or reaction. The threat is clear and present: the scope for analysis or deliberation constricts toward a zero-dimensional point, collapsing the speculative future into local immediacy. The dot has such persuasive force, for both shooter and target, because it indexes the high-tech hardware behind it, the industrialization of targeting that has guaranteed its lethal precision.[3] According to a 1974 advertisement for the American 180, for example, the promise of speed and exactitude ("Just put the red laser dot on the target and squeeze them off ... the rounds go exactly where you see the dot") is backed up by a regulated system of engineering expertise, innovation, and ingenuity ("This weapon is an all-new American design manufactured to stringent specifications") (Figure 17.1). Yet red dot sight is nothing merely technological, nor is it restricted to a particular configuration of marks or marksmen. Rather, it is an imaginary vantage in a scene of targeting, a contraction of the axis of sight to the point where both subject and object of targeting converge, as if occupying both sides of the dot at once. As we see in the American 180 advertisement, the photographic perspective situates the viewer in a foreshortened space—a constricted corridor, a flattened cone of vision centered by the red dot—looking at once forward and backward along an invisible radius that draws everything together in deadly intimacy, ahead of time: "This weapon commands instant respect without firing a shot." Significantly, it is the viewer of this scene whose respect is commanded—the viewer, the target audience, who is as much a target of red dot sight as the man on the stairs, as much a targeter as the policeman holding the gun. Whosoever sees the red dot is laser-locked, preemptively drawn into an all-new dimension of trouble: a proleptic future that orders everyone to fall in line, on the dot.

★ ★ ★

There are two predominant modes of red dot sight, each associated with a particular kind of weapon accessory: reflex sights and laser sights. Both are means of target acquisition, but a reflex sight works by reflection whereas a laser sight works by projection. Ever since their invention in 1975, reflex sights that use a red laser-emitting diode (LED) to generate an illuminated reticle—a dot reflected on a combining glass and visible only to the shooter—have been specifically called "red dot sights."[4] In contrast, laser sights emit a coherent beam of light that is visible as a small spot even at great distance. The media regime of red dot sight therefore comprises both a reflexive form, where only the shooter sees the red dot marking the target, and a projective form, where the red dot is potentially visible to the shooter and the target simultaneously.

Of course, there have been many other innovations, many other ways of weaponizing light since the 1970s. In addition to an assortment of red dot reflex sights and laser scopes, various other combat optics with similar features have appeared over the last 40 years. For example, the Advanced Combat Optical Gunsight, developed in 1987, provides rifle snipers with a highly magnified view of a target and a reticle illuminated by radioactive tritium. So too a significant amount of military R&D has focused on battlefield combat lasers (Freedman; Hecht; Seidel; Singer). In 2005, Sheldon Meth, a program manager for DARPA's Tactical Technology Office, claimed that "the age of the

Figure 17.1 Advertisement for the American 180, *Gun World*, February 1974

military laser is about to arrive" (191). While he noted at the time that most military uses of lasers were limited to sighting targets or guiding ordnance, he ventured that the future would see all manner of tactical laser weapons on the battlefield: "While I hesitate to admit that I am a Buck Rogers or Star Trek fan, I have to say it is fascinating how science fiction can anticipate reality" (191). Reassessing the status of military lasers and other directed energy weapons in 2010, the physicist and novelist Doug Beason, a retired U.S. Air Force colonel as well as the former Associate Laboratory Director for Threat Reduction at the Los Alamos National Laboratory, reiterated the current situation: "Directed energy is not science fiction. These are real weapons being tested in real scenarios" (12). Therefore, he suggested, the full implications are already inevitable: "National leaders will soon have the ability to instantly deter threats anywhere in the world with infinite precision at the speed of light" (10). While such an exquisite vision of full-spectrum deterrence may yet remain a twinkle in the eye, there are today a host of battlefield lasers beyond sights and guidance systems, including antimaterial lasers (lasers designed to disable vehicles or missiles), antisensor lasers (lasers that scan for optical sensors or signs of other lasers), and antipersonnel lasers (for example, blinding laser grenades, which were banned by the United Nations in 1995, or laser dazzlers, which disorient and cause temporary visual impairment) (McAulay; McCall; Zohuri). Many of these weapons and devices expand the regime of red dot sight, even though they may not involve red dots as such.

After all, regardless of its connections to any particular devices or technological genealogies, the projected image of the red dot epitomizes the promissory grammar of weaponized light, the entire discourse of high-tech optical targeting—precisely as a signifier of collapsed futurity. At this point, the red dot is a cliché, an image that everyone can call to mind and reference. Even as it has been separated from real material contexts, dislocated from actual battlefields or hunting grounds, the repetition of the red dot across any number of news reports, documentaries, marketing brochures, video games, television shows, and Hollywood films has made the logic of high-tech targeting visually comprehensible and ordinary, naturalized by the representational processes of popular media. Yet the familiarity of the red dot, the fact that it is a cliché, has not diminished its signifying capacities or its future-shaping effects. On the contrary, the regime of red dot sight depends on *recognition*. It requires recognition of the red dot's indexical function (i.e., pointing to some high-tech targeting apparatus), its metonymic function (i.e., designating the targeting circuit, the relation between the mark and the marksman, the object and subject of high-tech targeting), and its metaphorical function (i.e., implying a conditional future that will have been, its subjunctivity already falling behind the speed of actual events). To be sure, at the moment of recognition, the red dot already anticipates, or we might say premediates, the shot (cf. Grusin). It prefigures the shot to come by recollecting other red dots that have come before: an icon of the high-tech targeting industry and the militarization of light, as well as a warning, a foretoken image with the power to entrain the future through its promissory grammar alone.

In 1995, for example, when the New York transit police announced their Star Trek-like "experiment" with laser-equipped pistols, a police spokesman described their intended effect: "If you're a bad guy and you see the red dot on your chest, you'll probably realize you're in trouble. And you'll comply" (Lieutenant Valentino quoted in "Lasers to Be Tested"). In this speculative scenario, dreamed forth by police authorities, the imagined second-person target ("you") comes to realize the danger, the threat implied by the red dot, only to the degree that he simultaneously recognizes himself as a stock character in a conditional, subjunctive narrative ("if you're a bad guy"). Yet the compulsive force of the red dot, which seems to be the consequence or conclusion of this speculative story ("If you're a bad guy and you see the red dot ... you'll comply"), actually works retroactively, like a self-fulfilling prophecy. That is to say, if you see the red dot on your chest, you realize that you are already (presumed to be) the bad guy, in trouble even before the trouble starts. If you comply, you confirm that you were the bad guy all along—or rather, you acknowledge that you have been put in this role, whether you fit the description or not—and therefore prove yourself a legitimate target of red dot sight. If you do not comply ... well, you already know what follows the red dot.

The red dot is a technology of control for managing bodies and populations according to a "calculus of probabilities," which, as Gilles Deleuze noted in a 1986 lecture on biopolitics and Foucault, "is much better than the walls of a prison" (Deleuze quoted in Nail 256). Its purpose here is to introduce a certain fear and expectation, in other words, the calculus of risk ("you'll probably realise you're in trouble"). Yet in defining the zone of trouble—a sharp point of light at the center, that is, the origin of an expanding circle—the red dot takes command by reducing risk calculation to a simple algorithm: if compliance, continue; else, game over. Indeed, the power of the red dot to regulate the variables in a local zone of trouble was clear as soon as the first laser sights came on the market in the 1970s.[5] For example, in 1979, *Science Digest* described the capacity of the American 180 rifle to create a "risk reduced" environment, thanks to the red dot and its outsized "reputation with persons on both sides of the law" (Marsh 9–10). On the one hand, the dot disciplines the wild trigger fingers of law enforcement: as one police officer in Fort Lauderdale said, "We have pointed out that the laser beam is a safety feature because we fire only when the red dot is on the suspect and that eliminates bullets flying around the city" (George Long quoted in Marsh 11–12).

On the other hand, the dot reconfirms the futuristic image of the "Buck Rogers gun" and its "recognized damaging impact" (Marsh 10). As it moves around, preceded by its own reputation, the dot recodes a zone of trouble as a rule-bound space, almost like a game: "when inmates in a Utah prison were creating trouble, the red dot playing across the prisoners' chest sent them hurrying to their cells" (Marsh 12). Play along, follow the red dot. In the words of one corrections officer at Utah State Prison two years prior, "When I put that red dot on some of them … they got back in their cells but fast" (quoted in "Rifle With Laser Sight"). Or, as *Newsweek* recounted in July 1977, "one robbery suspect surrendered the moment he faced the red dot, even though he had a fully loaded automatic rifle at his side" ("Buck Rogers Gun").

As these examples indicate, red dot sight does not necessarily bring a particular future into being; it is not actually deterministic, insofar as the possibility of *not* shooting is innate in its structure. But it works as a deterrent by virtue of the belief in its machinic precision, the recognition of its fatalist grammar ("zap! It's instantaneous"). In this way, red dot sight concretizes the conditions of possibility for a particular enactment of the future. It reduces a complex system, all of the variables that make accuracy or predictability so fraught with uncertainty, and isolates it to a situation, a scene—a single dot—in which the outcome would seem absolute, a binary option: shot or not.

★ ★ ★

Paul Virilio has described the apparatus of global vision after World War II, when deterrence strategy came to be based on the "ubiquitous orbital vision of enemy territory" (2). It is not simply that the "war machine" and "watching machine" co-exist but that they have become mutually constitutive, even synonymous—a principle that has extended into the age of satellite surveillance and drone technologies (cf. Parks and Kaplan; Shaw). Yet deterrence strategies for the combat zones of the present have often emphasized precision targeting in contrast to orbital vision, which is to say the visualization of targets in areas that are not perfectly available to the regime of total illumination from above. The red dot thus trades the fantasy of total coverage for the virtuosity of precise coverage. The promise of precision targeting is that uncertainty and risk are contained, if not wholly eliminated. "The system is absolutely devastating. There is no way you can miss," concluded a counter-sniper expert in a 1982 U.S. Customs Service report on the Laser Products LPC-700 laser-aimed revolver (quoted in Vartabedian). "You're never going to hit the neighbor or the dog or the kids," averred Jack Kelley, the VP of marketing for Laser Products (now SureFire LLC), seemingly flush with enthusiasm at a moment when his company was on the brink of selling this weapon to a number of government agencies around the world. "With this you are performing neurosurgery. It really is a surgical instrument" (Kelley quoted in Vartabedian).

Questions of veracity aside, the overhyped precision of laser-assisted weapons conceals the more general and abstract nature of targeting, which occurs well before the line of sight has been established—the targeting before targeting. As Samuel Weber puts it, "The act of targeting is an act of violence even before any shot is fired" (105). The red dot creates a target literally on the spot. It anticipates what is to come but it also renders the apprehensive dimension of targeting—in other words, the identification of the enemy as such—visible and verifiable. In this respect, the practice of targeting must be understood as relational and differential, constructing a target within a larger system of other potential and actual targets. "To target," as McKenzie Wark suggests, "is to isolate something against the dense, tense fibers of the network, maybe to destroy it, but always to assign it a unique value" (149). The gamespace logic of targeting is discriminatory—each thing, node, piece defined in relation to other things. If the target is identified or classified by negation, if the target is marked as such in relation to that which is not a target, so too does the shooter stabilize as a subject in relation to its object. "Targeting turns time and space from a disconcerting experience of flux into conditions of self-awareness," snapping self and other into relational focus, locking them in position (Wark 128).

Despite whatever actual distance there may be between shooter and target, the red dot affords a fantasy of one-on-one combat. Yet the purported sensation of proximity, up close and personal—shooting as neurosurgery—serves as an alibi to disguise the depersonalized act of killing that is the particular hallmark of a regime of industrialized violence. As Slavoj Žižek argues, the mythologizing of embodied battle has the effect of allowing us not to see what warfare has actually become: "It is thus not the fantasy of a purely aseptic war run as a video game behind computer screens that protects us from the reality of the face to face killing of another person; on the contrary it is this fantasy of face to face encounter with an enemy killed bloodily that we construct in order to escape the Real of the depersonalized war turned into an anonymous technological operation" (77). Red dot sight, promoting the fantasy of the "perfect shot," obscures the automation of contemporary warfare by affirming the romance of a clean kill.

In that red dot sight isolates or reduces the complex networks of modern combat to a moment, a singular encounter, it offers the possibility of reinstating the human agent as the central figure of command and control. Yet to the degree that laser sight manages, directs, and focuses the faculty of human sight, it simultaneously renders distinctions between human and machine vision necessarily unstable (cf. Johnston; Virilio). Expertise—being a good shot—even seems strangely superfluous, at least in the exaggerated discourse of device manufacturers and enthusiasts. It is not simply that "there is no way you can miss" but that expertise becomes a particular affordance of the hardware, available to everyone. Charles Goff, when promoting the American 180, was reported to "thrust" the rifle upon the secretaries of potential buyers, "who often learn[ed] to handle it in fifteen minutes" ("The Buck Rogers Gun"). The practice of laser sighting—replicated through different devices, weapons, and media—reconfigures the embodied user, realigning skills and training to the projected beam. Here, too, we must consider Virilio:

> Weapons are tools not just of destruction but also of perception—that is to say, stimulants that make themselves felt through chemical, neurological processes in the sense organs and the central nervous system, affecting human reactions and even the perceptual identification and differentiation of object.
>
> *(6)*

But the reordering of perception around red dot sight is not produced by any weapon alone; in other words, it is nothing exclusively tied to the hardware. Rather, red dot sight refocuses sensory experience—in particular, it heightens the sense of apprehension, reconstituted as a twisted amalgam of control, militarism, and libidinal investment—exactly due to its grammar of anticipation, its proleptic futurism.

The appearance of the dot may thus even incite feelings of expectant arousal, a carnal sense of intimacy—in touch with the future. According to some gun enthusiasts, the primal scene shaping their interest in firearms, their general responsiveness to high-tech weapons, was the first sight of a laser sight: "Without a doubt, one of the most noteworthy 'gun porn' moments from my youth was when Arnold Schwarzenegger acquired 'the .45 longslide with laser sighting' in 1984's 'The Terminator'" (Cantrell). Red dot sight, seeing red, entails a kind of cyborg erotics. It is a form of militarized perception that, as Jordan Crandall suggests, fuses "technological innovation and the erotic charge of combat." It comes as no surprise then that manufacturers and marketers of laser scopes should elicit such feelings through the language and imagery of gunplay kink—the sight itself displayed as the ultimate hardware fetish: "This scope is as sexy as it gets" (2A4Life). Yet such an appeal to cyborg erotics, even if evidently figurative, nevertheless insists on the inadequacy of the present, encouraging a sensitivity to the human body as insufficiently precise, lacking accuracy, deficient in regard to the high-tech future. In the year 2013, one jokester summed it up like this: "It's 2013 scientists. Why do I still not have a laser sight on my penis?" (SkyWarpIsBetterThanStarScream). Whereas mere mortals may yearn for such enhancements, according to the secret lore of the Internet, certain superhuman icons may already be living this science fiction dream: "Chuck Norris has a Predator-style triple laser sight on his penis" (Chorris). Such jokes indicate how the regime of red dot sight fashions the laser scope not simply as an optical assist but as a prosthesis, a supplement to normal marksmanship that extends the body into the domain of speculative media as such.

For example, in 1988 the British company Imatronic released the LS45 Laser Aiming System on a wave of exuberant claims: "Tomorrow's sights … for today's handguns," offering the allure of "space age solutions to handgun aiming problems" (Milek). Since then, the appearance of the Imatronic LS45 in a variety of science fiction films—including *Terminator 2: Judgment Day* (1991), *Predator 2* (1990), *District 9* (2009), *Leprechaun 4: In Space* (1997), and *Universal Soldier* (1992)—has perpetuated the idea that this weapon upgrade puts users in touch with the future, redressing their "aiming problems" with "space age solutions." These films each suggest the increasing obsolescence of the human body under the regime of red dot sight. In *Universal Soldier*, for example, the resurrected supersoldier Luc Deveraux (played by Jean-Claude Van Damme), his cyborg hardware overheating, strips nude at a cheap motel just as a squad of other supersoldiers armed with LS45 laser-sighted weapons arrives to take him out. Moments later, recovered from his overheating, Deveraux hides in the same bed with a naked couple as another supersoldier enters the motel room, the red dot of his LS45 playing back and forth across their foreheads. The caress of the red dot, threatening instant death even as its passage means a reprieve, a little more life to come, maps this zone of trouble: a scene of copulation, conjuction, that is less about the juxtaposed bodies of the heterosexual couple than about the intercession of the cyborg supersoldier between them, desire interrupted by high-tech hardware. It allegorizes the way in which red dot sight invades even the most private spaces, the fantasy of the perfect shot to come retracing a militarization of flesh that has already occurred—the cyborg already hiding in the bed. It represents a condition of almost-thereness, endlessly deferred yet already here.

★ ★ ★

Red dot sight establishes the conditions by which a specific future might be precisely enacted: a kill. But at the same time, it remains open to the possibility of the kill not taking place, the residue of uncertainty accounting not only for the shooter's skill and other material variables (a misfire, a bad angle, an unexpected dust storm) but also for the fact that the target is likewise an agent in the system and participating in the calculus of risk, albeit from the other side.

Consider the film *Phone Booth* (2002), an 80-minute captivity narrative that unfolds in real time. The setting is the eponymous glass phone booth, one of only two that Verizon still owned at the time of filming. Stuart Shepard, a self-absorbed New York publicist played by Colin Farrell, is held hostage by an unseen sniper. We are meant to understand "Stu" from the start as a dubious character in need of some moral correction. Stu has sought out the phone booth in order to court a potential mistress, but is first interrupted by a pizza delivery man whom he quite sharply dismisses, before proceeding with the call that he has apparently been repeating daily, in the same booth. After his unsuccessful appeal for a date, the phone rings, he answers, and discovers almost immediately that the caller can see him and has been surveilling his calls (his surprise at which is almost as retro as the phone booth itself). The drama escalates when the mysterious caller announces that he has Stu in his sights, specifically in the telescopic sight of "a .30 caliber bolt action 700 with a Carbon 1 modification and a state-of-the-art handheld tactical scope," which is shortly confirmed with the sound of the rifle cocking. Just before he perceives the red dot on his chest, Stu is asked to sense the target: "Can you feel it?" the caller asks, "The heat of it?" "It," the red dot, signifies a threat that may not be realized. "You're doing so much better than the others," the caller tells him, referring to two previous victims, a pedophile and an inside trader, who failed to "come clean" or "make amends" and were therefore shot. The caller insists that the targets were somehow responsible for their own situation, their sitedness in the sights. This is the seemingly psychotic logic of the sniper as moral vigilante. Yet it is also an incisive emplotment of red dot sight, which collapses the distance between target and shooter as if they were virtually one and the same. All targets are made responsible for their own targeting; all shooters are now also targets. "Take a look at where I'm going," the caller says, and Stu looks at his chest to follow the movement of the red dot, to see and implicate himself as target.

In a pivotal moment, Stu is assailed by a pimp seeking to defend two women who work for him and had wanted the phone. The battle becomes triangulated: Stu is desperately pleading for his own release from the caller while at the same time pleading with the pimp to leave him alone in the booth. "Do you need help?" the caller asks in one moment and then, after the pimp has picked up a baseball bat and marches back toward the booth, demands, "Get rid of him!" We cut to a long shot of the pimp seen through a simulated reflex sight, as if the weapon and camera had fused, and hear the sound of the cocked rifle. The film then shifts to slow motion as the pimp begins his countdown to an assault. Stu sees to his horror the red dot clearly projected onto the pimp's white t-shirt—which is to say, he inhabits the perspective of red dot sight—and begins in that instant to regard not only his own safety but also the safety of others.

Stu seems to acknowledge responsibility, as if he were capitulating to the caller's insistence that this entire situation is Stu's own fault, that Stu—even though he is the primary target—is paradoxically his own sniper, and also responsible for looping the second man into the targeting circuit. The question of his culpability is introduced when the caller offers to shoot the pimp: "I can make him stop, just say the word." "Can you hear me?" he goes on to demand, to which Stu replies, "yes." Then: "What?" "Yes!" This moment of targeting is rife with hesitation (will Stu redirect the line of sight to himself? will the sniper pull the trigger?) and uncertainty, but it culminates in fulfillment: the sniper does indeed fire.[6] The sense of temporal foreshortening here—the pimp dies before he even sees the danger, before any onlookers realize that he had been targeted—certifies the ongoing deferral of Stu's own assassination as a structure of indebtedness, as if Stu were living on borrowed time.

Phone Booth reinforces the lethal certainty of red dot sight even while highlighting its conditionality, attesting to the way in which the dot re-dimensionalizes the scene of risk. There is no time, no space to flee. Stu is pinned down, his physical world reduced to the confines of the phone booth. Yet he is virtually linked to the unseen shooter: the red dot and the telephone line plot an axis between them, a radius of the zone of trouble. Along this line, the subject and object of targeting converge with surprising intimacy. As the dot plays over Stu's body, the caller goads him, "Come now, Stu, you can feel it." Locked in a circuit of recognition, Stu is made to believe that he has, in effect, made himself a target, that he has targeted himself because of his bad behavior (a literal character assassination), and the sniper at the other end of the red dot is merely the belated fulfillment, suturing the past and future together in the discrete red node on Stu's chest. To be sure, the actual identity of the sniper remains absolutely unknown: the threat is incorporated and then neutralized through the discovery of the body of the pizza delivery man left holding the gun, while the "real" sniper walks away from the scene, letting Stu know that he is still out there, still watching. The film thus ends with Stu continuing to see himself through the perspective of red dot sight, still potentially in the circuit of sniper and target. Which is to say, Stu complies—even though he is no longer directly under the gun.

When the red dot appears, the future contracts into absolute immediacy. After all, by the time you see that you are a target, you are as good as dead. It is a common joke in sniper media, of course. For example, in one iteration of the "Most Interesting Man in the World" online meme—based on the Dos Equis beer advertising campaign—the Interesting Man notes, "I don't always notice the sniper, but when I do it's too la—" (Figure 17.2). He cannot even complete the sentence, because the red dot means that time is up. Yet somehow, in this exact instant, he recognizes his own misrecognition as a pattern ("I don't always notice … but when I do …"). Indeed, this little joke reflexively shows how a crimson mote of light now signifies a fatal collapse of temporal

Figure 17.2 Anon, image macro created at I Can Has Cheezburger?, posted at Joy Reactor, 30 March 2010, http://joyreactor.com/post/567342

order—an imminent shot that may have already fired—precisely because its media repetition has given it this meaning. Red dot sight is therefore nothing merely technological, bound to the hardware. It describes a way of seeing that perceives precision targeting everywhere, prospectively and retroactively, even in situations where there is no gun at all.

This aspect of red dot sight is underscored in the final episode of the television drama *Breaking Bad* (2008–2013). Walter White, the notorious chemistry teacher-turned-crystal meth kingpin, has lost his drug empire. Knowing his own death to be imminent, he devises a plan to leave his remaining ill-gotten fortune to his son. He breaks into the house of his former colleagues Gretchen and Elliot and advises them of his scheme:

> On my son's eighteenth birthday, which is ten months and two days from today, you will give him this money in the form of an irrevocable trust. You will tell him that it is his to do with as he sees fit, but with the hope that he uses it for his college education and the betterment of his family.

To secure this arrangement, Walter draws attention to two red dots that have suddenly appeared on Gretchen and Elliot's chests. He says,

> Don't move. Don't, don't dare move a muscle, you don't want them to think that you're trying to get away. Just breathe. Just this afternoon I had an extra $200,000 … I gave it to the two best hitmen west of the Mississippi. Now, whatever happens to me tomorrow, they'll still be out there, keeping tabs. And if for any reason that my children do not get this money, a kind of countdown will begin. Maybe a day or so later. A week. A year. When you're going for a walk in Santa Fe or Manhattan or Prague, wherever. And you're talking about your stock prices without a worry in the world. And then, suddenly, you'll hear the scrape of a footstep behind you, but before you can even turn around—pop!
>
> ("Felina")

The scene is about securing compliance but also a kind of investment strategy—made crystal clear by Walter's reference to stock prices—which aims to control a speculative globality ("Sante Fe or Manhattan or Prague, wherever") through the rhetoric of prolepsis ("before you can even turn around—pop!"). The inculcation of red dot sight is a way of locking the future into place, pinning it to the once-and-future dot. It persists, in perpetuity. Yet Walter has not, in fact, hired the "two best hitmen west the Mississippi" to keep tabs for the rest of eternity, monitoring a perennial debt. This, it turns out, is a lie. Instead, Walter has provided his goofy stoner buddies Badger and Skinny Pete with simple office laser pointers, tools of corporate life that exactly reproduce the media regime of red dot sight—no bullets required. So we see that, if red dot sight relies on an *instantaneous* recognition of the sociotechnical meanings of the dot—the indexical, metonymic, and metaphorical aspects—it propagates without verification or substantiation as a *persistent* re-dimensionalization of the risk landscape, the zone of trouble, that leaves no room for discernment or reflection ("but when I do it's too la—").

For example, in one episode of the cartoon series *Family Guy*, the buffoonish protagonist Peter Griffin tackles a Hindu man after seeing his tilak: "Look out! Oh, I thought that dot on your head was from a sniper rifle." Peter does not perceive himself as the target of red dot sight, but he misidentifies himself in relation to it (Figure 17.3). Seeing the red dot, he reacts without hesitation; it may already be too late, but he tries to preempt the bullet. Of course, the narrative frame provides television viewers ironic distance: we know that Peter misrecognizes the tilak for a laser-scope beam, and we know that, had he paused and observed instead of springing to action, he would have discovered the threat was no threat. The same ironic distance then allows further meanings to become clear: a white man assaults a brown man due to a misunderstanding of religious practice; Peter injures the Hindu man while playing hero, saving him from a danger that is only in Peter's mind; the logic of preemption inadvertently leads to an actual violent act by trying to prevent an imaginary one; and so forth. And yet, even with ironic distance (knowing that Peter doesn't know), we only get the joke if we have already recognized the structure of red dot sight. Moreover, getting the joke may distract us from actual risk, a point emphasized by a deleted scene from that same episode: a follow-up joke, another turn of the ironic screw, in which the Hindu man comes back to Peter later with a bleeding hole in his head, announcing, "You were right!" before falling down dead. This deleted scene, which must be considered something of an alternate history in the world of *Family Guy* (a show that nevertheless abounds in contradictory narrative twists and canon-resistant cutaways), reinforces the sense that red dot sight necessarily compels a *virtual certainty* even within the domain of uncertainty, preemptively justifying action even when the nature of the risk is unrecognizable. Just because we didn't see the sniper, doesn't mean he wasn't there.[7] At least, this is how it seems under the purview of red dot sight.

Is it satire, or straight-up realism? On a Sunday evening in June 2000, a uniformed patrol officer responding to a call of "unknown trouble" in an apartment complex located in the Watts

Figure 17.3 "The Father, the Son, and the Holy Fonz," *Family Guy*, 2005

neighborhood of Los Angeles reportedly "observed a laser light targeted at his upper torso" (LAPD). The Los Angeles Police Department press release about this incident, which notes the address but not the neighborhood, implicitly invokes a racialized imaginary of risk to explain an encounter between a 26-year-old officer on the street and a "shadow of a figure at the window behind the laser light." The officer's purported "[fear] that he was being targeted" prompted him to shoot preemptively at the figure in the window: a security decision that enacted a particular risk calculus, the virtual certainty inherent to red dot sight.[8] But this was a scene of misrecognition, once again, another iteration of "I thought I saw": the presumed sniper revealed himself to be an unarmed juvenile who had been using a laser pointer in a mimetic performance of targeting. The red dot had been misinterpreted precisely as anticipated, its meanings predetermined—indeed, overdetermined. To see the dot is to recognize that a target has been acquired, even when it is simulacral. Under the regime of red dot sight, snipers are not anywhere, because they are everywhere.

★ ★ ★

Preemptive, proleptic, and overdetermined, the semiotic status of the dot seems quite secure—it presents itself as secure. It belongs to a closed circuit in that one knows what is to come. But red dot sight seems to offer a more static version of the future than is actually possible. That is, its anticipatory logic suggests a circuit that contains a temporal lag, an interval, in which the promise of attachment may be broken. The red dot may point, as it were, to something that is never to come. It contains the promise of attachment—the completion of the circuit, the firing of the shot—but we can always find slippages or misfires in the interval, in the moment of recognition, the terrain of the exploit.

The 2008 film *Wanted*, for instance, frenetically thematizes the potential to interrupt red dot sight. *Wanted* is manifestly concerned with targeting—and especially the figuration of targeting as a promissory contract—even in its very title. The narrative concerns a secret fraternity of assassins given kill assignments that have been encoded into fabric by a "loom of fate"; these are contractual "orders that must be executed." Wesley (played by James McAvoy) is a newbie assassin-in-training. As the supposed target of a rogue fraternity member said to have killed his father, Wesley is brought into the fold and trained to intercept the bullet that is coming for him. There is a familiar aspect to the story of an ordinary if somewhat abject guy who needs to be taught to discover his latent inner reserves—in this instance, to redirect his superhuman sensory perception so as to transcend the physical laws of time and space, to both evade and curve the trajectory of bullets. In its opening scene, the red dot is projected on top of a woman's bindi (recalling the conflicted semiotic registers of *Family Guy*); Mr. X sees the dot, but before he can fully complete the warning, "Get down!," she has been assassinated. It establishes the familiar zone of trouble, with all its temporal foreshortening. But the rest of the film is about the subversion, the denaturalization of red dot sight through the renovation of perception and the remediation of the body. As a member of the fraternity says at the start of his training, "I'm the repair man." Wesley asks, "What do you repair?" The answer is profound: "A lifetime of bad habits." Wesley's eventual ability to reroute the bullet and elude red dot sight is figured in terms of speculative fantasy, an impossible skill rendered plausible by the magic of special effects. But the capacity of potential targets to thwart or even seize the apprehensive force of the red dot, to turn its proleptic grammar back on itself, nevertheless inspires actual practices of circumvention—attempts to resist compliance—in contemporary zones of trouble.

For example, a tactical art project by Michael Naimark enacts a practice we might call counter-targeting (cf. Raley). Way back in 2002, Naimark was one of a small but growing number of art-activists working to draw public attention to what we can retrospectively understand to be a radical transformation in surveillance practices and technologies, as cameras became ever more ubiquitous and surveillance took different medial forms. With a nod to *Star Wars*, Naimark expressed concern with the "dark side" of these technological developments, the threat to privacy, and the emergence of a brave new world of lateral surveillance. His response was a project he called "camera zapping," which is both "robust metaphor" and actual technique. In his reflexive account of the formation of his research questions and subsequent development of an "anti-tool," he describes his discovery of the means by which one can repurpose, appropriate, or otherwise hack a laser pointer such that it can be used to interrupt the operation of a camera: "The results were striking. The tiny beam neutralized regions of the camera sensor far larger than the actual size of the beam. Properly aimed, it could block a far-away camera from seeing anything inside of a large window." In other words, "zap!"—a camera can be instantly, albeit temporarily, countervailed. On the basis of this discovery, mined from the "gold vein" of military literature, Naimark assembled a set of prototypes for tactical tools and tested the effects of different classes of lasers on cameras at distances up to 200 meters. He ended with a "rather serious" zapper comprised of a rifle scope, laser gun sight, and tripod, as well as a small, handheld device, in the event that "one wanted to scare away a news cameraperson": an elegant weapon for a more civilized age. His artist statement offers photographic documentation of failed photography (the potential frustration of a voyeur or policing agent) and gestures toward the project's more expansive purpose, namely, to imagine how one might circumvent or evade the targeting process and opt out of surveillance regimes. "One role of the artist in the contemporary world," he explained to the *New York Times*, "is to hold a mirror up to society ... and the artistic angle is in exposing and revealing and provoking things" (quoted in Markoff).

Performing exactly this function of critical speculum, the *Armored Dove of Peace*, an intervention attributed to the provocateur, guerrilla artist, and social critic Banksy, offers an altered perspective on the regime of red dot sight (Figure 17.4). Situated on the wall of the Palestinian Heritage Center in Bethlehem, it was originally claimed as part of Banksy's seasonal fund-raising exhibition, Santa's Ghetto. The artist moved the show from London to Palestine in December 2007 to help revitalize the area, which had seen a decline in tourism after construction began on the West Bank barrier

Figure 17.4 Banksy, *Armored Dove of Peace*, 2007
Source: Google Earth screen capture

wall. Communicating through representatives, he asserted at the time, "It would do good if more people came to see the situation here for themselves. If it is safe enough for a bunch of sissy artists then it's safe enough for anyone" (Frenkel). One of a series of stencil works sprayed on or near the wall, the *Armored Dove of Peace* is now one of the highlights of an unofficial Banksy Bethlehem art walk, which also includes his *Walled Off* hotel. The dove holds a green olive branch, after Pablo Picasso's *Dove of Peace*, and is—in the style of many of the anonymous artist's graffiti works—subtly but deeply biting. Wearing something like a flak jacket (the "armor" of the title), the dove is stationed unambiguously in the sights, its breast targeted by crosshairs and a red dot, a speculative line of fire that could be traced back across Manger Street to an approximate origin—a watchtower on the barrier wall.

How are we to regard this deployment of red dot sight? In this context, facing this wall, the indexical function of red dot sight is perhaps superfluous. We need no additional reminder of the structure of militarization and securitization that informs the red dot, its conditions of possibility. But we need also to take account of the armored vest, which the dove wears as if it, too, were aware of the security apparatus, apprehensive of the possibility of indiscriminate targeting and needing preemptively to guard itself against the possibility that snipers might take a shot.

The dove itself—or is it the artwork?—is positioned as a target. Indeed, the surface was "riddled with bullet holes" at the time the mural was painted, some of which have now been covered over with posters (Harrison). "Peace," then, as instantiated in the figure of the dove, is always under threat, threatened by its perception of itself as a target. What hope for peace if the dove needs to wear a protective vest? It is embedded from the outset in the very conflict from which it seemingly tries to escape. It matters not at all if the armored dove of peace reinforces or subverts the structure of red dot sight, because by the time it flies, aiming for an impossible future—peace as the target, wanted and in our sights—well, it is already too late....

Notes

1 On the role of science fiction in the discourse of laser weapons, see Fanning; Haley; Hecht; Slayton. On connections between science fiction and military technologies more generally, see Dedman; Franklin; Gannon; Gray; Milburn. One striking aspect of the early market for laser gun sights in the U.S. is that it included not only military and police customers but also survivalists. The Laser Products company, for example, advertised in survivalist publications and reinforced the survivalist anticipation of apocalyptic futures (Vartabedian).
2 On the history of military perception and the weaponizing of vision, see Bousquet; Crandall; Kaplan, *Arial Aftermaths*; Lenoir and Caldwell; Stahl; Terry and Kelly; Thornton; Virilio.
3 On the social construction of high-tech targeting and the rhetoric of speed, precision, and surgical strikes, see Chow; Cooper; Kaplan, "Precision Targets"; Phillips; Scarry; Slayton.
4 The Swedish company Aimpoint claims to be the "originator of the red dot sight." The letter "o" in their brand logo is even punctured by a red dot. In 1975, the company released the Aimpoint® Electronic reflexive sight, advertising it with campaigns focused on hunting. Today, Aimpoint promotes its red dot sights as sleek devices laden with a long history of scientific expertise: "We've done the science. You pull the trigger" (Aimpoint).
5 The zone of trouble conjured by red dot sight is one example of the displacement of temporal uncertainty (what does the future hold?) onto spatial management; see Aradau and van Munster, "The Time/Space of Preparedness." Such displacements have intensified over the last 40 years. "Precautionary risk" has now become a dominant spatializing logic of governmentality and securitization, especially after 9/11; see Aradau and van Munster, "Governing Terrorism Through Risk."
6 There are other aspects of uncertainty (was "yes!" a performative or an answer to the question?) and responsibility (the caller implicates Stu in the assassination by retroactively converting his assertion into a command: "you oughta be more careful with what you say").
7 On the ways in which snipers and sniper media cultivate paranoid forms of perception, see Shell.
8 On preemptive security practices as performative exercises in "routinizing the imagination," see de Goede et al; Thomas.

Works Cited

2A4Life. "3–9x40 Illuminated Tactical Scope with Red Laser & Holographic Dot Sight." 2A4Life, 2019, https://2a4life.com/products/illuminated-3-9x40-scope.
Aimpoint. "The Originator of the Red Dot Sight" [promo video]. Aimpoint website, June 6, 2016, https://us.aimpoint.com/about/the-company/originator/.
Aradau, Claudia and Rens van Munster. "Governing Terrorism Through Risk: Taking Precautions, (un) Knowing the Future." *European Journal of International Relations*, vol. 13, no. 1, 2007, pp. 89–115.
Aradau, Claudia and Rens van Munster. "The Time/Space of Preparedness: Anticipating the 'Next Terrorist Attack'." *Space and Culture*, vol. 15, no. 2, March 2012, pp. 98–109.
"Army Starts Testing 'Judge Dredd' Weapon." *Fox News*, May 29, 2009, www.foxnews.com/story/2009/05/29/army-starts-testing-judge-dredd-weapon.html.
Baldwin, Hanson. "Laser and Silent Plane Tested for Army of Future." *New York Times*, October 17, 1967, p. 4.
Beason, Doug. *The E-Bomb: How America's New Directed Energy Weapons Will Change the Way Future Wars Will Be Fought*. Da Capo Press, 2005.
Bousquet, Antoine. *The Eye of War: Military Perception from the Telescope to the Drone*. U of Minnesota P, 2018.
"The Buck Rogers Gun." *Newsweek*, July 1977, p. 56.
Cantrell, Jeremy. "Field Test: Mini Red Dot Sights for Concealed Carry." *Guns & Ammo*, December 10, 2014, www.gunsandammo.com/editorial/mini-red-dot-sights-concealed-carry/249531.
Chow, Rey. *The Age of the World Target*. Duke UP, 2006.
Chorris, Nuck. "Chuck Norris Fact/Joke No. 7006." *Chuck Norris Facts*, April 23, 2013, http://chucknorrism.com/chuck-norris-fact/7006.
Cooper, Melinda. *Life as Surplus: Biotechnology and Capitalism in the Neoliberal Era*. U of Washington P, 2008.
Crandall, Jordan. "Armed Vision." *Multitudes*, no. 15, 2004, www.multitudes.net/Armed-Vision/.
Dedman, Stephen. *May the Armed Forces Be with You: The Relationship between Science Fiction and the United States Military*. McFarland, 2016.
de Goede, Marieke, Stephanie Simon, and Marijn Hoijtink. "Performing Preemption." *Security Dialogue*, vol. 45, no. 5, 2014, pp. 411–422.

Fanning, William J., Jr. *Death Rays and the Popular Media, 1876-1939: A Study of Directed Energy Weapons in Fact, Fiction and Film*. McFarland, 2015.

"The Father, the Son, and the Holy Fonz." *Family Guy*, season 4, episode 18. Written by Danny Smith, directed by James Purdum. Fuzzy Door Productions and 20th Century Fox, 2005. In *Family Guy: Volume Four* (3-DVD set), 20th Century Fox Home Entertainment, 2006.

"Felina." *Breaking Bad*, season 5, episode 16. Written and directed by Vince Gilligan. High Bridge, Gran Via, and Sony Pictures Television, 2013. In *Breaking Bad: The Complete Series* (16 Blu-ray disc set), Sony Pictures Home Entertainment, 2014.

Franklin, H. Bruce. *War Stars: The Superweapon and the American Imagination*. Oxford UP, 1988.

Freedman, David H. "The Light Brigade." *Technology Review*, vol. 104, no. 6, July/August 2001, pp. 56–63.

Frenkel, Sheera Claire. "Let Us Spray: Banksy Hits Bethlehem." *The Times Online*, December 3, 2007, https://web.archive.org/web/20081013212221/www.timesonline.co.uk/tol/news/world/middle_east/article2988367.ece.

Gannon, Charles E. *Rumors of War and Infernal Machines: Technomilitary Agenda-Setting in American and British Speculative Fiction*. 2nd edition. Rowman and Littlefield, 2005.

Gibson, William. *Neuromancer*. 1984. Penguin, 2016.

Gray, Chris Hables. "'There Will Be War!': Future War Fantasies and Militaristic Science Fiction in the 1980s." *Science-Fiction Studies*, vol. 64, no. 3, 1994, pp. 315–336.

"Green Berets Will Receive Judge Dredd Computer Smart-Rifle." *Special Force*, May 9, 2019, https://web.archive.org/web/20110827175934/http://specialforce.info/302/green-berets-will-receive-judge-dredd-computer-smart-rifle/.

Grusin, Richard. *Premediation: Affect and Mediality After 9/11*. Palgrave Macmillan, 2010.

Haley, Christopher. "Science Fiction and the Making of the Laser." *Science Fiction and Organization*, edited by Martin Parker, Matthew Higgins, Geoff Lightfoot, and Warren Smith. Routledge, 2001, pp. 31–39.

Harrison, Rebecca. "Graffiti Artist Banksy Goes to the Holy Land." *Reuters*, December 3, 2007, https://uk.reuters.com/article/uk-palestinians-banksy/graffiti-artist-banksy-goes-to-the-holy-land-idUKL0233047720071203.

Hecht, Jeff. *Lasers, Death Rays, and the Long, Strange Quest for the Ultimate Weapon*. Prometheus Books, 2019.

Johnston, John. "Machinic Vision." *Critical Inquiry*, vol. 26, no. 1, Autumn 1999, pp. 27–48.

Kaplan, Caren. *Aerial Aftermaths: Wartime from Above*. Duke UP, 2018.

Kaplan, Caren. "Precision Targets: GPS and the Militarization of U.S. Consumer Identity." *American Quarterly*, vol. 58, no. 3, September 2006, pp. 693–714.

"Lasers to Be Tested by Transit Police." *New York Times*, January 6, 1995, p. B3.

Lenoir, Tim and Luke Caldwell. *The Military-Entertainment Complex*. Harvard UP, 2018.

Los Angeles Police Department. "Improper Use of Laser Pointer Results in an Arrest." LAPD Press Release, June 19, 2000, www.lapdonline.org/june_2000/news_view/29028.

Markoff, John. "Protesting the Big Brother Lens, Little Brother Turns an Eye Blind." *New York Times*, October 7, 2002, www.nytimes.com/2002/10/07/business/protesting-the-big-brother-lens-little-brother-turns-an-eye-blind.html.

Marsh, Thomas O. "Revolutionary, Laser-Sighted .22 Rifle Can Literally Put Criminals on the Spot." *Science Digest* 85, May 1979, 8–12, 67.

McAulay, Alastair D. *Military Laser Technology for Defense: Technology for Revolutionizing 21st Century Warfare*. Wiley, 2011.

McCall, Jack H., Jr. "Blinded by the Light: International Law and the Legality of Anti-Optic Laser Weapons." *Cornell International Law Journal*, vol. 30, no. 1, 1997, https://scholarship.law.cornell.edu/cilj/vol30/iss1/1.

Meth, Sheldon Z. "Disruptive High-Energy Laser Technology." *DARPATech 2005*, August 9–11, 2005, pp. 191–193, https://web.archive.org/web/20070412152429/www.darpa.mil/DARPAtech2005/presentations/tto/meth.pdf.

Milburn, Colin. *Mondo Nano: Fun and Games in the World of Digital Matter*. Duke UP, 2015.

Milek, Bob. "Tomorrow's Sights … for Today's Handguns." *Guns & Ammo*, February 1989, pp. 37–41.

Nail, Thomas. "Biopower and Control." *Between Deleuze and Foucault*, edited by Nicolae Morar, Thomas Nail, and Daniel W. Smith. Edinburgh UP 2016, pp. 247–263.

Naimark, Michael. "How to ZAP a Camera: Using Lasers to Temporarily Neutralize Camera Sensors." *Michael Naimark*, October 2, 2002, www.naimark.net/projects/zap/howto.html.

Parks, Lisa and Caren Kaplan, eds. *Life in the Age of Drone Warfare*. Duke UP, 2017.

Phillips, Amanda. "Shooting to Kill: Headshots, Twitch Reflexes and the Mechropolitics of Video Games." *Games and Culture*, vol. 13, no. 2, 2018, pp. 136–152.

Phone Booth. Directed by Joel Schumacher, performances by Colin Farrell and Kiefer Sutherland, 20th Century Fox, 2002.

Raley, Rita. *Tactical Media*. U of Minnesota P, 2009.

"Rifle With Laser Sight Attracting Wide Attention." *Los Angeles Times*, June 9, 1977, p. E12.

Scarry, Elaine. *Who Defended the Country?* Beacon Press, 2003.

Seidel, Robert W. "Glow to Flow: A History of Military Laser Research and Development." *Historical Studies in the Physical and Biological Sciences*, vol. 18, no. 1, 1987, pp. 111–147.

Shaw, Ian G.R. *Predator Empire: Drone Warfare and Full Spectrum Dominance*. U of Minnesota P, 2016.

Shell, Hanna Rose. *Hide and Seek: Camouflage, Photography, and the Media of Reconnaissance*. Zone Books, 2012.

Singer, P.W. *Wired for War: The Robotics Revolution and Conflict in the 21st Century*. Penguin, 2009.

SkyWarpIsBetterThanStarScream. "It's 2013 Scientists." *Imgur*, February 23, 2013, https://imgur.com/gallery/FTUKBvs.

Slayton, Rebecca. "From Death Rays to Light Sabers: Making Laser Weapons Surgically Precise." *Technology and Culture*, vol. 52, no. 1, January 2011, pp. 45–74.

Stahl, Roger. *Through the Crosshairs: War, Visual Culture, and the Weaponized Gaze*. Rutgers UP, 2018.

Terry, Jennifer and Raegan Kelly. "Killer Entertainments." *Vectors*, vol. 3, no. 1, Fall 2007, http://vectors.usc.edu/issues/5/killerentertainments.

Thomas, Lindsay. "Forms of Duration: Preparedness, the Mars Trilogy, and the Management of Climate Change." *American Literature*, vol. 88, no. 1, 2016, pp. 159–184.

Thornton, Pip. "The Meaning of Light: Seeing and Being on the Battlefield." *Cultural Geographies*, vol. 22, no. 4, 2015, pp. 567–583.

Universal Soldier. Directed by Roland Emmerich, written by Richard Rothstein, Christopher Leitch, and Dean Devlin. TriStar Pictures, 1992.

Vartabedian, Ralph. "Firm Setting High Sales Targets With Its Laser Gun Sight." *Los Angeles Times*, December 29, 1982, pp. OC_CA–B.

Virilio, Paul. *War and Cinema: The Logistics of Perception*. Verso, 1989.

Wanted. Directed by Timur Bekmambetov, written by Michael Brandt, Derek Haas, and Chris Morgan. Universal Pictures, 2008.

Wark, Mckenzie. *Gamer Theory*. Harvard UP, 2007.

Weber, Samuel. *Targets of Opportunity*. Fordham UP, 2005.

Žižek, Slavoj. *The Fragile Absolute*. Verso, 2000.

Zohuri, Bahman. *Directed Energy Weapons: Physics of High Energy Lasers (HEL)*. Springer, 2016.

18

THE SAFETY

Jordan Crandall

In "The Safety," Jordan Crandall speculates a future where a universal algorithmic culture regulates all human perception and cognition, behavior and action. Crandall presents a sci-fi scenario in which the automotive industry works in tandem with authoritarian civic institutions to integrate humans more fully into mobile machines. At a point when self-driving cars are imminent, the story invites readers to consider what its blueprints for "intelligent transit" mean for individual freedoms. The algorithmic calculus turns discrete aberrations and accidents into probable error patterns, which then calls for management through a regime of punishments and rewards. The ultimate goal is "safety," which drives the new control systems: the realignment of roads and cars, protocols and signals becomes lucrative business. Despite the dystopian risk scenario, Crandall places the corporeal, capricious, all-too-singular human body at the center of the story, a body whose motions, rhythms, and instincts scuttle the will to security.

★ ★ ★

1

Upon the narrow median strip formed at the interstice of two converging avenues, those crossing on foot have stopped to gather their wits, enjoy a brief respite on the island sanctuary before completing the agonizing scramble across the ten-lane stretch. We are *in median res*, entering the scene atop one of those midpoint stations experienced only by those who have the courage to hoof it—way stations that, in their absolute inclination toward departure, wholly neglect their preamble, excise their intake as the scope of attention leans on.

An entrant steps forth, her patience strained to the limit by the grueling wait. She, like many others who have come before, bolts across the stadium-wide stretch in a desperate attempt to make it before the light turns green and the great idling phalanx of automobiles rolls on.

Alas, it is not to be: the signal has changed midway and the driver of the DS sedan stationed before her now finds himself face to face with the luckless woman as she gapes at the waiting traffic mid-stride, caught in the throes of that perilous moment where options are narrowed, limits are amplified, and action is suspended so extensively as to be stopped, right there and then, in time: a stilled zone which he, this particular driver, has now been hailed, summoned out of the void to remain here, engine running, not yet in gear.

Those drivers on either side inch forward impatiently, riding the brakes. One of them advances into the crosswalk as if to taunt the poor woman. Her defenselessness has, in him, summoned the disproportionate. She is like a vulnerability so exposed that it arouses cruelty, a love that its declaring arouses scorn.

The crossing interlocks the disparities of intensive and extensive maneuver. The broadening of a margin introduces pressure. The overlap of signal timing, geared to permit safe passage through, can heighten the risk it is designed to outdo. Those at the curbside, pushed to the limit by the arduous wait, make a run for it; those behind the wheel, hoping to avoid a punishing delay, barrel through. The interlocking means of permission and constraint are machines you need to fine-tune. They are not merely what transport requires but the very ground on which it moves. The culture of the intersection resides within the dynamic, takes shape in the world of the risk.

Will it be there even when signals disappear? Vehicles slipping through the gaps in the cross-flows. Choreographies unnoticed within the overlaps. The steadiness of the course overriding the bound.

The driver of the DS sedan thinks about this for a while as he continues down the boulevard, turns down the access road and enters the onramp.

2

Along the state highway that passes beneath the interchange, circumvents the office park and ends, uneventfully, at the shopping district of old, lies the entrance of the Automotive Institute, a cavernous complex whose looming concrete supports, sloped floors and stone walls disclose its history as an underground parking garage.

Now that the facility has been repurposed as a research center, the structural features that once plagued it no longer seem to matter. The precipitously declining ramps, which once induced rapid shifts in momentum, are no longer used by cavalcades of circulating cars. The floor slab differentials, whose lack of transitioning led to the dreaded bottoming-out effect, where the front and rear wheels straddled the junction, producing drop, no longer hinder turnover efficiency. The inaccessible walkways, which once caused pedestrians to lumber along steep ramps intended solely for vehicles, often in search of their automobiles, which, due to the obscure organizational scheme, were often impossible to find, no longer pose ambulatory difficulty now that a battalion of mobility pods supplies the sole means of passage.

The only remaining pitfalls are the substandard acoustics, which are conducive to echo, and the unsteadying effect exerted by the floor slope, which can destabilize the footing and cause smooth objects to slide.

Compensatory actions have been taken in the primary meeting areas to counteract these effects. In the principal conference room for the Automotive Intelligence division, two massive steel forms have been installed on the end walls to provide visual and proprioceptive counterweights, arranged so as to lend the illusion of balance, thereby offsetting the destabilizing effect on the vestibular system otherwise exerted.

An embedded display panel stretched across the long wall offers a simulated vista, a ten-minute loop of sunrise and sunset over the metropolis from a high-level perspective, offering the illusion of dwelling high above the city in an observation tower rather than underground. The mid-city interchange looms front and center, its intricate network of sweeping bridges lent the tenor of the gothic. At sundown, when a golden mist bathes the freeways in a preternatural glow, the land below is transformed into something oceanic and uncanny, generating a slow, undulating lilt that heightens the effect it is designed to help alleviate, inducing a sense of roll along the axis of the floor slope.

The array of spotlights mounted above the conference table, as comprehensive as that of a theater, is arranged such that a single pinpoint beam falls upon each of the seats. It is intended to heighten the luminosity of each attendee, yet the harshness introduces a note of cruelty, lending each a dour look.

The leaders of the Consortium have assembled here to plan the media campaign, a series of news releases, promotional events, and public service advertisements geared to sway public opinion in favor of the planned Autocades. The most recent of these initiatives involves retrofitting a key section of the Crosstown, a corridor that stretches from the west side port to the eastern edge of the metropolitan region.

Such proposals, which restrict usage to autodriven vehicles alone, are understandably unpopular with those who still drive manually, a significant portion of the populace.

The exclusion is unavoidable if a complete synchronization of positions and speeds is to be achieved. All vehicles must be suitably equipped, able to interrelate and assemble into a cohesive system, engage in a choreography of actions attuned across distance and distinction.

It is understandable that manual drivers would find the prospect of giving up control unsettling, the Consortium realizes, given the modern sense of individuality that the vehicle has always been equated with. An ideology of self-determination that the automobile materializes in its very form. The symphony of aptitudes enabled by the machine is one they can no longer share, the realm of actionability no longer available to them, no longer reducible to any singular form at all. The ethic of an autonomous self imperiled, dissolved into a boundless sea.

The leaders of the Consortium understand the nature of the resistance and seek to counter it, transform it into something much more favorable. For them, there is no need for such a gloomy outlook—they see the developments of intelligent transit as wholly beneficial, empowering individuals to lead better lives, boosting valuable social qualities and enriching community bonds. Some recognize in the autocades an emerging form of empathy, the kind that comes into being through common procedures and rituals, customs shared among communities, recurrent programs and routines. Practices that have always been enabled by machines. Indeed there have been few practices in modern times more generative than driving: principles and techniques, instruments and imaginaries ingrained at the level of the body and all the way up, from the city itself to the larger symbolic horizon from which the whole experience of transit is drawn. The very means of conveyance, the capacity to move from place to place.

Of course there are going to be anomalies, the Consortium leaders allow. They are to be expected with any system of this level of complexity. Though they certainly have not made the task of convincing the public any easier. The manually-operating holdouts have been quick to seize on these incidents, blame them on software and systemic failing even as the Consortium's automotive and transport industry constituency—manufacturers, developers, engineers, researchers, entrepreneurs, investors, lobbyists, consultants and the like—have thoroughly revealed them, time and time again, to be the result of human error, the majority to these very same drivers fumbling with controls that they should not have to manage, controls that should be snatched from them entirely and integrated into the car itself.

Needless to say, these holdouts are not looked upon kindly. Indeed, while the Consortium is careful to project a benevolent front, the sentiment behind closed doors could hardly be less charitable to the organic operators with whom the machine is required to share the road, the fleshy counterparts with which the algorithms must reason if an efficient transport choreography is to be produced. The fact that the autodriven vehicle's primary objective is to avoid the heedless moves that these drivers tend to make—lurching into crosswalks, weaving in and out of lanes, cutting off pedestrians, barreling through intersections—makes the resistance all the more unbearable, especially when it results in accidents that could have easily been prevented.

The task of accommodating this mortal element is one that the logic of systems optimization is primed to reject. The body remains extricable from the machine, cognition from matter. If driving is to be posed as a problem, rendered addressable in ways that software can solve, then there is only one logical solution, only one possible course of action. It is the wild-eyed, paradoxical human at the helm that is to be shown the door: the indolent, drooling body perched at the wheel, capricious, fearful, and prone to distraction, easily riled by absurd, irrational needs, plagued by quizzical resentments and mindless delusions.

The only sensible way forward is algorithmic: logical operations unswayed by the vicissitudes of corporeal life.

A focus on safety issues has been deemed to have the best chance of success for the campaign, based on the assumption that, when push comes to shove, the reduction of injury and death is the concern that outweighs all others in the public mind. No one could dispute the priority of saving lives, especially when supported by data that is irrefutable, statistics that are inviolably clear.

The calculations have unequivocally demonstrated the benefits. They show how the reductions in risk will extend well beyond the highways themselves, benefitting every aspect of domestic and community life. There is no contesting the superiority of the response rates, which outperform the reaction time of even the most attentive human. Data pertaining to speed, position, heading, and environmental conditions shared, interpreted, cross-analyzed, and converted into action so fast that nearly any potential mishap can be evaded without consequence.

The advantages of massively distributed computation and control—from the interoperation implemented by control units for various internal subsystems to the larger urban coordinations actioned by traffic optimization agents—are so conclusive as to be absolute.

Indeed, they are so comprehensive as to be divine, as one of the founding members puts it, searching for the right media tagline:

They absolve the people. Save the people from themselves.

Selves, is repeated in the air.

Saviors! proclaims another of the senior members, a blunt equipment manufacturer who expresses his ideas in the style of a general, pummeling the listener in a series of sharp jabs.

Saviors—of the people!

The reverberation produced by the cavernous room, which can at times can introduce confusion as to who is actually speaking, no less the person being addressed, is conducive to expressions of a more direct nature, shorn of unnecessary appurtenance and put bluntly, often condensed into a brute imperative of some sort. As if they were geared for systemic efficiency, the circumvention of any ambiguity in the code. Much like the operator of a vessel might, under conditions where it might not be seen, honk its horn to boost its profile, clear up any ambiguity as to its whereabouts. The statements of the pummeling equipment manufacturer are an extreme case, his utterance functioning as artillery—communication by other means.

The executive next to him jumps in her seat whenever he speaks, as if he were firing a gun into the air.

Solved! adds the rotund head of a security firm, his hand protruding out the end of his arm brace like a claw.

The crisis of highway mortality—solved!

An industry analyst suggests that impermanence is the issue, not mortality; they can aim higher.

Her noble sentiment assumes an air of menace. Under the harsh glare of the pinpoint lights, even the most delicate assumes a monstrous overtone, the abrupt gesture cast in the tenor of the vengeful.

The only one spared is the Chair, whose monumental girth requires a sitting position much further back from the table, the overhead beam revealing no countenance save for, by means of the light bounce, the indirect semblance of a broad grin, its exceptional range and fixity suggesting an all-pervading enjoyment, a boundless and undifferentiated pleasure that is not meant for those around.

The effect is suggestive of an offscreen presence, the kind of atmospheric authority conveyed by those cinematic figures, obscured in a chiaroscuro of shadows, whose position outside the realm of visibility seems to heighten their influence, channel their authority into the vocal and increase it by means of the displacement. The inability to discern any expressive movement on the part of the Chair amplifies the effect; the use of a microphone makes the audio emanate from all corners of the room, generating some confusion as to the status of the voice that issues forth, whether it originates in the figure sitting there or whether it is even live.

What it proposes runs counter to the general sentiment:
They should not rely on logic, cannot rely on arguments if they hope to persuade.

The lack of a discernible echo lends the voice an otherworldly quality, as if it were somehow able to supersede the acoustic conditions of the room. As if the voice, rather than being projected not onto some unlikely counterpart in a ventriloquy of some sort, were instead being projected into a domain of articulation that had no visible agents whatsoever: an environmental realm whose voicing is no longer the privilege of any of the individuals assembled in the room but instead, a stratum from which they drew.

They should not equate safety with a banal sense of protection, an elementary barrier against danger, a buttress against an unruly and threatening exterior. Safety is not a shield. Protective measures should be generative of a proper engagement with the real.

The Chair's enormous presence at the lower end of the table seems to amplify the sense of tilt, as if at any moment the items on the surface might roll downward along the declivity. It stimulates an inherent sense of possessiveness, lends the sense that items in one's vicinity should be clutched. The fact that no one has ever witnessed the Chair out of the seat engenders a sense of incipient dread, a keen awareness of the potential repercussions of any such attempt to rise—the remote possibility, should the move be carried out, of a fundamental destabilization of the room's balance, with those at the high end susceptible to a precipitous drop. Especially as the voice elevates in pitch, as it does now, its agency linked to theirs in a unified field of address:

Does not our sensorium vibrate with the very threat that our thoughts would compel us to deny? That dangerous and irresolute outside that in our fascination we draw near, only to pull away again, as if in the throes of a machine. An engine to be fired up and oriented properly, paced adeptly, fueled proportionately. Data is but fuel for a vehicle already in motion.

A drink cart bursts through the door, followed by a server at the helm. The cart reverberates along the concrete floor with a crackling sound, like the crunch and pop of driving over gravel. After pulling to a stop at the table's north end, the server unsheathes a pair of tongs, clicks the ends together twice, removes the ice bucket lid and makes a hairpin turn. She bends her knees demurely, as if conducting a curtsy, kicks her right foot forward and shoots her left arm skyward. She then jumps to the side, places her free hand over her eyes and jumps back.

Here, here, says the accountant, an enormous man whose cervical collar compresses his jowls upward like a corset, squeezing his eyes shut.

Here is echoed twice.

A software official swats his arms in the air as if having a panic attack, his leg brace clumping against the table bottom.

The sunset has completed its cycle on the panoramic display, the first light of dawn now breaking over the city. The duration of the sunrise is compressed to a much greater degree than that of the converse, as if it were merely there to provide continuity for it, afford the illusion of an uninterrupted cycle. The excising of the intervening period generates for some the sense of euphoria, as if the hours were flying by; for others, it intensifies the anguish of time's passing. The golden haze burns off the highways with dizzying rapidity as a tangerine radiance is cast across the surfaces of the room, revealing the traces of long forgotten impacts, the chronicles of presence inscribed in density and tone, mass and speed differential.

The ceiling corrosion glistens like a fresco.

The polyurethane coating on the conference table refracts the light.

The clock chimes the hour.

The Chair's motionless profile illuminates briefly as the oratory, omnipresent as a voiceover, continues:

There are forces to be met, intimacies to be gained. Inclinations to affirm, choreographies to ascertain. To mount a default barrier is to relinquish the pursuit, withdraw from the knowledge of what we are up against. Abstract it through some kind of mystification that lets us off the hook.

Defer the transcendence that could have been ours to engage, allocating it to a world out of reach. Moving it from the environmental to the otherworldly, from the immediacy of experience to the ever-deferred unknown.

The chief of a marketing firm lurches toward the drink cart, sending his swivel chair rolling down the incline toward the massive steel ovoid that looms on the wall behind, the swirling lights of the highways along the skyline reflected upon its surface as the sunset commences yet again. The interchange, torturous and regenerative, fluctuates amid the vaporous swells.

Does not safety draw its resonance from the hazard that looms, the danger against which we could brush and whose variable force we might activate in a resurgent form? The unknowable encounter, from whose energetic undercurrent we could draw. The retraction from the instability we touch. That imperiling force, dangerous and irrational, at the basis of the transit world.

One of the company directors brings up the case of anti-rubbernecking screens, unfurled at crash scenes to block prying eyes, which, though helping to avoid bottlenecks, have been widely opposed by drivers as discriminatory, and for those with fundamentalist leanings, as morally unjustifiable as a condom.

From somewhere along the subterranean passageways, a faint squealing of tires.

Let us work the knife-edge ratio between fear and reward. One that could be fine-tuned with each installment.

A jocund company president veers side to side, seat base creaking like a metronome.

Close your eyes and imagine that exceptional moment when you, the everyday streetgoer, stride blithely into the road.

Someone is stirring a martini. Delicate taps on metal.

Trusting that even the most maniacal driver will stop in time, only to be caught in that perilous instant when you realize they might not.

Soft hum of the ventilation system.

Immobilized with the flash of a mortal terror so acute that it pierces the scrim, a horror so merciless that it shakes the soul.

Creaking of the seat.

Imagine that moment when you, the everyday viewer, have to avert your eyes from the impending calamity, only to be drawn back into its galvanizing center, its bonding swell of lurid fascination.

Rattling of a drip stand.

That horrifying scene from which you cannot flee.

Clinking of ice.

That roadside spectacle you cannot look at but must see.

Thrumming of wind.

In the uproar: an unmistakable desire for more.

More, is repeated.

At that point might we harness the power to convince, stoke the kind of arousal that sediments into belief.

Belief.

The kind that, once it gains momentum, sources what it needs for its powering and orients actions in accordance with its parameters and rules, however logical or illogical the tenets, as it gathers force, stabilizes into a platform, consolidates into a moving train that you now must sustain.

Only then might you then concede the point
that humans are the dangerous link in the chain.

3

From my desk near the classroom window I could see the safety patrol boys assembling on the corner outside. They checked in with the lieutenant, donned their harnesses, and fanned out to their assigned posts. I noticed the way their attitude changed from the moment they fastened those clasps, their movements assuming a newfound rigor, the hesitation that normally characterized them supplanted with a directness and authority—not just over others but over themselves, as if they had upgraded their ability, streamlined the rough edges and sharpened what was indistinct. Like when you wax your car or slick back your hair and you not only look but perform better.

I yearned for that sturdy optimization, that resolute sense of command, that unwavering resolve that would transport me into a world above the one that I knew.

I will never forget the day when I was finally old enough to join. Securing that bandolier around my body seemed to reorient me in the world, elevate me onto a stage, bind me to a source of aesthetic and ethical authority that demanded of me a change. A code that stretched far beyond the school halls, a domain that set the terms for how you moved about, along the hallways, sidewalks and roads outside. The lines of force that acted upon you, embodied in the concrete architecture of walkways and intersections, organized in the rhythms of ambulation, the relays of stops and starts—these now entered your purview, were now opened, expanded, and enlarged into a cosmos of sensation and regulation that you could now summon, as if out of nowhere.

From where did this power come? Somehow the terms were set for this theater in which you acted, in ways both apparent and not. Clustered at street corners and elongated in processions, in relationship to those who moved by. Condensed like snapshots in the window frames of car cabins. Blurred along the time-bound stretches of walkways. Corresponding at times, fitting tightly and falling in line, only to unravel, disband, and regroup.

Repertories of signs and devices influenced the movements of those on the street, adjusting the manner of their compliance. Their vocabulary of metallic and corporeal indicators, machine signals and hand gestures had all the grace, subtlety and precision of a sign language. You conjured it like a magician, but it also acted through you, as if it had swept you up in its fervor, called you to act on its behalf. It got activated as you shaped it from inside. You opened possibilities for coordinated action, immersed in loops of living performance, instilling form and timing, orientation and aim. Staged atop the curbstones and crossings, between the detection of states and the facilitation of conveyance, the integration of instruction and the exertion of force.

As well, the harness bound me to a lineage that stretched back in time, from the stately sword belts of military officers to the presidents and court justices, astronauts and gold medalists, generals and chief executives who had themselves donned the sash at my age. It bound you to a code of ethics shared by law enforcement officers and school board officials in the present day. Standards of responsibility and compliance, ritualized formalities and rewards. Insignias and equippings that together established the terms of the stage into which you entered, its arenas of expectation and esteem.

The variances I introduced into the safety repertoire had caused some degree of alarm among the school administrators. Volatility had arisen along the crosswalks, they said. Unpredictability come to light. There had been *close calls*.

I was sent to the school Principal.

The thought of having to see this man, the very incarnation of ruthless authority, filled me with dread, yet also with a strange excitement. Like some horrifying beast that lived in the dark and struck terror in your soul, but which had such a strong aura of transcendent power built up around it that you secretly hoped to encounter it, touch the immensity of its force in some way.

Our teacher called him Stalin, pointing out the resemblance to us in our illustrated history book. Indeed they looked exactly alike! She was soon fired, replaced with a woman half her size.

As I was saying, the very thought of this man—who I will continue to refer to as Stalin since most of us did (in secret)—caused us to tremble in fear. He was rarely seen, save for those occasional moments when he would suddenly appear out of nowhere, standing at the end of the hall in a dark suit, his eyes black and reptilian, his face cast with a diabolical pallor. Upon sight of him students would vacate the hall in a panic-stricken frenzy, scrambling over one another through the doors—a departure all the more treacherous due to the need to avoid the appearance of engaging in it. The unfortunates who remained had no choice but to stand there paralyzed with horror, or claw hysterically at the doorknob, unable to pull it.

Before I tell you about my visit to his office, it will be necessary to apprise you of an event that had occurred several weeks prior.

There had been a flurry of news reports about a local man who suffered an unfortunate accident, which the news bulletins described thus:

MAN RUNS OVER OWN HEAD.

Before I learned any of the details, a flurry of possibilities rushed through my mind—scenarios whose aims were more choreographic, one might say, than causal. I wondered whether the contortion implied by the headline was corporeal or rhetorical in nature. That is, whether the body at the wheel could have through some perverse extrusion hit its own head, or whether the operational programs were so umbilically tied to the driver that they could, for all intents and purposes, be said to constitute him even when he was standing on the pavement outside. Self-destructive undertones being present in this case if the operating composite deemed intentionally to roll over itself. In part.

The details reported in the article were minimal. While backing out of the driveway, the man apparently dropped a lit cigar down the front of his jacket, leapt from the car and fell to the ground as it continued to roll. No details were provided as to what happened from there. No identifying characteristics, other than the fact that he was local.

Under such conditions you could anticipate a great deal of speculation among the community, especially in a small town like ours where nothing much happens of any consequence and rumors spread like wildfire. As it so happened, the man was suspected to be none other than Stalin.

None of us believed this. We simply could not in our wildest dreams imagine our Principal as someone who could have done such a thing. It was as inconceivable as imagining his namesake, the despot, running over himself.

School board officials denied the hearsay. The official response they gave was: he was Away. Since we rarely saw him at school, we ourselves hardly ever knew whether he was here or Away. He was always in some sense both at the same time. You did not see him but sensed that he was there somewhere seeing you.

On the day I came to his office these rumors had run their course and I had forgotten about the episode entirely. I approached his door with the same degree of paralyzing fear that was the standard for all of us. My teeth chattered as I sat in the waiting room. My hair stood on end. I was about to enter a den of unspeakable torment, condemned on the spot or strapped to a harrow to prolong the anguish.

My knees buckled as his secretary bid me entry to the antechamber. A towering maternal figure, she had the kind of obscene, overbearing sexuality that at that age was utterly horrifying, even more so due to its happy voluptuousness. Her broad smile, which for some would likely assuage tension, in me only served to heighten it. Her large breasts swung over the top of my head; her torso, large as a sport utility vehicle, threatened to engulf.

I was shuttled into a long and narrow room. Two tracks of florescent lighting ran lengthwise from the entrance to the far end like a landing strip. Smoke hung thick in the air, obscuring the light. Behind an enormous desk at the end, in front of a wall-spanning road map, sat the figure of Stalin, encased in a shroud of orthotics, a rehabilitative apparatus of cement-white plaster and metallic rods that encircled his head and rose upward like rebar.

In that instant, the news report and the rumors rushed back to me and I knew that the speculation was true: he *was* the man. As if to drive home the point, the orthotic infrastructure in which he was encased brought to mind the front-end steering rack system of an automobile, as if the very apparatus that felled him was now the agent of his repair, its encircling wheel, rack, and pinion unit, control arm, mounting plates, and tie rods repurposed for exoneration and reconditioning.

Before I could catch myself, I expelled energy through my mouth in the form of words, like the last little sputter you sometimes got when you shut off the engine:

Man who ran over head.

He looked at me through the slots of the apparatus. A puff of smoke was emitted, and along with it a word:

Away, was what seemed to come out, but it was difficult to say as he intoned it with a hollow throttle, as if he were being garroted—a hideous noise that was even more alarming than his appearance, given the rich, booming baritone quality that I had always imagined it having, so large and omnipresent that it could hardly be sourced to an individual body let alone a single vocal organ.

The ensuing expressions were even more difficult to decipher. Were it not for the expectation of diction, one might not have thought them words at all. Yet even though I could not comprehend his speech, such as it was, I felt that we were achieving an implicit understanding of some sort, a commonality that did not require locution. An affinity, tender, and commiserating.

All at once, my fear vanished. I sensed that the punishment I expected to receive from him was not forthcoming, my so-called infraction not to be condemned.

I sensed that he too regarded the so-called *close call* as the necessary outcome of well-directed activity, something not to be avoided across the board but cultivated under the right conditions. He knew, as I did, that you had to provide for aggressive force, just as you did in a sport, channeling it into procedures, contouring its energetics through zones of permission and restriction, rhythmics of enabling constraint, lest it rise up and overwhelm you, catch you off guard. You had to harness its generative nature, work the upslope between the predictable and the improbable, what you presumed and what you did not expect.

These things he knew. He understood that the variances of gesture I introduced into the safety repertoire were of a low level, instilling a modicum of instability into the mix, hardly enough to wreak havoc. Those who waited on the curbstone rather than the sidewalk were already testing this boundary, pushing at the edge of the present. I was simply there working with them, helping advance their ability to manage what came. I restrained actions for those who were not ready, issuing for the distracted crosser a sharp rebuttal; for those who were alert I encouraged initiative, issued affirming challenge.

He understood this. Recognized the benefits, appreciated the need. He knew that protection had a dual orientation, instilling order and compelling you to push back. Safety devices were needed that were sufficient to hold firm without threat to life, but which also had resilience, such that reconstitution and adaptation could occur. You wanted to integrate these dynamics into the right program of rehabilitation and training. Of course he knew this—he himself was a living testament! The very embodiment of the endo-therapeutic imperative! He understood that you had to imperil the boundaries between self and world by introducing zones of pressure and velocity unforeseen. Forces that did not overwhelm, but which pushed against capacities to a point beyond the previous threshold, pushed against the limit of what a body could bear to the extent sufficient to induce a need for repair. The posture that emerged from the *close call* was just as relevant, and in some ways even more important than its casual counterpart, in that it responded to forces that were all too often ignored, all too readily normalized as so much benign surround.

Who could ignore the eruptive poignancy of arms flung in the air, the sudden hop, curve and side bend, eyes wide and legs akimbo, freeze-framed in the metallized glare of sun-lit cement? What sublime interplay of forces had wrought the driveway ballet in whose throes he himself had been caught, however through direct experience or oblique association with that unidentified man, that nameless figure who over his own head ran?

However inducted into the apparatuses of rehabilitation and reportage. However here, there or Away. However tightening or destabilizing the limitations of self-reference. However conducting similarity or difference.

Impersonation in one domain, extension in another. Shared platform, shared autonym. Bodily elongation, identification overlap.

I reached out to touch his casing. Hard as reinforced concrete it was. The rebar-like beam cage within which he was suspended, poised for reconditioning, replenishment and fill—how I admired its yield! The accident draws those around into its theater, loading and releasing pressure. Modifying rate, pliation, swivel. Restriction and stretch. Condensation and freeing. Elasticity and hardening.

Awareness of that which establishes the order of the world brings you closer in the knowledge of just how precarious it is.

Wherefore, our Principal? The integration of the body into rehabilitative systems makes the vulnerability difficult to locate, the gambit difficult to gauge. Outfittings stick out and in. Pipes, conduits, antennae, attachments, feelers: extensions and incursions make the support a topography, a structuring-registering baseline with no outside.

The demarcation of bodily form is subordinate to its securing. The outline, to the equipping. The delimitation of the frame gives way to the platform's gearing up.

I touched him, tenderly as I did my father. Away, I said, affirming intimacy in the remote, distance in the adjoining. Onward—into that which undercuts the limits of self-reference. Onward—into that which lays dormant at the threshold of the circumstance that roused it.

At that moment his secretary, keeper of the order, burst through the door as if delivering the very means of the advancement, facilitating transfer across the corridors of the drivetrain. Had she known that authority for whom she worked, or simply understood that it registered our presence and called us to act appropriately? Access to the knowledge of how order got made was not as important as addressing the challenges involved in maintaining it, the effort of meeting the demands imposed. One must delve deeply, touch injury. Find likeness at the limit, gain intimacy at the border of the life pushed against. I leapt beneath, fell upon the floor, rolled under.

19
TUNNEL RISK AND THE MEDIATION OF BORDER SECURITY SPECTACLE

Juan Llamas-Rodriguez

Writing for the libertarian think tank *The Reason Foundation*, contributor John Stossel makes a pointed argument against the U.S.-backed War on Drugs by explaining that it undermines harsher enforcement against what he deems "illegal" immigration. Stossel rightly notes that the U.S. government's involvement in cartel infighting has been responsible for exporting conflict to Central American nations and that, because of these conflicts, people from those places have been forced to migrate to the United States. In addition, the emphasis on drug policing grants this merchandise a premium, fostering incentives for traffickers to undertake innovative techniques that result in higher revenue. "Drug profits give smugglers the money to do what poverty-stricken immigrants can't: dig long, high-tech tunnels with lighting and ventilation systems," writes Stossel. "A border fence doesn't secure the border when immigrants—and criminals—can tunnel underneath it" (Stossel). The problem with the War on Drugs, as he sees it, is that it proves profitable for cartels, prompting them to build tunnels that not only further their profits but also open the possibility for other ways of violating state sovereignty. The issues raised by border tunnels are not only their current use for drug smuggling but also their *potential* for further ways of undermining the sovereignty of the United States.

Indeed, the threat of tunnels is pure potential. Reports from various U.S. agencies report that, by virtue of quantities, these structures are still relatively small sources of trafficking. These openings below the physical geopolitical boundary, with its fences, tracking technologies, and roaming vehicles, represent precisely that: an opening, in the sense of an opportunity, for the aboveground measures to be undone. Tunnels are foremost the grounds for uncertainty. From the perspective of the state, these infrastructural emergences must be contained. The threat of tunnels must be transformed from uncertainty into risk.

Tunnels, however, are unseen. As Stossel's op-ed makes it clear, the symbolic charge of border tunnels results from the fact that their very presence already implies a breach of sovereignty, where this breach is tied to a lack of visibility and control. In this manner, border tunnels are comparable to, yet contrast with, border walls. As Wendy Brown notes, these walls are "generative of [a] theological awe largely unrelated to their quotidian functions or failures" (26). These structures command attention because of their material might even before their functionality is taken into account. Both border walls and border tunnels "generat[e] significant effects in excess of or even counter to their stated purposes," and are expensive yet strikingly popular (Brown 27). Walls generate their theological awe because they are readily visible to anyone that visits the national borders. In contrast, tunnels remain inaccessible because they are built clandestinely and because, when found, they are shut down permanently by government agencies. The symbolic charge and political potential of narco-tunnels remains moored to their status as *infra*structure, as structuring materialities that lie just beneath the threshold of visibility. For state agencies, transforming these underground structures from uncertainty into containable risk requires simultaneous processes of revealing and concealing. The enactment of both these processes and the negotiation of the contradictions they subtend is best achieved through mediation, namely, by virtue of media productions that simultaneously enact this disclosure and concealment.

This chapter considers one such production that mediates the dual processes of tunnel visualization and concealment as well as the discrepant temporalities of emergence and capture: the 2014 video series *What Lies Beneath* created by the U.S. Customs and Border Protection to showcase the work of the Nogales Tunnel Task Force. This case study is representative of the operations of risk management performed by state-sanctioned media productions. In what follows, I analyze these media texts not only as elements in the discursive field of border securitizations but also as media productions themselves in order to foreground the affordances, as well as the pitfalls, of mediation for the state's management of border security. First, I consider the state's media productions as part of the larger "border security spectacle," drawing on the work of Nicholas De Genova, Peter Andreas, and Judith Butler to claim that much of border security is unthinkable without the processes of performativity and visualization enabled by mediation. Then, a close analysis of the videos in *What Lies Beneath* reveals the affordances and limitations that media productions have for circulating the work of border security beyond the publics immediately around the border. In particular, these videos reveal that mediation, while productive for the performance of border security, also provides openings for ideological negotiations and contradictions to emerge. Third, I argue that the mediation of tunnel security is self-referential, and it is because of this that uncertainty can be effectively transformed into risk. The chapter closes with the argument that this self-referentiality also lays the ground for the potential undoing of border security spectacle. By virtue of its reiterative performativity, the mediation of tunnel risk provides openings for further emergences, including its cooptation and critique.

Border Security as Mediated Spectacle

Border studies scholars have long argued that borders consist of complex social interactions and negotiations, constituted by tensions between practices of border crossing and border reinforcement (See Mezzadra and Neilson; Vila). Maintaining borders requires not only physical structures and acts of violence but also the continuous symbolic reassurance that those are implicated in the larger ideological investments of state sovereignty and national strength. Nicholas De Genova refers to these connections as the Border Spectacle, the persistent and repetitive implication of the "materiality of border enforcement practices in the symbolic and ideological production of a brightly lit scene of 'exclusion'" (De Genova, "The 'Crisis'"). Since bordering practices include a negotiation between inclusion and exclusion, the spectacle consists in foregrounding exclusionary tactics in a visually striking manner while maintaining the inclusionary ones within its shadow. The symbolic and ideological construction of this scene of exclusion demonstrates, validates, and legitimizes "the purported naturalness and putative necessity of [such] exclusion" (De Genova, "Spectacles" 1181). De Genova's commitments lie in theorizing the implications of these bordering practices for national politics and international policy surrounding human migration. His theoretical framework, however, also applies to other transnational flows. In the case of drug trafficking, border spectacle consists of visualizing the violent aspects of combating cartels and individual smugglers while effacing the fact that most of the drugs flowing into the United States pass unacknowledged through regular ports of entry because of bureaucratic inefficiency or systematic corruption. Departing from and extending De Genova's framework, this chapter pursues two claims about the constitution of border spectacle, particularly as it relates to securitization and the management of risk.

First, border security spectacle is a media spectacle. The enactment of this spectacle through media productions allows it to scale up its reach, stakes, and effects. The border spectacle De Genova names remains tied to the images that shape, form, and contour it. Further, as Guy Debord argues, "the spectacle is not merely a matter of images, nor even of images plus sounds. It is whatever escapes people's activity, whatever eludes their practical reconsideration and correction" (9). Mediation thus mobilizes the spectacle of border security for publics who are geographically removed from the border region. For one, these publics have no access to the material geopolitical border except through media. At the same time, these removed publics may not know of, or may not care about, the practicalities of border enforcement in everyday life. On some level, the mediation of border security functions to efface the material effects that such security measures have on border populations. Through media productions, state agencies and other stakeholders can foster the discourse of "national security" as tied to border enforcement techniques while ignoring the environmental, economic, and human consequences of these enforcement techniques.

Second, border security spectacle is performative in the sense defined by Judith Butler as a "discursive practice that enacts or produces that which it names" (13). The crucial insight derived from Butler's theorization is that power does not exist as such but emerges from reiterative action, which not only grants power but also signals its instability. Media becomes a useful tool in the performance of border security by re-producing the practices of enforcement and policing continuously and across dispersed publics. Border security practices acquire their "naturalized effect" by virtue of this reiteration, yet it is also because of such repetition that gaps and fissures "are opened up as the constitutive instabilities in such constructions" (Butler 10). Because border security is performative, it is bound to be fraught with inconsistencies and fissures. Its own constitutive performativity gives the lie of its undoing.

Political scientist Peter Andreas gestures toward the performative aspect of state securitization when he characterizes border policing as a "ceremonial practice," where policing is less a means to an end than an end in itself (11). Andreas argues that law enforcement, particularly at the border, includes an instrumental role concerned with the defense of physical boundaries and an expressive role tasked with reaffirming moral boundaries. Oftentimes the expressive role of such enforcement supersedes its instrumental goals. In fact, border enforcement campaigns can fail in their instrumental roles while remaining highly successful in their expressive ones. The rhetoric of border security championed by nativist movements and the politicians who cater to them exemplifies this privileging of expressive enforcement. In this manner, tunnel security stands as one endpoint within a long line of security spectacles that include heavy patrolling with vehicles and animals, brutal routine arrests, and inhumane incarceration practices. The measures proposed by such movements may be impractical or counterproductive, and their execution often faulty. Still, by going through the motions of performing border security, the state perpetuates the maxim about protecting its borders, a notion that then can trigger further mobilizations. The mediated construction of border security spectacle thus derives its effectiveness—its effects and its ability to deliver those effects—from the fact that it is performative.

Arguing for the performative, mediated ontology of border securitization does not imply that this practice belongs only to a semiotic realm. There are material consequences to all these security measures such as the destruction of precarious ecologies for nonhuman animals and the deaths of hundreds of migrants across the desert. None of these consequences, however, contribute to "national security" or the protection of sovereignty as defined by state agencies. Border securitization is foremost a spectacle and a performance even as the practical measures purported to achieve it have negative, and often tragic, externalities. Deconstructing the mediation of uncertainty into manageable risk within border security productions does not preclude addressing the physical consequences that security enforcements brings about. Instead, breaking down such mediations serves to begin articulating the fissures within the state security apparatus. As a limit case where the spectacularization of risk dwarfs the material importance of their threat, mediations of underground border tunnels unearth the ideological negotiations and contradictions contained within border security spectacle.

What Lies Beneath within Border Media Networks

What Lies Beneath is a 2014 video series created for the U.S. Customs and Border Protection's magazine *Frontline*, a digital publication that features stories about the agency in multimedia formats. The series showcases the work of the Nogales Tunnel Task Force, an interagency group dedicated specifically to tracking and shutting down tunnels around the border. It consists of six videos, three photo slideshows, and written excerpts from interviews with Kevin Hecht, the Deputy Patrol Agent in charge. Hosted on the Custom and Border Protection's website, each of these videos centers around one issue related to the Tunnel Task Force's efforts: experience of working on the team, the different team roles, job satisfaction, their use of technologies, the types of tunnels they find, and tunnel wildlife.

In and of itself, *What Lies Beneath* does not appear to have a wide reach, but this series of videos remains illustrative of the authorized messaging promoted by the state, a message that then extends further through its mediations across other channels. The message from the official state campaign becomes replicated in, for instance, local news reports on border tunnels from ABC and CBS affiliate stations as well as the National Geographic documentary television series *Border Wars* (2010–2015). Across these various other outlets, the same personnel, tropes, and, most importantly, ideological negotiations surface and circulate to a variety of media publics. Such recursivity gives life and shape to an expansive *border media network*, a system of institutions and media productions that circulate images about bordering practices and social relations. *What Lies Beneath*, like most government-sponsored media production, functions as an originary text that hopes to spread across media networks in order to foster particular discursive commitments. Analyzing this series of videos as a media production thus reveals the performative spectacle of border securitization while at the same time making salient the ideological contradictions inherent therein.

What Lies Beneath foregrounds the performative aspects of border security and enforcement by promoting the idea that the tunnel shutdown initiatives it showcases are solely responsible for a decrease in infiltration. Despite mentioning that "traffickers are nothing if not inventive," there is no allusion to the possibility that the reduced number of tunnel discoveries could be due to better circumvention practices. The performance of security captured in these videos purports to be reassuring in and of itself. The expressive role pursued by this media campaign is therefore performative in the sense that the work of this series of videos is "to enact or produce that which it names" (Butler 13) to bring about border securitization through its mediation. The performativity of mediated border security stands in for securitization itself.

The performative aspect of tunnel shutdown proves especially crucial because, quantitatively, tunnels are not the most significant form of drug smuggling into the United States. The former head of the Border Patrol's Nogales Station in Arizona, Gary Widner, readily admits that tunnel trafficking is but a fraction of the smuggling activities across the border. Although he has reinforced the importance of tunnel interdiction efforts in his multiple press interviews, he also notes that smuggling organizations adapt quickly and creatively to these efforts (Woodhouse). Furthermore, anthropologist Howard Campbell argues that the majority of drugs actually cross through ports of entry. Indeed, the 2017 Executive Orders to increase Border Patrol hires at the same time that Anti-Border Corruption Act protections are dismantled will likely result in more bribes to CBP officials and smoother trafficking through regular ports of entry (Frosch and Meckler; Raff). Campbell suggests that the Border Patrol's interest in finding and shutting down tunnels has less to do with the amount of drugs that pass through them than with their symbolic value: "[w]ith the Department of Homeland Security spending billions of dollars annually on agents and technology, smugglers outwitting their efforts with shovels and pickaxes doesn't look good" (qtd. in Woodhouse).

Given these practical considerations, tunnels prove a privileged structure for the mediation of risk for a number of reasons. Because of their material sophistication, the "theological awe" of tunnels is not only representational, but also partially grounded in their physical characteristics. One implication of this material–representational convergence is that tunnels allow a concrete problem-and-solution approach. A tunnel is found, a construction company is brought in, and the tunnel is shut down. Closing one tunnel can cost between 30 to 100,000 dollars, and involves using concrete with a high level of bonding. Because of this, local companies in the border cities normally cannot perform these jobs. National construction companies then bid for the highly lucrative contracts to shut down tunnels, and local companies must ally themselves with the right bidder to provide local support (Prendergast). For state institutions, this clear-cut, business-oriented approach proves beneficial as a security strategy. Although smuggling through ports of entry is more pervasive, addressing these problems requires broader, more complex, and more time-consuming solutions that are also less amenable to become spectacles of border security. The closure of each tunnel, instead, is always an open-and-shut occasion.[1]

A second implication is that tunnels allow the performance of border security as a preventive move. Municipal governments and CBP agents emphasize the "closing" of tunnels that are still inoperable, long from being finished. The closure of these tunnels becomes significant because of their potential use in the future. The potential threat of tunnels does not need to be assumed since there is an actual physical proto-structure that could eventually become a threat, and that these officials can render through media productions. Tunnel shutdowns provide a reassuring performance of prevention: they assume an ability to assess threats empirically, identify their causes, and provide testable solutions (Massumi 8). This practice likewise speaks to what Rey Chow calls "the preemptiveness of seeing as a means of destruction," a logic emerging from the post-World War II moment where visualization becomes tantamount to control under the regime of perpetual war (32). It is therefore not difficult to see why state investment in Tunnel Task Forces and tunnel detection technologies has increased even as their relatively low importance for trafficking remains the same (Office of National Drug Control Policy). *What Lies Beneath* exemplifies how mediation mobilizes the physical characteristics of tunnels in service of the spectacle of border security.

At the same time, these media productions contain multiple negotiations and contradictions embedded within their authorized messaging. For instance, by focusing on the Tunnel Task Force as an entry into exploring underground border tunnels, *What Lies Beneath* deflects the "technological awe" of trafficking tunnels from those who build them to those who shut them down. Sophisticated tunnels are complex structures designed and built by expert engineers trained in mining industries. Often, these structures include elevators, electric lights, ventilation ducts, and disguised entry and exit shafts; they can reach as deep as 70 feet; and they are tall enough for an adult to walk through. Thus, these take years to build and require substantial economic investment. However, there is no indication of this aspect in *What Lies Beneath*. Although one of the videos recites the Department of Homeland Security categorization of tunnels into rudimentary, sophisticated, and interconnected, overall the campaign ignores any details of how these tunnels differ in terms of composition and technical expertise. Instead, tunnels become structures that arise all on their own but must be shut down lest they actualize their potential threat. The mediation of tunnels within this campaign thus perpetuates myths about the asymmetry of technological innovation. By ignoring the complexity of the structures they seek to shut down, the state agents present themselves as cutting-edge technology users while narcotraffickers remain unsophisticated criminals with elementary tools.

Still, the specter of emergence haunts these mediated displays of control. The foregrounding of tunnel interdiction efforts begets a paradoxical stance: since these structures are underground and hidden, they must be made visible, but only briefly and only so that their shutdown becomes a significant event. Geographer Cynthia Sorrensen argues as much when she examines the content of press releases from national security agencies. Between 2003 and 2012, almost half these press releases repeated the total tally of tunnel discoveries every time, yet neglected to account for the widely aleatory numbers year to year. These reports also characterized the prevalence of tunnels as a response to the stronghold on surface border protection. Notably, almost all press releases included a detailed description of the structure of these tunnels: the reinforced wood paneling, the electric lines, the ventilation systems, the complex pulley entry/exit systems. From this content analysis, Sorrensen concludes that "since the subterranean space is less visible than the surface, security agencies [must] demonstrate knowledge and therefore security through descriptions of the physical characteristics of tunnels" (342). Mediating border security likewise consists of this two-part process. First, media makes the state of insecurity visible by shedding light on the fact that sophisticated tunnels exist. At the same time, the mediation of insecurity includes within itself the performance of security, such as the act of shutting down the tunnels that have just been made visible. This dynamic is evident in *What Lies Beneath* when visualizing tunnel shutdown presents the drop in the number of tunnels found as an effect of this demonstration of security. In doing so, however, these videos also serve as visual demonstrations of the sophistication and "technological awe" of the tunnel being shut down.

This distinction between tech savvy state agents and unsophisticated criminals does not segue into a deeper engagement with the technology itself. Instead, the campaign as a whole de-emphasizes the centrality of technology in favor of foregrounding labor. This aspect is particularly notable in the video titled "Tell Us About the Robots?" Although the video's framing question makes it seem like it focuses on the newly acquired robots for tunnel exploration, the voiceover and editing undermine this focus by foregrounding the Tunnel Task Force agents in action. In the voiceover, Deputy Agent Hecht states that, despite the advantages that robot scouting provides, the work that agents perform remains the same. At least one agent must go into the tunnel and verify that it reaches beyond the geopolitical border for the agency to take action in shutting it down. Likewise, the editing undermines the potential viewer's fascination with the robot's activities: brief shots from the robot's camera perspective are quickly intercut with shots of officers handling the machine, laying the cable for it, and operating the mobile unit controls (see Figures 19.1a and 19.b).

Decidedly non-technophilic, this video reinforces the idea that it is human agents who do the work of tunnel closure while the technology itself, no matter how advanced, are mere tools that remain useless without the intrepid agents.

Such foregrounding of labor over new technologies signals a tension within the production aims of these videos. State agencies have an interest in showcasing all sorts of border security measures, whether technological or human. The individual workers on the forefront of these measures, however, have a stake in reasserting their indispensability to the security apparatus. High-tech solutions to border surveillance and policing attract the attention of politicians and technophilic publications (Madrigal). Against such enthusiasm, these videos evidence the efforts of Border Patrol agents to cast their expertise by suggesting that only humans can perform the inordinate tasks of tunnel security. Agents restate the centrality of their work within the industry of border security to counter the narrative propagated by contractors that tunnel robots will bring about revolutionary changes in border policing (Lockheardt).

Of course, this anxiety over technological solutions replacing human labor is an issue for a great number of professions. As John Caldwell argues, media allows workers to become more self-reflexive about their roles in production at times when the pace of technologically motivated obsolescence accelerates (14). Media productions about production open up a space where workers can reinstate their indispensability within their industry. In the case of *What Lies Beneath*, this resistance to the displacement of labor by technologies occurs within the same productions aimed at showcasing the technologies for border policing. The mediation of border security enables these contradictions to coexist and circulate across border media networks.

What Lies Beneath thus functions as a "behind-the-scenes" feature, a type of programming that revolves around providing audiences with privileged access to the inner workings of an industry. While not new, behind-the-scenes features have multiplied in recent years because of the affordances of digital platforms for release of content. These features perform a marked form of industrial

Figures 19.1a and Figure 19.1b   *What Lies Beneath* foregrounds the labor of human agents even when promoting technologies (screengrabs)

reflexivity: they aid in the self-definition of the industry by showcasing the uniqueness of technical expertise and the industry insiders' complete control over finished product. Not unlike Hollywood's behind-the-scenes features, *What Lies Beneath* also aids in propagating the myth about "how hard it is to get into" a particular line of work (Caldwell 284–285). In the video centered on the job experience of Tunnel Task Force agents, Hecht's voiceover explains that crawling into tunnels to inspect them is mired with claustrophobia, darkness, and various unknowns that "play mind games with you." Throughout, images of cramped spaces and dark recesses of the tunnels reinforce his remarks (see Figure 19.2a). Hecht admits that it is not a job for everyone since some people naturally freeze. Instead, those agents that do participate must have "a desire to do it."

Figures 19.2a and 19.2b Camera position and framing convey the physical toll of shutting down tunnels, reinforcing the myth of exceptionality promoted by CBP agents (screengrabs)

Resonating with the agent's words about the job's "adrenaline rush," a shot includes a Tunnel Task Force agent climbing down a ladder to a tunnel then turning to look at the limitless drop below (see Figure 19.2b).

At once, this video foregrounds the mystery of border tunnels, evoking the agents' pleasure in exploring "what lies beneath," and perpetuates the myth of the extraordinary individual, depicting these agents as uniquely prepared to carry out these explorations.

The myth of exceptionality promoted by this series is unique to the work of finding and closing off underground tunnels. Agents can distinguish themselves from the vast, and growing, cohort of border security personnel. Propagating this notion about the exceptionality of the work of Tunnel Task Forces both upholds and undermines the effectiveness of border security spectacle. On one hand, this series upholds border security spectacle because it reinforces tunnels as a significant threat and the mediation of their closure as an effective means of securitization. On the other hand, propagating the myth of unique individuals undermines such spectacle by implying that the border security apparatus, as metonymically represented by its individual agents, may not always be prepared to deal with overhyped threat. By casting their expertise as tacit knowledge that cannot be found in all agents, the Tunnel Task Force further reveals the contingent aspect of tunnel security, dependent on finding unique individuals within the dwindling numbers of the Border Patrol. Amid reports that CBP has failed to meet the hiring increases mandated by the White House (Stenglein; Tanfani), the myth of the exceptional individual brings into relief the very obvious limitations of the organization as a whole. The dual upholding and undermining of the aims of border security spectacle, a contradiction without resolution, results from and circulates because of this spectacle's mediated nature.

The Age of the Border Security Spectacle

In *The Age of the World Target*, Rey Chow argues that a fundamental change in the production and circulation of knowledge occurred in the post-World War II moment. The logics behind the deployment of the atomic bomb as weaponized method as well as the Cold War era's impetus for dividing up the world resulted in an epistemic shift where visualizing—especially by technological means—became the foremost technique for the organization of control. These developments in conjunction carried implications for the reigning paradigms in theory, literature, and war, according to Chow. War in particular had become "an agenda that is infinitely self-referential," meaning that war would no longer primarily represent other longstanding or emerging struggles. Instead, war came to represent "war itself" (Chow 33). The self-referentiality of mediated spectacle continues to frame the analysis of global conflict, and it is a central feature of the mediation of border security.

The mediation of tunnel risk represents an exemplary case in the spectacle of border security because this type of risk often signifies only itself. Shutting down all existing underground tunnels will likely not impact in any significant way the movement of drugs into the United States, the trafficking of arms to cartels in Mexico, or the migration of people across both countries. Linking the tunnels to broader, systemic causes and effects of transnational narcotrafficking or human migration quickly reveals the relative insignificance of these structures within the networks that give rise to such phenomena. Instead, the mediation of tunnel risk works to contain such risk within the structures themselves, metonymizing complex interconnected processes therein. The Tunnel Task Force videos put forth the premise that underground border tunnels are a risk because their existence is a risk. This sort of tautology is only possible because of the reliance on mediated images, as Debord explains: "the tautological character of the spectacle stems from the fact that its means and ends are identical" (8). Media productions such as *What Lies Beneath* give rise to such risk at the same time that they foreclose it. The cyclical procedure of such mediations does little to affect the material conditions of the phenomenon that it references.

However, that the mediation of tunnel risk is self-referential is not to say that it achieves nothing. As John Stossel makes clear in the op-ed cited at the beginning of this chapter, tunnels are unbridled potential for fugitive flows. These structure's current use may be for trafficking drugs, but they also lay the infrastructure for other forms of unsanctioned movement across the geopolitical boundary. In this regard, the media productions around tunnel risk are also representative of another of the aims of border security spectacle: to foreclose futurities. Mediating the opening and closing of tunnels comes to represent the ability of the border security apparatus to address other potential threats. This process is a reassuring performance that every emergence will be met with its adequate form of control. *What Lies Beneath* allows for such reassuring performance because its focus and aim are narrow in scope. By centering the structures themselves, rather than the broader interconnecting networks that shape transnational trafficking, these media productions can figure the aims and means of border security. These short videos then feed into the border media networks sustained by local newscasts and television documentaries, among other forms of media. Through such extended networks, the potential of tunnels, and its mediated foreclosure, becomes emblematic of the work of border security spectacle for publics near and far away.

Finally, however, the mediation of tunnel risk provides openings for further emergences by virtue of its reiterative performativity. For the unbridled potential of tunnels to be transformed into risk—managed uncertainty—this risk has to be performed, over and over again, in order to grant it (and its performers) legitimacy. Tunnel Task Forces rely on the continued potential threat of tunnels and require further mediations about the forces' capabilities for shutting down these tunnels. Moving images give visibility to the risk of tunnels at the same time that they capture, code, and give it shape as risk. While participating in the formation of border security spectacle, these state media productions also give life to an even broader border media network, one that includes not only state-sanctioned productions but also mainstream film and television, digital projects, and activist artworks.[2] Maintaining the "technological awe" of underground border tunnels in the popular imagination represents a final contradiction in the mediation of border security spectacle: figuring security practices through media productions allows for such performative securitization to become co-opted, critiqued, and potentially undone.

Notes

1 Addressing tunnel closure in this manner parallels the cultural imaginary of tunnel prison escapes, where the tunnel closure reaffirms the impenetrability of the disciplinary fortress.
2 Such a broader "border media network" also includes different forms of border spectacles that transform other types of flows into risk. See, for instance, the chapter by Heller and Pezzani in this volume.

Works Cited

Andreas, Peter. *Border Games: Policing the U.S.-Mexico Divide*. Cornell UP, 2009.
Brown, Wendy. *Walled States, Waning Sovereignty*. Zone Books, 2010.
Butler, Judith. *Bodies that Matter: On the Discursive Limits of "Sex."* Routledge, 1993.
Caldwell, John. *Production Culture: Industrial Reflexivity and Critical Practice in Film and Television*. Duke UP, 2008.
Chow, Rey. *The Age of the World Target: Self-Referentiality in War, Theory, and Comparative Work*. Duke UP, 2011.
Debord, Guy. *The Society of the Spectacle*. Translated by Ken Knabb. Hobgoblin Press, 2002.
De Genova, Nicholas. "Spectacles of Migrant Illegality: The Scene of Exclusion, the Obscene of Inclusion." *Ethnic and Racial Studies*, vol. 36, no. 7, 2013, pp. 1180–1198.
De Genova, Nicholas. "The 'Crisis' of the European Border Regime: Towards a Marxist Theory of Borders." *International Socialism*, no. 150, 2016, http://isj.org.uk/the-crisis-of-the-european-border-regime-towards-a-marxist-theory-of-borders. Accessed November 22, 2017.
Frosch Dan and Laura Meckler. "In Rush for New Agents, Border Patrol Weighs Changing Polygraph Program." *Wall Street Journal*, April 13, 2017.
Lockheardt, Christopher. "Underground Radar Systems: Fighting Tunnels with Tunnels." *MITRE Publications*, September 2010.
Madrigal Alexis. "Bots vs. Smugglers: Drug Tunnel Smackdown." *Wired Magazine*, May 16, 2009.
Massumi, Brian. *Ontopower: War, Powers, and the State of Perception*. Duke UP, 2015.
Mezzadra, Sandro and Brett Neilson. *Border as Method, or the Multiplication of Labor*. Duke UP, 2013.
Office of National Drug Control Policy. "National Southwest Border Counternarcotics Strategy." *The White House*, 2013, www.whitehouse.gov//sites/default/files/ondcp/policy-and-research/southwest_border_strategy_2013.pdf. Accessed June 6, 2017.
Prendergast, Curt. "Drug Tunnel Filled with $50K in Concrete." *Nogales International*, 22 May 2014, www.nogalesinternational.com/news/drug-tunnel-filled-with-k-in-concrete/article_9814aadc-e1e1-11e3-b116-001a4bcf887a.html. Accessed November 22, 2017.
Raff, Jeremy. "The Border Patrol's Corruption Problem." *The Atlantic*, May 5, 2017, www.theatlantic.com/politics/archive/2017/05/not-one-bad-apple/525327/. Accessed November 22, 2017.

Sorrensen, Cynthia. "Making the Subterranean Visible: Security, Tunnels, and the United States-Mexico Border." *Geographical Review*, vol, 3, no. 104, July 2014, pp. 328–345.

Stenglein, Christine. "Struggling to Hang on to 20K Officers, Border Patrol Looks to Hire 5K More." *Brookings Institute*, July 7, 2017, www.brookings.edu/blog/fixgov/2017/07/07/struggling-to-hang-on-to-20k-officers-border-patrol-looks-to-hire-5k-more/. Accessed December 9, 2017.

Stossel, John. "The Drug War Makes Border Enforcement More Difficult." *Reason*, September 16, 2015, https://reason.com/archives/2015/09/16/the-drug-war-makes-border-enforcement-mo. Accessed November 22, 2017.

Tanfani, Josef. "In January, President Trump Vowed to Hire 5,000 New Border Patrol Agents. It Never Happened." *Los Angeles Times*, August 18, 2017, www.latimes.com/politics/la-na-border-security-20170818-story.html. Accessed November 22, 2017.

Vila, Pablo. *Border Identifications: Narratives of Religion, Gender, and Class on the US-Mexico Border*. U of Texas P, 2005.

Woodhouse, Murphy. "Nogales is Still Tunnel Capital, Despite Decline in Busts." *Nogales International*, October 2, 2015, www.nogalesinternational.com/news/nogales-is-still-tunnel-capital-despite-decline-in-busts/article_db33c082-6890-11e5-a3d4-b78ca081ea7c.html. Accessed November 22, 2017.

20
FLOATING ARCHITECTURES
Fantasies of Safety in Oceanic Riskscapes

Melody Jue

Floating islands abound in science fiction, modeling a variety of forms of sociality and structures for survival. The film *Waterworld* (1995), situated in a post-diluvian future where people have forgotten what land even looks like, features steampunk-like fortress islands of lashed-together scraps. Similar DIY recycled islands appear in China Mieville's novel *The Scar* (2002) and Neal Stephenson's cyberpunk classic *Snow Crash* (1992), while other fictions imagine forms of interconnected island voyaging. Set on alien ocean planets, Joan Slonczewski's *A Door Into Ocean* (1986), C.S. Lewis' *Perelandra* (1943), and Hal Clement's *Noise* (2003) explore the possibility of organically growing floating islands/rafts. Slonczewski's novel notably imagines an all-female socialist utopia of scientists who teach a male visitor how to live more sustainably with his environment. Each of these floating island narratives have significance beyond a simple escapist dream; more than just architectures, floating islands require authors to think through specific political and economic forms of life and their reproduction.

With the acceleration of global sea-level rise in recent years, the trope of the science fictional floating island has begun to seem less speculative and more necessary to the survival of low-lying island republics. Indeed, as Fredric Jameson aptly writes, "today, all politics is about real estate" (Jameson *Postmodernism*, 13). As coping strategies, oceanic peoples are facing a choice between relocation to countries with higher elevation and commissioning artificial islands.[1] Large international architectural firms have been quick to design futuristic-looking floating islands; for example, the island nation of Kiribati has considered artificial island proposals from Vincent Callebaut Architects (France) (Figure 20.1) and the Shimizu Corporation (Japan) (Figure 20.2). The Seasteading Institute (Silicon Valley) is working with the government of French Polynesia to work toward a new prototype of an artificial floating island, to be built off its coast in the near future. In each of these cases, floating architectures provide ways of mitigating the risks of sea-level rise, providing new and purportedly safer places for habitation.[2] Yet what forms of safety do artificial floating islands offer, and what forms of risk? If safety is imagined as a kind of groundedness, what happens when one runs out of soil?

This chapter explores the implications of theorizing risk as a kind of environment or milieu, which coheres in the recent neologism "riskscape." Whereas many scholars hold the terms "risk" and "environment" in productive tension, the term "riskscape" collapses the two into one t(r)opological figure. The riskscape has been theorized most extensively by Detlef Müller-Mahn and subsequently elaborated in the field of geography, a field that has often literalized the metaphorical term riskscape by producing maps that diagram particular sources of risk across regions. In this chapter, I trace the ways in which we figuratively and metaphorically speak about risk as something both abstract and material, cognitive and physical, that can manifest in particular environments but also itself constitute a kind of imaginary territory. By examining discourses in the field of geography, I show how spatial metaphors mediate perceptions of risk by turning it into an environment.

To anchor my analysis of the riskscape (a figuration which itself belies particular valuations of grounded stability), I turn to a variety of architectural proposals for artificial floating islands in the Pacific Ocean and their relationship to spatially imagined forms of risk (Somerville 25).[3] I contend that the creation of artificial floating islands is not only a geographic matter, but also entails the imagination of specific economic and political formations. I closely follow the role of metaphorical language used to naturalize capitalism as both an economic and political form, examining specifically how spatial and biological metaphors play a role in the imagination of risk. Many of the artificial islands designs internalize the paradigmatic architectures of capitalism: the shopping mall, the skyscraper, the cruise ship, and the oil rig. However, the entire notion of territoriality and risk becomes more complicated when considering sea-level rise, which involves the imagination of water and not just the landscape from which "riskscape" borrows its name. Yet risk also involves an orientation to the future—a state of preparedness often subsumed by practices of consumption. The Uncertain Commons writes that contemporary media play a critical role in channelling and intensifying perceptions of risk, "encouraging consumers to turn fear into preparedness: buy the pension plans for luxurious retirements, the vitamins for healthier, longer lives" (Uncertain Commons 577). In this case the refrain is, buy the artificial island for territorial security—an expensive solution to the threat of sea-level rise that comes at the cost of new levels of indebtedness.[4] I conclude with an example of floating architecture that takes inspiration from traditional Thai architectural forms and aims to incorporate indigenous rhythms of life and sociality, envisioning a self-determined future that breaks from neo-colonial structures of indebtedness.

Riskscape T(r)opologies

One of the more notable critical works that brings risk theory and environmental(ist) discourse into dialogue is Ursula Heise's seminal study *Sense of Place, Sense of Planet: The Environmental Imagination of the Global* (2008). Heise shows that risk perceptions have "galvanized the environmentalist movement from its beginnings," in recognizably cautionary accounts such as Rachel Carson's classic account of DDT use, *Silent Spring* (1962) (Heise 121). Yet as Heise argues, risk scenarios also take distinct and recognizable narrative forms such as the apocalyptic or pastoral. These overarching narrative templates, in turn, shape perceptions of ecological and technical risk, which "manifest themselves in both visual and verbal artifacts" and shape our "ways of inhabiting local, national, and global spaces and systems" (121, 123). Here, Heise is careful to keep risk and environment in tension, and does not go so far as to say that risk itself is a kind of environment, or milieu, that one might in habit. Instead, Heise sees risk as a plot, a narrative pattern, or a scenario that shapes one's perceptions of how to inhabit place. Risk is a story that we tell, having temporal dimensionality. If we inhabit risk, it is parallel to the way that we say we inhabit a fiction or narrative.

Whether the public perceives the plots of risk as realistic or not is a different question. Novelist Amitav Ghosh argues that the dominant form of literary realism since the nineteenth century has inhibited our ability to expect or perceive the risks of extreme weather phenomena that will accompany climate change. In *The Great Derangement*, Ghosh writes,

> I have come to recognize that the challenges that climate change poses for the contemporary writer ... derive ultimately from the grid of literary forms and conventions that came to shape the narrative imagination in precisely that period when the accumulation of carbon in the atmosphere was rewriting the destiny of the earth.
>
> *(7)*

In nineteenth century modes of literary realism (that we still cling to), the sudden disaster—tornado, hurricane, tsunami, etc.—is viewed as profoundly unrealistic, a kind of deus ex machina move imposed by the author. Against this, Ghosh argues that the sudden disaster and its possibility are precisely what we need to begin imagining, even though enduring literary standards of realism lull us into thinking such a thing would never happen.[5] Whereas Heise looks at the forms of genre that risk narratives take, Ghosh cautions that narrative conventions of depicting literary realism threaten to impede our ability to imagine environmental risk in the first place. Both arguments see risks to the environment as separate from the physical environment itself.

The metaphorical sense of risk as an environment or milieu emerges most explicitly in Detlef Müller-Mahn's edited collection, *The Spatial Dimension of Risk: How Geography Shapes the Emergence of Riskscapes*. Müller-Mahn traces a brief genealogy of the term in the field of geography, from Rachel Morello-Frosch's work on riskscapes in Southern California to Catherine Sutherland's work on riskscapes in communities in South Africa, to a hazard-mapping tool of the same name (http://riskscape.org.nz). In each of these texts, "riskscape" performs the work of making particular forms of vulnerability (to a variety of hazards) visible for geographers on a map, and thus available for intervention. Müller-Mahn defines the "riskscape" in a way that straddles both the material and imaginary:

> The notion of "riskscape" has a metaphoric meaning that combines the idea of a territory or a landscape with that of risk. A landscape in this sense is a territorial unit that is characterized by mutual interactions between its elements, whereas risks are regarded as structuring phenomena that shape the landscape into a riskscape.... Similar to a landscape, the physical elements of a "risky territory" form obstacles to and opportunities for the movement of people, and they are therefore part of their action frame of reference. The concept of the riskscape also allows the analysis of multiple risks and how people manage them. Riskscapes may therefore be understood as landscapes of multi-layered and interacting risks that represent both the materiality of real risks, and the perceptions, knowledge, and imaginations of the people who live in that landscape and continuously shape and reshape its contours through their daily activities.
>
> *(xvii–xviii)*

Throughout this passage, "risk" functions as both a noun ("multiple risks") and an adjective ("risky territory"); a thing and a description of things. The word has a grammatical flexibility that enables it to move through multiple parts of speech, a kind of unsettled movement. Müller-Mahn positions "riskscape" as cognate with "risky territory," shifting from risk as a noun to risk as an adjective. This raises an unresolved ontological question: does risk characterize the landscape, or is the landscape made of risk, or is risk itself a landscape?

The term "riskscape" also suggests a terrestrial bias through its etymological connection to "landscape" (as opposed to environments of ocean, polar ice, or air).[6] Müller-Mahn intentionally borrows his sense of riskscape from Arjun Appadurai's proliferation of kinds of landscape (ethnoscapes, mediascapes, technoscapes, financescapes, ideoscapes), which take inspiration from Benedict Anderson's concept of the imagined community (Appadurai 295–310). Each of these terms performs a spatialization of something both material and ideological, as a step toward orienting within the "bewildering" conditions of modernity.[7] What seems appealing about the riskscape, for Müller-Mahn, is its multiplicity: "Risk is not isolated or restricted to one place and one moment in time. Rather, risk is always multiple ... such as the combined risks of the earthquake-tsunami-nuclear meltdown" (Mahn 22). Yet orientation of the riskscape to landscapes only works to a point, perhaps most at a stretch in the phrase "multi-layered and interacting risks." Yet is the layer metaphor—reminiscent of geologic strata or paper maps—adequate to all the kinds of materiality of risk one might want to account for, from the toxicity of air pollution, to the residues of nuclear fallout post-Fukushima?

Curiously, Müller-Mahn also cites Linda Soneryd's theorization of "soundscape" as an inspiration for how he thinks about the riskscape—when soundscape itself borrows from the term landscape (Soneryd 740)! Both sound and risk operate in the non-visual register, and yet have real impacts on the ways that human beings navigate a particular space through phenomenological understanding. Müller-Mahn transposes Soneryd's schematizations of sound features as matters of attention (a sound might be part of the background, and not attended to; or it may stand out distinctly) in terms of the cognitive dimensions of risk.[8] Of course, Soneryd is not the first scholar to use the term "soundscape," which has a longer history in musicology and the emergent field of sound studies. As David Novak and Matt Sakakeehy point out in *Keywords in Sound Studies*, the term soundscape was theorized much earlier by R. Murray Schaffer, one of the founders of sound studies, in *The Tuning of the World*. Although "soundscape" is appealing to Soneryd—a geographer—it has come under criticism in the field of sound studies as such. Steven Feld, an enthomusicologist with decades of fieldwork in rainforests of Papua New Guinea, offers the alternative term "acoustemology," a concept that "refuses to sonically analogize or appropriate 'landscape,' with all its physical distance from agency and perception" and, "refuses to replace visualist ocularcentrism with sonocentrism as any sort of determining force of essentialist sensory master plans" (Feld 15). As a substitute for soundscape, Feld suggests "situated listening" as a relational practice dependent on the particular attunements, acculturations, and lived experiences of a listener in a particular milieu.

Riskscape, then, harbors a certain return to ocularcentrism and a fixation on land/earth over other kinds of multi-elemental habitats; yet it does perform a certain kind of work not achieved by other terms. By collapsing risk and landscape, the riskscape suggests relation between trope and topos, or the t(r)opological, a term that emphasizes the spatial qualities of metaphor (to orient, to collapse the distance between two unlike things, to displace) as well as metaphorical possibilities of figuring space. As Michel de Certeau reminds us, in modern Athens, public transportation vehicles are called metaphorai: "To go to work or come home, one takes a 'metaphor'—a bus or a train" (115). Paul de Man adds that, "tropes are not just travelers, they tend to be smugglers and probably smugglers of stolen goods at that (17)." In a similar vein, Paul Ricoeur asks,

> Is not the word "metaphor" itself a metaphor, the metaphor of a displacement and therefore of a transfer in a kind of space? What is at stake is precisely the necessity of these *spatial* metaphors about metaphor included in our talk about figures of speech, a spatiality in which things "which were remote now appear as close."
>
> *(145)*

Metaphor, then, has a certain navigational function; like maps, metaphors assist with cognitive and spatial orientation. What is perhaps of particular interest is the frequency with which scholars in the field of geography actually draw maps of risk as part of their studies—maps of famine areas, maps depicting conflict zones that overlay with famine areas, maps that trace the encroachment of invasive species. The term riskscape gives name to a literal practice of mapping risk that has already long been at work in geography and other fields.

I remain cautious about calling something a riskscape—for even to name a territory as a riskscape is to reify it. As Jameson cautions, theories that are too totalizing or inescapable lead to as sense of powerlessness: "Insofar as the theorist wins, therefore, by constructing an increasingly closed and terrifying machine, to that very degree he loses, since the critical capacity of his work is thereby paralyzed" ("An American Utopia" 5). Nonetheless, I find it useful as a heuristic to the extent that it opens to the question, what is left off the map? Müller-Mahn helpfully points out that mapping riskscapes can occlude other threats; for example, the riskscape of famine can itself risk "homogenizing the Horn of Africa as a riskscape of famine" and can silence other threats related to armed conflict, invasive species, and security that may be also be contributing to the problem of famine itself (32). We can take this lesson about the homogenizing power of the riskscape/map, and ask the same question of riskscapes of sea-level rise. Would artificial floating islands effectively insulate against risk, channelling paradisiacal fantasies of safety and security, or would they come with their own hidden risks? If the riskscape of sea-level rise presents one imagined version of living in risk, what new forms of risk will manifest within these new architectures?

Floating Architectures and Fantasies of Safety

Many low-lying islands in the Indian and Pacific Oceans are experiencing unprecedented levels of soil erosion and human displacement because of rising seas—a phenomenon exacerbated by global carbon emissions warming the Earth and melting glaciers. Rob Nixon's concept of "displacement in place"—where even though one has not moved geographically from one's ancestral home, the land beneath one's feet either poisoned or eroded away—aptly describes the consequences of sea-level rise (17). As a response to accelerating erosion and submersion, there has been a proliferation of designs for artificial floating islands. Most of these designs—periodically featured in newspapers like the *Guardian* and the *New York Times*—are from international companies and organizations such as Shimizu Corp (Japan), Vincent Callebaut Architects (France), Waterstudio (Netherlands), and the Seasteading Institute (U.S.A./Silicon Valley). Although these artificial islands are imagined as forms of risk mitigation, I caution that we should be skeptical of their promise. Artificial floating islands introduce other forms of risk related to structures of debt, class stratification, and new forms of economic colonialism. Artificial islands, in short, are not only about physical architectures, but also about living in particular social and economic forms.

Indeed, it is precisely economic and political risks that are obfuscated by the focus on sea-level rise as primarily a geographic problem, which has become the focus of a number of mapping projects and artistic interventions. For example, the National Ocean and Atmospheric Administration (NOAA—a prophetic acronym for a post-diluvian future) offers a Sea Level Rise Viewer that approximates the scale of future sea-level rise. In the application, you can zoom to any portion of the U.S. coastline and slide a scale to see how it will be affected by anywhere from one to six feet of sea-level rise. Climate Central's Surging Seas project offers a similar mapping application of risk zones, but at the scope of the whole world. In a more harrowing fashion, artist Michael Pinsky's project Plunge encircled monuments in London with a glowing blue ring to mark predicted sea-level rise for the year 3012. Each of these works necessarily addresses sea-level rise as a geographic problem of disappearing land. However, these risk assessments highlights only geographic dimensions of the problem of sea-level rise, but not the aftermath of how future architectures will shape the ways that displaced peoples work, socialize, and live.

What I aim to show through my focus on the imaginary architectures of floating islands is that the riskscape of sea-level rise is not only a geographic matter, but also an economic and political one. My focus on architecture as a symptom of the economic and political has its precedent in Jameson's classic analysis of the Bonaventura Hotel in *Postmodernism* (1984). "Of all the arts," Jameson writes, "architecture is the closest constitutively to the economic, with which, in the form of commissions and land values, it has a virtually unmediated relationship… grounded in the patronage of multi-national business" (5). Jameson argues that decisions about architecture are not merely aesthetic, but deeply related to economic relations and modes of production. For example, the ways that a building blends in with its surroundings, or stands out, or reflects the sky, or bewilders the visitor, can each tell us something about the present. In what follows, I argue that the architectural aesthetics of floating island designs (my version of the Bonaventura Hotel, in the Anthropocene) are a symptom of global capitalism, and not the innocent and "sustainable" solutions to sea-level rise that they purport to be.

Perhaps the innocent-seeming aesthetic of artificial islands stems from their emulation of natural forms (lily pads, hibiscus flowers, snowflakes) with artificial materials, creating sleek surfaces that appear unperturbed by surrounding ocean movement.⁹ Descriptions of artificial islands frequently draw on the rhetoric of sustainability or symbiosis, channelling these steady-states as ideals. Designers and venture capitalists envision artificial islands as having a low or non-existent carbon footprint, and in some cases, see artificial islands as hubs for creating carbon sinks (through kelp farming) or generating clean energy (wind or wave). Designs also tend to feature the colour white (see Figure 20.1 and 20.2), and evoke the sleek shapes of high-end yachts as luxury ships. They also feature the biomimetic emulation of natural forms (Figure 20.1), a commitment to sustainability in their architecture, and either independent living units or skyscraper-like towers (Figure 20.2). In artificial islands, the technological imitates natural forms in order to naturalize itself as a lived environment.[10]

However, the futuristic architecture of the naturalized technoscape can feel distant from the lived patterns of island life. In one interview, the President of Kiribati (Anote Tong) commented that,

> The last time I saw the models, I was like "wow it's like science fiction," almost like something in space. So modern, I don't know if our people could live on it. But what would you do for your grandchildren? If you're faced with the option of being submerged, with your family, would you jump on an oil rig like that? And [I] think the answer is "yes." We are running out of options, so we are considering all of them.
>
> *(Vidal)*

The situation is not ideal. Imagine that you live in a small one-story home in Kiribati, built by your grandfather, with a steep triangular thatched roof made of palm fronds that you periodically repair after storms. Your home is surrounded by lush vegetation, a small crop of papayas, and you can feel the sand beneath your feet. Imagine the distance between the rhythms of living in this way,

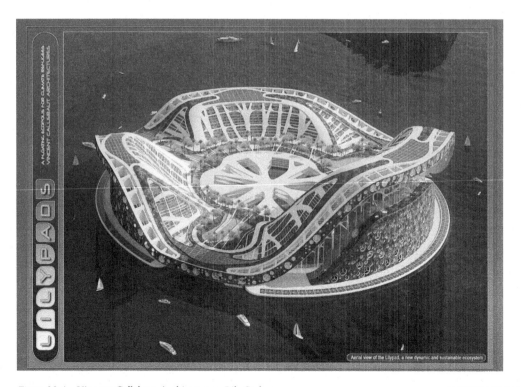

Figure 20.1 Vincent Callebaut Architectures, Lily Pad

Figure 20.2 Botanical City, Shimizu corporation

and the prospect of relocating to one of the new artificial islands that appear to concentrate all of the population in either a large shopping-mall like structure (Figure 20.1) or a large, skyscraper like tower (Figure 20.2). Such structures would alter the lived patterns of work, leisure, and socialization through their restructuring of the proximity of people to each other, a form of urbanization imposed at the scale of the island. What would be most foreign might not even be the "artificiality" of the island itself, so much as having to adjust to the spatial model of the city—a city which seems to take design inspiration from a yacht or shopping mall. As Jini Kim Watson argues, the postcolonial Asian cityscape is marked by the annihilation of traditional architectural forms in favor of Western architectures, and a shift from the horizontality of pre-colonial economic organization to the verticality of skyscrapers. Bishnupriya Ghosh adds that vertical buildings have been a subject of fascination in recent horror films; these films condition spectators to "psychic and economic investment in smart home security," but also disrupt this very sense of security through glitches, seepages, and the return of gravity as an anti-vertical force through which the "outside" returns to act on the insulated (73). Floating island architectures—which often feature towers and dense buildings—purport to offer security in architectural forms that emulate the high-rise or the cruise ship, structures deeply tied to the reproduction of capitalism at the expense of annihilating traditional architectures of inhabitation.

That floating islands reproduce capitalism (rather than their advertised role of providing sustainable homes for displaced peoples) is not a new thesis. Marxists scholars such as David Harvey, Henri Lefebvre, Edward Soja, and others (channelled by Watson in her excellent study of the new Asian city) have written extensively about the way that capitalism reproduces itself through geographic space and urbanization. Capitalism requires infrastructure to function—places of production (factories), distribution (roads, delivery, airports), and consumption (shopping malls). Space is both the product of capitalism and the medium for it (and other social activity). David Harvey offers a succinct argument: "Capital represents itself in the form of a physical landscape created in its own image" (35).

Perhaps no one understands the political and economic implications of creating artificial islands better than the Seasteading Institute, a group of Silicon Valley entrepreneurs poised to fund and create prototypes of these artificial islands. Funded in part by Peter Thiel, the Seasteading Institute is one of the most serious investors of artificial islands. It has recently approached the government of French Polynesia to host the first prototypes in its territorial waters. After signing a Memorandum of Understanding in January 2017 and arranging a planning meeting in May 2017, the Seasteading Institute was on the cusp of creating the first actual prototype of a floating island. In this memorandum, each partner agreed to prepare a "the special governing framework allowing the creation of the Floating Island Project located in an innovative special economic zone" ("Memorandum of Understanding"). The motivations were clear: French Polynesia would provide the territorial space for Seasteaders to create a prototype island, but leave them relative autonomy to develop it as they wish, crafting a libertarian enclave.

In *The Urbanism of Exception* (2017), Martin J. Murray writes that enclaves and autonomous zones are the paradigmatic spaces of global urbanism today (117). They are "durable yet malleable" instruments that can sponsor economic pursuits while operating "outside the glare of public oversight," with the capacity to "legally redefine" activities within a designated space (213). While the "archipelago" metaphor describes enclaves as "a distributed network of isolated satellite cities," some enclaves—like those imagined by Seasteaders—are literally islands (115).[11] Murray perceptively writes that these island enclaves "join the heterotopia of the oceangoing cruise ship with the historic idealization of the island," resulting in utopian fantasies of isolation and escape from regulation (240).

Seasteaders see the creation of floating islands as many things: freedom from government, freedom from regulation, freedom for experimentation, island paradises, and potential solutions to global climate change. These values are most clearly articulated in Joe Quirk's book, *Seasteading: How Floating Nations Will Restore the Environment, Enrich the Poor, Cure the Sick, and Liberate Humanity from Politicians*, a text with a superfluity of bad puns. Quirk imagines Seasteading as a neoliberal and libertarian project of freeing oneself from existing forms of government. In his vision of "seavilization," democracy, "a system by which majorities outvote minorities," would be "upgraded to a system whereby the smallest minorities, including the individual, could vote with their houses"— as if democracy were an operating system (Quirk location 100–108). These homes would be able to:

> detach at any time and sail to join another floating city, compelling ocean governments to compete for mobile citizens like companies compete for customers. A market of competing governments, a Silicon Valley of the sea, would allow the best ideas for governance to emerge peacefully, unleashing unimaginable progress in the rate at which we generate solutions to the oldest social problem: How do we get along?
>
> *(location 108)*

Here, the rhetoric of the tech company becomes the rhetoric of governance. Quirk uses such odd turns of phrase as "unleashing unimaginable progress" for the "social problem" of getting along, as if getting along could be conceptualized as a linear progress narrative. In neoliberal fashion, Quirk sees the invisible hand of market logic as governance itself, later lamenting "If only governance providers had to compete to keep mobile citizens as if they were customers!" (location 4279). Government is simply another form of technology that can be "upgraded"—a government 2.0, if you will. Seasteaders typically see themselves as outside ideology. As Quirk writes, "Seasteading is less an ideology than a technology"—a dubious statement if there ever was one (location 457). In their writings on the culture industry, Theodore Adorno and Max Horkheimer caution that, "the basis on which technology acquires power over society is the power of those whose economic hold over society is greatest. A technological rationale is the rationale of domination itself" (4).

Novelist China Mieville offers a more damning critique; while "Big Capital" has ample ways of avoiding paying taxes, libertarians are precisely those who find it hard to avoid their taxes because they "are too small, incompetent, or insufficiently connected to win Iraq-reconstruction contracts" and thus libertarianism betrays its fear of "actually existing capitalism, at which it cannot quite succeed" (Mieville "Floating Utopias").

The Seasteaders' model of self-governance draws on biological metaphors, envisioning the government–corporation and citizen–customer as natural life forms capable of creative evolution. In one notable phrase, Quirk envisions Seasteading as "a Cambrian explosion of governments,' a phrase that became a clarion call among Seasteaders" (location 496). Even though governmental forms are arguably human constructs, collectively shaped and agreed upon, Patri naively presumes that the people who make these new governments can return to a pre-ideological condition, or a pre-cultural state—that their own desires, values, and imagined forms of government and social organization are their own. Quirk images the global economy as an organism that must be sustained at any cost. Quirk writes that, "civilization still owes a great debt to Edward Robert Armstrong, whose design was applied to the global development of floating oil rigs, which pump lifeblood into our global economy" (352). No risks are accounted for, which is particularly surprising given that this book was written within recent memory of the 2011 BP oil spill, one of the worst environmental disasters in history (apart from the devastation wrought by nuclear weapons). The metaphorical collapse of biological evolution, economics, and government in Seasteading ideology constitutes an effort to naturalize neoliberal capitalism as the default mode of existence, a naturalization that intentionally obfuscates its ideological role by claiming to be purely technological.

For me, the prospect of building artificial floating islands raises the question of what happens to soil. Recent work in the humanities (or as Donna Haraway calls it, the "humusities") has turned to the soil as a critical site for the production and reproduction of forms of life. The soil is precisely what is shared in common by neologisms like the "Anthropocene," which presupposes a new geologic layer inflected by human activities, and Haraway's term "Chthulucene," which imagines worlding processes by multiple earthly or chthonic beings. In *Staying with the Trouble* (2016), Haraway's vision for the future is "not 'posthuman' but 'com-post,'" (11) a step toward the "detumescing project of a self-making and planet-destroying CEO" (32). Ecological Marxists have been quick to point out that Marx wrote his dissertation on the Greek philosopher Epicurus, as well as Lockean notions of property that involve humans mixing their labor with the soil (or other natural materials) (Foster). Indeed, one question with floating island designs is whether there would be any soil. Figures 20.1 to 20.3 each appear to have greenery, but it is unclear whether these plants would be grown hydroponically or whether the yacht-like structures of the floating islands would actually harbor containers of brown soil (and risk dirtying their white surfaces). Taken together, recent critical writings suggest that the loss of soil is nothing short of the loss of the ability to generate value and food, without external investment of capital.

Yet if we think of the ocean as a kind of "soil"—a site for the extraction of natural capital—then other questions arise around its future management. For example, there is the question of whether oceanic nations displaced by rising seas would be able to retain jurisdiction over the 200-mile Exclusive Economic Zone (EEZ) without physical geographic presence. Could the people of Kiribati, say, move to Fiji and retain exclusive fishing rights to their former geographic EEZ? This raises the important question of whether island nations would need to maintain geographic presence to retain their EEZ, although as yet there has been no legal precedent (Kraska).[12]

Conclusion: Lattices of Amphibious Survival

The question we are left with then, is: what kinds of architectures would island communities want that both protect against sea-level rise and preserve indigenous forms of life, living, and economic organization that do not form an umbilical cord of dependency to global capitalism? Jason Pomeroy of Pomeroy studios, an architectural firm based in Singapore, imagines waterborne communities as a solution to coastal urban pressures to expand city growth, while being sensitive to cultural heritage:

> [technology has] contributed to a transcendence of the corporation and consumer culture that arguably destroys the sense of identity of a people. A cultural sustainability that seeks to preserve traditional social and spatial practices potentially safeguards against the imposition of a modern built environment that lacks cultural relevance.
>
> *(Pomeroy 10)*

I conclude by turning to S+PBA's designs for a Wetropolis (Figure 20.3), which successfully incorporates elements of traditional Thai architecture that could be for all sorts of people—not just the wealthy.

S+PBA is a Bangkok-based architectural firm founded in 2005 by Ponlawat Buansiri and Songsuda Athibai. Their designs for a Wetropolis, exhibited at the AEDES Gallery in Berlin in 2011 in *Towards a Post-Diluvian Future*, address the acute problem of Bangkok's livability after the seas rise. The architects write,

> While most of the world follows the standard from dust to dust, ashes to ashes cycle, Bangkok prefers something wetter: from water to water. Almost 300 years after rising from the marshy banks of the Chao Phraya, it appears Bangkok will return to its watery origins.
>
> *(S+PBA, "A Post-Diluvian Future")*

Further,

> Bangkok has always been flooded… Once the city is submarine, can we even call this phenomenon flooding? Flooding implies a passing phase rather than a fixed environment, and yet, at the current juncture, water is much more predictable than land.

As a solution, the architects propose a floating architecture that takes the form of a mesh rather than an island, modifying indigenous architectural patterns (Figure 20.3). This meshwork structure borrows from Thailand's centuries-old traditions of "flood-conscious aquatecture into a contemporary, sustainable and visually stunning Wetropolis" (S+PBA "A Post-Diluvian Future"). Emulating the supra-marine stilt home community of Koh Pan Yii that hovers above the Andaman sea in Southern Thailand, S+PBA proposes modifying this traditional architectural form by adding mangrove forests alongside modest shrimp farming. S+PBA imagines a multi-level organization to the floating architecture network,

> derived from Thai traditional housing where the central courtyard/deck is used as a (family) common space on the upper floor. Furthermore, "Fah Lai" (fluid skin), a refined idea from vernacular architecture enables natural ventilation in and out of each individual space. It is adopted for the envelope to enable comfortable living conditions without fully relying on mechanical cooling systems.
>
> *(S+PBA "A Post-Diluvian Future" Wetropolis description)*

In this way, S+PBA makes a conscientious effort to organize living spaces according to traditionally-inspired forms. The "fluid skin" proposed seems responsive to not only the rising of the water below, but is also attentive to structural breathability with the humidity of the air.

Floating Architectures

Figure 20.3 Wetropolis, sky view. S+PBA Architects

The structural proximity to water in *Wetropolis* suggests a different relationship to risk—where the designed habitat is not aimed at excluding water/risk entirely out of the picture to absolute safety, but a situation of living with water/risk in a structurally porous way. Perhaps a more equitable future, one that resists replicating the structures of capitalism while retaining a historical memory of the past, might manifest in such amphibious structures of survival.

Acknowledgment

I would like to thank Bishnupriya Ghosh for her generous feedback on drafts of this chapter.

Notes

1 For example, in anticipation of sea-level rise, Kiribati has bought land in Fiji (Caramel).
2 One notable addition is China's expansion of small islands in the South China Sea, but I exclude this as an example because they are not floating structures; the islands are made by adding soil to existing shallow islands (Watkins).
3 I refer to the Pacific Ocean cautiously, since Somerville discusses the colonial history of how the Pacific Ocean came to be named as such is connected to war, empire, and attempted genocide.
4 The imagination of security—not the opposite of risk, but part of a similar episteme perhaps—also has spatial inflections. Michel Foucault writes that security involves the planning of milieu. Security

will try to plan a milieu in terms of events or series of events or possible elements, of series that will have to be regulated within a multivalent and transformable framework. The specific space of security refers then to a series of possible events.

(Foucault 20)

5 Although some writers of climate fiction, or CliFi, have argued that they have been doing the work of writing the castastrophe back into forms of realism, I agree with Ghosh's point that mainstream perceptions of catastrophe as unrealistic still hold sway. The solution, clearly, is more climate fiction.
6 I show how a terrestrial bias emerges through the ways we use orientational metaphors in ordinary language (Jue 87–105).
7 One of the words that frequently appears in Fredric Jameson's classic study *Postmodernism, or, the Cultural Logic of Late Capitalism* (1984) is "bewilderment." The Oxford English Dictionary defines bewilderment as the, "Confusion arising from losing one's way; mental confusion from inability to grasp or see one's way through a maze or tangle of impressions or ideas. To lose one's way," with an etymological connection to the wilderness.
8 Soneryd lists the following features of a soundscape: keynote sounds (recurring, repetitive, background sounds); soundfield (acoustic space generated by a sound source); soundmark (a well-defined sound with a clear source and symbolic connotations); signal (informative sound that stands out against the overall soundscape texture).
9 Science fiction was famously theorized by Darko Suvin as the genre of "cognitive estrangement," where (good) science fiction shocks or alienates us from the conditions of our existing present in some way, but shows us a world that might logically be possible within the bounds of our existing knowledge of physical laws/nature.
10 Although deconstructions of the natural/technical binary abound, I use the phrase in order to highlight the role of human intentionality: the biomimicry in floating architectures is extensively planned, and the final results will cost billions of dollars to finance.
11 See also Steinberg, "Atlas Swam" 1532–1550; Keith 190–204; Steinberg, "Liquid Urbanity" 2113–2122.
12 In an email correspondence with the author, Dr. Kraska wrote, "Bottom line is nobody knows for sure."

Works Cited

Adorno, Theodore and Max Horkheimer. "The Culture Industry," *The Consumer Society Reader*, edited by Juliet Schor and Douglas Holt, Norton, 2000, pp. 3–19.
Appadurai, Arjun. "Disjuncture and Difference in the Global Cultural Economy." *Theory, Culture, Society*, vol. 7, 1990, pp. 295–310.
Caramel, Lawrence. "Besieged by the Rising Tides of Climate Change, Kiribati Buys Land in Fiji." *Guardian*, June 30, 2014.
Carson, Rachel. *Silent Spring*. Mariner Books, 1962.
Clement, Hal. *Noise*. Tor Books, 2003.
De Certeau, Michel. *The Practice of Everyday Life*. UC Press, 1980.
De Man, Paul. "The Epistemology of Metaphor." *On Metaphor*, edited by Sheldon Sacks. U of Chicago P, 1978, pp. 11–28.
Feld, Steven. "Acoustemology." *Keywords in Sound Studies*, edited by David Novak and Matt Sakakeeny. Duke UP, 2015, pp. 12–21.
Foster, John Bellamy. *Marx's Ecology*. Monthly Review Press, 2000.
Foucault, Michel. *Security, Territory, Population*. Picador, 2004.
Ghosh, Amitav. *The Great Derangement*. U of Chicago P, 2016.
Ghosh, Bishnupriya. "The Security Aesthetic in Bollywood's High-Rise Horror." *Representations*, vol. 126, no. 1, 2014, pp. 58–84.
Haraway, Donna. *Staying with the Trouble*. Duke Press, 2016.
Harvey, David. "The Urban Process Under Capitalism: A Framework for Analysis." *The Blackwell City Reader 2nd edition*, edited by Gary Bridge and Sophie Watson. Wiley-Blackwell, 2010, pp. 32–39.
Heise, Ursula. *Sense of Place and Sense of Planet*. Oxford Press, 2008.
Jameson, Fredric. "An American Utopia." *An American Utopia*, edited by Fredric Jameson and Slavoj Zizek. Verso, 2016, pp. 1–96.
Jameson, Fredric. *Postmodernism, or, the Cultural Logic of Late Capitalism*. Duke Press, 1984.
Jue, Melody. "Vampire Squid Media." *Grey Room*, vol. 37, 2014, pp. 87–105.
Keith, Kent. "Floating Cities: A New Challenge for Transnational Law." *Marine Policy*, vol. 1, no. 3, 1977, pp. 190–204.

Kraska, James. Department of Ocean Law and Policy at the US Naval War College. Personal Interview. April 26, 2017.

Lewis, C.S. *Perelandra*. Scribner, 1996 [1943].

"Memorandum of Understanding." Government French Polynesia and the Seasteading Institute, January 17, 2017, www.seasteading.org/floating-city-project/. Accessed June 11, 2017.

Mieville, China. "Floating Utopias." http://inthesetimes.com/article/print/3328/floating_utopias. Accessed June 6, 2017.

Mieville, China. *The Scar*. Del Rey, 2002.

Morello-Frosch, Rachel. "Environmental Justice and Southern California's 'Riskscape': The Distribution of Air Toxics Exposures and Health Risks Among Diverse Communities." *Urban Affairs Review*, March 2001, 551–578.

Müller-Mahn, Detlef. *The Spatial Dimension of Risk: How Geography Shapes the Emergence of Riskscapes*. Routledge, 2013.

Murray, Martin J. *The Urbanism of Exception: The Dynamics of Global City Building in the Twenty-First Century*. Cambridge UP, 2017.

Nixon, Rob. *Slow Violence and the Environmentalism of the Poor*. Harvard, 2012.

Novak, David and Matt Sakakeeny, *Keywords in Sound Studies*. Duke Press, 2015.

Pinsky, Michael. "Plunge." www.michaelpinsky.com/project/plunge/. Accessed April 17, 2017.

Pomeroy, Jason, *P.O.G.: Pod Off-Grid: Explorations into Low-energy Waterborne Communities*. ORO Editions, 2016.

Quirk, Joe. *Seasteading: How Floating Nations Will Restore the Environment, Enrich the Poor, Cure the Sick, and Liberate Humanity from Politicians*. Free Press, 2017.

Ricoeur, Paul. "The Metaphorical Process as Cognition, Imagination, and Feeling," *On Metaphor*, edited by Sheldon Sacks. U of Chicago P, 1978, pp. 141–158.

RiskScape. http://riskscape.org.nz. Accessed April 17, 2017.

S+PBA. "A Post-Diluvian Future." http://spluspba.weebly.com/a-post-diluvian-future.html. Accessed April 26, 2017.

S+PBA. "A Post-Diluvian Future." Wetropolis description. Nd. TS.

Schaffer, R. Murray. *The Tuning of the World*. Random House, 1977.

Sea Level Rise Viewer. NOAA, https://coast.noaa.gov/slr/. Accessed April 17, 2017.

Slonczewski, Joan. *A Door Into Ocean*. Orb Books, 1986.

Somerville, Alice Te Punga. "Where Oceans Come From." *Comparative Literature*, vol. 69, no. 1 2017, pp. 25–31.

Soneryd, Linda. "Hearing as a Way of Dwelling: The Active Sense-making of Environmental Risk and Nuisance." *Environment and Planning D: Society and Space*, vol. 22, 2004, pp. 737–753.

Steinberg, Philip. "Atlas Swam: Freedom, Capital, and Floating Sovereignties in the Seasteading Vision." *Antipode*, vol. 44, no. 4, 2012, pp. 1532–1550.

Steinberg, Philip. "Liquid Urbanity: Re-engineering the City in a Post-terrestrial World." *Engineering the Earth: The Impacts of Mega-Engineering Projects*, edited by Stanley Brunn. Springer, 2011, pp. 2113–2122.

Stephenson, Neal. *Snow Crash*. Del Rey, 1992.

Surging Seas. Climate Central, http://sealevel.climatecentral.org/. Accessed April 17, 2017.

Suvin, Darko. *Metamorphoses of Science Fiction*. Peter Lang, 2016 [1979].

The Seasteading Institute, www.seasteading.org/tahiti-seasteading-gathering-2017-eng/. Accessed June 11, 2017.

Uncertain Commons. *Speculate This!* Duke UP, e-book, 2013.

Vidal, John. "Artificial Island Could be the Solution for Rising Pacific Sea Levels." *Guardian*, September 8, 2011.

Watkins, Derek. "What Has China Been Building in the South China Sea?" *New York Times*, October 27, 2015.

Watson, Jini Kim. *The New Asian City: Three-Dimensional Fictions of Urban Space*. Minnesota Press, 2016.

21
CORRECTIONS TO THE FIRST DRAFT OF HISTORY

Raqs Media Collective

In "Corrections to the First Draft of History," Raqs Media Collective offers a visual meditation on how our understanding of the world hinges on the ability to navigate between certainty and doubt. The visual essay takes its cues from the history of reading and learning languages, gesturing specifically to blackboards and early primers, to the forms and textures of letters, to the lengths and sounds of vowels. If writing seeks to express what one knows, it also bears the trace of what one cannot or does not know. Raqs focuses on time: in particular, how experiential time derails the duration and order—the very basis of historical understanding—imposed on it. Something unexpected, uninvited, and untimely, always arrives as stranger to scuttle the established measures of the world. Like the archaic sundial, the obdurate donkey, or the dapper pocket-watch intruding upon the well-ordered realm of stocks and shares. Such eruptions provoke other readings that "correct" the first draft of history.

The present volume seeks to move beyond the self-evident calculus of risk and to explore modes of apprehending uncertainty. In context of this collective project, speculation as open-ended play becomes significant as critical-cognitive practice. As a ludic performance, Raqs' "kinetic contemplation" propels its audience in the space between knowing and unknowing, inviting them to speculate on the limits of perception and representation, interpretation and knowledge.

★ ★ ★

Several words contain some silent letter or letters.

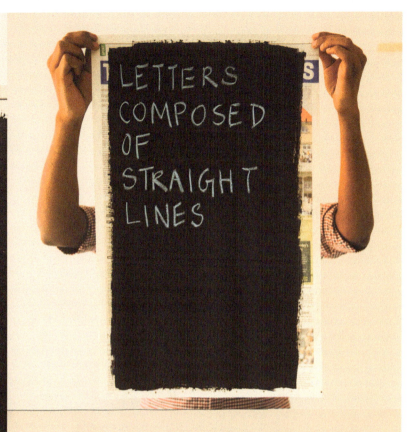

Let us read first, then.

A-TITHI

a guest is always
she comes without …
ointment, without …
agreement about da…
she changes the ro…
appears, un-annou…
un-expected.
It follows that ev…
always un-timel…

...tranger, an *atithi*...
...ing, without app-
..., notice, or prior
...*tithi*, of arrival.
... the moment she
..., un-called for,

... stranger is also

We do.
I go.

Do so to me.
Ye do so.

By me.

To be.

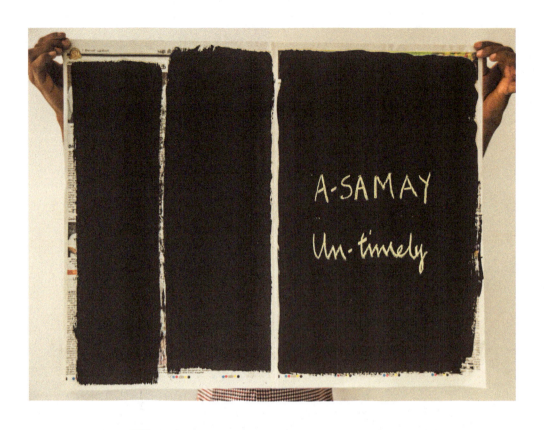

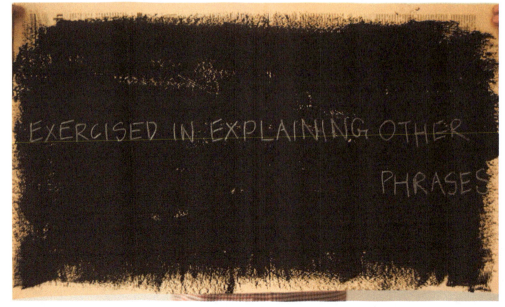

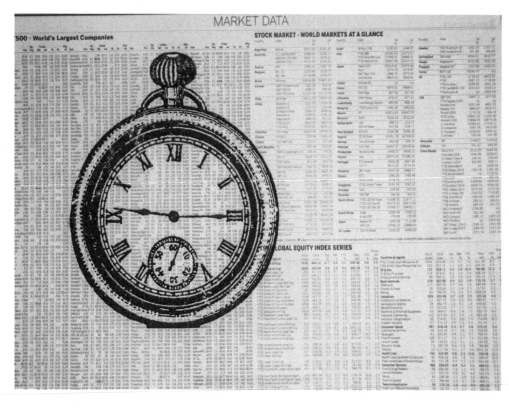

PART VI

AFFECT

22
SOCIAL MEDIA AND THE SOCIAL QUESTION

Speculations on Risk Media Society

Joshua Neves

Risk is an unusually sticky term. The *Oxford English Dictionary*, for example, lists no fewer than 24 couplings, including: risk aversion, risk-bearing, risk capital, risk-free, risk pooling, and risk taker, among others. These combinations highlight the paradoxical promiscuity of a concept that describes, even worries over, the possibility of exposure, loss, or injury—which extends to colloquialisms like run the risk or risky business. *Risk media* adds yet another combination. Media too are gooey, connective: from media darling, media events and media-saturated, to more academic terminology like media ecology, media infrastructure, algorithmic media, and so on. But more than this grammatology, media animate compound socio-techno encounters. As John Durham Peters puts it, each medium signals a what, how, and whom—a combination of "content, channel, and creature." He continues: "There is no form of communication, except for perhaps among angels as dreamt of by some theologians, without a medium" (Peters 267). To say that communication requires a medium—from that of the human body to the environment to social media platforms—is to say there is something essential about risk and exposure to mediation itself. Put simply: media are always risky; risk is always social (Beck).

This chapter is organized around distinct conjugations of risk media, paying particular attention to what has, in a short time, become intimately known as *social media*. Social media are historically rooted and spatially diverse, but they are also consolidated in current anxieties about everything from fake news and fractured publics to new aesthetic forms, social habits, and geospatialities. While I mean to open up debates about social media beyond "the social lives of networked teens" and popular technologies or platforms, it is worth pausing to consider familiar definitions (Boyd). One such explanation is a "group of Internet-based applications that build on the ideological and technological foundations of Web 2.0 and that allow the creation and exchange of user-generated content" (Kaplan and Haenlein 61). This notion is basically related to the rise of the Internet as a mass medium and to practical and discursive shifts regarding interactivity, labor, connectivity, data, smartness, and so on. It describes the fantasy of networked sociality as much as any actually existing Internet of people and things.

A related shift is that from mass media to a "social media logic."[1] As José van Dijck and Thomas Poell argue, social media platforms have "penetrated deeply into the mechanics of everyday life," transforming social interactions and public institutions—both online and offline—and ultimately becoming entangled with mass media in ways that change and intensify each (van Dijck and Poell 3). A telling example for van Dijck and Poell are the 2012 Facebook Riots in Haren, Netherlands. The riots, echoing similar irruptions elsewhere, began when a teenage girl's birthday invitation went viral on Facebook—inadvertently reaching thousands of invitees and subsequently gaining traction across other social media sites, as well as TV, radio, and print. This feedback loop included mundane social media contact, self-organized teens and trolls, on-site news coverage, and over 3000 people traveling to the Dutch suburb as part of "Project X Haren." For van Dijck and Poell, the events demonstrate how social media not only seep into mass media but enter into "all areas of public life," driving important changes in private, corporate, and state spheres.[2] Such transformations, in turn, become enmeshed with and amplify the familiar—reshaping media and sociality. Drawing on and reframing these debates, this chapter examines social media as risk media. It asks: what or where is *the social* in social media? Who or what can belong to it? How is (anti)sociality produced and managed? And what do "new" mediatized social relations tell us about *risk media society*?

Risk and Anxiety

Let's begin with a banal example. In a 2017 interview with the BBC's *Radio Times*, the British actress Daisy Ridley, recently catapulted to fame after being cast as Rey in the 2015 *Star Wars* reboot, described her decision to quit Instagram and social media altogether. She explained,

> I don't do social any more. I came off it last September and I will never get back on. The more I read about teenage anxiety, the more I think it's highly unhealthy for people's mental health. It's such a weird thing for young people to look at distorted images of things they should be.
>
> *(Lazarus)*

Ridley's reaction is not unique. Indeed, her co-star in 2017's *The Last Jedi*, Kelly Marie Tran, was forced off of social media after months of sexist and racist abuse ("Star Wars"). I highlight Ridley's comments here, in part, because Google's PageRank algorithm selected them for me. What is noticeable about the announcement is its familiar focus on youth and on gender (young women are routinely seen as most at risk), as well as both its interchangeability (it is one among many) and yet newsworthiness (from radio, to news sites, to social networking). More to the point, she poses a resonant concern about the risks of social media for mental health—especially what has come to be known as Social Media Anxiety Disorder (SMAD). As a recent article in *Teen Vogue* puts it, "SMAD can leave us wondering if we're good enough, pretty enough, popular enough—and that can suck up our time and stop us from healthier interactions" (Hovitz). One specialist quoted in the article likens the ups and downs of social media behaviors to drug addiction. Such stories are ubiquitous.[3] They are an important part of what we do when we do social media.

My aim here is less to dwell in this techno-pop paranoia, than to ask a parallel question about the relationship between risk and uncertainty, on the one hand, and anxiety and shock, on the other. This is a speculative analogy. But one, I think, that can help us to clarify an important aspect of *social-media-risk*. As developed in the introduction to this collection, Frank Knight's economic distinction between risk and uncertainty is crucial for cultural theories of risk media (Knight). If risk points to actuarial predictions and probability, the likeliness this or that may happen, uncertainty signals the limits of such epistemologies. This distinction was tragically popularized by the former U.S. Secretary of Defense, Donald Rumsfeld, in his assessment of Iraq's capacity to produce weapons of mass destruction. Using the language of strategic planning, Rumsfeld infamously distinguished between "known unknowns" and "unknown unknowns" (Courtney et al.). The former refers to risks you can anticipate, while the latter points to situations that are as yet unimaginable. The states are linked: risk attempts to manage uncertainty. And in so doing it tends to erase or minimize what is truly unknown. Rumsfeld plays with this uncertainty in order to justify both the lack of evidence and the imperative to intervene—transforming uncertainty into risk, and risk into militarized violence. In this way, uncertainty is both the problem posed by risk and its excess.

A century ago, Sigmund Freud offered an interesting parallel discussion to risk and uncertainty. In *Beyond the Pleasure Principle*, he famously delineates between three states of preparedness for danger: anxiety, fear, and fright. For Freud, these distinctions matter because they help us to understand trauma (such as "war neuroses"), repetition compulsion (such as repeatedly acting out traumatic events that are not consciously recognized), and thus situations where the subject remains a passive agent to her or his own experience. He defines anxiety as the state of expecting or preparing for danger, but where the exact danger itself is unknown. Similarly, fear relies on the expectation of danger and further specifies "a definite object of which to be afraid." In contrast to fear and anxiety—which can be understood as specifying degrees of risk—fright, or what Freud also terms surprise or shock, suggests a different vector. Fright "is the name we give to the state a person gets into when he has run into danger without being prepared for it" (Freud 6). It thus names the moment when uncertainty materializes as shock for those who experience it. What matters in this spectrum is that fear and anxiety do not lead to the traumatic behaviors that Freud observes in shell-shocked veterans, victims of industrial accidents, and the like. Instead, he argues, "there is something about anxiety that protects its subject against fright and so against fright-neuroses" (7).

If I opportunistically take up Freud's theory—leaving aside some of his main concerns, such as the pleasure principle itself—it is to reconsider his claims about anxiety and fright in light of risk media society. Distinct psychological, economic, or computational approaches share in stressing the paradoxical nature of risk management—which, on the one hand, identifies general and definite objects of danger, and on the other hand, attempts to anticipate what defies prediction. What interests me here is how risk media change the nature of danger and the dangerous. Or, to paraphrase Anthony Giddens: "there is a new riskiness to risk" media (4). This assertion is echoed by the felt experience that mediatized risk normalizes and intensifies anxiety—in everything from the Homeland Security Advisory System and TV news to cyberbullying, smart tech, and pharmaceutical disorderism. These systems of prediction, warning, and update legitimize protective claims, even scaremongering: managing risk makes us safe. Crucially, this works not primarily through prevention but through *preparation*—by preparing populations for the likelihood of risk, loss or injury. Risk media do more than domesticate danger: they make predictable and manage the production of affects like anxiety, fear, and even shock.

What is striking, and thus now anachronistic, in Freud's interpretation is that anxiety, fear, and fright are imagined to be atypical. They are associated with warfare, accidents, and moments of unusual danger or neuroses—not, that is, part of the texture of everyday life. This spectrum of encounters are important because they help to distinguish traumatic behavior from other afflictions and anxieties. Fright, unlike anxiety, is marked by the compulsion to repeatedly return to harrowing events in the hopes of mastering them and thus to return pleasure. Freud's account is thus both out of sync with risk media society and, at the same time, offers a useful starting point from which to theorize fractured subjectivities and the changing significance of repetition—including the new ways that unconscious experience seeps into conscious life. A century later we need to rethink Freud's understanding of risk and uncertainty by adding digital culture to the scene. Does anxiety continue to protect its subject? Or has it become something else entirely?

In contrast to shielding anxiety and traumatic fright, the social logic of risk media has itself become perilously routine—which is to say that it repeats differently. From the fear of missing out (FOMO) and "habitual new media" (Chun, *Updating*), to information addiction, dataveillance (Clarke), and the Internet of Things (IoT), anxiety no longer merely predicts, prepares, or protects: it overwhelms. The penetration of risk into all domains of human and nonhuman life acts not only to diminish shock—except when it does not—it also makes the banality of anxiety harrowing in its ubiquity. Put differently, risk society manages shock through resilience (Halpern et al. 121–124). Resilience is a mode of worldmaking that refuses stability or equilibrium—what we usually understand as key to healthy ecosystems—and instead embraces optimization and plasticity (Halpern et al. 121).[4] Subjects are not only prepared for the worst, but are also constantly updated. This is to signal the changing nature of automated anticipation and epistemologies as well as their import in shaping *the social* in social media. The simple point is this: risk media are not new or shocking—at least not in the old sense of surprise or fright—they are mundane, chronic. These "habitual" forms, as Wendy Hui Kyong Chun observes, are important because they "remain by disappearing from consciousness" (*Updating* x). They are what endures when novelty trucks on. My own thinking about risk media is indebted to this formulation. The ordinary and iterative pose vital, and vitally overlooked, risks. What once protected the psyche now exposes it; what was before technologically accidental is now the norm.

The Internet of People and Things

To that say that repetition has changed is to emphasize its provisional or "demo" logic. On the one hand, this is paradoxical because repetition must repeat itself in order to be so. On the other hand, it is crucial to understanding changes in the "technological unconscious." This, as Nigel Thrift argues, is "a different kind of repetition" (223).[5] For Thrift, the technological unconscious describes how the world shows up, addresses us, and is accepted as certain—it is about "*knowledges* of position and juxtaposition" (213). Echoing a range of scholars—including what Katherine Hayles terms the "cognisphere" or what Orit Halpern, Robert Mitchell, and Bernard Dionysius Geoghegan more recently have termed the "smartness mandate"—Thrift underscores how senses and capacities are remade since the 1960s. For example, he identifies the rise of *track and trace* technologies, and the mainstreaming of logistical systems and ubiquitous computing, as central to our changing technological cognizance (Thrift 219). Thrift sums up the shift in everyday experience as "a move of the 'social' 'atomic structure' from one model to another as a full-blown *standardization of space* takes hold, very similar in its ambitions and effects to the nineteenth century standardization of time" (214). In preliminary form, then, Thrift helps us to engage the plastic synchronization of the senses and environment that enable a new set of repetitions—a world—to materialize.

Beginning with these spaces of anticipation, my aim here is to explore two entangled aspects of social-media-risk: the Internet of People *and* the Internet of Things. While the Internet of Things (IoT) is a familiar concept describing the proliferation of smart/networked devices, and their embedding in everyday sites, the former moves in the opposite direction. The Internet of People emphasizes embodied actions and what I call technologies of intimacy (ToI). ToI describe the mundane habits, affects, and connectivities shored up by networked subjects and protocols. If one points to how technologies are made smart so that they can seamlessly aid and augment human interactions—how technologies become performatively human—then the other signals how people and social practices become technological: they are two sides of the same coin. Together they constitute the Internet of People and Things.

Not surprisingly, this assemblage has fostered a good deal of anxiety. Sherry Turkle's 2011 bestseller, *Alone Together*, is emblematic of this disquiet—and is framed by an increasing paranoia about the relationship between people and things (x). It begins, for example, by tracing the "turning points" in Turkle's work, which has shifted dramatically from the celebratory tone of *The Second Self* (1984) and *Life on Screen* (1995) to the present. Additionally, this narrative recalls Turkle's research before computers, where as a social scientist in Paris, she studied how the language of psychoanalysis entered people's everyday language and understandings of the self. Turkle's ethnographic engagement with psychoanalysis is important because it informs her subsequent approach to computer culture. She describes moving to Massachusetts Institute of Technology in the 1980s, because,

> I sensed that something similar was happening with the language of computers. Computational metaphors, such as "debugging" and "programming," were starting to be used to think about politics, education, social life, and—most central to the analogy of psychoanalysis—about the self.
>
> (x)

In other words, Turkle's research moved from a focus on the popular unconscious to what she refers to as the "inner history of devices" (x, xiii).

In addition to the tantalizing parallel between psychoanalysis and computation—itself an interesting invocation of a technological unconscious—what I find fascinating is Turkle's increasingly bleak view of digital life and, at the same time, the related nostalgia for a simpler past. From the heady excitement of 1984 to the anti-sociality of 2011's *Alone Together* and 2016's *Reclaiming Conversation: The Power of Talk in a Digital Age*, a rather different understanding of media's social risks emerges. As Turkle puts it: "we expect more from technology and less from each other" (*Alone Together* xii).[6] This line, which is also subtitle of the book, has become a kind of mantra and is repeated in the press, TED Talks (her video has over four million views), academic discourse, and across social media itself (see Turkle "Connected, but Alone"). The idea that we, especially the young among us, need to put down our devices and *live your life* is already cliché. Such colloquialisms also give a clear sense of how mediation is popularly understood: like a light switch—it is on or off.

The technological condition of being *alone together* is emblematic of current anxieties about the risks of social media: the fear that we are increasingly close with technology but are disconnected from other people. For example, Turkle describes teenage boys unable to make eye contact, silent family dinners where each person is tethered to a screen, the idea that texting has replaced talk, and both childcare and eldercare facilitated by screens and robots. Despite its determinism and bossy humanism, I want to take this provocation seriously. This is in part because her refrains have emerged as a kind of common sense about digital culture. But more importantly, I linger on Turkle's widely circulating arguments because, while purportedly focused on our intimate relations with technology, they largely ignore technologies themselves. People, not things, are the *we* who "bend to the inanimate with new solicitude" (*Alone Together* xii). A salient example for Turkle is how sociable robots—from ELIZA to Furbies—have shaped our artifactual relationships. For example, she is deeply suspicious of care robots, like Paro the seal, whose large blinking eyes and wiggly body is designed to comfort the elderly.[7] Turkle describes Paro's gaze as a form of "pretend empathy." Contrasting views that see such robots as social or medical breakthroughs, she notes: "That robot can't empathize. It doesn't face death. It doesn't know life" ("Connected, but Alone").[8] This and similar claims, in my view, not only misjudge our relationship with computers but ask us to reconsider intimacy itself. How, for instance, are human-centered notions of intimacy—where humans are the agents capable of close knowledge and feelings toward people, animals, ideas, things, and so on—contested or remade by emergent forms of computational intimacy (from cookies and facial recognition to neural networks)?

If the previous section emphasized the new risks of ordinary and calculative anxiety, my interest here is to add another dimension to risk media society: the condition of *being alone, with computers*. It's worth noting that since about 2010 the number of computers on the Internet has exceeded Earth's human population (Gershenfeld and Vasseur 60). And now that everyday things—from televisions to medical implants, stop lights to smart buildings—are web servers, capable of sending and receiving data, humans seemingly make up only a small part of the network. The idea that mundane things can go online is of course not new.[9] But recent years have seen an explosion of new devices, changes in Internet Protocol (IP), the rise of technologized urban forms, new policy and security concerns, and daily engagements with Siri, Fitbit, and a host of automated sensors and algorithms.

These relations are provocatively enlivened by artist Mark Leckey's 2010 *Green Screen Refrigerator Action*—a video and installation starring a Samsung smart refrigerator (Figure 22.1). In the video, the refrigerator moves seamlessly through time and space as an array of images fill the background and a synthesized voice addresses viewers and other technologies with refrains like: "see, we assemble" and "they ask, and they answer." Describing the video's production, the artist notes: "The Fridge stood on a green screen infinity cyc while I coaxed it into revealing its thoughts and actions."[10] The refrigerator dreams, reflects on its own design and inner-workings,

Figure 22.1 Mark Leckey's 2010 *GreenScreenRefrigeratorAction* provocatively engages the intimacies of the Internet of Things

imagines cosmic connections, and anticipates needs. What interests me about the work is how it enacts a technosphere that, while entangled with the human world, also projects a distinct form of networked consciousness. While the various images and ideas projected by the refrigerator originate in human activities—a refrigerator manual, product photos, renderings of kitchens, even social media-like sounds and images—the video also speculates about machine learning, knowing, and intimacy.

In this way, *GreenScreenRefrigerator* anticipates recent AI research projects like Google's Deep-Dream—a computer vision program that trains artificial neural networks to create patterns from "a sea of data" (Steyerl).[11] Google refers to these machine learning algorithms as "deep dreaming" or "inceptionism" because of their capacity to perceive patterns from randomness (Mordvintsev et al.). But, as Hito Steyerl argues in her analysis of contemporary forms of *apophenia*, this deep seeing is not chiefly hallucinatory. Rather, it is the result of specific technological protocols and ideologies.[12] What's more, she argues that DeepDream manages "to visualize the unconscious of prosumer networks" through the complex surveillance of user practices. Of particular interest is how this form of recognition—which, in popular examples, "sees" dogs and cats, spaghetti, lidless eyes, and other over-processed features—transforms terrifying changes in technologies of production and control into the banal and "cutesy" wallpaper of everyday life. Steyerl puts it baldly: "*You may own us*, they seem to say, *but we are going to inform on you. And guess what kind of creature we are going to recognize in you!*" (italics in original) (see Figure 22.2).

Deep dreaming and other machine learning software are basically related to changes in hardware, including the proliferation of the IoT. Consider the origins (or at least one origin story) of the IoT as recounted by the tech executive Kevin Ashton. Ashton claims the first usage of the phrase "Internet of Things" in a 1999 presentation at Proctor and Gamble, and argues against its by now too general usage. Referencing his initial presentation in a 2009 editorial, he writes:

> But what I meant, and still mean, is this: Today computers—and, therefore, the Internet—are almost wholly dependent on human beings for information. Nearly all of the roughly 50 petabytes (a petabyte is 1,024 terabytes) of data available on the Internet were first

Figure 22.2 Stilled YouTube video of "Google Deep Dream Zoom: 'Inside an Artificial Brain,'" is one of hundreds of such visualizations uploaded by users

captured and created by human beings—by typing, pressing a record button, taking a digital picture or scanning a bar code. Conventional diagrams of the Internet include servers and routers and so on, but they leave out the most numerous and important routers of all: people. The problem is, people have limited time, attention and accuracy—all of which means they are not very good at capturing data about things in the real world.

(Ashton)

This image of the thing-net, while familiar in certain respects, also dramatically extends the reach of the IoT beyond the simple efficiencies of networking previously stand-alone devices or popular anxieties about how machines enter everyday life and become intimate, animate. Ashton describes a world where we are able to track and trace every*thing*. The problem with existing information technology, in this view, is that it is too reliant on humans for generating data. This is not only because humans are prone to inattention and error, but also because these processes end up knowing "more about ideas than things" (Ashton). What is striking here is the tension between human knowledge and thing-knowledge—a tension provocatively captured by DeepDream and Leckley's smart fridge. Crucial to Ashton's vision of the IoT is to remove humans from the process of capturing data for networks, and to account for object relations rather than human quirks. Computers and other devices become vital agents in constructing a smart future that is basically tied to *computational epistemologies*. Ashton continues: "we need to empower computers with their own means of gathering information, so they can see, hear and smell the world for themselves…." The IoT, then, is not merely a network of smart devices but a mandate to account for and connect all things (and people). It fosters new forms of recognition or "pattern discrimination," to borrow the title of a recent book, where computers "hear and smell" for themselves (see Apprich et al.). This is also its chief contradiction: the IoT at once imagines total networked capture and assembly, and yet its resources are martialed for the comforts and control of people and populations.

Ashton describes a world making project—a particular entanglement of the Internet of People and Things—that is crucial for understanding contemporary social-media-risk. In this context,

Philip Agre's discussion of the "capture model" remains instructive. Two points are worth rehearsing here. First, computers can only capture what they can describe. And second, in order to describe humans or things—and thus to be able to gather, store, and augment—capture processes must institute new habits and protocols (click here!). As Agre argues, capture "describes the situation that results when *grammars of action* are imposed upon human activities, and when the newly reorganized activities are represented by computers in real time" (746; emphasis added). As I argue here, capture points to more than how human activities are given new syntax or standards. It also extends to the thingly and machinic (e.g., the IoT), suggesting, as Steyerl puts it, a "new totality of aesthetic and social relations."

In this logistical future, smart and sensuous technologies are coterminous with the world. One is here reminded of Borges' map, which is so important for Jean Baudrillard's theory of simulation: "the generation by models of a real without origin or reality: a hyperreal." (Baudrillard 166). But Baudrillard's model of simulation is also by now in tatters. The logic of the IoT is not about a real with no original—where pure simulation is untethered to reality. Instead, it has become intensely rooted in actuality in ways unimaginable by Baudrillard, among other prophets of the computer age. The promise of capture is the capacity to learn about and know, intimately, each user and thing—locations, habits, contacts, heart rate, anxieties, data. It also promises to create new standards for networked intimacy—now recast as knowledge or filtering of overwhelming data. This is why Figure 22.2 is not a hyperreal or hallucinatory image. Instead, it references the mundane practices and pulses that make up our everyday living with computers, and vice versa. If Baudrillard's simulation did away with quaint notions of truth, authentic experience, grand narratives about political relations, and the like, capture seeks to reinstate them on its own terms. Put differently, capture is a basic technique of risk media. It operates not only by managing uncertainty but also by instituting new forms of standardization and recognition that go beyond the spatial logics theorized by Thrift in his analysis of the technological unconscious. Indeed, we can add to that loose historical periodization, which identifies the nineteenth century with the standardization time and the twentieth century with the standardization of space, and consider how contemporary technologies of standardization takes the social as their object. This, and not Internet applications or two-way communication, is what is meant by social media across this chapter.

Social Media and the Social Question

Rather than the well-worn dichotomy whereby media either fracture or facilitate sociality—as with information bubbles or twitter revolutions—what must be accounted for is how media enter into and transform the idea of the social itself. Before returning to this question, I want to first consider the role of the social sphere in Hannah Arendt's foundational model of political action.[13] In *The Human Condition*, among other works, Arendt draws on the Greek polis to distinguish private, social, and political realms. Of the private and public, she writes "the distinction between a private and public sphere of life corresponds to the household and the political realms, which have existed as distinct, separate entities at least since the rise of the ancient city-state" (*The Human Condition* 28). This includes the well-established (and much critiqued) differentiation between the private space of necessity, nourishment, and reproduction (gendered as female and seen as prepolitical), and the public space of debate and concern for the common good (associated with the masculine, and political because it is free from the needs of private life).[14] My interest here is not to rehash critiques about Arendt's gendered division of labor and action—such critiques are important but well-digested. Rather, I want to explore Arendt's understanding of the social and its place within a larger political schema, including the "space of appearance" (199).

In addition to the private and public, Arendt identifies the rise of the social sphere as a third term in this model. She writes, "the emergence of the social realm, which is neither private nor public, strictly speaking, is a relatively new phenomenon whose origin coincided with the emergence of the modern age and which found its political form in the nation-state" (28). Further, she sees the maintenance of discrete private, social, and political spheres as crucial to democratic life. In contrast to the exclusive intimacy of the private, and the equality and action of the public, she associates social space with group preferences, taste and identity, and thus with discrimination. In a subsequent essay, she observes that discrimination

> is as indispensable a social right as equality is a political right. The question is not how to abolish discrimination, but how to keep it confined to the social sphere, where it is legitimate, and to prevent its trespassing on the political and personal sphere, where it is destructive.
>
> ("Reflections on Little Rock" 206; qtd. in Pang 74)

What troubles Arendt—and is only intensified in the present context—is that the lines of separation between these distinct spheres are increasingly blurred. The expansion of the social sphere, rather than protecting private and public domains, is instead crucial to their interpenetration: the private increasingly seeps into the social, and the social into the political. In particular, she notes the extension of the image of the family and "the rise of housekeeping" to the imagination of the nation-state (Arendt, *The Human Condition* 38).[15] Private customs begin to overwhelm political life. Such concerns lead the political theorist Hanna Pitkin to sum up Arendt's expanding and inescapable social as the *Attack of the Blob* (Pitkin 16).[16] While a more in-depth discussion of Arendt's political action is out of the scope of this chapter, what I want to emphasize is how earlier concerns regarding the widening of the social run parallel to contemporary debates about the risks of social media. Indeed, this seepage recalls van Dijck and Poell's claim, quoted at the outset, that social media "is gradually dissipating into all areas of public life." Arendt's hesitations about the social sphere both endure and are reimagined by present concerns.

Recent interventions by Laikwan Pang and Judith Butler are useful here. Both scholars return to Arendt to examine the increasingly blurred boundaries, and perhaps potentialities, between private emotions, expanding social domains, and public politics. Butler and Pang ask, albeit in different ways, if the *social* in social media is the *social* in social movements? What I take from these writings is that to understand meaningful assemblies—like the Umbrella Movement, Occupy or the Arab Spring, but also Charlottesville and surging rightwing populisms, among more mundane examples—requires a media theory of the social.

Referencing Pitkin's *blob*, Pang suggests a simple understanding of Arendt's social: "the intermediate space between the private and the public" (74). For Pang, the ambiguity and intermediary status of the social is what grants it potential. This definition is useful because it helps us to understand how social forms mediate between political concerns and private emotions. Rather than insisting upon rigid distinctions, Pang suggests that a more productive question to ask today might be "whether the social can reactivate the creative energy that human communities originally possessed by taking both the political and the private seriously" (87). This includes the many ways that current practices, like social media technologies and habits, bring the private into the political and vice versa. Pang's analysis, for example, centers on the role of social media applications, memes, and affective fans cultures in animating the 2014 Umbrella Movement in Hong Kong.

But beyond the pragmatic sense of social media—where virtual connection catalyzes real world action—Pang and Butler invite us to rethink the "space of appearance" as a basically mediated realm. This is both to loosen Arendt's categorical distinctions, even to insist on the volatility of social seepage and remediation, but also to link the politics of the street and the politics of sound and image in a different way. As Butler puts it, "What, then, does it meant to appear within contemporary politics, and can we consider this question at all without some recourse to the media?" (86) Butler's analysis takes seriously not only how media record and recirculate events, but become "part of the scene and the action" (91). This capacity to be both here and there transforms Arendt's intersubjective space of appearance—which relies not only on bodily appearance but upon mutual recognition. This latter aspect is interesting in regard to the much touted interactivity of Web 2.0. In this way, Butler both extends Arendt's notion of appearance to account for the material supports that are necessary and contested by the act of assembly, and also considers the imbrication of the protesting bodies and technologies in shoring up political actions.

The conjuncture of *street and media, here and there, us and them*, pressures our familiar sense of private, public, and social in useful ways. That is, more than the dual notion that social media either atomize or enliven communities—which isolates specific network effects—the aim is to turn to how people and technologies interlace. And to ask, as Butler does: "How does plurality form, and what material supports are necessary for that formation?" Without going further into Pang and Butler's useful interventions, what I want to emphasize here is this: the contemporary space of appearance is increasingly a media-enabled space—a distinct form, that is, of social media. But, as I argue above, this social media must be apprehended in relation to important changes in our technologized habitus. Here is where we can see certain limitations in Pang and Butler's arguments. While they are interested in new media forms, and how they transform understandings of the social and the space of appearance, they also remain tightly bound to a mass media logic. Butler's provocations, for example, while gesturing to the hand held and amateur projections, relies on an imagination of broadcast media and large-scale events. What we know about social media, however, is that neither of these elements need to be in place. Instead, circulation and address are fractured, targeted, and even invisible to human recognition. Similarly, Pang's analysis of social networks, memes, and actions is confined by a literal understanding of "the 'social' character of social media." This is reasonable given her focus on "retheorizing the social." But it does leave media as a supplemental term. As I suggested above contemporary social media point to more than an explosion of media devices or texts, or to new enfoldings of spatial practice. Rather, social media increasingly *intermediate* between private and public life, transforming familiar debates about an expanding the social realm that spills across intimate and political spheres. This is to say that the social describes a form of human organization that is deeply computational, (non)human, and networked. *Social* media must be recast to comprise this technologized coexistence—including new forms of social standardization, habits and affects, and the Internet of People and Things.

The recent fascination with Cambridge Analytica, Facebook data harvesting, and psychographics are illuminating in this context (see, for example, Granville). This example, while disingenuous in its surprise about data tracking and targeting, is important because it shifts the ground of action from street-level riots—which is a big part of what "appears" with familiar definitions of social media and examples like "Project X Heran"—to algorithmic encounters that only achieve the status of an event retrospectively (see Figure 22.3). That is, there were no riots and nothing that fits the usual understandings of an event took place with the Cambridge Analytica example. Election meddling, privacy breach, and fears of emotional manipulation by corporations and foreign governments only emerged after the fact to explain the failure of data analysis to predict populist ascendency. This suggests both a temporal shift and a reframing of eventfulness or the space of appearance. In terms of temporality, I have in mind the anachronistic role of computational processes that, in addition to acting in "real time," increasingly take on retrospective and predictive functions.[17] Like DeepDream, this challenges the legibility of actions because much of what takes place is not perceived by the human sensorium (such as in public space, in the news, etc.).[18] Instead, it relies upon computational processes to find meaning in countless past and future acts or data. What's more, these machine learning processes draw our attention to the peculiar feedback loop between learning about and modeling the world—what Matteo Pasquinelli terms *information becoming logic* (Pasquinelli). These asynchronous processes not only computationally map and model the present, but also animate new forms of uncertainty.

In this context, the Facebook scandal remains alarming even as its hoopla covers over broader shifts. This includes the elaboration of track and trace logics into all domains of social, economic,

Figure 22.3 The Facebook scandal is defined by Mark Zuckerberg's congressional testimony rather than years of privacy breaches or the company's role in shaping new interface intimacies

Source: *Guardian*, April 11, 2018

and political life. For example, psychographics—that is, using big data to map and precisely address specific groups according to psychological criteria—while clearly debatable, suggests an unsettling extension of the logic of inception to mundane digital practices (Halpern, "Cambridge Analytica"). Using the simple like button, for example, data experts claim to have developed powerful software capable of predicting the personal details of users with great certainty. One report notes that a mere 68 likes allows companies to predict skin color with 95 percent accuracy, sexual orientation with 85 percent accuracy, and so on. Further, associated researchers have claimed that 150 "likes" allows data profilers to know YOU better than your parents, and 300 "likes" better than ones spouse (Barbaro). More than the validity of these hyperbolic claims, they demonstrate the basic premise of programmability and how it increasingly coordinates people alongside goods. This is to say that social media are logistical: they attempt to organize social and technical practices so that they can be addressed and augmented, regulated, and remade.

Social media's collection and deployment of intimate data—the ways they enter into and exceed private and public realms—is, in part, what makes them risky. They generate new forms of networked and "algorithmic identity" that challenges existing models in important ways (Cheney-Lippold). It is not simply that private hierarchies or social discrimination intrudes into the sphere of political equality. Rather, our foundational political languages and repertoires of action—private, social, public—are being transformed. This is to recall Arendt's thinking, but it is also to begin to grapple with its utility in the present, especially, perhaps, to ask how Arendt's model can inform (social) media theory. While we tend to think of intimacy in terms of deeply personal relationships or knowledge, private space, close and shared experience, sex, and the like, our media technologies pose new questions about social and political action. How, for example, do we make sense of the increasing *programmability* of such affinities? (including the idea that Facebook "knows" you better than a parent or partner)? Programmability is one of the core elements that van Dijck and Poell associate with the social media logic (alongside: connectivity, popularity, and datafication). They distinguish between mass media's prior emphasis on "programming" and the current coding of technology and human agency (van Dijck and Poell 5–6). What makes this media *social* is not simply the two-way exchange between users and industries, but rather thickening relations between people and computers. The simple point is this: platformed sociality flattens prior distinctions between private, social, and public acts. And it does so both at the level of capture and in the production of a new space of appearance. Put differently, is Pitkin's *attack of the blob* the most relevant description of our present social and political realities? Or do we need new metaphors altogether?

While such examples stir fears of dystopic manipulation and total surveillance, the everyday textures of social-media-risk are much more normalized, efficient, and even apparently friendly. A crucial example of this algorithmic sociality is what sociologists have termed *homophily*. Homophily is the principle that "similarity breeds connection" (McPherson et al. 425). Paul Lazarsfeld and Robert K. Merton coined the term, in the 1950s, in their study of friendship networks and residential segregation in the Northeast of the United States. In it, they developed not only the idea of homophily, but the idea of heterophily as well. This fact is key to Chun's extension of homophily to social media networks ("We're All Living in Gated Communities"). In particular, she points to the problematic ways that homophily has been adopted as a default for technological infrastructures —rather than as one potential organization among many. In everyday life, we experience homophilic relations in the way mined data generates personalized recommendations, news, contacts, and the like—an Internet for each of us. It is also familiar in concerns over corporate surveillance, information silos, and new assaults on privacy. In this logic, it is not what "you" or other individuals do online that matters; rather it is *what people like you do* that is significant. As Chun echoes, homophily models homogeneity as a virtue: it segregates. She continues: "as homophily has moved from a problem to be solved to an answer to be used, we've become more and more virtually segregated" ("We're All Living"). As such, we find ourselves living in an increasingly (virtually) segregated world that, in turn, models the world itself.

The consolidation of homophily as a core logic of risk media society reaches back to redlining and the history institutionalized racism in the United States, among other racist formations globally. Importantly, these mundane and less-than-visible practices (like finding friends on the Internet or selecting a neighborhood to live in), are eclipsed by more spectacularly mediated dangers. In other words, current definitions of *social media* inhibit our understandings of the constitutive anti-sociality of networked life. Against fantasies of participation, connectivity, and user agency, this chapter has instead emphasized changes in the *computational unconscious*—especially, the affects, repetitions, and intimacies that make up and manage social-media-risk. This includes attending real and imagined incursions into our private, social and public lives, as well as examining how these familiar concepts are transformed by algorithmic processes. Crucial to these shifts are emergent forms of standardization that, beyond the temporal and spatial interventions noted by Thrift, among others, take the social as their object. Such a modest reframing turns our attention to the ways that network infrastructures reorganize humans and things, and, at the same time, reshape the languages and categories informing critical social theories. In this way, Arendt's cautioning about private and social spheres overwhelming the political domain still has much to teach us. My point here is not to uphold the conceptual rigidity at the heart of this model (or myth). Rather, what matters is how the discriminating tastes, practices, and identities that Arendt associated with the rise of the social— "housekeeping" and the nation-state—now animates the social itself as a technological formation. More sharply: platformed sociality does not simply seep into the private and public, it eliminates the categories altogether, positing new ones in their wake.

Acknowledgments: I would like to thank the editors, Bishnupriya Ghosh and Bhaskar Sarkar, for their guidance. I also want to thank Clemens Apprich, Michello Cho, Megan Fernandes, and J.P. Sniadecki for suggestions included in this chapter.

Notes

1 The authors adapt "social media logic" from Altheide and Snow.
2 According to van Djick and Poell, four basic elements undergird this platform sociality: programmability, popularity, connectivity, and datafiction (3).
3 See, for example, Molloy.
4 As Halpern et al. put it: "a smart infrastructure that can absorb constant shocks while maintaining functionality" (121).
5 The full paragraph on repetition is instructive:

> Thus what we see is a different kind of repetition which allows things to show up differently with different kinds of opportunities associated with them. Through the application of a set of technologies and knowledges (the two being impossible to separate), a style of repetition has been produced which is more controlled and also more open-ended, a new kind of roving empiricism which continually ties up and undoes itself in a search for the most efficient ways to use the space and time of each moment (223).

6 The full passage reads:

> These days, insecure in our relationships and anxious about intimacy, we look to technology for ways to be in relationships and protect ourselves from them at the same time. This can happen when one is finding one's way through a blizzard of text messages; it can happen when interacting with a robot. I feel witness for a third time to a turning point in our expectations of technology and ourselves. We bend to the inanimate with new solicitude. We fear the risks and disappointments of relationships with our fellow humans. We expect more from technology and less from each other" (xii).

7 For more information about Paro robots, see: www.parorobots.com/.
8 In "Connected, but Alone," for example, Turkle describes what she sees as the failure of sociable robots to care for the elderly. Describing her observations of an elderly woman with Paro, Turkle writes: "that woman was trying to make sense of her life with a machine that had no experience of the arc of a human life."
9 John Rothchild notes, for example, that Internet archaeologists recall a range of examples, including a Coke machine that grad students at Carnegie Mellon wired in 1982 so they could check soda inventory and coldness from their desks (1).
10 This claim and the video can be found on the Mark Leckey's YouTube page: www.youtube.com/watch?v=8X1QkseVjIY.
11 Steyerl also quotes the Google Research Blog, "Inceptionism: Going Deeper into Neural Networks," June 17, 2015:

> We train an artificial neural network by showing it millions of training examples and gradually adjusting the network parameters until it gives the classifications we want. The network typically consists of 10–30 stacked layers of artificial neurons. Each image is fed into the input layer, which then talks to the next layer, until eventually the 'output' layer is reached. The network's 'answer' comes from this final output layer.

12 As Steyerl puts it in "A Sea of Data," "Apophenia is defined as the perception of patterns within random data. The most common examples are people seeing faces in clouds or on the moon."
13 I begin here, in part, because of the continuing influence and rigor of Arendt's formulation, but also because several recent works return to Arendt in their examinations of social media and social movements (see Pang).
14 The gendered aspect of Arendt's thought is much criticized. For a nuanced discussion, see Judith Butler, *Notes Toward a Performative Theory of Assembly*. Butler describes Arendt's private sphere: "And the body in the private sphere is female, ageing, foreign, or childish, and always prepolitical" (72–75).
15 To open Chapter 6, Arendt writes:

> The emergence of society—the rise of housekeeping, its activities, problems, and organizational devices—from the shadowy interior of the household into the light of the public sphere, has not only blurred the old borderline between private and political, it has also changed almost beyond recognition the meaning of the two terms and their significance for the life of the individual and the citizen.

16 Laikwan Pang quotes from Pitkin's account in "Retheorizing the Social": "By 'the social' Arendt means a collectivity of people who—for whatever reason—conduct themselves in such a way that they cannot control or even intentionally influence the large-scale consequences of their activities" (74).

17 This is a much observed function of computational networks and contemporary forms of surveillance (see, for example, Lyon).
18 Steyerl opens her essay, "A Sea of Data," with a "secret" image from the Snowden files that shows only static. This image, she argues, is symptomatic because we cannot see anything: "Not seeing anything intelligible is the new normal."

Works Cited

Agre, Philip. "Surveillance and Capture: Two Models of Privacy." *The New Media Reader*, edited by Noah Wardrip-Fruin and Nick Monfort. The MIT Press, 2003, pp. 737–759.

Altheide David L. and Robert P. Snow. *Media Logics*. Sage Publications, 1979.

Apprich, Clemens et al. *Pattern Discrimination*. U of Minnesota P, 2018.

Arendt, Hannah. "Reflections on Little Rock." *Responsibility and Judgement*, edited by Jerome Kohn. Schocken Books, 2003.

Arendt, Hannah. *The Human Condition*. U of Chicago P, 1958.

Ashton, Kevin. "'That Internet of Things' Thing." *RFID Journal*, June 22, 2009, www.rfidjournal.com/articles/view?4986. Accessed January 10, 2018.

Barbaro, Michael. "The Data Harvesters." *The Daily (New York Times* podcast), March 21, 2018, www.nytimes.com/2018/03/21/podcasts/the-daily/cambridge-analytica-facebook-data.html. Accessed January 10, 2018.

Baudrillard, Jean. "Simulacra and Simulations." *Jean Baudrillard: Selected Writings*, edited by Mark Poster. Stanford UP, 1988.

Beck, Ulrich. *Risk Society: Toward a New Modernity*. Sage Publications, 1992.

Boyd, Danah. *It's Complicated: The Social Lives of Networked Teens*. Yale UP, 2014.

Butler, Judith. *Notes Toward a Performative Theory of Assembly*, Harvard UP, 2015.

Cheney-Lippold, John. "A New Algorithmic Identity: Soft Biopolitics and the Modulation of Control." *Theory, Culture & Society*, vol. 28 no. 6, 2011, pp. 164–181.

Chun, Wendy Hui Kyong. *Updating to Remain the Same*. The MIT Press, 2016.

Chun, Wendy Hui Kyong. "We're All Living in Gated Communities and Our Real-Life Relationships are Suffering." *Wired*, April 13, 2017, www.wired.co.uk/article/virtual-segregation-narrows-our-real-life-relationships. Accessed January 10, 2018.

Clarke, Roger. "Information Technology and Dataveillance." *Communications of the ACM*, vol. 31, no. 5, 1988, pp. 498–512. Also available: www.rogerclarke.com/DV/CACM88.html. Accessed January 10, 2018.

Courtney, Hugh et al. "Strategy Under Uncertainty." *The Harvard Business Review*, November–December 1997, https://hbr.org/1997/11/strategy-under-uncertainty. Accessed January 10, 2018.

Freud, Sigmund. *Beyond the Pleasure Principle (The Standard Edition)*. Translated by James Strachey. Liveright Publishing Corporation, 1961.

Gershenfeld Neil and J.P. Vasseur. "As Objects Go Online: The Promise (and Pitfalls) of the Internet of Things." *Foreign Affairs*, vol. 93, no. 2, March/April 2014, pp. 60–67.

Giddens, Anthony. "Risk and Responsibility." *The Modern Law Review*, vol. 62, no. 1, January 1999, pp. 1–10.

Granville, Kevin. "Facebook and Cambridge Analytica: What You Need to Know as Fallout Widens." *New York Times*, March 19, 2018, www.nytimes.com/2018/03/19/technology/facebook-cambridge-analytica-explained.html. Accessed March 30, 2018.

Halpern, Orit et al. "The Smartness Mandate: Notes Towards a Critique." *Grey Room*, no. 68, Summer 2017, pp. 121–124.

Halpern, Sue. "Cambridge Analytica and the Perils of Pyschographics." *The New Yorker*, March 30, 2018, www.newyorker.com/news/news-desk/cambridge-analytica-and-the-perils-of-psychographics. Accessed April 20, 2018.

Hayles, N. Katherine. "Unfinished Work: From Cyborg to the Cognisphere." *Theory, Culture & Society*, vol. 23, no. 7–8, December 1, 2006, pp. 159–166.

Hovitz, Helaina. "Social Media Anxiety Disorder, Explained." *Teen Vogue* online, September 8, 2017, www.teenvogue.com/story/social-media-anxiety-disorder. Accessed March 30, 2018.

Kaplan Andreas and Michael Haenlein. "Users of the World, Unite! The Challenges and Opportunities of Social Media." *Business Horizons*, vol. 53, no. 1, 2010, pp. 59–68.

Knight, Frank. *Risk, Uncertainty and Profit*. Sentry Press, 1964.

Lazarsfeld, Paul and Robert K. Merton. "Friendship as a Social Process: A Substantive and Methodological Analysis." *Freedom and Control in Modern Society*, edited by Morroe Berger. Van Nostrand, 1954, pp. 18–66.

Lazarus, Susanna. "Daisy Ridley Reveals Why She Quit Instagram." *RadioTimes*, December 7, 2017, www.radiotimes.com/news/film/2017-12-07/daisy-ridley-reveals-why-she-quit-instagram/. Accessed March 30, 2018.

Lyon, David. "Surveillance, Snowden, and Big Data: Capacities, Consequences, Critique." Big Data & Society, vol. 1, no. 2, 2014, pp. 1–13.

McPherson, Miller et al. "Birds of a Feather: Homophily in Social Networks." *Annual Review of Sociology*, vol. 27, 2001, pp. 414–444.

Molloy, Mark. "Facebook Addiction Activates Same Part of Brain as Cocaine." *Telegraph*, February 17, 2016, www.telegraph.co.uk/news/12161461/Facebook-addiction-activates-same-part-of-the-brain-as-cocaine.html. Accessed March 30, 2018.

Mordvintsev, Alexander et al. "Inceptionism: Going Deeper into Neural Networks." *Google AI Blog*, June 13, 2015, https://ai.googleblog.com/2015/06/inceptionism-going-deeper-into-neural.html. Accessed March 30, 2018.

Pang, Laikwan. "Retheorizing the Social: The Use of Social Media in Hong Kong's Umbrella Movement." *Social Text*, vol. 35, no. 3 (132), September 2017, pp. 71–94.

Pasquinelli, Matteo. "Machines that Morph Logic: Machine Learning and the Distorted Automation of Intelligence as Statistical Inference." *Site 1: Logic Gate, The Political and Artifactual Mind, Glass Bead*, 2017, pp. 1–17, www.glass-bead.org/journal/site-1-logic-gate-politics-artifactual-mind/?lang=enview. Accessed March 30, 2018.

Peters, John Durham. "Mass Media." *Critical Terms for Media Studies*, edited by W.J.T Mitchell and Mark B.N. Hansen. U of Chicago P, 2010.

Pitkin, Hanna Fenichel. *Attack of the Blob: Hannah Arendt's Concept of the Social*. U of Chicago P, 1998.

Rothchild, John A. "Net Gets Physical: What You Need to Know About the Internet of Things." *Business Law Today*, November 2014, pp. 1–5.

"Star Wars Actress Kelly Marie Tran Deletes Instagram Posts After Abuse." *BBC News*, June 6, 2018, www.bbc.com/news/world-asia-44379473. Accessed July 31, 2018.

Steyerl, Hito. "A Sea of Data: Apophenia and Pattern (Mis)Recognition." *e-flux*, no. 72, June 2016, www.e-flux.com/journal/72/60480/a-sea-of-data-apophenia-and-pattern-mis-recognition/. Accessed March 30, 2018.

Thrift, Nigel. *Knowing Capitalism*. Sage Publications, 2005.

Turkle, Sherry. *Alone Together: Why We Expect More From Technology and Less From Each Other*. Basic Books, 2011.

Turkle, Sherry. "Connected, but Alone." TED Talk, February 2012, www.ted.com/talks/sherry_turkle_alone_together. Accessed March 30, 2018.

van Dijck, José and Thomas Poell. "Understanding Social Media Logic." *Media and Communication*, vol. 1, no. 1, pp. 2–14.

23

YOUR BRAIN ON SCREENS
Neuronal Risk and Media Addiction

Thomas Lamarre

The term addiction is evoked so largely and loosely to describe our relation with contemporary media forms and platforms that it may prove difficult to take it seriously. We so regularly hear that we are addicted to smart phones, to the Internet, to social media, to television, and the term addiction is used so generally that it ceases to make an impression. Recently, for instance, in the context of denouncing Facebook's practices as a potential threat to democracy, Roger McNamee prefaces his remarks by establishing the fact of our addiction:

> We are all addicted one way or another to smartphones ... most people are conditioned to check it within a few minutes of waking up and will use it all day long, finishing only a few minutes before they go to sleep. If you can addict your user, they are a lot more valuable.
>
> *(McNamee and Simon)*

Despite their pervasiveness, such discourses on media addiction feel toothless and harmless, precisely because addiction remains undefined; they are mere discourse, so to speak. Indeed, the very notion of addiction is so fraught with social and cultural assumptions that it proves impossible to define scientifically without some reference to culture and society. Nonetheless, a growing number of accounts of media addiction draw heavily on scientific evidence, particularly on the neurosciences, to lend empirical support to the idea that we are at risk when we use media. This is where "mere discourse" on media addiction begins to turn into a discourse in the Foucauldian sense: a field of rationality emerges, stretched across a manner of speaking about addiction and ways of seeing and measuring it—that is, subjecting it to clinical observation and experimental methods. This is also where risk assessment comes into play: there is an effort to domesticate what is uncertain and unpredictable (due to social and cultural factors), to render it predictable by reference to scientific studies, as Frank Knight some time ago observed. The discourse on media addiction then gravitates toward questions of threshold: at what point do the pleasurable intoxicating effects of media cross the threshold, becoming genuinely toxic, putting users at risk, and tipping into allegedly dangerous forms of media addiction?

When mere discourses on media addiction begin to draw on neurosciences, they also pose a challenge to some of the received ways of thinking about the relation between sciences and social concerns. Generally speaking, humanistic studies tend to contest the idea that the empirical truths generated through scientific inquiry are unaffected by social concerns and cultural matters. The general tendency within risk communication studies, for instance, is to show how scientific truths are mobilized to reinforce existing social paradigms and popular discourses. It is true that many accounts of media addiction are content to mobilize neuroscientific research in order to shore up pre-existing cultural biases. Even when acknowledging the impact of technologies, for instance, accounts of media addiction will tend to place responsibility for managing media dosage on individuals and families, or make demands on media producers and distributors to tone down their products.

This way of establishing agency and responsibility tends to mobilize scientific studies largely to reconfirm our received understanding of social interaction, in quasi-legalistic terms. Scientific truths appear subordinated to social truths in advance. Put another way, a mechanistic or instrumentalist view of sciences is mobilized to shore up, however unwittingly, an instrumentalist view of sociality, agency, and responsibility. But it is worth taking a closer look at scientific studies without assuming their subordination to social interests. Instead, the sciences may pose challenges to received ways of thinking about risk and society, and about the social dimension of media technologies. Something else may be at risk—ways of thinking about the sociality of media beyond paradigms of sovereign subjects as bearers of agency and responsibility.

Media Addiction and Brain Health

I begin with some recent accounts of television addiction. Television may seem to be an odd point of departure, for it is often decidedly considered "old media" in contrast with newer media like smart phones, tablets, computers, and video games. Interestingly enough, however, accounts of addiction to new media frequently rely on research on television, and conversely, contemporary accounts of television addiction tend to expand rapidly in scope to include a range of media, such as game platforms and mobile phones. What is called in question, then, is not simply one kind of screen (such as the cathode ray tube screen) or one kind of platform (for instance the television set) but something closer to "screens in general" or "platforms in general." I will return to this tendency to generalize, to consider both its pitfalls and potential.

One striking feature of recent essays on television addiction is the historical shift in how they envision the ills of television. For instance, in their *Scientific American* article "Television Addiction Is No Metaphor," Robert Kubey and Mihaly Csikszentmihaly put it this way:

> Scientists have been studying the effects of television for decades, generally focusing on whether watching violence on TV correlates with being violent in real life…. Less attention has been paid to the basic allure of the small screen—the medium, as opposed to the message.
>
> *(76)*

Where prior studies of the effects of television focused primarily on how content affected social behavior (violence, anti-sociality, performance at school), newer studies place greater emphasis on the medium and, as if by extension, on the physiological effects of media, which means, above all, neurological effects. Simply put, the shift is from psychology to neurology. Implied, too, in the proposed shift from message to medium is a shift from sociology and cultural studies to media studies.

The prior tendency to study the effects of television on violence, anti-sociality, obesity, numbing of emotion, and reduced ability to learn, for instance, displayed concern for deviant behavior, as if television—or more precisely an excess of it—interfered with the processes of healthy development in accordance with received social norms. Such studies have not disappeared, of course, and will not soon disappear.[1] But with the shift from psychology to neurology, and from message to medium, a new concern is gaining ground, articulated clearly by Kubey and Csikszentmihaly's conclusion:

> Maintaining control over one's media habits is more of a challenge today than it has ever been. TV sets and computers are everywhere. But the small screen and the Internet need not interfere with the quality of the rest of one's life. In its easy provision of relaxation and escape, television can be beneficial in limited doses.
>
> *(Kubey and Csikszentmihaly 80)*

Media, then, are treated as intoxicants, comparable in effect to other everyday yet potentially harmful substances such as alcohol and cigarettes. Thus, the grounds for assessing the risk of television have shifted, from psychological health and degrees of social deviation to brain health and controlled intake. The danger of such a shift in emphasis is that it brackets questions about how culture may influence results. It is not that scientists are blissfully unaware of or indifferent to the ways in which culture hampers the process of isolating empirical data on addiction. They are well aware. A recent article in *Nature*, for instance, compares the difficulties faced by those who wish to conduct research on television with the difficulties faced by those who conducted research on the effects of smoking. On the one hand, objections to such research arise because it is seen as ethically intrusive, and effects are exceedingly difficult to track (Schnabel 767). On the other hand, culture gets in the way: not only do families resist studies because they feel their practices are acceptable, but there is also always the possibility of hidden factors not directly related to media exposure that interfere with solid results based on isolable effects (766).

As neurosciences gain in explanatory power and scope, however, discourses on media addiction have found new opportunities to dispel the shadows of uncertainty cast by social and cultural factors, which remain too numerous and volatile to assess. The neurosciences seem to herald new ways of accounting for media effects that cannot be reduced to psychological or cultural states. They seem to open new spaces for talking about physiological effects, neuronal effects. To build on neurosciences, then, discourses on media addiction need to find examples where cultural and social factors appear to be so minimal as to be negligible. It is for this reason that accounts of media addiction almost invariably gravitate toward the Pokémon Incident. The incident occurred on December 16, 1997, when the 38th episode of the *Pokémon* animated television series, "Dennō senshi Porigon" (Computer warrior Polygon), provoked photosensitive epileptic seizures across Japan.

The *Pokémon* franchise had enjoyed phenomenal popularity from the launch of its handheld console Nintendo game in 1996, and had already significantly expanded its base with the serialization of a *Pokémon* manga in the popular monthly magazine for children, *Korokoro Komikku* or *Corocoro Comic*. The debut of the animated television series on April 1, 1997 spurred the franchise to new heights of popularity. By the time the "Dennō senshi Porigon" episode went on the air, the animated series had already hit its stride, with a fairly distinctive look and feel, a recognizable set of characters, and a growing collection of brand products, such as manga, card games, foodstuffs, figures, and other toys. The broadcaster, TV Tokyo, aired the show in 27 prefectures in Japan, predicting that of the approximately ten million people who would watch it, over seven million would be schoolchildren.[2] The estimate was based on the show's ratings, which, at over 15 percent, were the highest in the 6:30 to 7:00 PM slot.

At about 6:50 PM, however, roughly two-thirds into the episode, a large number of viewers, especially children between the ages of 6 and 12 (the age group most prone to Portal Systemic Encephalopathy or PSE) experienced headaches, nausea, blurring of vision, convulsions, and other symptoms characteristic of photosensitivity. By 7:30 PM, 618 children had been taken to hospitals, and as word spread, several television stations replayed the flash sequence, which may have triggered additional cases. Ultimately, the Fire and Disaster Management Agency reported that 685 children (310 boys and 375 girls) were rushed to hospitals and were seen by physicians (Ishida et al. 1340). This figure has become the official count for Pokémon Shock, generally cited in subsequent news reports as "about 700 children." Of these children, however, hospitals only admitted about 150 to 200 children because symptoms cleared up in the other children either on the way to the hospital or at the hospital (Ishida et al.; Takahashi and Tsukahara).[3] In addition to this core group of children whose cases were actually reported at the time, subsequent surveys by doctors indicate that larger numbers of children experienced symptoms of neurological distress, running the gamut from headaches, blurred vision, loss of vision, nausea, vomiting, to abdominal pains (see Furusho et al., "Comparison Survey"). The affected population was probably much larger than actually reported through hospital cases. Some reports calculate that, because statistical analysis showed that about 5 percent of children viewers experienced neurological distress, even a conservative estimate would put the number of affected children closer to 100,000 among the over seven million school-age viewers (Furusho et al., "Patient Background"; Ishida et al. 1343).[4]

It is easy to understand why the Pokémon Incident is so widely cited in the literature on media addiction. It is as if broadcasters had inadvertently staged a randomized clinical trial of the neurophysiological effects of television on an exceedingly large population of viewers. Indeed, the sheer number of viewers offers a data set large enough for variations to be accounted for with some degree of statistical accuracy. What is more, the cause for the generated effects proved relatively easy to isolate, with a fairly high degree of confidence: a 12 Hz red–blue flicker. As such, although a handful of commentators strove to give priority to social and cultural factors in accounting for the incident, the evidence for a cause-and-effect structure—flicker effects inducing a neurophysiological response—is overwhelming. This is what continues to make the Pokémon Incident so appealing to those who are interested in scientific approaches to the effects of television: it is possible to bracket social and cultural factors with reference to the incident, that is, to eliminate them as *causes*. Once social and cultural factors are bracketed or eliminated, discussion may then place causal emphasis on the medium (rather than the message) as the key factor in assessing media risk.

In such accounts, however, no sooner is a case made for placing the emphasis on the medium than the medium is rapidly expanded to include a range of media, both forms and platforms. Again, Kubey and Csikszentmihaly's account of media addiction provides a prime example. They describe the Pokémon Incident as follows.

In 1997, in the most extreme medium-effects case on record, 700 Japanese children were rushed to the hospital, many suffering from "optically stimulated epileptic seizures" caused by viewing bright flashing lights in a Pokémon video game broadcast on Japanese TV. Seizures and other untoward effects of video games are significant enough that software companies and platform manufacturers now routinely include warnings in their instruction booklets. Parents have reported to us that rapid movement on the screen has caused motion sickness in their young children after just 15 minutes of play (80).

Note how quickly Kubey and Csikszentmihaly leap from the effects of television to video games. In their haste to connect the two, they even characterize the television broadcast as a video game broadcast! They are not entirely wrong to associate television and video games. On the one hand, strategies for multimedia franchising in Japan, frequently dubbed "media mix," encourage such an association, and after all, the *Pokémon* television anime series was conceived in tandem with the handheld Nintendo game. On the other hand, and more importantly, while the Pokémon Incident is indeed the largest incident of this kind, there were precedents for it. A number of incidents had occurred in which gamers experienced epileptic seizures while playing arcade games, console games, and Gameboys. In fact, prior to the Pokémon Incident, the association of seizures with Nintendo games had become so pronounced that such seizures were styled as Nintendo seizures in the American press in 1994, in the context of John Ledford's lawsuit against Nintendo. Ledford allegedly experienced his first grand mal seizure playing one of their games at a video arcade at age 27. In 2004, the BBC aired a documentary, *Outrageous Fortune*, which exposed evidence showing that Nintendo had deliberately suppressed knowledge of game-induced seizures.[5] In addition, a series of incidents in which Nintendo handheld consoles induced epileptiform phenomena led to the safety warnings mentioned by Kubey and Csikszentmihaly, which appear in pamphlets accompanying Nintendo handheld consoles and games played on them, and for consoles such as the Wii as well.

In addition, similar incidents had already occurred in the context of broadcast television. A British TV commercial provoked seizures in three individuals in 1993. This incident "prompted the Independent Television Commission (ITC)—the statutory regulatory body for all commercial TV in the U.K—to request the drafting of guidelines to prevent a recurrence," which led to the adoption of a similar code by the British Broadcasting Corporation (BBC) (Harding 265). What is more, something like the Pokémon Incident had already occurred earlier the same year (1997) in Japan: NHK's broadcast of an episode of *YAT Anshin! ūchū ryokō* or "Yamato Anshin Travel: Galactic travel, no worries!" apparently induced photosensitive epileptic seizures in some viewers, but on a lesser scale than the Pokémon Incident.[6]

In other words, there have been a wide variety of events in which media forms or platforms have induced epileptiform effects in users, ranging from nausea and dizziness to blackouts and seizures. In this respect, Kubey and Csikszentmihaly and other commentators are justified in expanding the scope of toxicity and risk from the television media ecology (cathode-ray tube screen and broadcast) to other media ecologies associated with different kinds of media such as video games and game consoles. What merits attention in such accounts of media risk, however, is the tendency to settle on one factor, to treat it as the cause in order to bracket social and cultural factors. The result is media determinism, in which the medium, or more precisely the effect of the medium, is isolated. But then the effect of the medium is generalized to comprise apparently comparable effects associated with other media. The result is the sense of a pervasive media risk, akin to environmental risk. As for social and cultural factors, they are placed in a secondary position; they are now assumed to follow from, and even to be caused by, media. Take, for instance, the research initiative launched in Japan in the first decade of the new century under the rubric "Brain Science and Education" (Koizumi, "Brain Science and Education"; Koizumi, "Concept of 'Developing the Brain'"). A review of international trends on brain science and neuroethics, published in *Neuroscience*, conveys the concerns of the Japanese initiative:

> One of the greatest societal demands in Japan is for accurate information about critical periods in brain development. When is the best time to begin teaching English? Or sports? What is the influence of video games, cell phones and "anime" (Japanese animations) on children? Many of the modern ills emerging among Japanese youth are attributed to excessive technology. Staggering increases in violent crimes, vagrancy and suicide among this sector of the population raise many questions about what can be done for children who burn out (known as "kireru"). In response, large cohort studies that will follow 10,000 Japanese children during the first several years of life have been launched under the rubric of "Brain Science and Education." This links pediatricians, educators, parents and scientists on a scale that has not previously been attempted.
>
> *(qtd. in Illes et al. 979)*

Not surprisingly since the context is Japan, the review is quick to add, "One need only consider the synchronized, photic seizures that were induced in almost 1,000 Japanese children by an episode of Pokémon to see the relevance of the basic biology of neural plasticity to humans" (qtd. In Illes et al., "International Perspectives," 979). At the same time, the reference to the Pokémon Incident is not deemed socially or culturally specific to Japan. It provides concrete evidence on a massive scale of media effects that are not socially or culturally determined. As such, the Pokémon Incident extends an invitation to posit neuroscience research as the key to understanding social ills.

The goal of the "Brain Science and Education" initiative is to establish the importance of brain research in understanding and improving educational practices. While it does not address media addiction per se, it presents a similar series of generalizations about neurosciences, media, and risk. The overall impression given by this account is that brains are more at risk than ever, especially children's brains. Naturally, because this account is an overview, a good deal of information is compressed into a few sentences, which gives it a suggestive, even provocative tone. Attention is suggestively focused in particular on risks stemming from *excessive technology*, characterized in terms of video games, cell phones, and anime, which is to say, both media platforms and forms. The account associates the contemporary excess of media forms and platforms with a variety of social ills, such as crime, vagrancy, burnout and suicide. The impact of media technologies takes the form of a linear, direct, determinism: media have the potential to damage brains (neuroplasticity), and damaged brains are responsible for social woes. Media excess makes for social excess. Indeed, because the authors already seem to know what the neuroscientific research will show, namely that excessive technologies are destroying youth, the actual research feels almost unnecessary. Something else is at stake: measuring excess, establishing thresholds. How much media is too much?

It is surely for this reason that the account makes exaggerated, even erroneous claims about Japanese society. In fact, crime has not shown staggering increases in Japan, and discourses to the contrary are demonstrably an ideological position adopted by an aging media elite of journalists and intellectuals; and vagrancy is more readily linked to socioeconomic inequality than to youth brain burnout (see Hurley; Slater; Toivonen). Given that the mission of the "Brain and Education" initiative is to promote neuroscience research, it makes sense that the emphasis does not fall on accurate social information related to crime, vagrancy, and suicide. Nor does it call for better accounts of social practices related to media technologies. Instead, there is a call for research on children's brains, with an emphasis on how excessive technologies produce excessive youth, because media pushes their plasticity and elasticity of their neurons to the snapping point (*kireru*).

In sum, when discourses on the effects of media turn toward the neurosciences (and conversely, when promotion of neurosciences takes up discourses on media effects), the result is a discourse in the Foucauldian sense—a field of rationality stretched across a manner of speaking about media excess (addiction and overuse) and ways of seeing and measuring it (neurosciences). The assessment of risk, based on the threshold for toxicity, becomes the hinge between the two. Note how the push to assess thresholds of risk encourages a determinist stance on media. It seems that media, however identified (form or platform), are causing social, psychic, and physiological transformations (usually deleterious ones), ensnaring humans in its web.

Interestingly enough, however, the diffuseness and pervasiveness of media allows them to escape being held responsible. Even though neurosciences discover a causal relation between media and brain effects, media are presented as if natural, environmental factors, not subject to regulation in themselves. It is true that the Pokémon Incident in Japan led to some new regulations for animators and broadcasters. But the principal outcome of the incident was an advisory warning that was to appear at the start of each episode of an animated television series (see Figure 23.1): "Please watch television animation in a well-lit room, and do not sit too close."

As this example attests, when it comes to dealing with the social dimension of media risk, the overall tendency is to place responsibility on individuals to negotiate their relationship to media forms and platforms. This is also what accounts of media addiction generally do: construe media in terms of an environmental risk, and enjoin users to monitor their threshold. In this way, the threshold effect evident in photoepileptiform seizures is transformed into a threshold between media use and media abuse. As Kubey and Csikszentmihaly recommend, we are encouraged to think of media in terms of controlled intake or doses, which puts the onus on individuals to determine their personal threshold and to regulate their intake.

The "Brain Science and Education" initiative implies mediation on the part of scientists, educators, and parents. Yet the site of mediation is the same: the relationship of the young individual to media forms and platforms. The upshot of thinking about media use in terms of brain health, risk, and addiction is incitement to personalize one's relation to media. The overall effect is increased emphasis on the individualization of media use. In this respect, discourses axed on assessing media risk do not pose a challenge or run counter to currently hegemonic media practices encouraging self-management, whose watchwords are personalize, individualize, responsibilize. The threat is

Figure 23.1 The 2014 anime series *Ai Tenchi Muyō* duly includes the television animation advisory over its opening sequence: "For the sake of your health, when you watch TV anime, please try not to approach the screen, and keep the room well illuminated"

clear: if you do not manage to manage your relation to media, you will snap, become dysfunctional; if you do not work on yourself through media, you will never find work (Figure 23.2).

Given that such discourses on media risk and addiction emerge and take on consistency through the combined forces of ways of speaking about media effects and ways of observing and measuring them, it would be wrong to lay the blame entirely at the feet of the neurosciences, to presume that they have nothing else to say. On the contrary, precisely because such discourses rely heavily on the authority of neurosciences, it is to the neurosciences that we need to turn if we wish to disturb

Figure 23.2 The 2015 anime series *Himouto! Umaru-chan* comically associates watching television up close in a darkened room with other excessive and addictive behaviors, such as junk food

Epileptiform Phenomena and Singularity

For over a century, flickering sunlight has been known to induce epileptic seizures in susceptible individuals, and similar effects have been observed with artificial light and striped patterns. Yet it is only in recent decades that PSE seizures have become associated with television and video games in particular (Kasteleijn-Nolst Trenité et al.). PSE has come to be measured in terms of an abnormal response, called photoparoxysmal response (PPR), provoked by intermittent photic stimulation during an electroencephalogram (EEG) (see Covanis; Fisher et al.; Kasteleijn-Nolst Trenité; and Verrotti et al.). What proved unusual about the Pokémon Incident is that many children who experienced actual seizures, which is indicative of PPR, did not test for PPR on the EEG. For instance, one research team found that of 685 children studied, 560 had actual seizures (Harding and Takahashi 46). Among those who experienced seizures, at least 70 percent had no history of epilepsy (Takahashi et al. 4), and 81 percent of these children showed no recurrence of epileptic seizures in a five-year follow-up study (Okumura, et al).

There are various ways to interpret such results. A team headed by Yamasaki Takao concludes that even healthy individuals may experience image-induced seizures, proposing "chromatic sensitive epilepsy" as a variant of PSE and recommending study of "the neural basis of latent color-luminance sensitivity in healthy people to prevent epileptic seizures occurring when watching TV" (Yamasaki et al. 1611). Takada Hiroyuki and colleagues, who conducted an extensive questionnaire survey in Aichi, also call for a shift of thinking about PSE: the previous belief in generalized seizures must be supplemented with attention to partial seizures. Their study concludes:

> Photosensitivity may not be an all-or-none phenomenon as has been believed. It may be possessed by any individual in whom a maximal visual stimulus can eventually produce abnormal paroxysmal discharges, as chemical convulsants or electric shock will do. The TV program may have been so highly epileptogenic as to induce epileptic seizures even in "subphotosensitive" persons.
>
> *(Takada et al. 1001)*

Likewise, Benjamin Zifkin and Dorothée Kasteleijn-Nolst Trenité found ways to produce effects akin to the Pokémon Incident in the laboratory. They write:

> The unusual potency of that particular Pocket Monsters sequence in causing photosensitive epileptiform EEG activity has been confirmed in other settings. One of us (D.K.N.T.) found that 25 or 35 known photosensitive patients (71%) were even sensitive to that specific 12 Hz colored flashing sequence segment when it was shown on a 100 Hz television, which generally reduces the chance of seizures triggered by the screen.
>
> *(1236)*

But they ultimately found that the Pokémon Incident calls for an expansion of our definitions to include more unusual and recently discovered forms of epileptic phenomenon. They point out that the lesser symptoms experienced by those who did not go to hospitals—"headache, nausea, vomiting, visual changes, and nonspecific abdominal symptoms"—are "highly suggestive of migraine or of photically-induced occipital seizures, a recently recognized and less common epileptic phenomenon that is difficult to discriminate from migraine" (Zifkin and Kasteleijn-Nolst Trenité 1235).

In sum, even as neuroscience research strives to determine the underlying physiological causes of the seizures observed during the Pokémon Incident, the incident is altering the definitions of seizures, effectively broadening them as they are more fully described, precisely because the experienced seizures did not fit the received forms of measurement. In the absence of a strictly measurable, isolable, and reproducible effect, it is not possible to localize the effect definitively in specific bodies. Even healthy teenagers, for instance, might be subphotosensitive and thus prone to partial seizures, which may involve a previously unrecognized form of epileptic phenomenon, akin to but mistaken for migraines.

This difficulty in localizing the cause for the effect is a sign that neurosciences are confronting a singularity.[7] In physics, a singularity is understood as a breakdown in the geometrical structure of space–time. Black holes, for instance, are often said to contain a space–time singularity at their center, but a singularity is not a thing that resides at some location. The singularity, sometimes described as a tear in space–time, brings with it notions of incomplete paths and missing points: when structures of location are torn, it is not possible to assign origins to movements. Put another way, particles function as intensities, not extensities. Consequently, in one interpretation of singularity, the relation between measurement (extensive) and intensity goes haywire: "For example, some measure of the intensity of the curvature ('the strength of the gravitational field') may increase without bound as one traverses the incomplete path" (Curiel and Bokulich). This is one way to explain the phenomenon of a black hole.

Similarly, scientific studies of epileptic phenomena in the context of the Pokémon Incident, while seeking to pin down the cause of the seizures, confront a singularity: the cause evades received forms of measurements (subphotosensitive), eludes definitive localization (even if seizures can be located in the occipital lobe, the phenomenon may entail partial seizures), and threatens to spread rapidly to populations not previously recognized as photosensitive. There is an underlying non-isolable "brain singularity" on the brink of exploding into a nova or contracting into a black hole, so to speak. Such a singularity does not undermine scientific procedures. Faced with singularities, sciences do not retreat. Nor do they deny them. They explore the intensities generated around singularities with an eye to those zones of intensities that may be understood in terms of recognizable, demonstrable, and reproducible facts.[8]

Because the singularity is, in effect, not reducible to a localizable cause, scientific understanding has to make do with the reproducibility of effects. Statistical understanding takes the place of etiological understanding, and attention is directed toward populations. Inquiries into the Pokémon Incident, for instance, introduced new possible populations: not only are children of a certain age more at risk, but also certain youths and maybe even some kinds of adult. As such, such inquiries lend themselves to what is commonly called biopolitics or the biopolitical—governance based on social distributions and real flows rather than on the segregation of individuals. But the neurosciences are not in or of themselves the biopolitical. It is not so simple as pressing (or repressing) the brain singularity into the service of biopolitical governance, for another singularity soon appears on the screen.

In addition to the brain singularity, the neurosciences discover a media singularity. In the neuroscientific studies on photosensitive epilepsy cited above, for instance, scientists proceed analytically. They begin with basic distinctions between media forms and platforms. They distinguish between television and video games when considering, for instance, the effects of light, color, and flicker. They also consider differences between kinds of screen technology such as cathode ray tube (CRT), liquid crystal display (LCD), plasma screens, and combinations thereof. The scientific results confirm that CRT screens and low-wavelength deep red flicker present the worst-case scenario for evoking seizures. At the same time, despite the distinctions drawn between media platforms and media forms in their research, they ultimately find that newer screen technologies and moving image techniques present similar risks. This discovery of a not-entirely-localizable cause at the level of media is not so surprising in light of what was discovered about the cause of the Pokémon Incident, the 12 Hz red–blue flicker. As it turned out, however, the 12 Hz flicker was not produced by animators. Animation at the time was still shot on film, with a frame rate of 24 frames per second, and because television is broadcast at 60 fields per second, the transfer of the film to television produced a new frame rate and frequency. As Takashi Takeo and Tsukahara Yasuo report: "Changing the film's two frames into the TV scene results in three red fields and two blue fields. The resultant alternating red/blue light frequency is therefore 12 Hz" (Takahashi and Tsukahara 632). In other words, the cause could not be localized in the media form (animation) or in the media platform (CRT TV). It arose across and through the media form and platform.

Neuroscientific research, then, arrives at two singularities: a media singularity and a brain singularity, and the one is not reducible to the other. The two singularities come to function for scientific inquiry like attractors, whose forces of attraction and repulsion give rise to a field—like the field formed between two unlike poles of magnets. A field of inquiry emerges, the neurosciences of media. This is why, on the one hand, research that begins with the givens of the Pokémon Incident gradually expands to include other platforms (handheld consoles, arcade games, television console), platform technologies (CRT, LCD, plasma screens), forms (animation frame rate, broadcast frequency, speed of motion), media delivery systems and reception (broadcast, cable, satellite, streaming), and even postures and stances of viewers, players, listeners, and users (how the platform is angled, its proximity). On the other hand, research gradually expands to consider populations other than the initially identified population at risk, of children aged six to 12.

From the perspective of the media singularity, then, commentators are not wrong to detect an opportunity to generalize across platforms and media. Empirically speaking, broadcast television and video games imply different media ecologies, and their effects differ. Still, the case of video games is like that of broadcast television in that the deleterious effects arise between the media form (animation) and media platform—and apparently, effects induced by arcade games, video consoles, and handheld consoles are analogous. Again, certain kinds of animated motion on the screen are not in themselves enough to produce the effect, but in conjunction with certain ways of using the platform, the effect arises. In the cases of both television and video games, then, the actual effect is generated between the media platform (television set or game console) and the media form (flicker or motion). The effect is not reducible to either. It arises between them or across them. Consequently, even if their discussion seems to move too rapidly from one media ecology to another and thus to confound them (the "video game broadcast"), Kubey and Csikszentmihaly are not entirely wrong to associate the effects induced via broadcast television with those induced through video games. The media singularity tends to deterritorialize the effect, distributing it across media forms and platforms.

The problem with discourses on media risk and addiction lies in their insistence on transforming singularity into causality, or more specifically, a cause-and-effect or action-and-reaction structure. In effect, they repress singularity, bringing structure to it in order to exploit it. This repression has to happen at both poles, acting upon both attractors of the neuroscience field—brain singularity and media singularity. The media singularity is made into the cause, and in both senses of the term cause, for, no sooner is the cause for the effect established than a social cause emerges—prophylactic techniques, regulatory measures, subjectifying statements begin to circulate around the physical cause. The brain singularity is placed in a linear relation to the cause. Despite the plasticity built into the notion of neuroplasticity, such plasticity now appears as a site of fragility to be protected from dangerous exposure, rather than as responsiveness or resilience. Such a gesture slides readily into neoliberal paradox: resilience is both the problem and the solution!

In sum, where neurosciences might be characterized in terms of a strategic use of singularity to generate a field of inquiry, discourses on media risk and addition may be characterized in terms of a massive repression of the challenges posed by emerging field of neuroscience research on the effects of media. But how to address the challenges implicit in neuroscientific studies?

As I mentioned at the outset, the dominant tendency within the humanities at present is to turn to media use, that is, to something like cultural studies. Charles Acland delineates the problem nicely in the context of screens when he writes:

> The concept of the "screen" stitches together an identifiable and meaningful array of artifacts" but "technical specifications—screen size, aspect ratio, resolution, frame and refresh rate, brightness, color scale—only [get] us so far in our job of actually understanding the related senses, sensibilities, and practices that form as a consequence of media use.
>
> (Acland 170)

As Acland points out, it is impossible to talk about screens in general or platforms in general due to their empirical diversity. Affordances multiply and proliferate. Yet the very concept of the screen tends to introduce a monolithic Screen that acts unilaterally on its putatively passive or exposed users. As such, it does indeed make sense to begin with use, and even in the manner of Marx in the first volume of *Capital* where the moment of exchange and circulation of the commodity is what brings the entire set of social relations into play.

Yet cultural studies focused on the use of media reach an impasse. Even when the subjectivity of users is considered, the constituency of users is posited in advance. Already constituted groups are the point of departure, and rarely are groups approached from the angle of their emergence. It is an impasse that troubled one of the first thinkers to dwell on cultural uses of media, Umberto Eco. Eco called for a departure from the questions that had, in his opinion, dominated the study of television, namely, "What do mass communications do to audiences?"(87) Instead he directs attention to what audiences do to (with) mass communications. And so he poses his provocative question: do audiences have bad effects on television?

Eco's analysis centered on the message and on what audiences do with the message. What interested him are those moments when people fail to understand the message in accordance with the senders' intentions (94–95). Yet failure to understand the television message did not signal for him a simple error that can be corrected by educating the audience or making the message clearer. Rather it shows that the message is, in fact, "a text on which converge messages based on different codes" (98). Simply put, sending a univocal unambiguous message is impossible. Failure to understand on the part of an audience, then, is not a passive misunderstanding. Eco thus called attention to a dimension of misunderstanding that is potentially active. Then, focusing on active refusal of television's messages, Eco looked for the emergence of new audiences or new constituencies, that is, audiences that would form new constituencies through their resistance to television's messages.

Initially, Eco's approach appears diametrically opposed to discourses on media risk and addition, which focus on the medium rather than the message. Yet it invites a delightfully unconventional reversal of emphasis: do brains hurt television? Does neuroplasticity pose a threat to media platforms? If such questions feel awkward, it is partly because Eco's model does not pave the way for them. While Eco radically departs from the univocal model of the message, he does not challenge the unidirectional model of the medium. At stake today is not only the polyvocal nature of messages. The "polydirectional" or "polyvalent" nature of media is also at stake. William Connolly is one thinker who has taken seriously the polyvalent challenge that the neurosciences pose to cultural studies. He writes,

> Although cultural theorists do have things to teach neuroscientists, some research by the latter can teach us a thing or two about the layered character of culture. It can show us how the inwardization of culture, replete with resistances and ambivalences, is installed at several different levels of being, with each level interacting with the others and marked by different speeds, capacities, and degrees of linguistic sophistication,
>
> (Connolly 7)

It may well be that neuroplasticity is harmful to television! After all, neurosciences find that media singularity and brain singularity are entangled from the outset.

In any event, if neuroscientific studies of photoepileptiform phenomena are not simply aligned with social discourses (as is common in cultural studies) or reduced to unidirectional cause-and-effect scenarios (as in technological determinism of discourses on media addiction), then their challenge comes of how they force cultural studies and media studies to address the politics of singularity.

Coda: The Expression of Singularity

Discourses on media addiction tend to naturalize a mode of subjectification or subject formation prevalent in contemporary media use—personalize, individualize, responsibilize. The first section of this essay showed how such discourses draw on scientific research in order to lay claim to neutrality, eliminating social and cultural factors from discussion while using empirical data to shore up dubious claims about media use. The basic problem might seem to be the false use of sciences, which implies that scientific truth may be disentangled from discursive constructions. My ultimate goal, however, is not to introduce a neat divide between discursive constructions and scientific facts, between the cultural and the natural. I turned to the complexity of the scientific process of generating facts about media effects, precisely to show that turning to culture or cultural uses of media does not really present a challenge to received ways of thinking subjectification, or more precisely, subjectivity. This is because when cultural studies turn to media uses, singularity is eliminated at the outset. As previously mentioned, cultures are generally imagined in terms of pre-existing constituencies. Brian Massumi puts it this way:

> As it is widely practiced, cultural studies falls short of singularity at both limits because it clings to the notion that *expression is of a particularity*. It realizes that expression is collective. But it takes the collectivity as already constituted, as a determinate set of actually existing persons (in common parlance, a constituency).
>
> (253)

The Pokémon Incident again furnishes a good example, for it defies reduction to the expression of a particularity, of a preconstituted set of actors, either Japanese people or children. It shows why it is that cultural studies of media may not be well equipped to counter discourses on media risk. Nor for that matter are area studies, for similar reasons. The incident happened in Japan but only due to the zoning of broadcasts, and the population seized by the incident does not correlate with the bounded territory of the nation. Moreover, while the 12 Hz flicker is statistically more likely to affect children between the ages of six and 12, it does not uniformly constitute this population as a particularity. It adds weight to Jyotsna Kapur's warnings about "inadequacy in assuming *children* to be a natural category, an audience that is simply found rather than constructed" (123). In this incident, familiar constituencies, such as children, parents, and nation, were brought into relation with other familiar constituencies, such as animators, broadcasters, scientists and doctors, but in entirely unfamiliar ways. It is precisely this emergent field that the cultural studies of media use—cultural analysis based on reading the event as an expression of received cultural positions—tend to overlook and betray. Such an event forces cultural studies and media studies to move beyond their reliance on expression of a particularity and grapple seriously with singularity, which means reckoning with neuroscientific findings. It renders untenable the reigning separation between the cultural studies question "what do audiences do with media or technologies?" and the sciences' question "what do media or technologies do to audiences?"

In sum, discourses on media risk and media addiction force a new kind of confrontation with the sciences, especially neurosciences, which are steadily replacing the psychological and psychoanalytic models of subjectivity in terms of explanatory force and social acceptance. This does not mean media scholars and cultural theorists need to accept the neurosciences at face value, as truth unadulterated. Rather an urgent new task has come to the fore, that of how to push neurosciences to the point of immanent critique, to apply pressure to the sites and moments where they help to counter the ongoing naturalization of the mode of subjectification that makes it seem that individualization, personalization, and self-responsibilization are the best, most rational and most natural ways of dealing with the pervasive pressure of media platforms.

The case of the Pokémon Incident, precisely because it is so stark and severe, raises the stakes for thinking in terms of singularities and intensities instead of particularity and measurable effects. When the incident is addressed in terms of measurable effects on particular constituencies, the outcome will be an emphasis on protecting yourself from harm, on managing risk. Addressed in terms of singularities and intensities, however, the same incident poses questions about dependency and vulnerability, which are not distributed homogeneously within a recognizable population (children, families). This is precisely what discourses on media addiction both presume and disavow: dependency. Recommendations to regulate dosage assume that users will not cease to use media, because they are somehow reliant on it. Yet that reliance or dependency, not only on media forms and platforms but also friends and family, is effectively denied as such. Instead everything hinges on autonomy, which is taken to be an overcoming of dependency, even if that overcoming entails continuous regulation. If friends and family are needed, it is in the guise of a collective overcoming of dependency and vulnerability that is figured in each individual. The scenario is like a Hobbesian security state. Dependency and vulnerability can never be acknowledged in a distributed, active form.

But such a possibility is implied in the Pokémon Incident: a collective becoming in which dependency and vulnerability are not overcome but are the point of departure for other ways of belonging together. What is more, this is such a salient and powerful theme in Japanese anime and games that one wonders how such a possibility is so resolutely eliminated from consideration in accounts hinging on such media forms. My point is not that we should simply return to content analysis or give messages precedence over media. On the contrary, neuroscientific studies direct attention to intensities and singularities in a manner that makes it impossible to impose a hierarchy on medium and message. Discourses on media addiction, however, act to reintroduce hierarchy: no sooner do they diffuse causal factors into a media environment (the pervasive pressure of platforms) than they reintroduce the subject who is to attain sovereign autonomy through the regulation and disavowal of dependency (protection of neuroplasticity). At the very moment when risk opens questions about collective becoming, it closes them. Perhaps it is time to think from the other side, in terms of situations in which user, platform, media, and infrastructures remain in play. After all, the Pokémon Incident remains in play today, not only in neurosciences but also in popular culture, in all its horror, affectively. Notions of media dependency and polyvalent vulnerability might afford a lure to reach the flipside of media addiction without endorsing the production of securitized and responsibilized individuals.

Acknowledgments

This essay builds on a line of inquiry running through several chapters of *The Anime Ecology: A Genealogy of Television, Animation and Game Media* that I was not able to fully develop in that context. I wish to thank the editors for the opportunity to expand and refine that strand of thought.

Notes

1 A good example is Desmurget, *TV Lobotomie*, which dwells on statistical documentation showing how television negatively affects health and academic performance and promotes violence and fear. While his study largely follows the social behavior model, he nevertheless draws a good deal from cognitive studies and neuroscientific research and concludes that, because television is everywhere at all times, we need to control our intake.

2 Furusho et al. *Pokémon* calculate schoolchildren as 55 percent of approximately 10 million viewers ("Patient Background" 553).
3 Takahashi and Tsukahara place the figure at 200; Ishida et al. place the figure at 150.
4 Ishida et al. calculate 55 percent of 10 million viewers, as does Furusho et al. (*Pokémon*).
5 For a summary of the documentary, see jsolodar.
6 On March 29, 1997, there was an incident involving the episode "The Mysterious Father" (Maboroshi No Oyaji) in which four children were taken to hospitals by ambulance after reportedly watching a scene in the episode with rapidly flashing red and white colors. Broadcasts were not suspended.
7 Deleuze's conceptualization of singularity is also pertinent here (63); Burns and Kaiser provide a precise overview of its geopolitical relevance (8–9); and see, too, Shaviro.
8 Brian Massumi puts it this way: "The processings of science run usefully from recognizability to reproducibility" (252).

Works Cited

Acland, Charles R. "Crack in the Electric Window." *Cinema Journal*, 51, no. 2 (2012), pp. 169–173.
Burns, Lorna and Birgit M. Kaiser. "Introduction: Navigating Differential Futures,(Un) making Colonial Pasts." *Postcolonial Literatures and Deleuze*. Palgrave Macmillan, 2012, pp. 1–17.
Connolly, William. *Neuropolitics: Thinking, Culture, Speed*. U of Minnesota P, 2002.
Covanis, Athanasios. "Photosensitivity in Idiopathic Generalized Epilepsies." *Epilepsia*, no. 46, 2005, pp. 67–72.
Curiel, Erik and Peter Bokulich. "Singularities and Black Holes." *Stanford Encyclopedia of Philosophy*, edited by Edward N. Zalta, Fall 2012 edition, http://plato.stanford.edu/. Accessed June 6, 2014.
Deleuze, Gilles. *Logic of Sense*. Bloomsbury Publishing, 2004.
Desmurget, Michel. *TV Lobotomie: La vérité scientifique sur les effects de la television*. Max Milo editions, 2011.
Eco, Umberto. "Does the Audience Have Bad Effects on Television?." *Apocalypse Postponed*, 1994, pp. 87–102.
Fisher, Robert S. et al. "Photic- and Pattern-induced Seizures: A Review for the Epilepsy Foundation of America Working Group." *Epilepsia*, vol. 46, no. 9, 2005, pp. 1426–1441.
Furusho, Junichi et al. "A Comparison Survey of Seizures and Other Symptoms of Pokemon Phenomenon." *Pediatric Neurology*, vol. 27, no. 5, 2002, pp. 350–355.
Furusho, Junichi et al. "Patient Background of the Pokemon Phenomenon: Questionnaire Studies in Multiple Pediatric Clinics." *Pediatrics International*, vol. 40, no. 6, 1998, pp. 550–554.
Harding, Graham. "TV Can Be Bad for Your Health." *Nature Medicine*, vol. 4, no. 3, 1998, pp. 265–267.
Harding, Graham F.A. and Takeo Takahashi. "Regulations: What Next?." *Epilepsia*, vol. 45, 2004, pp. 46–47.
Hurley, Adrienne Carey. *Revolutionary Suicide and Other Desperate Measures: Narratives of Youth and Violence from Japan and the United States*. Duke UP, 2011.
Illes, Judy et al. "International Perspectives on Engaging the Public in Neuroethics." *Nature Reviews Neuroscience*, vol. 6, no. 12, 2005, p. 977.
Ishida, Shigenobu et al. "Photosensitive Seizures Provoked While Viewing 'Pocket Mosnters,' a Made-for-Television Animation Program in Japan." *Epilepsia*, vol. 39, no. 12, 1998, pp. 1340–1344.
jsolodar, "Nintendo Knew About, Downplayed Seizure Risks: BBC Report." Seizures from Video Games, December 11, 2018, https://videogameseizures.wordpress.com/2013/02/20/nintendo-knew-about-downplayed-seizure-risks-bbc-report/. Accessed May 8, 2014.
Kapur, Jyotsna. "Out of Control: Television and the Transformation of Childhood in Late Capitalism." *Kids' Media Culture*, 1999, pp. 122–136.
Kasteleijn-Nolst Trenité, Dorothée. "Photosensitivity in Epilepsy. Electrophysiological and Clinical Correlates." *Acta neurologica Scandinavica. Supplementum*, no. 125, 1989, pp. 3–149.
Kasteleijn-Nolst Trenité, Dorothée et al. "Visual Stimuli in Daily Life." *Epilepsia*, vol. 45, 2004, pp. 2–6.
Knight, Frank H. *Risk, Uncertainty and Profit*. Houghton Mifflin Company, 1921.
Koizumi, Hideaki. "Brain Science and Education in Japan." *Neuroscience in Education: The Good, the Bad, and the Ugly*, 2012, pp. 319–332.
Koizumi, Hideaki. "The Concept of 'Developing the Brain': A New Natural Science for Learning and Education." *Brain and Development*, vol. 26, no. 7, 2004, pp. 434–441.
Kubey, Robert and Mihaly Csikszentmihalyi. "Television Addiction is No Mere Metaphor." *Scientific American*, vol. 286, no. 2, 2002, pp. 74–80.
Massumi, Brian. *Parables for the Virtual: Movement, Affect, Sensation*. Duke UP, 2002.

McNamee, Rodger and Scott Simon. "How Dangerous Is Misinformation On Facebook?" January 20, 2018, www.npr.org/2018/01/20/579330287/how-dangerous-is-misinformation-on-facebook. Accessed January 31, 2018.

Okumura, Akihisa et al. "Epilepsies after Pocket Monster Seizures." *Epilepsia*, vol. 46, no. 6, 2005, pp. 980–982.

Schnabel, Jim. "The Black Box: Assessing the Effects of Television on Young Children is Far from Easy. But, as Researchers Tell Jim Schnabel, That is No Reason Not to Try." *Nature*, vol. 459, no. 7248, 2009, pp. 765–769.

Shaviro, Steven. "What Are Singularities?" *Pinocchio Theory*, June 14, 2012, www.shaviro.com. Accessed January 11, 2018.

Slater, David H. "The Making of Japan's New Working Class." *Asia-Pacific Journal*, January 4, 2010, www.japanfocus.org. Accessed May 12, 2014.

Takada, Hiroyuki et al. "Epileptic Seizures Induced by Animated Cartoon, *Pocket Monster*." *Epilepsia*, vol. 40, no. 7, 1999, pp. 997–1002.

Takahashi, Takeo and Yasuo Tsukahara. "*Pocket Monster* Incident and Low Luminance Visual Stimuli: Special Reference to Deep Red Flicker Stimulation." *Pediatrics International*, vol. 40, no. 6, 1998, pp. 631–637.

Takahashi, Taeko et al. "Pokemon Seizures." *Neurological Journal of Southeast Asia*, vol. 4, 1999, pp. 1–11.

Toivonen, Tuukka. "Don't Let Your Child Become a NEET! The Strategic Foundations of a Japanese Youth Scare." *Japan Forum*, vol. 23, no. 3, 2011, pp. 407–429.

Verrotti, Alberto et al. "Photosensitivity: Epidemiology, Genetics, Clinical Manifestations, Assessment, and Management." *Epileptic Disorders*, vol. 14, no. 4, 2012, pp. 349–362.

Yamasaki, Takao et al. "Neural Basis of Photo/Chromatic Sensitivity in Adolescence." *Epilepsia*, vol. 49, no. 9, 2008, pp. 1611–1618.

Zifkin, Benjamin and Dorothée Kasteleijn-Nolst Trenité. "Pokemon Contagion: A Letter to the Editors." *Southern Medical Journal*, vol. 94, no. 12, 2001, pp. 1235–1236.

24
RISK'S FRAUGHT MEDIASCAPE
Jeff Scheible

Silence-Breaking: WikiLeaks and #MeToo

The aim of this chapter is quite modest. I simply want to consider a single scene in a film and to think about the work it is doing within the film. The film is *Risk*, a documentary about Julian Assange made by Oscar-winning filmmaker Laura Poitras that was released in 2017, and the specific scene that I'd like to turn to documents a memorable exchange between the notorious WikiLeaks editor and pop star Lady Gaga. While on one level, the scene offers light comic relief from a film that is otherwise quite serious, it simultaneously poses a series of more complex questions if we scratch at its surface. These questions speak to how celebrities and gender difference are conceptualized in the popular imaginary, and the cultural work such conceptualizations do in substituting for more difficult and messy problems of the risks tied to the utopian projects of global capitalism and the network society. These questions speak to how we are invited to take some

Figure 24.1 Lady Gaga interviews Julian Assange in *Risk*
Source: Laura Poitras, 2017

people—and the claims they make and the causes they fight for—more seriously than others. It is my argument here that such questions are not only about how we police discursive boundaries across genders but that they also figure into how we construct boundaries between genres (in this case comedy and documentary), shoring up epistemological limits in the ways that we understand cinema and media.

These issues seem especially important to reflect on in light of the momentum of #MeToo activism, the Trump administration's discursive and mediatized distortions, and related desires and political needs to not lose grip on truth, fact, and accountability. The 2016 U.S. presidential election spotlighted the pervasiveness of misogyny as a structuring ideology in American culture. As the first female to be the Democratic nominee for presidential candidate, Hillary Clinton was under intense scrutiny—for how she dressed, for how she used her email accounts, for her undeniable political competence. While Clinton was far from perfect (arguably not even as feminist an option as her Democratic competitor Bernie Sanders), Donald Trump, her Republican opponent, seemed to have been dealt a stack of get-out-of-jail-free cards, allowing him to proceed through the election campaign with only a few scars despite multiple accusations of sexual assault, alongside video footage released by *Access Hollywood* in which he vulgarly boasted of the way he treated women— "grab them by the pussy." Two days after this video was leaked, Clinton and Trump faced off in their second televised presidential debate, and each candidates' body language on the stage spoke volumes about the gendered power dynamics at stake. While Clinton stayed respectfully still as Trump talked, as she talked, he paced around her on the stage like a predatory lion preparing for a kill. Throughout their run-off, a global audience learned that even in the most esteemed posts, men are excused for bad behavior while women are scrutinized for activity, comportment, and utterances on scales not even comparable to those for which men receive free passes. We know how the rest of the story is going: Trump proceeded to win the election, further dividing the nation into xenophobes, racists, and sexists who have been empowered to openly voice their thoughts against leftists with more progressive ideologies who have been enflamed by the daily assaults on human rights and the duplicitous strategies and allegiances that Trump has forged on behalf of America on the world stage.

Less than one year after Trump was elected president via the nation's outdated mechanism of the electoral college, the Harvey Weinstein controversy broke. The *New York Times* published a story detailing decades of sexual assault allegations against Weinstein, a leading film producer in Hollywood. Scores of more women in the film industry spoke out—against Weinstein but also against a range of other prominent figures, in other industries, who abused their power and coerced women into uneven promises of success in exchange for sexual favors. Through a series of ongoing events, whose ramifications will surely be thought through and felt for years to come, Weinstein was swiftly exorcised from power—fired from his namesake company, ousted by the Academy, and criminally tried for sex act charges. In a symbolic departure from their customary decision to award the title to a single figure, *TIME Magazine* named the "silence breakers" their 2017 "person of the year." This move by *TIME* is suggestive on one hand of the rising wave of resistance toward accepting the sexually problematic behavior of men in power which has been accepted by American institutions for far too long, but on the other hand of the ways in which our responses to these power dynamics can be swiftly displaced, obscuring necessary critique and discomfort. To what extent, for example, in celebrating female victims coming forward, do we fail to come to terms with the monsters that run the world and have for decades controlled the images circulating on our screens by subjecting women to assault offscreen? And to what extent does this situation parallel the age-old fear that movies are a distraction from realpolitik—in other words, how does having it out with Weinstein inhibit us from having it out with Trump, the sexual predator who has been accused by multiple women of assault and yet walked away, so far, unscathed?

While populist ideologies and popular media tend to binarily compartmentalize complicated sets of relations in the national imaginary (good/bad; Democrat/Republican; real/fake; man/woman), risks are continually deferred. Beyond the displacement from Trump to Weinstein, a move which also reveals the impossibility of mapping gender politics onto party politics in light of Weinstein's contributions of about $300,000 to the Clinton Foundation, it seems that there lurks yet another series of displacements whose operations and flows are perhaps a bit less straightforward and have been less critically disentangled. *TIME*'s honoring of "silence breakers" is revealing of the displacement I have in mind. Among the many precursors to the women silence breakers in Hollywood in late 2017, and surely among the closest high-profile example in temporal proximity to it, are the widely covered accusations against Julian Assange that were separately brought forward by two Swedish women in 2010. The charges were dropped seven years later, on May 19, 2017, less than five months before the Weinstein story was front-page news. Assange himself is of course well known for being a "silence breaker" of a different sort; and in fact he was the readers' top choice for *TIME*'s person of the year in 2010, though the magazine very symbolically passed on him and instead decided to anoint the title to the safer and (at the time) less-controversial Facebook founder Mark Zuckerberg, who had received only a fraction of the votes Assange had. (Lady Gaga, I might note, was also in the running for the title, and also received more votes than Zuckerberg.)

In contrast to Weinstein or Trump, Assange is striking for his Jekyll-and-Hyde status as both a championed silence-breaker himself and a reviled and accused misogynist, often positioned in these dual poles of hero and villain by people of the same political persuasion. Trump of course is championed by plenty of people too, but not generally by the same people who disagree with his gender politics; though of course the question of his white female supporters does raise this issue. And indeed, the case of Assange perhaps more than Trump and Weinstein helps us see how a public figure can support contradictory attachments in a way that puts into perspective how we all have conflicting attachments to each one of these figures, if in different valences. Celebrities are figures that both enthrall and appall us—arguably on an ontological level.

Thus the example of Assange brings to the foreground several paradoxes that seem to apply to, or at least run parallel to, the silence breakers. Foremost among these is the question of information in the "new media" age—its availability and unavailability, its publicity and privacy, its truth and its deceptions. Jodi Dean has been one of the most compelling writers on these issues, arguing, following Slavoj Zizek, that disavowal is a central logic to how information is managed and contained. Running parallel to the logics identified in Timur Kuran's notion of "preference falsification," Dean writes that

> democratic politics has been formatted through a dynamic of concealment and disclosure, through a primary opposition between what is hidden and what is revealed. The fantasy of a public to which democracy appeals and the ideal of publicity at its normative core require the secret as their disavowed basis.
>
> *(Dean 625)*

In "the face of contemporary technoculture's pervasive cynicism," she notes, "unmasking is clearly pointless: cynicism already incorporates an ironic distance from official culture and everyday social reality. People know very well what they are doing, but they still do it" (627). At the same time that secrecy is a healthy and necessary component of a functioning democracy, the public is required to believe in the value of transparency. The public all the while also really suspects (if not knows) what the secrets are but puts them out of mind.

Mark Andrejevic addresses the role of journalism in relation to WikiLeaks and Assange more specifically:

> Assange is an information 'terrorist' precisely because he didn't tell us anything we did not already know. That is to say, he forced us to confront our disavowed knowledge (that US

soldiers are killing civilians; that, after toppling a regime in Iraq that tortures prisoners, the United States has created a regime that tortures; that the United States is engaged in covert warfare in Yemen; and so on).

(2623)

It is in the context of this impossible but real bind that the public forms contradictory attachments to Assange: by revealing secrets, he, perhaps too naively, impedes the functioning of democracy and is called by the well-liked former Vice President Joe Biden a "hi-tech terrorist," while others affirm that he is one of the most important figures of the twenty-first century, fighting for free speech in a repressive journalistic mediascape. The truth of course flows somewhere in the intermediation of these claims.

As Wendy Chun and Sarah Friedland observe, these paradoxes extend to the phenomenon of the leak:

> From Edward Snowden's revelations about the U.S. National Security Agency's (NSA) extensive data collection programs to images of unsuspecting 'sluts' that circulate on social media, from WikiLeaks to Facebook disasters, we are confronted everywhere with leaks. This leaking information is framed paradoxically as both securing and compromising our privacy, personal and national. Thanks to these leaks, we now understand the extent to which we are under surveillance; because of these leaks, we are exposed.
>
> *(Chun and Friedland 4)*

They make the powerful argument that leaks are not an effect of the new media environment but that the very operations of new media are, ontologically, leaky. "New media work by breaching, thus paradoxically sustaining, the boundary between private and public" they write (4). The work that digital networks do is constituted precisely through the exchange of information. The "secure transaction" is always fundamentally accompanied by the risk, a risk that in a sense very much echoes the logic of deconstruction's open-ended text. Once language is put into writing, it is given a form that is intended to travel and acquire future uses, whose meanings and interpretations always exceed whatever intention might exist in the inscription itself. The same claim can be made of information today—once it enters the network, it becomes open to any number of possible futures that go beyond its intended node of arrival.

My intention here is to suggest, through a reading of the Gaga–Assange interview in *Risk*, that the ideological contradictions and constitutive paradoxes of information in our new digital order play out not only through the technics of mediation, as Chun and Friedland suggest, but through celebrity and cultural form, or *genre*, as well. More specifically, the scene offers an opportunity to think about the compatibility and intersection of two modes that we might tend to think of, at least implicitly, as incommensurable: comedy and documentary. The intersection of these genres in fact is able to teach us much about the evolving landscape of journalism (precisely, as I will soon explain, the premise of *Risk*), in which so many people get their news through satire and in which mainstream news often seems to be a joke.

Risk's Production History and Gender Politics

Before I turn to the particulars of the scene, it might help to situate it with some context. Connected to Julian Assange through film programmer Charlotte Cook, a mutual acquaintance, Laura Poitras began filming the WikiLeaks founder soon after the not-for-profit organization received over 700,000 U.S. military and State Department documents in 2010, which were infiltrated by U.S. Army Private Bradley, now Chelsea, Manning. As many readers will likely remember, these leaks led to a string of headlines throughout 2010, beginning in April with the release of the notorious *Collateral Murder* video, 39 minutes of classified footage of two U.S. helicopters conducting an airstrike in Baghdad responsible for killing Iraqi civilians and two Reuters war correspondents. The headlines continued in July with the Afghan War Logs, in October with the Iraq War Logs, and then again one month later in November with Cablegate. The sexual allegations against him were brought forward in the midst of all of this, in August, and thus were interlinked with the WikiLeaks scandal almost immediately.

Poitras had begun shooting material for *Risk* with the general idea that the footage would make up the third part of a documentary trilogy examining the aftermath of 9/11, following her 2006 film *My Country, My Country* about U.S.-occupied Iraq and her 2010 film *The Oath*, about two men who had worked for bin Laden. This third documentary would focus on journalism and the surveillance state in the age of terrorism. With this objective, Poitras began following prominent figures including U.S. security-state journalist Glenn Greenwald and Internet activist Jacob Appelbaum. As soon as WikiLeaks released what the U.S. State Department called "the largest leak of classified documents in its history," Poitras was naturally drawn to the game-changing nature of this information's publicization for the field of journalism and turned her attention to Assange and his organization.

She continued following Assange intermittently for the next few years, including when in 2012 he was granted asylum in the Ecuadorian Embassy in London to avoid being extradited by Sweden (where he was facing charges of sexual assault and rape) to the U.S. (where he would face consequences for publishing a treasure trove of classified material). The film's original working title was "Asylum," but as Poitras attempted to grapple with the contradictions circling between Assange's actions and principles, the film gradually came to cover material well beyond the scope of its original focus, and the title changed accordingly. A key turning point in *Risk*'s production history, with which readers following contemporary documentary closely will likely be familiar, took place in January 2013, when Poitras received encrypted messages that would eventually be revealed to be from Edward Snowden. The National Surveillance Agency (NSA) contractor singled Poitras out, along with Glen Greenwald, as the journalists to whom he would entrust the responsibility of curating and publicly releasing massive amounts of classified documentation belonging to the NSA. The ensuing process, and Snowden's outing to the media, is captivatingly documented in Poitras's 2014 documentary *Citizenfour*, which replaced *Risk* to become the third film in her post-9/11 trilogy and won the Academy Award for Best Documentary.

Citizenfour thus began production after and was distributed before principal photography had even been completed on *Risk*, giving the two movies a palimpsestic relationship, not least of all because Assange seemed to feel betrayed by Poitras's (reasonable—and collaborative) decision to not release Snowden's information through WikiLeaks but instead to take it directly to more mainstream establishments like the *Guardian*. Poitras returned to filming Assange in 2015, but as she documents, their relationship grew increasingly strained, culminating in WikiLeaks sending Poitras a cease and desist letter attempting to censor the film after its 2017 Cannes premiere. Two weeks after *Risk*'s Cannes screening, accusations of sexual assault were mounted by women in the information security community against one of Poitras's key subjects, The Onion Router (TOR) founder Jacob Appelbaum, with whom Poitras herself had a fling. This revelation in particular prompted her to make pronounced formal alterations to the film, uneasily deciding to confront the sexual controversies of Assange and Appelbaum head-on. In order to do this, Poitras departed from her more standard verité approach to include narration from her production diaries. These late-addition voiceovers, while measured, decidedly push her own perspective and hesitations to the fore, and they articulate her ambivalent thoughts and feelings about Assange from the beginning of their filming relationship.

Upon seeing this cut, Assange texted Poitras with the message, read aloud by Poitras in the new voiceover ending the film, "presently the film is a severe threat to my freedom, and I am forced to treat it accordingly." The obvious irony in this response of course is that WikiLeaks privileges freedom of information above all else, and Assange undercuts this guiding principle in attempting to censor the film. Indeed, Assange is repeatedly critiqued precisely because in indiscriminately making information free he puts innocent people's lives at risk, and here he turns the tables, claiming this as a line of defense on his own behalf. As such Assange appears to betray the principle of transparency he has championed, challenging the spectator, like Poitras, to come to terms with his hypocrisy. This is made easier by reconsidering Assange's very first words that Poitras shares in the film: "Most people who have very strong principles, stances, don't survive for long. Actually we all want them to survive for long but they don't … Many times … I've had to be ruthlessly pragmatic."

Surely Assange's hesitations about the film's release, and his attempts to rationalize his request to censor it, stem from the objectionable manner in which he is depicted talking about the sexual allegations. One-third of the way into the documentary, Assange is seated on a couch, receiving counsel from a lawyer, Helena Kennedy, over how to handle the accusations of unlawful coercion and rape that have been filed against him. She essentially attempts to sensitize him to the importance of understanding patriarchal power, reviewing how to navigate the situation: gracefully affirming women's rights to come forward with accusations, while distancing himself from the position of perpetrator. Kennedy explains, for example, "it's about you getting your mind into not using language that sounds hostile to women" and that "you don't want to say it's all a mad feminist conspiracy," to which he boldly responds (on camera!), "not to say that publicly … "

In *Guardian* coverage anticipating the film's UK release, Simon Hattenstone notes that Kennedy's "look of despair" in response is "priceless." As Kennedy seemingly unsuccessfully tries wising Assange up, he talks over her (as he does many other interlocutors throughout the documentary), suggesting just how much he fails to understand the extent of, or to work on, his own imbrication in casual misogyny. This is perhaps the most damning scene of Assange, but it is important to emphasize that cinematically, it is purely observational filmmaking and contains no technical strategies that attempt to manipulate or distort the truth. As Kennedy helps Assange, the scene also offers a quick glimpse of the real ways in which women, too, can comply with misogyny, unsettling any easy binary logics that populism's political imaginary might stage.

Risk's focus on Assange precedes but is nevertheless roughly contemporaneous to the #MeToo movement, and therefore provides its audience an opportunity to reflect on one very prominent example of a celebrity facing ongoing sexual assault allegations that was simmering in the media landscape as the Weinstein revelations brought the movement to a boil in October 2017. The documentary will likely be impossible to not read against this backdrop, as it delivers a disquieting portrait of the abuse of power within the information security community that mirrors contradictions that constitute the unequal and sexist treatment of women in an even wider range of media institutions, industries, and communities. I offer this broader overview of the film's uncomfortable gender politics because it inflects and plays against the Gaga scene quite particularly.

Documentary Comedy and *Risk*'s Gaga Feminism

In general, Poitras' filmmaking style, with its seriousness and the connections it forges to urgent, political, real-world issues, aligns with what documentary film scholar Bill Nichols has called documentary's "discourse of sobriety." While in some senses the Gaga interview scene is continuous with the rest of the film (notably, we see Assange cut Gaga off just as he did with Kennedy earlier, for example), in other ways it has more affinities with a select couple of other moments in the film that register a notable tonal departure from its discourse of sobriety. These include a scene depicting Assange at a meeting in a secluded park, paranoid he is being spied upon and another when we witness him disguise himself with colored contact lenses, piercings, and dyed hair. Such moments, among the standout sequences of the film, break out of the logics of the film, recalling Jack Halberstam's discussion of "Gaga feminism," a mode of feminism modeled on Lady Gaga that takes the reorientation of established modes of relationalities and feminisms as its defining feature and political value. As Poitras herself says of the Gaga interview:

> I think it's such a great moment. She gets so much by pushing. When Julian says, "I don't care how I feel," that's such a brilliant moment of insight. Or when he says he's not a "normal person"; I love the scene for its humor, I love the scene for its insight, for how surreal it is, and what it reveals about both of them.

Critically spotlighting the scene also offers an opportunity to think about the under-studied relationship between comedy and documentary, usually conceived to be mutually exclusive modes, despite their increasing intersections across a range of contexts—from mockumentary and cringe-comedy TV to cable satire and what Jason Middleton refers to as Michael Moore's "awkward aesthetics." As a point of juxtaposition, we could briefly turn to a sequence from Moore's 2004 Palme d'Or-winning documentary on the Bush administration's foreign policies, *Fahrenheit 9/11*, to help think about this encounter in Poitras's film. In one of the film's most upsetting sequences, Moore presents an Iraqi woman standing in front of rubble. She directly addresses the camera and flails her arms back and forth as she emotionally protests the heartlessness and ignorance of the Americans who have just destroyed her uncle's home and killed civilians, including multiple family members. As she breaks down into tears, Moore cuts to an interview with Britney Spears donning a blonde wig, saying that we should "just trust our president and every decision that he makes."

Anna Fisher notes in her discussion of this sequence that the "film offers a complex bifurcation of Spears as female celebrity and uninformed American citizen" (305). She suggests that we are simultaneously positioned to side with Moore as he repurposes footage of Spears to represent the dumbing down of American society, yet at the same we are asked to *identify with Spears*, recognizing our complicity in blindly trusting the president as he led Americans into a war waged under false pretenses. Fisher writes, "How, we might ask, does a female celebrity like Spears come to be held as symbolically responsible for a war? How is it that Spears' so-called ignorance comes to seem more reprehensible than Bush's 'failed intelligence'" (304)? She goes on to draw parallels between the War in Iraq and the "War on Britney" as "two contemporaneous global media 'events' that have powerfully drawn together questions of excess and failure in the public sphere" (305). Key to the connection between these two seemingly different "wars" is the prominent place of "infotainment" in the evolving journalistic landscape, a portmanteau suggestive of how "serious" news is routinely mixed with lighter, often more feminized, strands of news about entertainment, pop culture, and, of course, celebrities. On the heels of this moment, Stephen Colbert's *Colbert Report* (Comedy Central, 2005–2014) emerged to satirize this mediascape, performing a stupid masculinity only to slyly affirm his own smart masculinity: drawing attention to but in its own way ultimately reaffirming easy dualisms.

Fisher offers a Baudrillardian argument, suggesting that the split between entertainment news and real news is a false binary, wherein the

> cultural obsession with Britney Spears during this period of national crisis did important political work for redirecting public attention to a spectacle far more within reach ... Spears was presented as a trainwreck to make the American public think that everything else was under control.
>
> (329)

I would argue that the public fascination with this same false binary is what makes the Gaga interview in *Risk* such a compelling sequence, if to a very different effect.

It does seem striking that in both of these documentaries aiming to educate viewers about the messy machinations of global politics, one finds turns to female pop stars. The two films document the logic of infotainment in which celebrities' latest outfits—or to recall the opening of Moore's *Capitalism: A Love Story* (2010), a cat flushing a toilet—are equally if not more newsworthy and fascinating as the government-sponsored killing of innocent civilians. It is worth noting that in both scenes it is not gossipy news about these pop stars that is featured so much as it is each one's explicit trespassing of the coordinates in the media ecology to which we are made to believe they must remain relegated, yet delight with surprise and schadenfreude as they inevitably, riskily, cross into the other half of infotainment. It is along these lines, I would argue, that many people, including Poitras herself, describe the Gaga scene as "surreal." An article on *The Daily Beast* identifies Gaga's interrogation of Assange as "the most surreal movie moment of the year."

Perhaps the biggest difference between these two scenes lies in the fact that Moore introduces Spears into the picture via Eisensteinian editing techniques: bringing together two seemingly unrelated pieces of footage taken from different places—to suggest a conceptual linkage, making his own rather heavy-handed argument, which is perhaps more polysemous and ambiguous than Moore accommodates for. By contrast, in *Risk*, the juxtaposition between these two halves of infotainment is occurring *in profilmic reality*. And indeed, it is hard to ignore the fact that, 13 years later, the intermingling of these two halves has been so thoroughly synthesized that a celebrity has become, once again, the American president—whose election, and reign, I would note, are also frequently felt to be "surreal."[1] An instructive index of this is Merriam-Webster's announcement that "surreal" was their 2016 word of the year. The dictionary's editor-at-large notes that "spikes of interest in a word are usually triggered by a single event," but in 2016 "what's truly remarkable … is that so many different stories led people to look it up" (Pengelly). These include the deaths of David Bowie and Prince and a terrorist attack in Nice, though Trump's election was credited by the outlet as being responsible for the single biggest spike. As such, it seems important to understand *Risk*'s "most surreal movie moment of the year" as capturing something of the zeitgeist—of the moment that sees boundary-crossing and logic-bending as routine. We must ask in turn: What is the risk of this epistemological confusion and normalization of surrealism? Does communicability spiral out of control, as per Baudrillard's diagnosis of the ecstatic proliferation of objects, messages, and events, which exhaust the subject of late capitalism into a state of "inertia"?

While I think it would be setting up yet another false celebrity binary to pit a bad Britney against a good Gaga, it does seem safe to say that Spears has been more of a victim of the media while Gaga has been more in control of it. And this extends to the differences in how their images operate in both documentaries. Poitras' observation that Gaga "gets so much by pushing" is telling of the different kind of celebrity that she is. As Halberstam notes in *Gaga Feminism*,

> Lady Gaga is a symbol for a new kind of feminism. Recognizing her power as a maestro of media manipulation, a sign of new world disorder, and a loud voice for different arrangements of gender, sexuality, visibility, and desire, we can use the world of Gaga to think about what has changed and what remains the same, what sounds different and what is all too familiar.…
>
> (xii)

Gaga has her fair share of problematic complicities—from performing in the Super Bowl to touring in Israel—yet her ability to rearrange gendered power dynamics are on full display in the scene included in *Risk*, as shown through her detailed attention to the mise-en-scene and her conversation with Assange.

Upon arriving, she establishes herself as not only the stand-in for the cinematographer with camera in hand, but also for the scene's wardrobe department, making Assange undress, changing him out of his suit and into a white tee-shirt: "I want it to look like you just took your shirt off and you're at home." He obliges, and they sit down face to face in a room, which, as Gaga observes, looks like a dorm room, while the camera reveals a Gillette can and a blue air mattress. The conversation included in the film emphasizes a variety of less political questions she poses to Assange. Gaga is in some sense engaging in impromptu role-play: instead of being the celebrity grilled about seemingly trivial questions by the press, she flips the script and becomes the interrogator, offering prompts such as "What's your favorite kind of food?"; "I just would really like for you to tell me how you feel" (Assange's response: "Why does it matter how I feel? Who gives a damn? I don't care how I feel"); or asking if he is ever emotionally overwhelmed: "*Do you ever feel like just fucking crying?*" Rewiring the logic of infotainment, Gaga foregrounds Assange's own celebrity status, while revealing that there are nevertheless gendered expectations attached to each one's role in the media ecology as she visibly forces Assange out of his comfort zone, while at the same time effectively eliciting and maintaining spectatorial identification—unlike, say, Michael Moore when he finally confronts Charlton Heston in *Bowling for Columbine* (2002). As Jason Middleton demonstrates in discussing this Heston–Moore face-off: "the viewer's embodied response to Heston's own embodied awkwardness and discomfort creates tension with our intended ideological alignment with Moore and corresponding desire to see Heston attacked" (45). In *Risk*, Gaga holds the camera, and though the footage we see obviously does not correspond to the footage that she shoots, the fact that she is holding the camera as she prods him encourages the spectator to identify with her, as she tries getting to better know this mysterious man.

The question of authenticity, and where it is located in this scene, also seems relevant. Lady Gaga has positioned herself within celebrity culture as something of a modern-day Andy Warhol—controlled, always performing, and in costume—whose own "true" self seems unknowable and out of reach. Recent exceptions to this mystique might be more readily available, with her personal 2016 album *Joanne*, which displays a more pared-down aesthetic and direct address to her family, alongside the 2017 Netflix documentary about her, *Gaga: Five Foot Two*, which marks a rare opportunity to see her in more natural states—vulnerable, without makeup, and inflicted by chronic back pain. Gaga's discussions in interviews about how hard it has been to shake the character she portrayed in *A Star Is Born* (2018) only further attest to this new, "authentic" turn. But in contrast to these more recent glimpses of authenticity, her interview in *Risk* took place in 2012 and belongs to an earlier phase in Gaga's chameleonic career; it feels more performative, and it is clear she is not willing to let her guard down for Assange. Halberstam's analysis could help us understand the significance of this display; for while Gaga undoubtedly appears to have a façade, dressed witch-like in all black, her encounter with Assange comes off as performance art, but performance art that nevertheless conveys a sense of genuine political purpose that is fitting with the rest of Gaga's persona in its refusal of normalization.

Poitras did not participate in filming this scene but bought the rights to it, and I would argue that Poitras' own exclusion from this scene could be understood as a structuring absence that parallels a series of other structuring absences—figures not present but evoked in or haunting this locked-up bedroom: one of course would be Pamela Anderson, who has been the subject of media attention for showing up to the embassy with take-out food for Assange and who has salaciously *not denied* being more than friends with Assange, further adding to Assange's figuration as celebrity by virtue of association. Yet perhaps an even more significant structuring absence in this scene is Chelsea Manning. As Mandy Merck notes in an analysis of the melodramatization of WikiLeaks in the documentary *We Steal Secrets* (2013), although both Manning and Assange

> take on the American state, Julian Assange becomes the villain—dominating, duplicitous, unfeeling, masculine.... Manning becomes the victim—vulnerable, honest, emotional, feminine. Assange seeks publicity. Manning is exposed by betrayal. They are no longer anonymous. Instead, they personify the split in the celebrity sign perceived by Marshall, its "tension between authentic and false cultural value."

(276)

Merck elucidates how Assange's gender politics have been more broadly narrativized by media, often as the bullying other to Manning. This aspect of his celebrity image of course extends even more recently to his sabotaging of the presidential campaign of Hillary Clinton, whom Assange and his female assistant are shown conspiratorially calling early in *Risk* when she was Secretary of State to warn of ramifications of leaks to come.

As Gaga and Assange struggle to find common language in *Risk*, it is tempting to view this scene as staging the same bifurcation Merck identifies between Assange and Manning. Indeed, it might be easy to forget Lady Gaga's very direct ties to Manning. Manning has explained,

> I would come in with music on a CD-RW labelled with something like "Lady Gaga" … erase the music … then write a compressed split file. No one suspected a thing.… [I] listened and lip-synched to Lady Gaga's "Telephone" while exfiltrating possibly the largest data spillage in American history.

Manning's use of Gaga—both as a cover-up and as a queer source of empowerment—is a useful reminder of the multidirectional and mutually constitutive paths traveled between WikiLeaks and mainstream media that variably gave one another momentum and that much of *Risk* documents. The documentary I would have preferred to *Risk* might have actually excavated this connection further—and, while we're at it, tied it back to the 2010 viral "Telephone Remake" video featuring U.S. army soldiers in Afghanistan lip-synching and doing choreographed dance to the song, and forward to the 2014 Australian musical *Gaga V Assange* written by Will Hannagan and billed as a "hypothetical romp with songs."[2] Tracing such a network of mediated connections would stand to offer a revealing, complicated portrait of the interpenetrations among gender politics, information security, popular culture, and state power that *Risk* has taken on belatedly, if admirably.

Gaga's very direct ties to WikiLeaks and the information security movement differentiate her as a celebrity in ways that foreground the question of the boundary between entertainment and politics, unsettling the false binary construction that pits them in mutually exclusive spheres—a false binary that parallels the same inability to think comedy and documentary, and real reality and performative reality, as compatible modes. As Jason Middleton has noted, however, if we look at a picture of the top-grossing nonfiction films of all time, we quickly realize that although comedic documentaries are seemingly few and far between, they account for a disproportionate amount of the most commercially successful nonfiction fare (*Jackass, Borat, Supersize Me*, several Michael Moore films)—suggesting that they serve and satisfy a spectatorial desire created by our social imaginary (12). This dynamic makes *Risk*'s interview sequence a compelling, unresolved snapshot of the endless, uneven deferrals at play between early twenty-first century popular culture and politics.

Notes

1 See for example, Pilkington and Gabbatt.
2 For an excellent discussion of this viral video, see Alford.

Works Cited

Alford, Robert. "'I Don't Wanna Talk Anymore': On the Queer Nonutility of 'Telephone Remake'." *Cultural Critique*, no. 93, Spring 2016, pp. 113–148.
Andrejevic, Mark. "WikiLeaks, Surveillance, and Transparency." *International Journal of Communication*, vol. 8, 2014, pp. 2619–2630.
Baudrillard, Jean. *Fatal Strategies*. Translated by Phil Beitchman and W.G.J. Niesluchowski. Semiotext(e), 1990.
Chun, Wendy Hui Kyong and Sarah Friedland. "Habits of Leaking: Of Sluts and Network Cards." *Differences*, vol. 26, no. 2, 2015, pp. 1–28.

Dean, Jodi. "Publicity's Secret." *Political Theory*, vol. 29, no. 5, October 2001, pp. 624–650.

Fisher, Anna Watkins. "We Love This Trainwreck!: Sacrificing Britney to Save America." *In the Limelight and Under the Microscope: Forms and Functions of Female Celebrity*, edited by Su Holmes and Diane Negra. Continuum, 2011.

Halberstam, Jack. *Gaga Feminism: Sex, Gender, and the Edge of Normal*. Beacon Press, 2012.

Hattenstone, Simon. "Laura Poitras on Her WikiLeaks Film *Risk*: 'I Knew Julian Assange Was Going to be Furious'." *Guardian*, June 29, 2017.

Kuran, Timur. *Private Truths, Public Lies: The Social Consequences of Preference Falsification*. Harvard UP, 1995.

Merck, Mandy. "Masked Men: Hacktivism, Celebrity, and Anonymity." *Celebrity Studies*, vol. 6, no. 3, 2015, pp. 272–287.

Middleton, Jason. *Documentary's Awkward Turn: Cringe Comedy and Media Spectatorship*. Routledge, 2014.

Nichols, Bill. "The Ethnographer's Tale." *Visual Anthropology Review*, vol. 7, no. 2, September 1991, pp. 31–47.

Pengelly, Martin. "Word of the Year 2016: For Merriam-Webster, 'Surreal' Trumps 'Fascism'." *Guardian*, December 19, 2016.

Pilkington, Ed and Adam Gabbatt. "How Donald Trump Swept to an Unreal, Surreal Presidential Election Win." *Guardian*, November 9, 2016.

Zizek, Slavoj. "Good Manners in the Age of WikiLeaks." *London Review of Books*, January 20, 2011.

PART VII

LEGITIMACY

25
"ONE LITTLE SEED BLOWING IN THE WIND"
Risk Media in Trans-species Biogovernance

John Shiga

Introduction

This chapter revisits legal and popular mediations of risks associated with agricultural biotechnologies in the 1990s and early 2000s to explore the ways in which patents, court decisions, and news stories operate as "risk media" that contribute to what Gerlach et al. call *biogovernance*, or the "set of management techniques aimed at tackling the risks of biotechnology in order to transform them into instruments of governance" (12). The chapter focuses on a legal dispute between a Saskatchewan farmer, Percy Schmeiser, and Monsanto Canada, which in the 1990s marketed a type of canola seed called Roundup Ready Canola that was genetically engineered to resist Roundup, an herbicide that was also marketed by Monsanto. Monsanto sued Schmeiser for infringing on its patent to Roundup Ready Canola, arguing that when Schmeiser saved the seeds produced by plants grown from Roundup Ready Canola seeds and replanted them the following year, Schmeiser had reproduced Monsanto's invention without authorization. Schmeiser denied Monsanto's claim that he had "used" the invention and argued that he was a victim of Monsanto's invention which "contaminated" his farm and many others across the country. The case attracted attention from news media around the world and brought into focus broad cultural anxieties about a wide range of potential risks posed by biotechnology, gene patents, and increasing corporate control over farming practices and the food system. As the legal dispute moved through all three levels of the Canadian legal system over the course of several years, it generated considerable discussion in academic and popular forums, much of which was focused on competing rights, specifically, the emerging property rights in genetically modified organisms (GMOs) versus the more established rights of farmers to save and reuse seeds. However, a key and often overlooked part of what is at stake in the discourse of risk in this case is the manner in which law and technical design merge in a way that increases the authority of material things, in this case a genetically engineered seed, to move through the environment, reproduce, and regulate the actions of farmers who encounter it. Schmeiser and his supporters put the emphasis on the irreversibility of the potential harms caused by the marketing and use of genetically engineered seeds. As he put it in a *World Watch* article in 2002, "One little seed blowing in the wind can contaminate a field in two years. We will never get rid of genetically altered canola in Canada now" ("Seeds of Discontent" 10). I suggest here that the case marked a significant turn in the cultural mediation of risk where the source of risk shifted from the actions of people and institutions to the new forms of agency and authority which were then being introduced into bioinformational materials.

With Roundup Ready Canola, Monsanto extended the logic of "regulation by design" from the electronics and software industry into the domain of biotechnology. As Michael Madison notes, this mode of regulation combines intellectual property, contracts (licenses, user agreements), and design so that using one object requires the use of (and payment for) a network or "ecosystem" of other objects produced by the same firm or consortium. When Monsanto began marketing Roundup Ready Canola, consumers and courts had already become accustomed to printers designed to work only with certain ink cartridges; garage door openers that would not open unless activated by the manufacturer's remote control; and DVDs that would only play on devices embedded with copy control software. Like their electronic precursors, Monsanto's seeds combined "governance and artifact" so that "the thing itself regulates. We move from ex post regulation via law to ex ante regulation via thing" (Madison 393). The "decomposability" of digital objects facilitates regulation by design since constraints around use can be engineered into the objects at various scales. Similarly, the biotechnology industry redefines life forms in terms of the trans-species mobility and determinative role of the gene; by moving genes between species, transgenic techniques produce new forms of vitality which in turn become the locus of speculative investment in biotechnology firms and their transgenic projects. In this context, the patent not only grants ownership rights in the existing or known properties of a genetic invention but also ensures control over all possible uses of the invention that may arise in the future, whether through transgenic techniques in the laboratory or the everyday interactions of people and things in particular fields of practice.

Mirroring the campaigns against piracy in the music and film industries, Monsanto's litigation campaign sought to bolster and expand the scope of its intellectual property rights to compensate for the apparent pliability of certain elements in the assemblage, as demonstrated by farmers like Schmeiser who were able to grow Roundup Ready Canola without paying for a license to "use" the invention. If the bioinformational thing—the patented DNA—was easily "plagiarized" or "stolen," then the solution appeared to be the expansion of the scope of the legal thing—the patent —to include not only the DNA but also biological cells, seeds, and plants containing the patented DNA. In its effort to persuade courts and the public to accept this broad interpretation of the patent claims, Monsanto promulgated an image of biopatent infringement as an economic threat not only to itself but to the viability of the biotechnology industry and to as-yet unrealized societal benefits that would eventually arise from biotechnological innovation. At the same time, in the legal and popular discourse surrounding the case, there were a number of competing definitions of risk, some of which emphasized ontological boundary confusion rather than economic risk as the primary threat. This notion of risk as ontological disruption became evident in the public debate about *Schmeiser*, particularly in the vexed question of how to separate informational DNA from the material cells, seeds, and plants.

Risk as ontological disruption is also legible in concerns about the implications that ownership of nonhuman reproduction as sources of biocapital might have for the eventual propertization of human reproduction. As Melinda Cooper argues, the "technological kinship" between human and nonhuman reproduction is "undeniable" and is a latent but persistent theme in the news coverage of *Schmeiser* and other biopatent disputes. Until recently, this risk of violating boundaries between the human and the nonhuman and between propertization and human reproduction has been mitigated through regulatory limits on the application of reproductive technologies. Although mass production techniques have long been applied to nonhuman biological reproduction in industrialized agriculture, the application of similar techniques to human reproduction (e.g., assisted reproduction technologies) tends to occur "within strict regulatory limits, precisely because it concerns the realm of *human* reproduction ... the differences between human reproductive medicine and the brute commodification of labor and tissues that prevails in the agricultural industry become difficult to maintain" (135).

Yet, in the domain of genetic engineering, the notion that regulatory mechanisms would shield human reproduction from processes of propertization and commodification had been undermined decades before *Schmeiser*. Indeed, the treatment of human bodies as sources of genetic biocapital can be traced at least as far back as 1976 to the case of John Moore, a patient who was being treated for hairy-cell leukemia at the University of California Medical Center (Boyle 22). Moore underwent a number of procedures whereby his doctors "took samples of every conceivable bodily fluid, including sperm, blood, and bone marrow aspirate" and eventually removed his spleen (22). The genetic information extracted from Moore's spleen was then patented by the University of California and used to mass produce human cell lines for use in research—a market valued at around $3 billion. The Supreme Court of California ruled that Moore did not own the cells or the genetic information contained within them, partly on the basis that ownership of one's body would hinder the free exchange of genetic information necessary for biomedical innovation. While the court rejected Moore's claim to ownership of his body, it granted the University of California patent rights to the genetic information in his cells because unlike the "natural" or "raw" cells taken from Moore's body, the court accepted the general view in the biotechnology industry that human cell lines generated from genetic information extracted from the body are the result of "human ingenuity" and "inventive effort" and are therefore patentable subject matter (as cited in Boyle 106). With *Moore*, the court upheld the notion that "biovalue" accrues to genetic information through the application of bioengineering knowledge and technique to generate what Catherine Waldby calls "fragmentary vitality"; value becomes less tied to the genes' presence and role in one's body. *Schmeiser* is an important part of this story since it operates as a test case for the capacity of biotechnology firms to reframe ownership rights in material things (plants, seeds) and agricultural practices of saving and replanting seeds as economic risks as well as the capacity of intellectual property rights to protect and exploit what Melinda Cooper calls the "speculative value" of biotechnologies (152).

While *Moore* appeared to settle the question of how "fragmentary vitality" acquires value (value is generated by the application of transgenic techniques to biological materials that would have otherwise become "waste"), *Schmeiser* reopened this question and engaged environmental groups, "conventional" farmers, and concerned citizens, among many other groups in this area of patent law. The widely reported lawsuit inadvertently ignited public debate around the question of whether Roundup Ready Canola could be legitimately recognized as an invention and how to isolate the source of value added to canola through its various transformations from laboratory to farm. Does this value arise exclusively from genetic engineering knowledge built into objects themselves? Or does the embodied knowledge of local ecologies required to use the seeds effectively and adapt them to particular contexts also add value to the seeds as material, communicative things?

Schmeiser emerged at a point in the development of biotechnology when it was becoming clearer that the use of biotechnology in the context of industrialized agricultural had important implications for human reproduction and, indeed, for the redefinition of life forms, including human bodies, as transgenic. The human body came to be seen as a potential source of, *but also a threat to*, the ability of firms to capture the speculative value of biotechnologies. I suggest that the case is significant in part because of the way it operated as a prototype for an emerging biopolitical regime based on the production and exploitation of new forms of molecular property through genetic engineering and the protection of speculative value through intellectual property. Whereas predominant notions of risk in the fields of risk management and risk communication tend to focus on the possibility of harm to health, security and other things that are valued by human subjects, what is distinct about the Schmeiser case is that risk is associated with uncertainty generated by biopatents about the agency, identity, and status of the human subject. What is significant about *Schmeiser* in the context of risk and media is that the court took the unusual step of engaging with the fundamental problem of how to represent and regulate the interaction of nonhuman and human bodies and populations in the transgenic landscape. Risk media are key to the production of truths about the biosubjects who interact with agricultural biotechnologies and other genetic inventions; biogovernance operates through the distribution of legal rights to molecular things but it also increasingly works by reshaping signifying systems, modes of perception, and cultural practices according to notions of individual responsibility for managing genetic risk. As Gerlach et al. argue, the Canadian government's response to biotechnology highlights the manner in which

> individuals are expected not only to discipline themselves, but to manage themselves and the risks they might pose to the wider social good; they must do so by accessing and mobilizing the resources and expertise at their disposal in the genetic marketplace.
>
> *(15)*

The chapter develops a concept of "risk media" in the broad sense of technologies, practices, and discourses that construct phenomena as risks and manage the threat which these risks may pose to the biopolitical order. Since risk media are powerful means for constructing objects and subjects as potential threats and enable those threats to be managed through surveillance and control, they are often integrated into strategies of governance to shape the actions and interactions of people and things. Risk media enable the exercise of biopower by distributing cognitive, affective, and technical resources across various possible definitions of risk in a given context for the purpose of identifying, deterring, and responding to a potential threat. Risk media are particularly important to the operation of biopolitical governance (or biogovernance), that is, strategies of power that operate simultaneously on the scales of human and nonhuman populations and bodies. What is significant about risk media in *Schmeiser* is not only the shifting context (the manner in which risk is projected into the domain of transgenic inventions), but also the way this new context redefines risk in relation to corporate investments in the speculative value of DNA. Similarly, the mobilization of patents as risk media in the agricultural biotechnology sector not only expands the scope of legal concepts of invention to life, regeneration, and biological reproduction, but also "reinvents the temporality of invention," as Cooper puts it, by granting ownership over future uses of the patented genes and cells as well as other possible forms of vitality and value that could emerge from the invention (186). While at first glance, *Schmeiser* may appear to be a dispute about the farmer's right to exploit the known properties of Roundup Ready Canola (its capacity to resist certain herbicides and in principle reduce the amount of herbicide used on crops), as risk media, the patent is actually key to capturing biovalue in the future, which "refers not to the stable and known properties of tissues but to the capacity of tissues to lead to new and unexpected forms of value" (Waldby and Mitchell 108).

In critical analysis of biotechnology, the concept of risk media has the advantage of drawing attention to the manner in which specialized and popular media contribute to the enactment of certain definitions of objects (for instance, the self-replicating invention) and subjects (such as the gene patent owner and the gene patent infringer or "agrarian plagiarist") of biopolitical control. In many instances, specialized media such as patents work together with news stories and other popular media to construct risk in biotechnology in similar ways. So, for example, both types of media tend to normalize the biotech industry's perception of biological entities as sources of biovalue that can only be realized through transgenic techniques as well as the parallel notion that other modes of reproduction such as cultivation or self-replication are "waste" in the sense that they are moments where biovalue cannot be captured by the biotechnology industry. In other instances, as in the process of responsibilization where the biotech industry attempts to pinpoint responsibility for managing the risk of wasted biovalue on the individual farmer, popular media tend to construct risk in ways that diverge from patents, court decisions, and other specialized media. As discussed in subsequent sections, the fragmentary and recombinant techniques of genetic engineering produce divisible bodies which in turn become the source of "fragmentary vitality" open to propertization, commodification, and other forms of economic and technical control. Biotechnology offers corporations and the state new means of detecting, tracking and intervening in risk problems at the levels of the individual body and the population. At the same time, these techniques displace the bounded subject characteristic of modernity with "contingent bodies" that can be a source of risk since they are not as easily identified, regularized, and predicted as those of bounded and sovereign subjects.

For their part, popular media circulate visual, aural, and narrative forms that can reinforce or challenge the ontological categories and epistemological frameworks through which institutions define, assess, and manage risk. Analysis of biotechnological risk needs to contend with the concepts, categories, narratives, and frames that construct risk in law and science as well as the manner in which this system of concepts enters public culture by way of popular media. I approach popular media not as secondary or supplementary to the operation of biopower via biotechnology and law but rather as key "elements of biopower strategies working to create new fields of subjectivity and sovereignty" (Gerlach et al. 10). This conceptualization of biopolitical strategy as an assemblage of specialized and popular media that produces truths about molecular being enables me to identify key characteristics of risk media central to Canadian biogovernance. I give particular attention to the role of affect generation in risk media and more specifically the manner in which risk media work upon cultural anxieties about interactions and exchanges between the human and nonhuman at the molecular level and render those anxieties useful in the production of truths about the objects and subjects of biogovernance.

This chapter focuses on five "risk mediators" outlined by Gerlach et al.—privatization, normalization, objectification, politicization, and responsibilization—which construct and incorporate risk into strategies of biogovernance. Together, the five mediators enable actors not only to articulate claims, facts, values, and data about biotechnological risk, but also to capture, diffuse, focus, and redeploy broader cultural anxieties about the intensification, rapidity, and increasing scale of the production of human–nonhuman assemblages. I highlight key components of risk media, economic, and technological infrastructures as well as processes and frameworks of perception and signification, that enable the production of truths about forms of molecular being produced through accidental, informal, and engineered human–nonhuman interactions and the risks associated with them. The context of food biotechnology highlights risks stemming from human–nonhuman interactions and the manner in which risk media open those interactions to strategies of biopolitical governance. From patents to legal decisions to popular news stories, risk media in the context of food biotechnology are instances of what Gwendolyn Blue and Melanie Rock call "trans-biopolitics," or "the classification and evaluation of life as it unfolds in complex, technologically-mediated networks with global reach" (354). *Schmeiser* was a landmark decision in Canadian patent law, but more importantly for my purposes is the way risk in this case becomes central to the "creation and exercise of power ... encompassing human as well as nonhuman populations, as well as constituent flesh, organs, tissues and cells" (354). In *Moore*, human cell lines were treated as the intellectual property of those who invest in their speculative value or potential for exchange, even if this attribution of value undermines the presumption of ownership of one's own body. *Schmeiser* goes a step further in the sense that the biopatent now regulates human interactions with nonhuman bodies and their reproductive processes in the name of securing the speculative value of genetically modified organisms. This logic of capturing future uses and configurations of the transgenic invention became particularly clear when Monsanto urged courts to recognize its patent claims not only in the genetic information but also in the biological materials (plants, seeds, cells) created in the future from that information, even if this conflicts with the property interests of farmers in the seeds and plants that are carried by wind, water, vehicles, and other means onto their farms. From this perspective, conventional farming practices do not add value to the invention; such practices are treated as hindrances to the creation and exploitation of biovalue and need to be deterred through litigation. *Schmeiser* in this sense builds on the notion of the patent as a means of capturing biovalue established in *Moore* and extends it to "open environments" beyond the laboratory where farmers, seeds, plants, herbicides, and countless other human and nonhuman entities interact in unpredictable ways, giving rise to potentially endless variations of the genetic invention. *Schmeiser* demonstrates how patents "optimize" the entire landscape of Canada as a circuit for biocapital and articulate forms of power that "move across and beyond human individuals and populations" (354–355). Whereas *Moore* renders the subject of biopower as a source or repository of patentable subject matters, *Schmeiser* repositions the subject as a potential user of transgenic inventions who is responsible for engaging "in self-techniques to manage their risk and susceptibility" to inadvertent patent infringement and interference in circuits of biocapital (Foster 374).

One of the central points of this chapter is that risk media in the context of the biotechnology industry normalize ways of seeing and knowing molecular being as manufactured or invented life which legitimates the exercise of power through intellectual property rights, surveillance, and the subjectivization of farmers as compliant, risk-managing biopatent users. The dominant discourse of agricultural biotechnology works to diffuse concerns about the political, ethical, ecological, and cultural implications of biotechnology by narrowing the meaning of biotechnological risk to quantifiable threats to the accumulation of biocapital. However, *Schmeiser* is also significant, I argue, because it demonstrates how risk media can in some instances enable marginal actors to problematize agricultural biotechnology and other elements of the emerging agricultural production system. Heller characterizes this system as "post-industrial agriculture" which is characterized by "a rationality that utilises genetic science, biological patents, product pairing, and neoliberal trade deregulation, as means through which to achieve more flexible, specialised and globally dispersed forms of agricultural production" (320–321). As a system of biogovernance, post-industrial agriculture tends to translate issues and concerns into quantifiable risks that affect the food industry, agro-food corporations, and consumers. In the Schmeiser case, a counterpublic contested this system of governance by mobilizing concepts of risk that emphasize and link together scientific uncertainty, negative affect, and unquantifiable threats. These alternative constructions of risk fall into two broad categories: epistemological risks associated with uncertainties stemming from the increasing scale and complexity of genetic inventions and their human and environmental interactions, and from the apparent unwillingness and inability of regulators to adequately manage "a hazard that is now, and perhaps always, hypothetical" (De Marchi and Ravetz 744); and ontological risks stemming from legal and scientific destabilizations of dominant body ontologies (the bounded subject based on bodily integrity) and the consequent anxiety about the status of human identity and agency in sociotechnical systems at the molecular scale.

Risk Mediator 1: Privatization

A characteristic element of risk media in the context of biotechnology is privatization, or the reconfiguration of economic structures and technical infrastructures of knowledge production so that risk definition, detection, and deterrence shift from the public sector to the private sector and become increasingly oriented toward market logic. Privatization is a configuration of technical, economic, regulatory, and communicative infrastructures that shapes the development and use of biotechnological knowledge and products, as well as the manner in which biotechnological risks are signified, perceived, and managed. The process of privatizing agricultural research and development has a long history in Canada and this is particularly clear in the case of canola. As discussed by Lawrence Busch and Keiko Tanaka, since the end of World War II, the Canadian government has worked with various industrial actors in Canada and internationally to transform rapeseed—a heterogeneous and unruly crop—into a commodity through the development of tests, classificatory schemes, and standards of "goodness" (for example, lower in saturated fat and able to withstand the Canadian winter) for both human and nonhuman entities involved in the canola commodity chain (Busch and Tanaka 6–7). Once considered a risky and unreliable crop, rapeseed was renamed "canola" and was modified through conventional breeding techniques to enhance Canadian food security and the health of the population while at the same time generating a new food commodity —canola oil—that is an important element of the processed and fast food industries. More recently, biotechnology firms have sought new markets for pesticides by pairing their use with crops that are genetically engineered to withstand powerful herbicides. Among the first transgenic plants to be marketed in this way was Monsanto's Roundup Ready Canola. The legal regulation of Roundup Ready Canola demonstrates the mediating role of law in privatizing biotechnological research, communication, and risk management and propertizing genetic information and biological materials containing that information. Privatization produces a narrow definition of biotechnical risk that enhances control by agro-food conglomerates of the conduct and interaction of genes, crops, fields, and farmers. At the same time, privatization is a disruptive force that generates uncertainty about potentially catastrophic biotechnological risk.

In addition to the late twentieth-century restructuring of scientific knowledge production according to market-based models, privatization also encompasses changes in law or in the way existing laws are used. In the biotechnology context, a key development in this regard is the application of patent law and contracts to regulate genetic inventions in agriculture. Patents and contracts act as risk media in that they establish an "in between" space for the exchange and translation of elements between biological and cultural reproduction. As Gerlach et al. note, "new technologies promise to bridge the divide between nature and culture by subjecting both to the same industrializing techniques" (14). Like genetics, patents can be understood as waypoints or contact zones for the convergence of previously distinct forms of reproductivity and their alignment with industrial organizations and market logic, enabling what has been learned about risk definition, detection, and deterrence in cultural reproduction to be imported into the domain of molecular biological reproduction (and vice versa).

As the central modality of biotechnological governance in Canada, private law, and patents in particular, not only authorizes and legally recognizes the convergence of biological and cultural reproduction occurring elsewhere (for instance in the biotech industry) but produces new linkages and categories across biological and cultural domains so as to "organize space, time, everyday life—even life itself" (Striphas and McLeod 122). Private law recodes molecular objects as "inventions" and as private property, subjects as owners or users of such property, and risks arising from the design and use of such objects as economic (rather than moral, ethical, political, etc.) in nature. In this way, law functions as a recognizing authority for innovations occurring in industry but also enacts symbolic and material changes in "life itself," which drive investment in biotechnological innovation and the reduction of financial risks associated with those investments.

As Laura Foster notes,

> Within the architecture of neoliberalism, nature becomes a public good best removed from the public domain and privatized in order to ensure its management through free market mechanisms and biopatents are crucial to the projection of neoliberal economic values onto nature at the molecular scale to render it as a circuit of biocapital.
>
> *(373)*

The movement toward intellectual property as a key modality in privatization of agricultural biogovernance arguably began on February 23, 1993 when Monsanto obtained Canadian patent no. 1,313,830 for an invention called "Glyphosate-Resistant Plants" (or "the '830 patent," as it was referred to in court proceedings) (*Monsanto v. Schmeiser*). As disclosed in the patent, Monsanto's invention consists of genes as well as cells containing those genes; once inserted into canola DNA, the genes produce canola plants that can withstand glyphosate, which normally destroys plant life by deactivating a gene involved in the production of enzymes essential for growth and survival. This novel protection against glyphosate is conferred by the insertion of two genes into canola DNA. The first is a glyphosate-tolerant mutant of an endogenous gene and the second is a gene taken for a soil bacterium. Canola grown from seed containing the Roundup Ready genes will survive glyphosate herbicide while weeds and other plants will die (Health Canada). Since Roundup Ready Canola has the same appearance as conventional canola, the only way to detect its presence is through a laboratory analysis of the plant's DNA or a "grow out test" in which Roundup is sprayed on the plants so that only Roundup Ready plants survive. The main use of Roundup Ready Canola is to produce oil that can be used in cooking or added as an ingredient to margarine, shortening, and other food products. According to Health Canada's assessment, there is no difference between Roundup Ready and conventional canola in terms of nutrition and safety and no basis for concerns about toxicity since the oil does not contain any genetic material. Health Canada published its decision approving the marketing and use of Roundup Ready as a "novel food" in November 1994.

Monsanto began marketing genetically modified seeds as Roundup Ready Canola in 1996 to farmers who, instead of spraying for weeds and then planting seeds, plant genetically modified (GM) seeds and then spray the entire crop so that all vegetation except canola will be eradicated. Since Roundup Ready Canola contains the patented gene, Monsanto can restrict its use by requiring farmers to sign a Technology Use Agreement (TUA) stating that the farmer agrees to Monsanto's rules for using the seeds and plants grown from them. The farmer is then bound by the agreement to buy and sell seed only through Monsanto's authorized dealers. The farmer cannot sell, give away, or save seed and must allow Monsanto to inspect the fields and take samples if it wishes to do so. The licensing fee for Roundup Ready Canola at the time Schmeiser was used was $15 per acre. Canola was and continues to be "Canada's most-planted commodity, accounting for more than one-fifth of all cropland" (Cotter).

Percy Schmeiser began growing canola in the 1950s, saving seeds to replant the next year, avoiding tilling diseased plants, spraying for weeds before planting and using Roundup only for areas around power poles and in ditches. Schmeiser described himself as a conventional farmer, using industrial farming techniques but not genetically modified seeds; he believed that he had developed his own strain of canola through conventional breeding techniques that was uniquely suited for the conditions in Bruno, Saskatchewan, where his farm was located. He claimed that he never purchased Roundup Ready Canola and had not signed Monsanto's TUA.

In 1996, a farmer grew Roundup Ready Canola in a field next to Schmeiser's canola crop from which he saved seed and replanted in 1997. In the summer of 1997, Schmeiser used Roundup to kill weeds around power poles and in the ditches between his fields and the main road into the town of Bruno. A few days later, he found that many canola plants had somehow survived the spraying. To figure out why, he performed a grow out test, spraying a three-acre swath of his crop near the road with Roundup. After a few days, he found approximately 60 percent of the plants were still alive, with high concentrations near the road and thinning inwards to his field. Schmeiser harvested the canola and, in the spring of 1998, had the seeds processed and then planted them in over 1,000 acres on his farm. He eventually sold the crop for $142,000.

Monsanto tested Schmeiser's 1997 crop and accused him of obtaining Roundup Ready Canola without authorization, but quickly withdrew its allegation of patent infringement. In 1998, Monsanto did more extensive testing on Schmeiser's fields, found a high percentage of Roundup Ready Canola plants, and promptly sued Schmeiser for using its invention without authorization. What was initially a test case for Monsanto's ability to enforce its monopoly rights granted by the 830 patent opened up a number of more fundamental questions about privatization as a condition of biogovernance. Schmeiser pushed the trial judge, the appeal judge, and then the Supreme Court of Canada to reconsider the validity of the patent claims, the meaning of "use" in regards to a gene patent, and the line between patentable and unpatentable subject matter. In this way, the trajectory of Roundup Ready Canola reopened the question of whether gene patents effectively confer intellectual property ownership over life generated by those genes.

The Supreme Court of Canada had already been divided on the issue of gene patents. In an earlier case, *Harvard College* v. *Canada*, the court upheld the Patent Commission's decision not to grant patent rights to the genes and cells that render mice susceptible to cancer (dubbed "Oncomouse," as such mice are useful in cancer research) because such a patent would grant rights to the mice themselves. Schmeiser's contestation of the validity of Monsanto's gene patent renewed this debate concerning the relation between genetic invention and living organism among jurists, environmental advocacy groups, government agencies, biotechnology industry representatives, bioethicists, and agricultural and legal scholars. If Schmeiser "used" Monsanto's invention by growing it, does it follow that any farmer who happens to have canola growing on his or her farm is a de facto "user" of the invention? Does any use of the plant—even unintentional uses—entail the "use" of Monsanto's patented gene that generates the plant? Moreover, if the invention in question is part of a mobile and self-replicating organism (and indeed is a crucial element of the species' capacities to reproduce and migrate), who exactly is using whom to spread such "inventions" from farm to farm and from farms to "wild" space? Since Monsanto had already been granted a patent to the transgenic canola, and since the Canadian government continued to avoid biotechnology issues, these matters would be addressed not so much in moral, ethical, or political terms through the legislative process, but in the legal–economic terms of patent infringement. As we will see, this has profound consequences for the way biotechnological risks are defined, perceived, and managed.

Risk Mediator 2: Normalization

Normalization refers to "a cluster of practices aimed at managing public discussion of biotechnology, rendering it legitimate, normal, and secure" (Gerlach et al. 14). In this mode, risk media aim "at controlling meaning-making before it reaches the controversial stage" (14). One of the means for deterring economic risks posed by biopatent infringement is engineering canola's reproductive capacity; in principle, biopatent "piracy" and other risks could have been programmed out of the Roundup Ready system by engineering the canola to produce sterile offspring. But given the strong public, academic, and activist responses against Genetic Use Restriction Technologies (GURTS) and other "hard coded" restrictions on agricultural resources in other countries, Monsanto shifted those controls into legal rather than genetic code when it marketed Roundup Ready products in Canada.

Normalizing certain ways of seeing and using genetic objects as property enables further mediations of biotechnological risk; for example, normalizing the notion of DNA as intellectual property would seem to facilitate the legitimation of "copy protection" built into seeds. Monsanto therefore sought to normalize property rights to gene sequences under the *Patent Act* (1985), whereas most other novel plant strains up until this point were protected by limited rights under the *Plant Breeders' Rights Act* (1990). While biopatenting has occurred in many jurisdictions around the world, the practice is arguably more central to the regulatory framework for biotechnology in Canada than it is elsewhere. In contrast to the biotechnology debate in the United States, for example, "both the Canadian government and the Canadian public have been either absent from, or very slow to act in, the political debates around the ways in which biotechnology should be implemented and governed" (Gerlach et al. 13). In recent years, Canadian courts have frequently asserted that their role is to interpret and apply law rather than to make it, but given the absence of policymaking around biotechnology in Canada, decisions in biopatent lawsuits can have far-reaching consequences.

Schmeiser illustrates the manner in which the reluctance of the Canadian state and the public to enter the biotechnology debate produces a governance gap that was "filled by the courts" who were now "in a position of ... deciding the policy issues" (Gerlach et al. 125). What is normalized in this context is certain definitions of molecular objecthood and of agrarian subjects who use molecular objects and monitor their own uses of such objects. In particular, the process outlined here tends to normalize the biotechnology industry's perception of biological entities as potentially limitless sources of fragmentary vitality that nevertheless require the application of transgenic techniques to render them as inventions—otherwise this transgenic potential is unrealized and the biological materials retain only their current properties and functions and are in this sense wasted as sources of biocapital. Patents further mediate biotechnological risks in the economic terms of private law where responsibilities and harms (or potential harms) become quantified as liabilities and damages.

Partly as a reflection of the importance granted to patent law in Canadian biogovernance, public discussion about biotechnology in popular media has been provoked by, but also remained tethered to, controversies around biopatent lawsuits, which tends to narrow risk discourse to issues related to Monsanto's intellectual property and normalizes a property-oriented perception of genetic objects as well as economic conceptualizations of biotechnological risk. The normalization of agricultural biotechnology was also assisted by privately funded communication channels such as social marketing, quasi-educational campaigns, and public exhibits produced by biotechnology firms and industry associations. New communications initiatives were launched to improve "public understanding" of biotechnology. One example was the development of the Guelph-based Food Biotechnology Communication Network (FBCN), which consisted of government officials, public relations experts, and industry representatives who enlisted "science-based groups" to persuade Canadians that food biotechnology is safe for humans and the environment. This is in line with the first risk mediator of privatization whereby private firms play a dominant role in genetic research, and the secrecy around research conducted in this manner leads state regulatory bodies to increasingly rely on industry experts to develop policy (Gerlach et al. 12). In *Schmeiser*, privatization affects the mode of normalization; public communication of biotechnological knowledge is organized as part of marketing-oriented knowledge commercialization/mobilization initiatives funded and operated by public–private partnerships such as the FBCN.

While industry attempted to manage public debate by controlling the way in which transgenic organisms were represented in public culture, in a number of instances, these strategies backfired as they became the subject of news stories. For example, a controversy about proposed changes to the GM labeling regime became a major news story in October 2001, when bill C-287 for the institution of a mandatory labeling regime in Canada was narrowly defeated in Parliament. Headlines in major Canadian dailies between 1999 and 2001 such as "Lines are fuzzy on GM foods," "Food fight," and "Local action brewing against GM giants" are suggestive of the growing unease and resistance to industry and government efforts to further undermine an already-difficult process of identifying and monitoring genetically modified elements in the food system (Paulson; Stewart; Walkom). The demise of mandatory labeling legislation compounded anxieties provoked by the contemporaneous "biotech sponsorship scandal," in which a Greenpeace-funded researcher found evidence that governmental regulators were funding pro-GM public relations campaigns in Canada, first reported by the *Montreal Gazette* in March 2000 (Abley).

As these stories developed in the news media, the figure of "contamination" came to represent not only the colonization of farms, bodies, and food systems by biotechnological inventions but also the suspected collusion between regulatory bodies and the institutions they were supposed to regulate, as well as the public communication of knowledge about GMOs which was presented as impartial but which encouraged a pro-industry view of GMOs as innocuous. The figure of contamination (of the environment and food system but also the media system that circulated information about biotechnology) became increasingly entrenched in popular media discourse. The public debate about risk came to center not so much on health, safety, or economic security, but rather, as Judith Roof argues, on "a generalized suspicion about the capabilities of genetic engineering," particularly in the context of the erosion of public trust in the governmental and industrial actors overseeing the application of genetic engineering techniques in agriculture (181).

Risk Mediator 3: Politicization

Politicization in this context refers to the articulation of competing and conflicting modes of constructing biotechnology and the risks associated with it. Issues around Roundup Ready Canola received wide and sustained media coverage due to the decade-long legal dispute between Monsanto and Schmeiser (along with their supporters) between August 1998, when the Monsanto filed its complaint against Schmeiser for patent infringement, and 2008, when Schmeiser won an out of court settlement with Monsanto for the removal of volunteers (stray plants) that Schmeiser claimed had contaminated his farm and compromised his status as a "non-GM" or conventional farmer. Despite significant private sector investment in privatization and normalization, and despite the state's reluctance to regulate biotechnology, the politicization process continued via the courts and popular media. There, the well-organized voices of Schmeiser and his allies were able to popularize a counter-discourse of biotechnological risk that focused on potential threats posed by genetic inventions and their producers to bodily, environmental, and informational integrity.

Key to the politicization of transgenic canola was the expansive notion of contamination that Schmeiser mobilized in court and in the news media. As a central concept in regulatory discourses of food safety in Canada and elsewhere, contamination typically refers to biological or chemical hazards in the food system. A key objective of the food safety regime in Canada is to minimize the risk that contaminants pose to human health by ensuring that contaminants do not exceed levels that health authorities consider to be acceptable. But whereas the dominant discourse of contamination focuses on risks posed by bacteria and other microorganisms, Schmeiser's counter-discourse focused on engineered genes as a biological hazard in the Canadian food system. The contamination of conventional and organic crops by genetically modified seeds also rendered farms and farmers vulnerable to control by the biotech industry through intellectual property and surveillance. In the wake of the Federal Court decision in *Schmeiser*, many news agencies highlighted Schmeiser's concern about crop contamination and the court's assertion that farmers have an obligation to alter their practices to avoid cultivating the patented gene. An example from BBC News demonstrates the way news stories underscored tensions in the exercise of power through agricultural biopatents:

> The judge said it was up to the farmer, who ought to know that once it appears there he must stop growing that crop. Mr. Schmeiser believes this is impractical: "How would a farmer know when you have a genetically altered canola plant, it looks exactly the same as another canola plant." He added that the unusual thing about this ruling is that the judge said if a seed blows onto a farmer's land, he has the right to use the seed from those plants the following year, except Monsanto's genetic altered seed. Mr. Schmeiser believes this gives the big companies complete control over farmers because if some of their seed blows onto a farmer's land, contaminates the seed and cross-pollinates, it then becomes the property of the big company.
>
> (BBC News)

The key tension here is between, on the one hand, the fact of crop contamination and the difficulty of identifying genetically modified plants and, on the other hand, the expectation that transgenic organisms will make themselves visible and that when this occurs farmers should know that they are in the presence of molecular property and are obliged to modify their practices.

A decade later, Schmeiser declared victory after Monsanto agreed to settle the matter of contamination out of court for $660, even though the Supreme Court of Canada determined that Schmeiser had indeed infringed upon Monsanto's patent. At that point, Schmeiser began to describe himself as well as his farm as contaminated. The link between contaminated objects (crops, farms, environments) and contaminated subjects (farmers, consumers) was initially made in a Reuters' story, parts of which were published in many Canadian newspapers. The Reuters report quoted without qualification Schmeiser's claim that his legacy was "poisoned" as a consequence of the "spreading noxious plant by natural means," an image of the genetic invention which bolstered Schmeiser's public image as an "international folk hero ... standing up for farmers' rights" (*Toronto*

Star A8). Schmeiser and his lawyer repeatedly articulated key elements of a new biojuridical subject—the "innocent bystander"—defined in relation to a biotechnological contaminant. The key elements of the contaminated biosubject were present in nearly every news report about the Federal Court decision: (1) the GM seeds came from Schmeiser's field; (2) his field was contaminated by pollen containing the patent genes; and, (3) this pollen originated in neighboring fields, traveling by wind or insects or falling off of trucks.

The politicization of GM canola emerged through Schmeiser's interventions in biosubjectivity and specifically in the framing of the contaminated farmer in terms of an absence of intent to "use" the invention and involuntary exposure to risks posed by the invention. The contaminated farmer (or the innocent infringer) is exposed to the legal and economic risks associated with crop contamination through the farmer's non-conscious, unintended interaction with the Roundup Ready gene in pollen, plants, and seeds. In news stories, the promiscuity of the GM plant was presented not so much as a way of extending patent law wherever the plant happened to multiply, but rather as an indication of Monsanto's inability to control the plant's behavior. "Schmeiser ... claimed Monsanto lost the right to control its patented genes when the seed arrived uninvited on his land" ("Farmer Fined in Fight with Biotech Giant" A4). To scaffold this emergent subject position of the contaminated farmer/innocent infringer, Monsanto's genetic modification of canola was reframed as a *source* of ecological and, from the point of view of conventional and organic farmers, economic risk because of the plant's capacity to replicate and spread. In an interview with *World Watch*, Schmeiser suggested that the trial judge may have lacked agricultural knowledge about the plant's reproductive and migratory behavior necessary to make an informed decision:

> I guess the judge maybe didn't understand the situation fully: canola is an open pollinate crop variety. It's very different from corn or soybeans and can spread quite easily. Canola requires cutting, like hay. And then it has to be put in rows to dry. Dried canola can act like tumbleweed and can blow for miles.... It's not uncommon for seeds to go five, ten miles. So, this is why canola can spread so easily. There is no stopping it.
>
> *("Seeds of Discontent" 8–9)*

In 2008, after Monsanto formally agreed to compensate Schmeiser for the removal of uninvited GM crops ("volunteers") on his farm, Schmeiser told reporters, "I really feel that if a farmer is now contaminated, he has a right to go after Monsanto for liability and to clean up the contamination" (Hartley). Schmeiser was not speaking metaphorically; like many of his supporters, he asserted that genetically modified seeds and plants like GM canola permanently contaminate the crops of conventional and organic farms which in turn taints farmers' claims to "conventional" or "organic" biosubjectivity and contaminates the food supply as well as the bodies of those who consume the contaminated food. "One little seed blowing in the wind," Schmeiser says, "can contaminate a field in two years. We will never get rid of genetically altered canola in Canada now" ("Seeds of Discontent" 10).

Schmeiser's strategies of politicization drew upon his agricultural knowledge as well as general knowledge of genetic engineering to construct the conventional farmer as an untenable subject position caught between the standards of purity in the Canadian food system and the contaminated molecular landscape. As Busch and Tanaka argue in their analysis of the construction of quality in Canadian canola economy, processing plants and certification organizations evaluate and classify farmers according to the qualities of their seeds and crops. When seeds are deemed to be "contaminated," the farm and farmer that produced them are also "contaminated." The construction of biotechnological contamination in Schmeiser's counter-discourse and its circulation in the language of a wide array of actors in the GM canola controversy underlines the manner in which anxieties about the reproductivity of transgenic organisms were channeled into alternative constructions of biotechnological risk and of the subjects exposed to it. These strategies of politicization were available to Schmeiser in part because of the circumstances of this encounter with GM canola; unlike other farmers who were sued around the same time by Monsanto, Schmeiser had not signed Monsanto's technology use agreement, he did not try to sell the seed, and he maintained that his infringement was an inevitable consequence of the irresponsible release of the gene, seed drift, and the broad terms of the patent.[1]

If privatization and normalization mediate risk in a filter-like manner, capturing a wide range of anxieties and concerns but reducing them to a singular frame such as economic risk, politicization works like a prism, beginning with what appears to be a singular, uniform definition of risk produced by privatization and normalization and then splitting it into competing risk definitions associated with a range of concerns, anxieties, and issues. Martina Newell-McGloughlin's analysis of public discourse about genetically modified organisms around the beginning of the *Schmeiser* saga highlights the broad range of concerns surrounding biotechnology, many of which were articulated as part of the definition of biotechnological risk produced by Schmeiser and his supporters (from grassroots organizations to the dissenting justices of the Supreme Court):

- ethics of genetic modification (interfering with nature);
- safety of food and of introducing genetically engineered organisms into the environment;
- the alleged radical novelty, unpredictability, or irreversibility of biotechnology;
- possible negative impacts on employment or small farms;
- trust or lack of trust of government regulatory agencies;
- enhancement of corporate power and ownership of intellectual property;
- possible exploitation of developing countries;
- possible mistreatment of animals.

(36)

Consistent with Newell-McGloughlin's study of the Swiss public, Heller found that when anti-GMO campaigns in France began in 1997 they were strongly tied to governmental discourses of food and environmental risk (for example, Greenpeace activists demonstrated in white biohazard suits) but by 1999 the campaigns used wider notions of food quality to include political and cultural concerns:

> While their early campaign tended to emphasise issues of food risk, appealing to the authority of science experts (a dominant trend in the overall debate during this period), their later discourse emphasised questions of food quality, drawing from their own forms of cultural expertise.
>
> *(325)*

In the Schmeiser dispute, the disparate set of concerns in Newell-McGloughlin's list eventually condensed into the specter of (bio)informational "contamination" rather than other political dimensions of genetic engineering such as the commodification life or mistreatment of organisms. Risk in popular media mobilized by the counterpublic was not so much about the economic risks for the biotechnology industry as it was about epistemological risk posed by biotechnological contamination to the capacity of farmers to know by visual inspection whether their crop is conventional or genetically modified, as well as the ontological risk posed by large-scale, complex techno-economic systems like gene patents to the coherence of "organic farmer" or "conventional farmer" as subject positions. As discussed below, this ontological risk in *Schmeiser* soon expanded as gene patents were articulated to the boundary between the human and the nonhuman.

Risk Mediator 4: Objectification

Though *Schmeiser* did not receive as much attention from bioethicists as similar cases involving animals, Roundup Ready Canola has significant implications for definitions of human and nonhuman life. Schmeiser's counter-discourse depended on the channeling of anxieties that such drastic revisions in the "correct" way of classifying and seeing the world tend to provoke. Of particular relevance here is the lower and higher life form dualism, which entered into the Canadian jurisprudence on biotechnology in *Harvard College* when the majority at the Supreme Court ruled that lower life forms can be property but higher life forms cannot—without providing much in the way of definitions for either category beyond the notion that lower life forms can be mass produced and cannot display emotion. Court decisions again operate as risk media but here they aim at what Gerlach et al. call "objectification" or "the production of the gene as a field of management, which includes such practices as mapping, testing, coding, banking, imaging, simulating, and representing" (14).

One particularly important example of objectification is the higher/lower life form dualism, imported into the Supreme Court's decisions in *Harvard College* and *Schmeiser* from other contexts (the Patent Office and the lower courts dealing with cases involving a different set of institutions and life forms) and installed by the court as an optic for discerning truths about the bodies of life forms, which in turn authorize trans-species interventions across human and nonhuman populations. While this type of risk mediation seems at first glance to address the broader definitions of biotechnological risk in public culture including the risk that surveillance, propertization, and fragmentation pose to human agency and identity, the Supreme Court refused to map the distinction between higher and lower life forms onto the categories of human and nonhuman. As a mode of objectifying the gene, the lower/higher life form dualism would seem to have the advantage of putting anxieties about biotechnological control to rest since it marks the human as out of bounds to patent ownership. Yet, the patenting of human genes and cell lines has become a key element of the life sciences industry since *Moore*, and in recent years led to the controversy about patents owned by Myriad Genetics which gave the Utah-based firm a monopoly on genetic tests and other user of the BRCA1 and BRCA2 genes, which are human genes linked to increased risk of ovarian and breast cancers (Balter). Interestingly, the growing opposition to the gene patents, culminating in the U.S. Supreme Court's unanimous decision in 2013 to invalidate the patents, centered not so much on the fact that the genes in question were human, but rather that the genes were identical to those found in all humans, were produced by cells and were thus "products of nature," and had not been sufficiently modified to add value (Chakrabarty 3). In this way, the U.S. Supreme Court appears to leave open the possibility of deriving biocapital from human genes if they are sufficiently modified from their natural state.

Similarly, the higher/lower life form optic in the Canadian context at first appears to function as a safeguard against the propertization of human genes but may in fact encourage an interpretation of human bodies as sources of patentable subject matter by rendering "humans kin to other mammals and multi-cellular, complex organisms. Singular human status is rejected for a model that does not deny the animal in the human. Humans and mice are equally biosubjects" (Gerlach et al. 123). The Supreme Court's lower/higher life form dualism produced a fuzzy line rather than a sharp divide between populations, which meant that in subsequent cases like *Schmeiser*, there was considerable uncertainty about where the line between patentable and non-patentable life would drawn next.

More than a mere test case for Monsanto's patent, *Schmeiser* raised the question as to how the state should respond when the same industrial logics and informational techniques begin to be applied to both biological and cultural reproductivity with profound consequences for ontological categories of being, ecological stability, and bodily integrity. As Striphas and McLeod suggest,

> The legal protections given to these [genetically modified] organisms signal an increasingly intensive, practical synthesis of cultural and agricultural production, or a blurring of

sorts that simultaneously resuscitates and transmogrifies an almost pre-modern understanding of culture as "the tending of something, basically crops or animals."

(122)

One of the key questions of law in this case—whether Monsanto's patent claims to genes and cells were valid—invited courts to operate as a recognizing authority for the application of existing forms of patent protection to the new objects and subjects produced by genetic engineering, which in turn generates new biojuridical objects and subjects. *Schmeiser* drew attention to new kinds of technoscientific boundary blurring between long-standing categories of life (i.e., species) that were considered to be relatively stable and crucial to modern understandings of human identity. This extension of patent law has the potential to enhance corporate control over genetic objects and subjects. At the same time, the molecular context of patent protection increases the complexity and scale of biojuridical intervention as well as the ontological disruptions and epistemological uncertainties associated with those interventions. These disruptions and uncertainties in turn amplify non-quantifiable risks around human identity and agency.

Schmeiser underscores this interplay between scientific uncertainty stemming from shifts in scale and complexity of engineered systems at the molecular level and legal uncertainty about the appropriateness of patent-based propertization as a mode of objectifying genetic things. One particularly interesting example of this articulation of uncertainty in the Supreme Court decision concerns the use of the term "higher life forms," which bifurcates the genetic gaze along the lines of species and extends patentability to molecular being, while at the same time marking some areas of this new domain as out of bounds for propertization. While the minority at the Supreme Court referred to "high life forms" 20 times, the majority used this term on only two occasions. While the majority criticized the minority for using the higher/lower life form distinction, which does not have a basis in the *Patent Act*, the minority argued that without this distinction, what seemed to be a mere application of the *Act* would actually extend rights beyond those granted by the *Act*. In this way, the minority opinion integrates the notion of risk proposed by Schmeiser and his supporters, that is, ontological risk generated by the interplay between legal categories of thingness (property) and the genetic things onto which those categories were being imposed.

In response to the potential disruption of boundaries between intellectual property and bodies, the minority articulated new classes of thingness, such as DNA in "isolated laboratory form" and DNA in a crop. These classes of biotechnological objects in turn affect the way biosubjects are constituted; the Federal Court of Appeal in *Schmeiser* argued, for example, that since the biotechnological invention is inaccessible to the senses and cannot be detected by farmers without laboratory analysis or a grow out test, intentional and unintentional infringement should be distinguished in cases of gene patent infringement. While Schmeiser's conduct suggests that he knowingly exploited Monsanto's invention, in other cases, the appeal court suggests, farmers might not be aware of the presence of the gene in their plants, or might be aware of it without attempting to cultivate it. The court hinted that in such cases, intentionality might be a factor in the determination of infringement. It thus points to a scenario in patent law in which intentions would matter, even though they are normally considered to be irrelevant in cases of patent infringement.

These new associations between human intentions and awareness of the genetic identity of plants in the crop, and the movement of genes between plants, crops, fields, and perhaps even legal jurisdictions, persists through to the Supreme Court decision in which the majority stated that the defendant's conduct can be used as evidence of intentional or willful use of the invention. Conversely, had Schmeiser tried to get rid of the Roundup Ready Canola rather than "actively cultivate" it, these actions could be taken as signs that he did not in fact "use" the canola's "stand-by" or insurance value (para. 86–87). As a mode of objectification, the decision identifies multiple forms of vitality that emerge from the different phases of the genetic invention's embodiment, in particular, the fragmentary vitality of isolated DNA in controlled laboratory environments and genes contained in the cells of plants in the open environment, which have the capacity to reproduce themselves without the awareness of farmers and biopatent owners. While this objectification of the genetic invention as an invisible, morphing, and self-replicating object seems to support a new defense in patent infringement lawsuits based on the defendant's lack of intent to "actively cultivate" the invention, this mode of objectification also attributes responsibility to farmers for managing risks associated with the potential presence of patented genes in crops and thus feeds into the final element of risk mediation: responsibilization.

Risk Mediator 5: Responsibilization

In the wake of *Harvard College*, it could be reasonably assumed that jurists would again attempt to police the boundaries of "thingness" in order to protect higher life forms from threats to their dignity, autonomy, and bodily integrity. If the court in *Schmeiser* followed the logic of *Harvard College*, the entanglement of higher life forms (humans, in the Schmeiser case) with patented lower life forms (plants in this instance) may not be particularly controversial insofar as lower life forms are objectified as property that can be framed as the product and/or instrument of human agency. But when this objectification process appears to be incomplete or unmanageable, the complexity and heterogeneity of genetic invention may confound conventional body ontologies structured according to the human/nonhuman dualism. In response to this inability to predict, know, or control all of the possible interactions between molecular objects and agrarian subjects, risk media work to construct new models of citizenship which emphasize responsibility rather than rights (Gerlach et al. 15). The fifth element of risk mediation can therefore be described as responsibilization, where the focus of risk media shifts from the assessment of various risks associated with biotechnology to the attribution of responsibility for monitoring and managing risk. "In other words, responsibilization individualizes social responsibility for managing the risks of biotechnology" (18).

While it was ultimately up to the court to decide who should bear responsibility for the risks, popular media again played a key role in normalizing the frames and establishing new habits of perception that guide the assignment of responsibilities for managing biotechnological risk. A divergence between the court decision (especially the majority opinion) and popular media becomes evident at this point. Whereas the court dealt primarily with the responsibility of the farmer for policing the economic risks stemming from conventional farming practices in the new molecular landscape, news media frequently emphasized the agency of nonhumans, and seeds in particular, which to some extent undermines the view that farmers can or should be responsible for the migrations and replications of biotechnological inventions occurring on their farms. Even Trish Jordan, Monsanto Canada's spokesperson throughout the Schmeiser dispute, noted that approximately 46 percent of the canola grown in Western Canada in 2007 was Roundup Ready, and, more importantly, admitted that 85 to 90 percent of all canola in the region would be classified as genetically modified since it would have herbicide-resistant traits (Lyons). The unmentioned implication here is that the vast majority of canola would contain the patented genes but around half of these plants would be second, third, or later generation "volunteers" rather than plants produced directly from seeds licensed by Monsanto to its farmers.

If Monsanto is the owner of a bioinformational life form, who is responsible for the restless, promiscuous actions of its materialized expressions? Ann Clark, a plant physiologist who submitted an affidavit on Schmeiser's behalf, suggested that "reproductive isolation" in the case of GM canola is impossible. Clark's argument that transgenic agricultural objects cannot be restrained troubles the manner in which *Schmeiser* pinpointed the humans responsible for the actions of a biotechnological assemblage: "how can farmers be held accountable for something which the seed trade itself cannot do?" (Steed). Transgenic inventions in *Schmeiser* were particularly disruptive of body ontologies because, depending on the setting and stage of reproduction, they appear as genes, cells, plants, crops, pollen, oil, and food, each of which presents different affordances and constraints to farmers in terms of their capacity to identify, intervene in, and assume responsibility for the actions of the genetic objects. While the isolated laboratory form of DNA is suitable for the application of transgenic techniques and thus to the creation of patentable genetic objects, *Schmeiser* reveals the crucial role that DNA in seeds plays in the exploitation of biopatents and the accumulation of biocapital. While biotech firms may encourage farmers to regard GM seeds as resources or tools for increasing the efficiency of agricultural production, the seeds also exert force on their environments as farmers begin using them. "To say that improved seed is a technique for increasing food production is only part of the story," argues Yapa (1993) in the context of the Green Revolution. "It has also been a bearer of the hegemonic culture of science, capital, and authority that subjugates tradition and the keepers of that knowledge" (267). In the contemporary shift toward fragmentary vitality as source of biocapital, Monsanto's patent works as a protective envelop around the seeds, setting boundaries on the practice of seed saving and creating a "need for external inputs" (267) such as technology user agreements, financing packages, branded herbicides, and the expertise and knowledge monopolized by biotechnology firms. As Street argues, "While it might at first appear odd to ascribe agency to non-humans such as seeds, it is these seeds' existence as active presences that provides a means of enrolling others into particular topologically extended social networks" (9). Seeds exert material force upon their environments but in *Schmeiser* seeds also work with patents and other media to alter the technological, cultural, social, and ecological conditions of farming. In short, the material agency of seeds and their capacity to transform the environments in which they circulate conflicts with Monsanto's attempt to attribute responsibility for managing biotechnological risk to the individual farmer.

Also complicating the instrumental notion of seeds and crops as resources that can be directed according to the intentions of the farmers is the agency of the patent. As Marianne de Laet argues, patents are "events that perform connections—and that bring about changes as they go along" between economic, technological, legal, and in this case, biological contexts (150). Key to the way the patent lawsuit operated as risk media was the court's conceptualization of "insurance value" as central to the meaning of "use" in the case of this particular genetic invention and the manner in which the majority at the Supreme Court concluded that Schmeiser had violated Monsanto's patents by "using" the invention's "insurance value"—that is, its "readiness" or resistance to Roundup should the need for spraying arise. However, since he did not spray Roundup on the Roundup Ready crop, the court concluded that Schmeiser did not profit from this "insurance value." The court in this way defines the value of the genetic invention in terms of its capacity to offset economic risks posed by the natural environment and in particular the unpredictable reproduction, movement, and emergence of unwanted plants.

In the end, the majority at the Supreme Court upheld the validity of Monsanto's patents and responsibilized Schmeiser and farmers like him with the construction of patent infringement as the cultivation of a plant which the farmer "knew or should have known" contained a genetic invention, the use of which required contractual agreement and payment. Key questions remained unresolved. For example, if the patent claims did not extend to plants, then how exactly could the use of plants on the farm constitute "use" of the invention? The Supreme Court's decision regarding damages and legal costs indicates this ambivalence: Schmeiser was not required to turn over profits from 1998 to Monsanto but he had to bear his own legal expenses which, according to Schmeiser's calculations, amounted to some $400,000.

Conclusion

In contrast to the narrowly defined economic risk posed by unauthorized reproduction in Monsanto's lawsuit and the court's concern with the way Monsanto's property claims stretch the zone of patentability, news reports suggested that the central question of the case revolved around the risk that this mix of genetic invention and patent law poses to farmers. Following the court's strategy of responsibilization, the news stories suggested that it *did* matter (despite the court's opinion that it did not) how the Roundup gene got into Schmeiser's crop in the first place: did

Schmeiser play a role in the plants' movement, or was the presence of Roundup Ready Canola due to the organism's own migratory and reproductive propensities? (McClelland). News stories typically presented the situation in terms of blame or celebration: either Schmeiser is an "innocent infringer," which points to the risk of biotechnological contamination and the incursion of corporate technoscience into farming via intellectual property, or he is an "active cultivator," which points instead to Schmeiser's failure as a biojuridical citizen to manage the risks that his conventional farming practices now pose in the molecular landscape (Tibbetts). In either case, these elements of risk media recode conventional farming practices from the future–anterior vantage point of a hypothetical legal–economic and/or ecological disaster where such previously acceptable practices such as seed saving become unacceptably risky and possibly even reckless.

Unlike economic risk, which biotech firms endeavor to contain by registering and enforcing patent rights, ontological risk, constructed by Schmeiser and by popular media as a form of molecular contamination, is presented as unpredictable and uncontainable due to the multiple scales and forms of embodiment of the invention (genes, cells, seeds, plants, populations) and due to the capacities of the invention to move, expand across space and replicate itself. In contrast to the austere representation of the genetic invention in Monsanto's patent claims and legal arguments as static, discrete, and precisely controlled, in news stories, the invention acquires a fluid-like material contingency, falling out of trucks (in the form of seeds) on the way to processing plants, cross-pollinating, and contaminating fields (in the form of plans and pollen), and, in complicity with the wind, insects, animals, and vehicles, flowing across property boundaries and perhaps geopolitical borders. If court decisions are risk media, then so too are news stories since they present court decision and patents as sources of ontological risk which impose new categories being that are not necessarily centred on the human (higher/lower life forms) and of epistemological risk since conventional modes of perceiving and knowing the farm are of limited use in carrying out one's responsibility for managing risks in the molecular landscape.

In some cases, news stories pointed out that no matter how the plants moved to Schmeiser's farm, Schmeiser's conduct would still constitute infringement (Leahy), but even in those instances the stories suggested that the case was complicated due to the agential properties of life forms, and specifically, their capacity to reproduce and move between farms ("Schmeiser Decision"). In news stories, the Ontario government appears to side with Schmeiser because of its concerns about the health costs of this "public nuisance" and the Council of Canadians similarly suggested that the ruling would have a negative impact not only on agriculture but on public health (Tibbetts). What Nisbet describes as the "Pandora's box/Frankenstein's monster/runaway science" frame in science news helped to construct biotechnological risks such as environmental contamination and an inability to meet other jurisdictions' standards of organic food quality (i.e., the absence of GMOs and chemical herbicides in the production process), which would in turn lead to a loss of international markets for Canadian canola (McClelland; Thibodeau). The centrifugal movement implied by runaway science and contamination points away from individual responsibility to a system-wide failure to recognize and address multiple, overlapping definitions of biotechnological risk.

News stories trace more fluid relationships than do court decisions between farms, farmers, plants, and genes and this has consequences for the type of risk that biotechnology seems to represent. Rather than the controllable and observable economic risks posed to firms or the biotech industry emphasized by Monsanto in its publicity around the case, news stories instead emphasize the uncontrollable, uncertain/unknown, and potentially global and long-term risks posed by GM contamination (Morgan et al. 11). This is congruent with the argument in Morgan et al.'s work that risk assessments by non-specialists often include factors that tend to be disregarded in formal risk assessments such as "how well the risk is understood, how equitably the risk is distributed across the population, how well individuals can control the risk they face, and whether the risk is assumed voluntarily or is imposed on people without their approval" (10). News stories appear to mediate biotechnological risk according to "lay" perceptions of risk; shifting the focus from economic damage to genetic contamination allows for a wider range of considerations to enter the definition of the risk problem including equity of exposure to risk, intentionality and consent to the exposure, and capacities to know about and control risk exposure.

What I find most significant about the mediation of risk in the Schmeiser case is that "conventional" or industrial farming—oriented toward the maximization of agricultural production in large-scale farming operations—now appears to be destabilized and devalued as prone to risk in the emerging paradigm of post-industrial agriculture with its emphasis on problems of consumption, including "consumer concerns regarding food safety and quality" (Heller 322). Conventional practices of saving seeds and breeding crops are marked as an aberration of newly established biojuridical responsibilities and as a failure to manage risks stemming from one's own conduct in the new agricultural milieu of ubiquitous genetic modification and biopatenting. While the biotech industry and the majority in the Supreme Court decision defined biotechnological risk in terms of economic loss, the counterpublic's strategies, which were circulated widely by news media, tended to focus on risks to the environment, to farmer's cultural rights, and to food quality. As Heller argues in the context of similar developments in France, these conceptualizations of risk in terms of "quality" (environmental and food) are already being incorporated into state and corporate strategies of biogovernance that "manage popular behaviour and attitudes" and strategies of trans-biopolitical governance which classify and evaluate relations between human and nonhuman genes, cells, bodies, and populations (322). The general trajectory of risk media that I have traced in this chapter is that the narrow risk definitions produced through normalization and diffusion strategies are suddenly joined by a much wider range of ethical, regulatory, political, and environmental issues as the controversy unfolded in popular media. This diversity of concepts of biotechnological risk then seems to narrow once more as depoliticized concepts of environmental risk and food quality become central to risk assessment frameworks of state and corporate institutions. We should therefore be cautious about the framing of biotechnological risk as "contamination" insofar as it ushers in "quality" as yet another biopolitical strategy that serves to legitimate the privatization of risk management and communication and other elements of trans-species, molecular biogovernance.

Note

1 See *Monsanto Co. v. McFarling*, 363 F.3d 1336 (Fed. Cir. 2004), wherein it was found that McFarling had signed Monsanto's TUA. *Pioneer Hi-Bred International, Inc. v. Ottawa Plant Food, Inc.*, 283 F. Supp. 2d 1018 (N.D. Iowa 2003), wherein defendant tried to resell patented product. *Monsanto Co. v. Trantham*, 156 F. Supp, wherein court rejected defendant's claim that Monsanto's patents were anti-competitive.

Acknowledgments

I am grateful to Sheryl Hamilton whose inspiration and advice shaped this chapter and my work on law, media and nonhuman others more broadly.

Works Cited

Abley, Mark. "Biotech Lobby Got Millions from Ottawa: Public Cash Used to Alter Image." *Montreal Gazette*, February 28, 2000, p. A1.
Balter, Michael. "Transatlantic War of BRCA1 Patent." *Science*, vol. 292, no. 5523, June 8, 2001.
BBC News. "Farmer Claims All Food Producers are Under Threat from Multi-national Seed Companies." April 4, 2001, www.bbc.co.uk/worldservice/business/story_fdh040401.shtml. Accessed June 8, 2017.
Blue, Gwendolyn and Melanie Rock. "Trans-biopolitics: Complexity in Interspecies Relations." *Health*, vol. 15, no. 4, 2010, pp. 353–368.
Boyle, James. *Shamans, Software, and Spleens: Law and the Construction of Information Society*. Harvard UP, 1996.
Busch, Lawrence and Keiko Tanaka. "Rites of Passage: Constructing Quality in a Commodity Subsector." *Science, Technology & Human Values*, vol. 21, no. 1, 1996, pp. 3–27.
Chakrabarty, Ananda M. "US Supreme Court's Decision on the Patent Ineligibility of Human Genes: BRCA1/BRCA2 as Products of Nature." *Journal of Commercial Biotechnology*, vol. 21, no. 4, 2015, pp. 3–7.

Cooper, Melinda. *Life as Surplus: Biotechnology and Capitalism in the Neoliberal Era*. U of Washington P, 2008.

Cotter, John. "King Canola, Fewer Cows, Aging Producers: Digging into the Agriculture Census." *CBC News*. May 10, 2017, www.cbc.ca/news/canada/calgary/more-cropland-larger-farms-stable-profits-census-of-agriculture-1.4109339. Accessed June 8, 2017.

De Laet, Marianne. 2000. "Patents, Travel, Space: Ethnographic Encounters with Objects in Transit." *Environment and Planning D: Society and Space*, vol. 18, no. 2, pp. 149–168.

De Marchi, Bruna and Jerome Ravetz. "Risk Management and Governance: A Post-normal Science Approach." *Futures*, vol. 31, no. 7, 1999, 743–757.

"Farmer Fined in Fight with Biotech Giant." March 30, 2001, *The National Post*, p. A4.

Foster, Laura, A. "Patents, Biopolitics, and Feminisms: Locating Patent Law Struggles over Breast Cancer Genes and the *Hoodia* Plant." *International Journal of Cultural Property*, vol. 19, 2012, 371–400.

Gerlach, Neil et al. *Becoming Biosubjects: Bodies, Systems, Technologies*. U of Toronto P, 2011.

Hartley, Matt. "Grain Farmer Claims Moral Victory in Seed Battle." *The Globe and Mail*, March 30, 2008, p. A3.

Health Canada. "Genetically Modified (GM) Foods and Other Novel Foods; Glyphosate Tolerant Canola, GT73." October 1, 1999, www.hc-sc.gc.ca/fn-an/gmf-agm/appro/ofb-094-325-a-eng.php. Accessed June 8, 2017.

Heller, Chaia. "Post-industrial 'Quality Agricultural Discourse': Techniques of Governance and Resistance in the French Debate over GM Crops." *Social Anthropology*, vol. 14, no. 3, 2006, pp. 319–334.

Leahy, Stephen. "Canada's Top Court Backs Monsanto against Farmer." *Inter Press Service*, May 21, 2004.

Lyons, Murray. "Small Victory for Schmeiser." *Saskatoon StarPhoenix*, March 20, 2008, www.pressreader.com/canada/saskatoon-starphoenix/20080320/282153581989324. Accessed June 8, 2017.

Madison, Michael J. "Law as Design: Objects, Concepts, and Digital Things." Case W. Res. L. Rev. 381, vol. 56, no. 2, 2005.

McClelland, Charles. "Canadian Supreme Court Rules against Farmer in Biotech Dispute." *USA Today*, May 21, 2004, http://usatoday30.usatoday.com/tech/news/techpolicy/2004-05-21-monsanto-wins-ruling_x.htm. Accessed June 8, 2017.

Morgan, Granger M. et al. *Risk Communication: A Mental Models Approach*. Cambridge UP, 2001.

Newell-McGloughlin, Martina. "Public Perceptions of Agricultural Biotechnology—A Non Social Science Perspective." *Medical Anthropology Quarterly*, vol. 15, 2001, pp. 34–37.

Nisbet, Matthew C. "Framing Science: A New Paradigm in Public Engagement." *Understanding Science: New Agendas in Science Communication*, edited by LeeAnne Kahlor and Patricia Stout. Routledge, 2009, pp. 40–67.

Paulson, J. "Local Action Brewing." *Star-Phoenix*, October 12, 2001, p. A1.

Roof, Judith. *Reproductions of Reproduction: Imaging Symbolic Change*. Routledge, 1996.

"Schmeiser Decision Causes Uproar around the World." *Canada Newswire*, May 21, 2004.

"Seeds of Discontent." *World Watch*, January/February 2002, pp. 8–10.

Steed, Judy. "Seeds of Conflict; Percy Schmeiser vs. Monsanto Reaches Canada's Supreme Court Early Next Year." *The Toronto Star*, November 5, 2003, p. D1.

Stewart, L. "Lines are Fuzzy on GM Foods." *Montreal Gazette*, April 5, 2002.

Street, Paul. "Stabilizing Flows in the Legal Field: Illusions of Permanence, Intellectual Property Rights and the Transnationalization of Law." *Global Networks*, vol. 3, no. 1, 2003, pp. 7–28.

Striphas, Ted and Kembrew McLeod. "Strategic Improprieties: Cultural Studies, the Everyday, and the Politics of Intellectual Properties: Introduction." *Cultural Studies*, vol. 20, no. 2–3, 2006, pp. 119–144.

Supreme Court of Canada. *Harvard College v. Canada* (Commissioner of Patents). 4 SCR 45, 2002 SCC 76, no. 28155, December 5, 2002.

Supreme Court of Canada. *Monsanto Canada Inc. v. Schmeiser*, 1 S.C.R. 902, 2004 SCC 34, no. 29437, 2004, para. 8.

Thibodeau, Wayne. "Island Farmers Divided over GMO Decision in Favour of Monsanto." *Guardian* (Charlottetown), *The Province*, May 22, 2004, p. A3.

Tibbetts, Janice. "Farmer Loses Final Court Battle." *CanWest News*, May 21, 2004.

Toronto Star. "Saskatchewan Farmer Loses Patent Fight against Biotech Giant; Fears He Could Lose Farm over Legal Bills in Monsanto Case." *Toronto Star*, March 30, 2001, p. A8.

Waldby, Catherine. "Stem Cells, Tissue Cultures, and the Production of Bio-value." *Health: An Interdisciplinary Journal for the Social Study of Health, Illness, and Medicine*, vol. 6, no. 3, 2002, pp. 305–323.

Waldby, Catherine and Robert Mitchell. *Tissue Economies: Blood, Organs, and Cell Lines in Late Capitalism*. Duke UP, 2006.

Walkom, T. "Food Fight." *Toronto Star*, August 22, 1999, p. 1.

Yapa, Lakshman. "What Are Improved Seeds? An Epistemology of the Green Revolution." *Economic Geography*, vol. 69, no. 3, 1993, pp. 254–273.

26
REFLECTIONS ON RISK, MEDIA, AND THE REASONABLE ANIMATED BY A TRIAL BY JURY

Lawrence Cohen

Seduction, Sociality, and Event (First Post)

From the beginning, this round of prospective jury duty was different. The previous times, I keyed in a phone number each evening for a week to find out if I needed to be at the court in San Francisco's civic center the following day. On each occasion, a recorded message spared me civic duty. But this time the phone offered no relief.[1]

The next morning, I took an early train and got to the court building before it opened. It was August 2015: the semester's teaching was about to start. I checked Yelp to find an open coffee shop, then walked some blocks to a Peet's. I bought the familiar coffee, found an empty seat, and tried to work on my syllabus. But I was grumpy, distracted by the interruption to routine. Most people at Peet's at that hour were schoolteachers. I found myself listening to their conversation. People were animated. Something had happened: the earth had moved and I had not noticed. At some point I got on Facebook and wrote something. This possibility, too, was new, this sense that what might have been a waste of a morning could with creativity, attention, and some self-love be realized as an event. Here is that first post:

> Sitting early morning in coffee shop next to courthouse, adjoining a school, awaiting my jury duty. Around me, government workers and teachers discussing the earthquake early this morning—"did you feel it?" … "We had just gotten on the bridge and paid our toll, and then I thought, oh shit!" … "I [didn't feel it but] woke up with a stomach ache … where did that come from?"

If you knew my demographics and profession, you might find the social grouping of the colleagues, friends, and family constituting the small public of my Facebook pronouncements predictable. After Gilles Deleuze and Felix Guattari, opening up the old debate between Émile Durkheim and Gabriel Tarde on the ontogeny of the social, you might call its sociality a *molar* one. And yet social media in its eventfulness appeared to offer all the seductions of the *molecular*, as Deleuze and Guattari termed their figure after Tarde of emergent and providential sociality. Facebook readers wrote back, immediately, allowing one to exult: look what we are creating, we masters of history. Though these affective reinforcements were usually of the familiar and molar, excited into attentiveness. At their most event-ratifying, they reinforced a sense of the in-group, something like Durkheimian effervescence or the *communitas* of Victor Turner, and far from any irruption into radical possibility.[2]

Actually, this first post provoked minimal reaction. My friend Pramod, a senior public health official in Iowa who I had known since we were both students in Varanasi, the north Indian city, referred to my academic profession in offering this: "Fun! If nothing else, a good place for an anthropologist to observe behaviors of a select few humans who are in flux." Indeed, I had been posting a series of reflections on fellow coffee shop users over that year on the social media site. Flux was an interesting, indeed Deleuzian, figure: Pramod had long questioned the status of some of my more fixed observations on his hometown, whether under the then regnant and competing molarities of culture or socio-economic class.

Where did that come from, one teacher had asked. The earthquake would come to presage the eventfulness of the day, or rather the trouble of constituting an event, for the jury yet to be assembled over at the courthouse, under law. Who and what is a jury and when is law eventful?

The event—around the status of which the court proceedings and jury deliberations would revolve—would over subsequent days in my own understanding appear something like this: woman, raising a daughter with multiple and serious physical disabilities, is reading a magazine.

The magazine had been sent by an association for parents of children with spina bifida, her daughter's diagnosis. She is reading, and then something happens. We might call that something a consciousness of risk, and of injury. It was sudden; it shook her. We could call it seismic. One might thus ask, as people do: where did that come from? And yet that question, as it turned out, was foreclosed.

Such magazines constitute a particular kind of Tardean public, one which after Paul Rabinow we might term biosocial in its being assembled around the knowledge, feeling, and self-organizing imperative of a shared diagnosis. But it is not only that the mediated diagnosis organizes a social entity. It organizes a reframing of risk.[3] She is at home—a jury would learn much about this home—and her eyes are reading, perhaps skimming over the surface of the print as mine often do. They alight upon a notice, an advertisement, boxed and distinct, suggesting the possibility of wrongdoing and the collection of damages for all parents of children with spina bifida. In that moment, she has as she would later claim a frisson, a shock, the sudden realization that her daughter's condition was not only the gift and grace of God that she had been assuming but additionally the effect of wrongdoing by a corporation that produced the medication she had taken which she had long understood to have played a role in causing the spina bifida.

She had this shock, this surfeit of sense, this sudden understanding that the risks one bears were not simply given by God and one's fate and one's doctors but that in addition and in exception to all that there might have been something else: an injury. In her account, the seismic moment was grounded in reading. At the risk of presuming a story, pushing toward its tragic conclusion—spoiler alert!—let me say that no one over the days of the trial that would follow, on either side, seemed to attend to that moment. Except her. Except me: I did mention self-love.

Perhaps it was self-love, in the sense of the familiar and modern anxiety of such scenes of women reading and being transported (Laqueur 263, 277, 302–320), that did not allow the trial to constitute the magazine as a legitimate and *reasonable* event, as a moral account of what the law terms discovery.

The Moral State (Second Post)

Syllabus unfinished, I walked back to the courthouse, passed through the metal detector, and went down to the basement to the juror selection room. At some point, the over 200 persons assembled were instructed by an official—I want to say a bailiff but I haven't a clue, really—to watch a video. The video introduced us to the process of jury selection and to its importance for the rule of law. The makers of the video were not, apparently, heeding the many law review articles examining the disappearance of the civil trial, including the jury trial, in the United States (Galanter "The Vanishing Trial"; Young) and the correlative disappearance of trial skills among litigators (McCormack and Bodnar). After it aired, I posted the following:

Watching video instructing our roomful of potential jurors in the value of trial by jury. It began with an extraordinary claim for an official document—"California is the greatest state in the Union"—and continued its series of normative caricatures, as when a juror recalls, based on no particular evidence, "I feel our system is better than that of other countries." Having just read the report in this morning's *NY Times* of continuing racial bias toward African Americans in jury selection, the boosterism seemed a bit perverse. But perhaps I am rehearsing my own hopeful inadmissibility as a juror.

I may wince, in hindsight, at the heroic narrator the genre encourages and I leapt to create, though I amplify the generic convention in writing this essay. My partner, who practices as a psychiatrist and psychoanalyst, would that evening trouble the presumption of the claim that I was rehearsing an exit. Was I more invested in getting on the jury than these repeated disavowals might indicate? Facebook friends, more numerous this second round, similarly read ambivalence in my desire for a way out. James, a colleague and former student, amplified the feeling:

> I was released from jury duty after the judge learned that I was a medical anthropologist, saying I was already doing my part for society. He and both attorneys then went on to confess that they all had wanted to be anthropologists. "Until you reclaimed your senses, obviously," [I thought] as I walked out the door with the feeling that I had just been selected out, not "excused."

Here the romance of anthropology carries a negative, Falstaffian charge. One grows up, and one reluctantly but necessarily disavows its pleasures. The anthropologist, to borrow J.L. Austin's (1956–1957) distinction, desires release from civic duty via the *excuse* and not the *justification*. That is, he or she does not want the release from civic service to be based on the presumption that an anthropologist has no role in fashioning the law as he or she always already done his or her good, his or her "part for society." He or she rather wants to be excused, based on the schedule of specialist teaching, or the much celebrated labor of fieldwork, but presuming a deferred commitment to the making of law.

Perhaps California was the best state. The woman who read the ad in the spina bifida magazine and claimed a sudden realization of the risk to which she had been unwittingly exposed by taking Depakote was from New Jersey. The law firm representing her was located in Texas. Abbott Laboratories, the corporation they were suing, was a larger entity, headquartered in Illinois. Its website, when I looked at it late in 2016, promoted the company's identity as a global institution: one was invited to click on any of a host of national flags to be transported to more localized information.[4] But the trial was held in California. What the prospective jurors learned, as the judge offered an outline of the case, was that California state law had a particular statute of limitations enabling the case to be brought. At stake in the trial, as at least one juror came to comprehend it, was a matter of timing, of when a reasonable person would have had cause to discover that a bodily condition was an injury allowing for redress through the courts.

Marc Galanter, the legal scholar whose assessment of the disappearance of the American jury trial I cited above, spent a year early in his career in India on a Fulbright scholarship. Despite the postwar frame of development, dominated by modernization theory, in which he came of age, Galanter became something other than a Cold War "India scholar" for whom the U.S. offered the exemplary model of India's legal future. Or rather, he broke from the particular ideal-typic commitments of modernization theory early on.

Galanter would recall his Fulbright year as itself a seismic shock to his legal training. As in George E. Marcus and Michael M.J. Fischer's discussion of the particular line of liberal thought in American anthropology in which the radical difference of what was usually comprehended as another culture becomes the ground of a "cultural critique" of American norms and institutions,

Galanter would write that India provided the moral and intellectual capacity for self-alienation: "immersion in another culture is a celebrated method for exposing our presuppositions and showing us that familiar arrangements are problematic rather than the way things have to be" (qtd. in Abel 562). What is striking here takes us beyond what hindsight may reveal as cliché, justification, and the workings of neo-colonial liberalism. Rather, and despite the classic holism of the American culture concept (Stocking, "Franz Boas") organizing this narrative of rendering the familiar strange, Galanter's cultural critique was in effect a critique of culture.[5] In a biographical essay, Richard Abel notes:

> Marc wrote that he came to India having been taught in America that law was "an integrated purposive system, residing in a hierarchy of agencies, moved by and applying a hierarchy of norms.... The study of India provided a series of lessons that undermined that picture by violating my expectations of continuity and correspondence between law and society."

In particular, Galanter applied a series of observations on law in India as an apparatus that could not be reduced to any generalized figure of culture (e.g., "law as a system of symbols diverges from the law as a system of operative controls") as the ground of a critical analysis of law in the United States (qtd. in Abel 563).

Let me stay with Galanter a bit longer. Despite his movement away from the evolutionary reason of modernization theory, Galanter was not interested in a philosophical relativism. First, the Indian system was rooted less in a historical anthropology of *karma* or *dharmashastra* than in a particular colonial condition. Thus the past Indian "century of indifference to tort remedies" given a "weak remedy system" that failed to recompense the expanding set of victims of industrial capitalism was primarily an effect of limits to civil litigation set up by the colonial state (Galanter "When Legal Worlds Collide") and not a radically incommensurate ontology of harm under the sign of culture (Evans-Pritchard). Second, neither the Indian system or the American typically benefitted the "have-nots" (Galanter "Why the 'Haves' Come Out Ahead"), though each comprised a distinctive apparatus of resources for and limitations to such benefit. Third, with the intensifying transnational circulation of risk, exemplified for Galanter in the mass death and morbidity unleashed in Bhopal in 1984 by Union Carbide's factory, subjects of risk and harm find themselves in intimate relation to multiple legal sovereignties (Galanter "When Legal Worlds Collide"). The question becomes not one of more or less modernized legal apparatuses but of the conditions and politics of global assemblage (Collier and Ong). The private U.S. tort lawyers that offered services to identified Bhopal victims exemplified not the magisterial power of modern legalism in a developed country but a particular apparatus of "strong remedy," high cost, and different forms of "have-not" exclusion than in the Indian system.

A shared feature of litigation across stronger and weaker tort-remedy systems as these were variably brought into global relation, for Galanter, was the growing asymmetry between litigants. Scenes of injury and contestations over remedies were less and less between neighbors than between individuals and large corporations.

In the courtroom in San Francisco, lawyers for a child with spina bifida and her parents (Galanter's "have-nots") would in a highly asymmetric trial be arguing with lawyers for a global pharmaceutical company, claiming their right to sue for damages under the delayed discovery rule of California's statute of limitations.

Feelings (Third Post)

Down in the juror assembly room, a group of two dozen potential jurors were called and sent upstairs. I was among them. We were given an overview of the case, which we were told was not a trial for damages but over whether such a trial could take place given when a reasonable person could have assumed the possibility of injury. This assumption was the *discovery* and the question of how long it could have taken a reasonable person to make the discovery of possible injury was the *delay*. More loquacious and not particularly attentive to the forthcoming trial, I again turned to Facebook when we broke for lunch and wrote of my fellow prospective jurors and the language organizing our selection:

> Ongoing notes from the jury selection process: lunch break now after the first group of us serially offered our name, education, occupation, occupation of adults we live with, and prior jury service to the judge. Of the first 24 of us to be considered for the jury (I am #23), almost no one in a city apparently being taken over and disemboweled by new technology appears to work for a tech company. There was one person who left college without finishing to go work for Uber, another who worked (along with her boyfriend) for Genentech, and a grad student in engineering at Berkeley. Before we got to offer our bona fides, the judge had further instructions on the matter of bias. Bias, we learned, was about feelings. We all have feelings, about this and that: the judge acknowledged he did as well. The issue was whether we could put our feelings to one side so as to give both parties to this trial a fair shake. I was struck by the predominantly affective language here, and by justice being framed as a process to determine who could be considered a subject able to control his or her feelings. My own feelings are unclear as I wait to find out whether my answers were a golden ticket, and to what.

I think my partner was right. I wanted to be on the jury. If I were not selected, what would I have to post about?

I was asked about conflicts of interest. I said I was unsure if the following were conflicts. (1) I had a friend, a biostatistician, who used to work for Abbott. (2) I taught courses in medical anthropology that included trying to understand the shifting place of the pharmaceutical industry and its regulation in matters of health, regionally and globally. The last potential conflict of interest was framed too carefully, my uncertain seduction of the legal teams. If I had wanted to be assured of getting off the jury I could have ratcheted up my feelings. Two of the potential jurors offered what seemed a calculated performance of being the angry women and men the judge was cautioning us could not further the course of justice. I watched them and watched the other potentials watch them, too. There was this emerging sense, as we all observed self and other, of being pulled into a movie or serial, perhaps a 1950s or 1960s teleplay.

The prospectives did not meet the family that day. We learned the minimum about the mother's history of mental illness. With my very limited training in psychiatry, as I listened the words mania and bipolar disorder came to mind. She, too, had feelings that were hard to control and indeed, that were threatening her life. A doctor prescribed Depakote. She became pregnant but did not immediately stop taking the drug. It was the first thing that had worked.

My partner said to me, months later, recalling my declared intention of getting off the jury: once you say you are a psychiatrist or psychologist, they immediately remove you. His point seemed to me to be that he had no recourse, ethically or conceptually, to the figure of the reasonable subject that was at stake in how the jurors were to interpret the delayed discovery rule. But during the juror selection process, I placed my own relation to feelings within a particular coding of rationalized analysis, one that in my training as a social scientist I had learned to call Weberian. That I did so may point to something beyond reason: a wish, a compulsion to get on the jury. To be pulled into something like television, like film, but more intense, better.

In Hindi and Urdu language popular film, the cinema with which I am most familiar, there are several genres of denouement that have interested me in which the future of lives and relations, often constituted through the marriage plot, is at stake. A director may stage this action in the anteroom to an operating theater, in a hospital. Family members or friends are present. Often an electric red sign announces the door past which they, and their entangled histories of affect and care, cannot go (Cohen). The door to the operating room is the barrier to feeling: beyond which they, and we, often cannot see. The sovereign gesture of narrative, granting life or death, is that of the surgeon, emerging back into the space of visibility, feeling, and care.

A second genre is set in the courtroom. Here the separation between the subject of life or death, or alternatively freedom or incarceration, and the entangled network of affect and care is the literal bar of the courtroom. Here sight is not occluded, but yet the play of affect is restrained to the particular rhetorical and formal demands of law. Here the sovereign gesture of narrative is the verdict, usually of the judge—this is not the telegenic American jury—offering life or death, return to or separation from the beloved and the family.

To write these words, I return to Facebook and to the comments responding to this post. "Love this!" is from Vanessa, a former and beloved student who was killed soon after the trial in a car accident. She wrote her senior thesis about the ethics and political economy of cooking, studying women who like herself were being trained at La Cocina, the "San Francisco incubator Kitchen." She went on to start a bakery in the Central Valley of California. Her friends have kept up her Facebook page. Its masthead now features bevies of white roses from her memorial, but when I found myself turning to it soon after hearing of her death I discovered a picture of her embracing the sky, on the roof somehow of my own house.

Esther, an anthropologist who tended to tell it like it is, warned "civil trials are boring from my limited experience." Bishnupriya, a literature and cultural studies scholar, wrote: "Oh my ... I'm scheduled for jury duty next week! I was hoping they NEVER take opinionated professors...." She and her partner Bhaskar would later ask me to consider writing a paper, and this experiment has resulted. I am not, perhaps obviously, a scholar of law or of risk or of media. It is only that I was called to jury duty in a time of the mediated incitement to eventfulness. I do not know if, the following week, Bishnupriya was taken.

During the process of our empanelment, the potentials sat both in the jury box and the public seats. We were temporarily on both sides of the bar. Our status as regulators of our feelings was not yet determined. We had not yet submitted to the convention that feelings could and were to be kept separate: by the force of reason, by the bar of the court, by the aseptic separation of the operating theater, or by the judicious use of Depakote.

Meta-drama (Fourth Post)

The juror interviews continued all afternoon, punctuated by a coffee break. In the hallway outside the courtroom, I wrote the following:

> Alas, I have not yet been excused from the day long process of jury selection. Another 10-minute break. The process—in that potential jurors are in effect asked to weigh in on questions of tort, causality, the chemical, the corporation, the nature of feelings (again and again), the nature of the law and one's relation to that, and the concept of instruction (here, the judge's instruction and what it means to be unable to follow it)—is intensely interesting. I am committed to being very polite and parsimonious but am emerging as a character, in this drama, particularly in my difficulty in answering questions about the category of a reasonable person and her relation to the question of the norm or 'average person': the two were sliding together in the questions to me by one of the lawyers. The lawyers were tailor-made for a made for TV drama, as I fear here am I.

I do not remember precisely what the lawyers asked. But I remember how they asked it and how they looked: sight, as in the Hindi film, is not occluded in the courtroom. All the lawyers, like the judge, the plaintiff's family, their daughter's caregiver, and perhaps half of the two dozen potential jurors, were white. The main lawyer for Abbott reminded me of the former vice-presidential (and later presidential) candidate Joe Lieberman. We were it seemed the two Jews in the room. He was compact and immaculately dressed.

There were two lawyers who spoke on behalf of the plaintiffs. The younger seemed in his early forties: dark-featured, a perennial five o'clock shadow, and a decent if less perfected suit. He seemed more sensible than his senior colleague but did not get to do much of the speaking. From the few occasions he did speak, I decided he was from my hometown of Boston despite his lack of the accent. In moments when the repeated questioning of the 24 prospectives seemed less interesting than I had reported, as Esther had warned, I would imagine doing it with him in the various spaces of the courtroom: on the bench, against the bar, in an emptied jury box. Esther, this seemed to relieve boredom.

The senior lawyer was perhaps what I had meant by tailor-made, though his light colored, wrinkled suits effected neither the perfected nor aspirational tailoring of the other two characters. He was a big man. He had a drawl. He joked. He was like us. He was not a corporate lawyer. He was from Texas. He told us so. The law was complicated, but the issues were not. He would not condescend to us. He would help us through. More than his fellow lawyers, his presumption of easy friendship through the thickets of tort law rubbed up against my structure of feeling, self-consciously suburban liberal, Harvard educated, San Francisco homosexual.

The senior lawyer was riveting, in a Jimmy Stewart in an *Anatomy of a Murder* fashion, repeatedly offering evidence upon objection declared inadmissible, as if like Stewart's character Paul Biegler he recognized that for a jury no evidence once heard could be struck from mind. As if he recognized that for the jury being empaneled this whole drama was like that experienced by Gore Vidal's Myra Breckenridge in her repeat performance in *Myron*, in which the titular character is sucked into her/his television set where the action plays out in an alternate, Hollywood-beamed-into-your living-room, universe.

This feel of being pulled into a different, something-like-television, world stayed with me, and in varied ways for my fellow prospectives as we got to know each other slightly over coffee breaks spent largely in the hallway outside, as if we dared not stray too far from the set. Remembering the feel, I am unclear of how to make sense of my knowing declarations at the time that we were all "made for TV." What else was possible?

Facebook Comments. Tulasi, friend and anthropologist, wrote "Law and Order: anthropologist. Da Dum!" This led to a cascade of comments from other friends. Lindsay wrote: "So hard not to picture this ... was trying to get Law and Order out of the picture, Tulasi." Tulasi offered a different script: "12 angry men?" Linda-Anne offered the following: she knew a "trial judge," who was

> a member of our congregation. He told me he always has to remind jurors that Law and Order and CSI are fiction; in real life most pieces of trace found are ordinary and show nothing, there are no fingerprints or DNA, and nothing is definitive.

What is definitive? Perhaps it is this feel, as in *Myron*, of having been pulled out of the everyday and into the set. It marks some of how many experience big events in our time. It marked the surreal of watching the twin towers fall, once woken up by a telephone call from my sister on the East Coast. It marked the upside-down-ness of Donald Trump's election victory. It did not mark my attending to the mass killings in Aleppo, or Fallujah, to the mass killings of students in Mexico, or to the pogroms against Muslims orchestrated by a future Indian prime minister in Ahmedabad. For these latter events, and perhaps troublingly, a sober realism was available. Perhaps, if despairingly, the distinction I was wrestling with is that between the sublime—here rendered as the sense of being sucked into the set—and its other, the word maybe or maybe not the beautiful, what I am marking here by the figure of all-too-realness.

What word is there when you are told, by the doctors during your future child's prenatal examination, that there is a serious problem, a likelihood of a severe condition known as spina bifida? Is it the suck of television? Or perhaps there are worlds beyond the split between the everyday and the event that Vidal authorizes in *Myron*. For this woman, as she would tell the camera during a deposition (I think it was a deposition, but I will err on such details), her struggle was to recognize the familiarity of God's grace in the diagnosis. If the Lord is invited, through the struggle and faith of His adherent, to inhabit a condition in which He was always present, can the event be called an injury? Could a reasonable person, aware of God's inhabitation, be expected to "discover" injury in such a moment? The question would haunt me, in the days that followed, though it was not present in any of the legal arguments. I would sit there, willing either Texas Daddy or Hunky Boston to bring knowledge of the divine into the proceedings, saving this woman and her family from the procedural sure-footedness of Most Excellent Joe.[6]

The Sorcerer (Fifth Post)

Why does the chronotope of the jury trial lend itself so easily to such figures of alterity, to other worlds, in my time to the world inside the TV set?[7] One could argue that this is a phenomenological rendering of the political theorist's state of exception: the necessity of being outside or in exception to the law in order to uphold the law. The literature produced by the empaneled—there is a weighty archive[8]—conveys this theme, that the deliberations of the jury far from being deadened to feeling are pickled in it. The axes of social distinction marking and differentiating the jury often underlie such descriptions of discord and drama that nonetheless converge into a decision. If the spirit of the law, as the judge instructed us, was to be found through an excision or bracketing of feeling, the sequestered jury is removed from the judge's presence and left to their own (human, divergent) devices in a zone of affective intensification. The narrative pay-off of this literature seems to be that out of the failure of law as feeling-control comes the law and its reason.

That evening, I returned to Facebook.

> I seem to have been impaneled, if that is the word, for a jury trial, despite my certainty throughout the day that I was wildly unimpanelable, as it were. As the lawyers called out juror after juror for the honor of being unacceptable, but not me, the horror began to sink in, rather suddenly.
>
> The perils of hubris, etc. Re. the specter of missed work, much worry, late nights, and more. But something else ... excitement? ... as I descend into the corporate body of the law. Must brush up on my Gilbert & Sullivan. Off FB for the duration.

The judge counseled the impaneled, jurors and alternates, that we were to communicate nothing of the trial to anyone outside of the courtroom. This post was a hand-washing. By now the reader is used to these pretensions of affective eventfulness. Numerous comments were generated. Alternate operettic references were offered. The next day, the trial began.

Within the specular logic of the courtroom the jury now got to see the family: mother, daughter, caregiver, and at a bit of remove, husband. The jury members were each provided with pens and notepads. I aggressively utilized a lifetime of note-taking, writing down each question, each response, each judicial direction. Pages flipped over rapidly. By the end of the day, a sense of the stakes for the opposed parties was emerging, in the jury box, along with a performance of my own distinction.

Much later, when the trial was over, the judge would tell us that we were now free to speak or write about the trial. I would keep my notepad. But over time I found the idea of returning to these notes a violation, a ratcheting up of the aggression.

The stakes, remembered: things of course hinged on delayed discovery. The judge provided careful wording for us, and I would return again and again to his words, circled on my pad. They were similar, perhaps identical, to the California Civil Jury Instructions one finds on the Internet.

455. Statute of Limitations—Delayed Discovery

[name of plaintiff]'s lawsuit was still filed on time if [name of plaintiff] proves that before that date, [name of plaintiff] did not discover, and did not know of facts that would have caused a reasonable person to suspect, that [he/she/it] had suffered harm that was caused by someone's wrongful conduct]....[9]

The trial came to hinge on two statements the mother appeared to make in a videotaped deposition: (1) that when she went for prenatal testing and learned that there was a significant risk her child would be born with spina bifida she was made aware that the Depakote could be a cause of the condition and that she consequently stopped the medication, and (2) that she was not aware of this risk when her psychiatrist prescribed her the medication. We were asked, again and again, what a reasonable person could suspect. The defense pointed us toward the psychiatrist as the source of possible wrongful conduct and to the prenatal test—years before the woman read the advertisement in the magazine and far outside the statute of limitations—as not only the reasonable but the all too clear moment of discovery.

As note-taker, I felt there were at least three problems with this argument: none of these were raised by the attorneys for the plaintiffs, however, and I struggled to find either evidence or instruction allowing me to make a case allowing for a claim of delayed discovery. Imagined contortions with Hunky Boston receded to make way for imagined arguments in the room where they would put the jury.

First: how could someone suffering from severe mental illness be expected to meet a reasonable person clause?

Second: if one's faith—at a moment when a prenatal examination comes with the presumption of reasonable abortion—constitutes an event as God's will, as opposed to as human injury, is there a place for such eventfulness within the law?

Third: if the woman under deposition notes her abiding trust in the physician who prescribed the Depakote, trust that constitutes the therapeutic relation at a time of severe crisis, is the failure to perceive injury irrational or the ground of necessary healing?

You ask for details. Notes placed to the side, I will not have enough. Here is an imaginary version of affairs, as if the two days of testimony and argument were structured as a single story.

Two people, a woman and a man, get married and have several children. They have money troubles. They have other troubles, call them psychological. They separate from time to time. Our focus is on the woman. She is in pain. She has all of the pressures of earning a living and taking care of a large family. She thinks of killing herself. She sees various people for help. She takes a series of medications. Years pass, like this. The children grow older. Things remain difficult. They get worse. She has limited health insurance. She sees a doctor at a clinic she can afford. He prescribes Depakote. She has no ability to pay for the medication: he gives her his stock of samples from the drug company representatives. These originally come, like all Depakote, in containers with a warning that taking this medication while pregnant could result in severe birth defects. All the lawyers would focus on the packaging: for Abbott, to argue that users were clearly instructed of the serious teratogenic effects to a fetus, for the plaintiff, continually alluding to inadmissible evidence of Abbott's non-disclosure of serious risks and a subsequent cover-up. But the marketing via charitable gift, if that is what it was, free sample pills moving from the drug company to the doctor and from the doctor to the woman, disaggregate the medicine from its packaging and warnings, putting aside the question of whether warnings on packages constitute adequately performing media for teratogenic risk. The onus is on the doctor. As the video deposition is many years after the woman came into his busy low fee New Jersey clinic, we might assume that he has no memory of the encounter and that his notes of the moment do not rise to an event. He tells the camera that he does not remember the visit but that his standard practice was to explain the risks of taking Depakote. The drug company lawyer seems to be searching for that sweet spot, assigning blame for non-disclosure neither to the woman with a sublimely sick child or to the hard-working doctor prescribing Abbott's product but leaving blame somewhere in between, and far from the company. Retrospective time advances. Depakote makes life less crazy and more manageable. Things can happen. The woman gets back together with her husband. The reunion is fruitful. The woman learns she is pregnant. She never expected, she says again and again, to get pregnant this late in her life: her children were behind her. One might limn what I was experiencing in hearing of that time as the motions of grace, molecularly advanced via the gift of $C^8H^{16}O^2$: a return to a form of life, of relationship, of the unexpected pleasures thereof, of the unexpected fruits thereof. Her thoughts she later says are not of risk to her daughter, but of a gift from God, a responsibility if that is the theologically correct word to that gift. Her thoughts are not of injury. She will contradict herself: in one deposition saying that she does not think her doctor, who she credits with saving her life, failed to instruct her on the risks, but later, perhaps given that this admission appears to harm the plaintiff case immeasurably, saying that she has no recollection of being warned of risks at that time. What is remembered? She will remember her prenatal examination and learning of the possibility of spina bifida. She will remember being told to stop the Depakote. Her understanding she will say was that the Depakote might do damage to her child going forward and not that injury, that figure here of necessity involving a party causing harm, had been done. But the jury is made to see, using the mother's words in her deposition against her current intent, that a reasonable person could and would ascertain, responsibly, of any possible injury at this point. Her daughter is born. We learn of the challenges faced by her and by all in her family. These are immense. We learn of how a form of care, precarious yet supple, is crafted. We learn of how the parents move on, less bound to each other than in the embrace of their reunion but more or less together. Years pass in stories of a hard childhood. Years move toward the moment, parents and daughter at home together, of the magazine, of a look for what is new in treatment, in science, in hope, of the ad from a law firm. This was the black box that called out injury and for the first time. Discussions follow, and then calls and then meetings with lawyers. The scene moves west from New Jersey, eventually to Texas, eventually here to California. Now details fall away: we do not know what resources the family has committed to this new consciousness of injury, or who these tort lawyers are. Now we are asked to assess a delay of discovery, now we are brought face to face with reason.

It was not *Trial By Jury* of the operettic canon that came to mind, but the one Gilbert and Sullivan production in which I had once performed, *The Sorcerer*, a story of two ambitious people convinced they can improve the world's lot by bringing the love they felt for one another as a couple to all who lacked similar grace, and calling in a sorcerer they see advertised to distribute a love philter, to disastrous effect. The sorcerer in my operetta was less the Texas lawyer promising magic, though the effects were in the end disastrous to the plaintiff family. In this production the sorcerer was myself, in the evenings after testimony and the hours before the closing arguments were concluded and the jury sequestered, again and again recalling the judge's rendition of the law's parameter to find a way to allow the facts of God's grace and the interruption or supplementation of that grace through the magazine ad to enable a delay of discovery. In the courtroom, where I had access to my trial notebooks—there were, by the end, several—I would go over my drawings and charts, trying alchemically to distill something from the days of testimony to delay under the terms of our instruction. What I was trying to conjure was a figure of reason, under the parts of law offered the jury and as instructed, that could not turn to a consciousness of injury under the totality of divine love necessary to live amid such pain and the risk of bipolar life, and once that form of consciousness was established, to show how the pleasure if that is the word of reading—the moment of encountering the ad in the magazine—might shock this God-beloved reason into a different consciousness of injury, whether supplemental or sequential to the reason of the subject cleaving to God. I felt as if I had to create something like *The Phenomenology of Spirit*, a form of argument that would begin with and only with the judge's instructions and the law provided to us and from that move out to God-consciousness and media-consciousness. I could not do it, and I had a sense in the final hours in the jury box of making a bit of a quiet scene, scribbling away. We know how the story ends.

No Way

There was a sixth post, and it included phrases like "heartbreaking," wince-worthy claims like "if justice was upheld by my wonderful fellow jurors and I it was not without some significant human cost," and a promise to write about it. I will spare myself.

The difference between me then and at the time of writing this now may only be this: that I was caught up then in such an intense commitment to the judge's instructions, something like love. I could not get out. The law is like a television set.

In the jury room, to which I brought my stack of notepads, there were some glances this way and that and I was then suggested as foreperson. With all due and fake humility I accepted. I was already imagining the Facebook posts: Oh, the Places You'll Go! I had not read the literature that would have told me that as the older of the two white men on the jury my being selected was all but a fait accompli.

I do not have a close account of the day we were sequestered. I did not take close notes on my fellow jurors in the small room where we sat together, but shifted into administrative mode as if I were chairing a faculty meeting, ensuring that everyone got to speak and that we had a steady eye on the goal. The goal was rendering the judge's charge to us into the grounds for deliberation, breaking it down into pieces to be fit to our varied sense of where the problems lay in what we had witnessed, problems that in our first go-around the table this or that juror felt needed to be resolved. I had a slightly paranoid sense that another of the jurors—the other white man—was a potential critic, that he had expected to be chosen, that I had to make good. There was a third juror, one of the two jurors that seemed older than me, an African American woman, who emerged as the closest thing to a collective spokesperson. My role settled into that of group secretary.

What was the collective speaking? That we wanted to support the plaintiff and her family. That she was not in a position to decline taking Depakote when she was seriously ill or to assess risks, that the figure of a reasonable person demanded by the law was hard to find in our apparently shared sense of severe mental illness. That the woman who came for her prenatal check-up, now well-medicated on Depakote, resembled the reasonable person of our instructed world. That one of the two alternate versions of her recounting of events, the initial version in the videotaped deposition, suggested that she understood that Depakote had likely injured her daughter in the womb and that her doctor had not informed her of the risk. That the second version of her testimony during the trial contradicted her earlier telling: now she did not understand the risk during the prenatal screening meeting. That we were inclined to accept the first, videotaped deposition we watched on the court television over the second, live one.

Here should have been my moment, just like in the courtroom dramas on TV, to tell my fellow jurors, no, no, we can save her. Her very assumption of reasonableness was a medicated, injurious condition: her survival was predicated upon the future destruction of her unexpected and unplanned daughter's health. The fact was unlivable, save through God's grace. The doctor that saved her life was beyond reasonable accusation. Memory of crazy life before Depakote was treacherous. It was only the later invitation to elite—legal—expertise that opened up a different terrain of risk and event. It was as if the impossible burden of accusation—against the doctor who saved her, against the self who was beyond easy reason, or against the husband who reappeared as a figure of promise and joy and the recognition of her good self and who enabled the entirely unexpected excess leading to pregnancy—was replaced by a form of reasonable injuriousness that was part of the elite pedagogy of biosocial participation.

I did not say any of this. The instructions bound and pleasured me. They bound me to the media of the first deposition. They did not allow a way to take God's grace into the scene of reason and law. They did not release me to attend only to the second moment, in which it was the magazine advertisement that offered a space of release from the burden of grace, a consciousness of injury and a secularization as it were of risk. Or perhaps the imagined other juror, who bore the authority of whiteness in my own story, was right: despite the weight of by note-taking, I failed to produce a *Phenomenology* for the situation.

Acknowledgments

Thanks to Bhaskar Sarkar and Bishnupriya Ghosh for the provocation, to one's unnamed fellow jurors for thinking during the trial, to Gabriel Coren, Eric Glassgold, and various Facebook friends for thinking before and after the trial, and to Kevin Karpiak, Katherine Lemons, Sally Falk Moore, and Laura Nader for conversation on law over the years.

Notes

1 One finds oneself committed to a given practice, call it method, and one may fail to recognize that readers may have other commitments, or find themselves uncommitted. A word then, as it were, on method. This chapter is based on "research" to the extent that anthropology's totalizing commitment to what it has conceived as its *field* (Gupta and Ferguson; Stocking "The Ethnographer's Magic") or to use a later and arguably post-totalizing figuration its *atmosphere* (Stewart), a legacy of totalization too obviously emergent from particular nineteenth-century species of holism, empiricism, and the assumption of imperial judgment (Bunzl; Said) but no less linked to twentieth-century conceptions of system and synesthesia, enables and for me demands a practice of life-as-fieldwork that loops back from the named field (for me, "India") to gather the presumptive non-field (see Fabian and Augé among others) into its operations of fetishism (that is, over-valuation, hyper-attentiveness, and repetition). This is no solution to the problems of the aforementioned nineteenth or twentieth centuries, let alone to those of the current time. A commitment is at best a provisional stance, if one harder and harder to escape.

  More to the point are particular practices of attentiveness within this commitment. Here, these lead me to focus on the media organizing time spent in and out of the courtroom and its regime of tort adjudication, and the ways these media appear to produce openings and demands. At stake in the essay is a particular magazine for families of children with a particular medical condition, and a particular invitation to an understanding of risk that magazine debatably offered one woman. One has little access to her reading or its moment: here, part of what I do is to attend to other invitations that clutter a possible telling of all this as a story.
2 See Durkheim; Durkheim and Tarde; Turner. Also see Latour.
3 If one were to adopt the group-grid analysis of Mary Douglas and Aaron Wildavsky from *Risk and Culture*, one might argue that the emergence of a biosociality of spina bifida familialism, here through the act of identification through reading, moves the woman from low-group to high-group orientation but at the same time, and given the capacity of patients-rights groups to challenge the established hierarchies of medicine, state regulation, and what we might call the established pharmaceutical order, moves her from a high-grid to a low-grid orientation. In these authors' much-discussed two-by-two table, the move is therefore from the upper-left position of the isolated subordinate to the lower-right position of the egalitarian enclave. Such a move would offer one rationale for the apparent shift that the trial would diagetically reveal in her relation to the risk-laden, from acceptance of and dependence on God's will to the challenging of big pharma.
4 The "global" website (www.abbott.com, downloaded December 20, 2016) addresses the variability of the pharmaceutical risk its products engender internationally (given differential regulation country by country), what Adriana Petryna terms ethical variability, by displacing this variability onto the media of different country-specific website links. Thus as one attempts to navigate the jump from the listing of "global sites" (www.abbott.com/global-sites.html) to, say, the site for India (www.abbott.in), one first receives the following alert:

  > Please be aware that the website you have requested is intended for the residents of a particular country or countries, as noted on that site. As a result, the site may contain information on pharmaceuticals, medical devices and other products or uses of those products that are not approved in other countries or regions.

  Of note, a medium is presumptively defined as having an "intended" addressee: to read the wrong medium is to enter into a culpable condition of self-injury.

5 Galanter frequently cites Sally Falk Moore, who formulated a broader critique of the American return to culture under Clifford Geertz and other variants of totalization (see Moore).
6 The inadmissibility of God's grace as the trial proceeded, preventing a literal *deus ex machina* that might have rescued the legitimacy of the woman's discovery of injury, cannot be explained by a rendering of the law as secular. As the editors Bishnupriya Ghosh and Bhaskar Sarkar remind me, questions of risk and injury are densely bound up across multiple universes of law with the question of divine agency: in particular, one confronts the familiar problem of Acts of God. Though the challenge these raise for an engagement with the secularization of risk—as this emerges in the unfolding of the case through an act of private reading—lies beyond the scope of this essay, one might note the formula *actus dei neminifacit injuriam*, that the law holds no one responsible for Acts of God (Hall 229). In this sense, the divine enables something like a membrane, enclosing what one might term secular injury as a space for the discovery of culpability, beyond which the distinction between culpable and blameless injury is incoherent. I find I am called, in reflecting on the proceedings here, to render God (and the classical figure of Nature taken in histories of law to precede God) not as an exception to a secular grammar of risk and due diligence (as in the Roman figure of *vis maior*), but as its founding condition and encompassment. That is, the ground of experience, and of its reason, for the woman is the certitude of eventfulness as divine. Within that certitude, a space opens up, a secular space, through the act of reading, within which another and additional account of injury becomes legible.
7 Not all readers will share the time or space of immersive television nor the particular conditions for possession by the set. And yet the sense of being pulled through the physical object of a medium into the other worlds that it encompasses is not specific to television.
8 The incitement to narrate one's jury duty "experience," as in my own case, appears to be strong. A frequent theme is the way the juror must bring her or himself to a decision, affirming the law's best intent, through (as opposed to in spite of) the failures of the trial, the law, and oneself. See for example, Powers.
9 I take the wording from www.justia.com/trials-litigation/docs/caci/400/455.html, downloaded December 17, 2016.

Works Cited

Abel, Richard. "How Marc Galanter Became Marc Galanter." *DePaul Law Review*, vol. 62, no. 2, Winter 2013, pp. 555–570.

Augé, Marc. *Non-Places: An Introduction to Supermodernity*. Translated by John Howe. Verso, 2008 [1995].

Austin, J.L. "A Plea for Excuses: The Presidential Address." *Proceedings of the Aristotelian Society*, vol. 57, 1956–1957, pp. 1–30.

Bunzl, Matti "Franz Boas and the Humboldtian Tradition: From *Volksgeist* and *Nationalcharakter* to an Anthropological Concept of Culture." *Volksgeist as Method and Ethic: Essays on Boasian Ethnography and the German Anthropological Tradition* (History of Anthropology), vol. 1, edited by George W. Stocking, Jr. U of Wisconsin P, 1996, pp. 17–78.

Cohen, Lawrence. "Foreign Operations: Reflections on Clinical Mobility in Indian Film and Beyond." *Critical Mobilities*, edited by Ola Söderström, Didier Ruedin, Shalini Randeria, Gianni D'Amato, and Francesco Panese. Routledge, 2013.

Collier, Stephen J. and Aihwa Ong. "Global Assemblages, Anthropological Problems." *Global Assemblages: Technology, Politics, and Ethics as Anthropological Problems*, edited by Aihwa Ong and Stephen J. Collier. Blackwell, 2005, pp. 3–21.

Deleuze, Gilles and Félix Guattari. *A Thousand Plateaus: Capitalism and Schizophrenia*. Translated by Brian Massumi. U of Minnesota P, 1987 [1980].

Douglas, Mary and Aaron Wildavsky. *Risk and Culture: An Essay on the Selection of Technological and Environmental Dangers*. U of California P, 1982.

Durkheim, Émile. *Elementary Forms of the Religious Life*. Translated by Karen E. Fields. Free Press, 1995 [1912].

Durkheim, Émile and Gabriel Tarde. "The Debate." Additional text by Louise Salmon, edited by Eduardo Viana Vargas, Bruno Latour, Bruno Karsenti, and Frédérique Aït-Touati. Translated by Amaleena Damlé and Matei Candea, 2008 [1893–1903], www.bruno-latour.fr/sites/default/files/downloads/TARDE-DURKHEIM-GB.pdf. Accessed December 20, 2016.

Evans-Pritchard, E.E. *Witchcraft, Oracles, and Magic among the Azande*. Clarendon Press, 1937.

Fabian, Johannes. *Time and the Other: How Anthropology Makes Its Object*. Columbia UP, 1983.

Galanter, Marc. "The Vanishing Trial: An Examination of Trials and Related Matters in Federal and State Courts." *Journal of Empirical Legal Studies*, vol. 1, no. 3, November 2004, pp. 459–570.

Galanter, Marc. "When Legal Worlds Collide: Reflections on Bhopal, the Good Lawyer, and the American Law School." *Journal of Legal Education*, vol. 36, no. 3, September 1986, pp. 292–310.

Galanter, Marc. "Why the 'Haves' Come Out Ahead: Speculations on the Limits of Legal Change." *Law and Society Review*, vol. 9, no. 1, Autumn 1974, pp. 95–160.

Gupta, Akhil and James Ferguson. "Discipline and Practice: 'The Field' as Site, Method, and Location in Anthropology." *Anthropological Locations: Boundaries and Grounds of a Field Science*, edited by Akhil Gupta and James Ferguson. U of California P, 1997, pp. 1–46.

Hall, C.G. "An Unsearchable Providence: The Lawyer's Concept of Act of God." *Oxford Journal of Legal Studies*, vol. 13, no. 2, 1993, pp. 227–248.

Laqueur, Thomas W. *Solitary Sex: A Cultural History of Masturbation*. Zone, 2003.

Latour, Bruno. *Reassembling the Social: An Introduction to Actor-Network Theory*. Oxford UP, 2005.

Marcus, George E. and Michael M.J. Fischer *Anthropology as Cultural Critique: An Experimental Moment in the Human Sciences*. U of Chicago P, 1986.

McCormack, Tracy Walters and Christopher J. Bodnar. "Honesty Is the Best Policy: It's Time to Disclose Lack of Jury Trial Experience." *The University of Texas School of Law, Public Law and Legal Theory Research Paper Series*, vol. 151, 2009.

Moore, Sally Falk. *Law as Process: An Anthropological Approach*. Routledge & Kegan Paul, 1978.

Petryna, Adriana. "Ethical Variability: Drug Development and Globalizing Clinical Trials." *American Ethnologist*, vol. 32, no. 2, 2005, pp. 183–197.

Powers, Scott. "Jury Duty: Tension, Division, Debate and Finally Agreement." *Orlando Sentinel*, June 16, 2015, www.orlandosentinel.com/opinion/os-ed-powers-jury-duty-20150615-story.html. Accessed January 2, 2017.

Rabinow, Paul. "Artificiality and Enlightenment: From Sociobiology to Biosociality." *Essays on the Anthropology of Reason*. Princeton UP, 1996, pp. 91–111.

Said, Edward. *Orientalism*. Pantheon, 1978.

Stewart, Kathleen. "Atmospheric Attunements." *Environment and Planning D: Society and Space*, vol. 29, no. 3, 2011, pp. 445–453.

Stocking, George W., Jr. "Franz Boas and the Culture Concept in Historical Perspective." *American Anthropologist*, vol. 68, no. 4, August 1966, pp. 867–882.

Stocking, George W., Jr. "The Ethnographer's Magic: Fieldwork in British Anthropology from Tylor to Malinowski." *Observers Observed: Essays on Ethnographic Fieldwork*, History of Anthropology, volume 1, edited by George W. Stocking, Jr. U of Wisconsin P, 1983, pp. 70–120.

Turner, Victor W. *The Ritual Process: Structure and Anti-Structure*. Aldine, 1969.

Vidal, Gore. *Myron*. Random House, 1974.

Young, William G. "Vanishing Trials, Vanishing Juries, Vanishing Constitution." *Suffolk University Law Review*, XL, vol. 1, 2006, pp. 67–94.

27

CRUISING RISK, SURVIVING DESIRE

Daren Fowler

In the summer of 1962, in Mansfield, Ohio, police began a two-month sting operation of an underground park restroom. After installing a one-way mirror on the restroom closet, police officers hid with a film camera to record any man who, according to the *Mansfield News-Journal*, "remained for long periods of time or acted in an abnormal manner" (Gaynor). On August 22, 1962, police arrested 17 men aged between 22 and 58, with the local paper publishing their names and addresses. Arrests continued throughout 1963 with at least 38 men charged and some 30 more identified (Biber and Dalton 244). All those charged were sent to Lima State Hospital for a 60-day psychiatric observation, as required by Ohio's sodomy laws, before at least 31 were convicted and sentenced from one to 20 years in prison ("9 Ordered to Lima"; Biber and Dalton).[1]

The now infamous Mansfield sting operation is one of many such moments in a long and full history of social fears and state violations of nonnormative sexualities, both public and private, real and assumed, but they speak to a fundamental intimacy between queerness, its desires, and risk. Risk regiments and orients sexuality and desire to "protect" and "sustain" the normative expectations of a culture (Foucault, *The Use of Pleasure* 117–118). The state produces impossibilities for queerness to contain and manage its "social contagion," to halt the paranoid fear of homosexuals "seeking continually to recruit others, particularly the youth, into their own deviate cult" (Jones 9). This fear drove a Central Intelligence Agency (CIA) memo from 1979 entitled "Homosexual Investigations." The memo provides suggestions and guidelines for ferreting out any secret homosexuals in the CIA for immediate expulsion. The memo is filled with terrifying, yet fascinating assumptions, ignorance, and contradictions made common, though not new, during the Cold War. Homosexuality is compared consistently to Communism within memos and reports since the 1950s, with both attached to drug use and "mental inadequacies." The connection to Communism is more than the suspicious, manipulative, and secretive assumed-nature of both Communism and homosexuality, but that homosexuals were seen as easy targets for Communist blackmail. As seen in a 1950 report to the U.S. Senate that would be the beginning of a series of reports used by Joseph McCarthy and others during the Red Scare, homosexuality was a risk to the state as a corrupting, contagious violation of decency and humanity; a morally and psychologically unstable force; and an internal threat to American global power and influence (U.S. Cong. Senate 3–5). "The Lavender Scare," a secondary focus of the larger Second Red Scare of the 1940s and 1950s, turned on paranoias and anxieties truly felt and performed as cover for social and political power (see Foertsch; Johnson).

The accumulation, projection, and production of fear and regimentation speak to the continual pointing to queerness by the state. As Michel Foucault argues in *The History of Sexuality*, the labor of repressing sexuality belies the immense investment in keeping sexual risk ever present (23).

The obsessive "policing of sexuality," in particularly of queerness, that McCarthy, the CIA, and Mansfield Police performed speaks to Lee Edelman's argument in his queer nihilistic opus, *No Future: Queer Theory and the Death Drive*, that queerness functions as the paradoxical vitalizing violation of heteronormativity. Edelman attempts to confront the continual presence of queerness in heterosexist rhetoric and the ways it becomes a perpetual threat that can never be resolved. Returning once more to the Mansfield Police, they chose to spy and record as opposed to raiding the restroom because of the danger of falsely accusing. However, more fundamentally, they chose not to arrest the men after they left the tearoom. Instead, they collected their information for a future spectacle. As Eve Sedgwick argues, the closet functions on the axis between "the closet viewed, the *spectacle of the closet*," and "the closet inhabited, the *viewpoint of the closet*" (222–223). The spectacle of the closet arrives both in the political potential and play of queerness performing within and beyond its containment, and in the violence inflicted on and through those that dare to take up space not given to them. The police used these excesses and masses of the closet to stage an *event*, a purposeful making-visible of a hidden queer sexuality to govern and maintain but also to reinforce the power and threat of norms (Berlant 5). That is, the police used the spectacular event of outing dozens of men to contain queerness while simultaneously mythologizing it as *the* danger and evil— its secret depravities tearing at the fabric of decent society.

Inspired by the carceral violence of the Mansfield Police sting and the much older history of queer regimentation, independent queer video game developer Robert Yang designed *The Tearoom* (2017), a cruising simulator set in a roadside restroom in 1962 Mansfield, Ohio. While the game reproduces the history of Mansfield, the labor and play of cruising, and the survival of state violence by queer people, it was also Yang's most explicit challenge to his own position within this history of moral panic. Yang is among the most banned video game developers on Twitch, a live video-streaming website ("Why I am"). Primarily focused on video games and video game culture (i.e., e-sports, speed runs, video game talk shows, and personal streams of video game playthroughs, or "Let's Plays"), Twitch ranks as the largest streaming service for video games, and among the most visited websites globally, reporting over 15 million unique daily viewers and two million unique monthly broadcasters producing content in 2017 (Perez). Of Yang's games on Twitch's incomplete list of prohibited games, Yang has the player make the best dick pic for a dating app that would then be uploaded to a Tumblr page (*Cobra Club*), help rinse a man in a gym shower (*Rinse and Repeat*), negotiate and perform consensual spanking (*Hurt Me Plenty*), erotically change a queer car's gears (*Stick Shift*), and help a "hunk" eat a popsicle (*Succulent*) ("List of Prohibited Games").[2] In his less sexual games, Yang has turned toward trauma and divorce (*Handle with Care*) and breakups during stargazes (*Polaris*). Yang's games, attempting to coopt the aesthetic of AAA games (major studio games with large production and marketing cost, the "blockbusters" of video games), circulate around the many facets of queer intimacy, and unlike AAA games, Yang centers the sexual and messy idiosyncrasies of queerness and its intimacies (Yang, "Radiator 2").

Yang's banning, as he has narrated in his writing, turns on the erotic nature of some of his games, but this fails to account for the ways similar, if not more explicit, sex and sexuality is allowed in other more heterosexual games, especially AAA games. Further, the rationale for any banning on Twitch is merely speculative. Developers are not notified when their games are banned, nor is an explanation given for their banning. As Yang writes:

> I have no idea, and that's the biggest problem: Twitch never says anything. No e-mail, no notification, no rationale, no reason, no pity tweet. Am I just supposed to keep refreshing the ban list page to see if they banned me, for every single game I make, forever?
>
> *("Why I am")*

Coupled with the incomplete list of banned games, Twitch leaves developers like Yang guessing as to what the fundamental issue is, and if they are interested in not being banned, unable to efficiently make changes that could make their games "appropriate" for Twitch. The vagueness and lack of transparency reads as quite purposeful. By keeping their guidelines open and malleable, Twitch can perform investment in "protecting" consumers from "inappropriate" content while making unstated exceptions for major studio games that drive much of Twitch's content.

In describing sexual content in games, Twitch lists "nudity and sexually explicit content or activities" in line with "content or activities that threaten or promote sexual violence and exploitation" in particular games, centering child exploitation ("Community Guidelines"). While *Cobra Club* makes use of images of penises, Yang's other explicitly banned games are erotic but not sexually explicit. Washing a man's chest in *Rinse and Repeat* becomes more threatening than two characters, with bodies exposed, fucking on a stuffed unicorn in *Witcher 3*, as well as the game mechanic that allows the player to initiate a sex scene with any sex worker in the game; and consensually spanking another is made equivalent to *Suck My Dick or Die!*, a "rape-themed" game whose gameplay is as its title states. In their banning, Twitch places Yang's games of queer intimacy alongside sexually explicit games about masculinist rape fantasies, explicit pornography, and child exploitation.[3] While I want to avoid challenging one moralistic argument with another, situating Yang's games within this definition, as Twitch does, narrates queer intimacy as inherently pornographic and socially deplorable—and pointedly continues the longstanding narrative of queerness as pedophilic. Twitch's guidelines and their banning of Yang's games participate in a history of moral panic around queerness. This also give context and propulsion for Yang's *The Tearoom*, a game that began as a response to the Yang's continual banning and grew into a larger historical reflection on queerness and the violence used to stop it.[4]

Inspired in part by Laud Humphreys's seminal and controversial ethnography, *Tearoom Trade: Impersonal Sex in Public Spaces* (1970), and William E. Jones's film *Tearoom* (2007), a "found documentary" of the Mansfield Police sting, Yang's *The Tearoom* uses a series of glances and negotiations to simulate the play, desire, and risk of cruising for male-on-male anonymous public sex.[5] The majority of the game takes place at the Hinsdale, the "Cadillac of urinals," with the player staring into its pristineness with an endlessly full bladder (Yang, "The Tearoom"). When another man enters the restroom, the player must decide how they want to engage. If they turn and look immediately, the man might get spooked and leave. If the player waits too long before turning—especially if they ignore the coughs and other attempts to get their attention—the other man will give up and leave. The player cannot hold the gaze too long either, or the other man will never reciprocate. What becomes clear during the first encounter is learning when to look and for how long. If the player succeeds in negotiating an encounter, the man walks over with his gun-dick hanging out. A timer appears on the screen as the playable character kneels in front of the flaccid gun-dick. Moving the mouse (visualized as a tongue) over the highlighted parts of the gun-dick will begin filling the magazine and arousing the gun-dick. Once full and erect, marked by changing from flesh-colored to gunmetal black, the gun-dick fires off its torrent of gun oil, creaming the player's face. A successfully unloaded gun-dick will be archived in the player's starting stall, flaccidly hanging from gloryholes. If the player fails to finish loading the magazine, the police will arrive, which will reset any progress made in collecting all the gun-dicks. In a distressingly erotic literalizing of masculinist penis-as-weapon metaphors, Yang puts the violent threat against queer life as the centerpiece of the erotic exchange of the game, and thus of queer play. To succeed, to find erotic play and relation, is to put a gun to your face. And yet, the gun-dick is also just an absurdly humorous visual gag, that speaks to the erotic thrill of public anonymous sex. That is, the gun-dick functions simultaneously as threat and desire, a playful fluidity that propels the critical thought of *The Tearoom* (Figure 27.1).[6]

The Tearoom continues the concerns that have played throughout Yang's career, but in turning to cruising, Yang offers a meditation on a fundamental aspect of queer intimacy—the negotiation of desire and risk. In its more clinical definitions, cruising is the search for public or semi-public sex. "Tearooms," or the British counterpart "cottages," are public restrooms where male cruising

Figure 27.1 Player-controlled tongue licking gun-dick to full magazine from Robert Yang, *The Tearoom*, 2017, video game

occurs. Whether it takes place in a public restroom, bathhouse, or park, cruising is a complicated and knowing process of signs, gestures, glances, and pauses—a kinesthetic desiring knowledge of space, another, and one's self.[7] Cruising requires bodies lingering in spaces meant to be moved through, and eyes staring for longer than appropriate on places that are private, even in their revealing—a repeating series of subtle gestures and glances, a bodily Morse code that propositions those in the know and reads as odd but potentially inoffensive to those on the outside. Awareness and control over one's body and a distant intimacy with the particularities of others and of the physical space allow cruising for sex to occur while also attempting to keep those participating safe from outsiders.

Before moving forward, it is important to pause on the use of cruising to consider queerness. José Esteban Muñoz cautions against mythologizing the queer potentials of cruising (*Cruising Utopia* 18). Cruising can easily become a vague marker of queer resistance, an eruptive political force, simply through two men having sex in public. Certainly, a dangerous and sometimes emotionally and physically necessary act, an unreflective use of (gay male) cruising can easily lead to the universalizing of queerness as gay men, and usually by extension, white, as well as privilege sex as the central orientation of queer politics, identity, and aesthetics. When considering a vibrant text such as Yang's *The Tearoom*, gay male cruising will necessarily be centered as the game, and Yang's works more generally, move around gay male desire. The aesthetic and affective work of these texts and the others considered here will focus on men who have sex with men; however, inspired by Muñoz's critical use of cruising as an aesthetic pedagogical tool of relation and history, where we "carefully cruis[e] for the varied potentialities that may abound," I wish to argue for using cruising not as a utopic vision of queer resistance but as a productive lens on the form and labor of queerness (Muñoz *Cruising Utopia* 18). Cruising, in its aesthetic multiplicity, centers the negotiation of risk and desire in the dangerous and playful tensions around visibility/invisibility, public/private, intimacy/anonymity, past/future. In theorizing queerness through the material labor of cruising (for instance, intimacy of anonymity, management of spatial knowledge, and relationality through kinesthetic feeling) can provide a valuable methodology of queer life, survival, and intimacy.

To begin working through this queer play of risk and desire, I turn to an early anecdote from Humphreys's *Tearoom Trade*—an ethnography set in the 1960s American Midwest—which centers on why men participate in public sex. A participant in Humphreys's study told a story of devotion to a favored tearoom:

> That was the greatest place in the park. Do you know what my roommate did last Christmas, after they tore the place down? He took a wreath, sprayed it with black paint, and laid it on top of the snow—right where the corner stall had stood ... he was really broken up!
>
> *(14)*

Humphreys uses this, and other stories of spatial devotion, as markers of displaced sentimentality. It is the one place that Humphreys allows emotional intimacy into the play of public sex. In part, this devotion comes from the process of finding and maintaining a tearoom—a production of a spatial knowledge. Public restrooms were studied for their location, condition, and frequency of use. Being underground meant that windows would be at feet level outside, allowing those inside to easily see someone coming while also making it difficult to see in from the outside. Being underground also meant stairs were needed. Metal stairs are louder, making it easier to hear if someone was coming. A restroom having graffiti would imply that teens—or "toughs"—may use the area and potentially harass those in the tearoom. Being in a public park could be good and bad. They were not frequented during weekday afternoons, a prime time for sex, and some restrooms were far enough away from the park entrances to be rarely used. However, kids are more likely at parks, and park security make rounds, sometimes on a schedule and sometimes not. Tearoom players would also make superficial changes to the restrooms, such as breaking a window to see and hear better outside or adjusting the door to creak (Humphreys 7–9). The vulnerability management of tearooms produced an intimate knowledge of a tearoom's material structure. The physical labor of making a restroom into a tearoom produced both a profound attunement to the spatial logic and rhythm of the restroom, and for Humphreys, makes the devotion found in the above anecdote "the normative response to the demand for privacy without involvement" (14). The affective attachment to the physical space of tearooms Humphreys found in the stories of the men he studied oriented his terming public sex acts "impersonal." That is, tearooms necessitate a displacement of desire, intimacy, and attachment onto the physical structure of the tearoom as a response to the nature of cruising.

The sex acts that Humphreys witnessed as a disguised observer were initiated in silence using gesture, glances, and an intuited knowledge of rules and roles. The sex itself was also lacking expected forms of emotional intimacy—eye contact, touching beyond the bare minimum, or speaking—instead, the sex was quick and almost mechanical, a rote process for getting off, and always on the verge of being cut short (12–14). Impersonality also functions as an interpretation of what was necessitated by the dangerous realities of cruising public restrooms where "straights" could arrive to disrupt the play and potentially out or physically harm the tearoom players.[8] Being caught meant arrest or attack—likely both. Arrest meant being publicly known as a deviant, effectively ending life as was known prior. This risk required the sex to be distant and the players to be anonymous and more aware of their surroundings than those they were with. Everyone involved had to be able to return to performing the "normal" functions of a restroom quickly should someone arrive and accept that the sex would rarely begin again. Humphreys's reading of the process and act of public sex hinged on a lack of human investment beyond the immediate sexual moment with a simultaneous hyper-investment in spatial surroundings for protection.

What Humphreys saw in the above anecdote of spatial devotion was the affective energy of sex projected away from the desiring body onto the structure that housed, protected, and enabled the potential for sex. It was a demonstration of the impersonal nature of public sex. Yang's game, while leaving behind the devotional blackened wreath, recreates the need for an intimate knowledge of space and bodies fundamental to tearoom play. As discussed above, in *The Tearoom*, the player, like those in the real tearooms, never knows when the encounter could be ended by the arrival of a "straight" or a cop, and thus must work quickly but not haphazardly. Speed is important in order to not waste time negotiating the encounter or in licking the gun-dick's erogenous zones for while some magazines only require six bullets, others need 30 or more. However, if the player focuses solely on the gun-dick's arousal and fails to be conscious of their surroundings, a cop can arrive and surprise the tearoom players. In *The Tearoom*, the play of public sex requires a consciousness of the erotic play of sex and the spatial threat of the public. This duel focus produces a frenetic, erotic, and anxious play. A gun-dick hangs before you, a weapon of desire and death, its firing can get you off but can also get you outed. The timer and the arrival of police that ends the round, and takes your collected gun-dicks, pushes the player more through threat and danger than just getting off.

This sort of play has a name in video games: predation play. These games purposefully put the player in impossible and threatening situations with hordes of enemies or overpowered bosses to challenge the player (Bertozzi 431). Critical to horror and shooting games, predation play attempts to overwhelm the player, producing stress and anxiety as the motivating energy of play (Perron). Predation games build on what Isabel Pinedo calls "recreational terror": the desire to be terrified, where stress becomes pleasure (106). Importantly for predation play, players are expected to fail. The gameplay is meant to push the player to the limit and demand they repeat, learn, and adapt (Bertozzi 431). Much like the tearoom players in Humphreys's study, players being hunted must come to learn the particularities of space and its inevitable threats to better maneuver and survive. Using predation play, what Yang's game makes central is that the desire to get another off must be managed with the threat of the state. The player can end any encounter should the police pull up or the player fears they won't finish in time, making every encounter potentially partial and oriented outwards. And this remains the critical distinction between *The Tearoom* and other predation play games, the predator remains a *potential* threat as opposed to an overwhelming present force. The omnipresent potentiality of violence—be it the state or another restroom user—restrains and suffocates tearoom play, and by extension queer desire and life. This shifts the primary mode for creating the feeling of risk and danger from movement through enemies to the management of space and time. It subsequently forces the player to be prepared to end any encounter, any progress, on their own—a self-collapsing of desire. Thus, by using predation play, *The Tearoom* positions queer intimacy (and life) as always partial, dangerous, and anxious—bound up in the necessary and precarious knowledge and management of space and in the critical contradictory reality that the fear and stress of risk drives the desire of play. That is, queerness via cruising can be understood as both a maneuvering through violent moral panic and a playful use of threat as arousing desire.

While Humphreys's conception of risk as desire for tearooms is a critical reference point for Yang's *The Tearoom*, the purpose of parsing the play between risk and desire through Humphreys arises from the fundamental role such a framing has played in the history of queer stories, anecdotal and artistic. Tim Dean argues in *Unlimited Intimacy: Reflection on the Subculture of Barebacking* (2009) that cruising, while still impersonal, offers access to a risky intimacy; that is, an intimacy built on trusting strangers, trusting the unknown. Cruising, according to Dean, "involve[s] a profound exposure to the other and thus an experience of vulnerability and trust with complete strangers" (175). As seen in Humphreys, cruising across its forms makes use of the protection and intimacy of anonymous play. The lack of knowing the other limits the ability to "name names," but also constructs a play of intimacy liberated from the normative requirements of familial and social structures. Cruising, as performed in queerness, asks strangers to love each other while staying strangers, an ethics of relation unburdened from the politics of connection and community. Removed from those regimented formations and in continuation of Leo Bersani's anti-social project of self-shattering *jouissance*, Dean advocates for intimacy across the sameness of desire that cruising makes possible (22–25). Dean demonstrates that the impersonal sex of cruising does not need to be bound to heterosexuality, a move critical to Humphreys's work on tearooms, to conceptualize how risk transforms into desire. Similar uses of risk as desire abound in Samuel Delany's memoirs, be it the erotic abjections of porn theaters in a transiting New York (*Times Square Red, Time Square Blue*, 1999), or the monochromatic desires of bathhouses (*The Motion of Light in Water*, 1988); a long history of queer readings of Proust's temporal, narcissistic peacocking as forms of the spectacular closet for Eve Sedgwick (*Epistemology of the Closet*, 1990) or as catastrophic ruptures of the self where desire becomes an obsessive fascination in difference for Bersani (*Homos*, 1995); and any review of the now-closed Craigslist personals section where an unending collection of anonymous desires, new gloryhole locations, and hoped for sexual repetitions show the desires for risky public play between men (Shadel 2018). While these are just a small fraction of works on queer desires for cruising's threat, what speaks across them is a view of cruising as a critical tool of queer desire making and its comingling with risk.

Director Joe Gage's 2004 gay porn epic *Mens Room: Bakersfield Station* offers the most erotic and playful example of queer risk transmuted into desire. Also set in an unnamed Midwestern town, *Mens Room* follows a young man (Danny Vox) returning home for the first time in years.[9] An opening narration marvels at how little has changed as our protagonist enters the local bus station to use the restroom. *Mens Room*'s restroom performs a deconstruction of the already unstable distinction of public and private in the restroom. Troughs stand on one wall, and a few stalls stand on the another. An unmanned shoe shining station lingers by the entrance's large and open staircase. The middle of the restroom contains two rows of unenclosed toilets that face toward the outer walls. Except for the stalls, there is no space for privacy or cover; the assumption of privacy in the public is shown to be a performative and erotic lie. When Danny Vox's character enters the empty restroom, he moves to the troughs, and the film performs its most common shot: a medium closeup of a penis waiting—to piss, to be sucked, to fuck, to cum. As Vox attempts to empty his always full bladder, two men enter (Kent Larson and Matt Major). They stand at opposite exposed toilets in the center of the room. The camera lingers on each man, erotically caressing them as they unzip their pants, pull out their dicks, and like Vox, begin releasing their endless piss. After minutes of roaming their bodies, the film cuts to over Major's shoulder to see Vox attempting to covertly gaze at Larson and Major. Caught by Larson, Vox turns back to his pissing. The film begins once more to cut back and forth across all three men and their exposed, pissing dicks. In a form that will define Gage's film, the montage of frozen bodies, faces, and dicks stretches out for minutes. The viewer, and Vox, anxiously wait to see what will happen next. The montage, like a Leone standoff or an Eisensteinian struggle, elongates time, amplifying both the potential threat and the potential release. When Larson and Major finally move to confront Vox, the threat continues to linger, the type of pornography about to be revealed. Major touches Vox's shoulder before pushing him down. Vox yields and moves to his knees. The propositioning glance, and the fantasy it holds, become fulfilled in the consensual rewriting of the public and exposed restroom into an intimate and pseudo-private tearoom of queer sexual desire.

Each new scene begins this same way: one or more men enter the restroom causing those mid-thrust and -suck to stop and look. With close-ups of affectless faces alongside spit- and lube-soaked dicks and asses, we see each man waiting for the new arrivals to either join the play or puncture the erotic bubble. These montages build desire and arousal through waiting and lingering in space. Each cut points to sexual encounters waiting to resume and to fantasized possibilities should the new men join, while simultaneously acknowledging that those encounters, imagined and paused, are precariously waiting to be destroyed and to irrevocably change the lives and futures of those involved (Figure 27.2). This three-hour epic deploys the paradoxical potential of the cut as an aesthetic rupturing, connecting, lingering play that affectively heightens the "aphrodisiacal effect of danger" (Humphreys 151). Like the erotic play of space, temporality, and risk recounted by Humphreys and coded by Yang, *Mens Room* displaces the queer desire of public sex onto space and the looming affect of risk.

To varying degrees, these real and fictional texts turn on the pleasurable play of risk and desire, producing those risks in the movement through the public to the pseudo-private. As Lauren Berlant

Figure 27.2 The erotic aestheticization of risk in *Mens Room: Bakersfield Station*, directed by Joe Gage, Titan Media, 2004

and Michael Warner have argued, it is through the cultivation of distinct spaces of public and private that the liberal subject comes to being. The reality of sodomy laws stretching the public into the private for queerness denies queerness access to liberal notions of subjectivity and citizenry (554). This normative prohibition applied almost exclusively to same-sex desires justified the violation of liberal devotion to the private sphere of the individual. Queerness, denied a private, must therefore move through and desire in the public. Like the normatively-required enunciation of coming out that produces a recording of queer people in Mansfield, Ohio, queer desires cannot exist safely or comfortably in the private without first being negotiated in the public (Cante and Restivo 143). Ultimately, queerness exists in the paradoxical position of having to be simultaneously visible and invisible, present and absent (Sedgwick 70, 90). It is a violation of normality that must be eradicated but is always present as a regulating threat to others that marks the limits of the acceptable and appropriate—the contouring risk of normativity (Edelman 25).

In response to the paradoxes produced for queerness, Berlant and Warner see queerness creating "kinds of intimacy that bear no necessary relation to the domestic space, to kinship, to the couple form, to property, or to the nation" (558). Or more pointedly, as Rich Cante and Angelo Restivo parse in their study of all-male pornography, queerness intrudes forms of the private into the public, remaking the normative streets into abnormal zones of queer desire (153). The immense labor Humphreys describes in the scouting and making of tearooms reorients the public space of the restroom into a queer counterpublic of precarious privacy. The production of roles and rules in the tearoom further maintains the access to desiring in public and allows for the rapid deconstruction of that counterpublic by the players to protect themselves and the space they have remade. In being forced into paradoxical positions of visibility and invisibility, presence and absence, forming and destroying, queerness produces the matter necessary for their survival—a transmutation of the world for the needs of queer life and desire. "Put simply, things can change or be made to change through queer labor" (Galt 96).

Despite the admittedly transformational work at play in Humphreys, Gage, and Dean, I am uneased by the conclusion of queer desire being its transmutation into or even consumption by risk. This relation of risk as desire in queerness requires a flattening of not only desire, but the lived realities of risk. While pleasurable, and even erotically joyful in the case of *Mens Room*, such forms must exist outside of history, or at the very least, minimize or marginalize queer history, a critical move Humphreys performs in centering heterosexuality for his study. In the Mansfield Police sting footage, found and presented by experimental filmmaker William E. Jones for his found documentary *Tearoom*, such a politics, aesthetics, and ethics becomes untenable. Presented with only a few minor edits from Jones, *Tearoom* gives an image to what Humphreys recounts, and while affirming the impersonal mood, undermines the form of risk and desire Humphreys claims.

The men in the footage are a different kind of affectless from *Mens Room*, a tableau that renders the future inaccessible in the face of present erotic threat. The men seen in *Tearoom* do not have a flat affect but an empty one. They stare blankly and move slowly; their touch is frantic not from desire or thrill but fear (Figure 27.3). While glances dominate the negotiation stage, the eyes rarely meet again once the sex starts. The impersonality Humphreys reads is present in *Tearoom*, but the desiring energy of risk is not. Like Gage's film, the footage from Mansfield is fractured and heavily cut. The police only filmed when suspicious or illegal activity occurred. Whenever someone uninvolved arrived, the police would turn off the camera just as the men having sex would quickly and with precision return to "properly" using the restroom. The rapid cuts, as opposed to stretching and heightening sexual encounters, breaks and ends them. What had begun in one shot cannot find its completion. In each cut is the fact of impending arrest and outing, not the playful, intimate rupture of *Mens Room*. Humphreys does account for these destructive ruptures and affectless encounters in defining impersonal sex. And so, the encounters on display can go to validate Humphreys's reading as they raise the question of why someone would take the risk of public male-on-male sex when its desirability is not self-evident. Such a reading, however, requires a denial of queer desire beyond sex. Humphreys demands a rationale for tearoom play, and while he acknowledges and makes use of gay male culture and language, Humphreys is unwilling to consider, even for heterosexual men, that the labor of tearoom play was for the access to connection, intimacy, and acknowledgment. Jones's *Tearoom* returns us to desire as risk, posing that the potentials of tearoom sex may lie beyond sex and toward intimacy and relation. Despite the historical value of Humphreys work, the decision to center heterosexuality minimizes, if not erases, the historical violence against queer people *as* queer—a critical reality driving the risk of tearooms.

Figure 27.3 The distancing glances and affects that blur the line between erotic caution and desperate fear from William E. Jones, *Tearoom*, 2007, film

Yang too destabilizes these assumptions of risk as desire. As discussed above, *The Tearoom* makes use of risk motivating and propelling the desire and play of the game. However, if played long enough, the player will encounter a hidden threat in the game: undercover police. When a potential sex partner comes in, the player can figure out quickly if they are there just to piss or to get off. An undercover cop, however, will play the game of coughing, pissing, waiting, and glancing. They perform the desiring negotiation. The only difference comes in eagerness. A cop will take less back and forth. Their desiring meter will increase faster and diminish slower than a regular john wanting to get off. Once revealed, this mechanic shifts the game's world and structure. The game was always concerned with the play of risk and desire, but the undercover cop introduces a different form of risk, a risk that forces a reconsideration of the game and the productive labor of the stranger; demanding the player become more suspicious, more anxious. The game slows down considerably as the player uses more time and effort to interpret the accuracy of the other man's use of cruising codes, and makes the player more willing to choose to end the encounter out of fear of a potential cop. The risk is no longer just displaced onto space, but onto the other men—the very people desired. Each man is simultaneously a source of desire and risk, which was always a truth of the encounter seen with the importance of anonymity but is now translated more fully onto the tearoom community's representative body. The real game in *The Tearoom* is not getting off in public but a careful negotiation of the blurred, not inverted or consumed, boundaries of desire and risk. Yang is not only invested in risk as Humphreys and Gage are, but also in how risk demands a different relation to public desire and the community of strangers that makes up the space of tearooms. The risk that drives the complexity of sexual exchange brings the player into closer intimacy with the bodies and spaces around them. To succeed and for their character to survive, the player must know intensely, personally, bodily, and spatially the form of glances, play of waiting, and norms of anxiety. Whereas the bodily labor of tearoom negotiations provides a rationale for Humphreys's investment in the impersonal, in Yang's deployment of the undercover cop, the kinesthetic labor of glances and nonverbal consent becomes a unique form of intimacy that makes the community of queer desire possible. Cruising, then, necessitates a bodily and affective labor of knowledge and relation that amplifies desire but also provides one of the strongest forms of risk management so that queer intimacy can labor and play. As opposed to cruising being impersonal and individualistic, which underlies theories of risk as desire, Yang's cruising is an intimate relationality between desire, bodies, and history to better negotiate and survive risk—the risk of the tearoom and the risk of queer life.

Yang's game, unlike Humphreys work, explicitly turns on the violent and humiliating history of queerness. His most challenging and productive design decision reflects this: no matter if the player "wins" (collects all eight gun-dicks) or "loses" (gets caught eight times), the outcome is the same. The game always ends with the back wall of the restroom opening to reveal that the police have been recording every encounter, while stills from the Mansfield footage are projected over the urinals, inserting the player's encounters into that same history. Such an ending can produce a sense of nihilistic closure that denies alternative modes forward. And yet, a belief in forward progress also requires an ignorance of history and the present. *The Tearoom* was released amid the unabashed white supremacy of President Donald Trump, record numbers of LGBT youth suicides, and a year that ended the upward trend of LGBT acceptance in the United States—a consistent 17-year increase assumed to be "lasting" only a year prior (Goodman; McKay 24). As every year sees more and more trans women murdered with little concern and the continuation of disproportionally high rates of queer youth homelessness, Yang offers a different problem altogether than anxieties over the future and progress (Durso and Gates; Talusan). Instead of a naïvely utopic faith in solving the puzzle of systemic violence or straightening the paradoxical knots of queerness, Yang shows that queerness, no matter how it moves and plays, will be at risk, but that this risk does not necessitate a rejection of desire and intimacy. As Elizabeth Freeman calls for, *The Tearoom* stages an encounter with queerness though erotically and intimately "negotiating with the past and producing [new] historical knowledge through visceral sensations" (123). These narratives and images of violation and desire contain a painful and humiliating history, but they also contain paradoxical power and erotics. Darieck Scott argues for making use of paradox, of finding a "capacity for action and creation" in the counterintuitive and damning (23, 14). Yang offers a "critical recycling" of history—evidentiary, affective, and gestural—to make a powerful, disidentificatory play. Trauma, stereotypes, and erasures are neither rejected nor taken on as identities but transformed into tools for intimate knowledge for survival (Muñoz *Disidentification* 58). As opposed to risk as desire or desire as risk, *The Tearoom* finds pleasure in the "amoral and perhaps immoral" intimacy of desire and risk that propels so much of queer life (Scott 28). In a historical moment where once again the traumatic past arrives in the present to undo assumed futures, a renewed call for playing with and in history is necessary. In *The Tearoom*, cruising offers a method of gestural play that brings risk and desire into relation, not to replace or overwhelm one with the other, but rather to produce a pleasurable, powerful, paradoxical intimacy that opens a space for reflection, connection, and survival.

Acknowledgments

I am immensely grateful to Georgia State University's *Playtest*, a deep, critical dive into game design and aesthetics organized by Cameron Kunzelman and Jenn Olive and hosted by the Creative Media Industries Institute, for providing me the opportunity to present my then highly speculative thoughts on Robert Yang and *The Tearoom*. The incisive and productive collective labor of those who attended my presentation helped shape what became this essay.

Notes

1 These numbers are treated as estimates here and in the other writings on the Mansfield Police sting because the official records from court documents are incomplete. Most numbers are a combination of court records and newspaper articles from the time.
2 While finishing this publication, Tumblr banned a wide variety of "adult" and "nonadult" content, including the Tumblr page that collected all of the dick pics made in *Cobra Club*, about 100,000 pictures over three years. This alongside Twitch's bans on Yang's games and PayPal cancelling the accounts of anyone who could potentially be associated with sex work (which includes Yang's sex games) speaks to the ever-expanding containment and erasure of sexual difference on the Internet, especially following the passage of SESTA/FOSTA. For more on PayPal and Yang, see his 2016 Game Developers Conference talk: "The Game Industry Needs to Get Laid and Just Chill Already."
3 Masculinist is a term I have added to clarify the reality of what these rape fantasy games center on: the domination and violation of women by and for men.
4 *The Tearoom* has not been added to Twitch's official list of prohibited games. However, as of July 2018, there are no available or recorded streams of *The Tearoom*. The assumption is that it too has failed the internal "quality" and "morality" control of Twitch. This happened simultaneously with numerous positive write ups from video game and mainstream magazines (*Kotaku*, *RockPaperShotgun*, the *Guardian*).
5 I will be referring to Humphreys, Jones, and Yang's similarly titled works throughout. Humphreys's ethnography will always be noted as *Tearoom Trade*. Jones' "found documentary" is simply *Tearoom*, and Yang's game is *The Tearoom*.
6 There is another essay to be written on Yang's use of guns in place of a penis. Continually banned from Twitch, no matter the content and gameplay of his work, Yang wanted to make a game that called attention to the absurdity of Twitch's system. As Yang writes in his artist statement, just by being in his game about state violence against queer people, the gun becomes an inappropriate object and one deserving censorship ("*The Tearoom* as a Record of Risky Business"). That is, *The Tearoom* is maybe the first game banned from Twitch for a gun—an object that is essential to many of the most profitable and streamed video games released every year.
7 This essay centers tearoom sex when parsing the particularities of cruising, which therefore privileges non-verbal consent performed in glances and gestures. When considering cruising in public parks, speaking and touching may be more crucial, and bathhouses may be even more open and intimate in their initiations. These differences, however, do not undermine the fundamental concern of risk and desire that propels cruising as a general form of semi-public sex.

8 "Straight" here does not necessarily refer to sexuality. This is the term from *Tearoom Trade* given to those who are using the restroom without any interest or knowledge of the tearoom. The language, like that of "tough," comes from the tearoom community that Humphreys entered.
9 There is much to be said on the consistent turning to the American Midwest in works on tearooms. What is striking about Gage's works on the Midwest is the erotic desire in the assumed bigotry and the potential for violence from the Midwest's blue collar, westerner whiteness. The risk that lead to the famous deaths of Matthew Shephard and Brandon Teena also leads the erotic fantasies of Gage and so many other gay pornographies. And a fundamental aspect of this will always be its whiteness—a concern lazily gestured to by Humphreys, left absent by Gage, and statistically-coded by Yang. The racial and racist component of this may not be confronted here but remains inescapable and inseparable from the questions and forms at play.

Works Cited

"9 Ordered to Lima: 60-Day Observation Period Provided." *Mansfield News-Journal*, August 23, 1962, p. 1.
Berlant, Lauren. *Cruel Optimism*. Duke UP, 2011.
Berlant, Lauren and Michael Warner. "Sex in Public." *Critical Inquiry*, vol. 24, Winter 1998, pp. 547–566.
Bersani, Leo. *Homos*. Harvard UP, 1996.
Bertozzi, Elena. "The Feeling of Being Hunted: Pleasures and Potentialities of Predation Play." *Games and Culture*, vol. 9, no. 6, 2014, pp. 429–441.
Biber, Katherine and Derek Dalton. "Making Art from Evidence: Secret Sex and Police Surveillance in the Tearoom." *Crime Media Culture*, vol. 5, no. 3, 2009, pp. 243–267.
Cante, Rich and Angelo Restivo. "The Cultural-Aesthetic Specificities of All-Male Moving-Image Pornography." *Porn Studies*, edited by Linda Williams. Duke UP, 2004, pp. 141–166.
"Community Guidelines." *Twitch*, https://help.twitch.tv/customer/portal/articles/983016#GamingContent. Accessed February 10, 2018.
Dean, Tim. *Unlimited Intimacy: Reflections on the Subculture of Barebacking*. U of Chicago P, 2009.
Delany, Samuel. *The Motion of Light in Water: Sex and Science Fiction Writing in the East Village*. Arbor House, 1988.
Delany, Samuel. *Time Square Red, Time Square Blue*. New York UP, 1999.
Durso, Laura E. and Gates, Gary J. *Serving Our Youth: Findings from a National Survey of Service Providers Working with Lesbian, Gay, Bisexual, and Transgender Youth who are Homeless or At Risk of Becoming Homeless*. The Williams Institute with True Colors Fund and The Palette Fund, 2012.
Edelman, Lee. *No Future: Queer Theory and the Death Drive*. Duke UP, 2004.
Foertsch, Jacqueline. *Enemies Within: The Cold War and the AIDS Crisis in Literature, Film, and Culture*. U of Illinois P, 2001.
Foucault, Michel. *The History of Sexuality: Volume 1: An Introduction*, 1978. Translated by Robert Hurley. Vintage Books, 1990.
Foucault, Michel. *The Use of Pleasure: The History of Sexuality, Volume 2*. 1985. Translated by Robert Hurley. Vintage Books, 1986.
Freeman, Elizabeth. *Time Binds: Queer Temporality, Queer History*. Duke UP, 2010.
Galt, Rosalind. *Pretty: Film and the Decorative Image*. Columbia UP, 2011.
Gaynor, Donn. "Hidden Movie Camera Used By Police TO Trap Sexual Deviates At Park Hangout: 17 Arrests Climax Probe." *Mansfield News-Journal*, August 22, 1962, p. 1.
Goodman, Matt. "GLAAD Unveils Study with the Harris Poll Showing Alarming Erosion of LGBTQ Acceptance at World Economic Forum in Davos, Switzerland and Calls for Change as President Trump Prepares to Address Forum." *GLAAD*, June 25, 2018, www.glaad.org/releases/glaad-unveils-study-harris-poll-showing-alarming-erosion-lgbtq-acceptance-world-economic. Accessed February 10, 2018.
Humphreys, Laud. *Tearoom Trade: Impersonal Sex in Public Places*. Aldine De Gruyter, 1975.
Johnson, David K. *The Lavender Scare: The Cold War Persecution of Gays and Lesbians in the Federal Government*. U of Chicago P, 2004.
Jones, William E. *Tearoom*. 2007, www.2ndcannons.com/tearoom-cover.html. Accessed March 10, 2018.
"List of Prohibited Games." *Twitch*, https://help.twitch.tv/customer/portal/articles/1992676. Accessed February 10, 2018.
McKay, Richard A. *Patient Zero and the Making of the AIDS Epidemic*. U of Chicago P, 2017.
Mens Room: Bakersfield Station. Directed by Joe Gage, Titan Media, 2004.
Muñoz, José Esteban. *Cruising Utopia: The Then and There of Queer Futurity*. New York UP, 2009.
Muñoz, José Esteban. *Disidentification: Queers of Color and the Performance of Politics*. U of Minnesota P, 1999.

Perez, Sara. "Twitch Now Has 27K+ Partners and 150K+ Affiliates Making Money from Their Videos." *Tech Crunch,* February 6, 2018, https://techcrunch.com/2018/02/06/twitch-now-has-27k-partners-and-150k-affiliates-making-money-from-their-videos/. Accessed February 20, 2018.

Perron, Bernard. "Coming to Play at Frightening Yourself: Welcome to the World of Horror Video Games." *Aesthetics of Play*, October 2005, Bergen, Norway, www.aestheticsofplay.org/papers/perron2.htm. Accessed November 20, 2018.

Pinedo, Isabel Cristina. "Postmodern Elements of the Contemporary Horror Film." *The Horror Film*, edited by Stephen Prince. Rutgers UP, 2004, pp. 85–117.

Scott, Darieck. *Extravagant Abjection: Blackness, Power, and Sexuality in African-American Literary Imagination*. New York UP, 2010.

Sedgwick, Eve Kosofsky. *Epistemology of the Closet*. U of California P, 2008.

Shadel, Jon. www.washingtonpost.com/news/soloish/wp/2018/03/27/as-craigslist-personal-ads-shut-down-were-losing-an-important-queer-space/?utm_term=.6d1ac7f6979c. Accessed November 20, 2018.

Tearoom. Directed by William E. Jones, 2007.

Talusan, Meredith. "Documenting Trans Homicides." *Mic.com*, December 8, 2016, https://mic.com/unerased. Accessed November 1, 2018.

U.S. Central Intelligence Agency. "Homosexual Investigations," April 21, 1980, www.cia.gov/library/readingroom/document/cia-rdp78-04007a000700110005-8. Accessed February 5, 2018.

U.S. Cong. Senate. "Committee on Government Operations. Employment of Homosexuals and Other Sex Perverts in Government; Interim Report Submitted to the Committee on Expenditures in the Executive Departments by Its Subcommittee on Investigations Pursuant to S. Res. 280, 81st Congress, a Resolution Authorizing the Committee on Expenditures in the Executive Departments to Carry out Certain Duties." 81st Cong., 2nd sess. S. Rept. 241, https://stacks.stanford.edu/file/druid:fd720pb8753/employment-homosexuals-serialset.pdf. Accessed February 5, 2018.

Yang, Robert. "Radiator 2 as Loud and Quiet." *Radiator Design Blog*, June 16, 2016, www.blog.radiator.debacle.us/2016/06/radiator-2-as-loud-and-quiet.html. Accessed February 10, 2018.

Yang, Robert. "The Game Industry Needs to Get Laid and Chill Already." *Radiator Design Blog*, March 23, 2016, www.blog.radiator.debacle.us/2016/03/the-game-industry-needs-to-get-laid-and.html. Accessed December 20, 2018.

Yang, Robert. *The Tearoom*. 2017, video game.

Yang, Robert. "The Tearoom as a Record of Risky Business." *Radiator Design Blog*, June 29, 2017, www.blog.radiator.debacle.us/2017/06/the-tearoom-as-record-of-risky-business.html. Accessed February 10, 2018.

Yang, Robert. "Why I am One of the Most-banned Designers on Twitch." *Polygon*, July 16, 2016, www.polygon.com/2016/7/14/12187898/banned-on-twitch. Accessed February 10, 2018.

28

SKIN OUT OF THE GAME
Virtual Gambling in Novel Spaces

Alexander Mirowski and Edward Castronova

In this chapter, we describe new manifestations of risk at the intersection of technology and games. The argument we defend here is that while games have a long and natural association with risk, that association is decisively modulated by technology. We support this view through the story of "skin gambling" in *Counter-Strike* (*CS*) over the period 2012–2016. A *CS* "skin" is the outermost layer of a game object, for example, the metal on a virtual gun or the shirt on a virtual soldier. Guns and soldiers can retain their basic shape but dramatically alter appearance by applying a different skin. Our tale explains that in *CS*, skins became a rare luxury item and a mark of high prestige. A lucrative market for *CS* skins emerged, as it always does in games with trading between players, and some of this trading migrated out of the game and onto third-party websites. There, the skins acquired the properties of real-world money. Skins were treated on these sites as a legitimate store of economic value. Soon afterwards, "skin gambling" emerged; players could wager their current skins in the hope of winning even better ones. Skin gambling quickly became a multibillion-dollar industry, and its success naturally led to skin gambling cheating. Thus was born a new arena of game-related risk-taking. It is an old pattern, but our story will highlight the many places where the technological changes of the last 20 years have played a decisive role: The games were played on computers connected through the Internet; the game design created the skins, made them rare, and enabled trading; streaming services connected rare skins to famous players, making those skins into prestige items; the World Wide Web enabled third-party trading sites; some third-party trading sites started automated gambling systems; and the concept of "virtual" value sheltered the practice from regulation, law, and taxation, allowing it to grow explosively. We conclude that skin gambling is an example of the way technology will always surprise us, giving rise to new risks where we would never expect them.

Risk, Games, and Technology

In taking a historical–institutional approach to manifestations of risk in games, we will tell the story of a form of gambling that emerged in (or, more accurately, as a result of) a specific videogame called *Counter-Strike*, or *CS* for short. The story proceeds in three distinct phases. First, we explain what a skin is, and how it came to be an item of value in the broader ecosystem of the game, which consists of the game itself and its designers, but also the player community, fan websites, trading websites, journalists, and even attorneys general. We then relate how the gambling practice succumbed to corruption in three senses: First, people cheated (of course). Second, this gambling might have been strictly illegal. Third, some actors in this drama could be accused of ethics violations. Whether these corruptions are genuine or not depends on such arcane issues as: does an item in a game have economic value? If people gamble using a company's products as tokens, is the company responsible? Is gambling with game items "real" gambling or only play-gambling? And so forth. We do not take a stand on these thorny issues of culture, practice, and law. Our only goal in telling the story is to give the reader an insight into the way technology tosses up new forms of risk for us to consider.

Of course, the assertion that risk follows gambling is not new, nor is the connection between gambling and virtuality. In the chapter that follows, we use "virtual" synonymously with "digital" or "computerized." In addition, we draw on another, older meaning of virtuality. Wolfgang Welsch asks us to recall Aristotle's use of the term, in which it was taken to mean "potential," or that which has not yet been actualized. So, the virtual is that which exists only as possibility and has yet to become real. Gambling, it can then be argued, has always held an element of virtuality, for it is the very act of wagering that a particular potential reality (the turn of an ace, the alignment of reels, or success in a competition) will come about. A third meaning of "virtual" comes into play here as well: that which exists but is removed in some way and set apart from whatever is considered the "real." Pat O'Malley writes that early attempts to curtail gambling in the West were "not associated with any condemnation of reliance upon *fortuna*. Rather, the nature of games was at issue" (238). He describes in particular concerns arising in eighteenth-century Britain about gambling's lack of a "material value or title to value, which in itself constitutes an essential element of advantage to commerce," which is to say it often wasn't a fair exchange of anything (239). O'Malley indicates that worries at this time were heightened by the insurance industry, which was too closely associated with the hazy area of speculation and gambling for the comfort of regulators. In other words, concerns were raised about the virtuality of speculative transactions, which were lacking the necessary "real" stuff of commerce and so were viewed with suspicion. Those speculative transactions are at the heart of gambling, in which significant real wealth is wagered upon what only might become real.

Given all of this, why should we be surprised about gambling taking hold in an environment that would seem to be fertile ground for such a practice? If gambling has always been a virtual pursuit of sorts, it would seem only natural that a virtual space with virtual currency equivalents would breed such activity. The answer may be that gambling and the risk associated with it are too perfect a match for the space around (and within) video games; the latter can camouflage the former. This is an environment that proved conducive to gambling while still managing to fall right on the border of all preexisting regulations and cultural norms of the activity. As this chapter will show, skin gambling was and is an extremely liminal practice, and it is precisely its existence at the edge of categories that made it problematic and that makes it an interesting case to examine.

Skins

On October 5, 2016, The State of Washington's Gambling Commission released a statement indicating that it had sent a cease and desist letter to a company self-described as "per employee … more profitable than Google or Apple" (Chiang). That company was Valve Corporation, a game developer and distributor headquartered in Bellevue, Washington. Valve is best known for its Steam platform, a digital distribution service that has become a dominant force in the video game industry. The platform serves as a game library for users, a social media hub, an online marketplace for the sale of games from a plethora of small and large developers, and a maker space for fans of games to create and distribute custom content for them. It thus came as a shock to many that the letter required Valve to stop facilitating illegal online gambling through the platform. But the Gambling Commission's letter came with good reason, as attention had been drawn to Valve by a recent scandal involving predatory behavior and a popular betting practice tied to Steam: skin gambling through the game *Counter-Strike: Global Offensive* (*CS:GO*). The Commission indicated that it had been assessing the practice and Valve's role in it since February of that year, but cited a lack of response from the developer as the impetus for the more stringent action. Valve responded quickly, arguing that it was not involved with any illegal activity and that "there [was] no factual or legal support for these accusations" (Grosso). The developer also highlighted efforts it had taken earlier in 2016 in an attempt to cut off the growing skin gambling presence. Publicity follows scandal, however, and coverage of this new form of betting ranged across media and spaces of public discussion alike, drawing attention to this previously niche practice. As a regulatory body, Washington's Gambling Commission became aware of skin gambling and proceeded to conduct a thorough investigation, which led eventually to its cease and desist order. Thus, a real-world regulatory body ordered a game company to change the behavior of its players in virtual spaces or face severe legal penalties.

How such a bizarre thing could happen begins with the concept of skins in video games and particularly with the game in question, *Counter-Strike*. *CS*, one of the flagship properties of Valve, was released in November 2000 and quickly created its own gaming ecosystem. It is a first-person shooter game, where a team of players fights another team for control of a map, using modern weapons (AK-47s, grenades, etc.). Several games were later released with the same theme, and a dedicated community of players arose around the series. Thus it is appropriate to think of *CS* not as a single game but rather as a franchise, with multiple games being released over a decade or more, a persistent fan community, a cadre of journalistic reporters and reviewers, competitive tournaments, and generations of superior "athletes" who play the game very well. The original *Counter-Strike* and its successor *Counter-Strike: Source* proved to be dominant both in the genre and in competitive gaming, with the former serving as a flagship game for one of the major sports leagues in the world (Walker). Benjamin Jörissen writes of the important contribution *Counter-Strike* made to the early computer gaming environment as a first-person shooter, citing it as "the beginning of a very particular online-gaming-culture" (Jörissen 26).

Unsurprisingly, *CS* spawned competitors; each new release in the series therefore had to add something new so as to maintain (or reacquire) the game's competitive advantage. Moreover, Valve was gradually changing its entire business model. One of the company's games, *Team Fortress 2* (*TF2*), made fascinating innovations in the design, provision, and trading of virtual items. For example, Valve allowed *TF2* players to own and trade hats for their characters. The hats had no gameplay effect and were intended simply as a goofy bonus. As it happened, however, player interest in hats exceeded all expectations. This must have alerted Valve to a previously unknown source of player interest and a strong motivational tool for continued player engagement with their games. In the early 2000s, Valve was also experimenting with digital content distribution, becoming one of the first game makers to move away from retailing in big box stores. Instead, the company launched its own digital storefront called Steam in 2003. Steam originally distributed only Valve games, but in 2005 the company opened Steam to other developers and paved the way for the platform's meteoric rise to its current dominance of the digital distribution market. Valve thus changed from being solely a game development company into serving as a digital content distributor as well. Over ensuing years, the company added many networking and community features to Steam, including friends lists, messaging, leaderboards, and server listings. Today, Steam is the most popular source for PC game content; as of this writing there are more than 14,000 games available on the service (Galyonkin). Thus, as Valve's *CS* franchise aged, the company saw new possibilities in the realm of virtual items and digital distribution.

This is where skins come in—a result of the release of *Counter-Strike: Global Offensive* in August 2012. The release came at a difficult point in the development of first-person shooters; there were many competitors and once again finding a unique draw for this offering in the genre proved complicated. The game did not experience a successful release, managing to keep less than 50,000 concurrent players after only a few months. The first-person shooter genre is very popular, so player numbers for highly anticipated games are usually much higher ("About CS:GO"; Barrett; "Call of Duty Peak Play Count Statistics"). (See Table 28.1 for context).

Table 28.1 FPS Game player numbers after their launches

Call of Duty Modern Warfare 2	100,000 concurrent players after 3 months.[1]
Overwatch	7 million concurrent players after 3 months.[2]
CS:GO	11 million concurrent players after the Arms Deal Update.[3]

Things changed quickly with the release of a 2013 update, entitled the "Arms Deal Update," which implemented a cosmetic item system much like the hats in *TF2*.

In *CS:GO*, however, the cosmetic items were not just one piece of apparel but rather a change to the entire look of an item. Game developers refer to the external look of an item as its skin, and the Arms Deal Update was notable in offering entirely new skins for the many items and objects in the game. These skins ranged from minor changes such as adding "battle scarring" to completely recoloring weapons (Leack). (See Figures 28.1a, 28.1b, and 28.1c). Images are screenshots by authors).

Figure 28.1a The original appearance of the AK-47 weapon
Source: Screenshot by authors

Figure 28.1b An unobtrusive skin for the AK-47
Source: Screenshot by authors

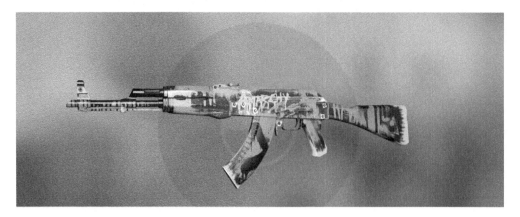

Figure 28.1c An ostentatious skin for the AK-47

Source: Screenshot by authors

The skins in *CS:GO* were not available to just anybody. They were acquired by opening Loot Crates, which were randomly given to players as they spent time in the game. Loot Crates could only be opened, however, with Keys, which could be acquired through a connected microtransaction store for US$2.50.[4] Moreover, skins could be traded or sold from player to player via the Steam platform, and a lively economy soon sprang up around them. Yamamoto and McArthur examine this economy and describe the processes by which individual skins today can be valued at over $20,000 (1).

This sort of exchange was facilitated by the Steam platform's API, or application program interface, which allows third-party sites to acquire publicly available information from Steam databases including the games that a particular player account owns; statistics about play for various games; and the items in a player's account "inventory," which holds items such as the weapon skins shown above. These third-party sites became prolific and today continue to serve important functions in the digital economy of the game, such as allowing inventory browsing and classified listing as well as facilitating the development of trust between potential traders. Beginning soon after the Arms Deal Update, however, a practice developed surrounding the *CS:GO* skin system and the Steam API that did not mirror previous developments in *TF2* and the platform that supports it: gambling.

The precise point at which skin gambling first appeared is difficult to ascertain. In the years after the 2013 Arms Deal Update in *CS:GO*, a variety of websites such as CSGO Lounge (allegedly the first), CSGO Jackpot, and CSGO Lotto began offering a mixture of games of chance that could be played by wagering the skins that players acquired from Loot Crates. The sites also offered the ability to bet on professional matches, which significantly increased viewer numbers and profit margins for those matches (Yu). It has been argued that the true impact of the Arms Deal Update on *CS:GO* popularity was not the cosmetic items themselves, but the uptick in the gambling of those items and the resultant increase in match viewership (Holden et al.). Using their Steam accounts, players transferred items to the sites, from which other skins could be withdrawn as prizes upon the winning of a game. The games themselves ranged from a simple binary choice in which players win by the outcome of a coin flip, to others that randomly distributed prizes from a large shared pot constituted by many players, similar to a roulette. The amount a player won in certain games was in large part determined by the value of the skin(s) a player bet, such that greater risk provided the potential for greater reward. This also benefitted the gambling sites themselves, which could rapidly accumulate skins with significant real currency valuation. A Bloomberg article in early 2016 cited estimates that in the previous year over $2.3 billion worth of skins were bet on professional matches alone (Brustein and Novy-Williams). It was also in 2016 that significant evidence of foul play in the already unregulated gambling market arose.

Scandal

To write of just one scandal surrounding *CS:GO* skin gambling is to mischaracterize the complicated history of the practice. In 2015, a story broke suggesting match fixing by a top U.S. competitive team in order to win high-stakes bets on their own games; the allegations were proven, and Valve banned the involved players from competitive play (Lewis). Indeed, Valve was also subject to multiple lawsuits over skin gambling, most notably a class action complaint filed on June 23, 2016: *Michael John McLeod et al. v. Valve Corporation*. The lawsuit alleged that Valve "knowingly allowed, supported, and/or sponsored illegal gambling" as the owner of both the game and the platform that jointly facilitated the practice. Other suits filed within approximately one month of the first allegations of various unlawful activity on the part of Valve related to the use of Steam and gambling services by minors and the violation "of more than 150 state gambling laws including at least one violation in every state" (Holden et al. 5). The majority of these cases did not achieve their desired outcomes, but sustained legal action, regardless of its merit or results, draws unwanted attention and here served to sully the reputation of a company looking to expand its offerings on a platform now associated with illegal activity.

One of the most widely publicized scandals, however, was that of CSGO Lotto, a gambling site that appeared in 2015, and it was likely this particular incident that encouraged more scrutiny of skin gambling as a whole. Founded in December of 2015, CSGO Lotto was another in the line of websites looking to profit from the rapidly proliferating skin gambling practice. Popular offerings on the site included the traditional coin flip and roulette games, and the site proved successful. Like many other gambling sites, it also became popular with streamers who could easily make back their losses on the site while entertaining their viewers. CSGO Lotto in particular appeared to attract big name streamers such as ProSyndicate and TmarTn. On July 3, 2016, however, popular YouTube channel h3h3 released a video detailing findings from another YouTuber, HonorTheCall, which revealed that the two streamers above were in fact the owners of CSGO Lotto, calling into question every wager they had placed on the site, as well as the fact that they had engaged in the illegal practice of self-promotion of a gambling service ("Deception, Lies, and CSGO"). The video further revealed that TmarTn had attempted to cover up his ties with CSGO Lotto, which generated significant outrage in the *CS:GO* community as well as critical media attention. CSGO Lotto was included in the McLeod suit, also for alleged allowance of gambling. The case did not succeed, however, due to the weakness of its sole federal claim: the Racketeer Influenced and Corrupt Organizations Act, or RICO. This sort of claim, originally developed to fight organized crime, argued that there existed an online enterprise of gambling providers who sought to defraud players and derive profits through illegal means. State claims were also made, but the court argued that it did not have the jurisdiction to take action (Balasbrumani).

The court did not dismiss the lawsuit until October of 2016, however, and negative press over the summer worsened sufficiently that Valve itself eventually released a statement. This was notable as the developer does not often comment on affairs regarding peripheral sites. Indeed, the announcement itself was unassumingly sandwiched between the much more common sale notices for software on its platform, in this case for a baseball game and benchmarking software. The weight of the statement was obvious, however. In no uncertain terms, Valve representative Erik Johnson indicated that the gambling businesses making use of the Steam API were doing so in violation of its terms of use and of Steam user agreements, and that Valve would be sending notices to cease operations to the skin gambling websites. The company did so, and multiple skin gambling sites entered a permanent "temporary closure" or closed down altogether.

The scandal reached even further as well, prompting the most popular game streaming site, *Twitch.tv*, to release its own statement in July of 2016. Despite their dubious legality, gambling streams, or those streams that included gambling elements, had been extremely profitable for *Twitch*. However, *Valve's* announcement was a powerful incentive to end such practices, and so the platform published on its blog a reminder that "broadcasters are not permitted to stream content that breaks the terms of service or user agreements of third-parties" ("Twitch and Third-party Terms of Service and User Agreements"). It is notable that the blog post explicitly bans violations of other entities' user agreements, which includes operation of gambling businesses for Valve. The post does not restrict gambling practices generally from being broadcast on *Twitch*; as this new media platform continues to grow, it is likely to encounter a conundrum faced by traditional media outlets: what draws the most attention and revenue is not always the most ethical broadcast option.

Scrutiny

This was the turbulent environment into which the State of Washington Gambling Commission's letter was released. As indicated above, the October 5 letter was not the first correspondence that the organization had sent to Valve, but it included a more forceful message: work to stop the illegal activity or there will be legal consequences. Valve did make efforts to do so over the summer of 2016, largely in response to publicity surrounding the scandal, but presumably also maintained an awareness that its home state's regulatory body had taken an interest. That effort on Valve's part was not enough to satisfy the Gambling Commission, however, as evidenced by an interview with the body's Chairman shortly after news of the letter to Valve broke. Conducted by game news site GameRevolution, the interview was intended to clarify the Commission's position in their action against skin gambling. The Chairman, Chris Stearns, indicated that the Commission's intent was clear: "Bottom line: Gambling is going on in Washington state ... [Valve's cease and desist letters] are nice; but they didn't end gambling. Valve hasn't solved the problem" (Kozanitis). The site's interviewer pushed for an answer as to what methods Valve should use to comply, and received an evidently unsatisfactory response to the effect that the Commission would look to Valve to implement its own solution. The whole transcript of the interview is not available, but the conclusion the interviewer drew from it was that the letter was

> intended to open up a dialog between Valve and the Washington State Gambling Commission so they can come to a solution together" given the gambling regulations currently in place in the state.
>
> *(Kozanitis)*

This insight into the Commission's thinking suggests that from a legal perspective, the body's inquiries to Valve were sound and quite simple: an illegal practice was being facilitated by the Steam platform, and it was desired that such practice be ended. It is in the technical implications of that desire that complexities arise. In fact, the conundrum clearly faced by the Commission and passed on to Valve raises larger questions about what regulation might look like for this nascent "gaming within gaming" space, and how the risk posed by this new gambling medium might be minimized while satisfying the significant demand for it.

John T. Holden, Ryan M. Rodenberg, and Anastasios Kaburakis provide a list of Statutes that might apply to skin gambling in the American context and find that key to the potential regulation of the practice is whether or not the play associated with it—competitive matches of *CS:GO* and other games—is considered a sport; were this the case, then skin gambling becomes open to a wide variety of existing and tested regulatory apparatuses including the Federal Wire Act of 1961, the Sports Bribery Act of 1964, and the Professional and Amateur Sports Protection Act of 1992. All of this legislation is designed to counter illegal activity, particularly that relating to gambling, surrounding traditional sports such as baseball and basketball. However, as the authors indicate, much of the activity that these and other acts are intended to prevent has already been witnessed in the digital context of skin gambling and related practices, which suggests that legal action upon these established bases is not out of the realm of possibility (Holden et al. 11–12). Valve has expanded its business through Steam into non-game software including development packages and various media editing utilities, as well as expanding into consumers' living rooms through its release of physical hardware such as the Steam Link, Steam Machine, and a Virtual Reality partnership with technology manufacturer HTC. These are expansions that might be described as falling within a "comfort zone" for Valve's development of software and services; becoming subject to the same regulations that apply to Major League Baseball and horse racing is, in comparison, likely an undesirable direction for the developer.

The global reach of the digital also poses problems for skin gambling as a nascent practice. The State of Washington Gambling Commission was the most immediate regulatory body to act as Valve is headquartered in its jurisdiction, but various international governments will have an interest in skin gambling activity if it and other game-related gambling practices maintain their popularity. Holden et al. examine the international context as well, indicating that multiple European countries including the U.K., France, and Germany have taken various steps toward the recognition and regulation of esports betting, under which skin gambling would fall (11–12). This attention from multiple governments assures that while there may be a framework in which such digital gambling is allowed, navigating any one particular offering to be in line with all legal requirements will not be easy.

A timely example of the complexities inherent in the international context is the case of the Czech Republic, which adopted at the turn of 2017 an updated set of gambling regulations in the form of a new Gambling Act. While these new regulations do not explicitly mention digital gambling practices, commentators were quick to examine the possibility of their allowing these practices and skin gambling in particular. An interested law firm found that none of the provisions of the new Gambling Act would prevent its definition of gambling to extend to digital spaces; critical to the acceptance of skin gambling in particular, the firm found, was whether the skins themselves would be defined as a "non-monetary deposit," as the Act prevents gamblers from wagering anything besides currency (Krasula). Thus, in this national context, there is the possibility of skin gambling and similar practices being legal and supported by regulation while definitions of relevant components of these betting practices remain indistinct; the gambling could be legal, but skins might not be. What would the penalty be, should this prove to be the case and skin gambling sites continue to operate in the country?

> Operators of such activities would not only risk being placed on the list of unlicensed online game providers, but they could also face severe fines, IP-blocking and payment blocking, and their revenues could also be subject to a high rate of tax.
>
> *(Krasula)*

These are serious punishments were they to be levied against Valve, since the availability of Steam to as many players as possible is critical to its profit margin. Wariness from those in any way affiliated with digital gambling practices, no matter how indirect, is therefore prudent.

In a twist of irony, the result of this saga and of efforts to curtail skin gambling may be a net increase in the amount of digital gambling that occurs around video games. Just as TmarTn's illegal promotion of CSGO Lotto drew significant public attention, so too did it draw the gaze of private entities with an interest in more legitimate betting practices. In July of 2016, a report on skin gambling was published by Narus Advisors, a consulting company for all manner of entities in or interested in the gambling market, from traditional casinos to esports providers. The report described itself in the following manner:

> This white paper provides a concise but comprehensive education on the fundamentals of skin betting, the size and nature of the market for skin betting, the legal landscape, and some key takeaways for commercial gambling stakeholders.
>
> *(Grove 2)*

It describes in detail the rapid growth of the market for skin gambling into "a multi-billion dollar industry by turnover [which] took a little over a year and happened in an almost completely organic fashion," an environment that Narus argues is ripe for the investment of traditional, experienced, and most importantly legal gambling industries (8). Indeed, one interpretation of the saga of skin gambling cannot fail to be that a significant amount of money was generated through the practice in a very short amount of time. And it is precisely this narrow time-to-money ratio that has caught the interest of casino operators in recent years. Natasha Dow Schüll has written extensively on the value casinos place on "accelerating play," in which gamblers are drawn into extended gambling sessions through careful design of gaming machines. Schüll quotes one gaming machine manufacturer who sums up his product thusly: "A gaming machine is a very fast, money-eating device…. The play should take no longer than three and a half seconds per game" (Schüll 55). The average skin gambling roulette game might last 20 seconds, while a coin flip game can be over in five seconds, a highly desirable time per game for the established gambling industry.

The report also indicates that "the slot machine format," the dominant form of gambling in casinos, "does not appear to resonate with esports fans" (8). The problem of player retention and market growth is one, too, that traditional casinos have been wrangling with. One proposed solution that has not yet caught on in the industry has been the integration of gambling with additional skill-based games. The archetypal form of these games has been poker, which occupies a bittersweet position within the casino environment. On the one hand, the possibility for profits is significant, as patrons can quickly wager (and lose) all of their available funds. However, the game is not determined solely by a set of probabilities developed by the house or its design partners. Instead, players can affect outcomes through technical skill (counting cards) or social skill (bluffing), which can lead to reduced returns for the casino. It is no mystery that slot machines have continued to encroach on the space previously allocated to this and similar table games. New models of integration with digital games such as *Counter-Strike*, or the markets surrounding them, have been slow to catch on but could be the future of an industry looking to capture a new market. The use of *CS:GO* skins in these new betting markets is somewhat arbitrary, and other games and game competitions have already seen gambling platforms and systems rise around them. One of the most successful has been UNIKRN, a startup founded in 2015 which allows for betting on popular competitive games such as *League of Legends, DOTA 2*, and *CS:GO*, and which drew venture funding from many established sources, including entrepreneur Mark Cuban (Morris).

Indeed, in all of these cases the gambling itself was not an immediate problem from the perspective of risk management. Rather, authorities were concerned about the Steam platform serving as a gateway for minors to begin betting, since there is no mechanism of enforcement if a user falsely states their age when creating an account on the service. The gambling sites themselves contribute to this by advertising rules of play which indicate that use of their services constitutes confirmation of one's legal age to gamble. But that confirmation is not always enough. Terms of service of any kind are, after all, notoriously unread. A second problem was the unethical behavior of those promoting their gambling services, because dishonest and false advertisement for gambling is unlawful. Finally, there were concerns over the circumvention of gambling regulations through the use of virtual currencies and other means.

Important in this debate and central to the argument made by Valve was that the Steam platform was a *neutral* part of the skin gambling enterprise. In the release described above, Johnson wrote of

> false assumptions about our involvement with these sites. We'd like to clarify that we have no business relationships with any of these sites. We have never received revenue from them. And Steam does not have a system for turning in-game items into real world currency.
>
> *(Johnson)*

While the statement is not false, implicit in all of these claims is the notion that the Steam platform simply *existed*, and that third parties with ill intentions made use of the affordances it provided to further their own ends. Tarleton Gillespie provides an excellent critique of platform "neutrality" by examining YouTube and other online services, and indicates that the use of the term "platform" is a precise form of "discursive positioning" that allows "YouTube and others [to] stage themselves … allowing them to make a broadly progressive sales pitch while also eliding the tensions inherent in their service" (347–364, 349). The skin gambling scandal brought this positioning to the fore for Valve, as Steam was suddenly indicted for its integration into a practice with decidedly polarizing associations. The degree to which Valve was or was not responsible for the proliferation of gambling on its platform notwithstanding, it is almost assured that similar situations will occur again in the future, as Steam continues to grow and be brought into new environments and new markets. Resting upon the defense of neutrality might be a feasible strategy in the short term, allowing game platforms to continue to diversify, but proactive efforts in combatting predatory practices might eventually become a necessity.

Conclusion

As we write, the future of skin gambling is difficult to discern. Some jurisdictions have welcomed the practice as a potential source of revenue, while others have attempted to crack down with the view that it could never be legitimate (Wood). As a practice, it problematizes the idea of a clean line between "game" and "real world" in ways that simply cannot be ignored, and serves as a reminder that such a line might never have existed to begin with. So, the question may be whether or not skin gambling constitutes risk-taking in the real-world sense. However, if some other hybrid answer is more appropriate, then law, policy, and culture need to change so as to create and recognize the new category, whatever it may be. Esports as an institution is growing; it is experiencing an increase in popularity, financial support, the construction of more physical and virtual infrastructure, and a dedicated betting market. This growth would seem to make developing a hybrid answer all the more crucial. Until that happens, however, skin gambling will continue to generate heated debates about both legal and personal culpability. This is so simply because skin gambling has surprised us. The technological foundations fell slowly into place and then, over the course of only a few years, this new version of an old practice suddenly emerged as a serious and utterly confusing problem. We might return to Pat O'Malley at this point, who as we have seen writes of a similar time when understandings of gambling and risk changed, and whose own conclusion mirrors that of this chapter: "The episodes with which this paper has dealt did not create this shift, but rather reflect a disturbance that generated new arguments concerning what constitutes the 'good of commerce'" (O'Malley 250). Similarly, skin gambling was at the nexus of changing conceptions of speculative action; its disturbance of the status quo, we argue, will have important ramifications for the way video games and gambling continue to intertwine in the years to come. Gambling is old; the ethics of gambling are old; the law of gambling is old; but what's new is the confluence of gambling between players A, on website B, with cosmetic virtual items produced by company C, with apparent market value D, in apparent contravention of the laws of jurisdiction E. This is a new arena of risk, produced in a unique way within this strange, ongoing era of light speed technological change.

Notes

1 "Call of Duty Peak Player Count Statistics." *Call of Duty View*, htt. Accessed April 9, 2017.
2 Barret Ben, "Overwatch Passes 25 Million Player Milestone, Just Getting Silly Now." *PGamesN*, January 27, 2017. www.pgamesn.com/overwatch/overwatch-sales-numbers. Accessed April 9, 2017.
3 "About CS: Go." *Valve*, http://blog.counter-strike.net/index.php/about/. Accessed April 9, 2017.

4 Microtransactions are an increasingly popular method of monetizing video games. They take the form of very small purchases (a single in-game item, an extra life, or a minor cosmetic change) that can be made within games using real currencies. These are often facilitated by "stores" that are proprietary marketplaces included in games that can be accessed as one plays.

Works Cited

"About CS:GO." *Valve*, http://blog.counter-strike.net/index.php/about. Accessed January 9, 2013.
Balasbrumani, Venkat. "Federal Court Rejects Online Gambling Lawsuit Against Valve-McLeod v. Valve." *Technology & Marketing Law Blog*, October 5, 2016.
Barrett, Ben. "Overwatch Passes 25 Million Player Milestone, Just Getting Silly Now." *PCGamesN*, 27 Jan. 2017, www.pcgamesn.com/overwatch/overwatch-sales-numbers. Accessed April 9, 2017.
Brustein, Joshua and Eben Novy-Williams. "Virtual Weapons are Turning Teen Gamers Into Serious Gamblers." *Bloomberg Businessweek*, April 20, 2016, www.bloomberg.com/features/2016-virtual-guns-counterstrike-gambling. Accessed March 20, 2017.
"Call of Duty Peak Player Count Statistics." *Call of Duty View*, www.callofdutyview.net/content/call-of-duty-peak-player-count-statistics. Accessed April 9, 2017, UP017.
Chiang, Oliver. "The Master of Online Mayhem." *Forbes*, February 2, 2011, www.forbes.com/forbes/2011/0228/technology-gabe-newell-videogames-valve-online-mayhem.html. Accessed January 12, 2017.
"Deception, Lies, and CSGO." *h3h3 Productions*, July 3, 2016, www.youtube.com/watch?v=_8fU2QG-lV0. Accessed March 20, 2017.
Galyonkin, Sergey. "Total Games on Steam." *Steamspy*, https://steamspy.com. Accessed April 13, 2017.
Gillespie, Tarleton. "The Politics of 'Platforms'." *New Media & Society*, vol. 12, no. 3, 2010, pp. 347–364.
Grosso, Robert. "Valve to Respond to Washington Gambling Commission After Given Deadline." *TechRaptor*, October 17, 2016, https://techraptor.net/content/valve-respond-washington-gambling-commission-given-deadline. Accessed March 9, 2017.
Grove, Chris. "Understanding Skin Gambling." Narus Advisors, July 26, 2016, p. 2.
Holden, John T et al. "Esports Corruption: Gambling, Doping, and Global Governance." *Maryland Journal of International Law*, vol, 32, no. 1, 2017, pp. 236–273.
Johnson, Erik. "In-Game Item Trading Update." *Valve*, July 13, 2016, http://store.steampowered.com/news/22883. Accessed March 19, 2017.
Jörissen, Benjamin. "Virtual Reality on the Stage. Performing Community at a LAN-party." *Envision. The New Media Age and Everyday Life*, edited by Patrik Hernwall. Stockholm University, 2004, pp. 23–40.
Kozanitis, James. "Interview: WA State Gambling Commission Doesn't Know What They Want Valve to Do." *GameRevolution*, October 5, 2016, www.gamerevolution.com/features/interview-wa-state-gambling-commission-doesnt-know-what-they-want-valve-to-do. Accessed March 18, 2017.
Krasula, Vladimir. "Skin Betting from a Czech Gambling Law Perspective." *Bird & Bird*, January 5, 2017, www.twobirds.com/en/news/articles/2017/global/skin-betting-from-a-czech-gambling-law-perspective. Accessed January 9, 2017.
Leack, Jonathan. "How Microtransactions Propelled Counter-Strike: Global Offensive to Stardom." *Game-Revolution*, January 12, 2017, www.gamerevolution.com/features/how-microtransactions-propelled-counterstrike-global-offensive-to-stardom. Accessed March, 8 2017.
Lewis, Richard. "New Evidence Points to Match-fixing at Highest Level of American Counter-Strike." *Dot Esports*, January 16, 2015, https://dotesports.com/counter-strike/match-fixing-counter-strike-ibuypower-netcode-guides-1256. Accessed March 20, 2017.
Morris, Chris. "Mark Cuban is Investing in this eSports gambling startup." *FORTUNE Tech*, June 30, 2016, http://fortune.com/2015/06/30/mark-cuban-esports-unikrn. Accessed March 8, 2016.
O'Malley, Pat. "Moral Uncertainties: Contract Law Distinction between Speculation, Gambling, and Insurance." *Risk and Morality*, edited by Richard V. Ericson and Aaron Doyle. University of Toronto Press, 2003, pp. 231–257.
Schüll, Natasha Dow. *Addiction by Design: Machine Gambling in Las Vegas*. Princeton UP, 2012.
"Twitch and Third-party Terms of Sservice and User Agreements." *Twitch*, July 13, 2016, https://blog.twitch.tv/twitch-and-third-party-terms-of-service-and-user-agreements-b9827599e0fc#.v7pvmthdb. Accessed March 19, 2017.
United States District Court of Connecticut. *Michael John McLeod v. Valve Corporation*, June 23, 2016, www.ctd.uscourts.gov. Accessed March 8, 2017.
Walker, Rob. "Double Fantasy." *New York Times Magazine*, February 5, 2006, www.nytimes.com/2006/02/05/magazine/double-fantasy.html. Accessed March 8, 2017.
Welsch, Wolfgang. "Virtual to Begin With." *Subjektivität und Öffentlichkeit*, 2000, pp. 25–61.

Wood, Joss. "Good News For Skin Betting, As Isle Of Man Amends Gaming Regulations To Allow It." *Esports Betting Report,* February 21, 2017, www.esportsbettingreport.com/isle-man-amends-gaming-regulations-allow-skin-betting. Accessed March 30, 2017.

Yamamoto, Kei'Ichiro and Victoria McArthur. "Digital Economies and Trading in Counter Strike Global Offensive: How Virtual Items are Valued to Real World Currencies in an Online Barter-free Market." *Games Entertainment Media Conference (GEM), 2015 IEEE,* IEEE, 2015.

Yu, Eric. "The Start of it all: Skin Gambling." *UNIKRN,* July 15, 2016, https://unikrn.com/news/the-start-of-it-all. Accessed March 20, 2017.

PART VIII

DISCIPLINARY MODULATIONS

29
RISK AS AESTHETIC VIRTUE

Vinzenz Hediger

In Western modernity, risk is an aesthetic virtue. "It's the very law of poetic expression," writes Gaston Bachelard, "to transcend our thinking." Reading Novalis, Shelley, Poe, Baudelaire, Rimbaud or Nietzsche creates the impression that the imagination is "one of the forms of human daring" (Bachelard 11f.). Audiences and critics judge the relevance of artworks for their novelty and originality, which in turn can be measured in terms of the risks the artist is willing to take, i.e., the degree to which she is willing to infringe upon and alter existing aesthetic (as well as social) norms (Farchy). In music and dance, performers earn admiration by braving the dangers of challenging partitas or choreographies, or by developing new forms, such as by making risk a core element of their artistic displays. In fashion, transcending the staid and conventional with breathtaking new creations earns a designer her standing as a leader in her field. In sports, from football (aka "soccer"), to surfing and mountain climbing, to motor racing and air shows, performances are evaluated according to the risks taken by the team or individual athletes, while artists and performers appreciate boldness and daring in their sources of inspiration. Risk-taking is one of the criteria that distinguishes the avant-garde from mainstream art. The Brazilian concrete poets of the 1950s paved the way for the Tropicália movement of the late 1960s because they "liberated our imagination for certain formal experiments that perhaps we wouldn't have otherwise risked," according to singer/songwriter Caetano Veloso (Dunn 69). Similarly, Hélio Oiticica, whose installation "Tropicália" gave the movement its name, defines modern art as "the commencement of the emergence of what I call the state of invention" (quoted in Small 2016). Conversely, artists who avoid risk and play it safe are ripe for critique.

In this contribution, I want to explore the concept of risk as aesthetic virtue in three steps. First, I want to provide a brief sketch of the economy of aesthetic risk. Like other forms of risk, aesthetic risk has social and financial rewards. This means that aesthetic risk, even where it stands in seeming opposition to it, remains inexorably tied to the modern market economy. I will then discuss how risk became an aesthetic virtue at the intersection of the parallel histories of art and globalized trade, with the main event being a transition from a metaphysics of providence to a one of probability. Taking avant-garde dance and the Hollywood film industry as examples, I discuss in a third step how risk works as an aesthetic virtue and argue that both examples may be understood in terms of an aesthetics of uncertainty.

Novelty and Originality: The Economy of Aesthetic Risk-Taking

A broad consensus, ranging from classical Indian Rasa theory and the third century to European aesthetics since the eighteenth century, stipulates that the object of aesthetics is an experience that is different and distinct from other types of experience, whether it is defined by the viewer's emotions (as in Rasa theory) or by a specific form of judgment (as in Kantian aesthetics). Aesthetic risk may thus be understood as the effort to create an experience without precedent—an experience not of the sublime and/or the beautiful, but of norms challenged, routines broken, and new terrain explored.

Like all forms of risk-taking, aesthetic risk involves an economy of risk and reward. Risk can be defined as the probability of something happening multiplied by the resulting cost or benefit if it does happen. In purely financial terms, there is the risk that an actual return on investment will be lower than the optimal return. That is, the risk lies in having an outcome with an expected loss. Faced with a world of uncertainty, risk-taking is a form of rational behavior. In a famous distinction proposed by economist Frank Knight in the 1920s, uncertainty is incalculable, whereas risk is calculable in terms of the probability of outcomes. Entrepreneurs take risks to reduce uncertainty, and a similar point can be made for artists and performers as well as for audiences. Aesthetic risks are taken for an audience, to find an audience, and at the risk of not finding, or losing an audience. For the audience, the risk is the potential loss of the time and money if the experience disappoints, and the reward is the experience and its invigorating effects. As Bachelard writes, cherishing the spectacle of risk fills the audience with a "dynamisme novateur," a force of renewal (12). A taste for risk primes one for innovation.

Aesthetic novelty in new works is the primary source of the infectious pleasure of the *dynamisme novateur*, but the experience can expand to include historical objects. What makes a cubist painting by George Braque relevant and secures its place on a museum wall today is not just its inherent artistic quality—whether we describe it in terms of the artist's mastery of the medium, the depth of its meaning, or its emotional impact—but its place in art history. It presents an innovation, which we can appreciate if we assess how much of a risk a given choice of artistic expression represented relative to the norms and standards of its time, or indeed of our time. On occasion, artists fade from view, while others return from oblivion. Correggio was considered a master on par with Raphael and Michelangelo at the beginning of the twentieth century, while Caravaggio was largely forgotten. Now, their ranks have been inverted. Similarly, nineteenth-century critics and artists elevated Rembrandt to his current status as a master of light and color by inscribing the Dutch master in a genealogy of modern painting (McQueen). To the critics, artists, and curators who re-discovered Rembrandt and Caravaggio, they appeared as contemporaries across time, whose innovations prefigure more recent advancements in the history of art.

For the artist, performer, or athlete, the primary reward for risk-taking is social recognition—honor, reputation, and status. As Correggio shows, recognition is ephemeral, which creates an incentive for risk-taking: the bigger the risk taken, the better the chances for enduring recognition. The secondary reward is financial and material. Social rewards are always abundant: The pool of potential admirers grows with the size of the audience. Financial rewards tend to be scarce. In poetry or avant-garde music, even the most recognized artists depend on scholarships or day-jobs. Paul Cézanne, the son of a banker, pursued his career secured by a large inheritance. Wallace Stevens and Charles Ives, the United States' foremost modernist poet and composer of the first half of the twentieth century, both worked in insurance, as did Franz Kafka until his early retirement in 1922. By contrast, in areas like the visual arts, pop music, sports, and film, remuneration can be abundant, whether through gallery sales and auctions or engagement contracts. In either case, remuneration is proportional to the size of the audience, while in classical music and opera, it may relate to the purchasing power of the average audience member.

If social and financial rewards do not always align, they are often at odds. Artists who openly seek to increase their audience in pursuit of profit run the risk of being treated as "sell-outs."

Conversely, it can pay to be "difficult," albeit usually only in terms of social recognition. Starting in the nineteenth century, there is an ethos of the artist working outside of and even in opposition to the market economy. The struggling artist, the artist as "ungrateful beggar," as French poet Léon Bloy liked to style himself, emerges as a heroic figure. Negating the commodity form of the artwork becomes the hallmark of modern art, as in the aesthetic theory of Theodor W. Adorno. Aesthetic risk becomes synonymous with the risk of forfeiting financial rewards.

A similar ostentatious, disdain for market considerations informs the modern Olympic movement. Founded by French nobleman Baron Pierre de Coubertin, the Olympic games combined the ancient myth of the noble amateur with an aristocratic ethos of leisure. Participation was originally limited to white men of certain means. Medal winners who were discovered to have accepted fees, in other words to have sold their labor for money, were stripped of their awards (Toohey and Veal 21). The rule persisted into the 1980s, long after television had turned the event into a global business. American college athletes are also barred from taking pay, unlike their coaches, who are usually the university's highest paid employees. Considering that most athletes are black, this has been described as a form of indentured labor (Hawkins). Until at least the late 1960s, however, college athletes and teams enjoyed a higher social standing and found larger audiences than professional athletes, based on the premise that college sports reject commercialization in favor of an unblemished experience of community.

But whether social and economic rewards align or are in conflict, aesthetic risk-taking remains inexorably tied to the market economy. A market economy can be understood as a system in which society is separated into an economic and a political sphere, and in which the exchange of commodities is expanded to include land, labor, and money (Polanyi 71ff.). Visual artists working in an era that predates the modern market economy, or more specifically, before the first half of the nineteenth century, usually worked on commission for the church (in Europe) or courts (both in Europe and Asia). They created their works within what philosopher Jacques Rancière describes as the "representative regime of art": In this regime, *poesis* and *aisthesis*, creation and perception, align. A relatively stable and limited set of genres and topics, like the *pietà* or the portrait of members of a royal family, serves to represent and reinforce the established social and political order (Rancière 102). By contrast, in a market economy, creation and perception are separated both temporally and structurally. Artists produce works in view of a future transaction, for instance the sale to an unknown buyer, be it through the intermediary of an art dealer or an auctioneer. Not unlike industrial entrepreneurs, modern artists are faced with a state of uncertainty about future demand. Finding an audience requires a double differentiation, both diachronically and synchronically. To expand on a point raised by philosopher Stanley Cavell, who argues that art in its modern understanding requires an historical consciousness (Cavell 68ff.): only by placing themselves within, and occasionally at odds with, a tradition and by connecting the past, the history of art, to a future marked by the uncertainty of demand, can artists produce works of originality and novelty. Industrial entrepreneurs create innovations that are substitutes for earlier products: The automobile makes the carriage obsolete. Cultural innovation, on the other hand, requires the continuing presence of archives of cultural meaning. Novelty only appears as such based on knowledge of the forms which the new work transcends. Only by placing themselves within, and in opposition to a tradition, and by connecting the past—the history of art—to a future marked by the uncertainty of demand, can artists produce novelty. At the same, they have to differentiate themselves from their current competitors through their originality.

In 1803, Friedrich Willhelm Schelling established a genealogy for modern art starting with Dante. "The sheer individuality of his poem, which has no comparison," writes Schelling, "is what makes Dante the creator of modern art, which is unthinkable without this arbitrary necessity and necessary arbitrariness (Schelling 38; translation by the author)." With this dialectical word play, Schelling defines the generative principle of modern art. "Arbitrary necessity" refers to a condition under which outcomes are no longer preordained, as fate, god's plan, and others strictures of tradition are supplanted with man-made and hence "arbitrary" forms of order. From this condition, for the artist the freedom to create unique artistic forms arises—the freedom to be arbitrary—but also the obligation to do so, the necessity to be arbitrary. The modern artist cannot choose to innovate, she must. To paraphrase Schelling's contemporary, Hegel: Her freedom arises from her acknowledgment that double differentiation, necessary arbitrariness in the face of arbitrary necessity, is her fate.

Or, to put it differently: Modernity describes a condition under which it is better to be new, original, and wrong than safe and right. As a consequence, rather than working within an established set of genres, modern artists systematically take occupational risks and engage in formal and thematic innovation (Menger). Like in the case of the industrial entrepreneur, innovation occurs through the recombination of preexisting elements (Schumpeter 66; Steiner 156). Mahler and Bartok's appropriations of folk music, or Charles Ives' *Symphony No. 4*, which uses multimetrics (different meters) and temporal a-synchronicities to juxtapose orchestral and choir elements, a technique that draws on both the Romantic and the Marching band repertoires, exemplify the uses of cultural archives for the purposes of artistic innovation (Burkholder 120, 134ff.).

It is important to note that the focus on novelty and originality is, to a certain extent, the hallmark of Western modernity. Chinese painters and poets from the fifth through the seventeenth century repeatedly stress the importance of originality. For instance, Su Shi (1037–1101), a painter, offered that there is "one basic rule in poetry and painting: natural genius and originality." (cited in Udden 2017, 7). In Japanese art, on the other hand, *honka-dori*, the "picking up of a melody," which in painting means the copying, imitation, and allusive variation of old masters, is a revered genre, while copying has mostly been relegated to a training exercise for students in Western art schools (Brougher and Müller-Tamm 245). One of the few comparable bodies of work in Western canonical modernism are Picasso's black-and-white variations on Velazquez' *Las Meninas* from 1957 and of other classical works of European painting. Significantly, these are generally considered to be a secondary element of his oeuvre (Galassi). But even in a context where copying is the ultimate gesture of reverence, archives of cultural meanings are indispensable for artistic achievement: for the copy to be appreciated, the original must be known.

Aesthetic risk-taking can thus be understood as the activity of (usually) a single individual responding to a condition of ineradicable uncertainty by searching to produce works and performances that have the potential to be recognized as novel and unique, as distinct in both a diachronical and synchronical perspective.

From Providence to Probability: How Risk Came to Be an Aesthetic Virtue

The term "risk" first enters the English language in the early seventeenth century. It can be traced back to the sixteenth century and the French "*risqué*," which derives from the thirteenth-century Italian "*rischio*" and the seventh-century Arabic term "*rizq*" ("God's provision").[1] The *Oxford English Dictionary* underlines that risk relates to the possibility of "damage to merchandise when transported at sea" (Levy 3). The first insurance companies were formed to enclose and spread the risks of maritime trade. The concept and experience of risk is thus tied to the expansion of global trade networks. As historian John Darwin argues, "the discovery of the sea as a global commons offering maritime access to every part of the world transformed the economics and geopolitics of empire" (6). The European empires, which first emerged in the sixteenth and seventeenth centuries, were the first empires in history not to be based primarily on the control of territory, but on logistics, particularly in regards to advanced shipping technologies and, later, railroads. The consensus among economic historians now suggests that the colonies did not contribute significantly to the wealth of Europe. But there is no question that the global trade networks established in the centuries prior to the Industrial Revolution were a precondition for the emergence of a globalized market economy and for the so-called "Great Divergence," the unprecedented economic growth of the industrialized West after 1800 relative to the rest of the world. In fact, modernity itself may best be understood in relation to these global trade networks. It is, as Darwin argues, "a comparative and a competitive stage." The best test of modernity is "the extent to which, in any given society, resources and people could be mobilized for a task and redeployed continuously as new needs arose or pressures were felt" (Darwin 27).

The first forays into the transatlantic trade, the discoveries of Columbus and Cabot, were financed by bankers from Florence, Italy. The Americas were named after an agent and explorer of the Medici bank, Amerigo Vespucci (1452–1512), also a native of Florence. The model for what was to become modern art history was developed two generations later by another Florentine, artist and writer Giorgio Vasari (1511–1574). The first artist biographies appear in late antiquity, often using stories of a mythical or miraculous nature to celebrate and explain individual achievement (Kris and Kurz). Revitalizing the genre after a millennial hiatus and with a focus on biographical detail rather than legend, Vasari's *Vite dei più eccellenti pittori, scultori e architetti* from 1568 underscores the idea that the life of the artist is a life apart, of particular richness and profundity. But distinctiveness is the organizing principle of the *Vite* in yet another sense: Artists find entrance into Vasari's canon based on the originality of their style and the novelty of their individual contributions.

For instance, in his contribution on the Florentine painter Masaccio (1401–1428), Vasari writes that "not only did he away with the primitive and cumbersome manners [*rozze e goffe maniere*] which had been maintained until then, but with his beautiful works, he incited and light up the souls of those who came after him." Vasari then goes on to specify the innovations that can be attributed to Masaccio and through which his works became contagious, carriers of what Bachelard, three and a half centuries later, proposes to call *dynamisme novateur*. For instance, "before anyone else," Masaccio put the feet of his figures on the ground and thus ended the "clumsiness [*goffezza*] of letting all figures stand on the tip of their feet," which had been prevalent in earlier painters. Most importantly, Masaccio, one of the first painters to absorb the lessons in perspective from Brunnelleschi and Alberti, "gave so much liveliness [*vivezza*] and so much depth [*rilievo*] to his paintings," that he deserved to be recognized as if he were the very inventor of the art of painting ("inventore della arte") (Vasari 267). Particularly in comparison with his competitors ("a comparazione de'suio concorrenti"), and those who tried to imitate him, his paintings were much more alive and true ("vive e vere") than forgeries of reality ("contrafatte"). Pliny the Elder relates the story of painters Zeuxis and Parrhasius striving for realism in a competition, in which Zeuxis paints grapes so realistic that birds pick at them, while Parrhasius paints a curtain so realistic that Zeuxis mistakes it for a real curtain (Bergmann). In this Roman legend about Greek painting, the competition evolves around the individual mastery between contemporaries. Masaccio is caught up in a competition which is about attaining honor through incontrovertible technical progress. As Vasari argues, Masaccio, like few others, showed us the "true way to progress to the highest level" ("la vera via di camminare al grado supremo") in art.

To summarize: Excellence in the arts is a matter of innovation; innovations are acquired in competition with other artists; innovations set standards behind which subsequent generations may not regress; and art history is a history of progress from lower to higher levels of technical and artistic achievement. Like the seafarers and discoverers of Vasari's time, the artists who deserve our appreciation are those who boldly go where no one has gone before. What drives this history of technical development and progress is not least an incipient form of what George Orwell would later, in his critique of nineteenth and twentieth century nationalism, describe as competitive prestige, the "purpose … to secure more power and more prestige, *not* for himself, but for the nation" (Orwell 866). For Vasari, artists thrive on the patronage of princes, which in turn is grounded in the "virtuosa ambizione delle republiche," the "virtuous ambition" of every state to outshine its neighbors and competitors (7).

Economic historian Joel Mokyr argues that we cannot understand the Industrial Revolution unless we account for the factor of culture. Mokyr argues that the "growth of useful knowledge" from the sixteenth century onward paved the way for the technological innovations that made the Industrial Revolution possible. This growth was initially driven by the "res publica literaria" or "republic of letters," a transnational assembly of scholars corresponding and sharing their insights starting in the Italian Renaissance and expanding to include northern Europe by way of the incipient postal networks in the seventeenth and eighteenth century. In this precursor to the modern scientific community, the freedom of thought and expression of the participants in the "republic of letters" was guaranteed by the patronage of competing states. Having fallen from grace in one state, scholars would simply move to the next and benefit from the "virtuous ambition" of their new host. Echoing a thought by Montesquieu, who traced the European "genius of liberty" to the competition between states, Mokyr argues that what drove the growth of practical knowledge was "that political fragmentation was coupled with an intellectual and cultural unity, an integrated market for ideas" (170).

While the antecedents of the "republic of letters" date back to the fourteenth century and the relocation of the papacy to Avignon, its most productive phase came in the seventeenth and eighteenth centuries, not least under the impact of Bacon's *Novum Organon*, published in 1620, and Newton's *Principia*, published in 1668. Predating the history of "republic of letters" by at least a century—the first entry in his collection of biographical sketches is dedicated to the Florentine painter Giovanni Cimabue (1240–1302)—the history of art as told by Vasari may similarly be understood as a history of progress in an integrated market for ideas. It is driven by political fragmentation—small states competing for prestige in a relatively restricted geographical space—coupled with intellectual and cultural unity, provided by the (self-) identification of all participants as "Italian" (and, by implication, Christian). To use a term proposed by Moykr, the artist–innovators who are the protagonists of Vasari's *Vite* could be characterized, rather than as mere artisans, as "cultural entrepreneurs" like Bacon and Newton, as takers of intellectual and cultural risk. Incidentally, "novel" and "unique" are also key criteria for relevance in modern scientific research (Stichweh). As Natalie Heinich writes, in the wake of Vasari, artists' biographies quickly became established across Europe as "models of excellence" and discursive analogues to the self-portrait, which served as a conduit for the consecration of the artist as a cultural producer in her own right (Heinich 120). In particular, they paved the way for the passage from the mere painter to the artist, which happens in France with the foundation of the *Académie royale de peinture et de sculpture* in 1648, 28 years after the publication of the *Novum organon* and 40 before the publication of the *Principia*.

Another driver of cultural entrepreneurism in the arts was the museum. If modernity, as Darwin suggests, is a measure of the degree to which a society is capable of circulating people, goods, and ideas, then the museum is a quintessentially modern institution. "The role of the museum in our relation to artworks is so important," writes André Malraux, "that we are at pains to think that it could not exist, and to imagine that it didn't exist in places where modern European civilization is and was unknown" (Malraux 205). One of the first public art museums was the Amerbachsammlung, which contains the world's largest collection of paintings from the Holbein family and which the city of Basel acquired in 1661 and opened to the public in 1671. The Louvre became a public institution after the French revolution in 1793, while the National Gallery in London was founded in 1824. While the Amerbachsammlung had a local connection—Holbein the elder spent most of his life in Basel—the collections of the Louvre contained artworks and objects from all over the world. Vivant Denon, the director of the museum from 1802 to 1814, used Napoleon's campaigns to stack the collections, justifying his collection policy with a mission to preserve artworks for future generations. Either way, André Malraux' observation is valid: "A roman crucifix was not, at first, a sculpture, the Madonna by Cimabue was not, at first, a painting, the *Pallas Athéné* by Phidias was not, at a first a statue." Only the transfer to the museum turned these artifacts into artworks, and their selection occurred according to a conception of art history as a history of innovation and progress, in which novelty and relevance are closely tied. But museums transform artifacts into valuable artworks not only retroactively, but proactively. An exhibition in a first-rate museum like the "Schaulager" in Basel virtually guarantees that prices paid for art works at auctions will be matched in a re-sale.[2] Museums are the central banks of the global art market, securing the risk of investors with their prestige.

The idea of history as human progress is itself tied to the global expansion of trade networks in the wake of the voyages of "discovery." In his inaugural lecture as professor of history at the University of Jena, delivered on May 28, 1789, German enlightenment playwright and poet Friedrich Schiller argues that the European experience of history as the spectacle of an upward movement playing out on successive stages of development, stems from "the discoveries, which our European seafarers made in far-away oceans and on remote coasts" (Schiller 754; translated by the author). Writing at a key moment in the "Sattelzeit," to quote Reinhart Koselleck's term, the threshold period at the dawn of modernity, Schiller argues that the experience of history in the modern understanding of the term, the development of a collective "we" toward an open-ended future (Koselleck XV), is grounded in a perception of the contemporaneity of the non-contemporaneous, for which the encounter with the "primitive" Other provides the template (Fabian). Vasari, a contemporary of the "discoveries," shows that this spatio-temporal distribution dates back at least to the sixteenth century. Masaccio's innovations become salient against the backdrop of the continuing presence of the more "primitive and cumbersome" works of his predecessors. "Art exists as an autonomous sphere of existence and production since History exists as a concept for collective life," writes Rancière (15). Vasari's conception of the history of art suggests that art and history are indeed coterminous. For Vasari, the history of art is a spectacle of the contemporaneity of the non-contemporaneous in a way that is structurally analogous to Schiller's "universal history," with historical antecedent taking the place of, and being interchangeable with, the "primitive" Other.

A similar spatio-temporal distribution reappears in Hegel's *Vorlesungen über Ästhetik*, which offers a philosophical account of the expression of the idea of the absolute spirit in art throughout human history. Hegel distinguishes between symbolic, classic, and romantic art, relegating non-European art to the role of a historical antecedent devoid of historical consciousness. Sheldon Pollock argues that Hegel's *Vorlesungen über Ästhetik* are "structured deeply, if with no self-awareness, by the inequity of colonial judgment" (Pollock 334). Like Schiller, Hegel considered global trade as an "educational asset," but while Schiller stressed the instructive effects of the spectacle of the Other for educated Westerners, Hegel focused on the educational benefits of the experience of trade for those who were "discovered" and deplored the "stagnation" of peoples "cut off from its dynamic contact" (Brennan 98). Non-European art similarly suffers from being cut off from the dynamics of the progression from symbolic to classic and Romantic art.

The lack of self-awareness that Pollock discerns in Hegel's aesthetics is not a bug, but a feature. While modern Western aesthetics shares with earlier conceptions such as Rasa theory the notions of the specificity of aesthetic experience, it emerges in the late eighteenth and early nineteenth century as the result of what may be described as a differentiation and purification of the sphere of aesthetic experience.[3] From Baumgarten to Kant and Schleiermacher, "aesthetic consciousness" appears as distinct from, and more subjective and ultimately epistemologically inferior to, scientific knowledge (Gadamer 283). This concept of aesthetic experience paves the way for the idea of the autonomy of art in modernity, as well as for the notion of advanced art as critique of social relations. In order to critically reflect on alienation in modern capitalist societies and provide a utopian sense of the alternative, art and the aesthetic sphere have to be separate from the sphere of economics. In that sense, the autonomy of the aesthetic realm mimetically rehearses the separation between the political and the economic sphere in modern market economies. Yet for autonomous art to critically reflect on the pathologies of the economic sphere, a connection, however dialectically, must persist. According to some philosophers of art, the spheres of art and non-art eventually re-converge. For Arthur Danto, for instance, Warhol's Brillo boxes mark the point where art and non-art become indistinguishable, at least to the extent that the distinction is based on inherent features of the artwork. But even such a neo-Hegelian conception of the end of art assumes that art in modernity evolved in an autonomous sphere and according to its own logic, rather than in constant communication with other areas of human agency. In fact, looking back over the historiography of art, one could argue that art in Western modernity not only evolves according to patterns of innovation that run parallel to those of technological, and by extension, economic development, but that the visual arts, as chronicled by Vasari and his many successors, appear as a laboratory in which specifically modern protocols of innovation take shape, which provide a template for innovation in other areas, including the development of scientific and practical knowledge.[4] And if modern aesthetics may be said to emerge from a set of operations of exclusion and purification, non-metropolitan avant-gardes remained very much aware of the connection between art, traffic, and trade. In his influential "Brazil-Wood Manifesto" from 1926, which together with the 1928 "Anthropophagy Manifesto" paved the way for the Brazilian avant-gardes of the 1920 and 1930s, as well as the "Tropicália" movement and the Cinema Marginal of the late 1960s, poet Oswaldo de Andrade argues for a "poetry for export" to counter the "poetry for import," which emanates from the cultural centers of the Northern hemispheres (259).

The standard accounts of the transition to artistic modernity in art history focus on features of formal innovation. Cubism and the move to abstraction, for instance, appear as seminal events. They signal the dawn of a register of art in which artworks not only conform to, but foreground their medium's specificity. The standard accounts in the philosophy of art and in social theory focus on changes in the social function of art works. Hegel marks the point where art emerges as an autonomous sphere by pointing out that we no longer bow our knees in front of a Madonna, but admire the artistic achievement. Similarly, in the second half the nineteenth century, writers such as Matthew Arnold, Oscar Wilde, and Stephane Mallarmé argued that art replaced religion as the site of spiritual aspirations (Schusterman). Against the backdrop of what Max Weber called the "disenchantement of the world," art thus promised to offer a secular re-enchantment, a substitute for religion. A more recent account of the "aesthetic revolution" at the threshold to modernity comes from Jacques Rancière's attempt to remarry the spheres of art and politics. According to Rancière, at the turn of the nineteenth century the representative regime of art transforms into an aesthetic regime of art, which is thoroughly democratic and in which anything and anyone can become the object of an artwork, a transformation that coincides with Foucault's transition from a classical to a modern *episteme*. However, if we focus on the notion of risk and on the history of risk, a different transition emerges—one that could be argued to combine the process of secularization with a major epistemological shift: A transition from providence to probability (or, in Schelling's phrasing, from necessity to arbitrariness and "arbitrary necessity").

In the transition to a globalized market economy in the nineteenth century, a metaphysics in which the vagaries of life follow a preordained divine plan, however little we may understand it, gives way to a metaphysics in which the vagaries of life are accidents occurring largely at random, that is under conditions of uncertainty, albeit with a calculable probability, as actuarial science. In a metaphysics of uncertainty, truth is no longer based on revelation or the discovery of the accordance of our knowledge with an ahistorical substance of being. Rather, as Henry James writes in *Pragmatism*, truth lives "for the most part on a credit system": "Our thoughts and beliefs 'pass', so long as nothing challenges them, just as banknotes pass so long as nobody refuses them." Verification is a form of trade: "You accept my verification of one thing, I yours of another. *We trade on each other's truth.*" As Jonathan Levy argues, for James "the uncertainty of a particular financial transaction modeled the fundamental metaphysical uncertainty of the universe" (260). Along the same lines Frank Knight argues in *Risk, Uncertainty, and Profit* that risk can never entirely eliminate uncertainty, and that uncertainty under capitalism is in a way "ineradicable." If Knight's metaphysics of uncertainty earn him a place "in the cannon of classic works in the American philosophy of pragmatism" (Levy 281), the distinction between risk (calculable) and uncertainty (incalculable and ultimately ineradicable) also informs Keynes' *General Theory of Employment, Interest and Money*, first published in 1936. In his *Pensées*, Pascal, one of the founding figures of probability, formulates an ironic question: "Is it *probable* that *probability* brings certainty?" (qtd. in Gray 13f) A fully developed market economy resoundingly answers that question with "no."

The metaphysics of uncertainty describe a condition of pure immanence structured by the fact of an open, indeterminate future. Against this backdrop, the biographical coincidence that Wallace Stevens, Charles Ives, and Franz Kafka, giants of twentieth-century modernism, all worked in insurance, acquires a new significance. In *Paradise Lost*, a transposition of the Biblical story of the fall from Grace into iambic pentameter, or Heroic English Verse, first published in 1667, John Milton takes it upon himself to "justify the ways of God to man." Echoing Homer's invocation of the muse at the beginning of the *Odyssey*, Milton opens the poem by asking the "Spirit" (i.e., the Holy Ghost), which "from the first was present," for instruction:

> What in me is dark
> Illumine, what is low raise and support;
> That to the height of this great Argument
> I may assert Eternal Providence
> And justify the ways of God to men.

While clad in bold formal innovation, this is poetry as theodicy, to quote Leibniz' term: Milton's ambition is to help his readers understand how God, despite being all-powerful, all-knowing, and infinitely benevolent, has allowed evil to come into the world and shape the lives of mere mortals. Among the achievements of Kant, apart from destroying classical metaphysics and laying the groundwork for the "aesthetic revolution" at the threshold of modernity, is a radical critique of theodicy, based on the logical impossibility of any proof of the existence of good.

Wallace Stevens, the insurance executive and modernist poet, once defined poetry as "a purging of the world's poverty and change and evil and death" (Szalay 49). At first, his project seems comparable to that of Milton: poetry addresses the existence of evil. Yet there is a difference between justifying the ways of God to man and setting out to purge the world of evil and death. Stevens' poetry engages not in theodicy. Rather, it covers the same contingencies as modern insurance: unemployment, accident, illness… With Stevens, poetry enters the framework of what economist Karl Polanyi described as the "double movement" that propelled nineteenth-century liberal capitalism forward: The "market expanded continuously, but this movement was met by a countermovement checking the expansion in definite directions" (136). The countermovement includes such institutions as labor unions, regulatory frameworks for labor and financial markets, but also the new financial instruments such as futures markets, the large corporation, and, most significantly on the level of individual risks, insurance (Levy). Yet perhaps paradoxically, what we might call Stevens' actuarial aesthetics yield not a poetry that is safe and secure in its choices. Quite to the contrary. His poetic expression transcends established ways of thinking quite as much as that of the nineteenth-century poets celebrated by Bachelard.

The difference between Milton and Stevens marks the transition from providence to probability, from the exegesis of revealed truth to a trade on verifications. Milton uses Heroic English Verse and the template of the Homeric epos to harmonize the experience of evil and adversity with a metaphysics of providence. Stevens' poetry deploys aesthetic experiment to purge evil in the face of extreme uncertainty and turns art into a privileged site for demonstrative risk-taking and its vicarious experience. In aesthetics, as in finance, the way to reduce uncertainty and to adjust to the probable is not to avoid risk, but to take risks.

The Heroics of Control Loss: How Risk Works as Aesthetic Virtue

Western philosophical aesthetics could be summarized in a paradox: It is as an attempt to establish objective criteria for something that is assumed to be essentially subjective, namely taste. One way to resolve the paradox is to look for intersubjective criteria of value and relevance for works and performances. To speak of risk as aesthetic virtue can be seen as one such attempt. Virtue, very broadly defined, is a trait of personal excellence which is recognized by others as the principle of individual or collective achievement. For Kant, virtue resides in the moral quality of the motivation for one's action: Actions are moral only if their motivation, their *Triebfeder*, is in accordance with a principle that could serve as the basis for a general legislation. Virtue in that sense is private: Someone who is perceived to act morally could in fact be motivated by selfish reasons, which are evident only to herself. A similar split, but in an inverse relation, traverses the incipient forms of modern economic thought. In the *Bee Fable*, a poem published in 1714, the Anglo-Dutch philosopher and satirist Bernard Mandeville anticipates many key principles of modern economic thought, from the division of labor to the "invisible hand," and introduces the "paradox of thrift," according to which consumption drives employment and growth. In Mandeville's famous turn of phrase, private vices, such as luxury and debauchery, amount to public virtues. Modern liberalism does away with Mandeville's irony and assumes, to varying degrees, that the pursuit of self-interest will eventually result in aggregate growth and social welfare. Aesthetic virtue may be rooted in private vice. Just think of all the complicated life stories of artist in modernity, and the license granted to the genius, a thoroughly modern figure, to be difficult. But it is a thoroughly public virtue. It aims for and thrives on recognition and honor, and it has collective benefits in the shape of aesthetic pleasure and the *dynamisme novateur* it engenders in audiences. It can of course also serve to generate competitive prestige.[5] To the extent that it is a public virtue, aesthetic risk requires recognition and validation in what cultural economist Michael Hutter proposes to call "arenas of information" (*Neue Medienökonomik*): i.e., showcases ranging from museums to gallery, theaters, festivals, sports tournaments, social media, review and fan websites, etc. Strictly speaking, novelty and uniqueness are not inherent in a work or performance. They result from the recognition and validation of risk-taking behavior in an arena of information.

In his autobiography *Before Pictures*, art historian and critic Douglas Crimp offers an illustration of how aesthetic virtue works in this sense. In a chapter on dance, Crimp reflects on "Farellitis," an obsession with Suzanne Farrell, Georges Balanchine's preferred prima-ballerina of the 1960s and 1970s. Documenting the "mad love Farrell inspired" (208) through the decades, Crimp contrasts Farrell with the dancer appearing in Jack Goldstein's *A Ballet Shoe*. This 19-second film shows a ballerina's foot in a ballet shoe, en point; two hands enter the frame and unfasten the shoe's ribbon, and the foot slowly lowers to the ground. As Crimp observes:

> The dancer in *A Ballet Shoe* is a fine technician. She is able to execute a gorgeously steady descent from pointe. But the difference between a perfect technician and a great ballet dancer is the latter's readiness to relinquish control, to move off-balance, to take unexpected risks. That was the marvel of watching Suzanne Farrell dance Balanchine's ballets. It's not that you were afraid she might fail. On the contrary, you had complete confidence in her, but her out-of-control risk-taking thrilled you and, visible, her as well. Goldstein's films, by contrast, create in the viewer "foreboding, premonition, suspicion, anxiety," as I wrote in "Pictures". I attributed those qualities to how his pictures were presented, staged, and structured. I would now add: controlled.
>
> *(269)*

Both performances share a high level of competence. But there is a difference that has enormous consequences in terms of the aesthetic experience: The difference between control and the readiness to relinquish control. The perception of control results in the viewer's "foreboding, premonition, suspicion, anxiety," while "out-of-control risk-taking" results in the viewer's excitement.

Originating from a queer context, Crimp's observations on "Farrellitis" and the "readiness to relinquish control" as the source of the viewer's excitement seem to apply to other arts and performances as well. Sociologist Mark Stranger makes a similar point for surfing, while gymnast Nadia Comaneci inspired excitement with the out-of-control risk-taking that earned her multiple gold medals with straight tens as a 14 year old at the 1976 Montreal Olympics.

Yet in one respect, the viewer's interest in out-of-control risk-taking remains inseparable from foreboding, premonition, suspicion and anxiety. The standard account of audiences distinguishes between mass and elite audiences according to their level of education. Economist Joelle Farchy argues that the difference is rather one between audiences who have the time and resources to properly acquaint themselves with the supply of programs, works, and performances, and those who don't. Her underlying assumption is that all audiences crave novelty and the excitement of demonstrative risk-taking, yet tend to avoid the risk of being disappointed. Or, to put it differently, while audiences appreciate the display of risk-taking as an aesthetic virtue, they are also looking for a form of insurance for themselves. And that propensity of the audience to minimize and avoid risk in their choices shapes aesthetic practice in modernity as much as search for novelty and the necessity of double differentiation. The Hollywood film industry is a case in point.

For going on a century now, Hollywood has been dominated by a limited number of between five to eight large corporations. Of the top ten public traded companies of the 1920s, only General Electric and General Motors survive. Of the eight large studios of the late 1920s, only RKO has disappeared. The seven others, Paramount, Universal, Warner Bros., Fox, Universal, MGM, and United Artists, still operate, albeit in the case of MGM and United Artists only as trademarks for other studios, while Disney, a niche producer until the 1970s, has become a major studio. Through their global distribution networks, which have been their institutional core since the 1920s, they dominate the world market for filmed entertainment. The only serious challenge to the hegemony of the studios arose recently when tech-based companies, the streaming platforms Amazon and Netflix, entered production. Yet the studios still dominate the theatrical market, which is the bottleneck a film has to pass on its way to long-term profitability in subsidiary markets (cable, DVD/blueray, streaming). While the Hollywood studios cultivate distinctive trademarks and are nominally fierce competitors, they also often cooperate. Aesthetically speaking, one of the most remarkable aspects of the industry is the relative lack of what I propose to call double differentiation: Films tend to reprise successful elements of previous films, such as stars and genre narratives, with little variation, and the industry's overall output is relatively homogeneous in terms of visual style, narrative structure, and production values.

We can argue that Hollywood's institutional continuity and the relative homogeneity of its output are closely related answers the same question: How can producers and moviegoers deal transform the extreme uncertainty that characterizes markets for information goods in general, and for cultural goods in particular into calculable risks?

The point of the corporation, according to Jonathan Levy, was to "organizationally 'insure' as best it could—without resort to actuarial knowledge—against dynamic risks" (280). The corporation answers the question of how risk can be socialized. Insurance answers the question of how risk can be mitigated and borne by the individual. The corporate structure of Hollywood is about socializing aesthetic risk, while the homogeneity of style is a form of insurance for the audience.

Economic theory assumes that actors in markets act out of rational self-interest: buyers know their preferences and search for the best product at the lowest price. In markets for cultural goods, it is structurally impossible to match one's preferences with the supply of goods. Since films are experiential goods, the audience will only be able to judge the film's quality after the fact. In the absence of proper knowledge, one has to rely on substitute sources of information, namely advertising and the preferences of others, as expressed in reviews, word-of-mouth and box-office results.

Faced with an overabundance of choices, one will tend to select the choice that offers the lowest risk, the choice with the best information. Offerings with caveats—unknown stars, directors, provenance—are likely to be shunned in favor of films that are recommended by critics and trustworthy friends. On the other hand, films that are already successful will tend to become more successful, since in the absence of other information success will be seen as an indicator of quality. As a consequence, the majority of films will fail to find an audience. Following a so-called Pareto distribution, roughly 80 percent of films are flops, meaning they fail to recoup their production costs, while 20 percent of films earn 80 percent of all revenue. In fact, the median box-office revenue of a Hollywood film is slightly lower than the median budget (Vany). And while there are always hits, they are impossible to predict. In markets for items like used cars, the seller will know more about the quality of the product than the buyer, which creates a situation of asymmetrical information. In contrast, markets for cultural goods are structured by what economist Arthur de Vany proposes to call "symmetrical ignorance," a situation where both buyer and seller cannot properly judge the quality of the product before the transaction. Or, as screenwriter William Goldman put it, in Hollywood, nobody—not the producers, nor the audience—knows anything.

Against this backdrop of a near-certainty of financial loss, producing a single film is not a rational form of behavior. Considering that only one in five films reliably makes money, and considering that it is impossible to predict which one of the five it will be, the only rational option is to produce packages of films and spread the risks over a larger portfolio. This is exactly what Hollywood studios do, what they were built for, and why there are so few of them. Hollywood studios are actually primarily global distribution networks. On the production side, Hollywood went from a factory system developed in the late 1910 to unit-producer to a package unit system in the 1950s, in which highly-paid free agents—stars, directors, technicians—team up for individual projects. On the exhibition side, Hollywood went from a cinema industry, which had the majority of its assets in real estate like theaters, to a copyright industry focused on the long-term valuation of copyrighted programs.[6] Distribution, on the other hand, is where the institutional continuity of Hollywood has been since the 1920. Distribution, to quote Douglas Gomery, is "the key to market control," as it stabilizes the kind of market access and minimum demand, which is required for the studios to find the surprise winners, the few hits, among their production portfolio (69).

The problem of symmetrical ignorance also helps us understand the homogeneity of style in the Hollywood studios' output. Symmetrical ignorance and its attendant uncertainty induce producers across the industry to engage in what we might call a dialectics of innovation and repetition, which include casting the same stars over and over in slightly different roles and developing genres from stealth remakes of successful. The relative lack of double differentiation serves an insurance of sorts, which allows the audience to manage its share of the risk.

It is now an acknowledged fact even in Hollywood that the director is the artist responsible for the film. The standard Directors' Guild of America contract has identified a film in the credits as "a [name of the director] film" since the 1990s, giving legal form to the auteur theory, the outlines of which the French devised in the 1920s to distinguish their cinema from that of Hollywood, and which Village Voice critic Andrew Sarris brought to America in the 1960s. Yet Hollywood continues to be a producers' business. The Oscar for the best film still goes to the producer, not the director. The genius of Hollywood, as French critic André Bazin put it, is the "genius of the system" (Bazin 143) Against this backdrop, the struggle of the director in Hollywood is always one for more double differentiation, or, as we could also describe it, a paradoxical struggle for control: a struggle to wrest control over the film from the producer in order to better be able to lose control and take aesthetic risks in the creative process. As a consequence, the paradigmatic story of aesthetic risk in Hollywood since the 1920s has been one of failure: The story of rebel *auteurs* like Erich von Stroheim, Orson Welles, Sam Peckinpah, or Michael Cimino, who wrest artistic control from their corporate overlords only to see their vision, and their careers, destroyed by pettiness and risk-adversity of upper studio management: Stroheim's *Greed* cut from five hours to 90 minutes, Welles' career diminished by the work of William Randolph Hearst's gossip column henchwoman, every single one of Peckinpah's films mutilated in post-production, Cimino's *Heaven's Gate* shelved before it got a fair hearing with the audience. Conversely, the status and enduring legacy of directors such as Hitchcock, Ford, and Kubrick derives in large part from the fact that knew how to play by the rule of the system while exerting almost complete artistic control over their films. The "director's cut," when it first emerged in the 1990s with, among others, Ridley Scott's extended version of his seminal 1984 film *Blade Runner*, was supposed to mark the belated artistic triumph of the director over the producer. But advanced capitalism reliably absorbs its contradictions, and the "director's cut" has now become another way of selling the same film twice or more (Davenport).

Hollywood's homogeneity of output has been decried as the hallmark of the "culture industry" by Adorno and Horkheimer in the *Dialectics of Enlightment*. Hollywood is the polar opposite of the avant-garde. The reductive, commodified experience offered by the culture industry alienates the spectator from herself and perpetuates the pathologies of capitalism, while the demonstrative aesthetic risk-taking of the avant-garde imparts a liberating *dynamisme novateur*.

Yet, as the tale of the heroic rebel *auteur* suggests, the desire to relinquish control, to run risks rather than avoid them, haunts even the corporate aesthetics of Hollywood. Again, the Oscars, the awards through which the industry speaks to itself about the way in which it wishes to be perceived, are an indicator. Honorary awards to *auteurs* from De Sica (who received the price for Sciuscia in 1947 and Ladri di biccilette in 1949), Orson Welles (1970), Jean Renoir (1973), Kurosawa Akira (1989), Satyajit Ray (1991), Federico Fellini (1992), Michelangelo Antonio (1994), and even Jean-Luc Godard (2010; Godard obviously failed to pick up the award), and Best Picture awards for edgy small films like *Moonlight* (2017) speak of a gap between who the industry are and who they wish to be, and of a continuing aspiration to go beyond the routine management of risk and the defensive actuarial aesthetics of the mainstream film. Once a year, Hollywood reminds itself that in filmmaking, too, like in the other arts, there is a point where the readiness to relinquish control turns anguish into excitement. And so, at least in the sense of a regulative idea, as Kant would call it, risk works as an aesthetic virtue across the spectrum, from the avant-garde to the culture industry, and from Balanchine to Hollywood.

Or, to put it in other words, in modernity, all aesthetics are aesthetics of uncertainty.

Notes

1 See Gaspar Mairal's contribution to this volume.
2 Art dealers and auctioneers consider a museum show in a venue like "Schaulager" as a "as a world-class legitimation" for an artist's work (Tully 153).
3 "Differentiation" is the key term in the sociological system theory of Niklas Luhmann, "purification" is a concept borrowed from Bruno Latour.
4 For this point, see also Hutter, *Ernste Spiele*.
5 Risk as aesthetic virtue may thus be understood as a virtue in both a classical and a modern sense, i.e., as a display of courage, but in the face of ineradicable uncertainty. Both aspects are in play when Nietzsche celebrates Beethoven and Goethe as creative geniuses and exemplars of virtue that elicit admiration through public displays of courage (cf. Nietzsche 501).
6 This shift occurred after the Paramount decree, an anti-trust measure from 1948, which forced the studios to divest from their theater chains.

Works Cited

Adorno, Theodor W. *Aesthetic Theory*. Bloomsbury, 2013.
Andrade, Oswald de. *Anthropophagies*. Translated and edited by Jacques Thiériot. Flammarion, 1982.
Bachelard, Gaston. "L'imagination est une des formes de l'audace humaine." Librairie José Corti, 1943.
Bazin, André. "La Politique des auteurs." *The New Wave*, edited by Peter Graham. Doubleday, 1968, pp. 137–155.

Bergmann, Bettina. "Greek Masterpieces and Roman Recreative Fiction." *Harvard Studies in Classical Philology*, vol. 97, 1995, pp. 79–120.
Bloy, Léon. *Le Mendiant ingrat (Journal de l'auteur) 1892–1895*. Mercure de France, 1946.
Brennan, Timothy. *Borrowed Light. Vico, Hegel, and the Colonies*. Stanford UP, 2014.
Brougher, Kerry and Pia Müller-Tamm, editors. *Hiroshi Sugimoto*. Hatje Cantz, 1948.
Burkholder, J. Peter. *All Made of Tunes: Charles Ives and the Uses of Musical Borrowing*. Yale UP, 2004.
Cavell, Stanley. *Must We Mean What We Say?* Cambridge UP, 2015.
Cimino, Michael. *Heaven's Gate*. Partisan Productions, 1980.
Crimp. Douglas. *Before Pictures*. Chicago UP, 2016.
Darwin, John. *After Tamerlane. The Rise & Fall of Global Empires, 1400–2000*. Penguin, 2008.
Davenport, Thomas H. et al. *The Return of Enterprise Solutions: The Director's Cut*. Accenture Institute, 2004, www.business.vu.edu.au/staff/paulhawking/return_of_enterprise_solutions.pdf.
Dunn, Christopher. *Brutality Garden. Tropicália and the Emergence of a Brazilian Counterculture*. U of North Carolina P, 2001.
Fabian, Johannes. *Time and the Other. How Anthropology Makes Its Object*. Columbia UP, 2014.
Farchy, Joëlle. "Le rôle de l'information dans la demande culturelle." *Iris*, no. 17, 1994, pp. 67–84.
Gadamer, Hans-Georg. *Truth and Method*. Continuum, 2004.
Galassi, Susan Grace. *Picasso's Variations on the Masters*. Harry Abrams, 1996.
Gomery, Douglas. "Corporate Ownership and Control in the Contemporary US Film Industry." *Screen*, vol. 25, no. 4–5, 1984.
Gray, John. "We Simply Don't Know!" *London Review of Books*, vol. 31, no. 22, 2009.
Hawkins, Billy. *The New Plantation. Black Athletes, College Sports and Predominantly White NCAA Institutions*. Palgrave Macmillan, 2013.
Heinich, Natalie. *Du peintre à l'artiste. Artisans et académiques à l'âge classique*. Les Éditions de Minuit, 1993.
Hutter, Michael. *Ernste Spiele. Geschichten vom Aufstieg des ästhetischen Kapitalismus*. Wilhelm Fink, 2015.
Hutter, Michael. *Neue Medienökonomik*. Fink, 2006.
Kant, Immanuel. "Über das Mißlingen aller philosophischen Versuche in der Theodizee." *Schriften zur Anthropologie, Geschichtsphilosophie, Politik und Pädagogik*, vol. 11. Suhrkamp, 1964, pp. 105–124. 12 vols.
Knight, Frank. *Risk, Uncertainty, and Profit*. Houghton Mifflin, 1921.
Koselleck, Reinhardt. "Einleitung." *Geschichtliche Grundbegriffe*, edited by Otto Brunner et al., vol. 1. Klett Cotta, 1979.
Kris, Ernst and Otto Kurz. *Legend, Myth and Magic in the Image of the Artist*. Yale UP, 1981.
Latour, Bruno. *We Have Never Been Modern*. Harvester Wheatsheaf, 1993.
Levy, Jonathan. *Freaks of Fortune. The Emerging World of Capitalism and Risk in America*. Princeton UP, 2012.
Malraux, André. *Les Voix du Silence. Oeuvres completes*. Translated by the author, vol. 4, no. 1. Gallimard, 2004.
McQueen, Alison. *The Rise of the Cult of Rembrandt: Reinventing an Old Master in 19th Century France*. Amsterdam UP, 2003.
Menger, Pierre-Michel. *The Economics of Creativity. Art and Achievement under Uncertainty*. Harvard UP, 2014.
Mokyr, Joel. *A Culture of Growth. The Origins of the Modern Economy*. Princeton UP, 2016.
Nietzsche, Friedrich. *Menschliches Allzu-Menschliches. Kritische Studienausgabe*, vol. 2. Walter de Gruyter/Deutscher Taschenbuchverlag, 1988.
Orwell, George. "Notes on Nationalism." *Essays*. Selected and Introduced by John Carey. Knopf, 1968, pp. 865–884.
Polanyi, Karl. *The Great Transformation. The Political and Economic Origins of Our Time*. Beacon Press, 2001.
Pollock, Sheldon. *A Rasa Reader. Classical Indian Aesthetics*. Translated and edited by Sheldon Pollock, Columbia UP, 2016.
Rancière, Jacques. *Aisthesis: Scenes from the Aesthetic Regime of the Art*. Verso Books, 2013.
Schelling, Friedrich Willhelm. "Über Dante in philosophischer Beziehung." *Kritisches Journal der Philosophie*. Translated by author. Tübingen, 1803.
Schiller, Friedrich. *Sämtliche Werke. Historische Schriften*. Translated by the author, vol. 4. Hanser, 2004.
Schumpeter, Joseph A. *Theory of Economic Development*. Harvard UP, 1934.
Schusterman, Richard. "Art and Religion." *The Journal of Aesthetic Education*, vol. 42, no. 3, 2008, pp. 1–18.
Scott, Ridley, director. *Blade Runner*. Director's cut, Warner Bros., 1992.
Small, Irene. *Hélio Oiticica: Folding the Frame*. U of Chicago P, 2016.
Steiner, George. *Grammars of Creation*. Faber & Faber, London, 2010, p. 156.
Stichweh, Rudolf. "The Sociology of Scientific Disciplines: On the Genesis and Stability of the Disciplinary Structure of Modern Science." *Science in Context*, vol. 5, no. 1, 1992, pp. 3–15.
Stranger, Mark. "The Aesthetics of Risk. A Study of Surfing." *International Review of Sports*, vol. 34, no. 2, 1999, pp. 265–276.

Stroheim, Erich von, director. *Greed*. Metro-Goldwyn-Mayer, 1924.

Szalay, Michael. "Wallace Stevens and the Invention of Social Security." *Modernism/modernity*, vol. 5, no. 1, 1998.

Toohey, Kristen and Anthony James Veal. *The Olympic Games. A Social Science Perspective*. CABI, 2000.

Tully, Judd. "Nachklänge einer bahnbrechenden Auktion." *Helden der Kunstauktion*, edited by Dirk Boll. Hatje Cantz, 2014.

Udden, James. *No Man an Island. The Cinema of Hou Hsiao Hsien*, 2nd edition. Hong Kong UP, 2017.

Vany, Arthur de. *Hollywood Economics. How Extreme Uncertainty Shapes the Film Industry*. Routledge, New York, 2003.

Vasari, Giorgio. *Le vite de` più eccellenti architetti, pittori, et scultori tialini, da Cimabue, insino a`tempi nostril*, vol. 1. Einaudi, 1986.

30
NOTES ON DISSENT AND RISK

Ricardo Dominguez

In his essay, Ricardo Dominguez presents a reflection on artistic interventions into state and corporate surveillance systems. He characterizes these interventions as "dissent," a practice that arises from both the subject's particular historical location and the desire to dis-embed from control systems that ensure docility in that location. Thus, *dissent is singular practice*: each life follows a trajectory based on personal history. This activist mode of artistic production brings the artist as well as the work into direct conflict with state apparatuses of securitization. In Dominguez' case, there have been charges of inappropriate use of public funds on research that challenge legal frameworks, as well as questions about the role of a university professor and the social function of new media art; he has been subjected to multiple investigations, a Congressional hearing, and a digital counter-strike by the U.S. Department of Defense. In short, the researcher-artist who questions the risk discourses of the security state has had to bear real material risks.

Dominguez locates himself in this autobiographical piece as a "screenal" child growing up amid the gambling phantasmagoria of Las Vegas, while watching the counter-cultural protests of the 1960s and 1970s on television. This early technological relation to control/dissent would prove formative. As co-founder of the Electronic Disturbance Theater (EDT), a group that developed *virtual sit-in* technologies in 1998 in solidarity with the Zapatista communities in the Chiapas, Dominguez has been a theorist and practitioner of "network-art-activism." The phone app Transborder Immigrant Tool has pushed performativity in the domain of art to a new level, deploying GPS technology to direct "illegal" immigrants to water sources in the desert borderlands. Dominguez' many notable collaborative interventions (with ACT-UP, EDT, and Critical Art Ensemble, among others) strive to "take back" technology as a common good so as to rewire one's machinic relation to the present data-driven governance of human thought and action.

★ ★ ★

dissent (v.)

early 15c., from Latin *dissentire* "differ in sentiments, disagree, be at odds, contradict, quarrel," from *dis-*"differently" (see *dis-*) + *sentire* "to feel, think" (see sense (n.)). Related: *Dissented*; *dissenting*. The noun is 1580s, from the verb.

risk (n.)

1660s, risque, from French risque (16c.), from Italian risco, riscio (modern rischio), from riscare "run into danger," of uncertain origin. The Englished spelling first recorded 1728.

Spanish riesgo and German Risiko are Italian loan-words. With run (v.) from 1660s. Risk aversion is recorded from 1942; risk factor from 1906; risk management from 1963; risk taker from 1892.

1.1 Dissent, as risk, is always about the location and dislocation of one's social sense or (ae)ffective condition in relation to the embedded real in which one finds oneself; that is the influence of where and when one is born or comes into being. My dissenting being emerges from the convolute of being from Las Vegas, Nevada—the land of risks and of the always/already gamble. My world was full of bright burning neon nukes going off down the road, casino capitalism playing the odds 24/7, strange alien areas run by military groups for unknown purposes, nuclear bombs, and the pragmatic platonic prayers of the Mormons running the state. I found myself under a simple formula that would soon run the whole neoliberal world:

Money+Mafia+Military+Mormons (+ a Mexican me) = the ruins yet to come.

1.2 I was a screenal child. The performative matrix of screenality became the site of learning dissent and risk on multiple scales and realities. It was on the screen that I witnessed assassination after assassination in the 1960s, the battle for civil rights, U.S. presidents commit crimes, Vietnam, the Pentagon Papers—the list is endless. The screenal condition also offered me the potential to feel otherwise, to see otherwise, to imagine otherwise, to act otherwise: by watching endless monsters created by ground zero politics destroy the world, by watching black power take down the man in *The Spook Who Sat by the Door*, by watching hippies dance into other worlds in countless groovy flicks—I could sense other worlds were possible. One could dissent otherwise. One could risk watching the watchers (like Cop Watch in Chicago).

1.2 I saw our dissenting sisters and brothers in the 1960s and 1970s driven insane by the surveillance state on TV. Many groups—the Black Panthers, the Brown Berets, the Yellow Pearl—were all under extreme surveillance. They had no proof at first, but it became overwhelmingly self-evident due the public leaking of the FBI's COINTELPRO documents and many other risky actions by dissenters that there indeed was a nation-state force aggressively seeking to keep track of them. So in the 1980s, for me and others, there was a sense of accepting that, "Yep, sure, they are surveying us-so what?"

1.3 ACTUP (AIDS Coalition to Unleash Power) was basically the on-the-ground dissent training for me and many others, where we tried to meld notions of media with notions of direct action to perform aggressive acts against the therapeutic state. I and other members of ACTUP/Tallahassee felt that our data bodies and real bodies had to manifest themselves in a radically transparent manner, without fear of what it might mean to be surveilled. Because often surveillance aggressively tried to bring you down because of your sexuality: "We're going to out this person now because we now have a letter he sent to his lover, who was a male or female or whatever." And thus the individual was broken because of this knowledge getting out. Obviously, when you're entering into queer spaces, where issues of sexuality are at the forefront, that begins to shift some of the oneness of what is available to the surveillance state to break you. Again, there was this move toward a certain level of acceptance of surveillance, an acceptance that one could counter surveillance by disallowing it to aggregate around what the surveillance state imagined to be sites of personal trespass that on a social scale could be used against one or one's community to disentangle it. I remember being the mediator for our local

ACTUP/Tallahassee, and the very first question that we were trained to ask was, "Hello, welcome. If there are any undercover agents, please raise your hands, or FBI or journalists, you're welcome to be here with us. Don't be afraid to come out."

1.4 I think I took a lot of that history with me when we started to assemble Electronic Disturbance Theater 1.0 in the 1990s, in terms of our choice to engage in radical transparency. Some of the actions that happened during that time were the jam ECHELON actions. ECHELON was a well-known global surveillance system established by the NSA. Remember, I grew up in the 1970s, during the Watergate scandal, the leaking of the Pentagon Papers and, at the end of that period, the 1982 publication of James Bamford's famous book, *The Puzzle Palace*. We knew the NSA had the ECHELON system, so in the 1990s we asked, "How can we imagine ECHELON's functions?" So we said, "Well, it probably picks up words and targets certain words: blow up, bomb, whatever." So, for Jam ECHELON Day, we asked all the communities who were involved with us on a global scale to take 50 words and paste them on every email that they sent out. In theory, we would jam ECHELON because it would be tracing all of these systems. The outcome was that the United Kingdom and other countries began to question the United States regarding where the ECHELON bases or stations were located in Europe.

1.5 Thus there was an awareness of the way in which surveillance would function within the paradigm of data body/real body in the days to come. Our response was to be transparent, to have the code available to anybody who wanted to look at it, and also to enunciate what we were going to do, how we were going to do it, why we were doing it, and so on. This really became part of a larger aesthetics of disturbance that manipulated the operations of surveillance by encompassing the surveillance state as part of its performative matrix. It wasn't that we were going to do something secretly because we didn't want to be surveilled, but our gesture was to have the surveillance state participate in—to help amplify—the gesture of disturbance.

1.6 Within the surveillance state, there is this kind of Roman empiricism of the law: "You are breaking this law [whatever law they say you are breaking] because your technology is effectively functioning within the paradigm of the law that we have established, and we have now aggressively gathered your emails, gathered your photographs, and we see you stating that you are going to use this technological add-on." To this we would respond, as part of the gesture of disturbance, "Yes, welcome surveillance state to the performance. We understood how the technological empiricism of law, which you are seeking to establish against us, works. But the technological aspect is on your side, in terms of breaking the law of trespass. On our side, nothing is happening. There is no weight of empirical technology on our end. We are less than script kitties [the lowest level of hackers]. Nothing about anything we do works. It does not function—or better said functions all too well. So you are all in this performative matrix that allows us to make visible the infrastructures of technology and the social structures of surveillance at play."

1.7 Part of the aesthetics is one in which the surveillance state and the hackers become confused—in what we in the Critical Art Ensemble in the 1980s called the "aesthetics of confusion." This then allowed us to have a different conversation with those entities on a different scale, and that scale would be the field of aesthetics of art production. Often we would have encounters where lawyers or FBI agents or others would say, "Are we part of the performance? Are we part of the artwork?" To which we would respond, "Yes, you are." I think that allowed us then to create an a/effective, visceral response around the theater of code and the empiricism of utilitarianism-effective society that condition the state's logics of surveillance and technology. It allowed for our dissenting gestures to risk blooming otherwise.

1.8 Leaping over the 1990s we land under the Post-9/11 engines of manufactured states of reality. Where the aesthetics of confusion were now being used to create policies for war beyond the nation and within the nation, a world where we were all potential "enemy combatants." One exemplary moment was a statement by the G.W. Bush administration reported in the *New York Times* on October 17, 2004 by Ron Suskind (who indicated later that it was Karl Rove who he was quoting):

> People like you are still living in what we call the reality-based community. You believe that solutions emerge from your judicious study of discernible reality. That's not the way the world really works anymore. We're an empire now, and when we act, we create our own reality. And while you are studying that reality—judiciously, as you will—we'll act again, creating other new realities, which you can study too, and that's how things will sort out. We're history's actors, and you, all of you, will be left to just study what we do.
> *www.nytimes.com/2004/10/17/magazine/faith-certainty-and-the-presidency-of-george-w-bush.html*

(Rove denies ever saying it.) Yet the trajectory of the statement framed the very core of the Bush presidency push for the second Iraq war via the construction of the "new realities" about the catastrophic push to start it because of the so called "truth" of weapons of mass destruction that needed to be dealt with. One can easily leap to post-contemporary moment of living with Trumpism's "alternative facts" land. Now the question of what tactical gesture needs to take place beyond the aesthetics of "truth" and "reality." We have to re-consider the potential of using the aesthetics of dislocation that is organized not by "reality" or "fact" but by focusing on the un-real, the un-truth or the un-fact via what scholar, poet and member of Electronic Disturbance Theater 2.0, Amy Sara Carroll has name as the un-documentary form in book *REMEX: Toward An Art History of the NAFTA ERA*. The un-documentary is a contestational gesture that seeks to establish an un-reality based community outside of the discourse of the U.S. Empire and its multiple collusions and risk creating practices that make visible the un-real frames its production in order to re-locate progressive social actions "not at the speed of technology, but at the speed of dreams" as the Zapatistas, in Chiapas, Mexico, like to sing.

31
TRIGGER WARNINGS AND THE DISCIPLINING OF CINEMA AND MEDIA PEDAGOGY

Lucas Hilderbrand

Trigger warnings are content advisories intended to alert readers, viewers, and/or students with post-traumatic stress disorder (PTSD) about representations or language that may "trigger" panic attacks, flashbacks, dissociation, the impulse to self-harm, or other disabling responses. Trigger warnings began as a feminist practice online, informing discussion board, blog, and fan fiction readers about the inclusion of discussions of rape, incest, sexual violence, domestic violence or other subjects likely to be personally sensitive; in this original context, the goal of trigger warnings was to be sensitive to survivors of traumatic experiences by allowing them to make informed decisions whether to continue reading and/or to prepare themselves mentally if they choose to do so. Variations on this practice have been adapted in a number of college and university courses, often in response to students' requests. The migration of trigger warnings from online venues to classrooms in the United States, however, has been controversial, to put it mildly. Since 2014, academic and popular press accounts of trigger warnings have suggested a generational battle of wills between students and faculty, with claims of coddled students and chilling effects on academic freedom among the most prominent talking points.

Advocates argue that trigger warnings allow students who experience PTSD to prepare themselves to engage sensitive course content but that the goal is not necessarily to allow students to opt out of required material; such verbal warnings provide minimal accommodation for students who would otherwise experience a form a disability that would prevent them from participating and learning. Although trigger warnings, in the proper sense, may have a specific meaning and intended purpose, their deployment and the debates about them exist in charged contexts that often blur boundaries between the trigger warnings and other issues. Trigger warnings are intended to address trauma, but they are often invoked in cases of offense: commentators, pro and con, agree that trigger warnings are not intended to protect students from being politically or personally offended in a way that would curtail ideological debate or grappling with structures of oppression. Yet a repeatedly expressed concern is that students conflate forms of being uncomfortable—being offended, being put on the spot, being accused, being disagreed with, being spoken to in a loud or stern voice, being called out, and having PTSD—with being triggered. Some advocates of trigger warnings suggest that they do not go far enough insofar as they give permission to perpetuate hateful language, worldviews, and violence as long as a trigger warning is given.[1] The conflict over trigger warnings is ultimately also about power: who decides what is and what can be said.[2]

The intensity of the debates about trigger warnings reveals a culture in which both students and instructors feel vulnerable. Students may feel vulnerable to the faculty who design course syllabi and to their classmates' comments, as well as to the world beyond the classroom. Faculty may feel vulnerable to student demands, to institutional policies, and to ever-more-precarious and laborious professional status. Multiple scales or forms of risk can be activated or felt in these situations: individual risk (based in trauma, mental health, and/or personal experiences and circumstances), institutional risk (subject to bureaucratic policies based in liability-adverse actuarial logics as much as due process), and social risk (the structural oppressions and inequalities that continue to shape—and misshape—power dynamics, including on campuses). In the humanities, we often seek to interrogate social risks through the lens of individual risk narratives or representations, which in turn we may hope students internalize for personal intellectual, political, even humanist transformation. But hoping our students are personally affected by course material obviously risks triggering experiences —and, in turn, risks our own professional security.

In this chapter, I review some of the language used in advocating for and cautioning against trigger warnings. I am less interested in defending or decrying the practice of offering trigger warnings than in understanding them as a symptom or index of broader institutional crises in higher education and as an opportunity to question our discipline-specific pedagogies.[3] As cinema and media studies continues to expand in its objects and methods, the field no longer retains a coherent sense of what the shared theoretical or formal lessons for our students must be. Although the accounts of trigger warnings have predominantly pertained to teaching in the humanities generally or to topics related to gender, sexuality, race, and ethnicities specifically—rather than cinema and media studies—the preponderance of images and media as the content that triggers poses important implications for our discipline.

I look to trigger warnings to examine the kinds of institutional critique that the debate around them helps us see, which the attention to trigger warnings at times misdirects or blurs. I also want to think more specifically about how the questions they raise can be discipline-specific, which the discussions of trigger warnings rarely examine. Although often framed as a scandal of intellectual freedom, I find it more productive to think of the trigger warning movement and the resistance to it as a struggle to define the purpose of higher education and renegotiate what should be taught or can be required of students. In the next section, I track back to frame trigger warnings as a symptom of broader structural problems on campuses; in the following section, I zoom back in to suggest that it may be time to question our own discipline's pedagogical goals.

Campuses in Crisis

Two of the most publicized campuswide policies for requiring trigger warnings appeared at the small prestigious liberal arts college Oberlin College and at the large public research institution the University of California, Santa Barbara (UCSB) in early 2014. Oberlin's administration imposed a controversial campuswide policy mandating trigger warnings on course syllabi, which was repealed after faculty resistance (see Flaherty). At UCSB, the call came from students, specifically the Associated Student Senate, which advanced "A Resolution to Mandate Warnings For Triggering Content in Academic Settings," calling for warnings in courses with content referencing or representing "Rape, Sexual Assault, Abuse, Self-Injurious Behavior, Suicide, Graphic Violence, Pornography, Kidnapping, and Graphic Depictions of Gore." The faculty academic senate at UCSB did not adopt or validate the student's resolution. The UCSB resolution begins by stating statistics for the incidence of sexual assault, rape, and domestic violence on college campuses and presents triggers as a symptom of post-traumatic stress syndrome, which is a recognized disability. The resolution requests that this disability be recognized by faculty so as not to interfere with academic performance and access: "Having memories or flashbacks triggered can cause the person severe emotional, mental, and even physical distress. These reactions can affect a student's ability to perform academically." The resolution also refutes the most prevalent academic critiques of such warnings:

Including trigger warnings is not a form of criticism or censorship of content. In addition, it does not restrict academic freedom but simply requests the respect and acknowledgement of the affect of triggering content on students with PTSD, both diagnosed and undiagnosed.[4]

Responding to the emergent movement, small and large collectives of faculty issued statements critiquing the basic premise of trigger warnings in 2014. A group taking the name 7 Humanities Professors, featuring a number of cinema and media studies scholars, offered a ten-point essay on why they would not use such warnings. I condense and summarize their points (with which I agree, point-by-point) below:

1. Faculty cannot predict triggers, and research on PTSD and trauma has not demonstrated that representations trigger.
2. Triggers cannot distinguish critical from sensationalistic representations.
3. Faculty are not trained to address student traumas.
4. PTSD is a disability and class accommodations are most appropriately handled through campus disability services offices rather than ad hoc by faculty.
5. Trigger warnings may prompt students to file complaints against individual faculty rather than seeking appropriate treatment.
6. Demands for trigger warnings may become pervasive rather than at the discretion of individual faculty.
7. Faculty of color, queer faculty, and faculty teaching in gender and sexuality studies are more likely to be targeted with complaints.
8. Untenured and adjunct faculty are more likely to experience a chilling effect in their choice of course materials and vulnerable to disciplinary fallout from student complaints.
9. Trigger warnings present the illusion that campuses are addressing sexual and/or racial aggression systematically when they may not be.
10. Trigger warnings can prompt increased Title IX investigations that have significant costs in terms of resources, labor, and faculty climate.

(see 7 Humanities Faculty)

As the 7 Humanities Faculty suggest, trigger warnings are misguided and ineffective because no systematic policy can address the nuances and specificities of personal trauma, faculty are not the appropriate people to handle students' mental health issues, and they disproportionately impact faculty who are most vulnerable to discrimination or employment precarity. The first two points, specific to questions of representation, would seem to draw most clearly from cinema and media studies insights, whereas latter institutional critiques come out of social justice commitments of gender and sexuality studies and critical race and ethnic studies. Students who request warnings or file complaints and the administrators who investigate complaints may not understand the pedagogical goals of the course content and may conflate being uncomfortable or merely offended with being triggered.

In August 2014, the American Association of University Professors (AAUP) issued a report on trigger warnings, declaring

> The presumption that students need to be protected rather than challenged in a classroom is at once infantilizing and anti-intellectual. It makes comfort a higher priority than intellectual engagement and—as the Oberlin list demonstrates—it singles out politically controversial topics like sex, race, class, capitalism, and colonialism for attention. Indeed, if such topics are associated with triggers, correctly or not, they are likely to be marginalized

if not avoided altogether by faculty who fear complaints for offending or discomforting some of their students. Although all faculty are affected by potential charges of this kind, non-tenured and contingent faculty are particularly at risk.

Furthermore, it contends

> The classroom is not the appropriate venue to treat PTSD, which is a medical condition that requires serious medical treatment. Trigger warnings are an inadequate and diversionary response. Medical research suggests that triggers for individuals can be unpredictable, dependent on networks of association. So color, taste, smell, and sound may lead to flashbacks and panic attacks as often as the mention of actual forms of violence such as rape and war. The range of any student's sensitivity is thus impossible to anticipate. But if trigger warnings are required or expected, anything in a classroom that elicits a traumatic response could potentially expose teachers to all manner of discipline and punishment.
> … The Americans with Disabilities Act contains recommendations for reasonable accommodation to be made on an individual basis. This should be done without affecting other students' exposure to material that has educational value.
>
> (AAUP)

Virtually all of the think pieces and reporting I've come across in the so-called liberal press and educational trade journals—*New Republic, Salon, The Atlantic, New York Times, Los Angeles Times, The Chronicle of Higher Education, Inside Higher Ed*—have resoundingly opposed trigger warnings, at times with a scandalized tone (see Blanchard, Daum, Gay, and Jarvie). Few such articles actually quote students; a *New Yorker* article, which is an exception to this trend, makes student complaints seem ridiculous (Heller). A controversial article in *The Atlantic* presented the rise in requests for trigger warnings and claims of microaggressions—which the authors call "vindictive protectiveness"—as the product of "coddling" and as harmful to students. As belittling as this article may appear, the authors connect students' pleas for trigger warnings to rising rates of mental distress. The authors reference numerous common cognitive disorders that likely exacerbate students' perceptions of hostility or triggering. They also cite a 2014 report that "54 percent of college students surveyed said that they had 'felt overwhelming anxiety' in the past 12 months"—an uptick of 5 percent over five years. If students are feeling increasingly anxious, so too are universities when it comes to liability. The authors signal that administrators have had reason to become more skittish about student claims because federal antidiscrimination statutes have lowered the bar for actionable speech from "objectively offensive" (in 2003) to merely "unwelcome" (in 2013). The authors offer governmental and administrative solutions to the crisis of oversensitivity and stifled speech, from raising the federal threshold for claims of harassment to teaching cognitive behavioral therapy techniques to incoming students during orientation—much the way cultural sensitivity is—to help give students the skills to deal with their distress (Lukianoff and Haidt). Although faculty may claim that we are "not therapists" to our students, such claims are at least partially disingenuous; our work *is* affective labor, and we *do* have to manage the affects of a student population with increasing neurodiversity and anxiety across a range of contexts—in the classroom, in office hours, and most difficultly (because tone and affect can be difficult to gauge) via email. Indeed, managing student distress can be the most draining part of our jobs.

Perhaps the most troubling anecdotal account arguing against trigger warnings that I have read came from an instructor who actually used them. In a piece for *Salon*, Rani Neutill recounted teaching a course on the history of sex in cinema and using trigger warnings in her syllabus and before specific clips. She states that she believed in trigger warnings, particularly as someone who had witnessed a friend's sexual assault, who volunteered at her local rape crisis center, and who worked as acting director of the Office of Sexual Assault Prevention Services. Despite her commitment to feminist community support and pedagogy, she recounts that students continued to abruptly leave the class in tears and to request ever-more explicit trigger warnings, including comprehensive advance emails detailing very potential triggers. She describes that the students did not do the assigned reading, which would have contextualized the clips in class, and refused or failed to grasp the goal of analyzing historical representations of sex—including racialized sex. One student demanded positive representations prior to being shown any troubling ones. Neutill suggests that trigger warnings only begat more trigger warnings, despite her feminist belief in them at the start of the term. The experience of the class prompted her to leave academia after a decade of teaching. What this widely circulated autobiographical think piece suggests is not only were trigger warnings ineffective in this case but that the students at times tried to dictate the content and the lessons to be learned from the course.

Of course, not all faculty oppose trigger warnings. But also importantly, others have tried to redirect the debate. Examining the rise of anxieties about trigger warnings in the U.S. concurrently with the increasingly bureaucraticization of British higher education, Sara Ahmed (who subsequently resigned from Goldsmiths College in protest of campus policies) has recognized the scapegoating of students as a common—and misguided—rhetorical refrain.

> The moral panic around trigger warnings is a very good pedagogic tool: we learn from it. Trigger warnings are assumed to be about being safe or warm or cuddled. I would describe trigger warnings as a partial and necessarily inadequate measure to enable some people to stay in the room so that "difficult issues" can be discussed....
>
> It seems to me that it is often students who are leading discussions of "difficult issues" on campus. But when students lead these discussions they are then dismissed as behaving like consumers or as being censorious....
>
> My own sense is that our feminist political hopes rest with over-sensitive students.
>
> Over-sensitive can be translated as: Sensitive to that which is not over.
>
> All of these ways of making students into the problem work to create a picture of professors or academics as the ones who are "really" oppressed by students....
>
> We are learning more here about professors (their investments, emotions, and strategies of dismissal) than we are learning about students.

Ahmed rightfully understands the trigger warning debates within a broader political context, but even her careful recuperation of such warnings reflects that the issue bleeds into more generalized frustrations with liberal "policing" and tensions between students and instructors over appropriate speech and course content. Faculty and students alike blur the distinctions between what might be properly understood as triggering trauma and what is offensive; although these may well overlap in specific instances, differentiating the two would surely present any number of "teachable moments."

The rise of trigger warnings has frequently been attributed in part to a generation gap between instructors and undergraduates, at times characterized as a new form of political correctness run amok—often code for dismissing the existence, experiences, and identities of already marginalized populations. Substantive communication that might clarify and negotiate generational differences seems to not be happening as the divides become entrenched in this controversy. Because students interface with their instructors most immediately and regularly, it should not be surprising that they often voice their distress to their instructors rather than to upper administration. Unfortunately, this often creates antagonisms between faculty and their students—and situates administrators as mediators—without addressing structural biases and institutional conservatism.

It may be easy to conflate—or, indeed, difficult to disentangle—the varied implications of a generational shift in students who seemingly do not want to be "challenged." Instructors routinely recount anecdotal frustrations that higher education has come like a kind of customer service in which students are "entitled" and don't have the focus or discipline to do the assigned readings but nonetheless expect inflated grades. It can be easy to experience this as pandering on the part of instructors and laziness on the part of students. Another issue is that many students have been raised in a K-12 educational model that has taught them how to take standardized texts or lower-division composition classes that teach them reductive five-paragraph essay formats. Such pedagogy has not given them the conceptual tools or intellectual freedom to think complexly or curiously, nor to see learning as valuable in unquantifiable/non-monetizable ways. Humanities education can mean trying to undo the entirety of students' prior training, which can be frustrating for all involved because the students may not understand such a shift in orientation, whereas faculty may not recognize the need to articulate such basic principles. Beyond such generalized pedagogical expectations and goals in which instructors and students may have conflicting perspectives, another goal of humanist education poses a challenge that is more threatening because it is more ideological, political, and personal: one of the goals of higher education is (or arguably should be) for students to encounter perspectives, experiences, and interpretations different from their own, which necessarily causes the unsettling process of prompting one to question one's given worldview.

Each of these kinds of discomfort for students is different from what precisely demands personalized trigger warnings. Yet each might also blur into the demands, frustrations, and debates around such warnings: instructors may feel that trigger warnings are just another consumerist demand, or they may not sufficiently explain the educational value of complex, ambivalent, or unfamiliar content. Students may not fully differentiate between course material that is threatening because it counters their ideological expectations and because it stimulates specific personal traumas.

The debates about trigger warnings appeared as a flashpoint amid a number of other crises facing U.S. campuses and cannot be understood without at least acknowledging some of these contexts (in no specific order):

- escalating tuition costs and student debt;
- decades of austerity and budget cuts for schools at all levels;
- politically motivated defunding of public education;
- the general privatization of education;
- the push toward online rather than in-person instruction;
- exploitative admissions practices of non-resident "net payer" students at public universities;
- U.S. educational investment in STEM fields at the costs of arts and humanities;
- assessment-driven educational policies;
- reliance upon underpaid and exploited adjunct and lecturer instructors instead of tenure-line faculty;
- the dismantling of tenure at some institutions;
- the growth of upper campus administration;
- the cutting of on-the-ground staffing and student services;
- academically under-prepared students during K-12;
- surveillant parenting styles that have not raised children to be self-reliant adults;
- admissions practices designed to recruit more diverse students without sufficient on-campus climate programs or critical masses of communities to make campuses non-alienating for minority students;
- increased attention to and backlash against trans students;
- high incidences and increased awareness of racist graffiti and racial tensions on campuses;
- increased attention to and backlash against the concept of microaggressions;
- invitations to and cancellations of appearances by politically controversial speakers, which spark debates about free speech on campuses;
- campus police brutality against student protestors;
- fatal shootings on or near campuses;

- woefully inadequate and understaffed campus counseling and mental health services;
- a survivor-led student movement to utilize Title IX protections to expose the high incidence of sexual assaults on campuses across the U.S.—and a broadening of the category of "sexual assault";
- pervasive non-response and cover-ups by college campuses for complaints about sexual assaults and investigations of harassments complaints that become their own forms of harassment—for both complainants and the accused;[5]
- the tendency to only address sex as a problem, rather than institutionalizing education and resources for developing our student's *positive* sexual health, curiosity, exploration, pleasure, and informed consent;
- administrative policies that serve to protect the college or university from liability, litigation, or loss of future revenues rather than to protect students, faculty, or staff;
- and, in the wake of the 2016 U.S. election, the precarious protections of campuses as "sanctuaries" for undocumented students (typically those brought to the U.S. as children without legal immigration status).

Individually and collectively, this laundry list of issues has created cultures of frustration, anxiety, and anger on college campuses. Social media platforms echo many of these issues: they have importantly allowed for such campus crises to be exposed and shared, but they also allow for trolling responses to self disclosures and social justice critiques. This reflects a classic double-bind: visibility for controversial issues or for marginalized people often renders them more vulnerable, even as visibility is necessary for political and personal enfranchisement. Aside from occasional publicity or activism, students and faculty alike often feel powerless to effect change on many of these fronts. Requesting trigger warnings may be one of the few resources students feel they can call upon amid so much insecurity and negativity—and in some instances may not be a response to PTSD exactly so much as generalized anxiety.

In many instances, being triggered has become conflated with being harassed; individuals tend to be targeted for punishment, rather than structural issues for change and prevention; and individual cases are being remediated through an expanded interpretation of Title IX (gender non-discrimination) protections. The situation has become so untenable that the AAUP issued a report on the "History, Uses, and Abuses of Title IX."[6] Among its findings, the Office of Civil Rights (OCR) had long affirmed that investigations of sexual harassment and other complaints must exist in tandem with protecting academic freedom; in 2011, the OCR's guidelines on Title IX investigations stopped including language about academic freedom (AAUP draft report, 16). In 2013, the OCR "broaden[ed] … the definition of sexual harassment to encompass any 'unwelcome conduct' (including speech)," which "create[d] a seemingly limitless definition of harassment." Furthermore, "In its policy documents and compliance investigation reports, OCR has given only limited attention to the due process rights of those accused of misconduct" (AAUP draft report, 17).[7] These processes ultimately serve to protect the college or university from liability and litigation more than to protect students or faculty. They also expose how the legalistic yet incoherent policies and procedures produce a kind of "administrative trauma" that exposes "the university's experience of its own vulnerability" (Doyle 9 and 24).[8] The AAUP report affirms that investigations and punishment based on Title IX complaints may have unintended consequences of silencing speech in women's, gender, and queer studies classes and in allied disciplines, as well as disproportionately impact faculty of color when bias informs allegations.

One of the common reactionary ways of dismissing requests for trigger warnings is to suggest that the world is not a "safe space"—so the classroom shouldn't be either. Although I agree that coddling and limitless exceptions (this applies to deadlines for assignments even more than anything else) deserve students for life skills beyond the classroom, this argument also misses the basic point of a safe space. A safe space is intended to precisely allow for students to engage with difficult, sensitive, or controversial material and to express and encounter different points of view openly without self-censoring or fears of retaliation. Much of the press coverage of trigger warnings seems to misunderstand safe spaces as censured classrooms where controversial topics and opposing viewpoints cannot be uttered. Although we perhaps most often see triggering as affecting those who are socially most oppressed—women, people of color, queer and trans students—such claims are also at times perversely taken up by straight white cis men who feel their own privilege under attack.

Trigger warnings are perhaps unique among these issues in that the primary site of tension occurs between students and teachers. The call for trigger warnings, which is about what gets taught and how, might on the one hand seem to reiterate a paradigm shift in academia and a struggle between the disempowered (students) and the power structure (faculty and instructors). Contested positions over curriculum are nothing new, but the goals that undergird trigger warnings might be: they indicate a shift away from broad identitarian debates over inclusion in the canon toward more personalized accommodation. One of the uncomfortable shifts marked by the invocation of trigger warnings is that, whereas debates about academic freedom a few decades ago fought for inclusion of multicultural and sexual course content against conservative moral censors, the more recent conflicts would seem to come from the same end of the ideological spectrum. Professors who consider themselves leftists are likely to be flummoxed and defensive when students confront their biases and privileges.

If the trigger warning debate caught fire in 2014, it may have reached its denouement—though without resolutions—in 2016. In August 2016, the Dean of Students at the University of Chicago provoked controversy in his welcome letter to incoming freshman by stating,

> Our commitment to academic freedom means that we do not support so-called trigger warnings, we do not cancel invited speakers because their topics might prove controversial and we do not condone the creation of intellectual safe spaces where individuals can retreat from ideas and perspectives at odds with their own.
>
> (Jaschik "U Chicago to Freshman")

More than 150 University of Chicago faculty signed a response letter published in the campus newspaper, stating in part,

> let there be no mistake: such requests often touch on substantive, ongoing issues of bias, intolerance, and trauma that affect our intellectual exchanges. To start a conversation by declaring that such requests are not worth making is an affront to the basic principles of liberal education and participatory democracy.
>
> ("Letter")

In the past 50 years, academia has seen a number of student protests and politicized upheavals that have sought to challenge what gets taught and how—from Marxists who questioned the dominant ideologies of a previously under-interrogated narrative of western civilization to feminists who taught us to recognize structural sexisms to cultural studies scholars who intervened in hierarchies of elite and popular texts to critical ethnic studies, postcolonial, queer, and other frameworks that have challenged our narratives of identity, cultural nationalism and nationhood, sovereignty, and norms (see Ferguson). Each of these movements encountered resistance and dismissal from the status quo, but some legitimation, recognition, and regression has also happened in fits and starts. Although overtly politicized, each was also—despite debates over recognizing the legitimacy of such scholarship—*academic* insofar as it sought to change what is taught, who gets hired and tenured, and ultimately how we interpret the world. Cinema and media studies are very much the product of each of these interventions and intellectual movements.

Cinema and Media Studies and the Pedagogy of Shock

At its most broadly conceived, cinema and media studies examine the production and dissemination of moving images and their formal, ideological, political, cultural–historical, and personal meanings for viewers. Spectatorship has been one of the core preoccupations of film theory, and reception has been one of the central topics of media studies. Trigger warnings attempt to anticipate audience's emotional and physical responses to specific representational moments or plot events. Thus, it might seem that cinema and media studies would be one of the most germane humanist disciplines to shed light on triggered responses. Yet, spectatorship and reception theories have primarily focused on pleasure, objectification, and normalizing ideologies—or on reading against the grain and appropriation. What our discipline teaches us is that audiences negotiate their own complex and idiosyncratic meanings from texts, rather than responding automatically to stimulation. The claims of texts' power to indoctrinate audiences has been challenged for decades. Therefore, the basic logic of trigger warnings counters our basic disciplinary tenets about how reception works. The turn to phenomenology and affect theory as a post-psychoanalytic method might be more productive for addressing triggered responses, yet the individualized nature of embodied responses and emotion frustrate generalizable (as opposed to autobiographical) theoretical frameworks. Even a recent theoretical work on viscerally difficult films offers a troublingly depoliticized and depersonalized focus on form (see Brinkema). One of the impasses of spectatorship theory is that it can never make effective universalizing claims, nor ever-comprehensive-enough affordances for different positions and experiences.[9]

Rather than attempt to explain triggered responses through theory, however, I want to focus instead on the pedagogical logics of our discipline. Among our longstanding—or at least once-common—disciplinary pedagogical assumptions has been that encountering shocking or challenging formal techniques is important for students to expand their understanding of the film medium. In "old school" film history (the era of the discipline's own struggle for institutional legitimation), shock was canonized as a defining strategy of the medium's aesthetic history in such films as *Electrocuting an Elephant*, *Battleship Potempkin*, *Un Chien Andalou*, *Psycho*, *La hora de los hornos*, and *Pink Flamingos*, to name just a handful of examples. Texts that pack a punch have also been the go-tos for teaching the elements of film form: the fight sequences in *Raging Bull*, for instance, are more likely to get students' attention when discussing editing than more subtle clips. For decades, seeing key difficult, viscerally assaultive films was treated as a rite of passage for film students—and, let's be honest, a source of lightly sadistic pleasure for instructors. But reactions to certain film texts has also long been more or less predictable; instructors can anticipate near-universal discomfort at seeing the slicing of an eyeball or the eating of dog shit. Among of the shifts introduced by trigger warnings are the expectation that instructors should anticipate more personalized responses and that full-disclosure itemized warnings (perhaps not dissimilar to allergen warnings on food) would essentially spoil the impact of the texts. And, of course, our canons reflect their own historical contexts. Although not "shocking" in the same way as the films mentioned above, I'm personally more uncomfortable when screening *Rashomon*—with its retelling of a sexual assault in which it appears that the woman likes it—in my film history survey class than when screening pornography in my electives.

As cinema studies pedagogy has expanded beyond a formalist aesthetic history or a psychoanalytic–semiotic theoretical lens to include other media and methods, fewer undergraduate programs' curricula appear to require year-long survey courses teaching students a linear canonical history of cinema, and therefore we appear to have moved away from a standardized expectation of what students know and what they've seen.[10] The logic of "and media" has, by and large, been an additive one—a strategy of coverage and inclusion—rather than actually contending with rethinking the core projects of our discipline. With important reorientations toward enfranchising media studies, non-Western cinemas, cultural studies, feminist studies, critical race studies, and queer studies, shock arguably became decentered as an aesthetic paradigm for the medium (increasingly understood as plural media) and was coincidentally repositioned as an originary historiographic paradigm through work on early cinema and modernity. I present this broader disciplinary context to understand the intellectual moment in which trigger warnings have emerged and the ways in which the pedagogy of "shock" has shifted.

Curiously, the very term "trigger" connotes gun violence and a connection to our conceptions of early cinema's technologies and impacts. A number of sources trace the concept of triggering to shellshock and PTSD in the wake of World War I. The related concepts of shock and post-traumatic stress likewise have roots in military settings. Wolfgang Schivelbusch traces the origins of "shock" in the modern strategies of war, when combat transitioned from person-to-person fighting to a barrage of bullets fired in unison without aiming at a singular target in order to kill as many people as possible at once; the risks and experiences of being struck without sensing the bullet's specific source and the resulting state of psychosomatic disorientation were termed "shock." This experience of shock became generalized as a condition of modern life, of which cinema has come to be understood as the exemplary sensational visual medium (see Charney and Schwartz; Gunning; Hansen; Singer).[11] As art historians often remind us, the early twentieth-century term "avant-garde" derives from the military "front lines" of battle, and Paul Virilio has suggested the interconnections of war and cinema itself.

Cinema and media studies have become ever-more decentered disciplines with numerous, largely separate fields of research. As I've discussed with various friends and colleagues in recent years, there is less than ever a sense that we share the same texts; for instance, it would be hard to claim that any book in our discipline published in the past decade can be assumed to have been read across the discipline. This decentering is most likely productive, but as we may need to recognize that there are no longer central debates—and possibly not even debates—in our discipline that give our work clear stakes and interventions, we need to then ask what we are trying to achieve.

My own attention to disciplinarity surely comes at least in part out of the fact my own institutional location: I am faculty in an interdisciplinary and interdepartmental graduate program (visual studies, constituted by film and media studies and art history) and regularly teach classes cross-listed between film and media studies and gender and sexuality studies. One of the lessons that I have learned is that different disciplines ask different questions and have different foundational assumptions; one of the most productive elements of interdisciplinarity is to recognize the structuring logics that bound one's one intellectual bubble. I have also (skeptically, grudgingly) written curriculum assessment reports at both undergraduate and graduate levels. If there is anything productive about those processes, it is being forced to articulate for oneself and one's students the goals of your pedagogy. The ways these goals must be articulated to the administration almost inevitably becomes so general—"teaching critical thinking and writing"—as to be unquantifiable, creating a tautological administrative exercise to rationalize an existing curriculum's existence.

But what if—for ourselves if not for the administration—we actually asked ourselves the big existential disciplinary questions? What would those questions be? Perhaps:

- What do we actually need to change in our teaching and in what (possibly new) ways do we need to be accountable to our students and learn what they need from us?
- What is the purpose of our core classes: are they for teaching a canon of films, industrial histories, and theories—in other words, of discipline-specific assumed or essential knowledge? Or are they for teaching a set of analytical skills? How are we communicating these goals to our students?
- Does the expansion of our discipline to be more inclusive mean that we need to rethink its central questions?
- Are we listening to what our students find useful and what they want or need to learn? How can we be responsive to these desires, even as we respectfully recognize they may not yet know what they need to learn or may not yet have the language to articulate it?
- How do we make cinema and media histories and theories relevant, rather than just things to be learned for their own academic sake? What are the stakes of what we're teaching?

- Is becoming more inclusive—by including works by women, by people of color, from beyond Europe and the U.S., of different media or platforms—sufficient? How do we work toward inclusion in meaningful rather than just tokenizing ways? Does validating historically under-recognized material by normalizing its inclusion in courses actually change how we understand cinema and media and change our discipline?
- Can our discipline ever be finished with addressing questions of representation—particularly if this framework continues to be among the first and most persistent kinds of questions students want to ask and for which they seek answers? Although I was trained in an era when questions of representation were often dismissed as passé, the allure, complexity, and shortcomings of representation remain central preoccupations within the industry and for audiences. Isn't every figural media text on some level about social identity, gender, sexuality, race, ethnicity, nationality, class, and sovereignty?
- How do we teach contemporary and recent media when our students have fewer and fewer common frames of reference as audiences consume a wider range of moving-image media across so many platforms at different times?
- Does medium specificity matter anymore? Should our classes teach across media, formats, and platforms? Should all classes be transmedial or start from the assumption of digital delivery?
- How do we adjust our pedagogy and our expectations to the specificities of our students; different schools serve different populations and student cultures, so a one size-fits-all curricular model would be ineffective.
- How do we teach our students to think critically, ideologically, and independently about media when they've been taught to take standardized tests in K-12 and have been raised in a culture that deskills them for problem solving?
- How can we be responsive to the underlying issues raised by trigger warnings within the specific context of cinema and media studies classes?
- Don't we risk under-serving our students if we don't ask ourselves these questions?[12]

I recognize that I am concluding with questions rather than answers. In part, this is because I don't have the answers—and don't believe that there are satisfying singular responses. But I also want my colleagues in the field to ask these questions of the discipline and of themselves. I imagine there would be a wide range of perspectives, just as there are and must be many forms and methods of media, feminism, and queer pedagogy.

Offering one way forward through the trigger warning debate that draws from media audience practices rather than more academic intellectual histories, Alexis Lothian looks to the content advisory notices common in fan fiction and fan conventions that predate more recent academic trigger warnings. Recognizing fan practice's orientation toward pleasure and creativity, such advisories were as much a signal to opt-in as to opt-out for fans. Lothian ponders,

> What if the praxis of warning, broadly conceived, can be a method not to avoid such [intensely affective] spaces and experiences, but to facilitate them? Fandom's history with warnings ... does suggest possibilities for creatively appropriating warnings discourse in order to shape the worlds we want to create....
>
> (745)

Lothian does not demonize trigger warnings but suggests, following fan practices, a discursive shift from "trigger *warnings*," which could predetermine interpretations, to the more neutral phrase "content *notes*" (753–755). In this, fan cultures have found productive ways to self-determine participation; even though class media and assignments are generally less than voluntary, this rhetorical shift may be helpful.

I still believe in the potential value of pedagogies of shock: of working through formally, politically, and/or viscerally challenging moving images.[13] But we also need to be sensitive to the complexities of such texts and of our students, attending both to the aesthetic and historical specificities of media and to the range of charged new reactions they might engender for our students. The classroom remains perhaps the best venue for talking through how and why some scenes have particular kinds of power, what motives the creation of troubling texts, and how our responses to them are more complicated than just personal taste. A classroom retains the immediacy and potential for a dynamic space of dialogue, for thinking differently. But instructors need to recognize that charged responses from students may reflect broader institutional anxieties, not just an encounter with a text or a classroom dynamic. We also have to be prepared to be uncomfortable and question our own assumptions and reactions, just as we expect students to do.

Postscript, September 2018

The mid-2010s debate about trigger warnings has waned as a number of recent events—most conspicuously the 2016 U.S. election and the 2017 #MeToo campaign—became more urgent and all-consuming. I wrote the above essay between summer and fall 2016 and have decided to maintain the text, aside from minor revisions, as a snaphot of the debate at a particular moment. I have added this brief postscript because I see these subsequent historical developments as expanding and intensifying attention to many of the same underlying issues and affects that animated the discussion of trigger warnings.

In the wake of the 2016 U.S. election, the new administration promised far-reaching crises for education funding, civil rights protections, mass deportation, and access to basic human services. Most directly relevant to the analysis above, in fall 2017 the Trump administration's Secretary of Education Betsy DeVos rescinded the Obama administration's Title IX guidelines, introduced in 2011 and 2014. DeVos's interim guidelines allowed individual campuses to determine their own standards of evidence, timeline, and appropriate resolutions; these changes were presented as reinstating more due process for the accused but were perceived as rollbacks by victims' rights advocates (see Kreighbaum).[14]

Also in fall 2017, #MeToo became a viral hashtag campaign that exposed the pervasive experiences of sexual harassment and sexual violence, with countless people disclosing themselves as survivors by posting "#MeToo" on social media. (The phrase was originally coined by Tarana Burke in 2006.) A number of powerful men in the entertainment industry and other fields were forced to resign in disgrace after their histories as sexual predators were exposed by the people they targeted. Through investigative journalism articles, the campaign also served to expose *institutional* structures of complicity and silence (see, for instance, Twohey et al.). In 2018, a high-profile sexual harassment case involving a senior female advisor and a male graduate student (both queer identified) at New York University effectively became the face of #MeToo in academia and produced polemical responses about abuses of power, star mentors, and queer pedagogy, among other issues (see Gessen for an overview). In the culture at large, #MeToo has put men (predominantly) on alert that they, too, may be called to accountability for past conduct. The #MeToo discourse has not only exposed clear-cut wrongful behavior but also, in certain cases, ambiguity and complexity; reception of the accusations against Aziz Ansari, in contrast to most other high-profile instances, produced little consensus because the detailed retelling of the encounter seemed to reveal mixed messages and differing expectations about what constitutes consent. We are effectively in a transitional period when new norms about sex, consent, and scales of accountability are being worked out—at times with diverging generational interpretations—but not yet agreed upon.

The rhetoric and policies of the Trump administration and the visibility and consequences of the #MeToo movement intensify the existing vulnerability and anxiety felt by students, staff, and faculty—what I suggest motivated the trigger warnings debate. As political and sexual speech have become more pitched in our present moment, they are also more essential than ever for rigorous analysis and open class discussion.

Notes

1. See, for instance, Jos Charles' contributions to Milks, "On Trigger Warnings: A Roundtable."
2. As anecdotal evidence of instantaneous backlash, sarcastic claims to being "triggered" also became colloquially used among my friends and colleagues during conversation.
3. To make my biases clear: I was strongly opposed to trigger warnings when I began researching this chapter, have become more sympathetic to their precise intended goals, but remain skeptical of their effectiveness in systematic use. In classes dealing with sexuality, I have included general content advisories on the syllabus but have not used specific trigger warnings in classes and have not had students request them.
4. www.as.ucsb.edu/senate/resolutions/a-resolution-to-mandate-warnings-for-triggering-content-in-academic-settings/.
5. For an account of the incidence of sexual assault and student mobilization in response to it, see the documentary *The Hunting Ground* (Kirby).
6. Signed into law in 1972, Title IX of the federal Education Acts states, "no person in the United States shall, on the basis of sex, be excluded from participation in, be denied the benefits of, or be subject to discrimination under any educational program or activity receiving Federal financial assistance." (AAUP "Executive Summary" 4.) "It encompasses ten key areas with regard to women's educational opportunities: access to higher education, athletics, career training and education, education for pregnant and parenting students, employment, the learning environment, math and science education, sexual harassment, standardized testing and technology." (AAUP "Executive Summary" 5).
7. In 2011, the OCR,

   > In a shift of enormous significance … prohibited the use of the standard calling for "clear and convincing" evidence (highly probable or reasonably certain), and replaced it with a lower standard: that there need be no more than a "preponderance of evidence" (more likely than not) to assess sexual violence claims and *all* sexual harassment claims.
   >
   > (AAUP "On Trigger Warnings" 18)

8. See also Laura Kipnis's articles for *The Chronicles of Higher Education* and her book, which expands upon them to offer broader critiques of Title IX overreach, lack of due process and transparency, and regressive feminism. For an important account of a feminist-identified mentor accused of sexual harassment two decades prior, see Gallop.
9. Masha Salazkina, however, offers a productive model of reflexive disciplinary and institutional analysis in tandem with introducing a collection of new work theorizing non-Western film and media.
10. In doing comparative undergraduate curricular review, I discovered that relatively few "peer institutions" require majors to take as many film history classes (a full year) as my home department.
11. For a more historically expansive aesthetic history of shock and trauma, see Lowenstein.
12. I later, separately have found myself asking variations on these questions in "The Big Picture."
13. I recognize that I assert this with the privilege and protection of tenure. We need to remember that tenure exists—where and for whom it exists—to protect risk-taking academic freedom, not to produce a deadening intellectual complacency. And that our privilege entails the responsibility to defend the academic freedom of those without job security.
14. As of this writing, the interim guidelines remain without permanent policies in place.

Works Cited

7 Humanities Faculty. "Essay by Faculty Members about Why They Will Not Use Trigger Warnings." *Inside Higher Ed*, May 29, 2014, www.insidehighered.com/views/2014/05/29/essay-faculty-members-about-why-they-will-not-use-trigger-warnings. Accessed September 30, 2018.

Ahmed, Sara. "Against Students." *The New Inquiry*, June 29, 2015, http://thenewinquiry.com/essays/against-students/. Accessed September 30, 2018.

American Association of University Professors (AAUP). "Executive Summary: The History, Uses, and Abuses of Title IX" (draft report), March 24, 2016, www.aaup.org/file/TitleIX-Report.pdf. Accessed September 30, 2018.

American Association of University Professors (AAUP). "On Trigger Warnings." August 2014, www.aaup.org/report/trigger-warnings. Accessed September 30, 2018.

Blanchard, Kathryn D. "Trigger Warnings: Not the Greatest Threat to Higher Education." *The Chronicle of Higher Education*, January 8, 2016, http://chronicle.com/article/Trigger-Warnings-Not-the/234778. Accessed September 30, 2018.

Brinkema, Eugine. *The Forms of the Affects*. Duke UP, 2014.

Charney, Leo and Vanessa R. Schwartz, eds. *Cinema and the Invention of Modern Life*. U of California P, 1995.

Daum, Megan. "Why 'Trigger Warnings'? We Already Live in a Hair-trigger World." *Los Angeles Times*, April 3, 2014, www.latimes.com/nation/la-oe-daum-trigger-warning-santa-barbara-20140403-column.html#axzz2ybI5UwVg. Accessed September 30, 2018.

Doyle, Jennifer. *Campus Sex/Campus Security*. Semiotext(e), 2015.

Ferguson, Roderick A. *We Demand: The University and Student Protests*. U of California P, 2017.

Flaherty, Colleen. "Trigger Unhappy." *Inside Higher Ed*, April 14, 2014, www.insidehighered.com/news/2014/04/14/oberlin-backs-down-trigger-warnings-professors-who-teach-sensitive-material#sthash.7F2fketT.dpbs. Accessed September 30, 2018.

Gallop, Jane. *Feminist Accused of Sexual Harassment*. Duke UP, 1997.

Gay, Roxane. "The Seduction of Safety, on Campus and Beyond." *New York Times*, November 13, 2015, www.nytimes.com/2015/11/15/opinion/sunday/the-seduction-of-safety-on-campus-and-beyond.html. Accessed September 30, 2018.

Gessen, Masha. "An NYU Sexual-Harassment Case Has Spurred a Necessary Conversation about #MeToo." *New Yorker*, August 25, 2018, www.newyorker.com/news/our-columnists/an-nyu-sexual-harassment-case-has-spurred-a-necessary-conversation-about-metoo. Accessed September 30, 2018.

Gunning, Tom. "An Aesthetic of Astonishment: Early Film and the [In]Credulous Spectator." *Art and Text*, vol. 34, Fall 1989, pp. 31–45.

Hansen, Miriam Brautu. *Cinema and Experience: Siegfried Kracauer, Walter Benjamin, and Theodor Adonro*. U of California P, 2012.

Heller, Nathan. "The Big Uneasy." *New Yorker*, May 30, 2016, www.newyorker.com/magazine/2016/05/30/the-new-activism-of-liberal-arts-colleges. Accessed September 30, 2018.

Hilderbrand, Lucas. "The Big Picture: On the Expansiveness of Cinema and Media Studies." *Cinema Journal*, vol. 57, no 2, winter 2018, 113–116.

Jarvie, Jenny. "Trigger Happy." *New Republic*, March 3, 2014, https://newrepublic.com/article/116842/trigger-warnings-have-spread-blogs-college-classes-thats-bad. Accessed September 30, 2018.

Jaschik, Scott. "The Chicago Letter and Its Aftermath." *Inside Higher Ed*, August 29, 2016, www.insidehighered.com/news/2016/08/29/u-chicago-letter-new-students-safe-spaces-sets-intense-debate. Accessed September 30, 2018.

Jaschik, Scott. "U Chicago to Freshmen: Don't Expect Safe Spaces." *Inside Higher Ed*, August 26, 2016, www.insidehighered.com/news/2016/08/25/u-chicago-warns-incoming-students-not-expect-safe-spaces-or-trigger-warnings.

Kipnis, Laura. "My Title IX Inquisition." *The Chronicle of Higher Education*, May 29, 2015, http://chronicle.com/article/My-Title-IX-Inquisition/230489. Accessed September 30, 2018.

Kipnis, Laura. "Sexual Paranoia Strikes Academe." *The Chronicle of Higher Education*, February 27, 2015, http://chronicle.com/article/Sexual-Paranoia-Strikes/190351/.

Kipnis, Laura. *Unwanted Advances: Sexual Paranoia Comes to Campus*. Harper, 2017. Accessed September 30, 2018.

Kirby, Dick. dir. *The Hunting Ground*. Chain Camera Pictures for CNN, 2015.

Kreighbaum, Andrew. "New Instructions on Title IX." *Inside Higher Ed*, September 25, 2017, www.insidehighered.com/news/2017/09/25/education-department-releases-interim-directions-title-ix-compliance.

"Letter: Faculty Respond To Ellison With A Letter Of Their Own." *The Chicago Maroon*, September 13, 2016, www.chicagomaroon.com/article/2016/9/13/letter-faculty-respond-ellison-letter/. Accessed September 30, 2018.

Lothian, Alexis. "Choose Not to Warn: Trigger Warnings and Content Notes from Fan Culture to Feminist Pedagogy." *Feminist Studies*, vol. 42, no. 3, 2016, pp. 743–756.

Lowenstein, Adam. *Shocking Representation: Historical Trauma, National Cinema, and the Modern Horror Film*. Columbia UP, 2005.

Lukianoff, Greg and Jonathan Haidt. "The Coddling of the American Mind." *The Atlantic*, September 2015, www.theatlantic.com/magazine/archive/2015/09/the-coddling-of-the-american-mind/399356/. Accessed September 30, 2018.

Milks, Megan. "On Trigger Warnings: A Roundtable. Part One: In the Creative Writing Classroom." *Entropy*, April 14, 2014, http://entropymag.org/on-trigger-warnings-part-i-in-the-creative-writing-classroom/. Accessed September 30, 2018.

Milks, Megan. "On Trigger Warnings: A Roundtable. Part Two: Generational Tensions." *Entropy*, April 16, 2014, http://entropymag.org/on-trigger-warnings-part-ii-generational-tensions/. Accessed September 30, 2018.

Milks, Megan. "On Trigger Warnings: A Roundtable. Part Three: Disability and Accommodation." *Entropy*, April 18, 2014, http://entropymag.org/on-trigger-warnings-part-iii-disability-and-accommodation/. Accessed September 30, 2018.

Neutill, Rani. "My Trigger-warning Disaster: '9 1/2 Weeks,' 'The Wire' and How Coddled Young Radicals Got Discomfort All Wrong." *Salon*, October 28, 2015, www.salon.com/2015/10/28/i_wanted_to_be_a_supporter_of_survivors_on_campus_and_a_good_teacher_i_didnt_realize_just_how_impossible_this_would_be/. Accessed September 30, 2018.

Salazkina, Masha. "Introduction: Film Theory in the Age of Neoliberal Globalization." *Framework*, vol. 56, no. 2, fall 2015, pp. 325–349.

Schivelbusch, Wolfgang. *The Railway Journey: The Industrialization of Time and Space in the 19th Century*. U of California P, 1987.

Singer, Ben. "Making Sense of the Modernity Thesis." *Melodrama and Modernity: Early Sensational Cinema and Its Contexts*. Columbia UP, 2001, pp. 101–130.

Twohey, Megan et al. "Weinstein's Complicity Machine" *New York Times*, December 5, 2017, www.nytimes.com/interactive/2017/12/05/us/harvey-weinstein-complicity.html. Accessed September 30, 2018.

Virilio, Paul. *War and Cinema*. Verso, 1989.

32

"A PATH SO TWISTED"

Staying Off the Straight and Narrow

Jack Halberstam

> Improvement makes straight roads; but the crooked roads without improvement are roads of genius.
>
> *William Blake*

A Path So Twisted

In the summer of 2014, puzzled after attending a queer friendly, performance studies conference where multiple scuffles broke out about potentially offensive and damaging representations of trans and queer bodies accompanied by calls for trigger warnings, I jotted down some ideas about a new culture of complaint and posted them on a blog (Halberstam "You Are Triggering Me!"). My remarks on trigger warnings, generational conflict in LGBT communities and the politics of injury, couched in a playful and jocular mode and relayed through some Monty Python scenes of absurdity and humor, were instantly received as either a timely summary of an exasperating phenomenon, or as a vicious and mean take down of a younger generation dealing with traumatic stress and struggling to stay afloat. The blog site that featured my opinion piece was flooded with comments and we received more hits in three days than we had ever seen in the whole history of the blog. My piece had gone viral.

But then, virality and triggers are somewhat connected in the sense that there is something contagious about the phenomenon I was trying to describe. People who discuss triggering can trigger others or can cause others to feel vulnerable in relation to their triggers. Discussions of triggering, as the name suggests, can set off chain reactions causing psychological response sequences that can be as damaging as an online virus and as seductive as a YouTube video of kittens cuddling elephants. And, attempts to write about triggering have tended to be polemical and so through the process of setting up a for/against response, the writing on triggering literally lights a virtual wildfire of responses through enraging or confirming the feelings of others. And so discussions that set out to be orderly and careful quickly become enflamed and rash. Consequently a response chain begins to burn online, there is little that can be done to stop it. If you dismiss trigger warnings then you give evidence of the very abuse that the advocates warn about and inflame them to action; if you write in support of trigger warnings then you run the risk of making others feel shut down, which, of course, prompts them to respond more strongly than they otherwise might!

My piece, coming as it did in the middle of some serious media attention to the phenomenon of trigger warnings, dropped into the center of a battle zone in which the weapons were language itself and a war on words was rapidly escalating. Add to this the fact that I suggested in my blog that *maybe* millennials were just too sensitive in the first place and that this brouhaha was generational, and you had a perfect storm of hot button issues, insensitivity to sensitivity, Oedipal conflict, and lots of Monty Python jokes. Right-wingers and left-wingers weighed in to say thank you or shut up or thank you now please shut up and the genuine confusion that had spurred me to write the piece in the first place now increased exponentially.

Within online communication and pedagogical exchange, what counts as censorship and what counts as sensitivity to the feelings of others? When are trigger warnings polite, when are do they police content? And what, if anything, can Monty Python teach us now about life, love, and the holy grail? Speaking of Monty Python, in *The Life of Brian* (directed by Terry Jones in 1979), a hilarious meditation on religion, ideology, political struggle, and false faith, the Python team gives us lots of ammunition to fight this war on words. In one priceless scene, the Pythons convey a healthy regard for slang terms, names that nowadays will be cast as "triggering": Brian is willing to take the words that the Romans have used to abuse the Jews and claim them as his own. And so, when his mother tries to tell him that he is really Roman by birth since his father was a centurion with whom she had sex (Brian: "you were raped?" Mother: "well, at first, yes …"), he refuses to renounce his Jewish identity and proudly tells her: "I'm not a Roman, Mum, and I never will be! I'm a Kike! A Yid! A Hebe! A Hook-nose! I'm Kosher, Mum! I'm a Red Sea Pedestrian, and proud of it!" Using a vernacular language made up variously of slang ("yid"), anti-Semitic caricature ("hook nose"), and myth ("Red Sea Pedestrian"), Brian both refuses to take on the identity of the oppressors, even when it is available to him, and he articulates his revolutionary identity, not by pushing back on the terms of his exclusion but by repurposing those same terms for uses that the Romans can never even imagine. By incorporating the terms of abuse into his own lexicon, Brian stymies the imperial assault and disarms it, humorously and with good intent.

Humorously and with good intent—this was the voice I tried to inhabit in my original blog on triggers and trigger alerts. But humor, it seems, has gone out of style. The kind of humor that Monty Python harnessed and channeled in the 1970s—absurd ("this parrot is deceased"), parodic ("blessed are the cheesemakers"), satirical ("Oh, what sad times are these when passing ruffians can say Ni at will to old ladies. There is a pestilence upon this land, nothing is sacred. Even those who arrange and design shrubberies are under considerable economic stress in this period in history."), and silly ("I fart in your general direction! Your mother was a hamster and your father smelt of elderberries!")—seems to have little purchase nowadays when earnestness has made a come back and activism has chosen sanctimonious litany over riotous speech. Humor, Lenny Bruce once said, "is the only honest art form." By which he meant that laughter is a response that we cannot really fake (laugh tracks notwithstanding). Humor in general has also been dependent all too often upon social differences for its material—men joke about women, Jews joke about Christians, black people joke about white people, and English people joke about hamsters and parrots.

And while humor loves a target, humorlessness thrives in the rarefied atmosphere of holier-than-thou political causes. We accuse a group of lacking a sense of humor when we want to portray them as rigid, focused upon the wrong things, trivial in their interests, piecemeal in their approach and so on. But what is the purpose of humor and when is humor a shrewd and effective weapon? When is humor an annoyance and when does it stifle rather than animate critique? What models of identity do the new modes of sensitivity betray and when does a critique of sensitivity clear the ground for other conversations, when does it join forces with a militaristic, pull yourself up by your bootstraps ethic? In what follows, I range from humor to horror, from complexity to complicity, from trauma to resilience, from triggers to giggles on behalf of a project on identity, memory, violence, and language. Along the way, I amplify some claims I made in *The Queer Art of Failure* about forgetting traditions of knowing, undoing disciplinary training and about getting lost on the way to actually experiencing the world anew.

The questions I hope to pursue, many of them influenced by Jacques Ranciere's attention to the importance of ignorance and unlearning are as follows:

1. Can we unlearn the political idioms and structures of knowing that currently keep us locked into our own private systems of pain and pleasure but simultaneously prevent us from seeing the potential and even the rightness of other systems of sharing and co-experiencing? Can we simultaneously open up to another logic of being through the activity that is not teaching or learning but, as Stefano Harney and Fred Moten put it in *The Undercommons*, "study." Study, according to them, is a mode of thinking with others separate from the thinking that the institution requires of you, and it prepares us to be embedded in what Harney calls "the with and for" and allows us to spend less time antagonized and antagonizing (*The Undercommons* 143).
2. Can we deploy some different strategies of articulation within critical thinking to extend and stretch our communications beyond the explicative and away from the performance of diagnosis—in other words, not what is wrong and why but what is right and how? Can we, for example, call upon rarely used affective registers in academia like comedy or passion, rage or teasing, in order to break away from the self-authorizing seriousness that mires us in what Harney and Moten call academic immiseration? In other words, how do we currently use pain to legitimate all kinds of claims and can we do without that legitimation or use something else—fun and fury for example—that would lead first and foremost to pleasure but lastly, and equally important, to inspired, improvised, emancipated engagement?
3. Finally, if as Ranciere proposes in *The Emancipated Spectator*, the spectator must not expect to be enlightened by an aesthetic text and the artist must not seek to teach the audience what he presumes they do not know, then how can we stage the kinds of intellectual adventures, to use one of Ranciere's terms, that allow for surprise, unanticipated outcomes, and unpredictable effects?

In the next section, I want to try to answer these questions by paying close attention to a queer film from 1980 that sheds light upon a very different approach to topics like hurt, injury, activism and culture, never mind feminism, queerness, youth and politics.

Defeated and Gifted

In this second section, I return to a "lost" queer film from the late 1970s, *Times Square* by Alan Moyle. In this film, produced by Robert Stigwood who also produced *Saturday Night Fever*, two teenage girls, Nicky Marotta (played by Robin Johnson) and Pammy (played by Trini Alvarado) get lost in a gritty, dirty New York City and search together for something that exceeds the claustrophobia of family (embodied by Pammy's politician father), the emptiness of mainstream media (represented here by TV and disco), and the well-meaning social workers and doctors. The two girls meet on a psych ward where they have been placed for different reasons. Pammy's politically ambitious father wants his daughter to be tamed and "cured" of her discontent; Nicky's social worker has had her hospitalized for evaluation after she gets arrested for vandalism, creating a disturbance outside a disco.

Rejecting the comfort of home, the predictability of programmed culture, and the recuperative efforts of youth services, Pammy and Nicky strike out on their own and to the accompaniment of the Ramones' "I Wanna Be Sedated." On their journeys, they find the perils of pre-gentrification Times Square to be far preferable to the dangerous safety of the various homes that seek to enclose and contain them. After leaving the hospital, the two girls wander the city, pick up some gigs as dancers in red light clubs, and scavenge for food. Picking through the rejected goods of a crumbling city, they make their way to the famous Chelsea piers and make an alternative home for themselves in one of the massive empty warehouses that were lined up along the Hudson river in the 1980s and provided shelter to gay runaways, drug addicts, homeless people, and queer youth. To a loud and very current 1980s punk soundtrack, Pammy and Nicky dance, sing, yell, and scream their way into a different reality and a potentially new configuration of rebellion, space, and power.

Times Square (1980) is missing from most contemporary histories of queer cinema, new or old. It does not appear in Ruby Rich's queer film histories or in her book *Chick Flicks* and it does not get mentioned alongside *Go Fish* (1994) or *Bound* (1996) that came out in the next decade, or even *The Killing of Sister George* that came some ten years earlier. Even more surprisingly, it is rarely placed in its own decade, the 1980s, alongside films like *Desert Hearts* (1985), *Lianna* (1983) and *Personal Best* (1982). One could imagine a narrative that places *Times Square* firmly at the beginning of a new era of representation, a post-Hayes code era of visibility and legibility. But instead, it seems to have been cast as part of the conclusion to decades of censorship; part of an inglorious era of coded messages, of mad and bad women, dangerous and predatory men and sad, lonely queers. Despite being overlooked, however, *Times Square*, a punk film that capitalized on the themes of youth, rebellion, and mayhem, has much to offer in terms of its refusal to capitulate to a politics of respectability.

Times Square was directed by Allan Moyle. Moyle, who went on to make another teenage rebellion film, *Pump Up the Volume* (1990) starring a young Christian Slater, apparently had some differences with the producers of *Times Square* when they removed a clear and explicit lesbian scene between the two heroines. The DVD audio commentary by Moyle tells of several conflicts between his screenplay, which he based on a found diary of a girl living on the streets, and Robert Stigwood's production strategy. Stigwood was primarily known for *Saturday Night Fever* at this point and he must have liked the idea of another New York film set to music and featuring the hard luck story of an Italian-American youth. However, Stigwood had not consented to a lesbian narrative with two very young actors and he insisted on removing key scenes that make the intimacy between the two leads explicit. Moyle also objected to Stigwood's additions of certain songs to the soundtrack (this explains the totally inappropriate Bee Gees track that closes out the film) and he left the crew before the film was complete. According to Robin Johnson and Moyle on the DVD commentary, the cuts made by Stigwood had a deleterious effect on sequencing and flow in the film and made it uneven and hard to follow.

Moyle's departure, one can only surmise, left *Times Square* adrift; while the acting is fine, the production values are good, and the plot itself is powerful, the film received a poor critical reception and was quickly consigned to the trash heap of film history. But this is unfortunate because, despite Stigwood's cuts, and despite the padding of the soundtrack to make it into a double album, the film actually stands up well over the years and remains a very compelling representation of youth rebellion, queer desire, and pre-gentrification New York City.

In a scene early in the film, set to the soundtrack of "Life During Wartime" by *The Talking Heads*, Nicky shows Pammy where she lives and with whom. In a long take characteristic of an earlier mode of cinema, the two girls walk and dance, shimmy and sashay down the street, weave in and out of the foot traffic, and interact with the other down and out denizens of *Times Square*. The scene, which lasts about three full minutes, is not about anything, it does not advance the plot, and it gives us no new information until the end when we see Pammy's picture on the side of a bus announcing that she is "missing." The scene, in other words, unwinds slowly and pans the city while unfurling the dimensions of the cinematic world we are entering. Nicky and Pammy interact with a diverse set of characters on the streets of New York. As in *Saturday Night Fever*, while there is an obvious deployment here of black bodies to represent the seamy, dangerous side of the city and an idiom of rebellion, the sequence simultaneously places Pammy and Nicky joyfully alongside that version of the city rather than fearfully surrounded by it. Identity here emerges from proximity and shared space, and it takes shape within a mutual choreography that allows bodies to dance together despite, rather than because, of their identities. Here identity emerges not from the shared conditions of embodiment but through the spatialization of marginalization.

Toward the end of the clip we get a glimpse of the porno theaters that made up Times Square before it became the sanitized, safe, tourist-centric mall that is today. Indeed, the whole film is an homage to the worlds that exist within the version of Times Square that the mayor and others seek to "clean up." Predicting Samuel Delany's love song to red and blue versions of Times Square and the subterranean ecosystems that thrived there, *Times Square* offers viewers a long, hard look at the good, the bad, and the ugly as they overlap in New York's mean streets. Standing on the street and surveying the movie marquees, the cheap sex arcades, and peep shows, Pammy glances up at a nearby movie house advertising *House of Psychotic Women*, a 1974 horror film about a serial killer. Pammy jokes that she and Nicky are the "psychotic women" and the two embrace the role that the straight world has handed to them—defeated, twisted, sick, and neurotic, if not psychotic, women. They slip past cops and duck into a peep show going in through a door marked "novelties" and out through a door marked "films" allowing us to read them under the sign of the new, the visual, and the sleazy all at once. The nod to the B movie is a quick glance at the history of representation that would, in the very recent past, have filed Nicky and Pammy under some designation like "psychotic." But it is also a look forward to a brave queer world where the choice is not between cleaving to one's diagnosis or clinging to one's normativity, but where the sheer absurdity of the either/or explodes within the laughter of the liberated.

When the two girls spot Pammy's face on an ad on the bus announcing her as "missing," a loaded term in a film about queer love, they draw a mask on Pammy's mug shot. The raccoon mask turns Pammy from a milk carton runaway to a purposeful outlaw, a saboteur who embodies why, where, and how, as Nicky puts it, "no sense makes sense." And so begins the trademark masking of the "Sleez Sisters" as they are now known, that allows them to build a community of "psychotics," united in anonymity, confirmed through defacement, and most present as "missing."

Times Square came out the same year as William Friedkin's *Cruising*, 1980, and like that film, it has missing sex sequences (let's hope James Franco does NOT try to restore them). Like *Cruising*, it depicts an underground culture that is both rebellious and subject to violent attempts to shut it down; and like *Cruising*, *Times Square* is committed to exploring a dark, dirty, unsanitized, and maverick version of New York City. *Cruising*, released on the very brink of the AIDS crisis, linked its gay sex drama to a narrative about a serial killer on the loose and then played a complex cat and mouse, cops and robbers game that deliberately confused the boundaries between an us and a them, the law and crime, sex and death. For making the connections between cruising and stalking, gay sex and criminality so clear, the film was protested by gay activists in New York City who went so far as to try to make gay bars off limits to the film's director and producers. Friedkin defended his film before it was released saying: "Anyone who knows me or knows anything about me knows that I am not antigay," he said. "I don't make a film because I'm against something. For that matter, I don't make a film because I'm for something—don't make propaganda. If anything, all the films I've made are enormously ambiguous" (Maslin "Friedkin Defends," 12). The film, however bad or wrong-headed it may be considered to be, has survived as a queer classic in a way that *Times Square* did not.

No protestors marched on the sets of *Times Square*. No activist groups turned up to speak out at its opening. In fact, no one showed up at all. The film was poorly received, the actors were ignored and had no significant roles thereafter, and the film played in a few queer film festivals before dropping out of sight. In her review for the *New York Times*, Janet Maslin told audiences to listen to the soundtrack and skip the movie. She wrote: "The action is so false … the characters so unsympathetic and uninteresting, that after a while the music begins playing the only dominant role" (Maslin "'Times Square' With a Beat"). David Denby also excoriated the film calling it "a true atrocity" (84) and Roger Ebert described it as "a good idea that fails." *Playboy*, meanwhile, gave *Times Square* two bunnies and described as a triumph of "sleaze over substance" (Williamson)!

My interest in the film lies first in its unrelenting commitment to rebellion and resistance; second in the way that the film predicts certain disruptive forms of queer activism that later became a big part of ACT UP and the Lesbian Avengers; and finally for the glimpse it gives us of a queer past that is neither "backwards," in Heather Love's terms, nor simply experimental, but rather it registers as utopian in the way that the late José Muñoz conceives of utopia—a horizon that beckons with possibility and a time that never comes. Let's consider another clip to get at this utopian sensibility—once the two girls have made a home in the piers, their relationship becomes much more serious. The piers that are so often represented as the domain of gay male sex and cruising, in this film become the backdrop to a very queer domesticity that Pammy and Nicky craft out of leftover furniture, abandoned goods, and the commitment of friendship. In this scene, they make a blood oath and Nicky pulls out a knife to slice into her hand and then Pammy's in order to exchange blood in a gesture that just a few years later would be unimaginable and would represent unsafe sex. But this blood bond means everything to the two girls who recognize in each other a new form of kinship and intimacy. Nicky now seals the bond by telling Pammy that in the future, if she is ever in trouble, she just has to call Nicky's name. The two girls yell and scream the name of the other outloud, filling the empty warehouse spaces with the echoes of their cries. The missing sex scene can be discerned in the loud, exuberant cries that bounce around the piers and announce their love to the world.

This scene registers for me the alternative landscape of identity, politics, space, desire, and utopia that the film beckons toward and situates as its future, a future, by the way, that we, the contemporary viewer, now know will never come. As Samuel Delany documented in *Times Square Red, Times Square Blue*, the developers and corporate interests won out handily over the denizens of the subterranean sex cultures that were razed in the sanitization of Times Square. But even as Delany mourns the lost worlds of gay cruising cultures, he fails to even see or recognize the landscape of lost girls that also gave *Times Square* its rough edges and its soundtrack. All the meaningful interactions between Nicky and Pammy happen here in this improvised domesticity, this do it yourself intimacy and this world within a world within a world that represents so much of queer and female subcultures.

The love that joins the two girls is rudely and abruptly interrupted, as it must be, by a radio DJ, played creepily by Tim Curry, among others. Their bond can survive the rigors of the streets but not the pressures brought to bear upon them by figures who represent the family (Pammy's father), compulsory heterosexuality (Tim Curry), and institutional punishment (a social worker). And while the film's fabulous denouement in an improvised concert in Times Square allows the girls to reunite and see their romance through, there is another scene where the two girls announce to the world, not simply their "forbidden love," but their forbidden identifications with the dispossessed or what we might call now, the undercommons. Nicky and Pammy play a punk song at the radio station where Tim Curry presides as King of New York. In this scene, the girls cleave to and claim the words that their culture has used against them and they make identity, as Harney and Moten might say, out of dispossession and brokenness. Just as they salvage furniture and dress in garbage bags, so they reclaim the rhetoric of the insult and make common cause with the insulted, the abandoned, the marginalized, and the criminalized. The song begins with Pammy telling her father and all of New York that he is a charlatan and a bigot. She lists the words for the city's abandoned night world denizens that her father sees as impediments to his project to clean up Times Square. "You know at home, I have heard you use these following words: spick, nigger, faggot psycho … well I just want you to know, your daughter is one!" And so the song counters the rhetoric of lifestyle, hygiene, sanity, and respectability with the violence it produces, the punishments it metes out, and the dispossession it requires. By claiming the very names that have been used to marginalize, diminish, instrumentalize, and pathologize, Pammy and Nicky recognize honor in defeat, power in perversion, and they delay, for a moment, the coming tide of positive images that sought, in the decade that followed, to rectify wrongs with rights, exclusions with inclusions, negatives with positives. *Times Square*, unlike all the positive-image films that followed, recognized that the either/or of positive/negative had nothing to offer in the way of redemption or retribution. It only sealed the deal on an assimilationist platform that made gay, lesbian, and transgender recognition the right and true goal of a social movement.

"Should I pursue a path so twisted?/ Should I crawl defeated and gifted?" So sings poet Patti Smith in the film's climactic moment of rupture. "Pissing in the River" rejects the language of improvement and rejects the straight and narrow preferring with Blake, one of her favorite poets, to take the path so twisted and the crooked roads of genius. I propose that we think again about giving up on words like tranny and about losing the connections forged through dispossession and loss. These bonds, as Christina Hanhardt's work in *Safe Space* shows, allowed queers in the 1970s to understand their political struggles as part and parcel of a more thoroughgoing critique of economic and racial policies. Once they gave way to an anti-violence and pro-gentrification gay agenda in San Francisco's Castro district, Los Angeles' West Hollywood, and NYC's Times Square, we lost the ability to imagine these different struggles as part of each other's fabric, as twisted or braided together through a shared sense of disaffection, abjection, refusal, and anger. Instead of trying to get this sense of a multidirectional politics back by creating check lists of political goals and identities and by snapping our fingers and applauding when we hear the rights words and phrases, we might want to return to the politics embedded in the curse or the insult and look to a horizon at the end of a path so twisted where we find not the heroes and the survivors but the defeated and the gifted.

Conclusion

According to the logic of this essay so far, it is probably time for another Monty Python interlude about speech and injury ("it's just a bloody flesh wound"). Despite the fact that his mother claims he is the son of a Roman, Brian does not abandon his Jewishness; despite the fact that he despises the blind faith of the crowd, he does not abandon the people; and, finally, despite the fact that he is not the messiah, he leads through earnest example and exhorts his followers to, well, "fuck off." *The Life of Brian* offers much satirical commentary on political organizing as the People's Front of Judea (PFJ) tries to overthrow the imperial force of the Romans. "What have the Romans ever done for us?" asks Reggie, the PFJ leader. "Aqueduct?" offers one unhelpful party member. "Well, yes, the aqueduct, ok, but part from the aqueduct. What have the Romans ever done for us?" "Sewage?" offers another. "Roads?" "Medicine?" In another scene, the revolutionaries talk about how talking is not enough, action is what they need. And they keep on talking about action, and talking about it and talking about it. And finally, when they do take action and try to kidnap the wife of Pontius Pilot, they find that their rivals, The Popular Front of Judea are doing the same thing. As the People's Front begins to fight with the Popular Front, our hero, Brian, tries to remind everyone that they have a common enemy and should focus their energies there. This sounds like a good plan for seriously scary political times. Rather than confronting each other, it may be time for a united front, a punk sensibility, and little more humor.

Works Cited

Bound. Directed by Lily and Lana Wachowski, Gramercy Pictures, 1996.
Cruising. Directed by William Friedkin. United Artists, 1980.
Delany, Samuel R. *Times Square Red, Times Square Blue*. New York UP, 1999.
Denby, David. "Times Square." *New York Magazine*, November 3, 1980, p. 84.
Desert Hearts. Directed by Donna Deitch. The Samuel Goldwyn Company, 1986.
Ebert, Roger. "Times Square." RogerEbert.com, November 17, 1980, www.rogerebert.com/reviews/times-square-1980. Accessed March 30, 2018.
Go Fish. Directed by Rose Troche. Samuel Goldwyn Company, 1994.
Halberstam, Jack. *The Queer Art of Failure*. Duke UP, 2011.
Halberstam, Jack. "You Are Triggering Me! The Neo-Liberal Rhetoric of Harm, Danger and Trauma." Bullybloggers, July 5, 2014, https://bullybloggers.wordpress.com/2014/07/05/you-are-triggering-me-the-neo-liberal-rhetoric-of-harm-danger-and-trauma/. Accessed March 30, 2018.
Hanhardt, Christina. *Safe Space: Gay Neighborhood History and the Politics of History*. Duke UP, 2013.

Harney, Stefano and Fred Moten. *The Undercommons: Fugitive Planning and Black Study*. Minor Compositions, 2013.
Lianna. Directed by John Sayles. United Artists Classics, 1983.
Love, Heather. *Feeling Backwards: Loss and the Politics of Queer History*. Harvard UP, 2007.
Maslin, Janet. "Friedkin Defends his '*Cruising*.'" *New York Times*, September 18, 1979.
Maslin, Janet. "'Times Square' With A Beat." *New York Times*, October 17, 1980, np.
Muñoz, José. *Cruising Utopia: The Then and There of Queer Utopia*. NYU Press, 2009.
Personal Best. Directed by John Sayles. Warner Bros., 1982.
Ranciere, Jacques. *The Emancipated Spectator*. Verso, 2011.
Rich, Ruby. *Chick Flicks: Theories and Memories of the Feminist Film Movement*. Duke UP, 1998.
The Killing of Sister George. Directed by Robert Aldrich. Cinerama Releasing Corporation, 1968.
The Life of Brian. Directed by Terry Jones. HandMade Films, 1979.
Times Square. Directed by Alan Moyle. EMI Films, 1980.
Williamson, Bruce. *Playboy*, vol. 28, no. 1, np, January 1981.

33

THE RISK OF TOLERANCE

Feminist Killjoys, the Creative Humanities, and the Belligerent University

Karen Redrobe

> Feminist killjoys: those who refuse to laugh at the right points; those who are unwilling to be seated at the table of happiness. Feminist killjoys: willful women, unwilling to get along, unwilling to preserve an idea of happiness.
>
> Sara Ahmed, *Willful Subjects*, 2

"Toleration"

About 12 miles from my workplace, the campus of the University of Pennsylvania, there's a statue buried deep in the woods of the Wissahickon Valley Park dedicated to the concept of "Toleration," a word derived from the Latin *tolerare*, meaning to endure (pain), to bear, or to put up with. The sculptor Herman Kirn's depiction of William Penn was erected in 1883 by the land-owner and U.S. Ambassador to Britain, John Welsh, on the brink of a precarious outlook known as "Mom Rinker's Rock" ("Structures & Landmarks"). Rather generic, this figure is perhaps most striking for the way he turns his back on those walking along Forbidden Drive, spatially insinuating the paradox that lies at the heart of tolerance: while toleration, or tolerance, describes the salutary and deliberate act of accepting "the feelings, behavior, or beliefs of someone," it can also involve a more passive and perhaps detrimental gesture of looking away, of allowing "something that is bad, unpleasant, etc. to exist, happen, or be done" (Merriam-Webster.com "Tolerate"). Welsh not only positioned this statue in a way that any person attempting to examine toleration head-on would have to risk falling off a rock, but also selected a rock with a particular political and gendered charge. Here, Molly "Mom" Rinker, a Philadelphia tavern owner, engaged in espionage for George Washington's Army during the Battle of Germantown, using the feminine craft of knitting as cover for the messages she passed at the end of her balls of yarn ("Rinker, Molly 'Old Mom'"). In this essay, I take Mom Rinker's Rock, a site where war, gender, creativity, and tolerance collide, as a catalyst for thinking about the risks and responsibilities involved in the practice of tolerance, from the specific perspective of a tenured feminist scholar working within the intertwined contexts of the arts and humanities in the twenty-first century United States research university.

A recent conversation between Wendy Brown and Rainer Forst productively explores some of the tensions that lie at the heart of tolerance, a concept central to the very idea of liberalism. Although Forst emphasizes tolerance as an "ethos of respect for others' right to exist" while Brown pursues the question of how tolerance wields political and normative power, these interlocutors share much common ground (16–17).[1] As Brown insists,

Figure 33.1 "Toleration" (Herman Kirn, 1883, Wissahickon Valley Park)
Source: Author photo

> [B]oth of us recognize that tolerance does not simply reduce conflict, or promote collective thriving. We're both aware that tolerance is not only or always what it says it is. We also share an appreciation of tolerance as a nested notion or practice, one that never stands by itself, but whose specific contextualization always matters for its operation and for its effects. And we share an appreciation, above all, of the inseparability of power from both the occasion of tolerance and the operation of tolerance.
>
> *(14)*

For Herbert Marcuse, whose 1965 essay "Repressive Tolerance" was the catalyst for Brown and Forst's exchange, the nature of tolerance is not stable but has morphed over time: "the political locus of tolerance has changed" (82, 117). Writing in the midst of the Vietnam War, Marcuse saw postwar tolerance as having departed from the active, authentically liberal protection of dissent toward a passive acceptance of governments, institutions, and "established policies" (Marcuse 82). Yet for Brown, the concept has always demanded a negotiation of the complexity of what constitutes passive and active modes of political being and participation at any given historical moment.

I am interested in addressing the risk of tolerating certain kinds of structures and modes of thought in the context of the contemporary research university, knowing that even the mention of not tolerating within the university context immediately raises questions about academic freedom. More specifically, I am interested in how the "nesting" of impact, innovation, the integration of knowledge, and the digital humanities—all key priorities for my home institution, as for many major research universities—helps to cultivate and sustain the faculty's tolerance of, and even enthusiasm for, an increasingly militarized system of higher education.[2] I take my home institution as a privileged example in this essay, partly because it is the example I know best, and because it is the institution in which I am deeply implicated. Rather than writing a polarizing and overly condemnatory polemic, I am more interested in considering what might be, in the words of Jean Bethke Elshtain, "the preconditions for important dialogue" about this issue, and in adopting an implicated critical approach, which Elshtain sees as necessary for avoiding the trap of always being "enraged about something" (Banac et al. 12, 16).[3] Nevertheless, Marcuse's essay insists that there are moments when one must take a stance in relation to intolerable forms of tolerance, by which he means tolerance that functions in a destructive way and that seeks to "protect false words and wrong deeds which demonstrate that they contradict and counteract the possibilities of liberation" (Marcuse 88).

For Marcuse, while the uncertain and chance-ridden quest for freedom "necessitates freedom of thought and expression as preconditions of finding the way to freedom—it necessitates *tolerance*," this tolerance "cannot be indiscriminate" (Marcuse 88). For him, indiscriminate tolerance seems justified only—"in harmless debates, in conversation, in academic discussion … in the scientific enterprise, in private religion"—but not in those arenas "where the pacification of existence, where freedom and happiness themselves are at stake" (88).[4] Here, the word "academic" seems to imply "having no practical importance: not involving or relating to anything real or practical" ("Academic"). And yet in the contemporary research university, the measurable "impact" of research on the so-called "real" world has become ever-more important to a media-oriented sense of what constitutes academic "success" as well as viable—rather than ostensibly irrelevant—academic work, including "pure" scientific research. At Penn, measurable "Impact," which often seems to involve plans for local gentrification and global penetration, constitutes one of three top presidential priorities within the institutional vision document known as "Penn Compact 2020."[5] Furthermore, one of the university's most celebrated areas of research impact lies in a realm that, according to Marcuse, should lie beyond the "merely academic": happiness, aka Authentic Happiness™ ("Authentic Happiness"). Penn's Authentic Happiness project, a future- and resilience-oriented psychology program to which I will return later, weaves together multiple arenas of the university under four major and mutually reinforcing categories: Creativity, Education, Military Resilience, and Prospective Psychology.[6] Under this rubric, the limits of what is humanly bearable in life are being pushed back, and extending these limits has become a top research priority. As suicide rates of students and soldiers rise, institutional and military mental health initiatives respond by seeking ways to increase resilience, yet perhaps we should be agitating for increased intolerance rather than resilience. Or, as Sara Ahmed puts it, "When we are not willing to adjust, we are maladjusted. Perhaps willfulness turns the diagnosis into a call: don't adjust to an unjust world!" (Ahmed *Wilful Subjects*, 157).

While the university's policies on academic freedom and faculty governance should guarantee a protected space within which tenured faculty might frankly debate different and arguably intolerable aspects of this or other research projects, it becomes important for understanding where and when the university claims the right to limit the information available to interested faculty members or curtail their participation in governance ("Appendix A: Policy on Consultation"). Though tenure is designed to protect academic freedom, scholars whose academic work draws attention to problematic institutional behavior within the university, resulting in an oppositional relationship with the university administration, and/or whose work opposes local, state, or federal government policies, run the risk of jeopardizing their job security even when they do have tenure. Ahmed, for example, draws attention to the way university diversity initiatives can screen rather than undo institutional racism, leading to trouble for diversity workers who actually seek structural change (Ahmed *On Being Included*, 29–50). For another example, at UC San Diego, in response to Electronic Disturbance Theater (EDT)'s use of a "Transborder Immigrant Tool" as well as EDT co-founder and performance artist Ricardo Dominguez's virtual sit-in against students' fees in the UC system and the dismantling of K-12 public education in California, Professor Dominguez's tenure was placed under review (Dominguez 343–354). While students, staff, and non-tenured or adjunct faculty exist in a more precarious position than tenured faculty when it comes to research-based institutional and government critique, it is important to note that tenured faculty members are also at risk from the consequences that can ensue from the humanistic impulse toward self-reflection and immanent critique.

A robust culture of faculty leadership that includes the voices of well-informed and engaged humanists may go a long way to protecting scholars' rights and responsibilities to speak publically about areas of concern that derive from their research realm and activity, a realm that for humanists, as for artists, can be practically limitless. But within the corporate university, the culture of faculty governance is increasingly in danger of being restricted to the point of toothlessness, especially when what are described as the "strategic interests" of the university are at stake—interests that often include good relationships with the government, donors, and other funders, as well as the protection of institutional priorities and investments. As Kwame Anthony Appiah argued during his term as Modern Language Association President, "the practice of faculty governance" constitutes one of two areas of the university most in need of "defending and revivifying." He noted, "Too many of the decisions that have reshaped the work of college teachers in the humanities over the past few decades have involved too little faculty consultation." While it is time-consuming and often boring to read the small print of our own institution's policies, to which changes often appear in small-print faculty newsletters that tend to be instantly recycled or deleted, it is here where we can often pinpoint the structures that exacerbate escalations of risk, including the risk involved in participating in certain kinds of humanistic and artistic thought, activity, and speech.

At Penn, which resembles many of its peers in this regard, the limits of faculty governance are dictated by the university's "Policy on Consultation Where the Administration Has Primary Decision-making Responsibility" (("Appendix A: Policy on Consultation"). This document distinguishes two separate realms within the university, explaining that only in the second of these do faculty members have equal or primary responsibility:

> In the decision-making areas to which this policy on consultation applies, ultimate decisional authority rests with the trustees and (pursuant to authority delegated by the trustees)

the president, in order that they may fulfill their responsibility to ensure the institutional and financial health of the University, as distinguished from its academic and scholarly mission, where the faculty holds primary responsibility under the trustees or, in some cases, shares such responsibility with the administration.

("Appendix A: Policy on Consultation" 1.f)

The line between these two areas is not always clear, however. On April 17, 2012, for example, Penn's Provost emailed the faculty to inform them that the university would be participating with Princeton, Stanford, and the University of Michigan in the MOOC platform of Coursera, a decision made by the administration and the Trustees without open consultation with the full faculty. If we understand this decision through the university's policy on consultation, one must deduce that Penn, in spite of the public rhetoric surrounding the democratic aspirations of online learning, regarded Coursera, at least at that moment, as most relevant not to "the academic and scholarly mission" of the university, but, at least potentially, to its "institutional and financial health." The policy leaves further room to avoid consultation in the case of research projects involving what is vaguely described as "strategic concerns." It states:

Except where strategic concerns actually and reasonably counsel little or no public knowledge or awareness of emergent policies or actions, it is the administration's duty to allow for full and open discussion, that is consistent with the democratic aspirations of the University.

("Appendix A: Policy on Consultation" 1.b)

As there are often financial incentives provided by the state for military-related research, there may be situations where the faculty is not consulted on morally complex research- and pedagogy-related issues for reasons that blur the line between strategic concern and financial gain, even when the grants do not require engagement of classified material (which Penn prohibits). Once strategic interests shape consultation policies, there is the potential for those aspects of academic life with the greatest impact on "freedom and happiness" to become the least visible and least discussed. Yet if faculty governance is to have any teeth at all, rigorous debate among the faculty at precisely such moments seems most important as research communities try to decide what is tolerable and intolerable within the research realm, and, if necessary, what form intolerance might most productively take.

Activism and Passivism in the Realms of Art and the Humanities

In considering the risks and responsibilities of tolerance from a humanistic perspective within the contemporary research environment, it is productive to pause and consider how tolerance resonates with notions of activity and passivity, thought and action, and at what cost or benefit. In its most passive form, tolerance hovers on the brink of indifference, and like indifference, it raises complicated questions about how accountability and responsibility should be attributed in relation to a mode of being that seems primarily to be about *not* doing something. Psychoanalytic feminist theorist Jacqueline Rose delves into the ethical dynamics of what one doesn't do or say in the particular context of South Africa's Truth and Reconciliation Commission, focusing in particular on an Indian woman who applied for amnesty for what she called her "apathy" (*On Not Being Able to Sleep* 217). The woman argued that "individuals can and should be held accountable by history for our lack of necessary action in times of crisis," leading Rose to examine the difficulty of talking about "the ways in which we do not implicate ourselves in the burden of history" (220). "How," Rose asks, do you at once recognize the fullness and extent of historical accountability and draw boundaries around it, how do you let it flow … while also keeping it in, if not its proper, then at least a definable, precisely *accountable*, place?

(224)

This question is asked not only of individual subjects in her essay, but also of institutions. In a section on "shortcomings," for example, the Commission's report highlights the fact that it did not investigate universities, an oversight that reminds us not to do the same in the context of America's current wars (231).

Yet while certain modes of inaction and silence risk rendering a subject or an institution guilty of apathy or injustice in times of violence, numerous feminist scholars, including Rose, Judith Butler, Rosalyn Deutsche, and Mignon Nixon, have simultaneously highlighted a different set of problems that arise from the demand for direct and assertive political action in times of war. Deutsche, for example, criticizes the editors of the academic art journal *October* for encouraging, through their questionnaire about the role of artists, activists, and academics in the war in Iraq, a "regression to heroic masculinism" (9–10).[7] This regression, Deutsche suggests, comes at the expense of more uncertain, ambivalent, and feminist modes of responsiveness that acknowledge "the inseparability of the social and the psychic" as well as the role of the unconscious in political life, and that seek to make the imbrication of these two dimensions visible in the forms of "action" they both invent and support (1–7). Here, Deutsche follows Maurice Blanchot in resisting criticism's tendency to become "warlike" itself as a result of what he describes as a "political impatience" that wins out in times of war "over the patience proper to the 'poetic'" (Blanchot 78).

Similarly, Rose has repeatedly explored the deep intertwining of authoritative knowledge, masculinity, and militarism, and has sought out possible alternatives to this configuration. For Rose, in dialogue with both Freud and Winnicott, the specific action of war allows us to "project on to the alien, or other, the destructiveness we fear in the most intimate relations or parts of ourself. Instead of trying to repair it at home, we send it abroad." Acting in this way, Rose argues, "saves us the effort of ambivalence, the hard work of recognizing that we love where we hate, that, in our hearts and minds at least, we kill those to whom we are most closely and intimately attached" ("Why War?" 19). Just as writing and the poetic offer Blanchot an alternative to warlike criticism, for Rose, the "effort of ambivalence" leads to mourning, a state of being she sees as actively enabling a speculative and dissociated form of thought that offers a significant and direct alternative to the absolute, total, and triumphalist knowledge so intimately bound to war: "It is not thought as assured knowledge, but a form of thinking unable, in any single or singular way, to own or possess itself" (20). This inability of thought to "own or possess itself" seems to fall short of contemporary demands for the measurable real-world impact of scholarship. While research universities increasingly defend themselves through carefully crafted displays of the linear movement from classroom learning to independent research to real-world results, this is not the form of the "action" or trajectory of humanistic thought. Drawing on a variety of thinkers, Elaine Scarry illustrates that the evidence-based arguments that humanists craft through a form of thinking that often limns the contours of the poetic resists the teleological and progress-oriented paradigms that contemporary university culture celebrates; deep thought often has more in common with stasis than rapid forward movement leading to measurable outcomes (103–104). Cultivating modes of learning and creating that are not outcome-oriented may constitute a form of both artistic and pedagogical activism. However, such a form of activism also arguably stands directly at odds with best-practices guidelines in pedagogical theory and state-based educational review standards, which persistently ask faculty members to identify clear goals in descriptions of majors and on course syllabi, and to describe in detail both expected outcomes and the criteria for evaluation. In many ways, this teleological approach to education seems reasonable in that it asks teachers to have some kind of accountability to students, and those opposing outcome assessment in the name of upholding core humanistic values can run the risk of losing institutional favor, and of seeming misguided, irresponsible, or, as Ahmed points out, simply crazy. The call for tolerance often arises in situations where there is a degree of moral complexity or ambiguity, and as humanists, our responsibilities might include refusing to oversimplify or obfuscate such complexity; struggling to find language to bring such contradictions and irresolvable tensions into the realm of thought and dialogue; and refusing what Marcuse describes as "Tolerance toward that which is radically evil" but which "now appears as good because it serves the cohesion of the whole on the road to affluence" (83).

For John Locke, as Scarry argues, "fast forward momentum" in the mind constitutes a form of "laziness"; indeed, he celebrates the moment when the argument "bottoms," a "thick" process that "clogs" one's studies in a way Locke admires (103–104). Similarly, Scarry describes how for John Dewey, thought acts as an uneasiness, an interruption, a sometimes-painful thing that must be "endured" as it resists the forward glide of the mind (104). Humanistic thinking at its best, like art and the poetic, leads to a kind of failure of masculine, authoritative, possessable knowledge. Rose celebrates this failure as being an—and perhaps even *the*—antidote to war: "Hang on to failure, hang on to derision—a failure and derision that would not invite a reactive triumphalism but preempt it—if you want to avoid going to war" ("Why War?" 37). These largely feminist lines of thought about what form intellectual and aesthetic political responsibility might best take in times of war and crisis resist the opposition between thought and action, but they also go further to distinguish among different types of thought, particularly regarding thought's relationship to activity and passivity, terms to which the political charge of tolerance is tethered.

While belligerent calls for proper responses to war from artists and academics usually stress action over words, Judith Butler, in dialogue with both Jean Laplanche and Emmanuel Levinas, develops an alternative theory of responsibility that is fundamentally passive in nature. Because a "passive relation to the other being" becomes the instrument through which the formation of the ego occurs, Butler argues, it is a mistake to think "that we can be responsible only for that which we have done, that which can be traced to our intentions, our deeds…. I am *not* primarily responsible by virtue of my actions," she continues, "but by virtue of the relation to the Other that is established at the level of my primary and irreversible susceptibility, my passivity prior to any possibility of action or choice" (88) And again: "responsibility is not a matter of cultivating a will, but of making use of an unwilled susceptibility as a resource for becoming responsive to the Other" (91).

Here, Butler's discussion of passive responsibility, which contains within it a taint of violence in the Other's unwilled occupation of the self, takes us one step beyond Rose's discussion of apathy and accountability. Both Butler and Rose argue for the centrality of the Other in their theories of responsibility; yet, at least when writing about the historically specific context of South African atrocities, Rose retains a sense of accountability as a deliberate act of the imagination on the part of a subject for whom the Other remains in her formulation largely outside of the self, in another pair of shoes. She writes, "Accountability halts at the barrier of identification. As does atrocity. All the evidence suggests that people do not kill if they can imagine themselves in the other person's shoes" (*On Not Being Able to Sleep* 234). By contrast, Butler's Levinasian version of responsibility posits a subject so fully intertwined with and vulnerable to the Other that it would be impossible for a subject to choose a way out of responsibility:

> none of us is fully bounded, utterly separate, but, rather, we are in our skins, given over, in each other's hands, at each other's mercy. This is a situation we do not choose. It forms the horizon of choice, and it grounds our responsibility.
>
> *(101)*

In contrast to the warlike mode of criticism that denigrates thought over action because of thought's apparent lack of action, this line of thinking establishes a powerful affinity among thought, passivity, otherness, and responsibility, and embraces the value of thought precisely *because of* these affinities. Blanchot writes of

> a passive that is thought—an always already past of thought—that which, in thought, cannot make itself present, or enter into presence, and is still less able to be represented or to constitute itself as a basis for representation.
>
> *(33)*

Thought emerges as close but outside of presence: "the other as thought" (33). In striking contrast to what Rose calls "assured knowledge" (19), Blanchot offers thought, like the Other, as radically unknowable. Consequently, to risk coming into a relationship with thought is to do so with the Other too:

> Of thought, it must first of all be said that it is the impossibility of sticking to anything definite—the impossibility, then, of thinking of anything determined—and that it is thus the permanent neutralization of all present thought at the same time that it is the repudiation of all absence of thought. Oscillation (paradoxical equality) is the risk run by thought which is abandoned to this double requirement and which does not know that it must be sovereignly patient—in other words, passive outside of all sovereignty.
>
> *(Blanchot 33)*

Passivity is not the same as apathy, or as choosing not to do something: "Passivity neither consents nor refuses: neither yes nor no, without preference, it alone suits the limitlessness of the neutral, the unmastered patience which endures time without resisting" (Blanchot 30).

These philosophical and pedagogical discussions provide a useful foundation for reflecting on how to make sense of one rapidly expanding area of interest in the U.S. research university: art. It makes sense, at least to me, to think about art in a manner that parallels the ways in which Blanchot articulates thought, writing, and the poetic; as an oscillating entity that is strange to itself and that resists militaristic and assured knowledge through the patience that its necessary unfamiliarity provokes. And yet at times of war and social crisis, it is common not only for the state to make use of art as propaganda, but also for antiwar discourse to elevate a heroic version of the artist, one who is above the fray of humankind, outside the realm of implication, a truth-teller and visionary able to see and articulate those things to which ordinary mortals are blind. Howard Zinn's *Artists in Times of War* exemplifies this attitude when he writes:

> So the word *transcendent* comes to mind when I think of the role of the artist in dealing with the issues of the day. I use that word to suggest that the role of the artist is to transcend the world of the establishment, to transcend the orthodoxy, to go beyond and escape what is handed down by the government or what is said in the media.... It is the job of the artist ... to think outside the boundaries of permissible thought and dare to say things that no one else will say.
>
> *(11, 14)*

While this version of the transcendent artist as clear-sighted and unencumbered by confusion or implication may seem reassuring, it stands at odds with a "connected" version of art that would resonate with Blanchot's sense of the poetic and not stand above or outside of violence and the conditions that give rise to it. For Zinn, the artist has a responsibility to speak the truth of a wartime situation, and he assumes both that "the truth" of a given situation can be accessed and that socially engaged art can ultimately be equated with political pamphlets (this conflation occurs in the final pages of his text). But such an emphasis on the potentially positive political impact of art in wartime risks supporting a notion of art as worthy because of its use value. While this is not the same as the product-oriented, monetizable, and "useful" creativity that is becoming increasingly fetishized within the twenty-first century research university, it inadvertently affirms a linear paradigm based on outcomes, measurable progress, and impact. This works against the temporality, passivity, oscillation, and frustration that lie at the heart of both Blanchot's poetic and humanistic approaches to thought—modes that can enable implicated, complex, and more nuanced possible responses to war.

Writing, the poetic, Blanchot suggests, "does not know what will become of it politically: this is its intransitivity, its necessarily indirect relation to the political." Blanchot continues, "This indirection makes us unhappy. We would like to proceed in a straightforward way toward the goal—the social transformation which it is in our power to affirm" (78). Extending Blanchot's paradigms for criticism and the poetic to the realm of contemporary art, we might argue for the importance of artistic responses to war that do not necessarily submit to what Blanchot calls "a desire for active commitment (engagement)," for responses that may seem "out of phase or belated," and that enliven "writing's being" understood as "incertitude or chance (and also invention)" (78). To respond in this way offers an alternative to either falling into the trap of belligerent masculine action or turning away in a gesture of intolerable tolerance. This capacity to provoke thought and uncertainty, to pause the forward movement of life, and to create opportunities for calling oneself personally and institutionally into question represents for me one of the most potent aspects of what the intertwining of the creative arts and the humanities have to offer the research university.

In a different response from Deutsche's to *October*'s questionnaire on the invasion and occupation of Iraq, the artist Coco Fusco underscores Deutsche's concerns about the danger of reductive political timelines when considering war, art, and activism, pointing out that it is

> somewhat difficult to conceive of these exhibitions [about the wars on terror] in terms of their efficacy. First of all, it is too early to tell. Second, it would be absurd to assume that antiwar efforts are ineffective just because the war persists.
>
> *("Questionnaire" 54–55)*

The critical impatience of the questionnaire and its interest in quantifying the impact of art is only one of a series of related problems that respondents identify. Deutsche describes the journal's suggestion that younger generations of artists and activists should identify with the "supposedly authentic antiwar politics" of the previous generation as a "paternal demand," and sees this regression in antiwar cultural criticism as mirroring the wars' own "regression to heroic masculinism" (38). In the book that develops out of her response, Deutsche argues that this critical approach, with its insistence on a heroic, political public subject, neglects the insights of both feminism and psychoanalysis, and "tries to divide the subjective and the material, the public and the private, and the social and the psychic as though war has nothing to do with mental life" (Deutsche 4). She responds by focusing on art that refuses the separation of public and private histories, and that seeks to develop what she calls "non-indifferent ways of seeing," something which, she suggests, "obliges us to call ourselves into question" (66).

Flattening the Topography: Between Art and Arms Races

But how might this act of calling oneself into question as a response to war operate within one's own local and specific scholarly context; what institutional and structural mechanisms inhibit open critical discussion of the relationship of art and the academy to war; how might one respond in the face of institutional inhibitors, and at what cost? In *Reassembling the Social*, Bruno Latour suggests that a "flattened topography" allows us "to go *continuously* from the local interaction to the many delegating actors" who act in realms beyond the local, and to resist what he calls the "folds" that make these continuous pathways invisible (174). I am keen to attempt this flattening across distinct spaces even as I seek out alternatives to the "warlike" mode of speech that often characterizes the language of institutional critique in the hope of encouraging a more critical, organic, and multidirectional interdisciplinarity, and a better notion of the research university than the one we currently inhabit.

In the digital humanities era, there is an increasing demand, and perhaps need, for humanists to develop a familiarity with skills traditionally thought to belong to the realm of engineering and computer science, and this is often accompanied by a parallel institutional emphasis on the monetization of creativity and research under the rubrics of innovation and knowledge integration. At Penn, the former has been most recently and explicitly underscored in the President's Innovation Prize, which rewards undergraduates with money for projects that "must seek to generate a profit" (Gutmann). (I was unaware that student motivation was lacking in this arena.)

Research university-based art activity, apparently on the rise, is increasingly being shepherded into this model of monetizable or at least transferable creativity, and while creative design is not a bad thing, there are significant risks in allowing it to stand in for art. As James Russell put it in a recent *New York Times* article, "[o]n elite campuses, the arts race is on." Russell's invitation to reflect on the relationship between "the arts" and "arms," though not pursued by him, is of crucial importance at this moment when universities seek to bring art and engineering into ever closer alignment. Russell writes:

> Art for art's sake is not discouraged, but departments collaborate in an entrepreneurial spirit: Engineering students sought out artists to improve the appeal of devices they had designed. The university drew attention when a student who will graduate with a degree in sculpture designed molds of silicon and foam that a university pediatric plastic surgeon used to reconstruct torsos for conjoined twins.[8]

Yet while universities frequently "[draw] attention" to applied artistic activity through its evermore sophisticated communication vehicles, there is markedly less excitement about the creative endeavors that generate critique, confusion, thought, disruption, historical understanding, or perhaps nothing at all. Indeed, there's even a surprisingly open jocular disdain for this aspect of culture. As Penn's Vice President for Communications put it when I went to talk with him about the absence of interesting arts and humanities stories in Penn's *Daily News*, he half-joked, "I don't want to hear about John Donne unless it's to tell me that he's an alien." At the time, I was flabbergasted to hear this position articulated by a Vice President of one of America's top-ranked research universities (still am). When I have tried to begin conversations about this statement and the communications policy—which reflects development priorities and therefore research funding —the result has usually been laughter. While part of me gets the joke, a larger part wants to "refuse to laugh" at this point (Ahmed *Wilful Subjects*, 2), and to do so in a deliberate way that makes visible what my non-laughter registers. If the consequences of this attitude to the arts and the humanistic study of them are rather intolerable, how might faculty members most effectively intervene?

In a gesture of intolerance, I want to begin by identifying three structural inhibitors to public discussion about the implications of Penn's institutional and intellectual priorities. First, the high profile distribution of centrally administered university funds, professorships, and awards that enable research and professional mobility has helped to create an imperial intellectual culture that rewards those who are, to adapt Sara Ahmed's phrase, willing to be willing (*Wilful Subjects*, 152–157).[9] As humanists, the knowledge that we rarely benefit from these incentives, and often don't need them in order to pursue our research, can liberate us from the pressure to conform to certain preferred forms and topics that such rewards attempt to exert. Second, in contrast to more horizontal models of interdisciplinarity that emerge unpredictably in response to research problems, aesthetic experience, and experimental thought, top-down initiatives tend to assign some schools and disciplines more value than others for strategic reasons that, while not always articulated, are perceptible through patterns over time. These preferences expand the influence of specific modes of thinking across the university, and it may be important to articulate and analyze these patterns. It may be important for us to pay more attention to the way that interdisciplinarity is being shaped in institutionally strategic ways amid all the discussion of individual creativity and getting out of our silos, and to ask what choices are being made about which types of knowledge to support, and by and for whom. (Mark McGurl put it succinctly at a conference I organized on the relationship between the arts and the humanities: "Capitalism loves creativity and hates history" ("Making it Up").) For example, while the Penn Integrates Knowledge (or "PIK") professorship program is ostensibly available for joint appointments across any two schools, these professorships almost always involve the Schools of Medicine, Engineering, or Business, sometimes in combination with each other; and they explicitly favor those scholars who possess "a drive to solve complex, real-world problems" ("PIK Professors").

While I don't doubt that the continued vibrancy of research depends on evolving intellectual borders, I am struck by the absence of friction and debate as academic priorities and trajectories are centrally announced. At Penn, interdisciplinarity is often replaced by the concept of "integration," a term that—along with "innovation" and "impact"—drives our development strategy.

The word "integration," whose use in English has escalated over the course of the twentieth century, speaks of coming together, equality, wholeness. According to the Merriam-Webster dictionary's primary definition of the word, integration also describes the "coordination of mental processes into a normal effective personality or with the environment." But how does the normalization and structural coordination of our mental processes with the environment relate to the challenges and aspirations of academic freedom? And given that a researcher's mandate involves being free, in the pursuit of truth, to depart from coordinated and normalized mental environments in cases when dominant thinking seems wrong or problematic, shouldn't the disintegration of knowledge be at least as important as its integration to the intellectual well-being of the university?

"Innovation" is the third mechanism I wish to highlight by which open critical discussion of the university's priorities among the faculty is managed, as a corporate version of cross-disciplinary exchange prioritizes those modes of thinking and creativity that lead to profit. Penn is, for example, one of four schools nationwide that art historian David Joselit singles out on this front in *After Art* (2013), in relation to exactly this issue. He writes: "In the realm of entrepreneurship, medical and high-tech research can generate significant revenue for universities like Stanford, the University of Pennsylvania, the University of Texas, or MIT, where laboratories serve as incubators for profitable start-up companies" (85). I understand the motivation for the rise of these entrepreneurial centers, particularly in the context of federal higher education cuts. I also think we underestimate the agency and intelligence of artists if we assume that their participation in these types of projects is necessarily worthless by virtue of such work occurring explicitly within the context of the corporate university's profit-generating wing. Nevertheless, I am troubled by the way in which the rise of an entrepreneurial mentality in one arena begins to dominate other areas of inquiry within the university, including the arts and humanities, often through the combined logic of innovation and integration, as if there were no competing models. This homogenization has the potential to marginalize or render laughable (as in the case of John Donne) the most powerful elements the arts and humanities have to offer, including "the poetic," as Blanchot describes it, and to favor, through an emphasis on team spirit, group thinking, and institutional branding, not only certain types of thought but also certain types of thinkers.

"Tolerance," Marcuse writes, "is extended to policies, conditions, and modes of behavior which should not be tolerated because they are impeding, if not destroying, the chances of creating an existence without fear or misery" (82) He continues, "Tolerance toward that which is radically evil now appears as good because it serves the cohesion of the whole on the road to affluence or more affluence" (83). Invoking the language of evil here may seem melodramatic, yet it is worth noting that when Penn's Board of Trustees decided not to divest from tobacco stocks, it did not shy away from the term, and indeed its decision was grounded in the absence of "a moral evil that creates substantial social injury" (Cohen). The Trustees did give examples of the kinds of things in which it would not be appropriate to invest—genocide and Apartheid—but isn't this a fairly low ethical bar for financial self-regulation? The 1980s example of the Divestment Action on South Africa by U.S. and Canadian colleges and universities, obliquely referenced in this response to Penn faculty and student requests for divestment from the tobacco industry, reminds us of a moment where change and collective action in response to critiques of the university as a financial institution seemed more possible than they do now (The Africa Fund). In order to sustain the possibility of such change, members of university communities need to pay more active attention to the streamlining of faculty leadership and expansion of leadership roles for those with a financial or political interest in university decisions.

These questions about the relationship between innovation in research and funding sources resonate with a growing interest among investigative journalists in the Department of Defense's role in shaping American higher education. While this is not a new topic, the dialogue is worth highlighting as we consider the issue of risk and the humanities. In a recent 2015 VICE News investigation entitled, "The Most Militarized Universities in America," William M. Arkin and Alexa O'Brien examine "university labs funded by US intelligence agencies, administrators with strong ties to those same agencies, and, most importantly, the educational backgrounds of the approximately 1.4 million people who hold Top Secret clearance in the United States."[10] In what may be the most important insight of the study, the journalists highlight how the nature of campus "militarization" has changed. They write:

> Today's national security state includes a growing cadre of technicians and security professionals who sit at computers and manage vast amounts of data; they far outnumber conventional soldiers and spies. And as the skills demanded from these digital warriors have evolved, higher education has evolved with them.
>
> (Arkin and O'Brien)

Working with a data set of 90,000 people, Arkin and O'Brien highlight some interesting trends. None of the top 100 Liberal Arts colleges in America appear on the list. Twenty of the 100 most militarized schools are primarily online schools. Several top-tier research universities are on the list, but only three Ivy Leagues: Harvard (#32), Cornell (#53), and Penn (#57). Changing government funding structures, especially in the sciences, have encouraged this move toward militarized research. In April 2015, for example, the House passed The America COMPETES Act, drafted by the House Science, Space and Technology Committee, chaired by Texas Republican Lamar Smith. This bill, which has been opposed by the Association of American Universities, the American Physical Society, and the Consortium of Social Science Associations, not only redirects money from the social sciences and climate and energy research to biology, computing, engineering, math, and physical sciences, but now also requires grant writers to "issue a written explanation of how a grant award meets the national interest" (Mulhere).

In a constrained funding climate, instrumentalized research starts to look more appealing than it otherwise might, even at places like Penn where there are measures in place, primarily related to transparency, to limit financial pressure on research choices. The Office of the Provost swiftly provided data about the university's history of Department of Defense funding (Penn received $15 million from the DoD in 2000; $50 million in 2014 and $48 million this year);[11] and Section 3.4 of our Sponsored Projects Handbook from the Office of Research states:

> The University does not possess a government security clearance and can not as a corporate entity possess classified material. It is the policy of the University not to accept agreements

which require access to classified data, require University employees to obtain security clearances, or restrict the dissemination of the results.

(University of Pennsylvania Office of Research Services)

Nevertheless, these safeguards have not prevented the university's intellectual identity from becoming very publicly intertwined with contemporary war and the weaponization of research for the purpose of global domination. This affects the climate in which faculty, staff, and students work. Just as South Africa's Truth and Reconciliation Commission realized that it should have investigated the role of research universities in Apartheid, so in our own belligerent moment, perhaps we share the responsibility of examining the role of research and teaching in making war, of identifying the intolerable now, not after the wars end (for we live in a climate of endless war), and to do so quite explicitly as poetically-aligned humanists.

Resisting Resilience

When Joe Biden spoke in 2013 at Penn's Commencement, before going on to stereotype the Chinese ("China's going to eat our lunch"), he began by celebrating in particular those graduates who were "going to be commissioned in the United States Military today," telling them, "You are about to join the finest group of warriors the world has ever seen" (Biden). His booming voice filled the stadium with the declaration that we have entered "an era of breathtaking change and progress," a claim supported by a giddy list that piled up fantasies of trauma reversed or undone, and of body parts engaging in leisure activities independently of any bodily whole. Addressing an audience that included the families of those students about to be enlisted, he paratactically raved of technology's power to undo or erase the damage war does to young bodies:

> 3-D printers able to restore tissue after traumatic injury and restore skin damaged by fire to unblemished skin. The ability to regenerate organs and limbs that have been damaged or lost, saving tens of thousands of lives and restoring our wounded warriors to their full capabilities…. Prosthetic legs that are able to climb mountains, prosthetic arms able to play the piano. I've watched just in the last four years, visiting well over 1,500 amputees, the radical change that is taking place, restoring them to full capacity, and it's only now just beginning."

(Biden)

Here, Biden relies on the verbs "to restore" and "to regenerate." Yet this dream of immortality is haunted by the specter of another word with the same prefix "re": "redeployment," a word unhappily familiar to contemporary U.S. service people impacted by the U.S. military's "stop-loss" policy, which allows the involuntary extension of active duty, which has well-documented adverse mental effects, and which depends, often unsuccessfully, upon the technologies of physical and mental restoration that Biden invokes.

Penn's research in the realm of Positive Psychology has played a central role in preparing American soldiers for redeployment in the Middle East. While psychiatrists elsewhere attempted to support redeployment efforts by experimenting with a pharmaceutical prophylactic treatment for post-traumatic stress disorder (PTSD) that used controversial "memory-blunting agents,"[12] Martin Seligman began working with the Army in 2009 to implement a mandatory resiliency program for all U.S. soldiers that aims to prevent the onset of PTSD known as the Comprehensive Soldier Fitness (CSF) program (Seligman 126–149).[13] A Working Paper published by the Coalition for an Ethical Psychology in May 2012 addressed the serious research-based problems associated with CSF, which received a $31-million no-bid Department of Defense grant. Citing the urgency of the problem, the Army adopted CSF as a mandatory program for soldiers without pilot testing, making it, as Roy Eidelson and Stephen Soldz point out, "a research study involuntarily imposed on troops without appropriate protections such as independent ethical review ... and informed consent." Furthermore, they suggest that CSF "may distract attention away from addressing the documented adverse effects of multiple and lengthy exposures," may inappropriately promote religion (the recent institutional appropriation and instrumentalization of the spiritual practice of mindfulness is pertinent here), and suffers from "insufficient examination of ethical questions posed by efforts to build 'indomitable' soldiers" (1). The challenge of fostering critical and open discussion about this research realm resembles the challenge of resisting pedagogical approaches that emphasize outcomes, in that there is a risk of seeming either ridiculous or perverse when one takes a position that ostensibly opposes resilience, mental peace, and well-being.

The War on/of Terror has generated a sense of an infinite temporality outside of the context of individual soldier's experience, a fantasy of deathless life, often with the aid of what have variously been described as "tactical media" (Rita Raley), "incriminated technologies" (Laura Kurgan), or "operational images" (Harun Farocki, in Paglen). While there has been much bemused discussion about what the actual research content of the digital and creative humanities should be, I find Laura Kurgan's urgent call for us to become visually literate in a new image age, a call made in response to the example of Colin Powell's images (supposedly) of weapons of mass destruction in Iraq, a compelling priority. She writes:

> [Powell's] presentation and its catastrophic results remind us that we need to be alert to what is being highlighted and pointed toward, to the ways in which satellite evidence is used in making assertions and arguments. We need to learn how to agree and disagree with those arguments, to challenge the interpretations made of images that are anything but objective or self-evident.
>
> *(26)*

It will soon be impossible, perhaps it is already so, to act as an informed citizen without this type of technological and visual literacy, and meaningful interdisciplinary exchange across the visual humanities and Engineering and Computer Science becomes of existential importance.

With the widespread recent emphasis on integrated knowledge, research universities like Penn should be well-poised to lead in this area, but open and critical cross-disciplinary and multidirectional debate and education about war technologies is hard to come by, not least when scholars involved with the development of such technologies become vulnerable and defensive in the face of actual or perceived attacks (HAIKU). A few of years ago, in an attempt to explore what a multidirectional and interdisciplinary conversation about drone technology might look like, for example, I asked the Director of Penn's GRASP (General Robotics, Automation, Sensing and Perception Laboratory) if I might bring the graduate students from my war and film seminar to his lab. The reply was friendly but resistant, explaining that as the lab focused on the basic research aspects of robotics, researchers there would not be the appropriate people to talk to about their use in war. I explained that while I understood the resistance to talking about the use of such technologies in war, I hoped that someone would be able to help my students understand something of robotic visual perception, but I received no further reply.

Penn's current Dean of Engineering, Vijay Kumar, a strong supporter of the "computational humanities," formerly served not only as the Director of Penn's GRASP lab but also as the assistant director of robotics and cyber physical systems at the White House Office of Science and Technology Policy. When asked about the use of drones in war, he has underscored the neutrality of basic research: "Any technology can be used for military purposes—you can't worry about where it will be used, otherwise no research on anything will ever be done" (Bhojani). And yet at this moment when engineers, humanists, and artists are becoming increasingly intimate through creative computational humanities initiatives that coordinate our mental processes across schools, what do humanists and artists have to offer the conversation if we must stop "worrying"—some might call it "thinking"—about how technologies will be used, are being used, and have been used, in case our thoughts get in the way of, or "clog," as Locke would say, applied research? How do we reconcile the individual researcher's protected right to academic freedom, regardless of possible consequences in either direction on the political spectrum, with the research university's escalating efforts to grease the flow of ideas between pure and applied realms for financial and strategic reasons?

As digital humanities initiatives take shape across the country, it strikes me as vital that humanists participate in conversations about how the technological turn impacts our methods as well as our thought processes, tempos, vectors, and indeed our lives, and reject any version of the digital humanities that involves a unidirectional flow of programming and expertise from the realm of engineering/computer science to the humanities, especially if it refuses to tolerate or deem relevant the questions and arguments that humanists produce through a systematic engagement with history and culture.

The Quadrators, or mini-drones, that Penn develops in the GRASP lab provide a perfect point of departure for one such exchange. For mini-drones, like many contemporary movies, rely on motion capture technology, and their creators seem keen to foreground the relationship between the product of drones, what PIK Professor Robert Ghrist calls "global knowledge about the properties of a space," and cinema (Hartnett 50–54). Take, for example, the music video produced by Penn's Office of Communications with former Penn students Alex Kushleyev and Daniel Mellinger to accompany Dean Kumar's 2012 TED talk. Quite brilliantly, these students programmed drones to perform Monty Norman's "James Bond theme" from the first of the Bond franchise, Terence Young's 1962 film, *Dr. No*.[14] Music here is instrumentalized in complex ways. On the one hand, the students' performance lightens the tone of the TED talk by framing drones in playful, pedagogical, and experimental rather than belligerent terms, distracting the audience away from the ethical and political debates that surround drone technology. Yet on the other hand, the music in question aurally places the audience in Bond's Cold War world, where good-guy gadgets prevent Dr. No from using his atomic-powered radio beam to disrupt the state's use of global vision technology. This is a fictional world where we never have to worry about the impact of precision technology on life, human or nonhuman. What could be wrong with mini-drones used only to hit the right notes, or indeed with James Bond himself? Who would even raise objections within this scene of creative play? A feminist killjoy might. She'd examine the work that music, cinema, and students are made to do in the context of this talk, which, by July 15, 2016, had been viewed 3,950,111 times; ask what kinds of wars our research universities support; explore how the arts contribute to making those wars tolerable and even entertaining; and request a digital humanities path that is more than just a one-way street.[15]

Notes

1 See also Brown, *Regulating Aversion: Tolerance in the Age of Identity and Empire*.

2 For Penn's embrace of "innovation" and "the integration of knowledge" as intertwined concepts, see "Penn Compact 2020," especially "Innovation" and "Impact."

3 For an example of this type of polemic and totalizing style of argument, see Allington et al. The overstatements of the article trouble me and often seem unsustainable (e.g., "Digital Humanities was born from disdain and at times outright contempt, not just for humanities scholarship, but for the standards, procedures, and claims of leading literary scholars"). The polarization of Digital Humanities as neoliberal and interpretive humanistic scholarship as more political in nature than other forms of scholarship also strikes me as unhelpful and reductive, even if some aspects of the argument raise important questions about the computational humanities. For Jean Bethke Elshtain's discussion of what she, quoting Christopher Lasch, names "pseudo-radicalism," see Banac et al. (11–18). For her, the vision of a "connected" rather than contemptuous critic is one of

> an intellectual who acknowledges that she is a part of that which she analyzes and explores and, from time to time, criticizes it. This critic is not apart from but a part of that which she is lifting up for analysis.

(12)

Yet as Sara Ahmed makes clear, it is easier for some than for other types of scholars to be perceived as calm (*Wilful Subjects*, 153–154).

4 It is worth noting that at this point in the essay, Marcuse switches his attention to the danger of "destructive tolerance" or "benevolent neutrality" toward art.

5 I benefit personally from this gentrification. My three children have all attended the Sadie Tanner Mossell Alexander University of Pennsylvania Partnership School (aka Penn Alexander), a public school that has intervened in the dire public school situation in the historically Black neighborhood of Cedar Park in West Philadelphia (which has been rebranded as "University City"), and that has in many ways been an engine of racial integration. The appeal of this school, however, has driven up rents, house, and property taxes in the areas, resulting in economic displacement of and pressure on long-term residents. The neighborhood is now majority white for the first time, and the percentage of African-American students in the Penn Alexander School fell to half what it once was (see Blumgart; "Penn Compact 2020 Impact"). Johns Hopkins president Ronald J. Daniels, former Provost at Penn, is now adapting Penn's strategies for the city of Baltimore, illustrating how major research universities seek to implement each other's economically successful strategies ("Daniels: Urban Universities Can Transform Local Communities"). This approach is not without resistance (see Hendrix).

6 Angela Duckworth's *Grit: The Power of Passion and Perseverance* illustrates how these categories support each other. While Duckworth, a 2013 McArthur Fellow, has (rightly) become increasingly associated with the role of grit and student success in the context of public school education, Chapter 1 opens thus: "By the time you set foot on the campus of the United States Military Academy at West Point, you've earned it" (3). Duckworth's grit research predicts success in three realms: the military, education, and business (12). I am interested in what it would take to disintegrate the naturalized alignment among these three realms.

7 In 2008, an *October* questionnaire asked a group of artists, curators, and scholars to respond to a series of questions about art, the academy, and the invasion and occupation of Iraq. The second of the six questions framed contemporary activism in comparison with earlier responses to the Vietnam War, and implied that today's artists and academics fall short by comparison:

> Are there examples of an active counter-public sphere in which protest against the war in Iraq is conducted with an intensity comparable to protests organized during the era of the Vietnam War? What, if anything, demotivates the current generation of academics and artists from assuming positions of public critique and opposition against the barbarous acts committed by the government of the United States against a foreign country?

8 For three important histories of the postwar creative turn, see Liu; McGurl, *The Program Era*; and Dutta et al., especially Anna Vallye's essay, "The Middleman: Kepes's Instruments" (144–185).

9 Alan Liu describes how the ideology of corporate culture infiltrates the work of artists thus: "they set the agenda and starve or reward individual practitioners" (Liu 323).

10 Thank you for this reference to Oliver Gaycken, who teaches at the nation's #1 ranked militarized university, The University of Maryland.

11 Thanks to Josie Rook for gathering this data.

12 See, for example, Vaiva et al. 947–949. For a discussion of the ethical issues around this treatment, see *Beyond Therapy* (President's Council on Bioethics).

13 A June 19, 2014 Department of the Army memo describes the policy on the training for the Comprehensive Soldier and Family Fitness Program, which is a risk reduction as well as a pre-emptive rehabilitation program ("Comprehensive Soldier and Family Fitness"). The program claims to build resilience in five areas: physical, emotional, social, spiritual, and family. The second of these areas fosters "emotional control," "good character in choices and actions," and the ability to approach "life's challenges in a positive, optimistic way."

14 Kushleyev and Mellinger went on to form the company KMel Robotics, which was acquired by Qualcomm Technologies, Inc. on February 2, 2015.

15 Software Studies scholar Matthew Fuller asks the following question on the FAQ page of the tactical media group, the Bureau of Inverse Technology:

> The way in which Art presents itself is moving increasingly to resemble Engineering. How do you negotiate the difference between art and Engineering? For instance, BIT is relatively capable of using art institutions—in a broad sense—to spread information about, conduct and fund its operations. Engineering on the other hand does not seem to be structured in away which allows or encourages trouble-making activity.

Works Cited

"Academic." *Merriam-Webster.com*, www.merriam-webster.com/dictionary/academic. Accessed June 27, 2016.

Ahmed. Sara. *On Being Included: Racism and Diversity in Institutional Life*. Duke UP, 2012.

Ahmed. Sara. *Willful Subjects*. Duke UP, 2014.

Allington, Daniel et al. "Neoliberal Tools (and Archives): A Political History of Digital Humanities." *The Los Angeles Review of Books*, May 1, 2016, lareviewofbooks.org/article/neoliberal-tools-archives-political-history-digital-humanities/. Accessed June 23, 2016.

"Appendix A: Policy on Consultation where the Administration has Primary Decision-Making Responsibility." *University of Pennsylvania Office of the Provost*, 1999, provost.upenn.edu/policies/faculty-handbook/other-policies/appendix-a. Accessed July 9, 2016.

Appiah, K. Anthony. "Ghosts in the Machine." *Modern Language Association, the Presidential Blog*, First published in the Summer 2016 MLA Newsletter, president.commons.mla.org/2016/04/19/ghosts-in-the-machine/. Accessed July 9, 2016.

Arkin, William M. and Alexa O'Brien. "The Most Militarized Universities in America: A VICE News Investigation." *VICE News*, November 6, 2015, news.vice.com/article/the-most-militarized-universities-in-america-a-vice-news-investigation. Accessed November 9, 2015.

"Authentic Happiness." The University of Pennsylvania, www.authentichappiness.sas.upenn.edu. Accessed June 11, 2017.

Banac, Ivo et al. (Moderator). "If We Say It, Will They Listen?" *The Humanities and Its Publics*, ACLS Occasional Paper no. 61, 2006.

Bhojani, Fatima. "Frontier of Drones." *Motherboard*, May 21, 2014, http://motherboard.vice.com/read/why-the-us-military-is-funding-tiny-autonomous-flying-robots. Accessed November 16, 2015.

Biden, Joseph R. "A Chance to Write a New Chapter." University of Pennsylvania Commencement Address, Monday, May 13, 2013, *University of Pennsylvania Almanac*, vol. 59, no. 33, May 21, 2013, www.upenn.edu/almanac/volumes/v59/n33/comm-biden.html#sthash.BkwuXHaN.dpuf. Accessed November 10, 2014.

Blanchot, Maurice. *The Writing of the Disaster*. University of Nebraska Press, 1995. Lincoln and London: University of Nebraska Press, 1995. First published in French in 1980.

Blumgart, Jake. "The Changing Streets of Cedar Park." *Philadelphia Magazine*, March 11, 2017, www.phillymag.com/news/2017/03/11/cedar-park-gentrification-west-philadelphia/. Accessed June 7, 2017.

Brown, Wendy. *Regulating Aversion: Tolerance in the Age of Identity and Empire*. Princeton UP, 2006.

Brown, Wendy and Rainer Forst. *The Power of Tolerance: A Debate*, edited by Luca di Blasi and Christoph F.E. Holzhey. Columbia UP, 2014.

Butler, Judith. *Giving an Account of Oneself*. Fordham UP, 2005.

Cohen, David L., Board Chair. "Statement Regarding Trustees of the University of Pennsylvania Position on Tobacco Divestment." June 20, 2014, secure.www.upenn.edu/secretary/TrusteeStatementonTobaccoDivestment-June-20-2014.pdf. Accessed July 1, 2018.

"Comprehensive Soldier and Family Fitness." Army Regulation 350–353, Department of the Army, June 19, 2014, www.army.mil/e2/downloads/rv7/r2/policydocs/r350_53.pdf. Accessed July 10, 2016.

"Daniels: Urban Universities Can Transform Local Communities." *HUB*, February 27, 2013, hub.jhu.edu/2013/02/27/daniels-community-saisphere/. Accessed July 1, 2018.

Deutsche, Roslyn. *Hiroshima After Iraq: Three Studies in Art and War*. Columbia UP, 2010.

Dominguez, Ricardo. "UCOP versus R. Dominguez: The FBI Interview. A One-Act Play à la Jean Genet." *The Imperial University: Academic Repression and Scholarly Dissent*, edited by Piya Chatterjee and Sunaina Maira. U of Minnesota P, 2014, pp. 343–354.

Duckworth, Angela. *Grit: The Power of Passion and Perseverance*. Scribner, 2016.

Dutta, Arindam et al., ed. *A Second Modernism: MIT, Architecture, and the "Techno-Social" Moment*. MIT Press, 2013.

Eidelson, Roy and Stephen Soldz. "Does Comprehensive Soldier Fitness Work? CSF Research Fails the Test." *Coalition for an Ethical Psychology*, Working Paper No. 1, May 2012, pp. 1–12.

Gutmann, Amy. "President's Innovation Prize Announcement." Received by Karen Redrobe, October 28, 2015.

HAIKU (The Humanities and the Arts in the Integrated Knowledge University) Conference, September 14–15, 2014, Rainey Auditorium, the Pennsylvania Museum of Art and Archaeology, University of Pennsylvania.

Hartnett, Kevin. "Pure to Applied." *The Pennsylvania Gazette*, June 23, 2015, http://thepenngazette.com/pure-to-applied/ 50–54. Accessed July 1, 2018.

Hendrix, Steve. "Johns Hopkins Hospital Inspires Mistrust and Fear in Parts of East Baltimore." *Washington Post*, February 2, 2017, www.washingtonpost.com/local/johns-hopkins-hospital-inspires-mistrust-and-fear-in-parts-of-east-baltimore/2017/01/25/a4f402c2-bbf3-11e6-91ee-1adddfe36cbe_story.html?utm_term=.28cd92341132. Accessed July 1, 2018.

"Integration." *Merriam-Webster.com,* www.merriam-webster.com/dictionary/integration. Accessed November 16, 2015.

Joselit, David. *After Art.* Princeton UP, 2013.

Kurgan, Laura. *Close Up at a Distance: Mapping, Technology, and Politics.* Zone Books, 2013.

Latour, Bruno. *Reassembling the Social: An Introduction to Actor-Network Theory.* Oxford UP, 2007.

Liu, Alan. *The Laws of Cool: Knowledge Work and the Culture of Information.* U of Chicago P, 2004.

Marcuse, Herbert. "Repressive Tolerance." *A Critique of Pure Tolerance,* Robert Paul Wolff, Barrington Moore, Jr. and Herbert Marcuse. Beacon Press, 1968.

McGurl, Mark. "Making It Up: Creative Writing, Literary Study and Digital Technologies" roundtable panel.

McGurl, Mark. *The Program Era: Postwar Fiction and the Rise of Creative Writing.* Harvard UP, 2009.

Mulhere, Kaitlin. "Out of Favor With House GOP." *Inside Higher Ed.* April 23, 2015, www.insidehighered.com/news/2015/04/23/house-committee-draws-criticism-again-proposed-cuts-social-sciences. Accessed November 9, 2015.

Paglen, Trevor. "Operational Images." www.e-flux.com/journal/59/61130/operational-images/. Accessed November 9, 2015.

"Penn Compact 2020." *University of Pennsylvania Office of the President, www.*upenn.edu/president/penn-compact/. Accessed June 27, 2016.

"PIK Professors." *Penn Impact 2020: The Power of Philanthropy,* www.giving.upenn.edu/givingopportunities/faculty-and-staff/pik-professors. Accessed July 10, 2016.

President's Council on Bioethics. *Beyond Therapy: Biotechnology and the Pursuit of Happiness.* Washington, DC, 2003. Full report: https://repository.library.georgetown.edu/bitstream/handle/10822/559341/beyond_therapy_final_webcorrected.pdf?sequence=1. Accessed November 11, 2014.

"Questionnaire." *October,* vol. 123, Winter 2008, pp. 9–10.

Raley, Rita. *Tactical Media.* U Minnesota P, 2009.

"Rinker, Molly 'Old Mom'." *An Encyclopedia of American Women at War: From the Home Front to the Battlefields,* edited by Frank, Lisa Tendrich, vol. 1. ABC CLIO, 2013.

Rose, Jacqueline. *On Not Being Able to Sleep: Psychoanalysis and the Modern World.* Princeton, 2003.

Rose, Jacqueline. "Why War?" *Why War?—Psychoanalysis, Politics, and the Return to Melanie Klein.* Blackwell, 1993.

Russell, James. "On Elite Campuses, an Arts Race." *New York Times,* November 13, 2013, AR1.

Scarry, Elaine. *Thinking In An Emergency.* W.W. Norton & Co., 2011.

Seligman, Martin E.P. *Flourish: A Visionary New Understanding of Happiness and Well-being.* Simon & Schuster, 2012.

"Structures & Landmarks." *Friends of the Wissahickon,* www.fow.org/visit-the-park/structures-landmarks/. Accessed June 15, 2016.

The Africa Fund. "Divestment Action on South Africa from US and Canadian Colleges and Universities." August 1988, http://kora.matrix.msu.edu/files/50/304/32-130-E6E-84-AL.SFF.DOCUMENT.acoa000194.pdf. Accessed June 7, 2017.

"Tolerate." *Merriam-Webster.com,* www.merriam-webster.com/dictionary/tolerate. Accessed June 15, 2016.

University of Pennsylvania Office of Research Services. "Sponsored Projects Handbook." www.upenn.edu/researchservices/manual/sponsoredprojectshandbook.html#_Toc84300121. Accessed November 9, 2015.

Vaiva, G et al. "Immediate Treatment with Propranolol Decreases Posttraumatic Stress Disorder Two Months after Trauma." *Biological Psychiatry,* vol. 54, 2003, pp. 947–949.

Zinn, Howard. *Artists In Times of War.* Seven Stories Press, 2003.

INDEX

Abbott Laboratories 13, 413
Abel, Richard 414
absolute spirit in art, idea of 459
accident and health insurance policies 46
Act of Quarantine (1721), Britain 43
Acute Radiation Sickness (ARS) 223
addiction 187, 201, 348–349, 362; *see also* media addiction
administrative trauma 478
Adorno, Theodor W. 322, 455, 465
Advanced Combat Optical Gunsight 278
adventure, narratives of 29, 33, 39, 48, 54, 56, 60, 80, 92, 97–98
aesthetic consciousness 459
aesthetic revolution 460–461
aesthetic risk-taking 21, 453–465; economy of 453, 454–456; European aesthetics 454; heroics of control loss 462–465; Kantian aesthetics 454; from providence to probability 456–461; social and financial rewards 453; Tropicália movement of 1960s 453
aesthetics of confusion 470–471
Aesthetics of Risk, The (2008) 6, 191, 194
agrarian plagiarist 394
Agre, Philip 354
agricultural biopatents 401
agricultural biotechnologies: dominant discourse of 396; risks associated with 391
agro-food conglomerates 397
agro-food corporations 396
Ahmed, Sara 476, 498, 501, 504
AIDS Coalition to Unleash Power (ACTUP) 469–470
Alarm Phone project 140, 142–143
Aldrich, Mark 97
alert fatigue 111
Alexievich, Svetlana 220–221
algorithm dispositif 118–126
algorithmic identity 357

algorithmic provocations 124–125
al-Khwarizmi, Muhammed Ibn Musa 37
Althusserian scenario of interpellation 125
Alvarez hypothesis 265
Alvarez, Luis 265
Alvarez, Walter 265
America COMPETES Act (2015) 506
American Arms International 277
American Association of University Professors (AAUP) 474, 478
American model of risk: concept of 30–32; implementation of 32–34
American Physical Society 506
American Recovery and Reinvestment Act (2009) 111
Amnesty International 138
amphibious survival, lattices of 323–325
Anderson, Benedict 166, 317
Andreas, Peter 304
Andrejevic, Mark 379
anecdotal evidence 12, 148, 150, 153, 155–158, 161
Ansell, Charles 86
Anthropocene 8, 199, 219, 227–228, 247, 319, 323
Anthropophagy Manifesto 460
anticipatory action 166
anti-nuclear movement 224
anxiety: banality of 349; Freud's interpretation of 349; risk and 348–350; Social Media Anxiety Disorder (SMAD) 348
apophenia 352
Appadurai, Arjun 317
Appiah, Kwame Anthony 498
Applebee's Original Weekly Journal 43
Arabic numerals 37
Arabic *rizq see* Quranic *rizq*
Arab Spring 18, 131–132, 143, 355
Arab uprisings *see* Arab Spring
arbitrary necessity 455–456, 460
Arendt, Hannah 354–358

Aristotle 54, 121, 123–124, 439; aesthetic hylomorphism 122, 124; *Metaphysics* 121; *Poetics* 58, 120; theory of substances 121
Arkin, William M. 506
Armageddon (film) 266
Armored Dove of Peace 288–289
Armstrong, Edward Robert 323
Arora, Payel 185, 187
Ars coniecturandi (1713) 55, 58
art and the humanities, activism and passivism in 499–503
artistic and pedagogical activism 500
artistic innovation, purposes of 456
artistic production, activist mode of 468
art market 459
art of navigation, development of 30
ashanka (trepidation) 177
Ashton, Kevin 352; vision of the IoT 353
Assange, Julian 377, 379, 382; *see also Risk* (documentary about Julian Assange)
Assises de Jérusalem 48
Austin, J.L. 413
Automotive Intelligence 294
Autonomous Marxism 140

Bachelard, Gaston 453, 454, 457, 461
Bacon's *Novum Organon* 458
Baldwin, Ralph 265
Bartolus of Saxoferrato 61
Baudrillard, Jean 354, 383–384; model of simulation 354
Baumgartner, Felix 97
BBC's *Radio Times* 348
Beason, Doug 279
Beck, Ulrich 3–6, 96, 100–101, 148, 178, 191, 197, 214, 224, 233–236, 251; model of reflexive modernization 224; risk society, concept of 11, 46, 233–234
Bee Fable (1714) 462
Before Pictures 462
Bengal Famine (1943) 10
Bergmann, Jesper 215
Berlant, Lauren 174, 431–432
Bernoulli, Jakob 55, 58; *Art of Conjecturing* 75
Bernstein, Peter 27
betting on lives, practice of 82
Beyond the Pleasure Principle 348
bhadralok (genteel folk) 183–184, 186
bhoot.com 185–186
Bhopal disaster 270
Biden, Joe 380, 507
big data 14, 19, 111–112, 178, 357
Bijoygarh refugees 183
Binzel, Richard 266–269
biocapital, sources of 392, 396–397, 400, 404, 407
bioelectromagnetic terrain 152
bioinformational life form, ownership of 406
biojuridical intervention 405
biological hazard 401
biomedical disease models 111

biopatenting 399, 409
biopatents: agricultural 401; disputes 392; infringement of 392, 399; piracy 399; risk-managing 396
biopolitical governance 370, 394–395, 409
biopolitics 58, 224, 280, 370
biopower, operation of 395
biosocial participation, pedagogy of 421
biotech industry 394, 397, 401, 408
biotechnological governance 397
biotechnological innovation 392, 397
biotechnological inventions 400, 405–406
biotechnological knowledge 396, 400
biotechnological risk: analysis of 395; framing of 409; notions of 409
biotechnology, public understanding of 400
biotech sponsorship scandal 400
bioterrorism 199
biovalue, notion of 393
Birth of Physics, The 262–263
bjects (NEOs) 264, 266, 268, 271–272
Blade Runner (film) 198, 465
Blair, David 194, 200, 201; anthropocenic project 203
Blair's Wax 196, 200
Blanchot, Maurice 500; paradigms for criticism 503; poetic and humanistic approaches to thought 503; sense of the poetic 502
Boccaccio, Giovanni: *Elegia di Madonna Fiametta* 72; *Filoloco* 53; *Il Filoloco* 72; *Teseida* 72
Bodel, Jean 56
bodies and lives, commodification of 80, 134
border, humanitarianization of 136
border media network 306–311, 312n2
Border Patrol 306, 308, 311
border policing 305, 308
border securitization 304–306; mediated ontology of 305
border security: Anti-Border Corruption Act 306; *Border Wars* (television series) 306; as mediated spectacle 304–305; mediation of 305; practicalities of 305; techniques for 305
border security spectacle, age of 311–312
border tunnels 303, 305–307, 310–312
Border Wars (television series) 306
Borthwick, Meredith 185
Bot-tola books 181–182
Bound (1996) 490
bounded rationality, notions of 94
Bowling for Columbine (2002) 385
"Brain Science and Education" initiative 366
brain singularity 370–372
Branson, Richard 97, 99, 100
Braque, George 454
Brazil-Wood Manifesto 460
British Broadcasting Corporation (BBC) 366
British insurance industry 79
Brodsky, Rosalind 194, 198–199, 201
Brown, Wendy 303, 495, 497
bubonic plague, epidemic of 40

Buck Rogers gun 277; futuristic image of 281; high-tech optical targeting 280; optics of threat perception 278; red dot sight 278, 285
Burgess, Adam 152
Burgess, Anthony 42
Bush, G.W. 383, 471; Bush Doctrine 175n13
Butler, Judith 100–101, 304–305, 355–356, 501

Cadillac of urinals 427
Calcutta 178, 180–188
Caldwell, John 308
California Civil Jury Instructions 418
Cambridge Analytica 356
"camera zapping" project 288
Campbell, Howard 306
campuses in crisis 473–479
Capitalism: A Love Story (2010) 384
capitalist individualism, ethic of 99
capitalist societies 3, 459
Cardano, Girolamo 27, 37–38; *Liber de Ludo Aleae (On Casting the Die)* 38
Carrera de las Indias 30, 32
Carson, Rachel 316
casinos 92, 445–446, 469
Castel, Robert 96
cathode ray tube (CRT) 363, 366, 370
Cavalcanti, Guido 59; formula *rischio di morte* 62; *Guata Manetto* 62–63, 70; sonnet *Voi che per li occhi* 64; theory of love 60, 66
Cavell, Stanley 125–126, 455
Ceccarelli, Giovanni 79
celebrity 153, 380, 382–386
cell phone regulation industry 155
cell tower radiation controversy 151, 153–154
Cellular Operators Association of India 154
cellular phone industry 159
Central Intelligence Agency (CIA): "Homosexual Investigations" memo 425
Chakrabarty, Dipesh 8, 187; discussions of the "subaltern pasts" 188
Chakraborty, Kabita 180
Chandrabindu (Bengali music band) 180
Chandrashekhar, T. 153
Chapman, Clark 265, 269–270
Chaudhuri, Sukanta 181–182
Chernobyl Herbarium 227
Chernobyl nuclear power plant (Ukraine): Acute Radiation Sickness (ARS) 223; anti-nuclear movement 224; bipolar military–industrial modernity 228; cancer fatalities 224; Chernobyl Forum 224; Chernobyl Tax 223; "Chornobylets" (Chernobyl sufferer) 223; containment and conspiracy 222–224; and Duga-3 international radar system 224; East Ural Radioactive Trace area 220; explosion of 219; exposure and the "stalking" of the zone 224–226; Heavenly Hundred 223; narrative of trauma and victimhood 223; Sputnik religion and nuclear aesthetic 220–222; Zone of Alienation 219; Zone of Estrangement 219; Zone of Exclusion 227

chhom-chhom (embodied foreboding) 177
Chick Flicks 490
Chow, Rey 311
chreokoinomia 28
Christian Crusades 28
Chun, Wendy 380
Cimabue, Giovanni 458
cinema: and media studies 480–483; spectatorship 480; trigger warnings 480–483
Citizenfour (documentary) 381
civil rights protections 483
Clark, Ann 406
Clarke, Arthur C. 92, 265
Clark, Geoffrey 82
clean energy, generation of 320
climate change: causation and social ecology 246–249; CO_2 emissions 235; critical tipping points 236; global warming 237–238, 241; greenhouse gas emissions 246; impacts of 235; Landmark Federal Climate Lawsuit 243; lawsuits on 232–233, 243; and livable future 241–243; ocean acidification 235; producing the future 250–253; and redressability in the context of nonknowledge 249–250; risk and catastrophe 234–241; stake of communities 248
"clinical" spaces, definition of 108
Clinton Foundation 379
Clinton, Hillary 378–379, 386
Coalition for an Ethical Psychology 507
Cobra Club 426–427
"cognitive maps" of risk attitudes and perceptions 15
Colbert Report 383
Colbert, Stephen 383
Cold War 118, 191, 195, 202, 219, 222, 223, 271, 311, 413, 425
Collateral Murder video 381
Columbus, Christopher 32; sea contract with Antón Mariño 30
Comet Shoemaker–Levy 9, 265–266
commenda 28–29; medieval Mediterranean *commendas* 30
communicate risk 3
community, Leiss' notion of 2
Comprehensive Soldier Fitness (CSF) program 507
computer ghost stories 18, 182–183; bhoot.com 185; *Bhooter Preme Bhoot Howa* 182, 183–186; *Calcutta Chromosome* 188; *Compiutar Bhoot (Computer Ghost)* 182; *Compiutare Bhoot Dhukechhe (A Ghost Has Entered the Computer)* 182; *Khudita Pashan (Hungry Stones)* 188
computers: domesticated risk and 178–179; ghost stories *see* computer ghost stories; imaginaries 179–181; information technology-related businesses 178; proliferation of 178; reliability of 178; shock of old media 181–183; uncanny risks 186–189
confusion, aesthetics of 471
connection and community, politics of 430
Connolly, William 372

Consortium of Social Science Associations 506
conspiracy culture 4, 222, 224, 382
contingent bodies 395
cooperative insurance schemes 86
cooperative societies 90n8
Cooper, Melinda 392
Cosmic Catastrophes 265, 269–270
counter-risk analysis 14, 136, 140
Counter-Strike (CS) 438, 440, 446
"creative destruction" of extant systems 3
creative–intellectual production, cultures of 21
Crimp, Douglas 462–463
Critical Art Ensemble (CAE) 194, 197, 468, 470
crop contamination 401–402
Cruising (1980) 491
cruising, act of 14, 425–435
crusades 28, 46, 52
Crusoe economy, concept of 94
Crusoe, Robinson 93
CSGO Lotto 442–443, 445
cultural entrepreneurism 458
culture industry 465
Curry, Tim 492
cyberbullying 18, 349
cybernetics, concept of 119, 121–124

Dante: on aspect of God's creation and man's fall 67; ballad *I' mi son pargoletta* 71; on boundary between *Inferno* and *Purgatorio* 71; Canto XXV 69; encounter with Beatrice 71; *Inferno* 65; *Paradiso* 63–64, 70; on Platonic theory of love 69; reading of Saint Paul's promise 68; and Saint John 67; on three cardinal virtues of the Christian faith 67; translation of the Greek word ἀγάπη in Canto XXVI 67
Danto, Arthur 459
da Pistoia, Cino 65, 70; *Guardando a voi* 62–63; sonnet CXXIII of 61
Darwin, John 456–458
data mining 3–4, 19
#datapolitik 119–120, 124; algorithmic provocations 124–125; forms of power emergent in 126; information 120–124; modes of existence of 126; police power of 125; power dynamics of 126
dataveillance 125–126, 349
David, F.N. 35
Davis, Devra 155
Davis, Doug 271
Dean, Tim 430
death, risk of 59–71
Debord, Guy 305
Deb, Siddhartha 181
de Coubertin, Baron Pierre 455
deep dreaming 352, 356
Deep Impact (film) 266
Defert, Daniel 96
Defoe, Daniel: on equity, solidarity, and the work of friendly societies 86–88; *Essay Upon Projects, An* (1696) 86–87; on Great Plague of 1665 41; *Journal of the Plague Year, A* (1722) 39–44; on natural disasters 39; nature of narrative tempos 41; printed newspaper 42; readings of insurance 80; *Storm, The* (1704) 39, 41
De Genova, Nicholas 6, 132, 304
de Laet, Marianne 407
Delany, Samuel 430, 491, 492
delegative democracy 153
Deleuze, Gilles 125, 135, 200, 280
de Mendoza, Juan de Escalante 30–31
democratic monarchy 251–252
de Morgan, Augustus: *Essay on Probabilities and On Their Application To Life Contingencies* 55; *Theory of Probabilities* (1845) 56
de Pisa, Leonardo 37; *Liber Abaci (Book of Calculation)* 37
Derrida, Jacques 192; disjunction of ontology and fable 194; "No Apocalypse, Not Now" essay 193
Desert Hearts (1985) 490
DeVos, Betsy 483
Dewey, John 95–96
Dialectics of Enlightment 465
dialogic democracy 153
Digital Baroque 191, 199
digital distribution market 440
digital health apps 2, 107, 112–115
digital health risk media, emergence of 107, 109
digital health technologies 108, 110, 112, 113
digital humanities initiatives 509
digital imagery 199
digital infrastructures, of quantified selves 12, 17, 107, 109–110, 188
digital warfare systems 193
disaster capitalism 17
disciplines, on risk and media 5–9
displacement in place, concept of 319
Divestment Action on South Africa 506
divine revelation, criteria of 57–58
division of labor 354, 462
doctor–patient interaction 108
documentary films 16, 40, 42, 154–155, 209, 220, 224, 233, 237–238, 306, 378, 381, 382–386, 433
dolce stil novo poetry 59–61, 71
domestication of risk 81, 178–179
domination through knowledge 167
Donne, John 504
Don Sanche d'Aragon (1650) 54
drug trafficking 14, 304
Du Cange's *Glossarium* 59
Duga-3 international radar system 224
Dutt, Barkha 153–154, 156
dynamisme novateur 454, 457, 462

early modern Britain, rise of risk in 80–82
Earth Guardians 232
Eastman, Crystal 97
East Urals Nature Reserve 220
ECHELON (global surveillance system) 470
ecological sacrifice zones 227
economic entrepreneurship 10
écotechnie 199–203

Edgerton, David 181
Edison, Thomas Alva 186–187
Eidelson, Roy 508
electroencephalogram (EEG) 369
electromagnetic pollution: anecdotal evidence of 150, 154, 155–158; arguments among experts on 154–155; BioInitiative Report (2007) 154; biological effects of 151, 155; cell antenna signals 151–152; cell tower radiation controversy 151; electromagnetic field (EMF) emissions 149; experts vis-à-vis laypersons 153–154; in Green Bank, West Virginia 152; harmful effects of 149–150; human body–mobile phone/cell tower barrier 152; ICNIRP guidelines on 151, 154; lay expertise 155–158; mediation of risks related to 148; NDTV's talk show on 153–154; non-thermal effects of 151; risk management 149, 158; scientific evidence of 150; Specific Absorption Rate (SAR) testing 155; "uncertain risks" from 151–152
Electronic Disturbance Theater (EDT) 468, 470–471, 498
electronic health records (EHRs) 5, 107, 111
Electronic Medical Records (EMR) 12, 19
electrosensitives 152
electrosmog 152
Elshtain, Jean Bethke 497
Emancipated Spectator, The 489
embedded journalists 132
emergency management 166, 169, 271
emotional intimacy 429
endo-therapeutic imperatives 301
enforcement discretion 113
Epicurus (Greek philosopher) 262, 323
Epstein, Steven 155
Escalante, Juan 30–31; *Itinerary of Navigation of Western Seas and Lands* 30–32
Essay Upon Projects, An (1696) 86–87
Estienne, Henri 72; *Deux Dialogues du nouveau language françois italianizé* 72
estimate of risk 31
ethics violations 438–439
European aesthetics 454
European border management 139
European "genius of liberty" 458
Eurosur (European Border Surveillance System) 136
Eustace, Alan 97–99
event's numerical occurrence, possibility of 38
Ewald, François 58, 79, 88, 96
Exclusive Economic Zone (EEZ) 323
expertise 5, 8, 10–12, 18, 19, 148, 155–158, 161, 282, 407, 421, 509
extra-medial ontologies 4
extraterrestrial "projectiles," threat of 270

Facebook scandal 165, 356–357, 380
Factory of the Sun 198, 200–201
faculty governance, practice of 498–499
faculty leadership 498, 506
fake news 165, 347

Farchy, Joelle 463
Farocki, Harun 193, 508
fear of missing out (FOMO) 349
Federal Wire Act (1961) 444
Ferrín, Ignacio 261
fiction 165
fictional films 208
financial self-regulation 506
Fischer, Michael M.J. 413
Fisher, Anna 383
floating islands 315; aesthetic of 319; architectures and fantasies of safety 319–323; creation of 322; designs for 319; Floating Island Project 322; forms of risk mitigation 319; as hubs for creating carbon sinks 320; political and economic implications of creating 322; prospect of building 323; risk assessments 319
foenus nauticum 47, 50–51
folk music 456
Food and Drug Administration (FDA), U.S. 108
food biotechnology 395, 400
Food Biotechnology Communication Network (FBCN) 400
food quality 403, 408–409
food safety 401, 409
food security 248, 396
Forensic Architecture project 133
Forensic Oceanography research project 132–133, 135, 140, 143
forensic science 132–133
Foster, Laura 397
Foucault, Michel 13, 58, 280; *History of Sexuality, The* 426
fragmentary vitality 393–394, 399, 405, 407
freedom of information 138, 382
freedom of movement 130, 135, 142–143
freedom of thought and expression 458, 497
French revolution 458
Freud, Sigmund 60, 177, 198, 348–349, 500
Friedkin, William 491
Friedland, Sarah 380
Frontex (European border agency) 138; definition of risk 140; integrated border management 139; push-back operation 142–143; "Risk Analysis" reports 139–140; Risk Analysis Unit 140; Triton operation 138–139
Frontline (magazine) 306
Fukushima accident (Japan) 224
futurity 15, 19, 35, 118, 191, 194, 196–197, 235, 280

Gage, Joe 431, 434
gambling: attempts to curtail 439; casinos 446; Gambling Act (1774), Britain 82; illegal online gambling 439; and life insurance 82; self-promotion of 443; skin gambling *see* skin gambling; Washington's Gambling Commission 439–440, 444–445
game-induced seizures 365
game-related risk-taking 438; historical–institutional approach to 438; technology and 438–439

games of chance 10, 34–38, 55, 442
Gandhi, Rajiv 178
Garg, Rabbani 153, 156–158
Geens, Stefan 261
gender 53–54, 348, 377, 379, 380–382, 386, 474, 478, 481–482, 495
gene patents 391, 394, 398–399, 403–405
Genesis 262
genetically modified organisms (GMOs) 391, 395, 398, 400, 403–404
genetic engineering 392–394, 400, 402–403, 405
genetic modification 402–403, 409
Genetic Use Restriction Technologies (GURTS) 399
Gessen, Keith 220
Ghosh, Amitav 17, 188, 316
ghost stories 188
Gibson, William 277
Giddens, Anthony 10, 178, 349
Gillespie, Tarleton 119, 447
global capitalism 319, 324, 377
global carbon emissions 319
globalization 251
global media: markets 14; rise of 197
global positioning systems (GPS) 109
global risk culture 224
global South 130
global technomodernity 179
global trade 10, 456–457, 459
global warming 234, 237–238, 241
glyphosate-tolerant mutant 397
God-consciousness 420
Goff, Charles 277, 282
Go Fish (1994) 490
Golinski, Jan 264
Gombaud, Antoine 55
Google: Deep-Dream project 352, 356; machine learning algorithms 352; PageRank algorithm 348
Gorbachev, Mikhail 220
Goswami, Anindita 182
governmental bureaucracy 166
government-funded organization 198
grammars of action 354
gray literature, concept of 174n4
"gray" media 166
Great Divergence 456
Great Hunger of 1932–1933 222
Great Patriotic War 222
Great Plague of 1655 40, 43
Greek *kubernētēs* 124
greenhouse gas emissions 246, 249
Greenpeace 224, 400, 403
GreenScreenRefrigeratorAction 351–352
Gregory IX, Pope 50–51
Grusin, Richard 5, 126
Guillory, John 120, 165, 167, 169
Gulf War 201–202
gun-dick 427, 430, 434
'gun porn' moments 282

habitual new media 349
Hacking, Ian 9, 38, 80, 96
Halpern, Orit 123, 350
Hanhardt, Christina 493
Hansen, James E. 232
Harney, Stefano 489, 492
Hartwell, William 265
Harvard College v. *Canada* 398, 404, 406
Hattenstone, Simon 382
hazardous individualism 10, 91–92, 94, 95–97, 98–100
"health and wellness" tools 108
health datafication, practices of 108
Health Information Portability and Accountability Act of 1996 (HIPAA) 108–110
health information technology (HIT) 111
Health Information Technology for Economic and Clinical Health (HITECH) 111–112
health surveillance 107–109, 115
hedge funds 11, 46
Hegel's *Vorlesungen über Ästhetik* 459
Heimer, Carol 80, 82
Heise, Ursula 316–317
herbicides 391, 394–395, 397, 406–408
Heston, Charlton 385
hierarchical theological system 72
higher education 473, 477, 497, 505–506; bureaucraticization of 476
high-risk behaviors 14
high-risk professions 87
high-tech weapons 282
Hindi films 416
Hiroyuki, Takada 369
HIV–AIDS crisis 1
Hobbesian moral psychology 118
Hobbesian security state 374
Hobbes, Thomas 88, 100, 119
hojas volantes (flyers) 33–34
Hollywood film industry 453, 463–464
Holocene 227–228
Holodomor 222
Homeland Security Advisory System 272, 349
Homeland Security Digital Library 166
Homeland Security Digital Library (HSDL) 166, 168
homo economicus 91–100
homo floresiensis 211
homophily, principle of 18, 358
honka-dori 456
Honken, Scott 113–114
Hot Spotting 113
House of Psychotic Women (1974) 491
House Science, Space and Technology Committee 506
human beings, psychology of 33, 72, 79–80, 84, 167, 318, 352–353
Human Condition, The 354–355
humanities education 477
human life, application of risk to 31, 72
human-machine interface 20
human medical errors 110

human–nonhuman assemblages, production of 395
human–nonhuman interactions 395
human–nonhuman relations 5
human–thing duality 192
Humphreys, Laud 427; conception of risk 430; *Tearoom Trade* 428–429
Hutter, Michael 462
hyper-actuarialized citizens 6
hyper-events 16, 219, 227–228
hyper-rationalism 96

"illegal" immigrants 303, 468
imagined community, concept of 317
Indian Department of Telecommunications (DoT) 151
Indian Rasa, theory of 454
Individual Air Burst Weapon System 277
industrial farming 398, 409
industrialized violence 282
Industrial Revolution 227, 456–458
information and communication technologies (ICTs) 107
information–energy kernel 123
information technologies 11, 111, 178, 192, 353
info-vitalism, invention of 121
injunctive relief 235, 237
innovation 3, 7, 20, 37, 42, 43, 119, 122–123, 181, 234, 251, 278, 282, 307, 392, 397, 440, 454–461, 497, 504, 505–506
Institute of Militronics and Advanced Time Interventionality, The (IMATI) 198
insurance 463; British practices of 79, 80–82; commodification and property in lives 88–89; defined 79; key feature of 88; life insurance *see* life insurance; marine insurance *see* maritime insurance; origins of 79; philosophical probability of 80; policies of 37; private and public benefits 81; rise of 79; Smith's and Defoe's readings of 80; as technology of risk 79
integrated border management 139
integration 3, 15, 108, 110, 222, 299, 446, 447, 497, 504, 505
intellectual dissent 21
intellectual engagement 474
intellectual property and surveillance 392, 401
intellectual property rights 20, 392–393, 396
International Astronomical Union 266
International Atomic Energy Agency 224
International Commission on Non-Ionizing Radiation Protection (ICNIRP) 151, 156
International Monitoring Programs for Asteroid and Comet Threat (IMPACT) 266
Internet of People 347, 350–354, 356
Internet of Things (IoT) 349, 350–354; Ashton's vision of 353
Internet Protocol (IP) 351
intimacy, human-centered notions of 351
Into Eternity (2010) 8, 16, 207, 209–211, 213–214
isqa 28
Italian *Mare Nostrum* operation 131, 136–139

Italian Renaissance 458
Itinerary of Navigation of Western Seas and Lands (Escalante) 30–31
Ives, Charles 454, 456

Jameson, Fredric 5, 315, 318–319
James, William 95
Jeu de Paume game 55
Jevons, William Stanley 91
jhunki (hazard) 177
job satisfaction 306
job security 498
Johnson, Erik 443
joint-stock insurance companies 80–81; Adam Smith on contempt for risk and role of 83–86
Jones, William E. 427
Joselit, David 505
journalism, emergence of 39
Journal of the International Meteor Organization 263
Journal of the Plague Year, A (1722) 39–44
Judge Dredd weapon 277
judicial conservatism 243
Jugend Rettet NGO 139
Juliana v. United States 232–236, 244
Juncker, Jean-Claude 139
Junger, Ernst 96
Justinian's *Codex Iuris Canonici* 50

K-12 educational model 477
Kaibab National Forest 248
Kant, Immanuel: *Conflict of the Faculties, The* 72–73; *Idea of a Human History from a Cosmopolitan Point of View* 75; *philosophia ancilla theologiae* 72
Kanuk, Nelson 238–239, 240
Kapur, Jyotsna 373
Kasliwal, Sudhir 160–161
Kennedy, Helena 108, 382
Keynes' *General Theory of Employment, Interest and Money* 461
Killing of Sister George, The (film) 490
Kirn, Herman 495
Klein, Naomi 17
Klein, Richard 193
Knight, Frank 94, 348, 362, 454
knowledge production 166; speculation as 167–170; via documents and documentation 167
Korokoro Komikku (Corocoro Comic) 364
Kumar, Girish 154
Kuran, Timur 379

Lakoff, Andrew 14, 22, 166
laser-assisted weapons 277, 281
laser-emitting diode (LED) 278
laser sight 277, 278, 280–283
La Suite du Menteur (1643) 54
Latour, Bruno 503
Lavender Scare 425
lawsuits 21, 232, 242, 246, 249, 253, 365, 393, 399–400, 407, 443
Lazarsfeld, Paul 358

learning and creating, modes of 500
Lecavellum, Georgius 29
Leckey, Mark 351
Ledford, John 365
"left-to-die boat" case 131–132, 141
legality 8, 443
legal standing 248–249
Levy, David 265
Levy, Jonathan 460, 463
LGBT communities: generational conflict in 487
liability-adverse actuarial logics 473
Lianna (1983) 490
liberal capitalism 92, 100, 194, 323, 461
liberal capitalist rationality 98
liberalism, idea of 495
life and morality, sense of 80
Life During Wartime 490
life insurance: development of 81; gambling 82; in modern English 81; rules of conduct 82; for slaves 81; social criticisms of 82; trade risk and 82
life insurance companies 94
Life of Brian, The 488, 493
Life on Screen (1995) 350
L'impromptu de Versailles (1663) 55
Lindsay, Jack 40
liquid crystal display (LCD) 370
literary realism, modes of 317
Living it Up (lifestyle program) 156–158
living with risk, modalities of 3
Locard, Edmond 132
Locke, John 52, 56, 72, 88, 501; *Essay Concerning Human Understanding* 58; methods of approaching the truth 58
London Courant, The 39
London Gazette 39
Louisiana Museum's Moon Exhibit 208
love: forms of 71; theory of 60, 65, 69
love poetry 5, 10, 65, 71–72; traditional rules of 71
Luhmann, Niklaus 27
Lukes, Stephen 91
Lyotard, Jean-François 196

McCarthy, Joseph 425–426
McCurdy, Howard 271
machine learning 352, 356
Macpherson, C.B. 91, 100, 101
Madison, Michael 207–215, 391
Maidan Revolution (2014) 222–223
Maker, Jacob 200
Malaysia Airlines Flight 17; downing of 223
male-on-male anonymous public sex 427
Malraux, André 458
Mandeville, Bernard 462
Mansfield News-Journal 425
Marcuse, Herbert 497
Marcus, George E. 413
Marder, Michael 227
Mare Nostrum operation 131, 136–139
marginal revolution of 1871 91–92
marginal utility, theory of 92–94

marine-related disasters 85
marine ventures 80
Mariño, Antón 30
maritime contracts 28–29, 37–38
maritime frontier, militarization of 130
maritime insurance 80; in Britain 81; codification of 80; corporate 82; policy of 29
maritime loans: contracts issued in Marseille and Genoa 59; philosophy of 46–58
maritime navigation 29–30, 32
marketing-oriented knowledge 400
Masaccio 457, 459
Masco, Joseph 173, 272
masculinist penis-as-weapon metaphors 427
Maslin, Janet 491
mass extinction, notion of 265
mass killings 417
Massumi, Brian 373
matière de Bretagne 56
Matthews, Rajan 154
Mead, Richard 41
Médecins Sans Frontiers (MSF) 137
media addiction: and brain health 363–369; discourses on 362; epileptiform phenomena and singularity 369–373; expression of singularity and 373–374; forms of 362; Pokémon Incident (1997) 364–365; risk assessment of 362
media-consciousness 421
media dependency, notion of 374
media industries, political economy of 14, 20, 159
medial fabulation 198–199, 203
media/mediation, overview of 4
media platforms 109, 150, 156, 158, 347, 367, 370, 371, 374, 444, 478
media spectacle 304
media technologies and infrastructures 4
mediation: concept of 152; phenomenological dimension of 156
medical care, reimbursement for 110
medical devices, regulation for use of 108
Medicare Access and CHIP Reauthorization Act 2015 (MACRA) 110
medicine, risk media in: clinical and metaclinical spaces 108–109; clinical risk media 110–111; data-driven healthcare 107; digital health apps 107; digital infrastructures of quantified selves 109–110; doctor–patient interaction 108; emergence of 110; human medical errors 110; information and communication technologies (ICTs) and 107; interpretations of 20; metaclinical risk media 107; metaclinical risk media interfaces 112–115; Omada Health 107; patient-centered care and 110; from personal to population health 110–111; procedure- to outcome-based care 111; and public health 110; redefining "the human" through 115; return on investment (ROI) 107; user stratification and 108; value-based care 110
medieval commerce and poetry, origin of: from maritime loan to philosophy 46–58; from poetry

to theology and finance 72–75; from risk of death to paradise 59–71
Mediterranean: *commendas* 30; map of 47; maritime trade 37, 52; Mediterranean Sea 28–29, 35, 142; mobility conflict 130–131, 143; origin of risk 27–29; phenomenon of migrants crossing and dying 130, 136–137, 139; regime of (in)visibility 131
Mellor, Felicity 269
Mens Room: Bakersfield Station 431, 433
mental illness 415, 419, 421
mental inadequacies 425
Merck, Mandy 385
Merton, Robert K. 358
metaclinical risk media interfaces 112–115
"metaclinical" spaces, definition of 108
meta-drama 416–418
meteor, fall of: always on alert against 270–273; Chelyabinsk meteor 261; Comet Shoemaker–Levy 9, 265–266; digital recordings of 260; doomsday scenario 270; Duende meteor 264; Earth-approaching asteroids and comets 265; explosion over Chelyabinsk Oblast, Russia 259–262; extraterrestrial "projectiles," threat of 270; International Monitoring Programs for Asteroid and Comet Threat (IMPACT) 266; media/meteor complex 262; NASA's Near-Earth Object Observations Program 264; near-Earth objects (NEOs) 264; probability of the Earth being struck by a large asteroid or comet 264–266; scaling the risk 266–270; Serres's philosophy of *meteōra* 262–264; time of *Meteōra* 262–264; Tunguska meteor 260
#MeToo campaign 14, 377–380, 383, 483
microtransactions, in monetizing video games 448n4
Middle Ages: economic order of 58; risk in 59
Middleton, Jason 383, 385–386
migration, perils of: acts of border-crossing and 133; Alarm Phone project and 142; areas of maritime crossings 142; "Blaming the Rescuers" report 139; border control and 132; counter-risk analysis of 131, 136–141; criminalization of nongovernmental rescue initiatives 139; disobedient gaze and 132–135; documenting of violence of policies 136–141; EU's policy on 136; Frontex's Triton operation 138–139; hotline supporting boats in distress 142; illegal border crossers 141; Italian *Mare Nostrum* operation 136–139; "left-to-die boat" case 131, 132–135, 137, 141; Mediterranean Boat Capsizing 137; Mediterranean mobility conflict 130–131; migrants' deaths at sea 141–143; NATO-led operation and 135; *not to see* migrants 132; phenomenon of 131; policies of non-assistance 139; "pull-factor" encouraging migration 138; regime of (in)visibility 131–132; rescue of migrants 138; SAR operation to mitigate 139; Search and Rescue (SAR) zones 134; secret routes and safe houses 141; violence of borders 144; visual exposure of illegalized migrants 132

military–corporate research agenda 198
military–industrial complex 194
military–industrial–digital complex 200
military–industrial–digital system, of technoscience 198
millennial capitalism 189
Mill, John Stuart 91
Milton, John 461
mind–body duality 192
mobile phones: harmful effects of 149; mobile phone radiation 152; public fears about 152; Specific Absorption Rate (SAR) testing 155
Mobilize (documentary film) 155
modern art, principle of 455
modern market economies 453, 455, 459
Mokyr, Joel 457–458
molecular biogovernance 409
Monsanto Canada 391–392; genetic modification of canola 402; Glyphosate-Resistant Plants 397; intellectual property 400; Roundup Ready Canola 391–392, 397, 401; *Schmeiser* case 401
Montreal Gazette 400
MOOC platform of Coursera 499
Moonlight (2017) 465
Moore, John 392
moral psychology 84–85, 118
moral rectitude, rules and practices of 80
Morrison, David 265, 269
Moskowitz, Joel 155
Moten, Fred 489
Moyle, Alan 489
Mukherjee, Siddhartha 151
Müller-Mahn, Detlef 315, 317–318
Muñoz, José Esteban 428, 492
Murray, Martin J. 322

Naimark, Michael 288
Nanovision 179
narco-tunnels: Nogales Tunnel Task Force 304; political potential of 303; shutdown of 306; tunnel visualization and concealment 304
narratives 9, 12, 27, 29–44, 51, 111, 120, 182–183, 188, 197, 209, 211–214, 222, 223, 228, 286, 316, 350, 395, 416, 435, 473, 490, 491
National Aeronautics and Space Administration (NASA): *absolute geospheric* security 272; Jet Propulsion Laboratory 265; Near Earth Object Hazard Index 12, 266; Near-Earth Object Observations Program 264, 266, 271; Planetary Defense Coordination Office (PDCO) 271; *Spaceguard Survey, The* 264–265; *total terrestrial* security 272
National Institute of Mental Health And Neuro Sciences (NIMHANS), India 187; Service for Healthy Use of Technologies (SHUT) 187
National Ocean and Atmospheric Administration (NOAA) 319
National Radio Quiet Zone (Green Bank), West Virginia 152
natural–social dualism 5

Near-Earth Objects: Finding Them Before They Find Us 268
negative feedback, idea of 119, 123–125
neo-classical economics 91
neo-colonial liberalism 414
neoliberal capitalism 194, 323
network-art-activism 468
neuroplasticity 367, 371, 372, 374
Neutill, Rani 475–476
Newell-McGloughlin, Martina 403
news media 153, 265, 268, 391, 400, 401, 406, 409
Newsweek magazine 277–278, 281
Newton's *Principia* 458
New World 34
New York Times 97, 288, 319, 378, 471, 491, 504
Nichols, Bill 382
Nixon, Rob 237, 241, 247, 319
No Future: Queer Theory and the Death Drive 426
nonhuman 4–5, 13, 119, 124, 126, 192, 227, 305, 349, 392–396, 404, 406, 409, 509
normative rationality 94
Novak, David 318
Novum organon 458
nuclearization of India, issue of 154
nuclear: accidents 12, 219, 224; power 12, 219–220, 223, 235; radiation 149, 151; war 193, 270–271

Obama, Barack 232, 483
Object Oriented Ontology (OOO) 192
O'Brien, Alexa 506
Observations Made upon the Bills of Mortality (1662) 40
ocean acidification 235–236
oceanic navigation, risk in 30–31, 33
October Revolution (Soviet Union) 221
Odessa, fight between Ukrainian and Russians in 223
offenses 472
Office of Civil Rights (OCR): guidelines on Title IX investigations 478
Ohio's sodomy laws 425
Oiticica, Hélio 453
Omada Health (digital health risk media program) 107, 111, 113; target customers 113; Top Three Habits of Innovative Health Plans 113
"On Danger" essay (1931) 96
online learning 499
On the Nature of Things 262
optically stimulated epileptic seizures 365
Orange Revolution of 2004 222
organic farmer 402–403
Orwell, George 457
out-of-control risk-taking 462–463
Outrageous Fortune 365
Oxford Gazette 42

Pacioli, Luca 27, 37–38
Paradise Lost 461
paradise, notion of 59–71
Pascal 53, 55, 58, 220, 461; *la géométrie d'hasard* 58
Patent Act (1985) 399, 405

patent-based propertization 405
patent infringement 392, 396, 398–399, 401, 405–407
patient-centered care 110, 112, 115
Patient Protection and Affordable Care Act 2010 (ACA) 110
pattern discrimination 353
Pavlov, Ivan 121; experiments on conditioned reflexes 122
pedagogy 21, 421, 476–477, 480–483, 499
Penn, William: Authentic Happiness project 497; Board of Trustees 506; *Daily News* 504; institutional and intellectual priorities 504; Kirn's depiction of 495; Penn Compact 2020 497; Penn Integrates Knowledge (PIK) professorship program 505; Provost 499
People's Front of Judea (PFJ) 493
perceptual fields, immateriality of 195–196
performativity, idea of 9, 14, 304–306, 312, 468
Personal Best (1982) 490
personalized risk mediation 2
Peters, John Durham 237, 347
Petrarca, Francesco 61
phanda (astrological risk) 177
Phenomenology of Spirit, The 420
Philosophy of Science 121, 262
Phone Booth (2002) 283–284
photoepileptiform phenomena 373
photoparoxysmal response (PPR) 369
Pinedo, Isabel 430
Pitkin, Hanna 355, 358
Planetary and Space Science 266
Plant Breeders' Rights Act (1990) 399
Plato: theory of justice 119; theory of love 65
Poell, Thomas 347–348, 355, 357–358
Poitras, Laura 14, 377, 380–385
Pokémon Incident (1997) 16, 364–366, 369–371, 373–374
police 14, 120, 124–125, 130, 132, 134, 182, 184, 209, 215, 277, 280, 287, 378, 425–427, 430, 433–434, 488
Pollock, Sheldon 459
polyvalent vulnerability, notion of 374
Pomeroy, Jason 324
Ponzi schemes 3
pornography 182, 427, 431–432, 473, 480
Poroshenko, Petro 223, 227
Portal Systemic Encephalopathy (PSE) 364
Porter, Theodore 178
Positive Psychology 507
possessive individualism 91, 100
post-industrial agriculture 396, 409
Postmodernism (1984) 315, 319
post-traumatic stress disorder (PTSD) 472, 475, 481, 507
Pound, Ezra 60
Powell, Colin 170–173, 508
PPL Montana, LLC v. *Montana* 242
praise poetry: classical topos of 60; traditional tropes of 63

predation games 430
predation play video games 430
preference falsification, notion of 379
preparedness documents: definition of 167; *Homeland Security Digital Library* (HSDL) 168; *Interim National Preparedness Goal* 168; *National Preparedness Goal* document 167–168, 170; official documentation 171; self-reflexive document 171; temporality of 167–170; threats for 174n3; as world-making project 170–174
primal love, truth of 68
printed newspaper, birth of 42
privacy, breach of 2, 107, 288, 356, 358, 379, 380, 429, 431–432
Proactive Member Surveillance 113
probabilistic regression analyses 114
probability: mathematical formulation of 37–38; notion of 37; outcomes in dice rolling 38; principle of 38
Professional and Amateur Sports Protection Act (1992) 444
Project X Heran 356
projukti ashokti, phenomenon of 187
protected health information (PHI) 108
Protestant Ethic and the Spirit of Capitalism, The 58
psychosomatic disorientation 481
pub-based sociality 86
public health works 110
public–private partnerships 400
public sex acts 429
Purgatorio 65, 71, 75
Python, Monty 487–488, 493

qirad (Arab) 10, 28–29
Queer Art of Failure, The 488
queer films 489–491
queer intimacy, games of 426, 427, 430, 434
queer readings, history of 431
queer youth homelessness 434
Quran 27
Quranic *rizq*: defined 27; European version of 29; transposition of 28

Rabinow, Paul 412
Racketeer Influenced and Corrupt Organizations Act (RICO) 443
radio waves: effects on human body 155; emitted by mobile phones 155
raison d'etre 11
Rancière, Jacques 131, 455, 460, 488
randomized, controlled trials (RCTs) 113
Rangaswamy, Nimmi 185, 187
Raqs Media Collective 17, 20, 328
rationalized uncertainties 96
reasonable foreseeability 13
Reassembling the Social 503
recreational terror 430
Red Scare 425
Reed, Arden 264
relaciones (accounts) 33

remote sensing 132–133, 143
Rendezvous with Rama 265
republic of letters, history of 458
Rescue 911 docudrama 239
rescue, notion of 134
resource allocation 248, 265
responsibility, theory of 501
retail medicine 110
return on investment (ROI) 107, 113, 454
revenge, thoughts of 60
Ridley, Daisy 348, 465
rischio di morte 62, 64, 69–71
risk: American concept of 30–32; and anxiety 348–350; Arab adoption of numerous innovations 37; definition of 140; etymology of 27; Freud's understanding of 349; Islamic–Arabic version of 27; in matter of navigation 30–31; Mediterranean origin of 27–29; narratives of 39; objects at 30; objects of 30; secularization of 29
Risk (documentary about Julian Assange) 377; Gaga feminism 382–386; production history and gender politics 380–382
risk communication 1, 4, 6, 12, 266, 268–269, 362, 393
risk egalitarianism 101
risk histories, narrativization of 9–11
risk institutions 11–13
risk management 2, 11, 31, 91, 349, 397; aesthetic dimensions of 6; institutional 96; institutions in Europe and the United States 96; media and 3–4; privatization of 409
risk media: concept of 347, 394; social logic of 349; technologies 107
risk mediation 4, 20; affect of 20; disciplinary modulations of 21; expertise in 19; historical perspectives of 18–19; legitimacy of 20–21; scale of 19; times of 19; virtuality of 19–20
risk mediators, types of 395; normalization 399–400; objectification 404–406; politicization 400–403; privatization 396–399; responsibilization 406–407
risk rationality, standards of 92
risk–reward rationality 92, 97, 99
riskscape: notion of 317; topologies of 316–319
risk society 3, 100, 178; concept of 11, 46; culture of uncertainties and 177
Risk Society: Towards a New Modernity (1992) 236
risk stratification 112
Risk, Uncertainty, and Profit (1921) 94, 460
risk worlds 15–18, 20
risky territory, elements of 317
"robust metaphor" project 288
Roof, Judith 400
Roosevelt, Theodore 95–96
Rose, Jacqueline 499
rota Vergilii 54
Roundup Ready Canola 391–394, 397–398, 401, 404, 405, 408
Route to the Indies (*Carrera de las Indias*) 30
Rove, Karl 471
Rukh organization 222

Rumsfeld, Donald 348
Russell, James 504
Russia: fighting in Odessa 223; Russian Revolution 201; takeover of Crimea 223
Russian Woodpecker, The 224

safety 12, 18, 31, 88, 97, 99, 111, 142, 153, 155, 209, 228, 280, 293–302, 315, 319–322, 365, 400, 403, 409, 489
Sakakeehy, Matt 318
same-sex desires 432
sangshay (uncertainty) 177
Saturday Night Fever (film) 489–490
Scarry, Elaine 500–501
Schelling, Friedrich Willhelm 455–456, 460
Schengen Agreement 130
Schiller, Friedrich 459
Schivelbusch, Wolfgang 481
Schmeiser case 391–409
Schmeiser, Percy 391, 398
Schumpeter, Joseph 3
Schwarzenegger, Arnold 282
science and technology studies (STS) 159
science fiction 188, 204, 208, 215, 224, 236, 237, 265, 277, 279, 283, 315, 320
Scientific American 363
Scott, Darieck 435
screen-based media interfaces 107
sea-level rise 315–316, 319; problem of 319
Sea Level Rise Viewer 319
Search and Rescue (SAR) zones 134
Seasteading Institute (Silicon Valley) 315, 322
Second Self, The (1984) 350
Sedgwick, Eve 426, 431
self-care, science-based 107
self-determination, ideology of 295
self-evidence, notion of 58
self-governance, Seasteaders' model of 323
self-reference, limits of 302
self-replicating invention 394
Seltzer, Mark 170
Sense of Place, Sense of Planet: The Environmental Imagination of the Global (2008) 316
Serres, Michel 262; philosophy of *mete ra* 263–264
sexuality, policing of 426
sexual predation 14
Shepard, Stuart 283
shiksha factory 184
Shimizu Corporation (Japan) 315
shock, pedagogy of 480–483
Shoni puja (pacificatory rituals) 188
Silent Spring (1962) 316
simulation, theory of 354
skin gambling 438, 439–442; acceptance of 445; *Counter-Strike: Global Offensive (CS:GO)* 439–442; Federal Wire Act (1961) 444; lawsuits over 443; scandal surrounding 443–444; scrutiny regarding 444–447; Sports Bribery Act (1964) 444; Valve's role in 440
Skinner, B.F. 119, 121–122

slave trade 46, 52; life insurance for slaves 81
smartness mandate 350
Smith, Adam 80, 95; analysis of insurance and risk 83; on contempt for risk and role of joint-stock insurance companies 83–86; readings of insurance 80; views on human psychology and risk behaviors 85; *Wealth of Nations, The* (1776) 83
Smith, Lamar 506
Snowden, Edward 380–381
Social Amplification of Risk Framework (SARF) 6, 15, 152, 161n2
social contagion 425
social discrimination 357
social justice 474, 478
social lives, of networked teens 347
social media 4, 347; collection and deployment of intimate data 357; logic of 358; networks 20; Project X Heran 356; rise of 358; Social Media Anxiety Disorder (SMAD) 18, 348; social-media-risk 348, 350; and social question 354–358; virtual connection 355
social mobility 180–181, 183–184
social movement studies (SMS) 159
social risk: perceptions of 7; social-media-risk 348
social solidarity 80, 88
societas 28
Socrates 60
Soldz, Stephen 508
Soneryd, Linda 158, 318
Sorcerer, The 418–420
Sorrensen, Cynthia 307–308
soundscape, theory of 318
South Africa's Truth and Reconciliation Commission 499, 507
Specific Absorption Rate (SAR) testing 155
speculation, as knowledge production 167–170
speculative documentary 16, 19, 209
speculative transactions, virtuality of 439
Stalker (film) 224–225
statistics 2, 6, 39, 43–44, 55, 58, 73–74, 296, 473
Steam (digital storefront) 440
Stevens, Wallace 454, 461
Stewart, Jimmy 417
Steyerl, Hito 194, 197, 200–201, 203, 352, 354
Stigwood, Robert 489–490
Stossel, John 303, 311
Stranger, Mark 463
strategic territorialism, idea of 135
Suck My Dick or Die! ("rape-themed" game) 427
Sunstein, Cass 11

tactical laser weapons 279
Takao, Yamasaki 369
Talking Heads, The 490
targeting 64, 115, 278, 280–281, 284–285, 287–289, 356
Tarkovsky, Andrei 224–225
Tearoom (2007) 427, 433
Tearoom Trade: Impersonal Sex in Public Spaces (1970) 427–429

techno-economic integration 3
technological innovations 20, 458
technological kinship, between human and nonhuman reproduction 392
technological unconscious 350–351, 354
techno-logie, notion of 202
technologies of intimacy (ToI) 350
technology addiction, instances of 187
Technology Use Agreement (TUA) 398, 403
techno-pop paranoia 348
téléaction, system of 196–198
Telecom Regulatory Authority of India (TRAI) 154
television 5, 12, 150, 153, 156–158, 196, 198, 233, 265, 272, 280, 286, 312, 362–372, 415, 417, 455, 468
terrorist attacks 166, 235, 384
theology 35, 38, 50–51, 58, 65, 72–75
Thompson, Hunter S. 99
thom-thom (foreboding atmosphere) 177
Three Mile accident 12
Thrift, Nigel 350, 354, 358
thunderstone 270
Tiffany, Daniel 262
time *contretemps*, creator of 263
TIME Magazine 265, 378
Times Square (film) 489–490, 492
Title IX 474, 478, 483, 484n6
tobacco industry 159, 506
To Damascus: A Film on Interpretation (2005) 207
tolerance, risk of 495–509; between art and arms races 503–507; concept of 495–499; from humanistic perspective 499; Penn Compact 2020 497; in realms of art and the humanities 499–503; resisting resilience and 507–509
Tomorrow People, The (English television series) 198
Torino Impact Hazard Scale 266–269, 272
trade risk 82; and life insurance 82
trade unions 90n8
trans-biopolitics 395
Transborder Immigrant Tool 468, 498
transgenic canola, politicization of 399, 401
transit camps 183
trans-species biogovernance: mediations of risks associated with 391–396; normalization of 399–400; objectification of 404–406; politicization of 400–403; privatization of 396–399; responsibilization of 406–407
Treatise on Friendly, Societies, A (1835) 86
treatises of navigation 30
Treister, Suzanne 194, 198–199, 201, 203
Trenité, Dorothée Kasteleijn-Nolst 369
trial by jury: feelings (third post) 414–416; meta-drama (fourth post) 416–418; moral state (second post) 412–414; no way (sixth post) 421–422; seduction, sociality, and event (first post) 411–412; sorcerer (fifth post) 418–420
Triebfeder 462
trigger warnings 472–473; AAUP report on 474; *Atlantic, The* 475; cinema and media studies 480–483; and claims of microaggressions 475; contested positions over curriculum 479; feminist community support and pedagogy 476; moral panic around 476; pedagogy of shock 480–483; postscript, September 2018 483–484; rise of anxieties about 476
Tropicália movement of 1960s 453, 460
Trump, Donald 193–194, 201–202, 378–379, 384, 417, 434, 483
truth, methods of approaching 58
Turkle, Sherry 350–351

Ukraine 221–228; Chernobyl nuclear power plant *see* Chernobyl nuclear power plant (Ukraine); media treatments of 219
Umbrella Movement (2014), Hong Kong 355
Uncertain Commons 7, 250, 316
uncertainty: aesthetics of 453; culture of 177; mediation of 305; notion of 38
United Nations (UN): Convention on the Laws of the Sea to Search and Rescue 134; High Commissioner for Refugees (UNHCR) 137; International Conference on Near-Earth Objects 266; Security Council 170
University of California 21, 207, 393, 473
university's policies on academic freedom and faculty governance 498
Unlimited Intimacy: Reflection on the Subculture of Barebacking (2009) 430
Urbanism of Exception, The (2017) 322
U.S. Customs and Border Protection: *Frontline* (magazine) 306; Nogales Tunnel Task Force 304, 306, 310–311; *What Lies Beneath* (video series) 304, 306–311
U.S. Homeland Security Advisory System 272
usury 50–52, 58, 72
utilitarianism-effective society 471

value-based care 110, 114
Value, Inc. 113–114
Valve Corporation 439–440; digital distribution market 440; non-game software development 445; Steam (digital storefront) 440
van Dijck, José 347–348, 355, 357–358
Vasari, Giorgio 457–460
Veblen, Thorstein 94
Velazquez' *Las Meninas* 456
Veloso, Caetano 453
venture capital 3, 56, 109, 320
Vernadsky, Volodymyr 220
Vespucci, Amerigo 457
video game broadcast 365, 371
video game industry 439
video games 204, 214, 226, 280, 363, 365–371, 426, 428, 430, 438, 439–440, 445, 447; microtransactions in 448n4
Vietnam War 497
Vincent Callebaut Architects (France) 315, 319
violence 4, 8, 33, 39, 96, 100, 131–135, 143, 203, 214, 281, 304, 363, 426, 430, 434, 473, 475,

violence *continued*
    492, 500, 502; carceral 426; criminal 222; domestic 472; gun violence 481; industrialized 282; militarized 348; of policies 136–137, 139; against queer people 433; sexual violence 427, 472, 483; slow violence 236, 241; specific episodes of 142
violent moral panic 430
Virilio, Paul 12, 192, 195, 281–282, 481
virtual reality 208, 445
"virtual" value, concept of 438
virtual warfare 193
virtual weapon systems 200
virtuous ambition 457–458
visual arts 454–455, 460
vital systems preparedness 14
VNS Matrix 194
Voices from Chernobyl 221
Vox, Danny 431

Walpole, Horace 43
Walters, William 136
war–cinema relationship 195; Virilio's *War and Cinema* 195
Warner, Michael 1–2, 22, 432
War on Drugs 303
War on/of Terror 508
Washington Environmental Council v. Bellon 241, 246
WatchTheMed network 141–142
Watergate scandal 470
Watson, Jini Kim 265, 321
WAXWEB 200
Wealth of Nations, The (1776) 10, 83–84
weapons of mass destruction (WMD) 170, 172–173, 348, 471, 508

web-based interface 113
Weber, Max 58, 95, 167, 460
Weber, Samuel 281
Weizman, Eyal 6, 133
Welsch, Wolfgang 439
We Steal Secrets (2013) 385
Western philosophical aesthetics 462
We the People (talk shows) 153–154, 156
What Lies Beneath (video series) 304; "behind-the-scenes" feature 308; within border media networks 306–311
WikiLeaks 377–380, 381, 385–386
Williams, Raymond 5
Witt, John Fabian 99
work safety movement 97
World at Risk (2007) 236
World Health Organization (WHO) 156
World Watch 391
Wormwood Forest: A Natural History of Chernobyl 226
writ of mandamus 251–252
Wynne, Brian 151, 155–156, 159

Yang, Robert 426–430
Yeomans, Donald 264, 268
Yersinia pestis bacillus 40
YouTube video 168, 212, 260–261, 443, 447, 487

Zifkin, Benjamin 369
Zinn, Howard 502; *Artists in Times of War* 502
Žižek, Slavoj 282
zone of affective intensification 418
zoning of broadcasts 373
Zuckerberg, Mark 357, 379
Zuluaga, Jorge 261